Mark Twain's
Library of
Humor

A BALLAD OF THE RHINE

"Shoost look at dese shpoons und vatches,
Shoost see dese diamont rings;
Coom down und full your bockets,
Und I'll giss you like avery dings."

MARK TWAIN'S LIBRARY OF HUMOR

Illustrated by E. W. Kemble

STEVE MARTIN

SERIES EDITOR

Introduction by Roy Blount, Jr.

THE MODERN LIBRARY

NEW YORK

2000 Modern Library Paperback Edition

Abridgment copyright © 2000 by Random House, Inc.
Series introduction copyright © 2000 by Steve Martin
Introduction copyright © 2000 by Roy Blount, Jr.

This edition is an abridgment of the 1888 original.

LIBRARY OF CONGRESS CATALOGING-IN-PUBLICATION IS AVAILABLE.
ISBN 0-679-64036-3

Modern Library website address: www.modernlibrary.com

Printed in the United States of America
2 4 6 8 9 7 5 3 1

Mark Twain

Mark Twain was born Samuel Langhorne Clemens on November 30, 1835, in Florida, Missouri; his family moved to the port town of Hannibal four years later. His father, an unsuccessful farmer, died when Twain was eleven. Soon afterward the boy began working as an apprentice printer, and by age sixteen he was writing newspaper sketches. He left Hannibal at eighteen to work as an itinerant printer in New York, Philadelphia, St. Louis, and Cincinnati. From 1857 to 1861 he worked on Mississippi steamboats, advancing from cub pilot to licensed pilot.

After river shipping was interrupted by the Civil War, Twain headed west with his brother Orion, who had been appointed secretary to the Nevada Territory. Settling in Carson City, he tried his luck at prospecting and wrote humorous pieces for a range of newspapers. Around this time he first began using the pseudonym Mark Twain, derived from a riverboat term. Relocating to San Francisco, he became a regular newspaper correspondent and a contributor to the literary magazine the *Golden Era*. He made a five-month journey to Hawaii in 1866 and the following year traveled to Europe to report on the first organized tourist cruise. *The Celebrated Jumping Frog of Calaveras County and Other Sketches* (1867) consolidated his growing reputation as humorist and lecturer.

After his marriage to Livy Langdon, Twain settled first in Buffalo,

New York, and then for two decades in Hartford, Connecticut. His European sketches were expanded into *The Innocents Abroad* (1869), followed by *Roughing It* (1872), an account of his Western adventures; both were enormously successful. Twain's literary triumphs were offset by often ill-advised business dealings (he sank thousands of dollars, for instance, in a failed attempt to develop a new kind of typesetting machine, and thousands more into his own ultimately unsuccessful publishing house) and unrestrained spending that left him in frequent financial difficulty, a pattern that was to persist throughout his life.

Following *The Gilded Age* (1873), written in collaboration with Charles Dudley Warner, Twain began a literary exploration of his childhood memories of the Mississippi, resulting in a trio of masterpieces—*The Adventures of Tom Sawyer* (1876), *Life on the Mississippi* (1883), and finally *The Adventures of Huckleberry Finn* (1885), on which he had been working for nearly a decade. Another vein, of historical romance, found expression in *The Prince and the Pauper* (1882), the satirical *A Connecticut Yankee in King Arthur's Court* (1889), and *Personal Recollections of Joan of Arc* (1896), while he continued to draw on his travel experiences in *A Tramp Abroad* (1880) and *Following the Equator* (1897). His close associates in these years included William Dean Howells, Bret Harte, and George Washington Cable, as well as the dying Ulysses S. Grant, whom Twain encouraged to complete his memoirs, published by Twain's publishing company in 1885.

For most of the 1890s Twain lived in Europe, as his life took a darker turn with the death of his daughter Susy in 1896 and the worsening illness of his daughter Jean. The tone of Twain's writing also turned progressively more bitter. *The Tragedy of Pudd'nhead Wilson* (1894), a detective story hinging on the consequences of slavery, was followed by powerful anti-imperialist and anticolonial statements such as "To the Person Sitting in Darkness" (1901), "The War Prayer" (1905), and "King Leopold's Soliloquy" (1905), and by the pessimistic sketches collected in the privately published *What Is Man?* (1906). The unfinished novel *The Mysterious Stranger* was perhaps the most uncompromisingly dark of all Twain's later works. In his last years, his financial troubles finally resolved, Twain settled near Redding, Connecticut, and died in his mansion, Stormfield, on April 21, 1910.

Introduction to the Modern Library Humor and Wit Series

Steve Martin

When I was asked to be the editor for the Modern Library Humor series, including books that had been written as far back as the mid–eighteenth century, I was shocked. I frankly was not aware that anything funny had been written before I started writing. I had indeed heard of S. J. Perelman, James Thurber, and the like, but I was also aware that they were heavily influenced by me, even lifting some of my ideas, backdating them, and carefully inserting them in magazines from the thirties with the clever use of a razor blade and glue.

That said, I have read the essays in the Modern Library's editions, and will give these authors credit in that they have been extremely nimble in adapting my ideas—for example, my use of the word "the" before nouns—and disguising it so there appears to be no plagiarism at all.

Unlike as in most of the arts, greatness in comedy is not necessarily judged by its ability to transcend generations. Comedy is designed to make people laugh now, not three generations later, and it would be a poor stand-up comedian who suggested waiting forty-five years for a joke to take hold. Have you ever seen cartoons from early-twentieth-century magazines? The ones with captions that are longer than the phone book?

"Eloise, it seems to me that the men should retire to the den for sport and that the ladies should remain in the dining area until that hour which it is deemed appropriate for the . . ." blah blah blah

What were they laughing at?

But just because it isn't funny now doesn't mean it wasn't funny then. And, even though you have probably burst into uncontrollable fits of hysteria several times already in the reading of this essay, that doesn't mean that this will be hilariously funny *one thousand years from now.*

In fact, I worry that my fantasy dinner party, at which Mark Twain, Benjamin Franklin, S. J. Perelman, and Nora Ephron hold court in my dining room, instead of being from-mouth-to-page publishable, might be a disaster. Would Ben utter a short, to-the-point epigram, Twain offer a witticism, Perelman deliver an exasperated self-deprecation, and Ephron observe a social irony, and then all of them sit there, separated by generations, wondering what the others were talking about?

So in choosing the books for this series, it was necessary to select works whose humor remains intact for us today. Generally, the ability for humor to last is explained away by saying that it appeals to something in us that is human and universal. This is a cheap, dopey explanation, and I'm upset that you suggested it. I prefer to think that transcendent humor is the product of funny people, and that's all there is to say. Who would you rather have at your party, someone human and universal, or someone who is deeply funny? This is why my fantasy dinner party would be swell, because all of these writers are deeply funny people. Although I must add that I know Nora Ephron personally, and I'm happy to say that she is also universal.

Sometimes, when I am feeling insecure about my chosen profession, I try to imagine a world without comedy—for example, the world that ducks live in. Try to imagine a political climate where an ironic comment is *seized upon by a humorless news media.* Or the world of entertainment minus the hilarious zing of celebrity interviews. It would be a sad, straight, strict world. Instead, we live in a world that is actually thriving on humor, and consuming it at an alarming rate. Comedy writers, who undoubtedly wake up in the morning with joy on their faces and a joke in their hearts, are more in demand than ever, partially because of their high suicide rate.

I suppose some kind of deeper commentary about humor is in order. I am overjoyed at the prospect of offering my very sophisticated views on humor, as I have been in the comedy world for over ... wait a minute. I am suddenly reminded of a phrase that circulates around my group of funny friends, which is generally expressed thus: The day you start analyzing humor is the day you cease to be funny. I think I'd rather be funny.

Good night.

INTRODUCTION

Roy Blount, Jr.

Old pieces of humor are like antique toys: Some of them still work and some don't, but they all have a certain fascination. Especially if we know that they worked for Mark Twain. And when you find one that does still work after, say, a century and a half, if you are like me you say things like "Look at that workmanship" to cover your wonderment at sharing inner-child glee with someone who was in the grave when your grandmother was born. To my surprise, I feel that way about a good many of the pieces in this book.

And then there are the pieces that are just so strange. Have you ever watched the Game Show Channel, Herb Shriner in the gray-and-white 1950s asking a young couple to name "different types of winds that blow" for $5 a pop on the Old Gold (that was a brand of cigarettes) Scoreboard? Talk about diversity—consider how different from *all* of us *everybody* was just forty-some-odd years ago. I was alive then, and still it is hard to realize that *people didn't even hold their mouths the same ways,* at least on television, back then, and yet we perceive some (shaky, but all the more stimulating for that) common ground, between us and them, for laughter. Reading this book is even better.

It was first published in 1888. For years I have had a copy of an out-of-print 1969 reprint edition on the shelf where I accumulate books by and about Mark Twain. Until recently, however, I had barely dipped into this juicy compendium—my assumption being that its still-risible content was low. This was in part, I now see, because I was too sure of my expertise as a shade-tree connoisseur of American humor. (John Phoenix? Richard Malcolm Johnston? Who knew?) But I had also been influenced by what Twain had to say, in his posthumously published autobiography, about a different book—a revised, promiscuously expanded collection, also entitled *Mark Twain's Library of Humor,* that Harper and Brothers published in 1906 without consulting him. This "great fat, coarse, offensive volume" so outraged him that he was reduced very nearly to mere huffiness:

> This book . . . reveals the surprising fact that within the compass of these forty years wherein I have been playing professional humorist before the public, I have had for company seventy-eight other American humorists. Each and every one of the seventy-eight rose in my time, became conspicuous and popular, and by and by vanished. . . .
>
> Why have they perished? Because they were merely humorists. Humorists of the "mere" sort cannot survive. Humor is only a fragrance, a decoration. Often it is merely an odd trick of speech and of spelling. . . . Humor must not professedly teach and it must not professedly preach, but it must do both if it would live forever. By forever, I mean thirty years. . . .
>
> I have always preached. That is the reason I have lasted thirty years. . . . I should have written the sermon just the same, whether any humor applied for admission or not. I am saying these vain things in this frank way because I am a dead person speaking from the grave. Even I would be too modest to say them in life. I think we never become really and genuinely our entire and honest selves until we are dead—and not then until we have been dead years and years. People ought to start dead and then they would be honest so much earlier.

Not to pick a quarrel with America's preeminent funny writer, but there are two reasons why that passage is of abiding interest: because he was, and is, America's preeminent funny writer, and because the second and third paragraphs wind up funny. Certainly Mark Twain was up to more than diverting the public, and he often dealt with matters of gravity (for instance, death), but no one's *preaching* lives on the page unless it is exciting to read, and Mark Twain is exciting to read because he wrote great, distinctively American prose driven by comic instinct. Acuity, daring, hardy experience, and edgy empathy were his vigor, but humor was his aesthetic, and *this* book, which limits itself to forty-five writers, shows that his was not the only humor he appreciated.

In 1880, a man named George Gebbie suggested a project along these lines to Twain, who thought that it had commercial potential but that Gebbie didn't. For collaborators he turned to two of his friends: a Hartford journalist, Charles H. Clark, and the prominent editor and novelist William Dean Howells. They did most of the preliminary gathering. In 1885 the publisher that was to have brought out the collection, the James R. Osgood Company, went out of business. Twain's own publishing house, Charles L. Webster and Company (Webster was his nephew by marriage), took it over. And Twain, after dragging his feet for several years, pitched in. Since Howells had an exclusive arrangement with another publisher, his name did not appear on the finished product, although he wrote the introduction signed "The Associate Editors." Howells later recalled that "when I had done my work according to tradition, with authors, times, and topics carefully studied in due sequence, he tore it all apart, and 'chucked' the pieces in wherever the fancy for them took him at the moment. He was right: we were not making a textbook, but a book for the pleasure rather than the instruction of the reader, and he did not see why the principle on which he had built his travels and reminiscences and tales and novels should not apply to it."

So what we have here is Twain's unpreachy, unteachy collage. It begins with the piece that made him famous and ends with his fanciful account of an earlier, wilder and woollier, editing experience. Scattered in between are eighteen others of his own pieces, well selected. There is nothing from his 1885 masterpiece, *The Adventures of Huckleberry Finn*, which is too bad, since that novel contains a much funnier dog-in-church episode than "A Dog in Church." But "Blue-Jays," from *Roughing It*, may be my own favorite bit of Twain. "Our Italian Guide" is the funniest part of *Innocents Abroad*. "The Cayote," also from *Roughing It*, is so full of kinetic relish that it makes the great Chuck Jones Road Runner cartoons (which in fact, according to Jones, were inspired by it) seem almost sedate, not to mention stacked against the coyote. "Lost in the Snow" manages to derive rich jocularity out of real jeopardy. When I came to the kicker of the last-named piece I was moved to write in the margin, "Mark! You the man!" And note how the snippet from Josh Billings that follows "Lost in the Snow" adds a philosophical tweak. A number of pieces by other contributors are improved by the montage. For instance, Clarence Dudley Warner's "Pie" in itself eludes me, but its juxtaposition to "Cannibalism in the Cars" is nice.

A great many of the other writers' pieces, however, are fine on their own. Richard Malcolm Johnston! "The Expensive Treat of Col. Moses Grice"! "You spotted-backed, striped-legged, streaked-faced, speckled-b-breasted, p'inted-hatted son-of-a-gun!" This story makes a person realize why running away to join the circus was once such a dream of American boys. Even allowing for the heavy-handed orthography, I still don't see why Artemus Ward was such a favorite of Abraham Lincoln's, but "On 'Forts'" has energy—Twain never got so white-hot-personal-absurd (perhaps because he never got quite so drunk) as Ward playing horse. I had only vaguely ever heard of George H. Derby, pseudonym "John Phoenix," whom the headnote by Howells identifies as "the first of the great modern humorists," but I am delighted now to have read "Tushmaker's Toothpuller," from which, if I am not mistaken, Twain later stole a skeleton-extraction joke. You could not have forced me to read anything entitled "Rev. Cream Cheese and the New Livery," by the long-forgotten George William Curtis, if I had not come upon it here, provocatively following Twain's "The Tomb of Adam." Both the foppish Rev. C. C. and his *ton*-coveting counselee Mrs. Potiphar live now in my memory.

To be sure, Mrs. Potiphar's husband, the burgherish (I see him played by Eugene Pallette) voice of reason, gets off light. Let us stipulate right off that nineteenth-century humor generally has far too easy a way with women and non-Anglo-Saxons, not to mention cats, dismemberment, and delirium tremens. This is preponderantly a white middle-class Protestant guy's book. But the female contributors get some ladylike licks in. I find it a shame, in the context of so much grand male rowdiness, that the thrust of Marietta Holley's "A Pleasure Exertion" is against pleasure-seeking adventure, but that thrust has a certain corrective value. Aside from James M. Bailey's blithely misogynistic "A Female Base-Ball Club," and Artemus Ward's even more egregious "Women's Rights," the one really terrible piece of writing in the book, to my taste, is Katherine Kent Child Walker's fluffy-arch, inverted-comma-bestrewn "The Total Depravity of Inanimate Things" (was Howells, who first published this piece in *The Atlantic*, sweet on her or something?). And it is interesting to note how facetious the abolitionist Harriet Beecher Stowe's take on an African American man of New England seems today. But (Mrs.) Francis Lee Pratt's tough-skinned and (yet?) oddly poignant sketch entitled "Captain Ben's Choice" is an insight into widows, widowers, and clueless male privilege that reveals a refreshing undercoat, I think, from beneath subsequent layers of gender grievance. The reissuing of this book rescues from oblivion the intelligent if outmoded textures of a different time, textures that would embarrass the sensibilities of early-twenty-first-century anthologists, and which render even me, who am in no very clear-to-me way responsible, considerably (if insufficiently) defensive. "Trying to Understand a Woman," by Howells, may raise contemporary women's hackles (full disclosure: I, with certain due reservations, liked it), but if Howells's gentlemanly bemusement is less heartily sympathetic than Twain's feeling for the coyote, it is, in its own genteel way, attentive. And "Kitty Answers," also by Howells, strikes me, what do I know, as lovely.

If this book has an *unexpected* blind spot, given that Mark Twain arose from the Southmidwestern frontier, it is reflected in Howells's introduction, where he says that American humor "has always been so racy of the soil that the native flavor prevails throughout; and whether Yankee, Knickerbocker, Southern Californian, refined or broad . . . it was and is always American." Notice any region missing? Well, I suppose there are two: the Midwest (whence Howells moved to New England) *and* the South, but it is the latter that interests me. Mark Twain's style is more than the crowning glory of the rough Southwestern "Big Bear" school of humor, but it is that, too, and that school is scantily represented here. No A. B. Longstreet, no Thomas Bangs Thorpe, no Bill Arp (Charles Henry Smith), and only one piece by George Washington Harris, whose Sut Lovingood tales Twain enjoyed and was influenced by. (So did and was William Faulkner.) Sut's heavy dialect resists modern appreciation, but the same can be said for Artemus Ward and James Russell Lowell, and Harris in Sut's voice was a scurrilous genius, the Richard Pryor of his day. Aside from Twain, whom Howells described as "the most desouthernized Southerner" he'd ever known, only four of the contributors here are Southerners or miners of Southern material, and only one of them, Joel Chandler Harris, is represented by as many as two pieces. That makes five Southern items altogether, which is less than the allotment of George T. Lanigan (a Canadian by birth, whose "The Centipede and the Barbaric Yak" is, well, striking) alone. It is interesting to note that in his diatribe against the unauthorized expanded library, Twain the transplanted New Englander reels off a list of Northern humorists he has outlasted and then mentions "three very popular Southern humorists whose names I am not able to recall."

Among the contributors to this collection published thirty-three years after the Civil War, only four fought in it: on the Union side, Robert J. Burdette, Ambrose Bierce, and the aforementioned Bailey; on the other (for two weeks) Twain. Thirteen other male contributors, none of them Southern, were between the ages of seventeen and thirty-five in 1861, but managed to stay out of harm's way. And good for them. But an excerpt or two from *"Co. Aytch": A Side Show of the Big Show,* by the Tennessean foot soldier Sam R. Watkins (the book that Mark Twain might have written if he had stuck with, and survived, the war), would have served as a better observance of that absurd, allegedly glorious bloodbath than the only piece in this book that deals with it: Ward's clunkily conciliatory letter from Richmond "after the city catterpitulated." But as I say, even the pieces that don't work have a certain fascination.

Sometimes I envy these guys. Their readers' attention span was indulgent. They didn't have to worry about so many different kinds of people's sensitivities. They could get away with names like Funny Joe Mungoozle. And rather than strain to find something droll about some obscure, as-yet-unexhausted aspect of the cuisine of some as-yet-underexplored region of some un-done-to-death country, they could, as Mark Twain does here, ridicule the food you get in Europe, generally. "European" hotels couldn't cook a chicken? They served, by American standards, weak coffee and "characterless" soup? I guess. Back then.

Anyway, this book is no characterless soup. If I were to guide you on a tour through this monument to premodern American jocularity, and along the way I were to point out, say, Q. K. Philander Doesticks, and you were to come on the wiseacre like Mark Twain in Italy, asking me,

"Is, ah—is he dead?" I wouldn't turn a hair. We should all be only that dead a century and a half, or so, from now.

Roy Blount, Jr., is the editor of *Roy Blount's Book of Southern Humor* and the author of numerous books, including *Crackers*, *Be Sweet*, and *Not Exactly What I Had in Mind*. He wrote the introduction to the Oxford University Press facsimile edition of Mark Twain's *The Celebrated Jumping Frog of Calaveras County, and Other Sketches*.

EDITORIAL NOTE

Compiler's Apology

=

Those selections in this book which are from my own works, were made by my two assistant compilers, not by me. This is why there are not more.

Mark Twain

Hartford   Jan. 1 1888.

INTRODUCTION

There is no one whom people wish out of the way more than some well-meaning person who insists upon formally making them acquainted with a company of old friends, and is so full of his own performance that he won't see they are on hand-shaking terms already, and all they want is a chance to get at one another. Now if there is any one class of their authors whom the American people do know rather better than any other, it is the American humorists, from Washington Irving to Bill Nye, and we are not going to repeat their names here, or lecture upon their qualities. We have tried to arrange our Library so as to include passages representative of every period and section, and we think that the chaotic order which we have chosen will be found to facilitate the course of those who like to come upon their favorite authors unexpectedly. For example, the reader accustomed to the cheap artifices of other editors will be surprised to meet, first, a selection from the chief compiler's own work, which he would naturally have expected to find in the small print of an appendix; but throughout, the compiler has subordinated his diffidence as an author to his taste as an editor, and has put in a piece of his literature as often as he thought the public would stand it. We need not say that, if he could have had his way throughout, this Library would have consisted solely of extracts from his own books. But he was afraid the public would not stand it, not because it did not like his books, but because it had them all by heart already. For this reason, he has followed upon the first selection from himself with selections from Messrs. Warner, Aldrich and Burdette, and he has not hesitated in other places to intersperse extracts from Mark Twain, with episodes from Mr. Lowell, or Dr. Holmes, or Mr. Harris, or Mr. Cable, or others. This has the effect of bewildering the reader, who thought it was going to be all Mark Twain, and perhaps of convincing him that there are other humorists besides his favorite author.

Another advantage in the arrangement adopted, is that the reader will often be obliged to go through the whole book before he discovers that some favorite author is not in it; and by this time he will have been so much amused that he will have forgotten all about his favorite author. We meant to put in everybody's favorite author, but the limits of the Library would not allow of this; and we had to be content with the hope that no one would finally remember their absence except the favorites themselves. To these we would say, in the intimacy of a public advertisement, that they may confidently look to find themselves in a future work. They are no worse than many, perhaps most, of the authors here represented; in making this compilation we have exercised, not only the disorder of chaos, but the blindness of fate.

Our work is not, however, a last judgment; and an appeal may be easily taken from it. In fact, it is not a judgment at all, but is a species of garden-party, where representative people from all epochs and parts of the country meet and say, "What! *You* here?" as people do when they had not expected to find one another in such good society. But we think the little entertainment is favorable to the enjoyment, and even the study, if you please, of the different kinds of American humor, from the days of Irving, when it still smacked of Goldsmith and Addison, onward. Smack of whom it would, it has always been so racy of the soil that the native flavor prevails throughout; and whether Yankee, Knickerbocker, Southern Californian, refined or broad, prose, verse or newspaper, it was and is always American. But it is interesting to compare the varieties and differences of the fruits of this perennial and indigenous plant, the one thing that we can certainly claim ours whatever else may be denied us; and we think our garden-party gives an excellent chance for this. We have been obliged to make a selection of authors, but here the work of discrimination ends, and the whole American public is cordially invited to attend. It is going to be a very distinguished affair, and, in our hospitable feeling about it, we should really be very sorry if any one of our sixty millions missed it.

THE ASSOCIATE EDITORS

CONTENTS

Index of Authors

Mark Twain's
Library of
Humor

THE NOTORIOUS JUMPING FROG OF CALAVERAS* COUNTY

S. L. CLEMENS (MARK TWAIN)

Samuel L. Clemens (Mark Twain) was born at Hannibal, Mo., in 1835, and after serving an apprenticeship to the printing business in his brother's office there, "learned the river," as pilot. In this profession he borrowed the phrase which became his pseudonym from the river custom of crying the soundings, "Mark one! Mark twain! Mark three!" etc. When piloting fell into the decay that overtook the whole commerce of the rivers, he went to Nevada, where he made his first attempts in journalism. He was afterwards connected with various newspapers in San Francisco, visited the Sandwich Islands as correspondent of one of them, and, on his return, gave his first lecture. His earliest book, "The Innocents Abroad," was the result of his experience and observation as a passenger on the *Quaker City* in her famous cruise to the Holy Land. His succeeding books continue the story of his own life, with more or less fullness and exactness. After his return from Palestine, he was for a year in Buffalo, N.Y., but has ever since lived in Hartford, Conn. His books have been nearly all published by subscription, through different houses.

In compliance with the request of a friend of mine, who wrote me from the East, I called on good-natured, garrulous old Simon Wheeler, and inquired after my friend's friend, Leonidas W. Smiley, as requested to do, and I hereunto append the result. I have a lurking suspicion that *Leonidas W.* Smiley is a myth; that my friend never knew such a personage; and that he only conjectured that if I asked old Wheeler about him, it would remind him of his infamous *Jim* Smiley, and he would go to work and bore me to death with some exasperating reminiscence of him as long and as tedious as it should be useless to me. If that was the design, it succeeded.

I found Simon Wheeler dozing comfortably by the bar-room stove of the dilapidated tavern in the decayed mining camp of Angel's, and

*Pronounced Ca-le-*va*-ras.

I noticed that he was fat and bald-headed, and had an expression of winning gentleness and simplicity upon his tranquil countenance. He roused up and gave me good day. I told him a friend of mine had commissioned me to make some inquiries about a cherished companion of his boyhood, named *Leonidas W.* Smiley—*Rev. Leonidas W.* Smiley—a young minister of the gospel, who he had heard was at one time a resident of Angel's Camp. I added that if Mr. Wheeler could tell me anything about this *Rev. Leonidas W.* Smiley, I would feel under many obligations to him.

Simon Wheeler backed me into a corner and blockaded me there with his chair, and then sat down and reeled off the monotonous narrative which follows this paragraph. He never smiled, he never frowned, he never changed his voice from the gentle-flowing key to which he turned his initial sentence, he never betrayed the slightest suspicion of enthusiasm; but all through the interminable narrative there ran a vein of impressive earnestness and sincerity which showed me plainly that, so far from his imagining that there was anything ridiculous or funny about his story, he regarded it as a really important matter, and admired its two heroes as men of transcendent genius in *finesse*. I let him go on in his own way, and never interrupted him once.

"Rev. Leonidas W. H'm, Reverend Le—well, there was a feller here once by the name of *Jim* Smiley, in the winter of '49, or maybe it was the spring of '50—I don't recollect exactly, somehow, though what makes me think it was one or the other, is because I remember the big flume warn't finished when he first come to the camp; but anyway, he was the curiousest man about, always betting on anything that turned up you ever see, if he could get anybody to bet on the other side; and if he couldn't, he'd change sides. Any way that suited the other side would suit *him*—any way, just so's he got a bet, *he* was satisfied. But still he was lucky, uncommon lucky; he most always come out winner. He was always ready, and laying for a chance; there couldn't be no solit'ry thing mentioned but that feller'd offer to bet on it, and take any side you please, as I was just telling you. If there was a horse-race, you'd find him flush or you'd find him busted at the end of it; if there was a dog-fight, he'd bet on it; if there was a cat-fight, he'd bet on it; if there was a chicken-fight, he'd bet on it; why, if there was two birds setting on a fence, he would bet you which one would fly first; or if there was a camp-meeting, he would be there reg'lar to bet on Parson Walker, which he judged to be the best exhorter about here; and so he was, too, and a good man. If he even see a straddle-bug start to go anywheres, he would bet you how long it would take him to get to—to wherever he was going to; and if you took him up, he would foller that straddle-bug to Mexico, but what he would find out where he was bound for, and how long he was on the road. Lots of the boys here has seen that Smiley, and can tell you about him. Why, it never made no difference to *him*—he'd bet *any* thing—the dangdest feller. Parson Walker's wife laid very sick once for a good while, and it seemed as if they warn't going to save her; but one morning he come in, and Smiley up and asked him how she was, and he said she was consid'able better—thank the Lord for his inf'nit mercy!—and coming on so smart that, with the blessing of Prov'dence, she'd get well yet; and Smiley, before he thought, says, 'Well, I'll resk two-and-a-half she don't, anyway.'

"Thish-yer Smiley had a mare—the boys called her the fifteen-minute nag, but that was only in fun, you know, because of course she was faster than that—and he used to win money on that horse, for all she was so slow, and always had the asthma, or the distemper, or the consumption, or something of that kind. They used to give her two or three hundred yards' start, and then pass her under way; but always at the fag-end of the race she'd get excited and desperate-like, and come cavorting and straddling up, and scattering her legs around limber, sometimes in the air, and sometimes out to one side amongst the fences, and kicking up m-o-r-e dust and raising m-o-r-e racket with her coughing and sneezing and blowing her nose—and *always* fetch up at the stand just about a neck ahead, as near as you could cipher it down.

"And he had a little small bull-pup, that to look at him you'd think he warn't worth a cent but to set around and look ornery, and lay for a chance to steal something. But as soon as money was up on him he was a different dog; his under-jaw'd begin to stick out like the fo'castle of a steamboat, and his teeth would uncover and shine like the furnaces. And a dog might tackle him and bullyrag him, and bite him, and throw him over his shoulder two or three times, and Andrew Jackson—which was the name of the pup—Andrew Jackson would never let on but what *he* was satisfied, and hadn't expected nothing else—and the bets being doubled and doubled on the other side all the time, till the money was all up; and then all of a sudden he would grab the other dog jest by the j'int of his hind leg and freeze to it—not chaw, you under-stand, but only just grip and hang on till they throwed up the sponge, if it was a year. Smiley always come out winner on that pup, till he har-nessed a dog once that didn't have no hind legs, because they'd been sawed off in a circular saw, and when the thing had gone along far enough, and the money was all up, and he come to make a snatch for his pet holt, he see in a minute how he'd been imposed on, and how the other dog had him in the door, so to speak, and he 'peared surprised, and then he looked sorter discouraged-like, and didn't try no more to win the fight, and so he got shucked out bad. He give Smiley a look, as much as to say his heart was broke, and it was *his* fault, for putting up a dog that hadn't no hind legs for him to take holt of, which was his main dependence in a fight; and then he limped off a piece and laid down and died. It was a good pup, was that Andrew Jackson, and would have made a name for hisself if he'd lived, for the stuff was in him and he had genius—I know it, because he hadn't no opportunities to speak of, and it don't stand to reason that a dog could make such a fight as he could under them circumstances if he hadn't no talent. It always makes me feel sorry when I think of that last fight of his'n, and the way it turned out.

"Well, this-yer Smiley had rat-tarriers, and chicken cocks, and tom-cats and all them kind of things, till you couldn't rest, and you couldn't fetch nothing for him to bet on but he'd match you. He ketched a frog one day, and took him home, and said he cal'lated to educate him; and so he never done nothing for three months but set in his back yard and learn that frog to jump. And you bet you he *did* learn him, too. He'd give him a little punch behind, and the next minute you'd see that frog whirling in the air like a doughnut—see him turn one summerset, or maybe a couple, if he got a good start, and come down flat-footed and all right, like a cat. He got him up so in the matter of ketching flies, and kep' him in practice so constant, that he'd nail a fly every time as fur as he could see him. Smiley said all a frog wanted was education, and he could do 'most anything—and I believe him. Why, I've seen him set Dan'l Webster down here on this floor—Dan'l Webster was the name of the frog—and sing out, 'Flies, Dan'l, flies!' and quicker'n you could wink he'd spring straight up and snake a fly off'n the counter there, and flop down on the floor ag'in as solid as a gob of mud, and fall to scratching the side of his head with his hind foot as indifferent as if he hadn't no idea he'd been doin' any more'n any frog might do. You never see a frog so modest and straightfor'ard as he was, for all he was so gifted. And when it come to fair and square jumping on a dead level, he could get over more ground at one straddle than any animal of his breed you ever see. Jumping on a dead level was his strong suit, you understand; and when it come to that, Smiley would ante up money on him as long as he had a red. Smiley was monstrous proud of his frog, and well he might be, for fellers that had traveled and been every-wheres, all said he laid over any frog that ever *they* see.

"Well, Smiley kep' the beast in a little lattice box, and he used to fetch him down-town sometimes and lay for a bet. One day a feller— a stranger in the camp, he was—come acrost him with his box, and says:

" 'What might it be that you've got in the box?'

"And Smiley says, sorter indifferent-like, 'It might be a parrot, or it might be a canary, maybe, but it ain't—it's only just a frog.'

"And the feller took it, and looked at it careful, and turned it round this way and that, and says, 'H'm—so 'tis. Well, what's *he* good for?'

" 'Well,' Smiley says, easy and careless, 'he's good enough for *one* thing, I should judge—he can outjump any frog in Calaveras County.'

"The feller took the box again, and took another long, particular look, and give it back to Smiley, and says, very deliberate, 'Well,' he says, 'I don't see no p'ints about that frog that's any better'n any other frog.'

" 'Maybe you don't,' Smiley says. 'Maybe you understand frogs, and maybe you don't understand 'em; maybe you've had experience, and maybe you ain't only a amature, as it were. Anyways, I've got *my* opin-ion, and I'll resk forty dollars that he can outjump any frog in Calav-eras County.'

"And the feller studied a minute, and then says, kinder sad like, 'Well, I'm only a stranger here, and I ain't got no frog; but if I had a frog, I'd bet you.'

"And then Smiley says, 'That's all right—that's all right—if you'll hold my box a minute, I'll go and get you a frog.' And so the feller took the box, and put up his forty dollars along with Smiley's, and set down to wait.

"So he set there a good while, thinking and thinking to hisself, and then he got the frog out and prized his mouth open, and took a tea-

HE COULDN'T BUDGE.

spoon and filled him full of quail shot—filled him pretty near up to his chin—and set him on the floor. Smiley he went to the swamp and slopped around in the mud for a long time, and finally he ketched a frog, and fetched him in, and give him to this feller, and says:

" 'Now, if you're ready, set him alongside of Dan'l, with his fore-paws just even with Dan'l's, and I'll give the word.' Then he says, 'One—two—three—*git!*' and him and the feller touched up the frogs from behind, and the new frog hopped off lively, but Dan'l give a heave, and hysted up his shoulders—so—like a Frenchman, but it warn't no use—he couldn't budge; he was planted as solid as a church, and he couldn't no more stir than if he was anchored out. Smiley was a good deal surprised, and he was disgusted too, but he didn't have no idea what the matter was, of course.

"The feller took the money and started away; and when he was going out at the door, he sorter jerked his thumb over his shoulder—so—at Dan'l, and says again, very deliberate, 'Well,' he says, '*I* don't see no p'ints about that frog that's any better'n any other frog.'

"Smiley he stood scratching his head and looking down at Dan'l a long time, and at last he says, 'I do wonder what in the nation that frog throw'd off for—I wonder if there ain't something the matter with him—he 'pears to look mighty baggy, somehow.' And he ketched Dan'l by the nap of the neck, and hefted him, and says, 'Why, blame my cats if he don't weigh five pound!' and turned him upside down, and he belched out a double handful of shot. And then he see how it was, and he was the maddest man—he set the frog down and took out after the feller, but he never ketched him. And——."

[Here Simon Wheeler heard his name called from the front yard, and got up to see what was wanted.] A turning to me as he moved away, he said: "Just set where you are, stranger, and rest easy—I ain't going to be gone a second."

But, by your leave, I did not think that a continuation of the history of the enterprising vagabond *Jim* Smiley would be likely to afford me much information concerning the Rev. *Leonidas W.* Smiley, and so I started away.

At the door I met the sociable Wheeler returning, and he button-holed me and re-commenced:

"Well, this-yer Smiley had a yaller one-eyed cow that didn't have no tail, only jest a short stump like a bannanner, and——"

However, lacking both time and inclination, I did not wait to hear about the afflicted cow, but took my leave.

WARM HAIR

MARK TWAIN

Talking about warm hair, a lady in Milwaukee, whose hair very nearly matches the brick in the Wisconsin Building, and who has been joked about her red hair until she goes around and shoots the last few thousand who make ancient remarks about it, says she heard a new thing on red hair the other day. A friend from the East said to her, "Mrs.——, I rather like this Skeneateles hair of yours." She didn't like to ask questions, but finally curiosity got the best of her, and she asked, "Well, what in the name of the thirteen apostles is Skaneateles hair?" "Oh," says he, as he got on the other side of the table, and held his elbow up over his head so the press board wouldn't hurt, "Skeneateles is about forty miles beyond Auburn, you know." He is now carried in a sling, and his friends have to get a pass from the matron of the hospital to see him.—*Newspaper.*

A FIGHT WITH A TROUT

CHARLES DUDLEY WARNER

Charles Dudley Warner was born at Plainfield, Mass., in 1829. His boyhood was spent in the country, but he received a collegiate training, and after some years' experience as surveyor in the West, he took up the study of the law, and entered upon its practice in Philadelphia. He removed thence to Chicago, and then returned to the East, and formed the connection with the Hartford *Courant*, which still continues. In this journal were published the papers "My Summer in a Garden," the first expression of his delicate and characteristic humor, which received general recognition. It was followed by the "Backlog Studies," his work in collaboration with Mr. Clemens, "The

Gilded Age," and his different volumes of travel—"Saunterings," "Winter on the Nile," etc. He contributed to American History a delightful monograph on "Captain John Smith," and has written a critical biography of Washington Irving.

Trout-fishing in the Adirondacks would be a more attractive pastime than it is, but for the popular notion of its danger. The trout is a retiring and harmless animal, except when he is aroused and forced into a combat; and then his agility, fierceness and vindictiveness become apparent. No one who has studied the excellent pictures representing men in an open boat, exposed to the assaults of long-enraged trout flying at them through the open air with open mouth, ever ventures with his rod upon the lonely lakes of the forest without a certain terror, or ever reads of the exploits of daring fishermen without a feeling of admiration for their heroism. Most of their adventures are thrilling, and all of them are, in narration, more or less unjust to the trout: in fact, the object of them seems to be to exhibit, at the expense of the trout, the shrewdness, the skill, and the muscular power of the sportsman. My own simple story has few of these recommendations.

We had built our bark camp one summer, and were staying on one of the popular lakes of the Saranac region. It would be a very pretty region if it were not so flat; if the margins of the lakes had not been flooded by dams at the outlets—which have killed the trees, and left a rim of ghastly dead-wood like the swamps of the under-world pictured by Doré's bizarre pencil—and if the pianos at the hotels were in tune. It would be an excellent sporting-region also (for there is water enough) if the fish commissioners would stock the waters, and if previous hunters had not pulled all the hair and skin off from the deers' tails. Formerly sportsmen had a habit of catching the deer by the tails, and of being dragged in mere wantonness round and round the shores. It is well known that, if you seize a deer by this "holt," the skin will slip off like the peel from a banana. This reprehensible practice was carried so far, that the traveler is now hourly pained by the sight of peeled-tail deer mournfully sneaking about the wood.

We had been hearing, for weeks, of a small lake in the heart of the virgin forest, some ten miles from our camp, which was alive with trout, unsophisticated, hungry trout: the inlet to it was described as *stiff* with them. In my imagination I saw them lying there in ranks and rows, each a foot long, three tiers deep, a solid mass. The lake had never been visited, except by stray sable-hunters in the winter, and was known as the Unknown Pond. I determined to explore it; fully expecting, however, that it would prove to be a delusion, as such mysterious haunts of the trout usually are. Confiding my purpose to Luke, we secretly made our preparations, and stole away from the shanty one morning at daybreak. Each of us carried a boat, a pair of blankets, a sack of bread, pork, and maple-sugar; while I had my case of rods, creel, and book of flies, and Luke had an axe and the kitchen utensils. We think nothing of loads of this sort in the woods.

Five miles through a tamarack-swamp brought us to the inlet of Unknown Pond, upon which we embarked our fleet, and paddled down its vagrant waters. They were at first sluggish, winding among *triste* fir-trees, but gradually developed a strong current. At the end of three miles a loud roar ahead warned us that we were approaching rapids, falls and cascades. We paused. The danger was unknown. We had our choice of shouldering our loads and making a *détour* through the woods, or of "shooting the rapids." Naturally we chose the more dangerous course. Shooting the rapids has often been described, and I will not repeat the description here. It is needless to say that I drove my frail bark through the boiling rapids, over the successive waterfalls, amid rocks and vicious eddies, and landed, half a mile below, with whitened hair and a boat half full of water; and that the guide was upset, and boat, contents and man were strewn along the shore.

After this common experience we went quickly on our journey, and, a couple of hours before sundown, reached the lake. If I live to my dying-day, I never shall forget its appearance. The lake is almost an exact circle, about a quarter of a mile in diameter. The forest about it was untouched by axe, and unkilled by artificial flooding. The azure water had a perfect setting of evergreens, in which all the shades of the fir, the balsam, the pine, and the spruce were perfectly blended; and at intervals on the shore in the emerald rim blazed the ruby of the cardinal-flower. It was at once evident that the unruffled waters had never been vexed by the keel of a boat. But what chiefly attracted my attention, and amused me, was the boiling of the water, the bubbling and breaking, as if the lake were a vast kettle, with a fire underneath. A tyro would have been astonished at this common phenomenon; but sportsmen will at once understand me when I say that the water *boiled* with the breaking trout. I studied the surface for some time to see upon what sort of flies they were feeding, in order to suit my cast to their appetites; but they seemed to be at play rather than feeding, leaping high in the air in graceful curves, and tumbling about each other as we see them in Adirondack pictures.

It is well known that no person who regards his reputation will ever kill a trout with anything but a fly. It requires some training on the part of the trout to take to this method. The uncultivated, unsophisticated trout in unfrequented waters prefers the bait; and the rural people, whose sole object in going a-fishing appears to be to catch fish, indulge them in their primitive taste for the worm. No sportsman, however, will use anything but a fly, except he happens to be alone.

While Luke launched my boat, and arranged his seat in the stern, I prepared my rod and line. The rod is a bamboo, weighing seven ounces, which has to be spliced with a winding of silk thread every time it is used. This is a tedious process; but, by fastening the joints in this way, a uniform spring is secured in the rod. No one devoted to high art would think of using a socket joint. My line was forty yards of untwisted silk upon a multiplying reel. The "leader" (I am very particular about my leaders) had been made to order from a domestic animal with which I had been acquainted. The fisherman requires as good a catgut as the violinist. The interior of the house-cat, it is well known, is exceedingly sensitive; but it may not be so well known that the reason why some cats leave the room in distress when a piano-forte is played is because the two instruments are not in the same key, and the vibrations of the chords of the one are in discord with the catgut of the other. On six feet of this superior article I fixed three artificial flies—a simple brown hackle, a gray body with scarlet wings, and one of my own invention, which I thought would be new to the most experienced fly-catcher. The trout-fly does not resemble any known species of insect. It is a "conventionalized" creation, as we say of ornamentation. The theory is, that, fly-fishing being a high art, the fly must not be a tame imitation of nature, but an artistic suggestion of it. It requires an artist to construct one; and not every bungler can take a bit of red flannel, a peacock's feather, a flash of tinsel thread, a cock's plume, a section of a hen's wing, and fabricate a tiny object that will not look like any fly, but still will suggest the universal conventional fly.

I took my stand in the centre of the tipsy boat; and Luke shoved off, and slowly paddled towards some lily-pads, while I began casting—unlimbering my tools, as it were. The fish had all disappeared. I got out, perhaps, fifty feet of line, with no response, and gradually increased it to one hundred. It is not difficult to learn to cast; but it is difficult to learn not to snap off the flies at every throw. Of this, however, we will not speak. I continued casting for some moments, until I became satisfied that there had been a miscalculation. Either the trout were too green to know what I was at, or they were dissatisfied with my offers. I reeled in, and changed the flies (that is, the fly that was not snapped off). After studying the color of the sky, of the water, and of the foliage, and the moderated light of the afternoon, I put on a series of beguilers, all of a subdued brilliancy, in harmony with the approach of evening. At the second cast, which was a short one, I saw a splash where the leader fell, and gave an excited jerk. The next instant I perceived the game, and did not need the unfeigned "dam" of Luke to convince me that I had snatched his felt hat from his head, and deposited it among the lilies. Discouraged by this, we whirled about, and paddled over to the inlet, where a little ripple was visible in the tinted light. At the very first cast I saw that the hour had come. Three trout leaped into the air. The danger of this manœuvre all fishermen understand. It is one of the commonest in the woods: three heavy trout taking hold at once, rushing in different directions, smash the tackle into flinders. I evaded this catch, and threw again. I recall the moment. A hermit thrush, on the tip of a balsam, uttered his long, liquid, evening note. Happening to look over my shoulder, I saw the peak of Marcy gleam rosy in the sky (I can't help it that Marcy is fifty miles off, and cannot be seen from this region: these incidental touches are always used). The hundred feet of silk swished through the air, and the tail-fly fell as lightly on the water as a three-cent-piece (which no slamming will give the weight of a ten) drops upon the contribution-plate. Instantly there was a rush, a swirl. I struck, and "Got him, by——!" Never mind what Luke said I got him by. "Out on a fly!" continued that irreverent guide; but I told him to back water and make for the centre of the lake. The trout, as soon as he felt the prick of the hook, was off like a shot, and took out the whole of the line with a rapidity that made it smoke. "Give him the butt!" shouted Luke. It is the usual remark in such an emergency. I gave him the butt; and, recognizing the fact and my spirit, the trout at once sank to the bottom, and sulked. It is the most dangerous mood of a trout; for you cannot tell what he will do next. We reeled up a little, and waited five minutes for him to reflect. A tightening of the line enraged him, and he soon developed his tactics. Coming to the surface, he made straight for the boat faster than I could reel in, and evidently with hostile intentions. "Look out for him!" cried Luke as he came flying in the air. I evaded him by dropping flat in the bottom of the boat; and when I picked my traps up, he was spinning across the lake as if he had a new idea: but the line was still fast. He did not run far. I gave him the butt again; a thing he seemed to hate, even as a gift. In a moment the evil-minded fish, lashing the water in his rage, was coming back again, making straight for the boat, as before. Luke, who was used to these encounters, having read of them in the writings of travelers he had accompanied, raised his paddle in self-defense. The trout left the water about ten feet from the boat, and came directly at me with fiery eyes, his speckled sides flashing like a meteor. I dodged as he whisked by with a vicious slap of his bifurcated tail, and nearly upset the boat. The line was of course slack; and the danger was that he would entangle it about me, and carry away a leg. This was evidently his game; but I untangled it, and only lost a breast-button or two by the swiftly moving string. The trout plunged into the water with a hissing sound, and went away again with all the line on the reel. More butt; more indignation on the part of the captive. The contest had now been going on for half an hour, and I was getting exhausted. We had been back and forth across the lake, and round and round the lake. What I feared was, that the trout would start up the inlet, and wreck us in the bushes. But he had a new fancy, and began the execution of a manœuvre which I had never read of. Instead of coming straight towards me, he took a large circle, swimming rapidly, and *gradually contracting his orbit.* I reeled in, and kept my eye on him. Round and round he went, narrowing his circle. I began to suspect the game; which was, to twist my head off. When he had reduced the radius of his circle to about twenty-five feet, he struck a tremendous pace through the water. It would be false modesty in a sportsman to say that I was not equal to the occasion. Instead of turning round with him, as he expected, I stepped to the bow, braced myself, and let the boat swing. Round went the fish, and round we went like a top. I saw a line of Mount Marcys all round the horizon; the rosy tint in the west made a broad band of pink along the sky above the tree-tops; the evening star was a perfect circle of light, a hoop of gold in the heavens. We whirled and reeled, and reeled and whirled. I was willing to give the malicious beast butt and line and all, if he would only go the other way for a change.

When I came to myself, Luke was gaffing the trout at the boatside. After we had got him in, and dressed him, he weighed three-quarters of a pound. Fish always lose by being "got in and dressed." It is best to weigh them while they are in the water. The only really large one I ever caught got away with my leader when I first struck him. He weighed ten pounds.

The Villager and the Snake

GEORGE THOMAS LANIGAN

George Thomas Lanigan, author of the "*World's* Fables," was born at St. Charles, P. Q., Canada, December 10, 1846. He was educated at the High School, Montreal, Canada, and was upon the editorial staff of the *New York World* from 1874 until 1883. In 1884 he joined the staff of the *Philadelphia Record*, and he was connected with that journal at the time of his death, which occurred at Philadelphia, February 5, 1886.

A Villager, one frosty day, found under a Hedge a Snake almost dead with cold. Moved with compassion, and having heard that Snake Oil was good for the Rheumatiz, he took it home and placed it on the Hearth, where it shortly began to wake and crawl. Meanwhile, the Villager having gone out to keep an Engagement with a Man 'round the Corner, the Villager's Son (who had not drawn a sober Breath for a Week) entered, and, beholding the Serpent unfolding its plain, unvarnished Tail, with the cry, "I've got 'em again!" fled to the office of the nearest Justice of the Peace, swore off, and became an Apostle of Temperance at $700 a week. The beneficient Snake next bit the Villager's Mother-in-law so severely that Death soon ended her sufferings—and his; then silently stole away, leaving the Villager deeply and doubly in its Debt.

Moral—A Virtuous Action is not always its only Reward. A Snake in the Grass is Worth two in the Boot.

How We Astonished the

Rivermouthians

THOMAS BAILEY ALDRICH

Thomas Bailey Aldrich, born at Portsmouth, N.H., November 11, 1836, is well known as poet, novelist, essayist and editor. His first writings were contributed to the local press, and early in life he achieved immediate and wide recognition through various New York journals, and through the successive volumes of verse, which have followed one another at intervals of a few years since the publication of the first in 1854. He was connected editorially with the New York *Evening Mirror*, the *Home Journal*, and the *Saturday Press* in New York; in 1866 he was invited by Messrs. Ticknor & Fields to take charge of their new publication, *Every Saturday*, and he has ever since resided in Boston. In 1881 he succeeded to the editorship of *The Atlantic Monthly*. One of Mr. Aldrich's stories has been translated into French, German, Italian, Spanish, Danish and Magyar, and all his prose books have enjoyed European popularity, two of his works having appeared serially in the *Revue des Deux Mondes*. His peculiar vein of humor prevails notably in the volumes, "Marjorie Daw and Other People," and in the "Story of a Bad Boy," but its flavor is felt in nearly every page of prose that he has written.

Sailor Ben's arrival partly drove the New Orleans project from my brain. Besides, there was just then a certain movement on foot by the Centipede Club which helped to engross my attention.

Pepper Whitcomb took the Captain's veto philosophically, observing that he thought from the first the governor wouldn't let me go. I don't think Pepper was quite honest in that.

But to the subject in hand.

Among the few changes that had taken place in Rivermouth during the past twenty years, there is one which I regret. I lament the removal of all those varnished iron cannon which used to do duty as posts at the corners of streets leading from the river. They were quaintly ornamental, each set upon end with a solid shot soldered into its mouth, and gave to that part of the town a picturesqueness very poorly atoned for by the conventional wooden stakes that have deposed them.

These guns ("old sogers," the boys called them) had their story, like everything else in Rivermouth. When that everlasting last war—the war of 1812, I mean—came to an end, all the brigs, schooners and barks fitted out at this port as privateers were as eager to get rid of their useless twelve-pounders and swivels as they had previously been to obtain them. Many of the pieces had cost large sums, and now they were little better than so much crude iron—not so good, in fact, for they were clumsy things to break up and melt over. The Government didn't want them; private citizen didn't want them; they were a drug in the market.

But there was one man, ridiculous beyond his generation, who got it into his head that a fortune was to be made out of these same guns. To buy them all, to hold on to them until war was declared again (as he had no doubt it would be in a few months) and then sell out at fabulous prices, this was the daring idea that addled the pate of Silas Trefethen, "Dealer in E. & W. I. Goods and Groceries," as the faded sign over his shop-door informed the public.

Silas went shrewdly to work, buying up every old cannon he could lay hands on. His backyard was soon crowded with broken-down gun-carriages, and his barn with guns, like an arsenal. When Silas's purpose got wind, it was astonishing how valuable that thing became which just now was worth nothing at all.

"Ha, ha!" thought Silas; "somebody else is tryin' tu git control of the market. But I guess I've got the start of *him.*"

So he went on buying and buying, oftentimes paying double the original price of the article. People in the neighboring towns collected all the worthless ordnance they could find, and sent it by the cart-load to Rivermouth.

When his barn was full, Silas began piling the rubbish in his cellar, then in his parlor. He mortgaged the stock of his grocery-store, mort-gaged his house, his barn, his horse, and would have mortgaged him-self, if anyone would have taken him as security, in order to carry on the grand speculation. He was a ruined man, and as happy as a lark.

Surely poor Silas was cracked, like the majority of his own cannon. More or less crazy he must have been always. Years before this he pur-chased an elegant rosewood coffin, and kept it in one of the spare rooms of his residence. He even had his name engraved on the silver-plate, leaving a blank after the word "died."

The blank was filled up in due time, and well it was for Silas that he secured so stylish a coffin in his opulent days, for when he died his worldly wealth would not have bought him a pine box, to say nothing of rosewood. He never gave up expecting a war with Great Britain. Hopeful and radiant to the last, his dying words were, *England—war— few days—great profits!*

It was that sweet old lady, Dame Jocelyn, who told me the story of Silas Trefethen; for these things happened long before my day. Silas died in 1817.

At Trefethen's death his unique collection came under the auction-eer's hammer. Some of the larger guns were sold to the town, and planted at the corners of divers streets; others went off to the iron-foundry; the balance, numbering twelve, were dumped down on a de-serted wharf at the foot of Anchor Lane, where, summer after summer, they rested at their ease in the grass and fungi, pelted in autumn by the rain, and annually buried by the winter snow. It is with these twelve guns that our story has to deal.

The wharf where they reposed was shut off from the street by a high fence—a silent, dreamy old wharf, covered with strange weeds and mosses. On account of its seclusion and the good fishing it af-forded, it was much frequented by us boys.

There we met many an afternoon to throw out our lines, or play leap-frog among the rusty cannon. They were famous fellows in our eyes. What a racket they had made in the heyday of their unchastened youth! What stories they might tell now, if their puffy metallic lips could only speak! Once they were lively talkers enough; but there the grim sea-dogs lay, silent and forlorn in spite of all their former growlings.

They always seemed to me like a lot of venerable disabled cars, stretched out on a lawn in front of a hospital, gazing seaward and mutely lamenting their lost youth.

But once more they were destined to lift up their dolorous voices— once more ere they keeled over and lay speechless for all time. And this is how it befell:

Jack Harris, Charley Marden, Harry Blake and myself were fishing off the wharf one afternoon, when a thought flashed upon me like an inspiration.

"I say, boys!" I cried, hauling in my line hand over hand. "I've got something!"

"What does it pull like, youngster?" asked Harris, looking down at the taut line and expecting to see a big perch at least.

"O, nothing in the fish way," I returned, laughing; "It's about the old guns."

"What about them?"

"I was thinking what jolly fun it would be to set one of the old sogers on his legs and serve him out a ration of gunpowder."

Up came the three lines in a jiffy. An enterprise better suited to the disposition of my companions could not have been proposed.

In a short time we had one of the smaller cannon over on its back and were busy scraping the green rust from the touch-hole. The mold had spiked the gun so effectually, that for awhile we fancied we should have to give up our attempt to resuscitate the old soger.

"A long gimlet would clear it out," said Charley Marden, "if we only had one."

I looked to see if Sailor Ben's flag was flying at the cabin door, for he always took in the colors when he went off fishing.

"When you want to know if the Admiral's aboard, jest cast an eye to the buntin', my hearties," says Sailor Ben.

Sometimes in a jocose mood he called himself the Admiral, and I am sure he deserved to be one. The Admiral's flag was flying, and I soon procured a gimlet from his carefully kept tool-chest.

Before long we had the gun in working order. A newspaper lashed to the end of a lath served as a swab to dust out the bore. Jack Harris blew through the touch-hole and pronounced all clear.

Seeing our task accomplished so easily, we turned our attention to the other guns, which lay in all sorts of postures in the rank grass. Borrowing a rope from Sailor Ben, we managed with immense labor to drag the heavy pieces into position and place a brick under each muzzle to give it the proper elevation. When we beheld them all in a row, like a regular battery, we simultaneously conceived an idea, the magnitude of which struck us dumb for a moment.

Our first intention was to load and fire a single gun. How feeble and insignificant was such a plan compared to that which now sent the light dancing into our eyes!

"What could we have been thinking of!" cried Jack Harris. "We'll give 'em a broadside, to be sure, if we die for it!"

We turned to with a will, and before nightfall had nearly half the battery overhauled and ready for service. To keep the artillery dry we stuffed wads of loose hemp into the muzzles, and fitted wooden pegs to the touch-holes.

At recess the next noon the Centipedes met in a corner of the school-yard to talk over the proposed lark. The original projectors, though they would have liked to keep the thing secret, were obliged to make a club matter of it, inasmuch as funds were required for ammunition. There had been no recent drain on the treasury, and the society could well afford to spend a few dollars in so notable an undertaking.

It was unanimously agreed that the plan should be carried out in the handsomest manner and a subscription to that end was taken on the spot. Several of the Centipedes hadn't a cent, excepting the one strung around their necks; others, however, were richer. I chanced to have a dollar, and it went into the cap quicker than lightning. When the club, in view of my munificence, voted to name the guns "Bailey's Battery" I was prouder than I have ever been since over anything.

The money thus raised, added to that already in the treasury, amounted to nine dollars—a fortune in those days; but not more than we had use for. This sum was divided into twelve parts, for it would not do for one boy to buy all the powder, nor even for us all to make our purchases at the same place. That would excite suspicion at any time, particularly at a period so remote from the Fourth of July.

There were only three stores in town licensed to sell powder; that gave each store four customers. Not to run the slightest risk of remark, one boy bought his powder on Monday, the next boy on Tuesday, and so on until the requisite quantity was in our possession. This we put into a keg, and carefully hid in a dry spot on the wharf.

Our next step was to finish cleaning the guns, which occupied two afternoons, for several of the old sogers were in a very congested state indeed. Having completed the task, we came upon a difficulty. To set off the battery by daylight was out of the question; it must be done at night; it must be done with fuses, for no doubt the neighbors would turn out after the first two or three shots, and it would not pay to be caught in the vicinity.

Who knew anything about fuses? Who could arrange it so the guns would go off one after the other, with an interval of a minute or so between?

Theoretically we knew that a minute fuse lasted a minute; double the quantity, two minutes; but practically we were at a standstill. There was but one person who could help us in this extremity—Sailor Ben. To me was assigned the duty of obtaining what information I could from the ex-gunner, it being left to my discretion whether or not to intrust him with our secret.

So one evening I dropped into the cabin, and artfully turned the conversation to fuses in general, and then to particular fuses, but without getting much out of the old boy, who was busy making a twine hammock. Finally, I was forced to divulge the whole plot.

The Admiral had a sailor's love for a joke, and entered at once and heartily into our scheme. He volunteered to prepare the fuses himself, and I left the labor in his hands, having bound him by several extraordinary oaths—such as "Hope-I-may-die," and "Shiver-my-timbers"—not to betray us, come what would.

This was Monday evening. On Wednesday the fuses were ready. That night we were to unmuzzle Bailey's Battery. Mr. Grimshaw saw that something was wrong somewhere, for we were restless and absent-minded in the classes, and the best of us came to grief before the morning session was over. When Mr. Grimshaw announced "Guy Fawkes" as the subject of our next composition, you might have knocked down the Mystic Twelve with a feather.

The coincidence was certainly curious, but when a man has committed, or is about to commit, an offense, a hundred trifles, which would pass unnoticed at another time, seem to point at him with convicting fingers. No doubt Guy Fawkes himself received many a start after he had got his wicked kegs of gunpowder neatly piled up under the House of Lords.

Wednesday, as I have mentioned, was a half-holiday, and the Centipedes assembled in my barn to decide on the final arrangements. These were as simple as could be. As the fuses were connected, it needed but one person to fire the train. Hereupon arose a discussion as to who was the proper person. Some argued that I ought to apply the match, the battery being christened after me, and the main idea, moreover, being mine. Others advocated the claim of Phil Adams, as the oldest boy. At last we drew lots for the post of honor.

Twelve slips of folded paper, upon one of which was written "Thou art the man," were placed in a quart measure, and thoroughly shaken;

then each member stepped up and lifted out his destiny. At a given signal we opened our billets. "Thou art the man," said the slip of paper trembling in my fingers. The sweets and anxieties of a leader were mine the rest of the afternoon.

Directly after twilight set in Phil Adams stole down to the wharf and fixed the fuses to the guns, laying a train of powder from the principal fuse to the fence, through a chink of which I was to drop the match at midnight.

At ten o'clock Rivermouth goes to bed. At eleven o'clock Rivermouth is as quiet as a country churchyard. At twelve o'clock there is nothing left with which to compare the stillness that broods over the little seaport.

In the midst of this stillness I arose and glided out of the house like a phantom bent on an evil errand; like a phantom I flitted through the silent street, hardly drawing breath until I knelt down beside the fence at the appointed place.

Pausing a moment for my heart to stop thumping, I lighted the match and shielded it with both hands until it was well under way, and then dropped the blazing splinter on the slender thread of gunpowder.

A noiseless flash instantly followed, and all was dark again. I peeped through the crevice in the fence, and saw the main fuse spitting out sparks like a conjurer. Assured that the train had not failed, I took to my heels, fearful lest the fuse might burn more rapidly than we calculated, and cause an explosion before I could get home. This, luckily, did not happen. There's a special Providence that watches over idiots, drunken men, and boys.

I dodged the ceremony of undressing by plunging into bed, jacket, boots and all. I am not sure I took off my cap; but I know that I hardly pulled the coverlid over me, when "BOOM!" sounded the first gun of Bailey's Battery.

I lay as still as a mouse. In less than two minutes there was another burst of thunder, and then another. The third gun was a tremendous fellow, and fairly shook the house.

The town was waking up. Windows were thrown open here and there, and people called to each other across the streets, asking what that firing was for.

"BOOM!" went gun number four.

I sprung out of bed and tore off my jacket, for I heard the Captain feeling his way along the wall to my chamber. I was half undressed by the time he found the knob of the door.

"I say, sir," I cried, "do you hear those guns?"

"Not being deaf, I do," said the Captain, a little tartly—any reflection on his hearing always nettled him—"but what on earth they are for I can't conceive. You had better get up and dress yourself."

"I'm nearly dressed, sir."

"BOOM! BOOM!"—two of the guns had gone off together.

The door of Miss Abigail's bedroom opened hastily, and that pink of maidenly propriety stepped out into the hall in her nightgown—the only indecorous thing I ever knew her to do. She held a lighted candle in her hand, and looked like a very aged *Lady Macbeth*.

"Oh, Dan'el, this is dreadful! What do you suppose it means?"

"I really can't suppose," said the Captain, rubbing his ear; "but I guess it's over now."

"BOOM!" said Bailey's Battery.

Rivermouth was wide awake now, and half the male population were in the streets, running different ways, for the firing seemed to proceed from opposite points of the town. Everybody waylaid everybody else with questions; but as no one knew what was the occasion of the tumult, people who were not usually nervous began to be oppressed by the mystery.

Some thought the town was being bombarded; some thought the world was coming to an end, as the pious and ingenious Mr. Miller had predicted it would; but those who couldn't form any theory whatever were the most perplexed.

In the mean while Bailey's Battery bellowed away at regular intervals. The greatest confusion reigned everywhere by this time. People with lanterns rushed hither and thither. The town-watch had turned out to a man, and marched off, in admirable order, in the wrong direction. Discovering their mistake, they retraced their steps, and got down to the wharf just as the last cannon belched forth its lightning.

A dense cloud of sulphurous smoke floated over Anchor Lane, obscuring the starlight. Two or three hundred people, in various stages of excitement, crowded about the upper end of the wharf, not liking to advance farther until they were satisfied that the explosions were over. A board was here and there blown from the fence, and through the openings thus afforded a few of the more daring spirits at length ventured to crawl.

The cause of the racket soon transpired. A suspicion that they had been sold gradually dawned on the Rivermouthians. Many were exceedingly indignant, and declared that no penalty was severe enough for those concerned in such a prank; others—and these were the very people who had been terrified nearly out of their wits—had the assurance to laugh, saying that they knew all along it was only a trick.

The town-watch boldly took possession of the ground, and the crowd began to disperse. Knots of gossips lingered here and there near the place, indulging in vain surmises as to who the invisible gunners could be.

There was no more noise that night, but many a timid person lay awake, expecting a renewal of the mysterious cannonading. The Oldest Inhabitant refused to go to bed on any terms, but persisted in sitting up in a rocking-chair, with his hat and mittens on, until daybreak.

I thought I should never get to sleep. The moment I drifted off in a doze I fell to laughing, and woke myself up. But towards morning slumber overtook me, and I had a series of disagreeable dreams, in one of which I was waited upon by the ghost of Silas Trefethen with an exorbitant bill for the use of his guns. In another, I was dragged before a court-martial, and sentenced by Sailor Ben, in a frizzled wig and three-cornered cocked hat, to be shot to death by Bailey's Battery—a sentence which Sailor Ben was about to execute with his own hand, when I suddenly opened my eyes and found the sunshine lying pleasantly across my face. I tell you I was glad!

That unaccountable fascination which leads the guilty to hover about the spot where his crime was committed, drew me down to the wharf as soon as I was dressed. Phil Adams, Jack Harris and others of the conspirators were already there, examining with a mingled feeling of curiosity and apprehension the havoc accomplished by the battery.

The fence was badly shattered, and the ground ploughed up for several yards round the place where the guns formerly lay—formerly lay, for now they were scattered every which way. There was scarcely a gun that hadn't burst. Here was one ripped open from muzzle to breech, and there was another with its mouth blown into the shape of a trumpet. Three of the guns had disappeared bodily, but on looking over the edge of the wharf we saw them standing on end in the tide-mud. They had popped overboard in their excitement.

"I tell you what, fellows," whispered Phil Adams, "It is lucky we didn't try to touch 'em off with punk. They'd have blown us all to flinders."

The destruction of Bailey's Battery was not, unfortunately, the only catastrophe. A fragment of one of the cannon had carried away the chimney of Sailor Ben's cabin. He was very mad at first, but having prepared the fuse himself, he didn't dare complain openly.

"I'd have taken a reef in the blessed stove-pipe," said the Admiral, gazing ruefully at the smashed chimney, "if I had known as how the flag-ship was agoin' to be under fire."

The next day he rigged out an iron funnel, which, being in sections, could be detached and taken in at a moment's notice. On the whole, I think he was resigned to the demolition of his brick chimney. The stove-pipe was a great deal more shipshape.

The town was not so easily appeased. The selectmen determined to make an example of the guilty parties, and offered a reward for their arrest, holding out a promise of pardon to any one of the offenders who would furnish information against the rest. But there were no faint hearts among the Centipedes. Suspicion rested for a while on several persons—on the soldiers at the fort; on a crazy fellow, known about town as "Bottle-Nose;" and at last on Sailor Ben.

"Shiver my timbers!" cried the deeply injured individual, "Do you suppose, sir, as I have lived to sixty years, an' aint got no more sense than to go for to blaze away at my own upper riggin'? It doesn't stand to reason."

It certainly did not seem probable that Mr. Watson would maliciously knock over his own chimney, and Lawyer Hackett, who had the case in hand, bowed himself out of the Admiral's cabin, convinced that the right man had not been discovered.

People living by the sea are always more or less superstitious. Stories of spectre ships and mysterious beacons, that lure vessels out of their course and wreck them on unknown reefs, were among the stock legends of Rivermouth; and not a few people in the town were ready to attribute the firing of those guns to some supernatural agency. The Oldest Inhabitant remembered that when he was a boy a dim-looking sort of schooner hove to in the offing one foggy afternoon, fired off a single gun, that didn't make any report, and then crumbled to nothing, spar, mast and hull, like a piece of burnt paper.

The authorities, however, were of the opinion that human hands had something to do with the explosion, and they resorted to deep-laid stratagems to get hold of the said hands. One of their traps came very near catching us. They artfully caused an old brass field-piece to be left on a wharf near the scene of our late operations. Nothing in the world but the lack of money to buy powder saved us from falling into the clutches of the two watchmen, who lay secreted for a week in a neighboring sail-loft.

It was many a day before the midnight bombardment ceased to be the town-talk. The trick was so audacious, and on so grand a scale, that nobody thought for an instant of connecting us lads with it. Suspicion, at length, grew weary of lighting on the wrong person, and as conjecture—like the physicians in the epitaph—was in vain, the River-mouthians gave up the idea of finding out who had astonished them.

They never did find out, and never will, unless they read this veracious history. If the selectmen are still disposed to punish the malefactors, I can supply Lawyer Hackett with evidence enough to convict Pepper Whitcomb, Phil Adams, Charley Marden and the other honorable members of the Centipede Club. But, really, I don't think it would pay now.

THE LEGEND OF MIMIR

ROBERT JONES BURDETTE

Robert Jones Burdette was born at Greenesborough, Pa., July 30, 1844. His family removed to Illinois, where he received an education in the Peoria public schools, and where he enlisted for the war in 1862. Some years after his return he became associate editor of the *Burlington Hawkeye*, with which his name is identified. He is well known as a humorous lecturer and author.

It is a beautiful legend of the Norse land. Amilias was the village blacksmith, and under the spreading chestnut treekjn, his village smithophjken stood. He the hot iron gehammered and sjhod horses for fifty cents all round please. He made tin hjelmets for the gjodds, and stove pjipe trousers for the hjeroes.

Mimir was a rival blacksmith. He didn't go in very much for defensive armor, but he was lightning on two-edged Bjswords and cut-and-slash svjcutlassssses. He made chyjeese knives for the gjodds, and he made the great Bjsvsstnsen, an Arkansaw toothpick that would make a free incision clear into the transverse semi-colon of a cast-iron Ichthyosaurus, and never turn its edge. That was the kind of a Bhjairpin Mimir said he was.

One day Amilias made an impenetrable suit of armor for a second-class gjodd, and put it on himself to test it, and boastfully inserted a card in the *Svensska Norderbjravisk jkanaheldesplvtdenskgorodovusaken*, saying that he was wearing a suit of home-made, best chilled Norway merino underwear, that would nick the unnumbered saw teeth in the pot metal cutlery of the iron-mongery over the way. That, Amilias remarked to his friend Bjohnn Bjrobinssson, was the kind of a Bdjucckk he was.

When Mimir spelled out the card next morning, he said, "Bjjj!" and went to work with a charcoal furnace, a cold anvil, and the now iso-morphic process, and in a little while he came down-street with a sjword, that glittered like a dollar-store diamond, and met Amilias down by the new opera-house. Amilias buttoned on his new Bjarmor and said:

"If you have no hereafter use for your chyjeese knife, strike."

Mimir spat on his hands, whirled his skjword above his head and fetched Amilias a swipe that seemed to miss everything except the empty air, through which it softly whistled. Amilias smiled, and said "go on," adding that it "seemed to him he felt a general sense of cold iron somewhere in the neighborhood, but he hadn't been hit."

"Shake yourself," said Mimir.

Amilias shook himself, and immediately fell into halves, the most neatly divided man that ever went beside himself.

"That's where the boiler-maker was away off in his diagnosis," said Mimir, as he went back to his shop to put up the price of cutlery 65 per cent in all lines, with an unlimited advance on special orders.

Thus do we learn that a good action is never thrown away, and that kind words and patient love will overcome the harshest natures.

Tushmaker's Toothpuller

JOHN PHŒNIX

George H. Derby, the first of the great modern humorists, who made his pseudonym of "John Phœnix" a household word, was born in Norfolk County, Mass., in 1824, of an old Salem family. He was graduated at West Point (where his peculiar gift frequently showed itself) in 1846, and he saw active service as Captain of Engineers in the Mexican War. He was wounded at Cerro Gordo, and at the conclusion of the war he was stationed in California. It was here that he published (first in the San Diego *Herald*) the humorous pieces which won him immediate celebrity throughout the country.

He was sunstruck while building lighthouses on the Florida coast; softening of the brain ensued, and he died in an insane asylum at New York in 1861.

Dr. Tushmaker was never regularly bred as a physician or surgeon, but he possessed naturally a strong mechanical genius and a fine appetite; and finding his teeth of great service in gratifying the latter propensity, he concluded that he could do more good in the world, and create more real happiness therein, by putting the teeth of its inhabitants in good order, than in any other way; so Tushmaker became a dentist. He was the man that first invented the method of placing small cogwheels in the back teeth for the more perfect mastication of food, and he claimed to be the original discoverer of that method of filling cavities with a kind of putty, which, becoming hard directly, causes the tooth to ache so grievously that it has to be pulled, thereby giving the dentist two successive fees for the same job. Tushmaker was one day seated in his office, in the city of Boston, Massachusetts, when a stout old fellow, named Byles, presented himself to have a back tooth drawn. The dentist seated his patient in the chair of torture, and, opening his mouth, discovered there an enormous tooth, on the right hand side, about as large, as he afterwards expressed it, "as a small Polyglot Bible." I shall have trouble with this tooth, thought Tushmaker, but he clapped on his heaviest forceps, and pulled. It didn't come. Then he tried the turn-screw, exerting his utmost strength, but the tooth wouldn't stir. "Go away from here," said Tushmaker to

Byles, "and return in a week, and I'll draw that tooth for you, or know the reason why." Byles got up, clapped a handkerchief to his jaw, and put forth. Then the dentist went to work, and in three days he invented an instrument which he was confident would pull anything. It was a combination of the lever, pully, wheel and axle, inclined plane, wedge and screw. The castings were made, and the machine put up in the office, over an iron chair rendered perfectly stationary by iron rods going down into the foundations of the granite building. In a week old Byles returned; he was clamped into the iron chair, the forceps connected with the machine attached firmly to the tooth, and Tushmaker, stationing himself in the rear, took hold of a lever four feet in length. He turned it slightly. Old Byles gave a groan and lifted his right leg. Another turn; another groan, and up went the leg again. "What do you raise your leg for?" asked the doctor. "I can't help it," said the patient. "Well," rejoined Tushmaker, "that tooth is bound to come out now."

He turned the lever clear round with a sudden jerk, and snapped old Byles's head clean and clear from his shoulders, leaving a space of four inches between the severed parts! They had a *post-mortem* examination—the roots of the tooth were found extending down the right side, through the right leg, and turning up in two prongs under the sole of the right foot! "No wonder," said Tushmaker, "he raised his right leg." The jury thought so too, but they found the roots much decayed; and five surgeons swearing that mortification would have ensued in a few months, Tushmaker was cleared on a verdict of "justifiable homicide." He was a little shy of that instrument for some time afterward; but one day an old lady, feeble and flaccid, came in to have a tooth drawn, and thinking it would come out very easy, Tushmaker concluded, just by way of variety, to try the machine. He did so, and at the first turn drew the old lady's skeleton completely and entirely from her body, leaving her a mass of quivering jelly in her chair! Tushmaker took her home in a pillowcase. She lived seven years after that, and they called her the "India-Rubber Woman." She had suffered terribly with the rheumatism, but after this occurrence, never had a pain in her bones. The dentist kept them in a glass case. After this, the machine was sold to the contractor of the Boston Custom-house, and it was found that a child of three years of age could, by a single turn of the screw, raise a stone weighing twenty-three tons. Smaller ones were made on the same principle, and sold to the keepers of hotels and restaurants. They were used for boning turkeys. There is no moral to this story whatever, and it is possible that the circumstances may have become slightly exaggerated. Of course, there can be no doubt of the truth of the main incidents.

THE TOMB OF ADAM

MARK TWAIN

The Greek Chapel is the most roomy, the richest and the showiest chapel in the Church of the Holy Sepulchre. Its altar, like that of all the Greek churches, is a lofty screen that extends clear across the chapel, and is gorgeous with gilding and pictures. The numerous lamps that hang before it are of gold and silver, and cost great sums.

But the feature of the place is a short column that rises from the middle of the marble pavement of the chapel, and marks the exact *centre of the earth*.

To satisfy himself that this spot was really the centre of the earth, a skeptic once paid well for the privilege of ascending to the dome of the church, to see if the sun gave him a shadow at noon. He came down perfectly convinced. The day was very cloudy, and the sun threw no shadows at all; but the man was satisfied that if the sun had come out and made shadows, it could not have made any for him. Proofs like these are not to be set aside by the idle tongues of cavilers. To such as are not bigoted, and are willing to be convinced, they carry a conviction that nothing can ever shake.

If even greater proofs than those I have mentioned are wanted, to satisfy the headstrong and foolish that this is the genuine centre of the earth, they are here. The greatest of them lies in the fact that from under this very column was taken the *dust from which Adam was made*. This can surely be regarded in the light of a settler. It is not likely that the original first man would have been made from an inferior quality of earth, when it was entirely convenient to get first quality from the world's centre. This will strike any reflecting mind forcibly. That Adam was formed of dirt procured in this very spot, is amply proven by the fact that in six thousand years no man has ever been able to prove that the dirt was *not* procured here whereof he was made.

It is a singular circumstance that right under the roof of this same great church, and not far away from that illustrious column, Adam himself, the father of the human race, lies buried. There is no question that he is actually buried in the grave which is pointed out as his—there can be none—because it has never yet been proven that that grave is not the grave in which he is buried.

The tomb of Adam! How touching it was, here in a land of strangers, far away from home and friends and all who cared for me, thus to discover the grave of a blood relation! True, a distant one, but still a relation. The unerring instinct of nature thrilled its recognition. The fountain of my filial affection was stirred to its profoundest depths, and I gave way to tumultuous emotion.

I leaned upon a pillar and burst into tears. I deem it no shame to have wept over the grave of my poor dead relative. Let him who would sneer at my emotion close this volume here, for he will find little to his taste in my journeyings through Holy Land. Noble old man—he did not live to see me—he did not live to see his child. And I—I—alas, I did not live to see *him.* Weighed down by sorrow and disappointment, he died before I was born—six thousand brief summers before I was born. But let us try to bear it with fortitude. Let us trust that he is better off where he is. Let us take comfort in the thought that his loss is our eternal gain.

REV. CREAM CHEESE AND

THE NEW LIVERY

A Letter from Mrs. Potiphar to Miss Caroline Pettitoes

GEORGE WILLIAM CURTIS

George William Curtis was born at Providence, R. I., February 24, 1824, but his father removed to New York when the son was fifteen, and he spent the next year in a counting-house. In 1842 he became a member of the famous

Brook Farm community. Four years later he went to Europe and the East, and on his return published his two books of travel—"Nile Notes of a Howadji," and "The Howadji in Syria," shortly after followed by a book of American summer travel and sojourn, "Lotus Eating." This was originally printed in the New York *Tribune*, on which he was for a while a writer. He became editor of *Putnam's Magazine*, and lost his whole private fortune in the effort to save its creditors when it failed. Then he devoted himself to popular lecturing, and achieved almost unrivaled success. At the time of the Kansas troubles, he threw himself ardently into politics on the side of the Republican party, then forming, and he has ever since continued an active, influential and conscientious member of that organization, lending his whole strength to reform within it, and struggling to keep it to its original ideals. For twenty years his services as editor of *Harper's Weekly* have been inestimable in this direction. He has written every month the essays of the Easy Chair in *Harper's Magazine*, and he is the author of "Trumps: A Novel." "The Potiphar Papers," in which his humorous gift is chiefly shown, are a series of sketches and stories scourging the follies of New York society in 1854. "Prue and I," a book of romantic essays, is one of the loveliest books in the language.

NEW YORK, *April.*

MY DEAR CAROLINE:—Lent came so frightfully early this year, that I was very much afraid my new bonnet, *à l' Impératrice*, would not be out from Paris soon enough. But fortunately it arrived just in time, and I had the satisfaction of taking down the pride of Mrs. Crœsus, who fancied hers would be the only stylish hat in church the first Sunday. She could not keep her eyes away from me, and I sat so unmoved, and so calmly looking at the Doctor, that she was quite vexed. But, whenever she turned away, I ran my eyes over the whole congregation, and would you believe that, almost without an exception, people had their old things! However, I suppose they forgot how soon Lent was coming. As I was passing out of church, Mrs. Crœsus brushed by me.

"Ah!" said she, "good morning. Why, bless me! you've got that pretty hat I saw at Lawson's. Well, now, it's really quite pretty; Lawson has some taste left yet; what a lovely sermon the Doctor gave us. By-the-by, did you know that Mrs. Gnu has actually bought the blue velvet? It's too bad, because I wanted to cover my prayer-book with blue, and she sits so near, the effect of my book will be quite spoiled. Dear me! there she is beckoning to me: good-by, do come and see us; Tuesdays, you know. Well, Lawson really does very well."

I was so mad with the old thing, that I could not help catching her by her mantle and holding on while I whispered, loud enough for everybody to hear:

"Mrs. Crœsus, you see I have just got my bonnet from Paris. It's made after the Empress's. If you would like to have yours made over in the fashion, dear Mrs. Crœsus, I shall be so glad to lend you mine."

"No, thank you, dear," said she; "Lawson won't do for me. By-by."

And so she slipped out, and, I've no doubt, told Mrs. Gnu that she had seen my bonnet at Lawson's.

I've so many things to tell you that I hardly know where to begin. The great thing is the livery, but I want to come regularly up to that, and forget nothing by the way. I was uncertain for a long time how to have my prayer-book bound. Finally, after thinking about it a great deal, I concluded to have it done in pale blue velvet, with gold clasps, and a gold cross upon the side. To be sure, it's nothing very new. But what *is* new nowadays? Sally Shrimp has had hers done in emerald, and I know Mrs. Crœsus will have crimson for hers, and those people who sit next us in church (I wonder who they are: it's very unpleasant to sit next to people you don't know; and, positively, that girl, the dark-haired one with large eyes, carries the same muff she did last year; it's big enough for a family) have a kind of brown morocco binding. I must tell you one reason why I fixed upon the pale blue. You know that aristocratic-looking young man, in white cravat and black pantaloons and waistcoat, whom we saw at Saratoga a year ago, and who always had such a beautiful, sanctimonious look, and such small white hands; well, he is a minister, as we supposed, "an unworthy candidate, an un-profitable husband," as he calls himself in that delicious voice of his. He has been quite taken up among us. He has been asked a good deal to dinner, and there was hope of his being settled as colleague to the Doctor, only Mr. Potiphar (who can be stubborn, you know) insisted that the Rev. Cream Cheese, though a very good young man, he didn't doubt, was addicted to candlesticks. I suppose that's something awful. But could you believe anything awful of him? I asked Mr. Potiphar what he meant by saying such things.

"I mean," said he, "that he's a Puseyite, and I've no idea of being tied to the apron-strings of the Scarlet Woman."

Dear Caroline, who *is* the Scarlet Woman! Dearest, tell me, upon your honor, if you have ever heard any scandal of Mr. Potiphar.

"What is it about candlesticks?" said I to Mr. Potiphar. "Perhaps Mr. Cheese finds gas too bright for his eyes; and that's his misfortune, not his fault."

"Polly," said Mr. Potiphar—who *will* call me Polly, although it sounds so very vulgar—"please not to meddle with things you don't understand. You may have Cream Cheese to dinner as much as you choose, but I will not have him in the pulpit of my church."

The same day, Mr. Cheese happened in about lunch-time, and I asked him if his eyes were really weak.

"Not at all," said he; "why do you ask?"

Then I told him that I had heard that he was so fond of candlesticks.

Ah! Caroline, you should have seen him then. He stopped in the midst of pouring out a glass of Mr. P.'s best old port, and, holding the decanter in one hand and the glass in the other, he looked so beautifully sad, and said in that sweet low voice:

"Dear Mrs. Potiphar, the blood of the martyrs is the seed of the church." Then he filled up his glass, and drank the wine off with such a mournful, resigned air, and wiped his lips so gently with his cambric handkerchief (I saw that it was a hemstitch), that I had no voice to ask him to take a bit of the cold chicken, which he did, however, without my asking him. But when he said, in the same low voice, "A little more breast, dear Mrs. Potiphar," I was obliged to run into the drawing-room for a moment, to recover myself.

Well, after he had lunched, I told him that I wished to take his advice upon something connected with the church (for a prayer-book *is*, you know, dear), and he looked so sweetly at me, that, would you believe it, I almost wished to be a Catholic, and to confess three or four times a week, and to have him for my confessor. But it's very wicked to wish to be a Catholic, and it wasn't real much, you know: but somehow I thought so. When I asked him in what velvet he would advise me to have my prayer-book bound, he talked beautifully for about twenty minutes. I wish you could have heard him. I'm not sure that I understood much of what he said—how should I?—but it was very beautiful. Don't laugh, Carrie, but there was one thing I did understand, and which, as it came pretty often, quite helped me through: it was, "Dear Mrs. Potiphar;" you can't tell how nicely he says it. He began by telling me that it was very important to consider all the details and little things about the church. He said they were all timbales, or cymbals—

or something of that kind; and then he talked very prettily about the stole, and the violet and scarlet capes of the cardinals, and purple chasubles, and the lace edge of the Pope's little short gown; and—do you know it was very funny—but it seemed to me, somehow, as if I was talking with Portier or Florine Lefevre, except that he used such beautiful words. Well, by and by he said:

"Therefore, dear Mrs. Potiphar, as your faith is so pure and childlike, and as I observe that the light from the yellow panes usually falls across your pew, I would advise that you cymbalize your faith (wouldn't that be noisy in church?) by binding your prayer-book in pale blue; the color of skim-milk, dear Mrs. Potiphar, which is so full of pastoral associations."

Why did he emphasize the word "pastoral"? Do you wonder that I like Cream Cheese, dear Caroline, when he is so gentle and religious—and such a pretty religion, too! For he is not only well-dressed, and has such aristocratic hands and feet, in the parlor, but he is so perfectly gentlemanly in the pulpit. He never raises his voice too loud, and he has such wavy gestures. . . .

You can imagine how pleasantly Lent is passing since I see so much of him; and then it is so appropriate to Lent to be intimate with a minister. He goes with me to church a great deal; for Mr. Potiphar, of course, has no time for that, except on Sundays; and it is really delightful to see such piety. He makes the responses in the most musical manner; and when he kneels upon entering the pew, he is the admiration of the whole church. He buries his face entirely in a cloud of cambric pocket-handkerchief, with his initial embroidered at the corner; and his hair is beautifully parted down behind, which is very fortunate, as otherwise it would look so badly when only half his head showed. . . . How thankful we ought to be that we live now with so many churches, and such fine ones, and such gentlemanly ministers as Mr. Cheese. And how nicely it's arranged that, after dancing and dining for two or three months constantly, during which, of course, we can only go to church Sundays, there comes a time for stopping, when we are tired out, and for going to church every day, and (as Mr. P. says) "striking a balance;" and thinking about being good, and all those things. We don't lose a great deal, you know. It makes a variety, and we all see each other just the same, only we don't dance. . . .

I asked Mr. Cheese what he thought of balls, whether it was so very wicked to dance, and go to parties, if one only went to church twice a day on Sundays. He patted his lips a moment with his handkerchief, and then he said—and, Caroline, you can always quote the Rev. Cream Cheese as authority—

"Dear Mrs. Potiphar, it is recorded in Holy Scripture that the King danced before the Lord."

Darling, *if anything should happen*, I don't believe he would object much to your dancing.

What gossips we women are, to be sure! I meant to write you about our new livery, and I am afraid I have tired you out already. You remember, when you were here, I said that I meant to have a livery; for my sister Margaret told me that when they used to drive in Hyde Park, with the old Marquis of Mammon, it was always so delightful to hear him say,

"Ah! there is Lady Lobster's livery."

It was so aristocratic. And in countries where certain colors distinguish certain families, and are hereditary, so to say, it is convenient and pleasant to recognize a coat-of-arms, or a livery, and to know that the representative of a great and famous family is passing by.

"That's a Howard, that's a Russell, that's a Dorset, that's De Colique, that's Mount Ague," old Lord Mammon used to say as the carriages whirled by. He knew none of them personally, I believe, except De Colique, and Mount Ague, but then it was so agreeable to be able to know their liveries.

Now, why shouldn't we have the same arrangement? Why not have the Smith colors, and the Brown colors, and the Black colors, and the Potiphar colors, etc., so that the people might say, "Ah! there go the Potiphar arms."

There is one difficulty, Mr. P. says, and that is, that he found five hundred and sixty-seven Smiths in the Directory, which might lead to some confusion. But that was absurd, as I told him, because everybody would know which of the Smiths was able to keep a carriage, so that the livery would be recognized directly the moment that any of the family were seen in the carriage. Upon which he said, in his provoking way, "Why have any livery at all, then?" and he persisted in saying that no Smith was ever *the* Smith for three generations, and that he knew at least twenty, each of whom was able to set up his carriage and stand by his colors.

"But then a livery is so elegant and aristocratic," said I, "and it shows that a servant is a servant."

That last was a strong argument, and I thought that Mr. P. would have nothing to say against it; but he rattled on for some time, asking me what right I had to be aristocratic, or, in fact, any body else; went over his eternal old talk about aping foreign habits, as if we hadn't a right to adopt the good usages of all nations, and finally said that the use of liveries among us was not only a "pure peacock absurdity," as he called it, but that no genuine American would ever ask another to assume a menial badge.

"Why?" said I, "is not an American servant a servant still?"

"Most undoubtedly," he said; "and when a man is a servant, let him serve faithfully; and in this country especially, where to-morrow he may be the served, and not the servant, let him not be ashamed of serving. But, Mrs. Potiphar, I beg you to observe that a servant's livery is not, like a general's uniform, the badge of honorable service, but of menial service. Of course, a servant may be as honorable as a general, and his work quite as necessary and well done. But, for all that, it is not so respected nor coveted a situation, I believe; and, in social estimation, a man suffers by wearing a livery, as he never would if he wore none. And while in countries in which a man is proud of being a servant (as every man may well be of being a good one), and never looks to anything else, nor desires any change, a livery may be very proper to the state of society, and very agreeable to his own feelings, it is quite another thing in a society constituted upon altogether different principles, where the servant of to-day is the senator of to-morrow. Besides that, which I suppose is too fine-spun for you, livery is a remnant of a feudal state, of which we abolish every trace as fast as we can. That which is represented by livery is not consonant with our principles."

How the man runs on, when he gets going this way! I said, in answer to all this flourish, that I considered a livery very much the thing; that European families had liveries, and American families might have liveries; that there was an end of it, and I meant to have one. Besides, if it is a matter of family, I should like to know who has a better right? There was Mr. Potiphar's grandfather, to be sure, was only a skillful blacksmith and a good citizen, as Mr. P. says who brought up a family in the fear of the Lord.

How oddly he puts those things!

But *my* ancestors, as you know, are a different matter. Starr Mole, who interests himself in genealogies, and knows the family name and crest of all the English nobility, has "climbed our family tree," as Staggers says, and finds that I am lineally descended from one of those two brothers who came over in some of those old times, in some of those old ships, and settled in some of those old places somewhere. So you see, dear Caroline, if birth give any one a right to coats of arms and liveries, and all those things, I feel myself sufficiently entitled to have them.

But I don't care anything about that. The Gnus, and Crœsuses, and Silkes, and the Settem Downes have their coats of arms, and crests, and liveries, and I am not going to be behind, I tell you. Mr. P. ought to remember that a great many of these families were famous before they came to this country, and there is a kind of interest in having on your ring, for instance, the same crest that your ancestor two or three centuries ago had upon her ring. One day I was quite wrought up about the matter, and I said as much to him.

"Certainly," said he, "certainly; you are quite right. If I had Sir Philip Sidney to my ancestor, I should wear his crest upon my ring, and glory in my relationship, and I hope I should be a better man for it. I wouldn't put his arms upon my carriage, however, because that would mean nothing but ostentation. It would be merely a flourish of trumpets to say that I was his descendant, and nobody would know that, either, if my name chanced to be Boggs. In my library I might hang a copy of the family escutcheon, as a matter of interest and curiosity to myself, for I'm sure I shouldn't understand it. Do you suppose Mrs. Gnu knows what *gules argent* are? A man may be as proud of his family as he chooses, and, if he have noble ancestors, with good reason. But there is no sense in parading that pride. It is an affectation, the more foolish that it achieves nothing—no more credit at Stewart's—no more real respect in society. Besides, Polly, who were Mrs. Gnu's ancestors, or Mrs. Crœsus's, or Mrs. Settem Downe's? Good, quiet, honest and humble people, who did their work, and rest from their labor. Centuries ago, in England, some drops of blood from 'noble' veins may have mingled with the blood of their forefathers; or, even, the founder of the family name may be historically famous. What then? Is Mrs. Gnu's family ostentation less absurd? Do you understand the meaning of her crest, and coats of arms, and liveries? Do you suppose she does herself? But in forty-nine cases out of fifty, there is nothing but a similarity of name upon which to found all this flourish of aristocracy."

My dear old Pot is getting rather prosy, Carrie. So, when he had finished that long speech, during which I was looking at the lovely fashion-plates in *Harper*, I said:

"What colors do you think I'd better have?"

He looked at me with that singular expression, and went out suddenly, as if he were afraid he might say something.

He had scarcely gone before I heard:

"My dear Mrs. Potiphar, the sight of you is refreshing as Hermon's dew."

I colored a little; Mr. Cheese says such things so softly. But I said good morning, and then asked him about liveries, etc.

He raised his hand to his cravat (it was the most snowy lawn, Carrie, and tied in a splendid bow).

"Is not this a livery, dear Mrs. Potiphar?"

And then he went off into one of those pretty talks, in what Mr. P. calls "the language of artificial flowers," and wound up by quoting Scripture—"Servants, obey your masters."

That was enough for me. So I told Mr. Cheese that, as he had already assisted me in colors once, I should be most glad to have him do so again. What a time we had, to be sure, talking of colors, and cloths, and gaiters, and buttons, and knee-breeches, and waistcoats, and plush, and coats, and lace, and hatbands, and gloves, and cravats, and cords, and tassels, and hats. Oh! it was delightful. You can't fancy how heartily the Rev. Cream entered into the matter. He was quite enthusiastic, and at last he said, with so much expression, "Dear Mrs. Potiphar, why not have a *chasseur*?"

I thought it was some kind of French dish for lunch, so I said:

"I am so sorry, but we haven't any in the house."

"Oh," said he, "but you could hire one, you know."

Then I thought it must be a musical instrument—a panharmonicon, or something like that, so I said in a general way—

"I'm not very, very fond of it."

"But it would be so fine to have him standing on the back of the carriage, his plumes waving in the wind, and his lace and polished belts flashing in the sun, as you whirled down Broadway."

Of course I knew then that he was speaking of those military gentlemen who ride behind carriages, especially upon the Continent, as Margaret tells me, and who, in Paris, are very useful to keep the savages and wild-beasts at bay in the *Champs Elysées*, for you know they are intended as a guard.

But I knew Mr. P. would be firm about that, so I asked Mr. Cheese not to kindle my imagination with the *chasseur*.

We concluded finally to have only one full-sized footman, and a fat driver.

"The corpulence is essential, dear Mrs. Potiphar," said Mr. Cheese. "I have been much abroad; I have mingled, I trust, in good, which is to say, Christian society: and I must say, that few things struck me more upon my return than that the ladies who drive very handsome carriages, with footmen, etc., in livery, should permit such thin coachmen upon the box. I really believe that Mrs. Settem Downe's coachman doesn't weigh more than a hundred and thirty pounds, which is ridiculous. A lady might as well hire a footman with insufficient calves, as a coachman who weighs less than two hundred and ten. That is the minimum. Besides, I don't observe any wigs upon the coachmen. Now, if a lady set up her carriage with the family crest and fine liveries, why, I should like to know, is the wig of the coachman omitted, and his cocked hat also? It is a kind of shabby, half-ashamed way of doing things—a garbled glory. The cock-hatted, knee-breeched, pastebuckled, horse-hair-wigged coachman is one of the institutions of the aristocracy. If we don't have him complete, we somehow make ourselves ridiculous. If we do have him complete, why, then!"—

Here Mr. Cheese coughed a little, and patted his mouth with his cambric. But what he said was very true. I *should* like to come out with the wig—I mean upon the coachman; it would so put down the Settem Downes. But I'm sure old Pot wouldn't have it. He lets me do a great deal. But there is a line which I feel he won't let me pass. I mentioned my fears to Mr. Cheese.

"Well," he said, "Mr. Potiphar may be right. I remember an expression of my carnal days about 'coming it too strong,' which seems to me to be applicable just here."

After a little more talk, I determined to have red plush breeches, with a black cord at the side—white stockings—low shoes, with large buckles—a yellow waistcoat, with large buttons—lappels to the pockets—and a purple coat, very full and fine, bound with gold lace—and the hat banded with a full gold rosette. Don't you think that would look well in Hyde Park? And, darling Carrie, why shouldn't we have in Broadway what they have in Hyde Park?

When Mr. P. came in, I told him all about it. He laughed a good deal, and said, "What next?" So I am not sure he would be so very hard upon the wig. The next morning I had appointed to see the new footman, and as Mr. P. went out he turned and said to me, "Is your footman coming to-day?" "Yes," I answered.

"Well," said he, "don't forget the calves. You know that everything in the matter of livery depends upon the calves."

And he went out laughing silently to himself, with—actually, Carrie—a tear in his eye.

But it was true, wasn't it? I remember in all the books and pictures how much is said about the calves. In advertisements, etc., it is stated that none but well-developed calves need apply; at least it is so in England, and, if I have a livery, I am not going to stop half-way. My duty was very clear. When Mr. Cheese came in, I said I felt awkward in asking a servant about his calves, it sounded so queerly. But I confessed that it was necessary.

"Yes, the path of duty is not always smooth, dear Mrs. Potiphar. It is often thickly strewn with thorns," said he, as he sank back in the *fauteuil*, and put down his *petit verre* of *Marasquin*.

Just after he had gone, the new footman was announced. I assure you, although it is ridiculous, I felt quite nervous. But when he came in, I said calmly:

"Well, James, I am glad you have come."

"Please ma'am, my name is Henry," said he.

I was astonished at his taking me up so, and said, decidedly:

"James, the name of my footman is always James. You may call yourself what you please; I shall always call you James."

The idea of the man's undertaking to arrange my servants' names for me!

Well, he showed me his references, which were very good, and I was quite satisfied. But there was the terrible calf business that must be attended to. I put it off a great while, but I had to begin.

"Well, James!" and there I stopped.

"Yes, ma'am," said he.

"I wish—yes—ah!" and there I stopped again.

"Yes, ma'am," said he.

"James, I wish you had come in knee-breeches."

"Ma'am!" said he, in great surprise.

"In knee-breeches, James," repeated I.

"What be they, ma'am? What for, ma'am?" said he, a little frightened, as I thought.

"Oh! nothing, nothing; but—but—"

"Yes, ma'am," said James.

"But—but I want to see—to see—"

"What, ma'am?" said James.

"Your legs," gasped I; and the path *was* thorny enough, Carrie, I can tell you. I had a terrible time explaining to him what I meant, and all about the liveries, etc. Dear me, what a pity these things are not understood; and then we should never have this trouble about explanations. However, I couldn't make him agree to wear the livery. He said:

"I'll try to be a good servant, ma'am, but I cannot put on those things and make a fool of myself. I hope you won't insist, for I am very anxious to get a place."

Think of his dictating to me! I told him that I did not permit my servants to impose conditions upon me (that's one of Mrs. Crœsus's sayings), that I was willing to pay him good wages and treat him well, but that my James must wear my livery. He looked very sorry, said that he should like the place very much—that he was satisfied with the wages, and was sure he should please me, but he could not put on those things. We were both determined, and so parted. I think we were both sorry; for I should have to go all through the calf-business again, and he lost a good place.

However, Caroline, dear, I have my livery and my footman, and am as good as anybody. It's very splendid when I go to Stewart's to have the red plush and the purple and the white calves springing down to open the door, and to see people look and say, "I wonder who that is?" And everybody bows so nicely, and the clerks are so polite, and Mrs. Gnu is melting with envy on the other side, and Mrs. Crœsus goes about saying: "Dear little woman, that Mrs. Potiphar, but so weak! Pity, pity!" And Mrs. Settem Downe says, "Is that the Potiphar livery? Ah, yes! Mr. Potiphar's grandfather used to shoe my grandfather's horses!" (as if to be useful in the world were a disgrace—as Mr. P. says); and young Downe and Boosey and Timon Crœsus come up and stand about so gentlemanly and say, "Well, Mrs. Potiphar, are we to have no more charming parties this season?" And Boosey says, in his droll way, "Let's keep the ball a-rolling!" That young man is always ready with a witticism. Then I step out, and James throws open the door, and the young men raise their hats, and the new crowd says: "I wonder who that is!" and the plush and purple and calves spring up behind, and I drive home to dinner.

Now, Carrie, dear, isn't that nice?

CARRIE'S COMEDY

WILLIAM LIVINGSTONE ALDEN

William Livingstone Alden made his reputation as the humorous editor of the *New York Times.* He was born at Williamstown, Mass., in 1837, received a collegiate education, and then studied law. He has published some eight volumes, mostly of a humorous character.

Dr. Bartholomew, of Towanda Falls, Penn., is the proud possessor of an extremely precocious child. Miss Carrie Bartholomew is only ten years old, but, nevertheless, she is a young person of extraordinary acquirements and conspicuous culture. At the age of six she could read with great ease, and before reaching her eighth birthday she had developed a marked taste for novel-reading. About the same period she made her first attempt at authorship, and soon achieved an enviable reputation in several local nurseries, where her fairy tales were recited with immense applause. In her ninth year she wrote a novel—of which, unfortunately, no copies are now in existence—and begun an epic in six books upon "St. Bartholomew's Day"—which sanguinary event she classed among the ancestors of her family. The epic was discontinued after the completion of the second book, owing to the premature extermination of the Huguenots, but the young author lashed the Catholic party with great vigor, and denounced Charles IX. as the scarlet person mentioned in the Apocalypse. The latest effort of Miss Bartholomew was, in all respects, her crowning work. It was a drama in blank verse and in five acts, entitled "Robinson Crusoe; or the Exile of Twenty Years," and it was publicly performed in the Baptist lecture-room by a company of children drilled by the author. The proceeds of the entertainment were designed for the conversion of the heathen, and it was attended by a large and hilarious audience.

The entire work of mounting the drama fell upon the shoulders of the author. The stage was beautifully ornamented with borrowed shawls; and three fire-screens, covered with wall-paper and with tree and flower patterns, did duty as scenery. The costumes were unique and beautiful, and a piano ably played by a grown-up lady supplied the place of an orchestra. The curtain rose at the appointed time, and displayed *Crusoe* in his English home in the act of taking tea with his wife. A cradle in the corner held a young *Crusoe*—played with much dignity by Miss Bartholomew's best doll—and a wooden dog reposed on the hearth-rug. *Crusoe*, after finding fault with the amount of sugar in his tea—a touch that was recognized as wonderfully true to life—announced that he was to sail the next morning on a voyage to South America. *Mrs. Crusoe* instantly burst into tears, and remarked:

"Our wedded life has scarce begun!
But three months since you led me to the altar,
And now you leave me, friendless and forlorn!"

Crusoe, however, soon comforted his wife, and bidding her teach her surprisingly precipitate infant to revere his absent father, put on his ulster, and after a last passionate embrace, departed for South America.

The second act presented *Crusoe* in his island home, clad chiefly in seal-skin jackets, and much given to pacing the ground and soliloquizing. According to his account, he had now been on the island three years, and was beginning to feel rather lonesome. He referred in the most affectionate terms to the sole comrade of his joys and sorrows, his gentle goat—which animal, hired for the occasion, from a Towanda Falls Irishman, was conspicuously tethered in the background, and would obviously have butted *Crusoe* into remote futurity if he could have broken loose. Presently *Crusoe* heard a faint yell in the distance, and decided that it was made by a cannibal picnic party, whereupon he announced that he would go for his gun and sweep the wicked cannibals into the Gulf.

Act three was brought to an unexpected but effective climax. It opened with the entrance of a dozen assorted cannibals dragging two helpless prisoners, who were securely bound. After an effective war-dance, one of the prisoners was killed with a club, and was placed on a painted fire. Just as the chief cannibal had announced that the dinner was nearly cooked, *Crusoe's* goat, which had managed to escape from the green-room, burst upon the cannibals. Two of them were knocked over into the audience, where they wept bitterly; others were strewn over the stage, while a remnant escaped behind the scenes. The prisoner, in spite of the fact that he was dead and roasted, fled at the first onset of the goat, and the curtain was dropped amid wild applause. After the goat had been captured by some male members of the audience, and *Crusoe* himself had explained that his proposed massacre of the cannibals had been unintentionally anticipated, the stage was set for the fourth act, and the play went on.

This particular act was a magnificent proof of the author's originality. The rising of the curtain displayed *Crusoe* sitting on a grassy bank, surrounded by four children, whom he calmly alleged to be his own. Beyond vaguely alluding to them as the gift of heaven sent to cheer his lonely hours, that astonishing father did not offer to account for their origin. The author's chief object in introducing them was, however, soon disclosed. *Friday*, who presently appeared, and whose lack of any ostensible origin was doubtless due to the recent interference of the goat, was requested to sit down and undergo instruction in the West-minster Catechism. The scene that followed was closely modeled after the exercises of an ordinary Sunday-school; and *Crusoe's* four inexplic-able children sang songs to an extent that clearly proved that singing was the object of their remarkable creation. Lest this scene should appear somewhat too solemn, the author judiciously lightened it by the happy expedient of making *Friday* a negro, who constantly said, "Yes! Massa," and "Yah, yah!" and who always spoke of himself as "dis child." Altogether, the act was a delightful one, and whenever *Crusoe* alluded to his "dear children," and regretted that they had never seen their dear mamma, the audience howled with rapture.

How *Crusoe* and his interesting family escaped from the island the author omitted to mention. The fifth and last act depicted his arrival home and his final reunion with the bride of his youth. *Mrs. Crusoe* was sitting at her original tea-table, precisely as she was in the habit of doing twenty years earlier, when there was a knock at the door, and *Crusoe* entered, followed by his four children, and *Friday* carrying a large carpet-bag and a bundle of shawls. Mutually exclaiming, " 'Tis he!" and " 'Tis she!" the long-separated husband and wife rushed into each other's arms. After the first greetings were over, *Crusoe* remarking in the most elegant blank verse that though he had brought neither gold nor gems, he had nevertheless returned rich, presented in evidence thereof his four children. Whereupon that noble woman, remarking that she, too, had been wonderfully blest, brought in seven children from the next room and told them to kiss their father. After which the drama was brought to a graceful end by the singing of "Home, Sweet Home," by the entire strength of the Crusoe family.

For originality and rare dramatic genius, it is clear that this play has never been equaled by any previous American dramatist; and we may be sure Miss Carrie Bartholomew will in future look back upon it with at least as much wonder as pride.

To Correspondents

JOSH BILLINGS

Henry W. Shaw, the well-known wit and satirist, "Josh Billings," was born at Lanesborough, Mass., in 1818, of a family of politicians, his father and grandfather having both been in Congress. He went early in life to the West, where for twenty-five years he was a farmer and auctioneer. He did not begin to write for publication till he was forty-five years old. He has been one of the most popular of popular lecturers. Mr. Shaw died at Monterey, Cal., Oct. 14, 1885.

"*Benzine.*"—Men who hav a grate deal to do with hosses, seem tew demoralize faster than the hosses do.

Hosses are like dice, and kards; altho they are virteuous enuff themselves, how natural it iz tew gambol with them.

Hosses luv the society ov man, and being susceptable ov grate deceit, they will learn a man how to cheat and lie before he knows it.

I know lots ov folks who are real pius, and who are honest enuff tew work up into united estate accessors, and hav sum good-sized moral chunks left over, but when they cum tew tork hoss, they want az mutch look after az a case ov dipthery.

"*Benvolio.*"—In writing for yu an analasiss ov the frog, i must confess that i hav coppied the whole thing, "verbatus ad liberating," from the works ov a selebrated French writer on natural history, ov the 16th sentry.

The frog iz, in the fust case, a tadpole, aul boddy and tail, without cuming tew a head.

He travels in pond holes, bi the side ov the turnpike, and iz accellerated bi the acktivity ov his tail, which wriggles with uncommon limberness and vivacity. Bi and bi, pretty soon before long, in a few daze, his tail iz no more, and legs begin to emerge from the south end ov the animal; and from the north end, at the same time, may be seen a disposition tew head out.

In this cautious way the frog iz built, and then for the fust time in his life begins tew git his head abuv water.

His success iz now certain, and soon, in about five daze more, he may be seen sitting down on himself bi the side ov the pond hole, and looking at the dinner baskets ov the children on their way tew the distrikt skoolhous.

Az the children cum more nearer, with a club, or chunk ov a brickbat in his hand tew swott him with, he rares up on his behind leggs, and enters the water, head fust, without opening the door.

Thus the frog duz bizzness for a spell of time, until he gits tew be 21, and then his life iz more ramified.

Frogs hav 2 naturs, ground and water, and are az free from sin az an oyster.

I never knu a frog tew hurt ennyboddy who paid his honest dets and took the daily papers.

I don't reckoleckt now whether a frog has enny before leggs or not, and if he don't it ain't enny boddy's bizzness but the frog's.

Their hind legs are used for refreshments, but the rest ov him won't pay for eating.

A frog iz the only person who kan live in a well, and not git tired.

The Worst Man and the Stupidest Man in Turkey

SAMUEL S. COX

Samuel Sullivan Cox was born at Zanesville, O., September 30, 1824, and grew up in his native State. He entered journalistic life after graduating from Brown University, and has achieved distinction in politics as well as literature; his public services, in Congress and diplomacy, are as well-known as his books.

Several years ago the dragoman of our American Legation at Constantinople was asked to act as arbitrator in a dispute between a foreigner and an old Turkish doctor in law and theology. After several meetings with them, the dragoman concluded that the doctor was an ill-natured and unmanageable person. The latter had served for some years as cadi of the Civil Court at Smyrna. The dragoman related a story for his instruction. The story as to its place was in old Stamboul. As to its time, it does not matter much. Its moral is for every place and for all time. But it took place at the end of the sixteenth century, when the Turkish power was well established and growing. In other words, it was during the reign of Amurath III., the sixth emperor of the Ottomans, and grandson of Suleïman the Magnificent. This Sultan was not, as the sequel of the story shows, the worst of the Ottoman emperors. He was a tall, manly man, rather fat and quite pale, with a thin long beard. His face was not of a fierce aspect, like other Sultans. He was no rioter or reveler. He punished drunkards, and as for himself he indulged only in wormwood wine. His people knew that he loved justice, and although, according to an old chronicle, he caused his brothers to be strangled, "at which so tragicall a sight that he let some teares fall, as not delighting in such barbarous crueltie, but that the state and manner of his gouernment so required," still, he was, as the time was, a good prince.

But to the dragoman's story. Its moral had its uses, as the sequel reveals. This is the story, as it was told in one of the leisure hours at the Legation last summer:

"There was a man, Mustapha by name, who lived near the Golden Gate. He was well off, and when about to die, he called his son to him and said:

" 'My dear boy, I am dying. Before I go, I want to give you my last will. Here are one hundred pounds. You will give it to the worst man you can find. Here are one hundred pounds more. This you will give to the stupidest man you can discover.'

"A few days after, the father died. The son began to search for the bad man. Several men were pointed out, but he was not satisfied that they were the worst of men. Finally he hired a horse and went up to Yosgat, in Asia Minor. There the population unanimously pointed out their cadi as the worst man to be found anywhere. This information satisfied the son. He called on the cadi. He told the story of the will, and added:

" 'As I am desirous that the will of my father be accomplished, I beg you to receive these hundred pounds.'

"Said the cadi, 'How do you know that I am so bad as I am represented?'

" 'It is the testimony of the whole town,' said the son.

" 'I must tell you, young man,' said the cadi, 'that it is contrary to my principles to accept any bribe or present. If I ever receive money, it is only for a con-sid-er-a-tion. Unless I give you the counter-value of your money, I cannot accept it.'

"This reply of the cadi seemed just. It puzzled the young man. However, as he desired to fulfill his father's will, he continued to urge the cadi:

" 'Mr. Judge,' said he, 'if you sell me something, could not the will of my father be fulfilled?'

" 'Let me see,' said the cadi, looking around to find out what on earth he could sell to the youth, without destroying the spirit of the will. He reflected for a long time. Then all at once he was struck with a bright idea. Seeing that the courtyard of his house was filled with snow, about two feet deep, he said to the youth:

" 'I will sell you yonder snow. Do you accept the bargain?'

" 'Yes,' said the youth, seeing that there was nothing of value in the snow.

"The cadi then executed a regular deed, the fees of which were paid, of course, by the purchaser. The son then paid the hundred pounds for the snow.

"The boy went home; but he was not quite certain that he had strictly fulfilled the will of his father; for, after all, the cadi did not appear to him to be so very bad. Had he not decidedly refused to accept the money without a legal consideration?

"His perplexity was of short duration.

"The second day, early in the morning, the scribe of the cadi called on the youth and told him that the cadi wished to see him.

" 'Well, I will go,' said the youth.

" 'No,' said the scribe; 'I am ordered to take you there.'

"The youth resisted, and the scribe insisted. Finally the youth was compelled to submit, and went.

" 'What do you want of me, Cadi Effendi,' said the boy.

" 'Ah! you are welcome,' responded the cadi; 'I wanted you to come, because you have some snow in the courtyard which bothers me a great deal. The authorities cannot shoulder such a responsibility. Is not the deposit exposed? Can it be put under lock like other property? Besides, does it not occupy the road, to which the people have the right of easement? What follows? The result is, that your snow will be trampled or stolen, or it will melt, and then all the responsibility will rest on me. I am not prepared to assume it. I request you to carry away your snow.'

" 'But, Cadi Effendi,' said the boy, 'I do not care. Let it melt; let it be stolen; let it be trampled on; I will make no claim for its value.'

" 'Nothing of the kind,' said the cadi. 'You have no right to close the public way in that manner. Unless you take away your snow, I will confine you in prison, and make you answer for the nuisance, and for the decay of the property, which may be claimed by your heirs at some future time.'

" 'Let it be swept out,' said the youth; 'I will defray the expense.'

" 'Nonsense!' indignantly responded the cadi. 'Am I your servant? Besides, will it not take a great deal of money to have the snow swept out?'

" 'I will pay the expense, whatever it is,' said the youth.

" 'Well, it requires twenty pounds,' said the cadi.

" 'I will pay that sum,' said the youth.

"Thus the cadi squeezed out twenty pounds more from the son of the deceased.

"The youth is, however, content. He is glad to find in this cadi a man of the meanness so indispensable to the fulfillment of the will of his father.

———

"After this experience the youth goes in search of the stupid man. He must filially fulfill the second clause of the will.

"While engaged in this search for stupidity, the son limits his efforts to his own fair city of Stamboul. He is on the street leading up to the Sublime Porte. He hears a band of music. It is moving toward the Sublime Porte. He is curious to know what it all means. He walks toward the music. When at a short distance he discovers a grand procession, with a display of soldiers. He notices a comparatively old man riding a white Arabian horse. He is dressed in a magnificent uniform. His breast is covered with decorations of every size, color and description. The trappings of the horse are covered with gold embroideries. The old man is surrounded by a dozen high officials of the government of Amurath III. They, too, are dressed finely; they have recently returned from the Caucasus laden with riches, and they display their grand robes and jewels. They have gorgeously embroidered uniforms and ride splendid horses. They are followed by an immense crowd. All Galata, as well as Stamboul, is afoot to see the sight. Murmurs in three-score dialects rise on the sunny air. The son of Mustapha follows the crowd. He asks a pedestrian in a green turban, who sits by the fountain:

" 'What is the procession about?'

"He is informed that the old man is the newly appointed Grand Vizier of Amurath. The Vizier is going to take possession of his post. He is thus escorted with the usual solemnity.

"When the procession arrives at the gate of the Sublime Porte, the Grand Vizier dismounts on the foot-stone in front of the entrance, and, strange to say, there on that very foot-stone is a big tray; and on the tray, a human head freshly decapitated.

"The sight is blood-curdling. The youth is struck dumb with horror. Then, recovering his senses, he finds out the meaning of the usage. He is told that the bloody head is that of the preceding Grand Vizier, who had acted wrongfully, and was therefore beheaded.

" 'Will his successor succeed him in the tray also?' asks the youth, of a zaptieh who was standing near to police the procession.

" 'Nowadays it is difficult to escape it,' is the answer of the policeman.

"After this answer, the youth makes immediate inquiries. He discovers the 'Kiahaja' of the new Grand Vizier, for every Grand Vizier has a *factotum.* He goes to the Kiahaja and requests him to deliver to the Grand Vizier the hundred pounds which his father had willed. The Kiahaja, after inquiring the name of the youth and his whereabouts, receives the money. Later on, he takes the hundred pounds to the Grand Vizier. This high official is puzzled.

" 'Who,' he inquires, 'is the friend that left the money to me, and why?'

"He calls for the youth. The youth comes. The Grand Vizier asks him about his father. The boy replies:

" 'His name was Mustapha. He lived near the Golden Gate; but you did not know him, my lord!'

" 'But he knew me?'

" 'No, my lord, he did not.'

" 'Then why this bequest to me?

"The youth then gives the Grand Vizier the story, and adds that he could not expect to find a more stupid man or a greater idiot than the Grand Vizier; therefore, he concludes that the hundred pounds are due to that official, under his father's will.

"This puzzles the Grand Vizier, who says:

" 'How do you know that I am a stupid man? Neither you nor your father knew me.'

" 'Your acceptance of the position of Grand Vizier,' says the youth, 'in the presence of the dead head of your predecessor, speaks for itself. It needs no explanation.'

"The Grand Vizier can make no rational answer. He takes hold of his beard, strokes it, and considers for a minute.

"Then he says to the youth: 'Son of the good and wise Mustapha, will you not be my guest for to-night? To-morrow morning I must talk with you.' The boy accepts the invitation.

"In the morning the Grand Vizier calls the youth. He informs him that he is going to the palace of Amurath at the Seraglio Point. He desires the youth to accompany him. The boy objects. It is no use. The Grand Vizier compels him to go with him.

"They reach the palace. The Grand Vizier goes straightway to the Chief Eunuch, and thus addresses that beautiful Arabian:

" 'Your Highness: I am aware that His Majesty, in bestowing on me the responsible and confidential position of Grand Vizier, did me the greatest honor a man can ever expect in this world. I am grateful to him for such a rare distinction. But, Highness, here is a young man who came to see me yesterday, and spoke to me in such a wonderful way that I feel bound to tender my resignation. After my conversation with him, I feel incapable of sustaining the dignity which His Majesty deserves.'

"The Eunuch is thunderstruck. Up to that time no Grand Vizier had ever dared to resign. But the action of the Vizier seems so strange to the Eunuch, that the latter at once goes and reports it to the Sultan. The Sultan is amazed and indignant. He demands the presence of the Grand Vizier and the youth. When they appear they find that Amurath is not in one of his best moods. The Janizaries have been threatening him. His wife, sister and mother, on whom he relies for comfort in his poor health and mental distress, have in vain endeavored to placate and pacify him. His pale face grows scarlet with anger. He hotly addresses the Grand Vizier:

" 'How is it, sirrah! that you presume to dare to tender your resignation?'

" 'Your Majesty,' says the Grand Vizier, 'I know that I am doing a bold act; but it is this boy,' pointing out the simple youth, 'who compels me to do it. If your Highness wants to know the reasons, the boy will give them to you. I am sure that after hearing them you will acknowledge that, as I am considered the most stupid man in your empire, it is not becoming to your dignity to retain me as your immediate representative.'

"The boy is then called. He gives his story. The Sultan smiles. His innate sense of justice returns. He issues an iradé that henceforth no Grand Vizier shall be beheaded."

FIRST-CLASS SNAKE STORIES

BROOKLYN EAGLE

"Do you want some items about snakes?" asked an agriculturally-rural-looking gentleman of the *Eagle's* city editor the other day.

"If they are fresh and true," responded the city editor.

"Exactly," replied the farmer. "These items are both. Nobody knows 'em but me. I got a farm down on the island a piece, and there's lots of snakes on it. Near the house is a pond, about six feet deep. A week ago my little girl jumped into the pond, and would have drowned if it hadn't been for a snake. The snake seen her, went for her, and brought her ashore. The particular point about this item is the way he did it."

"How was it?" asked the city editor.

"It was a black snake, about thirty feet long, and he just coiled the middle of himself around her neck so she couldn't swallow any water, and swum ashore with his head and tail. Is that a good item?"

"First-class."

"You can spread it out, you know. After they got ashore the girl patted the snake *on the* head, and it went off pleased as Punch. Ever since then he comes to the house regular at meal-times, and she feeds him on pie. Think you can make anything out of that item?"

"Certainly. Know any more?"

"Yes. I got a baby six months old. He's a boy. We generally sit him out on the grass of a morning, and he hollers like a bull all day; at least he used to, but he don't any more. One morning we noticed he wasn't hollering, and wondered what was up. When we looked, there was a rattlesnake coiled up in front of him scanning his features. The boy was grinning and the snake was grinning. Bimeby the snake turned his tail to the baby and backed his rattle right into the baby's fist."

"What did the baby do?"

"Why, he just rattled that tail so you could hear it three-quarters of a mile, and the snake lay there and grinned. Every morning we found the snake there, until one day a bigger snake came, and the baby played with his rattle just the same till the first snake came back. He looked thin, and I reckon he had been sick and sent the other to take his place. Will that do for an item?"

"Immensely," replied the city editor.

"You can fill in about the confidence of childhood and all that, and you might say something about the blue-eyed cherub. His name is Isaac. Put that in to please my wife."

"I'll do it. Any more snake items?"

"Lemme see. You've heard of hoop-snakes?"

"Yes, often."

"Just so. Not long ago we heard a fearful row in our cellar one night. It sounded like a rock-blast, and then there was a hiss and things was quiet. When I looked in the morning the cider barrel had busted. But we didn't lose much cider."

"How did you save it?"

"It seems that the staves had busted out, but before they could get away, four hoop-snakes coiled around the barrel and tightened it up and held it together until we drew the cider off in bottles. That's the way we found 'em, and we've kept 'em around the house ever since. We're training 'em for shawl-straps now. Does that strike you favorably for an item?"

"Enormously!" responded the city editor.

"You can fix it up so as to show how quick they was to get there before the staves were blown off. You can work in the details."

"Of course. I'll attend to that. Do you think of any more?"

"Ain't you got enough? Lemme think. O yes! One Sunday me and my wife was going to church, and she dropped her garter somewhere. She told me about it, and I noticed a little striped snake running alongside and listening to her. Bimeby he made a spring and just wound himself around her stocking, or tried to, but he didn't fetch it."

"Why not?"

"He wasn't quite long enough. He jumped down and shook his head and started off. We hadn't gone more'n a quarter of a mile, when we see him coming out of the woods just ahead of us. He was awful hot and tired, and he had another snake with him twice as big as he was. They looked at my wife a minute and said something to each other, and then the big snake went right to the place where the garter belonged. He wrapped right around it, put his tail in his mouth and went to sleep. We got him yet. We use him to hold the stove-pipe together when we put the stove up. Is that any use as an item?"

"Certainly," said the city editor.

"You can say something about the first snake's eye for distances and intellectuality, when he found he wouldn't go 'round. You know how to do that better than me."

"I'll give him the credit he deserves. Can you tell us any more?"

"I don't call any to mind just at present. My wife knows a lot of snake items, but I forget 'em. By the way, though, I've got a regular living curiosity down at my place. One day my oldest boy was sitting on the back stoop doing his sums, and he couldn't get 'em right. He felt something against his face, and there was a little snake coiled up on his shoulder and looking at the slate. In four minutes he had done all them sums. We've tamed him so he keeps all our accounts, and he is the lighteningest cuss at figures you ever seen. He'll run up a column eight feet long in three seconds. I wouldn't take a reaper for him."

"What kind of a snake is he?" inquired the editor, curiously.

"The neighbors call him an adder."

"O, yes, yes!" said the city editor, a little disconcerted. "I've heard of the species. When did all these things happen?"

"Along in the fore part of the spring, but I didn't say anything about 'em, 'cause it wasn't the season for snake items. This is about the time for that sort of thing, isn't it?"

"Yes," chipped in the exchange editor, "you couldn't have picked out a better time for snake stories."

His First Day at Editing

EUGENE FIELD

Eugene Field, journalist, was born in Boston, Mass., in 1850. He received a classical education, settled in Chicago, and engaged in journalism on the *Chicago News*. He has published "Culture's Garland" (Ticknor & Co, Boston, Mass., 1887), several fairy tales, poems, and a number of dramatic criticisms, including one on Modjeska that is widely and favorably known.

Yesterday morning, Mr. Horace A. Hurlbut took formal possession of *The Chicago Times*, in compliance with the mandate of justice making him receiver of that institution. Bright and early he was at his post in *The Times* building; and the expression that coursed over his mobile features, as he lolled back in the editorial chair and abandoned himself to pleasing reflections, was an expression of conscious pride and ineffable satisfaction.

"I have now attained the summit and the goal of earthly ambition," quoth Mr. Hurlbut to himself. "Embarking in the drug-business at an early age, I have progressed through the intermediate spheres of real estate, brokerage and money-lending, until finally I have reached the top round of the ladder of fame, and am now the head of the greatest daily newspaper on the American continent. I expect and intend to prove myself equal to the demands which will be made upon me in this new capacity. I have my own notions about journalism— they differ somewhat from the conventional notions that prevail, but that is neither here nor there; for, as the dictator of this great newspaper, I shall have no difficulty in putting my theories into practice."

"Here's the mornin' mail, major," said the office-boy, laying innumerable packages of letters and circulars on the table before Mr. Hurlbut.

"Why do you call me major?" inquired Mr. Hurlbut, with an amused twinkle in his eyes.

"Oh! we always call the editors majors," replied the office-boy. "Major Dennett made that a rule long time ago."

"It is not a bad idea," said Major Hurlbut, "for it gives one a dignity and prestige which can never maintain among untitled civilians. So this is the morning mail, is it?"

Major Hurlbut picked up one of the letters, scrutinized the superscription, heaved a deep sigh, picked up several other letters, blushed, frowned, and appeared much embarrassed.

"Can you tell me," he asked, "whether there are any reporters about this office by the names, or aliases, or nom de plume, or pseudonym of 'M33,' and 'X14,' or 'S5,' or 'G38'? I find numerous letters directed in this wise, and I mistrust that some unseemly work is being done under cover of these bogus appellations. I will make bold to examine one of these letters."

So Major Hurlbut tore open one of the envelopes, and read as follows:

"G38, *Times* Office: I have a nice, quiet, furnished room. Call after eight o'clock P.M., at No. 1143 Elston Road."

"As I suspected," cried Major Hurlbut, with a profound groan. "Under these strange pseudonyms, the reporters of this paper are engaging in a carnival of vice! But the saturnalia must end at once. From this moment *The Times* becomes a moral institution. I shall ascertain the names of these reporters, and have them peremptorily discharged!"

"H'yar's a package for you, sah," said the dusky porter, Martin Lewis, entering, and placing a small bundle before Major Hurlbut.

"Ah, yes! I see," quoth the major, "they are the new cards I ordered last Saturday. We editors have to have cards, so as to let people know we are editors."

With this philosophic observation, the major opened the bundle, and disclosed several hundred neat pasteboard cards, printed in red and black as follows:

HORACE A. HURLBUT,

Receiver and Editor, "Chicago Times."

Real Estate A Specialty.
Drug Orders Promptly Filled.

Loans Negotiated without Publicity.

"They are very handsome," said Major Hurlbut, "but I am sorry I did not have the title of Major prefixed to my name. However, I will take that precaution with the next lot I have printed."

"Majah Dennett would like to speak with you, sah," said Martin, the porter.

"Although I am very busy with this mail, you may show him in," remarked Major Hurlbut.

Major Dennett pigeon-toed his way into the new editor's presence, and was loftily waved to a chair, in which he dropped, and sat with his toes turned in. Major Hurlbut heaved a weary sigh, ran his fingers through his hair, and regarded his visitor with a condescending stare.

"This is a busy hour with us editors," said Major Hurlbut, "therefore I hope you will state your business as succinctly as possible."

"I merely called to receive orders," explained Major Dennett, with an astonished look.

"Orders for what?" cried Major Hurlbut. "Perhaps you forget, sir, that I am out of the drug business, and am an editor. Permit me, sir, to hand you one of my professional cards."

"You mistake me, sir," replied Major Dennett; "I am connected with this paper, and have been managing editor for years."

Major Hurlbut's manner changed instantly. His cold reserve melted at once, and he became docile as a sucking-dove.

"My dear Major," he exclaimed cordially, "I am overjoyed to meet you. Draw your chair closer, and let us converse together upon matters which concern us both. Each of us has the interests of this great paper at heart; but I, as the head of the institution, have a fearful responsibility resting upon my shoulders. It behooves you to assist me; and, as the first and most important step, I must beg of you to inform me what is expected of me as an editor. I am willing and anxious to edit, but how can I?"

Major Dennett undertook to explain a few of the duties which would fall upon the editor's shoulders, and would have continued talking all day, had not the venerable Major Andre Matteson been ushered into the room, thereby interrupting the conversation. Upon being formally introduced to the new editor, Major Matteson inquired what the policy of *The Times* would be henceforward touching the tariff, the civil service, the war in the Soudan, and the doctrine of the transmigration of souls.

"I have not decided fully what the policy of the paper will be in these minor matters," quoth Major Hurlbut, "except that we shall favor the abolition of the tariff on quinine, cochineal, and other drugs and dyestuffs. I have made up my mind, however, to advocate the opening of a boulevard in Fleabottom subdivision; and, as you are one of the editorial writers, Major Matteson, I would like to have you compose a piece about the folly of extending the Thirtieth Street sewer through the Bosbyshell subdivision. And you may give the firm of Brown, Jones & Co. a raking over, for they have seriously interfered with the sale of my lots out in that part of the city."

Major George McConnell and Major Guy Magee filed into the

room at this juncture, and were formally presented to editor Hurlbut, who looked impressive, and received them with a dignity that would have done credit to a pagan court.

"I had hoped to be in a position to boom the city department of the paper," said Major Magee, "but I find that three of the reporters are sick with headache to-day."

"Sick? What appears to be the matter?" asked the editor.

"I did'nt ask them," replied Major Magee; "but they said they had headaches."

"They should try bromide of potassium, tincture of valerian, and aromatic spirits of ammonia," observed Major Hurlbut. "By the way, whenever any of our editors or reporters get sick, they should come to me; for I can give them prescriptions that will fix them up in less than no time."

"I presume the policy of the paper touching the theatres will remain unchanged?" inquired Major McConnell.

"That reminds me," said Major Hurlbut: "who gets the show-tickets?"

"Well, I have attended to that detail heretofore," replied Major McConnell.

"We get as many as we want, don't we?" asked Major Hurlbut.

"Certainly," said Major McConnell.

"Well, then, we must give the shows good notices," said the editor; "and, by the way, I would like to have you leave six tickets with me every morning; they will come in mighty handy, you know, among friends. Do we get railroad-passes too?

"Yes, all we want," said Major Dennett.

"I am glad I am an editor," said Major Hurlbut, softly but feelingly. The foreman came in.

"Shall we set it in nonpareil to-night?" he asked.

"Eh?" ejaculated Editor Hurlbut.

"Does nonpareil go?" repeated the foreman.

"What has he been doing?" inquired Editor Hurlbut.

"The minion is so bad that we ought to put the paper in nonpareil," exclaimed the foreman.

"It must be understood," thundered Major Hurlbut, "that no bad minions will be tolerated on the premises. If there is any minion here who is dissatisfied, let him quit at once."

"Then I am to fire the minion?" asked the foreman.

"No," said Major Hurlbut, "do not fire him, for that would constitute arson; discharge him, but use no violence."

We deeply regret that this astute mandate was followed by an interchange of sundry smiles, nods and winks between the foreman and the members of the editorial staff, which, however, Major Hurlbut did not see, or he most assuredly would have reproved this unseemly and *malapropos* levity.

And so they talked and talked. And each moment Major Hurlbut became more and more impressed with the importance and solemnity of the new dignity he had attained, and each moment he became more and more impressive in his mien and conversation. And each moment, too, he silently and devoutly thanked High Heaven that in its goodness and mercy it had called him to the ennobling profession of journalism.

ABELARD AND HELOISE

MARK TWAIN

Among the thousands and thousands of tombs in Père la Chaise, there is one that no man, no woman, no youth of either sex ever passes by without stopping to examine. Every visitor has a sort of indistinct idea of the history of its dead, and comprehends that homage is due there, but not one in twenty thousand clearly remembers the story of that tomb and its romantic occupants. This is the grave of Abelard and Heloise—a grave which has been more revered, more widely known, more written and sung about and wept over for seven hundred years than any other in Christendom, save only that of the Saviour. All visitors linger pensively about it; all young people capture and carry away keepsakes and mementoes of it; all Parisian youths and maidens who are disappointed in love come there to bail out when they are full of tears; yea, many stricken lovers make pilgrimages to this shrine from distant provinces to weep and wail and "grit" their teeth over their heavy sorrows, and to purchase the sympathies of the chastened spirits of that tomb with offerings of immortelles and budding flowers.

Go when you will, you find somebody snuffling over that tomb. Go when you will, you find it furnished with those bouquets and immortelles. Go when you will, you find a gravel-train from Marseilles arriving to supply the deficiencies caused by memento-cabbaging vandals whose affections have miscarried.

Yet who really knows the story of Abelard and Heloise? Precious few people. The names are perfectly familiar to everybody, and that is about all. With infinite pains I have acquired a knowledge of that history, and I propose to narrate it here, partly for the honest information of the public, and partly to show that public that they have been wasting a good deal of marketable sentiment very unnecessarily.

STORY OF ABELARD AND HELOISE

Heloise was born seven hundred and sixty-six years ago. She may have had parents. There is no telling. She lived with her uncle Fulbert, a canon of the Cathedral of Paris. I do not know what a canon of a cathedral is, but that is what he was. He was nothing more than a sort of mountain howitzer, likely; because they had no heavy artillery in those days. Suffice it, then, that Heloise lived with her uncle, the howitzer, and was happy. She spent the most of her childhood in the convent of Argenteuil. (Never heard of Argenteuil before, but suppose there was really such a place.) She then returned to her uncle, the old gun—or son of a gun, as the case may be—and he taught her to write and speak Latin, which was the language of literature and polite society at that period.

Just at this time Pierre Abelard, who had already made himself widely famous as a rhetorician, came to found a school of rhetoric in Paris. The originality of his principles, his eloquence, and his great physical strength and beauty created a profound sensation. He saw Heloise, and was captivated by her blooming youth, her beauty and her charming disposition. He wrote to her; she answered. He wrote again; she answered again. He was now in love. He longed to know her—to speak to her face to face.

His school was near Fulbert's house. He asked Fulbert to allow him to call. The good old swivel saw here a rare opportunity; his niece, whom he so much loved, would absorb knowledge from this man, and it would not cost him a cent. Such was Fulbert—penurious.

Fulbert's first name is not mentioned by any author, which is unfortunate. However, George W. Fulbert will answer for him as well as any other. We will let him go at that. He asked Abelard to teach her.

Abelard was glad enough of the opportunity. He came often and stayed long. A letter of his shows in its very first sentence that he came under that friendly roof like a cold-hearted villain, as he was, with the deliberate intention of debauching a confiding, innocent girl. This is the letter:

> "I cannot cease to be astonished at the simplicity of Fulbert; I was as much surprised as if he had placed a lamb in the power of a hungry wolf. Heloise and I, under pretext of study, gave ourselves up wholly to love, and the solitude that love seeks our studies procured for us. Books were open before us; but we spoke oftener of love than philosophy, and kisses came more readily from our lips than words."

And so, exulting over an honorable confidence, which, to his degrading instinct, was a ludicrous "simplicity," this unmanly Abelard seduced the niece of the man whose guest he was. Paris found it out. Fulbert was told of it—told often—but refused to believe it. He could not comprehend how a man could be so depraved as to use the sacred protection and security of hospitality as a means for the commission of such a crime as that. But when he heard the rowdies in the streets singing the love-songs of Abelard to Heloise, the case was too plain—love-songs come not properly within the teachings of rhetoric and philosophy.

He drove Abelard from his house. Abelard returned secretly and carried Heloise away to Palais, in Brittany, his native country. Here, shortly afterward, she bore a son, who, from his rare beauty, was surnamed Astrolabe—William G. The girl's flight enraged Fulbert, and he longed for vengeance, but feared to strike lest retaliation visit Heloise—for he still loved her tenderly. At length Abelard offered to marry Heloise, but on a shameful condition: that the marriage should be kept secret from the world, to the end that (while her good name remained a wreck, as before) his priestly reputation might be kept untarnished. It was like that miscreant. Fulbert saw his opportunity, and consented. He would see the parties married, and then violate the confidence of the man who had taught him that trick; he would divulge the secret, and so remove somewhat of the obloquy that attached to his niece's name. But the niece suspected his scheme. She refused the marriage, at first; she said Fulbert would betray the secret to save her;

and, besides, she did not wish to drag down a lover who was so gifted, so honored by the world, and who had such a splendid career before him. It was noble, self-sacrificing love, and characteristic of the pure-souled Heloise, but it was not good sense.

But she was overruled, and the private marriage took place. Now for Fulbert. The heart so wounded should be healed at last; the proud spirit so tortured should find rest again; the humbled head should be lifted up once more. He proclaimed the marriage in the high places of the city, and rejoiced that dishonor had departed from his house. But lo! Abelard denied the marriage! Heloise denied it! The people, knowing the former circumstances, might have believed Fulbert, had only Abelard denied it, but when the person chiefly interested—the girl herself—denied it, they laughed despairing Fulbert to scorn.

The poor canon of the Cathedral of Paris was spiked again. The last hope of repairing the wrong that had been done his house was gone. What next? Human nature suggested revenge. He compassed it. The historian says:

"Ruffians, hired by Fulbert, fell upon Abelard by night, and inflicted upon him a terrible and nameless mutilation."

I am seeking the last resting-place of those "ruffians." When I find it I shall shed some tears on it, and stack up some bouquets and immortelles, and cart away from it some gravel whereby to remember that, howsoever blotted by crime their lives may have been, these ruffians did one just deed, at any rate, albeit it was not warranted by the strict letter of the law.

Heloise entered a convent, and gave good-bye to the world and its pleasures for all time. For twelve years she never heard of Abelard—never even heard his name mentioned. She had become prioress of Argenteuil, and led a life of complete seclusion. She happened one day to see a letter written by him, in which he narrated his own history. She cried over it, and wrote him. He answered, addressing her as his "sister in Christ." They continued to correspond, she in the unweighed language of unwavering affection, he in the chilly phraseology of the polished rhetorician. She poured out her heart in passionate, disjointed sentences; he replied with finished essays, divided deliberately in heads and sub-heads, premises and argument. She showered upon him the tenderest epithets that love could devise; he addressed her from the North Pole of his frozen heart as the "Spouse of Christ!" The abandoned villain!

On account of her too easy government of her nuns, some disreputable irregularities were discovered among them, and the Abbot of St. Denis broke up her establishment. Abelard was the official head of the monastery of St. Gildas de Ruys at that time, and when he heard of her homeless condition a sentiment of pity was aroused in his breast (it is a wonder the unfamiliar emotion did not blow his head off), and he placed her and her troop in the little oratory of the Paraclete, a religious establishment which he had founded. She had many privations and sufferings to undergo at first, but her worth and her gentle disposition won influential friends for her, and she built up a wealthy and flourishing nunnery. She became a great favorite with the heads of the Church, and also the people, though she seldom appeared in public. She rapidly advanced in esteem, in good report and in usefulness, and Abelard as rapidly lost ground. The Pope so honored her that he made her the head of her order. Abelard, a man of splendid talents, and ranking as the first debater of his time, became timid, irresolute and distrustful of his powers. He only needed a great misfortune to topple him from the high position he held in the world of intellectual excellence, and it came. Urged by kings and princes to meet the subtle St. Bernard in debate and crush him, he stood up in the presence of a royal and illustrious assemblage, and when his antagonist had finished, he looked about him and stammered a commencement; but his courage failed him, the cunning of his tongue was gone; with his speech unspoken, he trembled and sat down, a disgraced and vanquished champion.

He died a nobody, and was buried at Cluny, A.D. 1144. They removed his body to the Paraclete afterward, and when Heloise died, twenty years later, they buried her with him, in accordance with her last wish. He died at the ripe age of 64, and she at 63. After the bodies had remained entombed three hundred years, they were removed once more. They were removed again in 1800, and, finally, seventeen years afterward, they were taken up and transferred to Père la Chaise, where they will remain in peace and quiet until it comes time for them to get up and move again.

History is silent concerning the last acts of the mountain howitzer.

Let the world say what it will about him, *I* at least shall always respect the memory, and sorrow for the abused trust and the broken heart and the troubled spirit of the old smooth-bore. Rest and repose be his!

Such is the story of Abelard and Heloise. Such is the history that Lamartine has shed such cataracts of tears over. But that man never could come within the influence of a subject in the least pathetic without overflowing his banks. He ought to be damned—or leveed, I should more properly say. Such is the history—not as it is usually told, but as it is when stripped of the nauseous sentimentality that would enshrine for our loving worship a dastardly seducer like Pierre Abelard. I have not a word to say against the misused, faithful girl, and would not withhold from her grave a single one of those simple tributes which blighted youths and maidens offer to her memory, but I am sorry enough that I have not time and opportunity to write four or five volumes of my opinion of her friend, the founder of the Parachute, or the Paraclete, or whatever it was.

The tons of sentiment I have wasted on that unprincipled humbug in my ignorance! I shall throttle down my emotions hereafter, about this sort of people, until I have read them up, and know whether they are entitled to any tearful attentions or not. I wish I had my immortelles back, now, and that bunch of radishes.

A Family Horse

F. W. COZZENS

F. W. Cozzens, author of the "Sparrowgrass Papers," which first appeared in *Putnam's Magazine* in 1856, and gave him immediate reputation, was born at New York in 1818, and spent his life in that city and its neighborhoods, dying in 1869. He was the author of a charming book of travel in Nova Scotia, "Acadia," and of many humorous sketches and magazine papers, as well as a number of peculiarly lovely poems. These productions were the fruit of such leisure as he could find amidst the cares of his business, which was that of a wine merchant.

"It rains very hard," said Mrs. Sparrowgrass, looking out of the window next morning. Sure enough, the rain was sweeping broadcast over the country, and the four Sparrowgrassii were flattening a quartette of noses against the window-panes, believing most faithfully the man would bring the horse that belonged to his brother, in spite of the elements. It was hoping against hope: no man having a horse to sell will trot him out in a rainstorm, unless he intend to sell him at a bargain— but childhood is so credulous! The succeeding morning was bright, however, and down came the horse. He had been very cleverly groomed, and looked pleasant under the saddle. The man led him back and forth before the door. "There, squire, 's as good a hos as ever stood on iron." Mrs. Sparrowgrass asked me what he meant by that. I replied, it was a figurative way of expressing, in horse-talk, that he was as good a horse as ever stood in shoeleather. "He's a handsome hos, squire," said the man. I replied that he did seem to be a good-looking animal, but, said I, "he does not quite come up to the description of a horse I have read." Whose hos was it?" said he. I replied it was the horse of Adonis. He said he didn't know him, but, he added, "there is so many hosses stolen, that the descriptions are stuck up now pretty common." To put him at his ease (for he seemed to think I suspected him of having stolen the horse), I told him the description I meant had been written some hundreds of years ago by Shakespeare, and repeated it

> "Round-hooft, short-joynted, fetlocks shag and long,
> Broad brest, full eyes, small head, and nostril wide,
> High crest, short ears, strait legs, and passing strong,
> Thin mane, thick tail, broad buttock, tender hide."

"Squire," said he, "that will do for a song, but it ain't no p'ints of a good hos. Trotters nowadays go in all shapes, big heads and little heads, big eyes and little eyes, short ears or long ones, thick tail and no tail; so as they have sound legs, good l'in, good barrel, and good stifle, and wind, squire, and speed well, they'll fetch a price. Now, this animal is what I call a hos, squire; he's got the p'ints, he's stylish, he's close-ribbed, a free goer, kind in harness—single or double—a good feeder." I asked him if being a good feeder was a desirable quality. He replied it was; "of course," said he, "if your hos is off his feed, he ain't good for nothin'. But what's the use," he added, "of me tellin' you the p'ints of a good hos? You're a hos man, squire: you know"— "It seems to me," said I, "there is something the matter with that left eye." "No, *sir*," said he, and with that he pulled down the horse's head, and, rapidly crooking his forefinger at the suspected organ, said, "See thar—don't wink a bit." "But he should wink," I replied. "Not onless his eye are weak," he said. To satisfy myself, I asked the man to let me take the bridle. He did so, and so soon as I took hold of it the horse started off in a remarkable retrograde movement, dragging me with him into my best bed of hybrid roses. Finding we were trampling down all the best plants, that had cost at auction from three-and-sixpence to seven shilling apiece, and that the more I pulled, the more he backed, I finally let him have his own way, and jammed him stern-foremost into our largest climbing rose that had been all summer prickling itself, in order to look as much like a vegetable porcupine as possible. This unexpected bit of satire in his rear changed his retrograde movement to a side-long bound, by which he flirted off half the pots on the balusters, upsetting my gladioluses and tube-roses in the pod, and leaving great splashes of mold, geraniums and red pottery in the gravel walk. By this time his owner had managed to give him two pretty severe cuts with the whip, which made him unmanageable, so I let him go. We had a pleasant time catching him again, when he got among the Lima bean-poles; but his owner led him back with a very self-satisfied expression. 'Playful, ain't he, squire?" I replied that I thought he was, and asked him if it was usual for his horse to play such pranks. He said it was not. "You see, squire, he feels his oats, and hain't been out of the stable for a month. Use him, and he's as kind as a kitten." With that he put his foot in the stirrup, and mounted. The animal really looked very well as he moved around the grass plot, and, as Mrs. Sparrowgrass seemed to fancy him, I took a written guarantee that he was sound, and bought him. What I gave for him is a secret; I have not even told Mrs. Sparrowgrass.

It is a mooted point whether it is best to buy your horse before you build your stable, or build your stable before you buy your horse. A horse without a stable is like a bishop without a church. Our neighbor, who is very ingenious, built his stable to fit his horse. He took the length of his horse and a little over, as the measure of the depth of his stable; then he built it. He had a place beside the stall for his Rockaway carriage. When he came to put the Rockaway in, he found he had not allowed for the shafts! The ceiling was too low to allow them to be erected, so he cut two square port-holes in the back of his stable and run his shafts through them, into the chicken-house behind. Of course, whenever he wanted to take out his carriage, he had to unroost all his fowls, who would sit on the shafts, night and day. But that was better than building a new stable. For my part, I determined to avoid mistakes by getting the horse and carriage both first, and then to build the stable. This plan, being acceptable to Mrs. Sparrowgrass, was adopted, as judicious and expedient. In consequence, I found myself with a horse on my hands, with no place to put him. Fortunately, I was acquainted with a very honest man who kept a livery stable, where I put him to board by the month, and in order that he might have plenty of good oats, I bought some, which I gave to the ostler for that purpose. The man of whom I bought the horse did not deceive me when he represented him as a great feeder. He ate more oats than all the rest of the horses put together in that stable.

It is a good thing to have a saddle-horse in the country. The early morning ride, when dawn and dew freshen and flush the landscape, is comparable to no earthly innocent pleasure. Look at yonder avenue of road-skirting trees. Those marvelous trunks, yet moist, are ruddy as obelisks of jasper! And above—see the leaves blushing at the east! Hark to the music! interminable chains of melody linking earth and sky with its delicious magic. The little, countless wood-birds are singing! and now rolls up from the mown meadow the fragrance of cut grass and clover.

> "No print of sheep-track yet hath crushed a flower;
>   The spider's woof with silvery dew is hung
>   As it was beaded ere the daylight hour:
>   The hookèd bramble just as it was strung,
>   When on each leaf the night her crystals flung,
>   Then hurried off, the dawning to elude."

> —

> "The rutted road did never seem so clean,
>   There is no dust upon the way-side thorn,
>   For every bud looks out as if but newly born."

Look at the river with its veil of blue mist! and the grim, gaunt old Palisades, as amiable in their orient crowns as old princes, out of the direct line of succession, over the royal cradle of the heir apparent!

There is one thing about early riding in the country; you find out a great many things which, perhaps, you would not have found out under ordinary circumstances. The first thing I found out was, that my horse had the heaves. I had been so wrapt up in the beauties of the morning that I had not observed what perhaps everybody in that vicinity had observed, namely, that the new horse had been waking up all the sleepers on both sides of the road with an asthmatic whistle of half-a-mile power. My attention was called to the fact by the village teamster, old Dockweed, who came banging after me in his empty cart, shouting out my name as he came. I must say I have always disliked old Dockweed's familiarity; he presumes too much upon my good-nature, when he calls me Sparrygrass before ladies at the depot, and by my Christian name always on the Sabbath, when he is dressed up. On this occasion, what with the horse's vocal powers and old Dockweed's, the affair was pretty well blown over the village before breakfast. "Sparrygrass," he said, as he came up, "that your hos?" I replied that the horse was my property. "Got the heaves, ain't he? got 'em bad." Just then a window was pushed open, and the white head of the old gentleman who sits in the third pew in front of our pew in church was thrust out. "What's the matter with your horse?" said he. "Got the heaves," replied old Dockweed, "got 'em bad." Then I heard symptoms of opening a blind on the other side of the road, and as I did not wish to run the gauntlet of such inquiries, I rode off on a cross-road; but not before I heard, above the sound of pulmonary complaint, the voice of old Dockweed explaining to the other cottage, "Sparrygrass—got a hos—got the heaves—got 'em bad." I was so much ashamed, that I took a roundabout road to the stable, and instead of coming home like a fresh and gallant cavalier, on a hard gallop, I walked my purchase to the stable, and dismounted with a chastened spirit.

"Well, dear," said Mrs. Sparrowgrass, with a face beaming all over with smiles, "how did you like your horse?" I replied that he was not quite so fine a saddle-horse as I had anticipated, but I added, brightening up, for good-humor is sympathetic, "he will made a good horse, I think, after all, for you and the children to jog around with in a wagon." "Oh, won't that be pleasant!" said Mrs. Sparrowgrass.

Farewell, then, rural rides, and rural roads o' mornings! Farewell, song birds and jasper colonnades; farewell, misty river and rocky Palisades; farewell mown honey-breath, farewell stirrup and bridle, dawn and dew; we must jog on at a foot pace. After all, it is better for your horse to have a pulmonary complaint than to have it yourself.

I had determined not to build a stable, nor to buy a carriage, until I had thoroughly tested my horse in harness. For this purpose, I hired a Rockaway of the stable-keeper. Then I put Mrs. Sparrowgrass and the young ones in the double seats, and took the ribbons for a little drive by the Nepperhan River road. The Nepperhan is a quiet stream that for centuries has wound its way through the ancient dorp of Yonkers. Geologists may trace the movements of time upon the rocky dial of the Palisades, and estimate the age of the more modern Hudson by the foot-prints of sauriæ in the strata that fringe its banks, but it is impossible to escape the conviction, as you ride beside the Nepperhan, that it is a very old stream—that it is entirely independent of earthquakes—that its birth was of primeval antiquity—and, no doubt, that it meandered through Westchester valleys when the Hudson was only a fresh water lake, land-locked somewhere above Poughkeepsie. It was a lovely afternoon. The sun was sloping westward, the meadows

———— "were all a-flame
In sunken light, and the mailed grasshopper
Shrilled in the maize with ceaseless iteration."

We had passed Chicken Island, and the famous house with the stone gable and the one stone chimney, in which General Washington slept, as he made it a point to sleep in every old stone house in Westchester County, and had gone pretty far on the road, past the cemetery, when Mrs. Sparrowgrass said suddenly, Dear, what is the matter with your horse?" As I had been telling the children all the stories about the river on the way, I had managed to get my head pretty well inside the carriage, and, at the time she spoke, was keeping a look-out in front with my back. The remark of Mrs. Sparrowgrass induced me to turn about, and I found the new horse behaving in a most unaccountable manner. He was going down-hill with his nose almost to the ground, running the wagon first on this side and then on the other. I thought of the remark made by the man, and turning again to Mrs. Sparrowgrass, said, "Playful, isn't he?" The next moment I heard something breaking away in front, and then the Rockaway gave a lurch and stood still. Upon examination I found the new horse had tumbled down, broken one shaft, gotten the other through the check-rein so as to bring his head up with a round-turn, and besides had managed to put one of the traces in a single hitch around his off hind leg. So soon as I had taken all the young ones and Mrs. Sparrowgrass out of the Rockaway, I set to work to liberate the horse, who was choking very fast with the check-rein. It is unpleasant to get your fishing-line in a tangle when you are in a hurry for bites, but I never saw a fishing-line in such a tangle as that harness. However, I set to work with a penknife, and cut him out in such a way as to make getting home by our conveyance impossible. When he got up, he was the sleepiest looking horse I ever saw. "Mrs. Sparrowgrass," said I, "won't you stay here with the children until I go to the nearest farm-house?" Mrs. Sparrowgrass replied that she would. Then I took the horse with me to get him out of the way of the children, and went in search of assistance.

The first thing the new horse did when he got about a quarter of a mile from the scene of the accident, was to tumble down a bank. Fortunately the bank was not over four feet high, but as I went with him, my trousers were rent in a grievous place. While I was getting the new horse on his feet again, I saw a colored person approaching, who came to my assistance. The first thing he did was to pull out a large jack-knife, and the next thing he did was to open the new horse's mouth and run the blade two or three times inside of the new horse's gums. Then the new horse commenced bleeding. "Dah, sah," said the man, shutting up his jack-knife, "ef 't hadn't been for dat yer, your hos would ha' bin a goner." "What was the matter with him?' said I. "Oh, he's on'y jis got de blind staggers, das all. Say," said he, before I was half indignant enough at the man who sold me such an animal, "say, ain't your name Sparrowgrass?" I replied that my name was Sparrowgrass. "Oh," said he, "I knows you; I brung some fowls once down to you place. I heerd about you and you hos. Dats de hos dats got de heaves so bad, heh! heh! You better sell dat horse." I determined to take his advice, and employed him to lead my purchase to the nearest place where he would be cared for. Then I went back to the Rockaway, but met Mrs. Sparrowgrass and the children on the road coming to meet me. She had left a man in charge of the Rockaway. When we got to the Rockaway we found the man missing, also the whip and one cushion. We got another person to take charge of the Rockaway, and had a pleasant walk home by moonlight.

Does any person want a horse at a low price? A good, stylish-looking animal, close-ribbed, good loin, and good stifle, sound legs, with only the heaves and blind-staggers, and a slight defect in one of his eyes? If at any time he slips his bridle and gets away, you can always approach him by getting on his left side. I will also engage to give a written guarantee that he is sound and kind, signed by the brother of his former owner.

A GENUINE MEXICAN PLUG

MARK TWAIN

I resolved to have a horse to ride. I had never seen such wild, free, magnificent horsemanship outside of a circus as these picturesquely clad Mexicans, Californians and Mexicanized Americans displayed in Carson streets every day. How they rode! Leaning just gently forward out of the perpendicular, easy and nonchalant, with broad slouch-hat brim blown square up in front, and long *riata* swinging above the head, they swept through the town like the wind! The next minute they were only a sailing puff of dust on the far desert. If they trotted, they sat up gallantly and gracefully, and seemed part of the horse; did not go jiggering up and down after the silly Miss Nancy fashion of the riding-schools. I had quickly learned to tell a horse from a cow, and was full of anxiety to learn more. I was resolved to buy a horse.

While the thought was rankling in my mind, the auctioneer came skurrying through the plaza on a black beast that had as many humps and corners on him as a dromedary, and was necessarily uncomely; but he was "going, going, at twenty-two!—horse, saddle and bridle at twenty-two dollars, gentlemen!" and I could hardly resist.

A man whom I did not know (he turned out to be the auctioneer's brother) noticed the wistful look in my eye, and observed that that was a very remarkable horse to be going at such a price; and added that the saddle alone was worth the money. It was a Spanish saddle, with ponderous *tapidaros*, and furnished with the ungainly sole-leather covering with the unspellable name. I said I had half a notion to bid. Then this keen-eyed person appeared to me to be "taking my measure;" but I dismissed the suspicion when he spoke, for his manner was full of guileless candor and truthfulness. Said he:

"I know that horse—know him well. You are a stranger, I take it, and so you might think he was an American horse, maybe, but I assure you he is not. He is nothing of the kind; but—excuse my speaking in a low voice, other people being near—he is, without the shadow of a doubt, a Genuine Mexican Plug!"

I did not know what a Genuine Plug was, but there was something about this man's way of saying it that made me swear inwardly that I would own a Genuine Mexican Plug or die.

"Has he any other—er advantages?" I inquired, suppressing what eagerness I could.

He hooked his forefinger in the pocket of my army-shirt, led me to one side, and breathed in my ear impressively these words:

"He can out-buck anything in America!"

"Going, going, going—at *twent-ty*-four dollars and a half, gen—"

"Twenty-seven!" I shouted, in a frenzy.

"And sold!" said the auctioneer, and passed over the Genuine Mexican Plug to me.

I could scarcely contain my exultation. I paid the money, and put the animal in a neighboring livery-stable to dine and rest himself.

In the afternoon I brought the creature into the plaza, and certain citizens held him by the head, and others by the tail, while I mounted him. As soon as they let go, he placed all his feet in a bunch together, lowered his back, and then suddenly arched it upward, and shot me straight into the air a matter of three or four feet! I came as straight down again, lit in the saddle, went instantly up again, came down almost on the high pommel, shot up again, and came down on the horse's neck—all in the space of three or four seconds. Then he rose and stood almost straight up on his hind feet, and I, clasping his lean neck desperately, slid back into the saddle, and held on. He came down, and immediately hoisted his heels into the air, delivering a vicious kick at the sky, and stood on his forefeet. And then down he came once more, and began the original exercise of shooting me straight up again. The third time I went up I heard a stranger say:

"Oh, *don't* he buck, though!"

While I was up, somebody struck the horse a sounding thwack with a leathern strap, and when I arrived again the Genuine Mexican Plug was not there. A Californian youth chased him up and caught him, and asked if he might have a ride. I granted him that luxury. He mounted the Genuine, got lifted into the air once, but sent his spurs home as he descended, and the horse darted away like a telegram. He soared over three fences like a bird, and disappeared down the road toward the Washoe Valley.

I sat down on a stone with a sigh, and by a natural impulse one of my hands sought my forehead, and the other the base of my stomach. I believe I never appreciated, till then, the poverty of the human machinery—for I still needed a hand or two to place elsewhere. Pen cannot describe how I was jolted up. Imagination cannot conceive how disjointed I was—how internally, externally and universally I was unsettled, mixed up and ruptured. There was a sympathetic crowd around me, though.

One elderly looking comforter said:

"Stranger, you've been taken in. Everybody in this camp knows that horse. Any child, any Injun, could have told you that he'd buck; he is the very worst devil to buck on the continent of America. You hear *me*. I'm Curry. *Old* Curry. Old *Abe* Curry. And moreover, he is a simon-pure, out-and-out, genuine d—d Mexican plug, and an uncommon mean one at that, too. Why, you turnip, if you had laid low and kept dark, there's chances to buy an *American* horse for mighty little more than you paid for that bloody old foreign relic."

I gave no sign; but I made up my mind that if the auctioneer's brother's funeral took place while I was in the Territory I would postpone all other recreations and attend it.

After a gallop of sixteen miles the Californian youth and the Genuine Mexican Plug came tearing into town again, shedding foam-flakes like the spume-spray that drives before a typhoon, and, with one final skip over a wheelbarrow and a Chinaman, cast anchor in front of the "ranch."

Such panting and blowing! Such spreading and contracting of the red equine nostrils, and glaring of the wild equine eye! But was the imperial beast subjugated? Indeed he was not. His lordship the Speaker of the House thought he was, and mounted him to go down to the Capitol; but the first dash the creature made was over a pile of telegraph poles half as high as a church; and his time to the Capitol—one mile and three-quarters—remains unbeaten to this day. But then he took an advantage—he left out the mile, and only did three-quarters. That is to say, he made a straight cut across-lots, preferring fences and ditches to a crooked road; and when the Speaker got to the Capitol he said he had been in the air so much he felt as if he had made the trip on a comet.

In the evening the Speaker came home afoot for exercise, and got the Genuine towed back behind a quartz wagon. The next day I loaned the animal to the Clerk of the House to go down to the Dana silver mine, six miles, and *he* walked back for exercise, and got the horse towed. Everybody I loaned him to always walked back; they never could get enough exercise any other way. Still, I continued to loan him to anybody who was willing to borrow him, my idea being to get him crippled, and throw him on the borrower's hands, or killed, and make the borrower pay for him. But somehow nothing ever happened to him. He took chances that no other horse ever took and survived, but he always came out safe. It was his daily habit to try experiments that had always before been considered impossible, but he always got through. Sometimes he miscalculated a little, and did not get his rider through intact, but *he* always got through himself. Of course I had tried to sell him; but that was a stretch of simplicity which met with little sympathy. The auctioneer stormed up and down the streets on him for four days, dispersing the populace, interrupting business, and destroying children, and never got a bid—at least never any but the eighteen dollar one he hired a notoriously substanceless bummer to make. The people only smiled pleasantly, and restrained their desire to buy, if they had any. Then the auctioneer brought in his bill, and I withdrew the horse from the market. We tried to trade him off at private vendue next, offering him at a sacrifice for second-hand tombstones, old iron, temperance tracts—any kind of property. But holders were stiff, and we retired from the market again. I never tried to ride the horse any more. Walking was good enough exercise for a man like me, that had nothing the matter with him except ruptures, internal injuries, and such things. Finally I tried to *give* him away. But it was a failure. Parties said earthquakes were handy enough on the Pacific coast—they did not wish to own one. As a last resort I offered him to the Governor for the use of the "Brigade." His face lit up eagerly at first, but toned down again, and he said the thing would be too palpable.

Just then the livery-stable man brought in his bill for six weeks' keeping—stall-room for the horse, fifteen dollars; hay for the horse, two hundred and fifty! The Genuine Mexican Plug had eaten a ton of the article, and the man said he would have eaten a hundred if he had let him.

I will remark here, in all seriousness, that the regular price of hay during that year and a part of the next was really two hundred and fifty dollars a ton. During a part of the previous year it had sold at five hundred a ton, in gold, and during the winter before that, there was such scarcity of the article that in several instances small quantities had brought eight hundred dollars a ton in coin! The consequence might be guessed without my telling it: people turned their stock loose to starve, and before the spring arrived Carson and Eagle valleys were almost literally carpeted with their carcases! Any old settler there will verify these statements.

I managed to pay the livery bill and that same day I gave the Genuine Mexican Plug to a passing Arkansas emigrant whom fortune delivered into my hand. If this ever meets his eye, he will doubtless remember the donation.

Now whoever has had the luck to ride a real Mexican plug will recognize the animal depicted in this chapter, and hardly consider him exaggerated—but the uninitiated will feel justified in regarding his portrait as a fancy sketch, perhaps.

A VISIT TO BRIGHAM YOUNG

ARTEMUS WARD

Charles F. Browne (Artemus Ward) was born at Waterford, Me., April 23, 1834. He was a printer by trade, and was a compositor in the office of the *Boston Carpet Bag*, a comic journal, to which he contributed his first humorous efforts. As a journeyman printer he wandered westward, but seems to have spent the greater part of his time in Ohio, where about the year 1858 he became the "local editor" of the *Cleveland Plaindealer*. In the "local column" of this newspaper his humorous paragraphs began to attract notice, and he invented, for the amusement of its readers, the character of Artemus Ward, the Showman, with which he soon became thoroughly identified. He was invited to New York, at the breaking out of the war, to take charge of *Vanity Fair*, a humorous weekly, which did not survive the serious mood of the time. When it died, he visited Utah and California, and then launched himself upon the public as a comic lecturer, and achieved brilliant success in this country and in England, where perhaps he was even more popular, and where he became a regular and favorite contributor to *Punch.* His collected sketches, lectures, extravaganzas, etc., in three volumes, respectively entitled "Artemus Ward: His Book," "Artemus Ward: His Travels," and "Artemus Ward in London," are published in New York. Shortly after his arrival in England Browne's health gave way; he fell into consumption, and died at Southampton, May 6, 1867.

It is now goin on 2 (too) yeres, as I very well remember, since I crossed the Planes for Kaliforny, the Brite land of Jold. While crossin the Planes all so bold I fell in with sum noble red men of the forest (N. B.—This is rote Sarcasticul. Injins is Pizin, whar ever found), which thay Sed I was their Brother, & wanted for to smoke the Calomel of Peace with me. Thay then stole my jerkt beef, blankits, et-settery, skalpt my orgin grinder & scooted with a Wild Hoop. Durin the Cheaf's techin speech he sed he shood meet me in the Happy Huntin Grounds. If he duz, thare will be a fite. But enuff of this ere. *Reven Noose Muttons,* as our skoolmaster, who has got Talent into him, cussycally obsarved.

I arrove at Salt Lake in doo time. At Camp Scott there was a lot of U.S. sogers, hosstensibly sent out thare to smash the Mormins but really to eat Salt vittles & play poker & other beautiful but sumwhat onsartin games. I got acquainted with sum of the officers. Thay lookt putty scrumpshus in their Bloo coats with brass buttings onto um, & ware very talented drinkers, but so fur as fitin is consarned I'd willingly put my wax figgers agin the hull party.

My desire was to exhibit my grate show in Salt Lake City, so I called on Brigham Yung, the grate mogull amung the Mormins, and axed his permishun to pitch my tent and onfurl my banner to the jentle breezis. He lookt at me in a austeer manner for a few minits, and sed:

"Do you bleeve in Solomon, Saint Paul, the immaculateness of the Mormin Church and the Latter-day Revelashuns?"

Sez I, "I'm on it!" I make it a pint to git along plesunt, tho I didn't know what under the Son the old feller was drivin at. He sed I mite show.

"You air a marrid man, Mister Yung, I bleeve?" sez I, preparin to rite him sum free parsis.

"I hev eighty wives, Mister Ward. I sertinly am marrid."

"How do you like it, as far as you hev got?" sed I.

He sed, "Middlin," and axed me wouldn't I like to see his famerly, to which I replide that I wouldn't mind minglin with the fair Seck & Barskin in the winnin smiles of his interestin wives. He accordinly tuk me to his Scareum. The house is powerful big, & in a exceedin large room was his wives & children, which larst was squawkin and hollerin enuff to take the roof rite orf the house. The wimin was of all sizes and ages. Sum was pretty & sum was Plane—sum was helthy and sum was on the Wayne—which is verses, tho sich was not my intentions, as I don't 'prove of puttin verses in Proze rittins, tho ef occashun requires I can Jerk a Poim ekal to any of them *Atlantic Munthly* fellers.

"My wives, Mister Ward," sed Yung.

"Your sarvant, marms," sed I, as I sot down in a cheer which a red-heded female brawt me.

"Besides these wives you see here, Mister Ward," sed Yung, "I hav eighty more in varis parts of this consecrated land which air Sealed to me."

"Which?" sez I, getting up & staring at him.

"Sealed, Sir! sealed."

"Whare bowts?" sez I.

"I sed, Sir, that they was sealed!" He spoke in a tragerdy voice.

"Will they probly continner on in that stile to any grate extent, Sir?" I axed.

"Sir," sed he, turning as red as a biled beet, "don't you know that the rules of our Church is that I, the Profit, may hev as meny wives as I wants?"

"Jes so," I sed. "You are old pie, ain't you?"

"Them as is Sealed to me—that is to say, to be mine when I wants um—air at present my sperretooul wives," sed Mister Yung.

"Long may thay wave!" sez I, seein I shood git into a scrape ef I didn't look out.

In a privit conversashun with Brigham I learnt the following fax: It takes him six weeks to kiss his wives. He don't do it only onct a yere, & sez it is wuss nor cleanin house. He don't pretend to know his children, thare is so many of um, tho they all know him. He sez about every child he meats call him Par, & he takes it for grantid it is so. His wives air very expensiv. Thay allers want suthin, & ef he don't buy it for um thay set the house in a uproar. He sez he don't have a minit's peace. His wives fite among theirselves so much that he has bilt a fiting room for thare speshul benefit, & when too of 'em get into a row he has em turned loose into that place, where the dispoot is settled accordin to the rules of the London prize ring. Sumtimes thay abooz hisself individooally. Thay hev pulled the most of his hair out at the roots, & he wares meny a horrible scar upon his body, inflicted with mop-handles, broom-sticks, and sich. Occashunly they git mad & scald him with biling hot water. When he got eny waze cranky thay'd shut him up in a dark closit, previshly whippin him arter the stile of muthers when thare orfspring git onruly. Sumtimes when he went in swimmin thay'd go to the banks of the Lake & steal all his close, thereby compellin him to sneek home by a sircootius rowt, drest in the Skanderlus stile of the Greek Slaiv. "I find that the keers of a marrid life way hevy onto me," sed the Profit, "& sumtimes I wish I'd remaned singel." I left the Profit and startid for the tavern whare I put up to. On my way I was overtuk by a lurge krowd of Mormins, which they surroundid me & statid they were goin into the Show free.

"Wall," sez I, "ef I find a individooal who is goin round lettin folks into his show free, I'll let you know."

"We've had a Revelashun biddin us go into A. Ward's Show without payin nothin!" thay showted.

"Yes," hollered a lot of femaile Mormonesses, ceasin me by the cote tales & swingin me round very rapid, "we're all goin in free! So sez the Revelashun!"

"What's Old Revelashun got to do with my show?" sez I, gettin putty rily. "Tell Mister Revelashun," sed I, drawin myself up to my full hite and lookin round upon the ornery krowd with a prowd & defiant mean—"tell Mister Revelashun to mind his own bizness, subject only to the Konstitushun of the United States!"

"Oh, now, let us in, that's a sweet man," sed several femailes, puttin thare arms round me in luvin style. "Become 1 of us. Becum a Preest & hav wives Sealed to you."

"Not a Seal!" sez I, startin back in horror at the idee.

"Oh stay, Sir, stay," sed a tall, gawnt femaile, ore whoos hed 37 summirs hev parsd—"stay, & I'll be your Jentle Gazelle."

"Not ef I know it, you won't," sez I. "Awa, you skanderlus femaile, awa! Go & be a Nunnery!" *That's what I sed,* JES SO.

"& I," sed a fat, chunky femaile, who must hev wade more than too hundred lbs., "I will be your sweet gidin Star!"

Sez I, "Ile bet two dollars and a half you won't!" Whate ear I may Rome Ile still be troo 2 thee, Oh Betsy Jane! [N. B.—Betsy Jane is my wife's Sir naime.]

"Wiltist thou not tarry here in the promist Land?" sed several of the meserabil critters.

"Ile see you all essenshally cussed be 4 I wiltist!" roared I, as mad as I cood be at thare infernal noncents. I girdid up my Lions & fled the Seen. I packt up my duds & Left Salt Lake, which is a 2nd Soddum & Germorrer, inhabited by as theavin & onprincipled a set of retchis as ever drew Breth in eny spot on the Globe.

THE SIMPLE STORY OF G. WASHINGTON

ROBERT J. BURDETTE

Only yesterday, a lady friend on a shopping excursion left her little tid toddler of five bright summers in our experienced charge, while she pursued the duties which called her down-town. Such a bright boy; so delightful it was to talk to him! We can never forget the blissful half-hour we spent looking that prodigy up in his centennial history.

"Now listen, Clary," we said—his name is Clarence Fitzherbert Alençon de Marchemont Caruthers—"and learn about George Washington.

"Who's he?" inquired Clarence, etc.

"Listen," we said; "he was the father of his country."

"Whose country?"

"Ours; yours and mine—the confederated union of the American people, cemented with the life blood of the men of '76, poured out upon the altars of our country as the dearest libation to liberty that her votaries can offer!"

"Who did?" asked Clarence.

There is a peculiar tact in talking to children that very few people possess. Now most people would have grown impatient and lost their temper when little Clarence asked so many irrelevant questions, but we did not. We knew, however careless he might appear at first, that we could soon interest him in the story, and he would be all eyes and ears. So we smiled sweetly—that same sweet smile which you may have noticed on our photographs, just the faintest ripple of a smile breaking across the face like a ray of sunlight, and checked by lines of tender sadness, just before the two ends of it pass each other at the back of the neck.

And so, smiling, we went on.

"Well, one day George's father—"

"George who?" asked Clarence.

"George Washington. He was a little boy then, just like you. One day his father—"

"Whose father?" demanded Clarence with an encouraging expression of interest.

"George Washington's; this great man we were telling you of. One day George Washington's father gave him a little hatchet for a—"

"Gave who a little hatchet?" the dear child interrupted, with a gleam of bewitching intelligence. Most men would have got mad, or betrayed signs of impatience, but we didn't. We know how to talk to children. So we went on:

"George Washington. His—"

"Who gave him the little hatchet?"

"His father. And his father—"

"Whose father?"

"George Washington's."

"Oh!"

"Yes, George Washington. And his father told him—"

"Told who?"

"Told George."

"Oh, yes, George."

And we went on just as patient and as pleasant as you could imagine. We took up the story right where the boy interrupted, for we could see that he was just crazy to hear the end of it. We said:

"And he told him that—"

"George told him?" queried Clarence.

"No, his father told George—"

"Oh!"

"Yes; told him that he must be careful with the hatchet—"

"Who must be careful?"

"George must."

"Oh!"

"Yes; must be careful with the hatchet—"

"What hatchet?"

"Why, George's."

"Oh!"

"Yes; with the hatchet, and not cut himself with it, or drop it in the cistern, or leave it out on the grass all night. So George went round cutting everything he could reach with his hatchet. And at last he came to a splendid apple-tree, his father's favorite, and cut it down, and—"

"Who cut it down?"

"George did."

"Oh!"

"But his father came home and saw it the first thing, and—"

"Saw the hatchet?"

"No! saw the apple tree. And he said: 'Who has cut down my favorite apple-tree?'"

"Whose apple-tree?"

"George's father's. And everybody said they didn't know anything about it, and—"

"Anything about what?"

"The apple-tree."

"Oh!"

"And George came up and heard them talking about it—"

"Heard who talking about it?"

"Heard his father and the men."

"What was they talking about?"

"About this apple-tree."

"What apple-tree?"

"The favorite apple-tree that George cut down."

"George who?"

"George Washington."

"Oh!"

"So George came up, and he said, 'Father, I cannot tell a lie. It was—'"

"His father couldn't?"

"Why, no, George couldn't."

"Oh! George? Oh, yes!"

" 'It was I cut down your apple-tree; I did—'

"His father did?"

"No, no, no; said he cut down his apple-tree."

"George's apple-tree?"

"No, no; his father's."

"Oh!"

"He said—"

"His father said?"

"No, no, no; George said, 'Father, I cannot tell a lie. I did it with my little hatchet.' And his father said: 'Noble boy, I would rather lose a thousand trees than have you to tell a lie.'

"George did?"

"No; his father said that."

"Said he'd rather have a thousand trees?"

"No, no, no; said he'd rather lose a thousand apple-trees than—"

"Said he'd rather George would?"

"No; said he'd rather he would than have him lie."

"Oh! George would rather have his father lie?"

We are patient, and we love children, but if Mrs. Caruthers, of Arch Street, hadn't come and got her prodigy at that critical juncture, we don't believe all Burlington could have pulled us out of the snarl. And as Clarence Fitzherbert Alençon de Marchemont Caruthers pattered down the stairs, we heard him telling his ma about a boy who had a father named George, and he told him to cut an apple-tree, and he said he'd rather tell a thousand lies than cut down one apple-tree. We do love children, but we don't believe that either nature or education has fitted us to be a governess.

THE COURTIN'

JAMES RUSSELL LOWELL

James Russell Lowell, whose "Biglow Papers" placed America inapproachably first in humorous literature, was born at Cambridge, Mass., in 1819, and was graduated at Harvard in 1838. He was admitted to the bar two years later, but never practiced his profession, having already given proofs of his poetic genius and transcendent wit. He early dedicated himself to the anti-slavery cause; and these literary efforts that made his fame were for a long time more or less in its interest. After some years' travel and study in southern Europe, he took the chair vacated by Longfellow's resignation, of Professor of Modern Languages and Belles Lettres in Harvard, which he held till appointed Minister to Spain in 1877. He was transferred to the English Court in 1880. He was the first editor of *The Atlantic Monthly*, and was afterwards editor of *The North American Review*.

> God makes sech nights, all white an' still
>   Fur 'z you can look or listen,
> Moonshine an' snow on field an' hill,
>   All silence an' all glisten.
>
> Zekle crep' up quite unbeknown
>   An' peeked in thru' the winder,
> An' there sot Huldy all alone,
>   'Ith no one nigh to hender.
>
> A fireplace filled the room's one side
>   With half a cord o' wood in—
> There warn't no stoves (tell comfort died)
>   To bake ye to a puddin'.
>
> The wa'nut logs shot sparkles out
>   Towards the pootiest, bless her,
> An' leetle flames danced all about
>   The chiny on the dresser
>
> Agin the chimbley crook-necks hung,
>   An' in amongst 'em rusted
> The ole queen's-arm thet gran'ther Young
>   Fetched back from Concord busted.
>
> The very room, coz she was in,
>   Seemed warm from floor to ceilin',
> An' she looked full ez rosy agin
>   Ez the apples she was peelin'.
>
> 'T was kin' o' kingdom-come to look
>   On sech a blessed cretur,
> A dog-rose blushin' to a brook
>   Ain't modester nor sweeter.

He was six foot o' man, A 1,
    Clean grit an' human natur';
None couldn't quicker pitch a ton
    Nor dror a furrer straighter.

He'd sparked it with full twenty gals,
    He'd squired 'em, danced 'em, druv 'em,
Fust this one, an' then thet, by spells—
    All is, he couldn't love 'em.

But long o' her his veins 'ould run
    All crinkly like curled maple,
The side she breshed felt full o' sun
    Ez a south slope in Ap'il.

She thought no v'ice hed sech a swing
    Ez hisn in the choir;
My! when he made Ole Hunderd ring,
    She *knowed* the Lord was nigher.

An' she'd blush scarlit, right in prayer,
    When her new meetin'-bunnet
Felt somehow thru' its crown a pair
    O' blue eyes sot upon it.

Thet night, I tell ye, she looked *some!*
    She seemed to've gut a new soul,
For she felt sartin-sure he'd come,
    Down to her very shoe-sole.

She heered a foot, an' knowed it tu,
    A-raspin' on the scraper—
All ways to once her feelins flew
    Like sparks in burnt-up paper.

He kin' o' l'itered on the mat,
    Some doubtfle o' the sekle,
His heart kep' goin' pity-pat,
    But hern went pity Zekle.

An' yit she gin her cheer a jerk
    Ez though she wished him furder,
An' on her apples kep' to work,
    Parin' away like murder.

"You want to see my Pa, I s'pose?"
 "Wal. . . . no. . . . I come dasignin' "—
"To see my Ma? She's sprinklin' clo'es
 Agin to-morrer's i'nin'."

To say why gals acts so or so,
 Or don't, 'ould be presumin';
Mebby to mean *yes* an' say *no*,
 Comes nateral to women.

He stood a spell on one foot fust,
 Then stood a spell on t'other,
An' on which one he felt the wust
 He couldn't ha' told ye nuther.

Says he, "I'd better call agin";
 Says she, "Think likely, Mister";
Thet last word pricked him like a pin,
 An'. . . . Wal, he up an' kist her.

When Ma bimeby upon 'em slips,
 Huldy sot pale ez ashes,
All kin' o' smily roun' the lips
 An' teary roun' the lashes.

For she was jes' the quiet kind
 Whose naturs never vary,
Like streams that keep a summer mind
 Snowhid in Jenooary.

The blood clost roun' her heart felt glued
 Too tight for all expressin',
Tell mother see how metters stood,
 And gin 'em both her blessin'.

Then her red come back like the tide
 Down to the Bay o' Fundy,
An' all I know is they was cried
 In meetin' come nex' Sunday.

'TIS ONLY MY HUSBAND

JOSEPH C. NEAL

Joseph C. Neal, author of the once famous "Charcoal Sketches," was born in Greenland, N. H., in 1807, and died in 1847 at Philadelphia, where he passed nearly two-thirds of his life in connection with different journals. He was the author of two other volumes: "The City Worthies," and "Peter Ploddy and other Oddities."

"Goodness, Mrs. Pumpilion, it's a gentleman's voice, and me such a figure!" exclaimed Miss Amanda Corntop, who had just arrived in town to visit her friend, Mrs. Pumpilion, whom she had not seen since her marriage.

"Don't disturb yourself, dear," said Mrs. Pumpilion, quietly, "it's nobody—'tis only my husband. He'll not come in; but if he does, 'tis only my husband."

So Miss Amanda Corntop was comforted, and her agitated arrangements before the glass being more coolly completed, she resumed her seat and the interrupted conversation. Although, as a spinster, she had a laudable and natural unwillingness to be seen by any of the masculine gender in that condition so graphically described as "such a figure," yet there are degrees in this unwillingness. It is by no means so painful to be caught a figure by a married man as it is to be surprised by a youthful bachelor; and, if the former be of that peculiar class known as "only my husband," his unexpected arrival is of very little consequence. He can never more, "like an eagle in a dove cote, flutter the Volsces." It is, therefore, evident that there exists a material difference between "my husband" and "only my husband;" a difference not easily expressed, though perfectly understood; and it was that understanding which restored Miss Amanda Corntop to her pristine tranquility.

"Oh!" said Miss Corntop, when she heard that the voice in question was that of Mr. Pumpilion. "Ah!" added Miss Corntop, intelligently and composedly, when she understood that Pumpilion was "only my husband." She had not paid much attention to philology but she was perfectly aware of the value of that diminutive prefix "only."

"I told you he would not come in, for he knew there was some one here," continued Mrs. Pumpilion, as the spiritless footsteps of "only my husband" passed the door, and slowly plodded upstairs. He neither came in, nor did he hum, whistle, or bound three steps at a time; "only my husband" never does. He is simply a transportation line; he conveys himself from place to place, according to order, and indulges not in episodes and embellishments.

Poor Pedrigo Pumpilion! Have all thy glories shrunk to this little measure? Only my husband! Does that appellation circumscribe him who once found three chairs barely sufficient to accommodate his frame, and who, in promenading, never skulked to the curb or hugged the wall, but, like a man who justly appreciated himself, took the very middle of the *trottoir*, and kept it?

The amiable but now defunct Mrs. Anguish was never sure that she was perfectly well, until she had shaken her pretty head to ascertain if some disorder were not lying in ambush, and to discover whether a headache were not latent there, which, if not nipped in the bud, might be suddenly and inconveniently brought into action. It is not too much to infer that the same reasoning which applies to headaches and to the physical constitution, may be of equal force in reference to the moral organization. Headaches being latent, it is natural to suppose that the disposition to be "only my husband" may likewise be latent, even in him who is now as fierce and uncontrollable as a volcano; while the desire to be "head of the bureau" may slumber in the mildest of the fair. It is by circumstance alone that talent is developed; the razor itself requires extraneous aid to bring it to an edge; and the tact to give direction, as well as the facility to obey, wait to be elicited by events. Both greymareism and Jerry-Sneakery are sometimes latent, and like the derangements of Mrs. Anguish's caput, only want shaking to manifest themselves. If some are born to command, others must certainly have a genius for submission—we term it a genius, submission being in many cases rather a difficult thing.

That this division of qualities is full of wisdom, none can deny. It requires both flint and steel to produce a spark; both powder and ball to do execution; and, though the Chinese contrive to gobble an infinity of rice with chopsticks, yet the twofold operation of knife and fork conduces much more to the comfort of a dinner. Authority and obedience are the knife and fork of this extensive banquet, the world; they are the true *divide et impera*; that which is sliced off by the one is har-pooned by the other.

In this distribution, however, nature, when the "latents" are made apparent, very frequently seems to act with caprice. It is by no means rare to find in the form of a man a timid, retiring, feminine disposition, which, in the rough encounters of existence, gives way at once, as if like woman, "born to be controlled." The proportions of a Hercules, valenced with the whiskers of a tiger, often cover a heart with no more of energy and boldness in its pulsations than the little palpitating af-fair which throbs in the bosom of a maiden of bashful fifteen; while many a lady fair, before marriage—the latent condition—all softness and graceful humility, bears within her breast the fiery resolution and the indomitable will of an Alexander, a Hannibal, or a Doctor Francia. The temperament which, had she been a man, would, in an extended field, have made her a conqueror of nations, or, in a more contracted one, a distinguished thief-catching police officer, by being lodged in a female frame renders her a Xantippe—a Napoleon of the fireside, and pens her hapless mate, like a conquered king, a spiritless captive in his own chimney-corner.

But it is plain to be seen that this apparent confusion lies only in the distribution. There are souls enough of all kinds in the world, but they do not always seem properly fitted with bodies; and thus a corporal construction may run the course of life actuated by a spirit in every respect opposed to its capabilities; as at the breaking up of a crowded *soirée*, a little head waggles home with an immense castor, while a pumpkin pate sallies forth surmounted by a thimble; which, we take it, is the only philosophical theory which at all accounts for the frequent acting out of character with which society is replete.

Hence arises the situation of affairs with the Pumpilions. Pedrigo Pumpilion has the soul which legitimately appertains to his beloved Seraphina Serena, while Seraphina Serena Pumpilion has that which should animate her Pedrigo. But, not being profound in their re-searches, they are probably not aware of the fact, and perhaps would not know their own souls if they were to meet them in the street; al-though, in all likelihood, it was a mysterious sympathy—a yearning of each physical individuality to be near so important a part of itself, which brought this worthy pair together.

Be that, however, as it may, it is an incontrovertible fact that, before they did come together, Pedrigo Pumpilion thought himself quite a model of humanity; and piqued himself upon possessing much more of the *fortiter in re* than of the *suaviter in modo*—a mistake, the latter quality being latent, but abundant. He dreamed that he was brimming with valor, and fit, not only to lead squadrons to the field, but likewise to remain with them when they were there. At the sound of drums and trumpets, he perked up his chin, stuck out his breast, straightened his vertebral column, and believed that he, Pedrigo, was precisely the individual to storm a fortress at the head of a forlorn hope—a greater mistake. But the greatest error of the whole troop of blunders was his making a Pumpilion of Miss Seraphina Serena Dolce, with the decided impression that he was, while sharing his kingdom, to remain supreme in authority. Knowing nothing of the theory already broached, he took her for a feminine feminality, and yielded himself a victim to sympathy and the general welfare. Now, in this, strictly considered, Pedrigo had none but himself to blame; he had seen manifestations of her spirit; the latent energy had peeped out more than once; he had entered unexpectedly, before being installed as "only my husband," and found Miss Seraphina dancing the grand rigadoon on a luckless bonnet which did not suit her fancy—a species of exercise whereat he marveled, and he had likewise witnessed her performance of the remarkable feat of whirling a cat, which had scratched her hand, across the room by the tail, whereby the mirror was infinitesimally divided into homœopathic doses, and whereby pussy, the patient, was most allopathically phlebotomised and scarified. He likewise knew that her musical education terminated in an operatic crash, the lady having in a fit of impatience demolished the guitar over the head of her teacher; but, in this instance, the mitigating plea must be allowed that it was done because the instrument "wouldn't play good," a perversity to which instruments, like lessons "which won't learn," are lamentably liable.

These little escapades, however, did not deter Pumpilion. Confiding in his own talent for governing, he liked his Seraphina none the less for her accidental displays of energy, and smiled to think how, under his administration, his reproving frown would cast oil upon the waves, and how, as he repressed her irritability, he would develop her affections, results which would both save the crockery and increase his comforts.

Of the Pumpilion *tactique* in courtship some idea may be formed from the following conversation. Pedrigo had an intimate associate, some years his senior—Mr. Michael Mitts, a spare and emaciated bachelor, whose hawk nose, crookedly set on, well represented the eccentricity of his conclusions, while the whistling pucker in which he generally wore his mouth betokened acidity of mind rendered sourer by indecision. Mitts was addicted to observation, and, engaged in the drawing of inferences and in generalizing from individual instances, he had, like many others, while trimming the safety lamp of experience, suffered the time of action to pass by unimproved. His cautiousness was so great as to trammel up his "motive power," and, though long intending to marry, the best part of his life had evaporated in the unproductive employment of "looking about." His experience, therefore, had stored him with that species of wisdom which one meets with in theoretical wooers, and he had many learned saws at the service of those who were bolder than himself, and were determined to enter the pale through which he peeped.

As every one in love must have a confidant, Pedrigo had selected Mitts for that office, knowing his peculiar talent for giving advice, and laying down rules for others to act upon.

"Pedrigo," said Mitts, as he flexed his nose still further from the right line of conformity to the usages of the world, and slacked the drawing-strings of his mouth to get it out of pucker—"Pedrigo, if you are resolved upon marrying this identical individual—I don't see the use, for my part, of being in a hurry—better look about a while; plenty more of 'em—but if you are resolved, the first thing to be done is to make sure of her. That's undeniable. The only difference of opinion, if you won't wait and study character—character's a noble study—is as to the *modus operandi*. Now, the lady's not sure because she's committed; just the contrary—that's the very reason she's not sure. My experience shows me that when it's not so easy to retract, the attention, especially that of young women, is drawn to retraction. Somebody tells of a bird in a cage that grumbled about being cooped up. It's clear to me that the bird did not complain so much because it was in the cage, as it did because it couldn't get out—that's bird nature, and it's human nature too."

"Ah, indeed!" responded Pumpilion, with a smile of confidence in his own attractions, mingled, however, with a look which spoke that the philosophy of Mitts, having for its object to render "assurance double sure," did not pass altogether unheeded.

"It's a fact," added Mitts; "don't be too secure. Be as assiduous and as mellifluous as you please before your divinity owns the soft impeachment; but afterwards comes the second stage, and policy commands that it should be one rather of anxiety to her. You must every now and then play Captain Grand, or else she may perform the part herself. Take offense frequently; vary your *Romeo* scenes with an occasional touch of the snow-storm, and afterwards excuse yourself on the score of jealous affection; that excuse always answers. Nothing sharpens love like a smart tiff by way of embellishment. The sun itself would not look so bright if it were not for the intervention of night; and these little agitations keep her mind tremulous, but intent upon yourself. Don't mothers always love the naughtiest boys best? Haven't the worst men always the best wives? That exemplifies the principle; there's nothing like a little judicious bother. Miss Seraphina Serena will never change her mind if bothered scientifically."

"Perhaps so; but may it not be rather dangerous?"

"Dangerous! not at all; it's regular practice, I tell you. A few cases may terminate unluckily; but that must be charged to a bungle in the doctor. Why, properly managed, a courtship may be continued, like a nervous disease, or a suit at law, for twenty years, and be as good at the close as it was at the beginning. In nine cases out of ten, you must either perplex or be perplexed; so you had better take the sure course, and play the game yourself. Them's my sentiments, Mr. Speaker;" and Michael Mitts caused his lithe proboscis to oscillate like a rudder, as he concluded his oracular speech, and puckered his mouth to the whistling place, to show that he had "shut up" for the present. He then walked slowly away, leaving Pumpilion with a "new wrinkle."

Seraphina Serena, being both fiery and coquettish withal, Pumpilion, under the direction of his preceptor, tried the "Mitts system of wooing," and although it gave rise to frequent explosions, yet the quarrels, whether owing to the correctness of the system or not, were productive of no lasting evil. Michael Mitts twirled his nose and twisted his mouth in triumph at the wedding, and set it down as an axiom that there is nothing like a little insecurity for rendering parties firm in completing a bargain; that, had it not been for practicing the system, Pumpilion might have become alarmed at the indications of the "latent system"; and that, had it not been for the practice of the system, Seraphina's fancy might have strayed.

"I'm an experimenter in mental operations, and there's no lack of subjects," said Mitts to himself; "one fact being established, the Pumpilions now present a new aspect."

There is, however, all the difference in the world between carrying on warfare where you may advance and retire at pleasure, and in prosecuting it in situations which admit of no retreat. Partisan hostilities are one thing, and regular warfare is another. Pumpilion was very well as a guerilla, but his genius in that respect was unavailing when the nature of the campaign did not admit of his making an occasional demonstration, and of evading the immediate consequences by a retreat. In a very few weeks he was reduced to the ranks as "only my husband," and, although no direct order of the day was read to that effect, he was "respected accordingly." Before that retrograde promotion took place, Pedrigo Pumpilion cultivated his hair, and encouraged its sneaking inclination to curl until it woollied up quite fiercely; but afterwards his locks became broken-heartedly pendant, and straight with the weight of care, while his whiskers hung back as if asking counsel and comfort from his ears. He twiddled his thumbs with a slow, rotary motion as he sat, and he carried his hands clasped behind him as he walked, thus intimating that he couldn't help it, and that he didn't mean to try. For the same reason, he never buttoned his coat, and wore no straps to the feet of his trousers; both of which seemed too energetically resolute for "only my husband." Even his hat, as it sat on the back part of his head, looked as if Mrs. Pumpilion had put it on for him (no one but the wearer can put on a hat so that it will sit naturally), and as if he had not nerve enough even to shake it down to its characteristic place and physiognomical expression. His *personnel* loudly proclaimed that the Mitts method in matrimony had been a failure, and that the Queen had given the King a check-mate. Mrs. Pumpilion had been triumphant in acting upon the advice of her friend, the widow, who, having the advantage of Mitts in combining experience with theory, understood the art of breaking husbands *à merveille*.

"My dear madam," said Mrs. Margery Daw, "you have plenty of spirit; but spirit is nothing without steadiness and perseverance. In the establishment of authority and in the assertion of one's rights, any intermission before success is complete requires us to begin again. If your talent leads you to the weeping method of softening your husband's heart, you will find that if you give him a shower now and a shower then, he will harden in the intervals between the rain; while a good sullen cry of twenty-four hours' length may prevent any necessity for another. If, on the contrary, you have genius for the tempestuous, continued thunder and lightning for the same length of time is irresistible. Gentlemen are great swaggerers, if not impressively dealt with and early taught to know their places. They are much like Frisk," continued the widow, addressing her lap-dog. "If they bark, and you draw back frightened, they are sure to bite: stamp your foot, and they soon learn to run into a corner. Don't they, Frisky dear?"

"Ya-p!" responded the dog, and Mrs. Pumpilion, tired of control, took the concurrent advice.

———

"To-morrow," said Pumpilion, carelessly and with an of-course-ish air, as he returned to tea from a stroll with his friend, Michael Mitts, who had just been urging on him the propriety of continuing the Mitts method after marriage—"to-morrow, my love, I leave town for a week to try a little trout fishing in the mountains."

"Mr. Pumpilion!" ejaculated the lady, in an awful tone, as she suddenly faced him. "Fishing?"

"Y-e-e-yes," replied Pumpilion, somewhat discomposed.

"Then I shall go with you, Mr. Pumpilion," said the lady, as she emphatically split a muffin.

"Quite *on*possible," returned Pumpilion, with decisive stress upon the first syllable; "it's a buck party, if I may use the expression—a buck party entirely—there's Mike Mitts, funny Joe Mungoozle—son of old Mungoozle—Tommy Titcomb, and myself. We intend having a rough and tumble among the hills to beneficialize our wholesomes, as funny Joe Mungoozle has it."

"Funny Joe Mungoozle is not a fit companion for any married man, Mr. Pumpilion; and it's easy to see, by your sliding back among the dissolute friends and dissolute practices of your bachelorship, Mr. Pumpilion, by your wish to associate with sneering and depraved Mungoozles, Mitts and Titcombs, Mr. Pumpilion, that the society of your poor wife is losing its attractions," and Mrs. Pumpilion sobbed convulsively at the thought.

"I have given my word to go a-fishing," replied Pedrigo, rather rue-fully, "and a-fishing I must go. What would Mungoozle say?—why, he would have a song about it, and sing it at the 'free and easies.' "

"What matter? let him say—let him sing. But it's not my observa-tions—it's those of funny Joe Mungoozle that you care for—the affec-tions of the 'free and easy' carousers that you are afraid of losing."

"Mungoozle is a very particular friend of mine, Seraphina," replied Pedrigo, rather nettled. "We're going a-fishing—that's flat!"

"Without me?"

"Without you—it being a buck party, without exception."

Mrs. Pumpilion gave a shriek, and falling back, threw out her arms *fitfully*—the tea-pot went by the board as she made the tragic move-ment.

"Wretched, unhappy woman!" gasped Mrs. Pumpilion, speaking of herself.

Pedrigo did not respond to the declaration, but alternately eyed the fragments of the tea-pot and the untouched muffin which remained on his plate. The *coup* had not been without its effect; but still he faintly whispered, "Funny Joe Mungoozle, and going a-fishing."

"It's clear you wish to kill me—to break my heart," muttered the lady, in a spasmodic manner.

" 'Pon my soul, I don't—I'm only going a-fishing."

"I shall go distracted!" screamed Mrs. Pumpilion, suiting the action to the word, and springing to her feet in such a way as to upset the table, and roll its contents into Pedrigo's lap, who scrambled from the *débris*, as his wife, with the air of the Pythoness, swept rapidly round the room, whirling the ornaments to the floor, and indulging in the grand rigadoon upon their remains.

"You no longer love me, Pedrigo; and without your love what is life? What is this, or this, or this?" continued she, a crash following every word, "without mutual affection? Going a fishing!"

"I don't know that I am," whined Pumpilion; "perhaps it will rain to-morrow."

Now it so happened that there were no clouds visible on the occa-sion, except in the domestic atmosphere; but the rain was adroitly thrown in as a white flag, indicative of a wish to open a negotiation and come to terms. Mrs. Pumpilion, however, understood the art of war better than to treat with rebels with arms in their hands. Her military genius, no longer "latent," whispered her to persevere until she obtained a surrender at discretion.

"Ah, Pedrigo, you only say that to deceive your heart-broken wife. You intend to slip away—you and your Mungoozles—to pass your hours in roaring iniquity, instead of enjoying the calm sunshine of domestic peace, and the gentle delights of fireside felicity. They are too tame, too flat, too insipid, for a depraved taste. That I should ever live to see the day!" and she relapsed into the intense style, by way of a specimen of calm delight.

Mr. and Mrs. Pumpilion retired for the night at an early hour; but until the dawn of day, the words of reproach, now passionate, now pathetic, ceased not; and in the very gray of the morning, Mrs. P. marched down stairs *en dishabille*, still repeating ejaculations about the Mungoozle fishing-party. What happened below is not precisely ascertained; but there was a terrible turmoil in the kitchen, it being perfectly clear a whole "kettle of fish" was in preparation, that Pedrigo might not have the trouble of going to the mountains on a piscatorial expedition.

He remained seated on the side of his bed, like Marius upon the ruins of Carthage, meditating upon the situation of affairs, and balancing between a surrender to petticoat government and his dread of Mungoozle's song at the "free and easies." At length he slipped down. Mrs. Pumpilion sat glooming at the parlor window. Pedrigo tried to read the *Saturday News* upside down.

"Good morning, Mr. Pumpilion! Going a-fishing, Mr. Pumpilion? Mike Mitts, funny Joe Mungoozle and Tommy Titcomb must be waiting for you, you know," continued she, with a mocking smile; "you're to go this morning to the mountains on a rough and tumble for the benefit of your wholesomes. The elegance of the phraseology is quite in character with the whole affair."

Pedrigo was tired out; Mrs. Margery Daw's perseverance prescription had been too much for the Mitt method; the widow had overmatched the bachelor.

"No, Seraphina, my dearest, I'm not going a-fishing, if you don't desire it, and I see you don't."

Not a word about it's being likely to rain—the surrender was unconditional.

"But," added Pedrigo, "I should like to have a little breakfast."

Mrs. Pumpilion was determined to clinch the nail.

"There's to be no breakfast here—I've been talking to Sally and Tommy in the kitchen, and I verily believe the whole world's in a plot against me. They're gone, Mr. Pumpilion—gone a-fishing, perhaps."

The battle was over—the victory was won—the nail was clinched. Tealess, sleepless, breakfastless, what could Pedrigo do but sue for mercy, and abandon a contest waged against such hopeless odds? The supplies being cut off, the siege-worn garrison must surrender. After hours of solicitation, the kiss of amity was reluctantly accorded; on condition, however, that "funny Joe Mongoozle" and the rest of the fishing party should be given up, and that he, Pedrigo, for the future should refrain from associating with bachelors and widowers, both of whom she *tabooed*, and consort with none but staid married men.

From this moment the individuality of that once free agent, Pedrigo Pumpilion, was sunk into "only my husband"—the humblest of all humble animals. He fetches and carries, goes errands, and lugs band-boxes and bundles; he walks the little Pumpilions up and down the room when they squall o' nights, and he never comes in when any of his wife's distinguished friends call to visit her. In truth, Pedrigo is not always in a presentable condition; for as Mrs. Pumpilion is *de facto* treasurer, he is kept upon rather short allowance, her wants being paramount, and proportioned to the dignity of head of the family. But although he is now dutiful enough, he at first ventured once or twice to be refractory. These symptoms of insubordination, however, were soon quelled—for Mrs. Pumpilion, with a significant glance, inquired:

"*Are you going a-fishing again, my dear?*"

A Day's Work

MARK TWAIN

Saturday morning was come, and all the summer world was bright and fresh, and brimming with life. There was a song in every heart; and if the heart was young the music issued at the lips. There was cheer in every face and a spring in every step. The locust-trees were in bloom, and the fragrance of the blossoms filled the air. Cardiff Hill, beyond the village and above it, was green with vegetation, and it lay just far enough away to seem a Delectable Land, dreamy, reposeful and inviting.

Tom appeared on the sidewalk with a bucket of whitewash and a long-handled brush. He surveyed the fence, and all gladness left him, and a deep melancholy settled down upon his spirit. Thirty yards of board fence nine feet high! Life to him seemed hollow, and existence but a burden. Sighing he dipped his brush and passed it along the topmost plank; repeated the operation; did it again; compared the insignificant whitewashed streak with the far-reaching continent of unwhitewashed fence, and sat down on a tree-box discouraged. Jim came skipping out at the gate with a tin pail, and singing "Buffalo Gals." Bringing water from the town pump had always been hateful work in Tom's eyes, before, but now it did not strike him so. He remembered that there was company at the pump. White, mulatto and negro boys and girls always were there waiting their turns, resting, trading playthings, quarreling, fighting, skylarking. And he remembered that although the pump was only a hundred and fifty yards off, Jim never got back with a bucket of water under an hour—and even then somebody generally had to go after him. Tom said:

"Say, Jim, I'll fetch the water if you'll whitewash some."

Jim shook his head and said:

"Can't, Mars Tom. Ole missis, she tole me I got to go an' git dis water an' not stop foolin' roun' wid anybody. She say she spec' Mars Tom gwine to ax me to whitewash, an' so she tole me go 'long an' 'tend to my own business—she 'lowed *she'd* 'tend to de whitewashin'."

"Oh, never you mind what she said, Jim. That's the way she talks. Gimme the bucket—I won't be gone only a minute. *She* won't ever know."

"Oh, I dasn't, Mars Tom. Ole missis she'd take an' tar de head off'n me. 'Deed she would."

"*She!* She never licks anybody—whacks 'em over the head with her thimble—and who cares for that, I'd like to know. She talks awful, but talk don't hurt—anyways, it don't if she don't cry. Jim, I'll give you a marvel. I'll give you a white alley!"

Jim began to waver.

"White alley, Jim! And its a bully taw."

"My! Dat's a mighty gay marvel, *I* tell you! But, Mars Tom, I's powerful 'fraid ole missis—"

"And besides, if you will, I'll show you my sore toe."

Jim was only human—this attraction was too much for him. He put down his pail, took the white alley, and bent over the toe with absorbing interest while the bandage was being unwound, In another moment he was flying down the street with his pail and a tingling rear, Tom was whitewashing with vigor, and Aunt Polly was retiring from the field with a slipper in her hand and triumph in her eye.

But Tom's energy did not last. He began to think of the fun he had planned for this day, and his sorrows multiplied. Soon the free boys would come tripping along on all sorts of delicious expeditions, and they would make a world of fun of him for having to work—the very thought of it burnt him like fire. He got out his worldly wealth and examined it—bits of toys, marbles and trash; enough to buy an exchange of *work*, maybe, but not half enough to buy so much as half an hour of pure freedom. So he returned his straightened means to his pocket, and gave up the idea of trying to buy the boys. At this dark and hopeless moment an inspiration burst upon him! Nothing less than a great, magnificent inspiration.

He took up his brush and went tranquilly to work. Ben Rogers hove in sight presently—the very boy, of all boys, whose ridicule he had been dreading. Ben's gait was the hop-skip-and-jump—proof enough that his heart was light and his anticipations high. He was eating an apple, and giving a long, melodious whoop, at intervals, followed by a deep-toned ding-dong-dong, for he was personating a steamboat. As he drew near, he slackened speed, took the middle of the street, leaned far over to starboard and rounded to ponderously and with laborious pomp and circumstance—for he was personating the *Big Missouri*, and considered himself to be drawing nine feet of water. He was boat, and captain, and engine-bells combined, so he had to imagine himself standing on his own hurricane-deck giving the orders and executing them:

"Stop her, sir! Ting-a-ling-ling!" The headway ran almost out, and he drew up slowly toward the sidewalk.

"Ship up to back! Ting-a-ling-ling!" His arms straightened and stiffened down his sides.

"Set her back on the stabbord! Ting-a-ling-ling! Chow! ch-chow-wow! Chow!" His right hand, meantime, describing stately circles—for it was representing a forty-foot wheel.

PUTTING IT IN A NEW LIGHT.

"Let her go back on the labbord! Ting-a-ling-ling! Chow-ch-chow-chow!" The left hand began to describe circles.

"Stop the stabbord! Ting-a-ling-ling! Stop the labbord! Come ahead on the stabbord! Stop her! Let your outside turn over slow! Ting-a-ling-ling! Chow-ow-ow! Get out that headline! *Lively* now! Come—out with your spring-line—what're you about there! Take a turn round that stump with the bight of it! Stand by that stage, now—let her go! Done with the engines, sir!' Ting-a-ling-ling! *Sh't! sh't! sh't!*" (trying the gauge-cocks).

Tom went on whitewashing—paid no attention to the steamboat. Ben stared a moment and then said:

"Hi-*yi! You're* up a stump, ain't you!"

No answer. Tom surveyed his last touch with the eye of an artist; then he gave his brush another gentle sweep and surveyed the result, as before. Ben ranged up alongside of him. Tom's mouth watered for the apple, but he stuck to his work. Ben said:

"Hello, old chap, you got to work, hey?"

Tom wheeled suddenly and said:

"Why, it's you, Ben! I warn't noticing."

"Say—*I'm* going in a-swimming, *I* am. Don't you wish you could? But of course you'd druther *work*—wouldn't you? Course you would!"

Tom contemplated the boy a bit, and said:

"What do you call work?"

"Why, ain't *that* work?"

Tom resumed his whitewashing, and answered carelessly:

"Well, maybe it is, and maybe it ain't. All I know, is, it suits Tom Sawyer."

"Oh come, now, you don't mean to let on that you *like* it?"

The brush continued to move.

"Like it? Well, I don't see why I oughtn't to like it. Does a boy get a chance to whitewash a fence every day?"

That put the thing in a new light. Ben stopped nibbling his apple. Tom swept his brush daintily back and forth—stepped back to note the effect—added a touch here and there—criticised the effect again—Ben watching every move and getting more and more interested, more and more absorbed. Presently he said:

"Say, Tom, let *me* whitewash a little."

Tom considered, was about to consent; but he altered his mind:

"No—no—I reckon it wouldn't hardly do, Ben. You see, Aunt Polly's awful particular about this fence—right here on the street, you know—but if it was the back fence I wouldn't mind, and *she* wouldn't. Yes, she's awful particular about this fence; it's got to be done very careful; I reckon there ain't one boy in a thousand, maybe two thousand, that can do it the way it's got to be done.

"No—is that so? Oh, come, now—lemme just try. Only just a little—I'd let *you*, if you was me, Tom."

"Ben, I'd like to, honest injun; but Aunt Polly—well, Jim wanted to do it, but she wouldn't let him. Sid wanted to do it, and she wouldn't let Sid. Now don't you see how I'm fixed? If you was to tackle this fence and anything was to happen to it——"

"Oh, shucks, I'll be just as careful. Now lemme try. Say—I'll give you the core of my apple."

"Well, here—. No, Ben, now don't. I'm afeared—"

"I'll give you *all* of it!"

Tom gave up the brush, with reluctance in his face but alacrity in his heart. And while the late steamer *Big Missouri* worked and sweated in the sun, the retired artist sat on a barrel in the shade close by, dangled his legs, munched his apple, and planned the slaughter of more innocents. There was no lack of material; boys happened along every little while; they came to jeer, but remained to whitewash. By the time Ben was fagged out, Tom had traded the next chance to Billy Fisher for a kite, in good repair; and when *he* played out, Johnny Miller bought in for a dead rat and a string to swing it with—and so on, and so on, hour after hour. And when the middle of the afternoon came, from being a poor poverty-stricken boy in the morning, Tom was literally rolling in wealth. He had, besides the things before mentioned, twelve marbles, part of a jew's-harp, a piece of blue bottle-glass to look through, a spool cannon, a key that wouldn't unlock anything, a fragment of chalk, a glass stopper of a decanter, a tin soldier, a couple of tadpoles, six fire-crackers, a kitten with only one eye, a brass door-knob, a dog-collar—but no dog—the handle of a knife, four pieces of orange-peel, and a dilapidated old window-sash.

Trying to Understand a Woman

W. D. Howells

Wm. Dean Howells was born at Martin's Ferry, Belmont County, O., March 1, 1837. He is a printer by trade and inheritance, and he early entered newspaper life. He is the author of many novels, sketches, criticisms, dramatic studies, poems and travels.

The last hues of sunset lingered in the mists that sprung from the base of the Falls with a mournful, tremulous grace, and a movement weird as the play of the Northern Lights. They were touched with the most delicate purples and crimsons, that darkened to deep red, and then faded from them at a second look, and they flew upward, swiftly upward, like troops of pale, transparent ghosts; while a perfectly clear radiance, better than any other for local color, dwelt upon the scene. Far under the bridge the river smoothly swam, the undercurrents forever unfolding themselves upon the surface with a vast rose-like evolution, edged all round with faint lines of white, where the air that filled the water freed itself in foam. What had been clear green on the face of the cataract was here more like rich verd-antique, and had a look of firmness almost like that of the stone itself. So it showed beneath the bridge and down the river, till the curving shores hid it. These, springing abruptly from the water's brink, and shagged with pine and cedar, displayed the tender verdure of grass and bushes intermingled with the dark evergreens that climb from ledge to ledge, till they point their speary tops above the crest of bluffs. In front, where tumbled rocks and expanses of naked clay varied the gloomier and gayer green, sprung those spectral mists; and through them loomed out, in its manifold majesty, Niagara, with the seemingly immovable white gothic screen of the American Fall, and the green massive curve of the Horse-Shoe, solid and simple and calm as an Egyptian wall; while behind this, with their white and black expanses broken by dark-foliaged little isles, the steep Canadian rapids billowed down between their heavily wooded shores.

The wedding-journeyers hung, they knew not how long, in rapture on the sight; and then, looking back from the shore to the spot where they had stood, they felt relieved that unreality should possess itself of all, and that the bridge should swing there in mid-air like a filmy web, scarce more passable than the rainbow that flings its arch above the mists.

On the portico of the hotel they found half a score of gentlemen smoking, and creating together that collective silence which passes for sociality on our continent. Some carriages stood before the door, and within, around the base of a pillar, sat a circle of idle call-boys. There were a few trunks heaped together in one place, with a porter standing guard over them; a solitary guest was buying a cigar at the newspaper stand in one corner; another friendless creature was writing a letter in the reading-room; the clerk, in a seersucker coat and a lavish shirt-bosom, tried to give the whole an effect of watering place gayety and bustle, as he provided a newly arrived guest with a room.

Our pair took in these traits of solitude and repose with indifference. If the hotel had been thronged with brilliant company, they would have been no more and no less pleased; and when, after supper, they came into the grand parlor, and found nothing there but a marble-topped centre-table, with a silver-plated ice-pitcher and a small company of goblets, they sat down perfectly content in a secluded window-seat. They were not seen by the three people who entered soon after, and halted in the centre of the room.

"Why, Kitty!" said one of the two ladies who must be in any traveling-party of three, "this is more inappropriate to your gorgeous array than the supper-room, even."

She who was called Kitty was armed, as for social conquest, in some kind of airy evening dress, and was looking round with bewilderment upon that forlorn waste of carpeting and upholstery. She owned, with a smile, that she had not seen so much of the world yet as she had been promised; but she liked Niagara very much, and perhaps they should find the world at breakfast.

"No," said the other lady, who was as unquiet as Kitty was calm, and who seemed resolved to make the most of the worst, "it isn't probable that the hotel will fill up over night; and I feel personally responsible for this state of things. Who would ever have supposed that Niagara would be so empty? I thought the place was thronged the whole summer. How do you account for it, Richard?"

The gentleman looked fatigued, as from a long-continued discussion elsewhere of the matter in hand, and he said that he had not been trying to account for it.

"Then you don't care for Kitty's pleasure at all, and you don't want her to enjoy herself. Why don't you take some interest in the matter?"

"Why, if I accounted for the emptiness of Niagara in the most satisfactory way, it wouldn't add a soul to the floating population. Under the circumstances, I prefer to leave it unexplained."

"Do you think it's because it's such a hot summer? Do you suppose it's not exactly the season? Didn't you expect there'd be more people? Perhaps Niagara isn't as fashionable as it used to be."

"It looks something like that."

"Well, what under the sun do you think *is* the reason?"

"I don't know."

"Perhaps," interposed Kitty, placidly, "most of the visitors go to the other hotel now."

"It's altogether likely," said the other lady eagerly. "There are just such caprices."

"Well," said Richard, "I wanted you to go there."

"But you said that you always heard this was the most fashionable."

"I know it. I didn't want to come here for that reason. But fortune favors the brave."

"Well, it's too bad! Here we've asked Kitty to come to Niagara with us, just to give her a little peep into the world, and you've brought us to a hotel where we're—"

"Monarchs of all we survey," suggested Kitty.

"Yes, and start at the sound of our own," added the other lady, helplessly.

"Come, now, Fanny," said the gentleman, who was but too clearly the husband of the last speaker, "you know you insisted, against all I could say or do, upon coming to this house; I implored you to go to the other, and now you blame me for bringing you here."

"So I do. If you'd let me have my own way without opposition about coming here, I dare say I should have gone to the other place. But never mind; Kitty knows whom to blame, I hope. She's *your* cousin."

Kitty was sitting with her hands quiescently folded in her lap. She now rose, and said that she did not know anything about the other hotel, and perhaps it was just as empty as this.

"It can't be. There can't be *two* hotels so empty," said Fanny. "It don't stand to reason."

"If you wish Kitty to see the world so much" said the gentleman, "why don't you take her on to Quebec with us?"

Kitty had left her seat beside Fanny, and was moving with a listless content about the parlor.

"I wonder you ask, Richard, when you know she's only come for the night, and has nothing with her but a few cuffs and collars! I certainly never heard of anything so absurd before!"

The absurdity of the idea then seemed to cast its charm upon her; for, after a silence, "I could lend her some things," she said, musingly. "But don't speak of it to-night, please. It's *too* ridiculous. Kitty!" she called out, and, as the young lady drew near, she continued, "How would you like to go to Quebec with us?"

"O Fanny!" cried Kitty, with rapture; and then, with dismay, "How *can* I!"

"Why, very well, I think. You've got this dress, and your traveling-suit, and I can lend you whatever you want. Come!" she added joyously, "let's go up to your room, and talk it over!"

The two ladies vanished upon this impulse, and the gentleman followed. To their own relief the guiltless eavesdroppers, who had found no moment favorable for revealing themselves after the comedy began, issued from their retiracy.

"What a remarkable little lady!" said Basil, eagerly turning to Isabel for sympathy in his enjoyment of her inconsequence.

"Yes, poor thing!" returned his wife; "it's no light matter to invite a young lady to take a journey with you, and promise her all sorts of gayety, and perhaps beaux and flirtations, and then find her on your hands in a desolation like this. It's dreadful, I think."

Basil stared. "O, certainly," he said. "But what an amusingly illogical little body!"

"I don't understand what you mean, Basil. It was the only thing that she could do, to invite the young lady to go on with them. I wonder her husband had the sense to think of it first. Of *course* she'll have to lend her things."

"And you didn't observe anything peculiar in her way of reaching her conclusions?"

"Peculiar? What *do* you mean?"

"Why, her blaming her husband for letting her have her own way about the hotel; and her telling him not to mention his proposal to Kitty, and then doing it herself, just after she'd pronounced it absurd and impossible." He spoke with heat at being forced to make what he thought a needless explanation.

"O," said Isabel, after a moment's reflection, "*That!* Did you think it so very odd?"

Her husband looked at her with the gravity a man must feel when he begins to perceive that he has married the whole mystifying world of womankind in the woman of his choice, and made no answer. But to his own soul he said: "I supposed I had the pleasure of my wife's acquaintance. It seems I have been flattering myself."

A FEMALE BASE-BALL CLUB

JAMES M. BAILEY

James Montgomery Bailey, so widely known as the *Danbury News* MAN, was born at Albany, N. Y., September 25, 1841, and after receiving a common-school education, learned the carpenter's trade. He fought through the war in a Connecticut regiment, and settled in Danbury at the close as editor of the *News.*

The only attempt on record of Danbury trying to organize a female base-ball club occurred last week. It was a rather incipient affair, but it demonstrated everything necessary, and in that particular answered every purpose. The idea was cogitated and carried out by six young ladies. It was merely designed for an experiment on which to base future action. The young ladies were at the house of one of their number when the subject was brought up. The premises are capacious, and include quite a piece of turf, hidden from the street by several drooping, luxuriant, old-fashioned apple-trees. The young lady of the house has a brother who is fond of base-ball, and has the necessary machinery for a game. This was taken out on the turf under the trees. The ladies assembled, and divided themselves into two nines of three each. The first three took the bat, and the second three went to the bases, one as catcher, one as pitcher, and the other as chaser, or, more technically, fielder. The pitcher was a lively brunette, with eyes full of dead earnestness. The catcher and batter were blondes, with faces aflame with expectation. The pitcher took the ball, braced herself, put her arm straight out from her shoulder, then moved it around to her back without modifying in the least its delightful rigidity, and then threw it. The batter did not catch it. This was owing to the pitcher looking directly at the batter when she aimed it. The fielder got a long pole and soon succeeded in poking the ball from an apple-tree back of the pitcher, where it had lodged. Business was then resumed again, although with a faint semblance of uneasiness generally visible.

The pitcher was very red in the face, and said "I declare!" several times. This time she took a more careful aim, but still neglected to look in some other direction than toward the batter, and the ball was presently poked out of another tree.

"Why, this is dreadful!" said the batter, whose nerves had been kept at a pretty stiff tension.

"Perfectly dreadful!" chimed in the catcher, with a long sigh.

"I think you had better get up in one of the trees," mildly suggested the fielder to the batter.

The observations somewhat nettled the pitcher, and she declared she would not try again, whereupon a change was made with the fielder. She was certainly more sensible. Just as soon as she was ready to let drive, she shut her eyes so tight as to loosen two of her puffs and pull out her back comb, and madly fired away. The ball flew directly at the batter, which so startled that lady, who had the bat clinched in both hands with desperate grip, that she involuntarily cried, "Oh, my!" and let it drop, and ran. This movement uncovered the catcher, who had both hands extended about three feet apart, in readiness for the catch, but being intently absorbed in studying the coil on the back of the batter's head, she was not able to recover in time, and the ball caught her in the bodice with sufficient force to deprive her of all her breath, which left her lips with earpiercing shrillness. There was a lull in the proceedings for ten minutes, to enable the other members of the club to arrange their hair.

The batter again took position, when one of the party, discovering that she was holding the bat very much as a woman carries a broom when she is after a cow in the garden, showed her that the tip must rest on the ground and at her side, with her body a trifle inclined in that direction. The suggester took the bat and showed just how it was done, and brought around the bat with such vehemence as to almost carry her from her feet, and to nearly brain the catcher. That party shivered, and moved back some fifteen feet.

The batter took her place, and laid the tip of the bat on the ground, and the pitcher shut her eyes again as tightly as before, and let drive. The fielder had taken the precaution to get back of a tree, or otherwise she must have been disfigured for life. The ball was recovered. The pitcher looked heated and vexed. She didn't throw it this time. She just gave it a pitching motion, but not letting go of it in time it went over her head, and caused her to sit down with considerable unexpectedness.

Thereupon she declared she would never throw another ball as long as she lived, and changed off with the catcher. This young lady was somewhat determined, which augured success. Then she looked in an altogether different direction from that to the batter.

And this did the business. The batter was ready. She had a tight hold on the bat. Just as soon as she saw the ball start, she made a tremendous lunge with the bat, let go of it, and turned around in time to catch the ball in the small of her back, while the bat, being on its own hook, and seeing a stone figure holding a vase of flowers, neatly clipped off its arm at the elbow and let the flowers to the ground.

There was a chorus of screams, and some confusion of skirts, and then the following dialogue took place:

No. 1. "Let's give up the nasty thing."

No. 2. "Let's."

No. 3. "So I say."

No. 4. "It's just horrid."

This being a majority, the adjournment was made.

The game was merely an experiment. And it is just as well it was. Had it been a real game, it is likely that some one would have been killed outright.

WOMAN

JOSH BILLINGS

Woman iz the glass ware ov kreashun. She iz luvly, and brittle, but she hez run up everything we really enjoy in this life from 25 cents on the dollar to par. Adam, without Eve, would hav been az stupid a game az playing checkures alone. Thare haz been more butiful things sed in her praze than thare haz ov enny other animate thing, and she is worthy ov them all. She is not an angell tho, and i hope she wont never go into the angell bizzness. Angells on earth dont pay. The only mistake that woman haz ever made iz to think she iz a better man than Adam.

THE ROBIN AND THE WOODPECKER

AMBROSE BIERCE

Ambrose Bierce, author of "Bierce's Fables," was born in Akron, O., in 1843. He served as a soldier in the war, and in 1865 went to San Francisco, where he was in newspaper work until 1872. Then he went to London, where he had great success, and published "Bierciana." With the younger Tom Hood he founded *London Fun*. He returned to California in 1877, and is now an editor of the San Francisco *Examiner*.

A woodpecker, who had bored a multitude of holes in the body of a dead tree, was asked by a robin to explain their purpose.

"As yet, in the infancy of science," replied the woodpecker, "I am quite unable to do so. Some naturalists affirm that I hide acorns in these pits; others maintain that I get worms out of them. I endeavored for some time to reconcile the two theories; but the worms ate my acorns, and then would not come out. Since then I have left science to work out its own problems, while I work out the holes. I hope the final decision may be in some way advantageous to me; for at my nest I have a number of prepared holes which I can hammer into some suitable tree at a moment's notice. Perhaps I could insert a few into the scientific head."

"No-o-o," said the robin, reflectively, "I should think not. A prepared hole is an idea; I don't think it could get in."

MORAL.—It might be driven in with a steam-hammer.

I DON'T reckolekt ov ever doing ennything that i waz just a little ashamed ov, but what sum one waz sure to remember it, and every once in a while put me in mind of it.

JOSH BILLINGS

THE TAR BABY

UNCLE REMUS

Joel Chandler Harris was born at Eatonton, Ga., December 9, 1848, and learned the printing business in the office of *The Countryman*, a paper published on a plantation, ten miles from any railroad. He there acquainted himself with the negro folk-lore, which he afterwards used in the "Nights with Uncle Remus." These sketches, now of a world-wide celebrity, first appeared in the *Atlanta Constitution*.

I.

One evening recently, the lady whom Uncle Remus calls "Miss Sally" missed her little seven-year-old. Making search for him through the house and through the yard, she heard the sound of voices in the old man's cabin, and, looking through the window, saw the child sitting by Uncle Remus. His head rested against the old man's arm, and he was gazing with an expression of the most intense interest into the rough, weather-beaten face that beamed so kindly upon him. This is what "Miss Sally" heard:

"Bimeby, one day, arter Brer Fox bin doin' all dat he could fer ter ketch Brer Rabbit, en Brer Rabbit bin doin' all he could fer ter keep im fum it, Brer Fox say to hisse'f dat he'd put up a game on Brer Rabbit, en he ain't mo'n got de wuds out'n his mout twel Brer Rabbit come a lopin' up de big road, lookin' des ez plump en ez fat en ez sassy ez a Moggin hoss in a barley-patch.

" 'Hol' on, dar, Brer Rabbit,' sez Brer Fox, sezee.

" 'I ain't got time, Brer Fox,' sez Brer Rabbit, sezee, sorter mendin' his licks.

" 'I wanter have some confab wid you, Brer Rabbit,' sez Brer Fox, sezee.

" 'All right, Brer Fox; but you better holler fum whar you stan'. I'm monstus full er fleas dis mawnin',' sez Brer Rabbit, sezee.

" 'I seed Brer B'ar yistiddy,' sez Brer Fox, sezee, 'en he sorter rake me over de coals kaze you en me ain't make frens en live naberly; en I tole 'im dat I'd see you.'

"Den Brer Rabbit scratch one year wid his off hine-foot sorter jub'usly, en den he ups en sez, sezee:

" 'All a settin', Brer Fox. Spose'n you drap roun' ter-morrer en take dinner wid me. We ain't got no great doin's at our house, but I speck de ole 'oman en de chilluns kin sorter scramble roun' en git up somp'n fer ter stay yo' stummuck.'

" 'I'm 'gree'ble, Brer Rabbit,' sez Brer Fox, sezee.

" 'Den I'll 'pen' on you,' sez Brer Rabbit, sezee.

"Nex' day, Mr. Rabbit an' Miss Rabbit got up soon, 'fo' day, en raided on a gyarden, like Miss Sally's out dar, en got some cabbiges, en some roas'n years, en some sparrer-grass, en dey fix up a smashin' dinner. Bimeby, one er de little Rabbits playin' out in de back-yard, come runnin' in, hollerin', 'Oh, ma! oh, ma! I seed Mr. Fox a comin'!' En den Brer Rabbit he tuck de chilluns by der years en make um set down; en den him en Miss Rabbit sorter dally roun' waitin' for Brer Fox. En dey keep on waitin', but no Brer Fox ain't come. Atter 'while Brer Rabbit goes to de do', easy like, en peep out, en dar, stickin' out fum behine de cornder, wuz de tip-een' er Brer Fox's tail. Den Brer Rabbit shot de do' en sot down, en put his paws behime his years en begin fer ter sing:

> " 'De place wharbouts you spill de grease,
>   Right dar youer boun' ter slide,
>   An' whar you fine a bunch er ha'r,
>   You'll sholy fine de hide.'

"Nex' day, Brer Fox sent word by Mr. Mink, en skuze hisse'f, kase he wuz too sick fer ter come, en he ax Brer Rabbit fer ter come en take dinner wid him, en Brer Rabbit say he wuz 'gree'ble.

"Bimeby, w'en de shadders wuz at der shortes', Brer Rabbit he sorter brush up en santer down ter Brer Fox's house, en w'en he got dar, he yer somebody groanin', en he look in de do' en dar he see Brer Fox settin' up in a rockin'-cheer all wrop up wid flannil, en he look mighty weak. Brer Rabbit look all 'roun', he did, but he ain't see no dinner. De dish-pan wuz settin' on de table, en close by wuz a kyarvin'-knife.

" 'Look like you gwinter have chicken fer dinner, Brer Fox,' sez Brer Rabbit, sezee.

" 'Yes, Brer Rabbit, deyer nice en fresh en tender,' sez Brer Fox, sezee.

"Den Brer Rabbit sorter pull his mustarsh, en say: 'You ain't got no calamus root, is you, Brer Fox? I done got so now dat I can't eat no chicken 'ceptin she's seasoned up wid calamus root.' En wid dat, Brer Rabbit lipt out er de do' and dodge 'mong de bushes, en sot dar watchin' fer Brer Fox; en he ain't watch long, nudder, kaze Brer Fox flung off de flannel en crope out er de house en got whar he could close in on Brer Rabbit, en bimeby Brer Rabbit holler out: 'Oh, Brer Fox! I'll des put yo' calamus root out yer on dish yer stump. Better come git it while it's fresh,' an' wid dat Brer Rabbit gallop off home. En Brer Fox ain't never kotch 'im yit, en w'at's mo', honey, he ain't gwineter."

II.

"Didn't the fox *never* catch the rabbit, Uncle Remus?" asked the little boy the next evening.

"He come mighty nigh it, honey, sho's you bawn—Brer Fox did. One day, atter Brer Rabbit fool 'im wid dat calamus root, Brer Fox went ter wuk en got 'im some tar, en mix it wid some turkentime, en fix up a contrapshun wat he call a Tar-Baby, en he tuck dish yer Tar-Baby en he sot 'er in de big road, en den he lay off in de bushes fer ter see wat de news wuz gwineter be. En he didn't hatter wait long, nudder, kaze bimeby here come Brer Rabbit pacin' down de road—lippity-clippity, clippity-lippity—dez ez sassy ez a jay-bird. Brer Fox, he lay low. Brer Rabbit come prancin' 'long twel he spy de Tar-Baby', en den he fotch up on his behime legs like he wuz 'stonished. De Tar-Baby, she sot dar, she did, en Brer Fox, he lay low.

" 'Mawnin'!' sez Brer Rabbit, sezee—'nice wedder dis mawnin',' sezee.

"Tar-Baby ain't sayin' nuthin', en Brer Fox, he lay low.

" 'How duz yo' sym'tums seem ter segashuate?' sez Brer Rabbit, sezee.

"Brer Fox, he wink his eye slow, en lay low, en de Tar-Baby, she ain't sayin' nuthin'.

" 'How you come on, den? Is you deaf?' sez Brer Rabbit, sezee. 'Kaze if you is, I kin holler louder,' sezee.

"Tar-Baby stay still, en Brer Fox, he lay low.

" 'Youer stuck up, dat's w'at you is,' says Brer Rabbit, sezee, 'en I'm gwineter kyore you, dat's w'at I'm gwineter do,' sezee.

"Brer Fox, he sorter chuckle in his stummuck, he did, but Tar-Baby ain't sayin' nuthin'.

" 'I'm gwineter larn you howter talk ter 'specttubble fokes ef hit's de las' ack,' sez Brer Rabbit, sezee. 'Ef you don't take off dat hat en tell me howdy, I'm gwineter bus' you wide open,' sezee.

"Tar-Baby stay still, en Brer Fox, he lay low.

"Brer Rabbit keep on axin' 'im, en de Tar-Baby, she keep on sayin' nuthin', twel present'y Brer Rabbit draw back wid his fis', he did, en blip he tuck 'er side 'er de head. Right dar's whar he broke his mer-lasses jug. His fis' stuck, en he can't pull loose. De tar hilt 'im. But Tar-Baby, she stay still, en Brer Fox, he lay low.

" 'Ef you don't lemme loose, I'll knock you agin,' sez Brer Rabbit, sezee, en wid dat he fotch 'er a wipe wid de udder han', en dat stuck. Tar-Baby, she ain't sayin' nuthin', en Brer Fox, he lay low.

" 'Tu'n me loose, fo' I kick de natal stuffin' outen you,' sez Brer Rab-bit, sezee, but de Tar-Baby, she ain't sayin' nuthin'. She des hilt on, en den Brer Rabbit lose de use er his feet in de same way. Brer Fox, he lay low. Den Brer Rabbit squall out dat ef de Tar-Baby don't tu'n 'im loose he butt 'er cranksided. En den he butted, en his head got stuck. Den Brer Fox, he sa'ntered fort', lookin' des ez innercent ez wunner yo' mammy's mockin'-birds.

" 'Howdy, Brer Rabbit,' sez Brer Fox, sezee. 'You look sorter stuck up dis mawnin',' sezee, en den he rolled on de groun', en laft en laft twel he couldn't laff no mo'. 'I speck you'll take dinner wid me dis time, Brer Rabbit. I done laid in some calamus root, en I ain't gwineter take no skuse,' sez Brer Fox, sezee."

Here Uncle Remus paused, and drew a two-pound yam out of the ashes.

BRER RABBIT CAUGHT.

"Did the fox eat the rabbit?" asked the little boy to whom the story had been told.

"Dat's all de fur de tale goes," replied the old man. "He mout, en den agin he mountent. Some say Jedge B'ar come 'long en loosed 'im—some say he didn't. I hear Miss Sally callin'. You better run 'long."

DICK BAKER'S CAT

MARK TWAIN

One of my comrades there—another of those victims of eighteen years of unrequited toil and blighted hopes—was one of the gentlest spirits that ever bore its patient cross in a weary exile: grave and simple Dick Baker, pocket-miner of Dead House Gulch. He was forty-six, gray as a rat, earnest, thoughtful, slenderly educated, slouchily dressed and clay-soiled, but his heart was finer metal than any gold his shovel ever brought to light—than any, indeed, that ever was mined or minted.

Whenever he was out of luck and a little down-hearted, he would fall to mourning over the loss of a wonderful cat he used to own (for where women and children are not, men of kindly impulses take up with pets, for they must love something). And he always spoke of the strange sagacity of that cat with the air of a man who believed in his secret heart that there was something human about it—may be even supernatural.

I heard him talking about this animal once. He said:

"Gentlemen, I used to have a cat here by the name of Tom Quartz, which you'd a took an interest in I reckon—most any body would. I had him here eight year—and he was the remarkablest cat *I* ever see. He was a large gray one of the Tom specie, an' he had more hard, natchral sense than any man in this camp—'n' a *power* of dignity—he wouldn't let the Gov'ner of Californy be familiar with him. He never ketched a rat in his life—'peared to be above it. He never cared for nothing but mining. He knowed more about mining, that cat did, than any man *I* ever, ever see. You couldn't tell *him* noth'n' 'bout placer diggin's—'n' as for pocket-mining, why he was just born for it. He would dig out after me an' Jim when we went over the hills prospect'n', and he would trot along behind us for as much as five mile, if we went so fur. An' he had the best judgment about mining ground—why you never see anything like it. When we went to work, he'd scatter a glance around, 'n' if he didn't think much of the indications, he would give a look as much to say, 'Well, I'll have to get you to excuse *me*,' 'n' without another word he'd hyste his nose into the air 'n' shove for home. But if the ground suited him, he would lay low 'n' keep dark till the first pan was washed, 'n' then he would sidle up 'n' take a look, an' if there was about six or seven grains of gold *he* was satisfied—he didn't want no better prospect 'n' that—'n' then he would lay down on our coats and snore like a steamboat till we'd struck the pocket, an' then get up 'n' su-perintend. He was nearly lightnin' on superintending.

"Well, bye an' bye, up comes this yer quartz excitement. Everybody was into it—everybody was pick'n' 'n' blast'n' instead of shovelin' dirt on the hill-side—everybody was put'n' down a shaft instead of scrapin' the surface. Noth'n' would do Jim but *we* must tackle the ledges, too, 'n' so we did. We commenced put'n' down a shaft, 'n' Tom Quartz he begin to wonder what in the dickens it was all about. *He* hadn't ever seen any mining like that before, 'n' he was all upset, as you may say— he couldn't come to a right understanding of it no way—it was too many for *him*. He was down on it, too, you bet you—he was down on it powerful—'n' always appeared to consider it the cussedest foolishness out. But that cat, you know, was *always* agin new-fangled arrange- ments—somehow he never could abide 'em. *You* know how it is with old habits. But bye an' bye Tom Quartz begin to git sort of reconciled a little, though he never *could* altogether understand that eternal sinkin' of a shaft an' never pannin' out anything. At last he got to comin' down in the shaft hisself, to try to cipher it out. An' when he'd git the blues, 'n' feel kind o' scruffy, 'n' aggravated 'n' disgusted— knowin', as he did, that the bills was runnin' up all the time an' we warn't makin' a cent—he would curl up on a gunny sack in the corner an' go to sleep. Well, one day when the shaft was down about eight foot, the rock got so hard that we had to put in a blast—the first blast'n' we'd ever done since Tom Quartz was born. An' then we lit the fuse 'n' clumb out 'n' got off 'bout fifty yards—'n' forgot 'n' left Tom Quartz sound asleep on the gunny sack. In 'bout a minute we seen a puff of smoke bust up out of the hole, 'n' then everything let go with an awful crash, 'n' about four million ton of rocks 'n' dirt 'n' smoke 'n' splinters

GOING UP.

shot up 'bout a mile an' a half into the air, an' by George, right in the dead centre of it was old Tom Quartz a goin' end over end, an' a snortin' an' a sneez'n', an' a clawin' an' a reachin' for things like all possessed. But it warn't no use, you know, it warn't no use. An' that was the last we see of *him* for about two minutes 'n' a half, an' then all of a sudden it begin to rain rocks and rubbage, an' directly he come down kerwhop about ten foot off f'm where we stood. Well, I reckon he was p'raps the orneriest lookin' beast you ever see. One ear was sot back on his neck, 'n' his tail was stove up, 'n' his eye-winkers was swinged off, 'n' he was all blacked up with powder an' smoke, an' all sloppy with mud 'n' slush f'm one end to the other. Well, sir, it warn't no use to try to apologize—we couldn't say a word. He took a sort of a disgusted look at hisself, 'n' then he looked at us—an' it was just exactly the same as if he had said—'Gents, maybe *you* think it's smart to take advantage of a cat that 'ain't had no experience of quartz minin', but *I* think *different*'—an' then he turned on his heel 'n' marched off home without ever saying another word.

"That was jest his style. An' maybe you won't believe it, but after that you never see a cat so prejudiced agin quartz mining as what he was. An' bye an' bye when he *did* get to goin' down in the shaft agin, you'd 'a been astonished at his sagacity. The minute we'd tetch off a blast 'n' the fuse'd begin to sizzle, he'd give a look as much as to say: 'Well, I'll have to git you to excuse *me*,' an' it was surpris'n' the way he'd shin out of that hole 'n' go f'r a tree. Sagacity? It ain't no name for it. 'Twas *inspiration!*"

I said, "Well, Mr. Baker, his prejudice against quartz-mining *was* remarkable, considering how he came by it. Couldn't you ever cure him of it?"

"*Cure him!* No! When Tom Quartz was sot once, he was *always* sot—and you might a blowed him up as much as three million times, 'n' you'd never a broken him of his cussed prejudice agin quartz mining."

AVOIDING eccentricity: "No," said the bank cashier, "I didn't need the money. I wasn't speculating. I had no necessity for stealing it. But, hang it, I didn't want to be called eccentric."

—BOSTON POST

THE HAUNTED ROOM

R. J. BURDETTE

Once, in the dead heart of the pitiless winter, I had drawn my good two-handed Lecture with the Terrible Name, and was smiting all the coasts of Pennsylvania with it, sparing neither (pronounced nyther) young nor old, and wearing at my belt the scalps of many a pale-face audience. One night I reached Erie the pleasant, just as the clock in the Lord Mayor's castle struck twenty-one. It was bitter, biting, stinging cold, and there was no ambulance at the station, while there was a good hotel there. I went in and registered, and a man of commanding presence, tailor-built clothes and a brown beard of most refined culture, followed me, and under my plebeian scrawl, made the register luminous with his patrician cognomen. I stood a little in awe of this majestic creature, and when in a deep, bass, commanding voice he ordered a room, I had a great mind—something I always carry with me when I travel—to go out and get him one. The gentlemanly and urbane night clerk, who also seemed to be deeply impressed—as is the habit of the night clerk—with the gentleman's responsible to any amount toot on sawmbel, said he was sorry, but he had but one vacant room, and it contained but one bed. "Still," he said, as became a man who was bound to stand for his house if it hadn't a bed in it, "it was a wide bed, very wide and quite long. Two gentlemen could sleep in it quite comfortably, and if——." But the Commanding Being at my side said that was quite altogether out of the question entirely. Quite. He was sorry for the—here he looked at me, hesitated, but finally said—gentleman, but He couldn't share His room with him. He was sorry for the—gentleman, and hoped he might find comfortable lodgings, but He couldn't permit him to occupy even a portion of His bed. Then the clerk begged pardon, and was sorry, and all that, but this other gentleman had registered first, and it was for him to say what disposition should be made of this lonely room and solitary bed. I hastened to assure the majestic being that it was all right; he was welcome to two-thirds of the room, all of the looking-glass and one-half of the bed. "No," he said, very abruptly, "I will sit here by the stove and sleep in my chair. I thank you, sir, but I would not sleep with my own brother. I prefer a room to myself." I meekly told him that I didn't know what kind of a man his brother was, but no doubt he did, and therefore I must conclude that he wasn't a fit man to sleep with. But his brother was out of the question, and if he wanted part of my couch, he might have it and welcome, and I would agree not to think of the brother. "No, sir," he said, "I will sleep in no man's bed." I said I wouldn't either, if I wasn't sleepy, but when I was sleepy, I didn't care; I'd sleep with the King of England or the President, and wouldn't care a cent who knew it.

Well, I went to bed. I curled up under the warm, soft blankets, and heard the wind shriek and wail and whistle and yell—how like all creation the wind can blow in Erie—and as the night grew colder and colder every minute, I fell asleep and dreamed that heaven was just forty-eight miles west of Dunkirk. About 2:30 or 3 o'clock there came a thundering rap at the door, and with a vague, half-waking impression in my dream that somebody from the other place was trying to get in, I said:

"What is it?"

"It is I," answered a splendid voice, which I recognized at once. "I am the gentleman who came on the train with you."

"Yes," I said, "and what is the matter?"

The splendid voice was a trifle humble as it replied:

"I have changed my mind about sleeping with another man."

"So have I?" I howled so joyously that the very winds laughed in merry echo. "So have I! I wouldn't get out of this warm bed to open that door for my own brother!"

I will close this story here. If I should write the language that went down that dim, cold hall outside my door you wouldn't print it. And when next morning I went skipping down-stairs as fresh as a rose, and saw that majestic being knotted up in a hard arm-chair, looking a hundred years old, I said:

"Better is a poor and wise child than an old and foolish king, who knoweth not how to be admonished. For out of prison he cometh to reign; whereas, also, he that is born in his kingdom becometh poor." This is also vanity.

A Restless Night

MARK TWAIN

We were in bed by ten, for we wanted to be up and away on our tramp homeward with the dawn. I hung fire, but Harris went to sleep at once. I hate a man who goes to sleep at once; there is a sort of indefinable something about it which is not exactly an insult, and yet is an insolence; and one which is hard to bear, too. I lay there fretting over this injury, and trying to go to sleep; but the harder I tried, the wider awake I grew. I got to feeling very lonely in the dark, with no company but an undigested dinner. My mind got a start, by and by, and began to consider the beginning of every subject which has ever been thought of; but it never went further than the beginning; it was touch and go; it fled from topic to topic with a frantic speed. At the end of an hour my head was in a perfect whirl and I was dead tired, fagged out.

The fatigue was so great that it presently began to make some head against the nervous excitement; while imagining myself wide awake, I would really doze into momentary unconsciousnesses, and come suddenly out of them with a physical jerk which nearly wrenched my joints apart—the delusion of the instant being that I was tumbling backwards over a precipice. After I had fallen over eight or nine precipices, and thus found out that one half of my brain had been asleep eight or nine times without the wide-awake, hard-working other half suspecting it, the periodical unconsciousnesses began to extend their spell gradually over more of my brain-territory, and at last I sank into a drowse which grew deeper and deeper, and was doubtless on the very point of becoming a solid, blessed, dreaming stupor, when—what was that?

My dulled faculties dragged themselves partly back to life and took a receptive attitude. Now out of an immense, a limitless distance, came a something which grew and grew, and approached, and presently was recognizable as a sound—it had rather seemed to be a feeling, before. This sound was a mile away, now—perhaps it was the murmur of a storm; and now it was nearer—not a quarter of a mile away; was it the muffled rasping and grinding of distant machinery?

No, it came still nearer; was it the measured tramp of a marching troop? But it came nearer still, and still nearer—and at last it was right in the room: it was merely a mouse gnawing the wood-work. So I had held my breath all that time for such a trifle!

Well, what was done could not be helped; I would go to sleep at once and make up the lost time. That was a thoughtless thought. Without intending it—hardly knowing it—I fell to listening intently to that sound, and even unconsciously counting the strokes of the mouse's nutmeg-grater. Presently I was deriving exquisite suffering from this employment, yet maybe I could have endured it if the mouse had attended steadily to his work: but he did not do that; he stopped every now and then, and I suffered more while waiting and listening for him to begin again than I did while he was gnawing. Along at first I was mentally offering a reward of five—six—seven—ten—dollars for that mouse; but toward the last I was offering rewards which were entirely beyond my means. I close-reefed my ears—that is to say, I bent the flaps of them down and furled them into five or six folds, and pressed them against the hearing-orifice—but it did no good: the faculty was so sharpened by nervous excitement that it was become a microphone, and could hear through the overlays without trouble.

My anger grew to a frenzy. I finally did what all persons before have done, clear back to Adam—resolved to throw something. I reached down and got my walking shoes, then sat up in bed and listened, in order to exactly locate the noise. But I couldn't do it; it was as unlocatable as a cricket's noise; and where one thinks that that is, is always the very place where it isn't. So I presently hurled a shoe at random, and with a vicious vigor. It struck the wall over Harris's head and fell down on him; I had not imagined I could throw so far. It woke Harris, and I was glad of it until I found he was not angry; then I was sorry. He soon went to sleep again, which pleased me; but straightway the mouse began again, which roused my temper once more. I did not want to wake Harris a second time, but the gnawing continued until I was compelled to throw the other shoe. This time I broke a mirror—there were two in the room—I got the largest one, of course. Harris woke again, but did not complain, and I was sorrier than ever. I resolved that I would suffer all possible torture, before I would disturb him a third time.

The mouse eventually retired, and by and by I was sinking to sleep, when a clock began to strike; I counted, till it was done, and was about to drowse again when another clock began; I counted; then the two great Rathhaus clock angels began to send forth soft, rich, melodious blasts from their long trumpets. I had never heard anything that was so lovely, or weird, or mysterious—but when they got to blowing the quarter-hours, they seemed to me to be overdoing the thing. Every time I dropped off for a moment, a new noise woke me. Each time I woke I missed my coverlet, and had to reach down to the floor and get it again.

At last all sleepiness forsook me. I recognized the fact that I was hopelessly and permanently wide awake. Wide awake, and feverish and thirsty. When I had lain tossing there as long as I could endure it, it occurred to me that it would be a good idea to dress and go out in the great square and take a refreshing wash in the fountain, and smoke and reflect there until the remnant of the night was gone.

I believed I could dress in the dark without waking Harris. I had banished my shoes after the mouse, but my slippers would do for a summer night. So I rose softly, and gradually got on everything—down to one sock. I couldn't seem to get on the track of that sock, any way I could fix it. But I had to have it; so I went down on my hands and knees, with one slipper on and the other in my hand, and began to paw gently around and rake the floor, but with no success. I enlarged my circle, and went on pawing and raking. With every pressure of my knee, how the floor creaked! and every time I chanced to rake against any article, it seemed to give out thirty-five or thirty-six times more noise than it would have done in the daytime. In those cases I always stopped and held my breath till I was sure Harris had not awakened— then I crept along again. I moved on and on, but I could not find the sock; I could not seem to find anything but furniture. I could not re- member that there was much furniture in the room when I went to bed, but the place was alive with it now—especially chairs—chairs everywhere—had a couple of families moved in, in the meantime? And I never could seem to *glance* on one of those chairs, but always struck it full and square with my head. My temper rose, by steady and sure degrees, and as I pawed on and on, I fell to making vicious com- ments under my breath.

Finally, with a venomous access of irritation, I said I would leave without the sock; so I rose up and made straight for the door—as I supposed—and suddenly confronted my dim spectral image in the unbroken mirror. It startled the breath out of me for an instant; it also showed me that I was lost, and had no sort of idea where I was. When I realized this, I was so angry that I had to sit down on the floor and take hold of something to keep from lifting the roof off with an explosion of opinion. If there had been only one mirror, it might possibly have helped to locate me; but there were two, and two were as bad as a thousand; besides, these were on opposite sides of the room. I could see the dim blur of the windows, but in my turned-around condition they were exactly where they ought not to be, and so they only confused me instead of helping me.

I started to get up, and knocked down an umbrella; it made a noise like a pistol-shot when it struck that hard, slick, carpetless floor; I grated my teeth and held my breath—Harris did not stir. I set the umbrella slowly and carefully on end against the wall, but as soon as I took my hand away, its heel slipped from under it, and down it came again with another bang. I shrunk together and listened a moment in silent fury—no harm done, everything quiet. With the most painstaking care and nicety I stood the umbrella up once more, took my hand away, and down it came again.

I have been strictly reared, but if it had not been so dark and solemn and awful there in that lonely vast room, I do believe I should have said something then which could not be put into a Sunday-school book without injuring the sale of it. If my reasoning powers had not been already sapped dry by my harassments, I would have known better than to try to set an umbrella on end on one of those glassy German floors in the dark; it can't be done in the daytime without four failures to one success. I had one comfort, though—Harris was yet still and silent; he had not stirred.

The umbrella could not locate me—there were four standing around the room, and all alike. I thought I would feel along the wall and find the door in that way. I rose up and began this operation, but raked down a picture. It was not a large one, but it made noise enough for a panorama. Harris gave out no sound, but I felt that if I experimented any further with the pictures I should be sure to wake him. Better give up trying to get out. Yes, I would find King Arthur's Round Table once more—I had already found it several times—and use it for a base of departure on an exploring tour for my bed; if I could find my bed I could then find my water pitcher; I would quench my raging thirst and turn in. So I started on my hands and knees, because I could go faster that way, and with more confidence, too, and not knock down things. By and by I found the table—with my head—rubbed the bruise a little, then rose up and started, with hands abroad and fingers spread, to balance myself. I found a chair; then the wall; then another chair; then a sofa; then an alpenstock, then another sofa; this confounded me, for I had thought there was only one sofa. I hunted up the table again and took a fresh start; found some more chairs.

It occurred to me now, as it ought to have done before, that as the table was round, it was therefore of no value as a base to aim from; so I moved off once more, and at random, among the wilderness of chairs and sofas—wandered off into unfamiliar regions, and presently knocked a candlestick off a mantel-piece; grabbed at the candle-stick and knocked off a lamp; grabbed at the lamp and knocked off a water-pitcher with a rattling crash, and thought to myself, "I've found you at last—I judged I was close upon you." Harris shouted "murder," and "thieves," and finished with "I'm absolutely drowned."

The crash had roused the house. Mr. X. pranced in, in his long night garment, with a candle, young Z. after him with another candle; a procession swept in at another door, with candles and lanterns; landlord and two German guests in their nightgowns, and a chambermaid in hers.

I looked around; I was at Harris's bed, a Sabbath day's journey from my own. There was only one sofa; it was against the wall; there was only one chair where a body could get at it—I had been revolving around it like a planet, and colliding with it like a comet half the night.

I explained how I had been employing myself, and why. Then the landlord's party left, and the rest of us set about our preparations for breakfast, for the dawn was ready to break. I glanced furtively at my pedometer, and found I had made forty-seven miles. But I did not care, for I had come out for a pedestrian tour anyway.

Rip Van Winkle

Washington Irving, author of the "Knickerbocker History of New York,"
"Life of Columbus," "Conquest of Granada," "Sketch Book," "Bracebridge
Hall," and many other famous works, was born at New York in 1783, and
early showed his aptitude for literature, although he studied law and expected to make it his profession. His reputation as a light satirist was already established when he wrote the "Knickerbocker History," which gave
him fame. In 1817 he went to Europe, and remained there till 1834, publishing many of his works in England, where his success was very great. He
held the post of Secretary of Legation in London, and Minister at Madrid.
In 1846 he returned finally to America, and died at Sunnyside on the Hudson in 1859.

Whoever has made a voyage up the Hudson must remember the
Kaatskill Mountains. They are a dismembered branch of the great Ap-
palachian family, and are seen away to the west of the river, swelling up
to a noble height, and lording it over the surrounding country. Every
change of season, every change of weather, indeed, every hour of the
day, produces some change in the magical hues and shapes of these
mountains, and they are regarded by all the good wives, far and near, as
perfect barometers. When the weather is fair and settled, they are
clothed in blue and purple, and print their bold outlines on the clear
evening sky; but, sometimes, when the rest of the landscape is cloudless, they will gather a hood of gray vapors about their summits, which,
in the last rays of the setting sun, will glow and light up like a crown of
glory.

At the foot of these fairy mountains, the voyager may have descried
the light smoke curling up from a village, whose shingle-roofs gleam
among the trees, just where the blue tints of the upland melt away into
the fresh green of the nearer landscape. It is a little village of great antiquity, having been founded by some of the Dutch colonists, in the
early times of the province, just about the beginning of the government of the good Peter Stuyvesant, (may he rest in peace!) and there
were some of the houses of the original settlers standing within a few

years, built of small yellow bricks brought from Holland, having lat-
ticed windows and gable fronts, surmounted with weather-cocks.

In that same village, and in one of these very houses (which, to tell
the precise truth, was sadly time-worn and weather-beaten), there
lived many years since, while the country was yet a province of Great
Britain, a simple good-natured fellow of the name of Rip Van Winkle.
He was a descendant of the Van Winkles who figured so gallantly in
the chivalrous days of Peter Stuyvesant, and accompanied him to the
siege of Fort Christina. He inherited, however, but little of the martial
character of his ancestors. I have observed that he was a simple, good-
natured man; he was, moreover, a kind neighbor, and an obedient, hen-
pecked husband. Indeed, to the latter circumstance might be owing
that meekness of spirit which gained him such universal popularity;
for those men are most apt to be obsequious and conciliating abroad,
who are under the discipline of shrews at home. Their tempers, doubtless, are rendered pliant and malleable in the fiery furnace of domestic tribulation; and a curtain lecture is worth all the sermons in the
world for teaching the virtues of patience and long-suffering. A termagant wife may, therefore, in some respects, be considered a tolerable blessing; and if so, Rip Van Winkle was thrice blessed.

Certain it is that he was a great favorite among all the good wives of
the village, who, as usual with the amiable sex, took his part in all family squabbles, and never failed, whenever they talked those matters
over in their evening gossipings, to lay all the blame on Dame Van
Winkle. The children of the village, too, would shout with joy whenever he approached. He assisted at their sports, made their playthings,
taught them to fly kites and shoot marbles, and told them long stories
of ghosts, witches and Indians. Whenever he went dodging about the
village, he was surrounded by a troop of them, hanging on his skirts,
clambering on his back, and playing a thousand tricks on him with impunity; and not a dog would bark at him throughout the neighborhood.

The great error in Rip's composition was an insuperable aversion to
all kinds of profitable labor. It could not be from the want of assiduity
or perseverance; for he would sit on a wet rock, with a rod as long and
heavy as a Tartar's lance, and fish all day without a murmur, even
though he should not be encouraged by a single nibble. He would
carry a fowling-piece on his shoulder for hours together, trudging

through woods and swamps, and up hill and down dale, to shoot a few squirrels or wild pigeons. He would never refuse to assist a neighbor even in the roughest toil, and was a foremost man at all country frolics for husking Indian corn, or building stone-fences; the women of the village, too, used to employ him to run their errands, and to do such little odd jobs as their less obliging husbands would not do for them. In a word, Rip was ready to attend to anybody's business but his own; but as to doing family duty, and keeping his farm in order, he found it impossible.

In fact, he declared it was of no use to work on his farm: it was the most pestilent little piece of ground in the whole country; everything about it went wrong, and would go wrong, in spite of him. His fences were continually falling to pieces; his cow would either go astray, or get among the cabbages; weeds were sure to grow quicker in his fields than anywhere else; the rain always made a point of setting in just as he had some out-door work to do; so that, though his patrimonial estate had dwindled away under his management, acre by acre, until there was little more left than a mere patch of Indian corn and potatoes, yet it was the worst conditioned farm in the neighborhood.

His children, too, were as ragged and wild as if they belonged to nobody. His son Rip, an urchin begotten in his own likeness, promised to inherit the habits with the old clothes of his father. He was generally seen trooping like a colt at his mother's heels, equipped in a pair of his father's cast-off galligaskins, which he had much ado to hold up with one hand, as a fine lady does her train in bad weather.

Rip Van Winkle, however, was one of those happy mortals, of foolish, well-oiled dispositions, who take the world easy, eat white bread or brown, whichever can be got with least thought or trouble, and would rather starve on a penny than work for a pound. If left to himself, he would have whistled life away in perfect contentment; but his wife kept continually dinning in his ears about his idleness, his carelessness and the ruin he was bringing on his family. Morning, noon and night her tongue was incessantly going, and everything he said or did was sure to produce a torrent of household eloquence. Rip had one way of replying to all lectures of the kind, and that, by frequent use, had grown into a habit. He shrugged his shoulders, shook his head, cast up his eyes, but said nothing. This, however, always provoked a fresh volley from his wife; so that he was fain to draw off his forces, and take to the outside of the house—the only side which, in truth, belongs to a hen-pecked husband.

Rip's old domestic adherent was his dog Wolf, who was as much hen-pecked as his master; for Dame Van Winkle regarded them as companions in idleness, and even looked upon Wolf with an evil eye, as the cause of his master's going so often astray. True it is, in all points of spirit befitting an honorable dog, he was as courageous an animal as ever scoured the woods—but what courage can withstand the ever-during and all-besetting terrors of a woman's tongue? The moment Wolf entered the house his crest fell, his tail dropped to the ground, or curled between his legs, he sneaked about with a gallows air, casting many a sidelong glance at Dame Van Winkle, and at the least flourish of a broom-stick or ladle, he would fly to the door with yelping pre-cipitation.

Times grew worse and worse with Rip Van Winkle as years of mat-rimony rolled on; a tart temper never mellows with age, and a sharp tongue is the only edged tool that grows keener with constant use. For a long while he used to console himself, when driven from home, by frequenting a kind of perpetual club of the sages, philosophers, and other idle personages of the village; which held its sessions on a bench before a small inn, designated by a rubicund portrait of His Majesty George the Third. Here they used to sit in the shade through a long lazy summer's day, talking listlessly over village gossip, or telling end-less sleepy stories about nothing. But it would have been worth any statesman's money to have heard the profound discussions that some-times took place, when by chance an old newspaper fell into their hands from some passing traveler. How solemnly they would listen to the contents, as drawled out by Derrick Van Bummel, the schoolmas-ter, a dapper, learned little man, who was not to be daunted by the most gigantic word in the dictionary; and how sagely they would deliberate upon public events some months after they had taken place!

The opinions of this junto were completely controlled by Nicholas Vedder, a patriarch of the village, and landlord of the inn, at the door of which he took his seat from morning till night, just moving sufficiently to avoid the sun and keep in the shade of a large tree; so that the neigh-bors could tell the hour by his movements as accurately as by a sun-dial. It is true he was rarely heard to speak, but smoked his pipe incessantly. His adherents, however (for every great man has his adherents), perfectly understood him, and knew how to gather his opinions. When anything that was read or related displeased him, he was observed to smoke his pipe vehemently, and to send forth short, frequent and angry puffs; but when pleased, he would inhale the smoke slowly and tranquilly, and emit it in light and placid clouds; and sometimes, taking the pipe from his mouth, and letting the fragrant vapor curl about his nose, would gravely nod his head in token of perfect approbation.

From even this stronghold the unlucky Rip was at length routed by his termagant wife, who would suddenly break in upon the tranquillity of the assemblage and call the members all to naught; nor was that august personage, Nicholas Vedder himself, sacred from the daring tongue of this terrible virago, who charged him outright with encouraging her husband in habits of idleness.

Poor Rip was at last reduced almost to despair; and his only alternative, to escape from the labor of the farm and clamor of his wife, was to take gun in hand and stroll away into the woods. Here he would sometimes seat himself at the foot of a tree, and share the contents of his wallet with Wolf, with whom he sympathized as a fellow-sufferer in persecution. "Poor Wolf," he would say, "thy mistress leads thee a dog's life of it; but never mind, my lad, whilst I live thou shalt never want a friend to stand by thee!" Wolf would wag his tail, look wistfully in his master's face, and if dogs can feel pity, I verily believe he reciprocated the sentiment with all his heart.

In a long ramble of the kind on a fine autumnal day, Rip had unconsciously scrambled to one of the highest parts of the Kaatskill Mountains. He was after his favorite sport of squirrel shooting, and the still solitudes had echoed and re-echoed with the reports of his gun. Panting and fatigued, he threw himself, late in the afternoon, on a green knoll, covered with mountain herbage, that crowned the brow of a precipice. From an opening between the trees he could overlook all the lower country for many a mile of rich woodland. He saw at a distance the lordly Hudson, far, far below him, moving on its silent but majestic course, with the reflection of a purple cloud, or the sail of a lagging bark, here and there sleeping on its grassy bosom, and at last losing itself in the blue highlands.

On the other side he looked down into a deep mountain glen, wild, lonely and shagged, the bottom filled with fragments from the impending cliffs, and scarcely lighted by the reflected rays of the setting sun. For some time Rip lay musing on this scene; evening was gradually advancing; the mountains began to throw their long blue shadows over the valleys; he saw that it would be dark long before he could reach the village, and he heaved a heavy sigh when he thought of encountering the terrors of Dame Van Winkle.

As he was about to descend, he heard a voice from a distance hallooing, "Rip Van Winkle! Rip Van Winkle!" He looked round, but could see nothing but a crow winging its solitary flight across the mountain. He thought his fancy must have deceived him, and turned again to descend, when he heard the same cry ring through the still evening air; "Rip Van Winkle! Rip Van Winkle!"—at the same time Wolf bristled up his back, and giving a low growl, skulked to his master's side, looking fearfully down into the glen. Rip now felt a vague apprehension stealing over him; he looked anxiously in the same direction, and perceived a strange figure slowly toiling up the rocks, and bending under the weight of something he carried on his back. He was surprised to see any human being in this lonely and unfrequented place, but supposing it to be some one of the neighborhood in need of his assistance, he hastened down to yield it.

On nearer approach he was still more surprised at the singularity of the stranger's appearance. He was a short, square-built old fellow, with thick bushy hair, and a grizzled beard. His dress was of the antique Dutch fashion—a cloth jerkin strapped round the waist—several pair of breeches, the outer one of ample volume, decorated with rows of buttons down the sides, and bunches at the knees. He bore on his shoulder a stout keg, that seemed full of liquor, and made signs for Rip to approach and assist him with the load. Though rather shy and distrustful of this new acquaintance, Rip complied with his usual alacrity; and mutually relieving one another, they clambered up a narrow gully, apparently the dry bed of a mountain torrent. As they ascended, Rip every now and then heard long rolling peals like distant thunder, that seemed to issue out of a deep ravine, or, rather, cleft, between lofty rocks, toward which their rugged path conducted. He paused for an instant, but supposing it to be the muttering of one of those transient thunder-showers which often take place in mountain heights, he proceeded. Passing through the ravine they came to a hollow, like a small amphitheatre, surrounded by perpendicular precipices, over the brinks of which impending trees shot their branches, so that you only caught glimpses of the azure sky and the bright evening cloud. During the whole time Rip and his companion had labored on in silence; for though the former marveled greatly what could be the object of carrying a keg of liquor up this wild mountain, yet there was something strange and incomprehensible about the unknown, that inspired awe and checked familiarity.

On entering the amphitheatre, new objects of wonder presented themselves. On a level spot in the centre was a company of odd-looking personages playing at nine-pins. They were dressed in a quaint outlandish fashion; some wore short doublets, others jerkins, with long knives in their belts, and most of them had enormous breeches, of similar style with that of the guide's. Their visages, too, were peculiar: one had a large beard, broad face, and small piggish eyes: the face of another seemed to consist entirely of nose, and was surmounted by a white sugar-loaf hat set off with a little red cock's tail. They all had beards, of various shapes and colors. There was one who seemed to be the commander. He was a stout old gentleman, with a weather-beaten countenance; he wore a laced doublet, broad belt and hanger, high-crowned hat and feather, red stockings and high-heeled shoes, with roses in them. The whole group reminded Rip of the figures in an old Flemish painting, in the parlor of Dominie Van Shaick, the village parson, and which had been brought over from Holland at the time of the settlement.

What seemed particularly odd to Rip was, that though these folks were evidently amusing themselves, yet they maintained the gravest faces, the most mysterious silence, and were, withal, the most melancholy party of pleasure he had ever witnessed. Nothing interrupted the stillness of the scene but the noise of the balls, which, whenever they were rolled, echoed along the mountains like rumbling peals of thunder.

As Rip and his companion approached them, they suddenly desisted from their play, and stared at him with such fixed statue-like gaze, and such strange, uncouth, lack-lustre countenances, that his heart turned within him, and his knees smote together. His companion now emptied the contents of the keg into large flagons, and made signs to him to wait upon the company. He obeyed with fear and trembling; they quaffed the liquor in profound silence, and then returned to their game.

By degrees Rip's awe and apprehension subsided. He even ventured, when no eye was fixed upon him, to taste the beverage, which he found had much of the flavor of excellent Hollands. He was naturally a thirsty soul, and was soon tempted to repeat the draught. One taste provoked another; and he reiterated his visits to the flagon so often that at length his senses were overpowered, his eyes swam in his head, his head gradually declined, and he fell into a deep sleep.

On waking, he found himself on the green knoll whence he had first seen the old man of the glen. He rubbed his eyes—it was a bright sunny morning. The birds were hopping and twittering among the bushes, and the eagle was wheeling aloft, and breasting the pure mountain breeze. "Surely," thought Rip, "I have not slept here all night." He recalled the occurrences before he fell asleep: the strange man with a keg of liquor—the mountain ravine—the wild retreat among the rocks—the woebegone party at nine-pins—the flagon— "Oh! that flagon! that wicked flagon!" thought Rip—"what excuse shall I make to Dame Van Winkle!"

He looked round for his gun, but in place of the clean, well-oiled fowling-piece, he found an old firelock lying by him, the barrel incrusted with rust, the lock falling off, and the stock worm-eaten. He now suspected that the grave roysters of the mountain had put a trick upon him, and, having dosed him with liquor, had robbed him of his gun. Wolf, too, had disappeared, but he might have strayed away after a squirrel or partridge. He whistled after him and shouted his name, but all in vain; the echoes repeated his whistle and shout, but no dog was to be seen.

He determined to revisit the scene of the last evening's gambol, and if he met with any of the party, to demand his dog and gun. As he rose to walk, he found himself stiff in the joints, and wanting in his usual activity. "These mountain beds do not agree with me," thought Rip, "and if this frolic should lay me up with a fit of the rheumatism, I shall have a blessed time with Dame Van Winkle." With some difficulty he got down into the glen: he found the gully up which he and his companion had ascended the preceding evening; but to his astonishment a mountain stream was now foaming down it, leaping from rock to rock, and filling the glen with babbling murmurs. He, however, made a shift to scramble up its sides, working his toilsome way through thickets of birch, sassafras and witch-hazel and sometimes tripped up or entan-

AWAKING FROM A LONG SLEEP.

gled by the wild grapevines that twisted their coils or tendrils from tree to tree, and spread a kind of network in his path.

At length he reached to where the ravine had opened through the cliffs to the amphitheatre; but no traces of such opening remained. The rocks presented a high impenetrable wall over which the torrent came tumbling in a sheet of feathery foam, and fell into a broad deep basin, black from the shadows of the surrounding forest. Here, then, poor Rip was brought to a stand. He again called and whistled after his dog; he was only answered by the cawing of a flock of idle crows, sporting high in air about a dry tree that overhung a sunny precipice; and who, secure in their elevation, seemed to look down and scoff at the poor man's perplexities. What was to be done? the morning was passing away, and Rip felt famished for want of his breakfast. He grieved to give up his dog and gun; he dreaded to meet his wife; but it would not do to starve among the mountains. He shook his head, shouldered the rusty firelock, and, with a heart full of trouble and anxiety, turned his steps homeward.

As he approached the village he met a number of people, but none whom he knew, which somewhat surprised him, for he had thought himself acquainted with every one in the country round. Their dress, too, was of a different fashion from that to which he was accustomed. They all stared at him with equal marks of surprise, and, whenever they cast their eyes upon him, invariably stroked their chins. The constant recurrence of this gesture induced Rip, involuntarily, to do the same, when, to his astonishment, he found his beard had grown a foot long!

He had now entered the skirts of the village. A troop of strange children ran at his heels, hooting after him, and pointing at his gray beard. The dogs, too, not one of which he recognized for an old acquaintance, barked at him as he passed. The very village was altered; it was larger and more populous. There were rows of houses which he had never seen before, and those which had been his familiar haunts had disappeared. Strange names were over the doors—strange faces at the windows—everything was strange. His mind now misgave him; he began to doubt whether both he and the world around him were not bewitched. Surely this was his native village, which he had left but the day before. There stood the Kaatskill Mountains—there ran the silver

Hudson at a distance—there was every hill and dale precisely as it had always been—Rip was sorely perplexed—"That flagon last night," thought he, "has addled my poor head sadly!"

It was with some difficulty that he found the way to his own house, which he approached with silent awe, expecting every moment to hear the shrill voice of Dame Van Winkle. He found the house gone to decay—the roof had fallen in, the windows shattered, and the doors off the hinges. A half-starved dog that looked like Wolf was skulking about it. Rip called him by name, but the cur snarled, showed his teeth, and passed on. This was an unkind cut indeed—"My very dog," sighed poor Rip, "has forgotten me!"

He entered the house, which, to tell the truth, Dame Van Winkle had always kept in neat order. It was empty, forlorn, and apparently abandoned. This desolateness overcame all his connubial fears—he called loudly for his wife and children—the lonely chambers rang for a moment with his voice, and then all again was silence.

He now hurried forth, and hastened to his old resort, the village inn—but it too was gone. A large rickety wooden building stood in its place, with great gaping windows, some of them broken and mended with old hats and petticoats, and over the door was painted, "The Union Hotel, by Jonathan Doolittle." Instead of the great tree that used to shelter the quiet little Dutch inn of yore, there now was reared a tall naked pole, with something on the top that looked like a red night-cap, and from it was fluttering a flag, on which was a singular assemblage of stars and stripes—all this was strange and incomprehensible. He recognized on the sign, however, the ruby face of King George, under which he had smoked so many a peaceful pipe; but even this was singularly metamorphosed. The red coat was changed for one of blue and buff, a sword was held in the hand instead of a sceptre, the head was decorated with a cocked hat, and underneath was painted in large characters, GENERAL WASHINGTON.

There was, as usual, a crowd of folk about the door, but none that Rip recollected. The very character of the people seemed changed. There was a busy, bustling, disputatious tone about it instead of the accustomed phlegm and drowsy tranquillity. He looked in vain for the sage Nicholas Vedder, with his broad face, double chin, and fair long pipe, uttering clouds of tobacco-smoke instead of idle speeches; or

Van Bummel, the schoolmaster, doling forth the contents of an ancient newspaper. In place of these, a lean, bilious-looking fellow, with his pockets full of handbills, was haranguing vehemently about rights of citizens—elections—members of Congress—liberty—Bunker's Hill—heroes of Seventy-six—and other words, which were a perfect Babylonish jargon to the bewildered Van Winkle.

The appearance of Rip, with his long grizzled beard, his rusty fowling-piece, his uncouth dress, and an army of women and children at his heels, soon attracted the attention of the tavern politicians. They crowded round him, eyeing him from head to foot with great curiosity. The orator bustled up to him, and, drawing him partly aside, inquired "on which side he voted?" Rip stared in vacant stupidity. Another short but busy little fellow pulled him by the arm, and, rising on tiptoe, inquired in his ear, "Whether he was Federal or Democrat?" Rip was equally at a loss to comprehend the question; when a knowing, self-important old gentleman, in a sharp cocked hat, made his way through the crowd, putting them to the right and left with his elbows as he passed, and planting himself before Van Winkle, with one arm akimbo, the other resting on his cane, his keen eyes and sharp hat penetrating, as it were, into his very soul, demanded in an austere tone, "what brought him to the election with a gun on his shoulder, and a mob at his heels, and whether he meant to breed a riot in the village?"—"Alas!" gentlemen," cried Rip, somewhat dismayed, "I am a poor quiet man, a native of the place, and a loyal subject of the king, God bless him!"

Here a general shout burst from the by-standers—"a tory! a tory! a spy! a refugee! hustle him! away with him!" It was with great difficulty that the self-important man in the cocked hat restored order; and, having assumed a tenfold austerity of brow, demanded again of the unknown culprit what he came there for, and whom he was seeking? The poor man humbly assured him that he meant no harm, but merely came there in search of some of his neighbors, who used to keep about the tavern.

"Well—who are they?—name them."

Rip thought himself a moment, and inquired, "Where's Nicholas Vedder?"

There was a silence for a little while, when an old man replied, in a thin piping voice, "Nicholas Vedder! why, he is dead and gone these eighteen years! There was a wooden tombstone in the church-yard that used to tell all about him, but that's rotten and gone too."

"Where's Brom Dutcher?"

"Oh, he went off to the army in the beginning of the war; some say he was killed at the storming of Stony Point—others say he was drowned in a squall at the foot of Antony's Nose. I don't know—he never came back again."

"Where's Van Bummel, the schoolmaster?"

"He went off to the wars too, was a great militia general, and is now in Congress."

Rip's heart died away at hearing of these sad changes in his home and friends, and finding himself thus alone in the world. Every answer puzzled him too, by treating of such enormous lapses of time, and of matters which he could not understand: war—Congress—Stony Point—he had no courage to ask after any more friends, but cried out in despair, "Does nobody here know Rip Van Winkle?"

"Oh, Rip Van Winkle!" exclaimed two or three, "Oh, to be sure! that's Rip Van Winkle yonder, leaning against the tree."

Rip looked, and beheld a precise counterpart of himself, as he went up the mountain: apparently as lazy, and certainly as ragged. The poor fellow was now completely confounded. He doubted his own identity, and whether he was himself or another man. In the midst of his bewilderment, the man in the cocked hat demanded who he was, and what was his name?

"God knows," exclaimed he, at his wit's end; "I'm not myself—I'm somebody else—that's me yonder—no—that's somebody else got into my shoes—I was myself last night, but I fell asleep on the mountain, and they've changed my gun, and every thing's changed, and I'm changed, and I can't tell what's my name, or who I am!"

The by-standers began now to look at each other, nod, wink significantly, and tap their fingers against their foreheads. There was a whisper, also, about securing the gun, and keeping the old fellow from doing mischief, at the very suggestion of which the self-important man in the cocked hat retired with some precipitation. At this critical moment a fresh, comely woman pressed through the throng to get a peep at the gray-bearded man. She had a chubby child in her arms, which, frightened at his looks, began to cry. "Hush, Rip," cried she, "hush, you little fool; the old man won't hurt you." The name of the child, the air of the mother, the tone of her voice, all awakened a train of recollections in his mind. "What is your name, my good woman?" asked he.

"Judith Gardenier."

"And your father's name?"

"Ah, poor man, Rip Van Winkle was his name, but it's twenty years since he went away from home with his gun, and never has been heard of since—his dog came home without him; but whether he shot himself, or was carried away by the Indians, nobody can tell. I was then but a little girl."

Rip had but one question more to ask; but he put it with a faltering voice:

"Where's your mother?"

"Oh, she too had died but a short time since; she broke a blood-vessel in a fit of passion at a New-England peddler."

There was a drop of comfort, at least, in this intelligence. The honest man could contain himself no longer. He caught his daughter and her child in his arms. "I am your father!" cried he—"Young Rip Van Winkle once—old Rip Van Winkle now! Does nobody know poor Rip Van Winkle?"

All stood amazed, until an old woman, tottering out from among the crowd, put her hand to her brow, and peering under it in his face for a moment, exclaimed, "Sure enough! it is Rip Van Winkle—it is himself! Welcome home again, old neighbor—why, where have you been these twenty long years?"

Rip's story was soon told, for the whole twenty years had been to him as one night. The neighbors stared when they heard it; some were seen to wink at each other, and put their tongues in their cheeks: and the self-important man in the cocked hat, who, when the alarm was over, had returned to the field, screwed down the corners of his mouth, and shook his head—upon which there was a general shaking of the head throughout the assemblage.

It was determined, however, to take the opinion of old Peter Vanderdonk, who was seen slowly advancing up the road. He was a descendant of the historian of that name, who wrote one of the earliest accounts of the province. Peter was the most ancient inhabitant of the village, and well versed in all the wonderful events and traditions of the neighborhood. He recollected Rip at once, and corroborated his story in the most satisfactory manner. He assured the company that it was a fact, handed down from his ancestor the historian, that the Kaatskill Mountains had always been haunted by strange beings; that it was affirmed that the great Hendrick Hudson, the first discoverer of the river and country, kept a kind of vigil there every twenty years, with his crew of the *Half-Moon*, being permitted in this way to revisit the scenes of his enterprise, and keep a guardian eye upon the river, and the great city called by his name; that his father had once seen them in their old Dutch dresses playing at nine-pins in a hollow of the mountain; and that he himself had heard, one summer afternoon, the sound of their balls, like distant peals of thunder.

To make a long story short, the company broke up, and returned to the more important concerns of the election. Rip's daughter took him home to live with her; she had a snug, well-furnished house, and a stout cheery farmer for a husband, whom Rip recollected for one of the urchins that used to climb upon his back. As to Rip's son and heir, who was the ditto of himself, seen leaning against the tree, he was employed to work on the farm; but evinced an hereditary disposition to attend to anything else but his business.

Rip now resumed his old walks and habits; he soon found many of his former cronies, though all rather the worse for the wear and tear of time; and preferred making friends among the rising generation, with whom he soon grew into great favor.

Having nothing to do at home, and being arrived at that happy age when a man can be idle with impunity, he took his place once more on the bench at the inn door, and was reverenced as one of the patriarchs of the village, and a chronicle of the old times "before the war." It was some time before he could get into the regular track of gossip, or could be made to comprehend the strange events that had taken place during his torpor. How that there had been a Revolutionary war—that the country had thrown off the yoke of old England—and that, instead of being a subject of his Majesty George the Third, he was now a free citizen of the United States. Rip, in fact, was no politician; the changes of states and empires made but little impression on him; but there was one species of despotism under which he had long groaned, and that was—petticoat government. Happily that was at an end; he had got his neck out of the yoke of matrimony, and could go in and out whenever he pleased, without dreading the tyranny of Dame Van Winkle. Whenever her name was mentioned, however, he shook his head, shrugged his shoulders, and cast up his eyes; which might pass either for an expression of resignation to his fate, or joy at his deliverance.

He used to tell his story to every stranger that arrived at Mr. Doolittle's hotel. He was observed, at first, to vary on some points every time he told it, which was, doubtless, owing to his having so recently awakened. It at last settled down precisely to the tale I have related, and not a man, woman or child in the neighborhood, but knew it by heart. Some always pretended to doubt the reality of it, and insisted that Rip had been out of his head, and that this was one point on which he always remained flighty. The old Dutch inhabitants, however, almost universally gave it full credit. Even to this day they never hear a thunderstorm of a summer afternoon about the Kaatskill, but they say Hendrick Hudson and his crew are at their game of nine-pins; and it is a common wish of all hen-pecked husbands in the neighborhood, when life hangs heavy on their hands, that they might have a quieting draught out of Rip Van Winkle's flagon.

THE OSTRICH AND THE HEN

GEO. T. LANIGAN

An Ostrich and a Hen chanced to occupy adjacent apartments, and the former complained loudly that her rest was disturbed by the cackling of her humble neighbor. "Why is it," he finally asked the Hen, "that you make such an intolerable noise?" The Hen replied, "Because I have laid an egg." "Oh, no," said the Ostrich, with a superior smile, "it is because you are a Hen, and don't know any better."

Moral.—The moral of the foregoing is not very clear, but it contains some reference to the Agitation for Female Suffrage.

WOMEN'S RIGHTS

ARTEMUS WARD

I pitcht my tent in a small town in Injianny one day last seeson, & while I was standin at the dore takin money, a deppytashun of ladies came up & sed they wos members of the Bunkumville Female Reformin & Wimin's Rite's Associashun, and thay axed me if thay cood go in without payin.

"Not exactly," sez I, "but you can pay without goin in."

"Dew you know who we air?" said one of the wimin—a tall and feroshus lookin critter, with a blew kotton umbreller under her arm—"do you know who we air, Sur?"

"My impreshun is," sed I, "from a kersery view, that you air females."

"We air, Sur," said the feroshus woman—"we belong to a Society whitch beleeves wimin has rites—whitch beleeves in razin her to her proper speer—whitch beleeves she is indowed with as much intelleck as man is—whitch beleeves she is trampled on and aboozed—& who will resist hense4th & forever the incroachments of proud & domineering men."

Durin her discourse, the exsentric female grabed me by the coatkollor & was swinging her umbreller wildly over my head.

I hope, marm," sez I, starting back, "that your intensions is honorable! I'm a lone man hear in a strange place. Besides, I've a wife to hum."

"Yes," cried the female, "& she's a slave! Doth she never dream of freedom—doth she never think of throwin of the yoke of tyrrinny & thinkin & votin for herself?—Doth she never think of these here things?"

"Not bein a natral born fool," sed I, by this time a little riled, "I kin safely say that she dothunt."

"Oh, whot—whot!" screamed the female, swinging her umbreller in the air. "O, what is the price that woman pays for her expeeriunce!"

"I don't know," sez I; "the price of my show is 15 cents pur individooal."

"& can't our Sosiety go in free?" asked the female.

"Not if I know it," sed I.

"Crooil, crooil man!" she cried, & bust into teers.

"Won't you let my darter in?" sed anuther of the exsentric wimin, taken me afeckshunitely by the hand. "O, please let my darter in—shee's a sweet gushin child of natur."

"Let her gush!" roared I, as mad as I cood stick at their tarnal nonsense—"let her gush!" Where upon they all sprung back with the simultanious observashun that I was a Beest.

"My female friends," sed I, "be4 you leeve, I've a few remarks to remark; wa them well. The female woman is one of the greatest institooshuns of which this land can boste. It's onpossible to get along without her. Had there bin no female wimin in the world, I should scarcely be here with my unparaleld show on this very occashun. She is good in sickness—good in wellness—good all the time. O woman, woman!" I cried, my feelins worked up to a hi poetick pitch, "You air a angle when you behave yourself; but when you take off your proper appairel & (mettyforically speaken)—get into pantyloons—when you desert your firesides, & with you heds full of wimin's rites noshuns go round like roarin lions, seekin whom you may devour someboddy—in short, when you undertake to play the man, you play the devil and air an emphatic noosance. My female friends," I continued, as they were indignantly departin, "wa well what A. Ward has sed!"

NOTHING TO WEAR

WILLIAM ALLEN BUTLER

William Allen Butler, born at Albany, N. Y., in 1825, is best known by his poem of "Nothing to Wear," which he published in 1857, and which attained at once the most extraordinary currency and celebrity. He was the author of other poems, and various humorous papers, which he threw off in such leisure as his profession of lawyer allowed him, but none are comparable to the satire which won him fame, and, with the exception of "Two Millions," would now hardly be remembered. He was a versatile and accomplished man, whose advantages and opportunities had been great.

Miss Flora M'Flimsey, of Madison Square,
Has made three separate journeys to Paris,
And her father assures me, each time she was there,
That she and her friend Mrs. Harris
(Not the lady whose name is so famous in history,
But plain Mrs. H., without romance or mystery)
Spent six consecutive weeks, without stopping,
In one continuous round of shopping—
Shopping alone, and shopping together,
At all hours of the day, and in all sorts of weather,
For all manner of things that a woman can put
On the crown of her head, or the sole of her foot,
Or wrap round her shoulders, or fit round her waist,
Or that can be sewed on, or pinned on, or laced,
Or tied on with a string, or stitched on with a bow,
In front or behind, above or below;
For bonnets, mantillas, capes, collars and shawls;
Dresses for breakfasts, and dinners, and balls;
Dresses to sit in, and stand in, and walk in;
Dresses to dance in, and flirt in, and talk in;
Dresses in which to do nothing at all;
Dresses for Winter, Spring, Summer and Fall;
All of them different in color and shape,
Silk, muslin and lace, velvet, satin and crape,
Brocade and broadcloth, and other material,
Quite as expensive and much more ethereal;
In short, for all things that could ever be thought of,
Or milliner, *modiste* or tradesman be bought of,
 From ten-thousand-franc robes to twenty-sous frills;
In all quarters of Paris, and to every store,
While M'Flimsey in vain stormed, scolded and swore,
 They footed the streets, and he footed the bills!
The last trip, their goods shipped by the steamer Arago,
Formed, M'Flimsey declares, the bulk of her cargo,
Not to mention a quantity kept from the rest,
Sufficient to fill the largest-sized chest,
Which did not appear on the ship's manifest,
But for which the ladies themselves manifested
Such particular interest, that they invested

Their own proper persons in layers and rows
Of muslins, embroideries, worked under-clothes,
Gloves, handkerchiefs, scarfs, and such trifles as those;
Then, wrapped in great shawls, like Circassian beauties,
Gave *good by* to the ship, and *go by* to the duties.
Her relations at home all marveled, no doubt,
Miss Flora had grown so enormously stout
     For an actual belle and a possible bride;
But the miracle ceased when she turned inside out,
     And the truth came to light, and the dry-goods beside,
Which, in spite of Collector and Custom-House sentry,
Had entered the port without any entry.
And yet, though scarce three months have passed since the day
This merchandise went, on twelve carts, up Broadway,
This same Miss M'Flimsey of Madison Square,
The last time we met was in utter despair,
Because she had nothing whatever to wear!

—

Nothing to wear! Now, as this is a true ditty,
     I do not assert—this, you know, is between us—
That she's in a state of absolute nudity,
     Like Powers' Greek Slave or the Medici Venus;
But I do mean to say, I have heard her declare,
     When at the same moment she had on a dress
     Which cost five hundred dollars, and not a cent less,
     And jewelry worth ten times more, I should guess,
That she had not a thing in the wide world to wear!

—

I should mention just here, that out of Miss Flora's
Two hundred and fifty or sixty adorers,
I had just been selected as he who should throw all
The rest in the shade, by the gracious bestowal
On myself, after twenty or thirty rejections,
Of those fossil remains which she called her "affections."
And that rather decayed but well-known work of art,
Which Miss Flora persisted in styling her "heart."
So we were engaged. Our troth had been plighted,
Not by moonbeam or starbeam, by fountain or grove,
But in a front parlor, most brilliantly lighted,

Beneath the gas-fixtures, we whispered our love.
Without any romance, or raptures, or sighs,
Without any tears in Miss Flora's blue eyes,
Or blushes, or transports, or such silly actions,
It was one of the quietest business transactions,
With a very small sprinkling of sentiment, if any,
And a very large diamond imported by Tiffany.
On her virginal lips while I printed a kiss,
She exclaimed, as a sort of parenthesis,
And by way of putting me quite at my ease,
"You know I'm to polka as much as I please,
And flirt when I like—now, stop, don't you speak—
And you must not come here more than twice in the week,
Or talk to me either at party or ball,
But always be ready to come when I call;
So don't prose to me about duty and stuff,
If we don't break this off, there will be time enough
For that sort of thing; but the bargain must be
That, as long as I choose, I am perfectly free—
For this is a kind of engagement, you see,
Which is binding on you, but not binding on me."

———

Well, having thus wooed Miss M'Flimsey and gained her,
With the silks, crinolines, and hoops that contained her,
I had, as I thought, a contingent remainder
At least in the property, and the best right
To appear as its escort by day and by night;
And it being the week of the STUCKUPS' grand ball—
    Their cards had been out a fortnight or so,
    And set all the Avenue on the tiptoe—
I considered it only my duty to call,
    And see if Miss Flora intended to go.
I found her—as ladies are apt to be found,
When the time intervening between the first sound
Of the bell and the visitor's entry is shorter
Than usual—I found; I won't say—I caught her,
Intent on the pier-glass, undoubtedly meaning
To see if perhaps it didn't need cleaning.
She turned as I entered—"Why, Harry, you sinner,

I thought that you went to the Flashers' to dinner!"
"So I did," I replied, "but the dinner is swallowed,
     And digested, I trust, for 't is now nine and more,
So, being relieved from that duty, I followed
     Inclination, which led me, you see, to your door;
And now will your ladyship so condescend
As just to inform me if you intend
Your beauty, and graces, and presence to lend
(All of which, when I own, I hope no one will borrow)
To the STUCKUPS', whose party, you know, is to-morrow?"
The fair Flora looked up, with a pitiful air,
And answered quite promptly, "Why, Harry, *mon cher*,
I should like above all things to go with you there,
But really and truly—I've nothing to wear."
"Nothing to wear! go just as you are;
Wear the dress you have on, and you'll be by far,
I engage, the most bright and particular star
     On the Stuckup horizon—" I stopped, for her eye,
Notwithstanding this delicate onset of flattery,
Opened on me at once a most terrible battery
     Of scorn and amazement. She made no reply,
But gave a slight turn to the end of her nose
     (That pure Grecian feature), as much to say,
"How absurd that any sane man should suppose
That a lady would go to a ball in the clothes,
     No matter how fine, that she wears every day!"
So I ventured again: "Wear your crimson brocade";
(Second turn up of nose)—"That's too dark by a shade."
"Your blue silk"—"That's too heavy." "Your pink"—
     "That's too light."
"Wear tulle over satin"—"I can't endure white."
"Your rose-colored, then, the best of the batch"—
"I haven't a thread of point-lace to match."
"Your brown *moire antique*"—"Yes, and look like a Quaker"
"The pearl-colored"—"I would, but that plaguy dress-maker
Has had it a week." "Then that exquisite lilac,
In which you would melt the heart of a Shylock";
(Here the nose took again the same elevation)—
"I wouldn't wear that for the whole of creation."

"Why not? It's my fancy, there's nothing could strike it
As more *comme il faut*"—"Yes, but, dear me, that lean
    Sophronia Stuckup has got one just like it,
And I won't appear dressed like a chit of sixteen."
"Then that splendid purple, the sweet Mazarine;
    That superb *point d'aiguille*, that imperial green,
    That zephyr-like tarletan, that rich *grenadine*"—
"Not one of all which is fit to be seen,"
Said the lady, becoming excited and flushed.
"Then wear," I exclaimed, in a tone which quite crushed
Opposition, "that gorgeous *toilette* which you sported
In Paris last spring, at the grand presentation,
When you quite turned the head of the head of the nation,
    And by all the grand court were so very much courted."
    The end of the nose was portentously tipped up,
And both the bright eyes shot forth indignation,
As she burst upon me with the fierce exclamation,
"I have worn it three times, at the least calculation,
    And that and most of my dresses are ripped up!"
Here I *ripped out* something, perhaps rather rash,
    Quite innocent, though; but to use an expression
More striking than classic, it "settled my hash,"
    And proved very soon the last act of our session.
"Fiddlesticks, is it, sir? I wonder the ceiling
Doesn't fall down and crush you—you men have no feeling;
You selfish, unnatural, illiberal creatures,
Who set yourselves up as patterns and preachers,
Your silly pretense—why, what a mere guess it is?
Pray, what do you know of a woman's necessities?
I have told you and shown you I've nothing to wear,
And it's perfectly plain you not only don't care,
But you do not believe me" (here the nose went still higher).
"I suppose, if you dared, you would call me a liar.
Our engagement is ended, sir—yes, on the spot;
You're a brute, and a monster, and—I don't know what."
I mildly suggested the words Hottentot,
Pickpocket, and cannibal, Tartar, and thief,
As gentle expletives which might give relief;
But this only proved as a spark to the powder,

And the storm I had raised came faster and louder;
It blew and it rained, thundered, lightened and hailed
Interjections, verbs, pronouns, till language quite failed
To express the abusive, and then its arrears
Were brought up all at once by a torrent of tears,
And my last faint, despairing attempt at an obs-
Ervation was lost in a tempest of sobs.

Well, I felt for the lady, and felt for my hat, too,
Improvised on the crown of the latter a tattoo,
In lieu of expressing the feelings which lay
Quite too deep for words, as Wordsworth would say;
Then, without going through the form of a bow,
Found myself in the entry—I hardly know how,
On doorstep and sidewalk, past lamp-post and square,
At home and up-stairs, in my own easy-chair;
    Poked my feet into slippers, my fire into blaze,
And said to myself, as I lit my cigar,
"Supposing a man had the wealth of the Czar
    Of the Russias to boot, for the rest of his days,
On the whole, do you think he would have much to spare,
If he married a woman with nothing to wear?"

Since that night, taking pains that it should not be bruited
Abroad in society, I've instituted
A course of inquiry, extensive and thorough,
On this vital subject, and find, to my horror,
That the fair Flora's case is by no means surprising,
    But that there exists the greatest distress
In our female community, solely arising
    From this unsupplied destitution of dress,
Whose unfortunate victims are filling the air
With the pitiful wail of "Nothing to wear."

Researches in some of the "Upper Ten" districts
Reveal the most painful and startling statistics,
Of which let me mention only a few:
In one single house on the Fifth Avenue,
Three young ladies were found, all below twenty-two,

Who have been three whole weeks without anything new
In the way of flounced silks, and thus left in the lurch
Are unable to go to ball, concert or church.
In another large mansion near the same place,
Was found a deplorable, heart-rending case
Of entire destitution of Brussels point-lace.
In a neighboring block there was found, in three calls,
Total want, long continued, of camel's-hair shawls;
And a suffering family, whose case exhibits
The most pressing need of real ermine tippets;
One deserving young lady almost unable
To survive for the want of a new Russian sable;
Still another, whose tortures have been most terrific
Ever since the sad loss of the steamer Pacific,
In which were ingulfed, not friend or relation
(For whose fate she, perhaps, might have found consolation,
Or borne it, at least, with serene resignation),
But the choicest assortment of French sleeves and collars
Ever sent out from Paris, worth thousands of dollars.
And all as to style most *recherché* and rare,
The want of which leaves her with nothing to wear,
And renders her life so drear and dyspeptic
That she's quite a recluse, and almost a sceptic,
For she touchingly says, that this sort of grief
Cannot find in Religion the slightest relief,
And Philosophy has not a maxim to spare
For the victims of such overwhelming despair.
But the saddest, by far, of all these sad features
Is the cruelty practiced upon the poor creatures
By husbands and fathers, real Bluebeards and Timons,
Who resist the most touching appeals made for diamonds
By their wives and their daughters, and leave them for days
Unsupplied with new jewelry, fans or bouquets,
Even laugh at their miseries whenever they have a chance,
And deride their demands as useless extravagance;
One case of a bride was brought to my view,
Too sad for belief, but, alas! 't was too true,
Whose husband refused, as savage as Charon,
To permit her to take more than ten trunks to Sharon.

The consequence was, that when she got there,
At the end of three weeks she had nothing to wear;
And when she proposed to finish the season
At Newport, the monster refused, out and out,
For his infamous conduct alleging no reason,
Except that the waters were good for his gout;
Such treatment as this was too shocking, of course,
And proceedings are now going on for divorce.

But why harrow the feelings by lifting the curtain
From these scenes of woe? Enough, it is certain,
Has here been disclosed to stir up the pity
Of every benevolent heart in the city,
And spur up Humanity into a canter
To rush and relieve these sad cases instanter.
Won't somebody, moved by this touching description,
Come forward to-morrow and head a subscription?
Won't some kind philanthropist, seeing that aid is
So needed at once by these indigent ladies,
Take charge of the matter? Or won't Peter Cooper
The corner-stone lay of some new splendid super-
Structure, like that which to-day links his name
In the Union unending of Honor and Fame,
And found a new charity just for the care
Of these unhappy women with nothing to wear,
Which, in view of the cash which would daily be claimed,
The *Laying-out* Hospital well might be named?
Won't Stewart, or some of our dry-goods importers.
Take a contract for clothing our wives and our daughters?
Or, to furnish the cash to supply these distresses,
And life's pathway strew with shawls, collars and dresses,
Ere the want of them makes it much rougher and thornier,
Won't some one discover a new California?

O ladies, dear ladies, the next sunny day,
Please trundle your hoops just out of Broadway,
From its whirl and its bustle, its fashion and pride,
And the temples of Trade which tower on each side,
To the alleys and lanes, where Misfortune and Guilt

Their children have gathered, their city have built;
Where Hunger and Vice, like twin beasts of prey,
    Have hunted their victims to gloom and despair;
Raise the rich, dainty dress, and the fine broidered skirt,
Pick your delicate way through the dampness and dirt.
    Grope through the dark dens, climb the rickety stair
To the garret, where wretches, the young and the old,
Half starved and half naked, lie crouched from the cold;
See those skeleton limbs, those frost-bitten feet,
All bleeding and bruised by the stones of the street;
Hear the sharp cry of childhood, the deep groans that swell
    From the poor dying creature who writhes on the floor;
Hear the curses that sound like the echoes of Hell,
    As you sicken and shudder and fly from the door;
Then home to your wardrobes, and say, if you dare—
Spoiled children of fashion—you've nothing to wear!

And O, if perchance there should be a sphere
Where all is made right which so puzzles us here,
Where the glare and the glitter and tinsel of Time
Fade and die in the light of that region sublime,
Where the soul, disenchanted of flesh and of sense,
Unscreened by its trappings and shows and pretence,
Must be clothed for the life and the service above,
With purity, truth, faith, meekness and love,
O daughters of Earth! foolish virgins, beware!
Lest in that upper realm you have nothing to wear!

ILLUSTRATED NEWSPAPERS

JOHN PHŒNIX

A year or two since a weekly paper was started in London, called the
Illustrated News. It was filled with tolerably executed wood-cuts, representing scenes of popular interest, and though perhaps better calculated for the nursery than the reading-room, it took very well in

England, where few can read, but all can understand pictures, and soon attained an immense circulation. As when the inimitable *London Punch* attained its world-wide celebrity, supported by such writers as Thackeray, Jerrold and Hood, would-be funny men on this side of the Atlantic attempted absurd imitations—the "Yankee Doodle," the "John Donkey," etc.—which, as a matter of course, proved miserable failures; so did the success of this Illustrated affair inspire our money-loving publishers with hopes of dollars, and soon appeared from Boston, New York and other places, Pictorial and Illustrated Newspapers, teeming with execrable and silly effusions, and filled with the most fearful wood-engravings, "got up regardless of expense," or anything else; the contemplation of which was enough to make an artist tear his hair and rend his garments. A Yankee named Gleason, of Boston, published the first, we believe, calling it "Gleason's Pictorial (it should have been Gleason's Pickpocket) and Drawing-Room Companion." In this he presented to his unhappy subscribers, views of his house in the country, and his garden, and, for aught we know, of "his ox and his ass, and the stranger within his gates." A detestable invention for transferring Daguerreotypes to plates for engraving, having come into notice about this time, was eagerly seized upon by Gleason for farther embellishing his catchpenny publication, duplicates and uncalled-for pictures were easily obtained, and many a man has gazed in horror-stricken astonishment on the likeness of a respected friend, as a "Portrait of Monroe Edwards," or that of his deceased grandmother, in the character of "One of the Signers of the Declaration of Independence." They love pictures in Yankeedom; every tin peddler has one on his wagon, and an itinerant lecturer can always obtain an audience by sticking up a likeness of some unhappy female, with her ribs laid open in an impossible manner, for public inspection, or a hairless gentleman with the surface of his head laid out in eligible lots, duly marked and numbered. The factory girls of Lowell, the professors of Harvard, all bought the Pictorial. (Professor Webster was reading one when Dr. Parkman called on him on the morning of the murder.) Gleason's speculation was crowned with success, and he bought himself a new cooking-stove and erected an out-building on his estate, with both of which he favored the public in a new wood-cut immediately.

Inspired by his success, old Feejee-Mermaid-Tom-Thumb-Woolly-Horse-Joyce-Heth-Barnum forthwith got out another Illustrated Weekly, with pictures far more extensive, letter-press still sillier, and engravings more miserable, if possible, than Yankee Gleason's. And then we were bored and buffeted by having incredible likenesses of Santa Anna, Queen Victoria and poor old Webster thrust beneath our nose, to that degree that we wished the respected originals had never existed, or that the art of wood-engraving had perished with that of painting on glass.

It was, therefore, with the most intense delight that we saw a notice the other day of the failure and stoppage of *Barnum's Illustrated News*; we rejoiced thereat greatly, and we hope that it will never be revived, and that Gleason will also fail as soon as he conveniently can, and that his trashy Pictorial will perish with it.

It must not be supposed from the tenor of these remarks that we are opposed to the publication of a properly conducted and creditably executed Illustrated paper. "On the contrary, quite the reverse." We are passionately fond of art ourselves, and we believe that nothing can have a stronger tendency to refinement in society, than presenting to the public chaste and elaborate engravings, copies of works of high artistic merit, accompanied by graphic and well-written essays. It was for the purpose of introducing a paper containing these features to our appreciative community, that we have made these introductory remarks, and for the purpose of challenging comparison, and defying competition, that we have criticised so severely the imbecile and ephemeral productions mentioned above. At a vast expenditure of money, time and labor, and after the most incredible and unheard-of exertion on our part, individually, we are at length able to present to the public an Illustrated publication of unprecedented merit, containing engravings of exceeding costliness and rare beauty of design, got up on an expensive scale, which never has been attempted before, in this or any other country.

We furnish our readers this week with the first number, merely premising that the immense expense attending its issue will require a corresponding liberality of patronage on the part of the public, to cause it to be continued.

PHŒNIX'S PICTORIAL,

And Second Story Front Room Companion.

Vol. I.] 　　　San Diego, October 1, 1853. 　　　**[No. I.**

Portrait of His Royal Highness Prince Albert.—Prince Albert, the son of a gentleman named Coburg, is the husband of Queen Victoria of England, and the father of many of her children. He is the inventor of the celebrated "Albert hat," which has been lately introduced with great effect in the U. S. Army. The Prince is of German extraction, his father being a Dutchman and his mother a Duchess.

Mansion of John Phœnix, Esq., San Diego, California.

House in which Shakespeare was born, in Stratford-on-Avon.

Abbotsford, the residence of Sir Walter Scott, author of Byron's Pilgrim's Progress, etc.

The Capitol at Washington.

Residence of Governor Bigler, at Benicia, California.

Battle of Lake Erie (*see remarks*, p. 96).

[p. 96]

The Battle of Lake Erie, of which our Artist presents a spirited engraving, copied from the original painting, by Hannibal Carracci, in the possession of J. P. Haven, Esq., was fought in 1836, on Chesapeake Bay, between the U. S. frigates Constitution and Guerriere and the British troops under General Putnam. Our glorious flag, there as everywhere, was victorious, and "Long may it wave, o'er the land of the free and the home of *the slave.*"

Fearful accident on the Camden & Amboy Railroad!!
Terrible loss of life!!!

View of the City of San Diego, by Sir Benjamin West.

Interview between Mrs. Harriet Beecher Stowe and the Duchess of Sutherland, from a group of Statuary, by Clarke Mills.

Bank Account of J. Phœnix, Esq., at Adams & Co., Bankers, San Francisco, California.

Gas Works, *San Diego Herald* Office.

Steamer Goliah.

View of a California Ranch—Landseer.

Shell of an Oyster once eaten by General Washington, showing
the General's manner of opening Oysters.

There!—this is but a specimen of what we can do, if liberally sustained.
We wait with anxiety to hear the verdict of the Public before proceeding
to any farther and greater outlays.

Subscription, $5 per annum, payable invariably in advance.

INDUCEMENTS FOR CLUBBING.

Twenty copies furnished for one year, for fifty cents. Address John
Phœnix, office of the *San Diego Herald.*

JACK DOWNING IN PORTLAND

SEBA SMITH

Seba Smith, the author of the "Jack Downing Letters," which had immense vogue in their day, was born at Buckfield, Me., in 1792, and died at Patchogue, L. I., in 1868. He entered upon newspaper life in Portland, Me., and his "Letters," which were mainly political satires, were first printed there. He wrote several other books, which are now little known: "Way Down East," "My Thirty Years Out of the Senate," and "Dew Drops of the Nineteenth Century."

In the fall of the year 1829 I took it into my head I'd go to Portland. I had heard a good deal about Portland, what a fine place it was, and how the folks got rich there proper fast; and that fall there was a couple of new papers come up to Downingville from there, called the Portland Courier and Family Reader; and they told a good many queer kind of things about Portland and one thing another; and all at once it popped into my head, and I up and told father, and says I, I'm going to Portland whether or no; and I'll see what this world is made of yet. Father stared a little at first, and said he was afraid I should get lost; but when he see I was bent upon it, he give it up; and he stepped to his chist and opened the till, and took out a dollar and give to me, and says he, Jack, this is all I can do for you; but go, and lead an honest life, and I believe I shall hear good of you yet. He turned and walked across the room, but I could see the tears start into his eyes, and mother sot down and had a hearty crying spell. This made me feel rather bad for a minute or two, and I almost had a mind to give it up; and then again father's dream came into my mind, and I mustered up courage, and declared I'd go. So I tackled up the old horse and packed in a load of ax handles and a few notions, and mother fried me some dough-nuts and put 'em into a box along with some cheese and sassages, and ropped me up another shirt, for I told her I didn't know how long I should be gone; and after I got all rigged out, I went round and bid all the neighbors good bye, and jumped in and drove off for Portland.

Ant Sally had been married two or three years before and moved to

Portland, and I inquired round till I found out where she lived, and went there and put the old horse up and eat some supper and went to bed. And the next morning I got up and straightened right off to see the Editor of the Portland Courier, for I knew by what I had seen in his paper that he was just the man to tell me which way to steer. And when I come to see him I knew I was right; for soon as I told him my name and what I wanted, he took me by the hand as kind as if he had been a brother; and says he, Mr. Downing, I'll do any thing I can to assist you. You have come to a good town; Portland is a healthy, thriving place, and any man with a proper degree of enterprise may do well here. But says he, Mr. Downing, and he looked mighty kind of knowing, says he, if you want to make out to your mind, you must do as the steam boats do. Well, says I, how do they do? for I didn't know what a steam boat was, any more than the man in the moon. Why, says he, they *go ahead*. And you must drive about among the folks here just as though you were at home on the farm among the cattle. Don't be afraid of any of 'em, but figure away, and I dare say you will get into good business in a very little while. But says he, there's one thing you must be careful of, and that is, not to get into the hands of them are folks that trades up round Huckler's Row; for there's some sharpers up there, if they get hold of you, would twist your eye teeth out in five minutes. Well, after he had gin me all the good advice he could I went back to Ant Sally's again and got some breakfast, and then I walked all over the town, to see what chance I could find to sell my ax handles and things, and to get into business.

After I had walked about three or four hours I come along towards the upper end of the town, where I found there were stores and shops of all sorts and sizes. And I met a feller, and says I, what place is this? Why, this, says he, is Huckler's Row. What, says I, are these stores where the traders in Huckler's Row keep? And says he, yes. Well then, thinks I to myself, I have a pesky good mind to go in and have a try with one of these chaps, and see if they can twist my eye teeth out. If they can get the best end of a bargain out of me, they can do what there aint a man in Downingville can do, and I should jest like to know what sort of stuff these ere Portland chaps are made of. So in I goes into the best looking store among 'em. And I see some biscuit lying on the shelf, and says I, Mister, how much do you ax apiece for them are biscuit? A cent apiece, says he, Well, says I, I sha'n't give you that, but if you've a mind to, I'll give you two cents for three of 'em, for I begin to feel a little as though I should like to take a bite. Well, says he, I wouldn't sell 'em to any body else so, but seeing it's you I don't care if you take 'em. I knew he lied, for he never see me before in his life. Well he handed down the biscuits and I took 'em, and walked round the store awhile to see what else he had to sell. At last, says I, Mister, have you got any good new cider? Says he, yes, as good as ever you see. Well, says I, what do you ax a glass for it? Two cents, says he. Well, says I, seems to me I feel more dry than I do hungry now. Ain't you a mind to take these ere biscuits again and give me a glass of cider? And says he, I don't care if I do; so he took and laid 'em on the shelf again, and poured out a glass of cider. I took the cider and drinkt it down, and to tell the truth it was capital good cider. Then, says I, I guess it's time for me to be a going, and I stept along towards the door. But, says he, stop Mister. I believe you haven't paid me for the cider. Not paid you for the cider, says I, what do you mean by that? Didn't the biscuit that I give you jest come to the cider? Oh, ah, right, says he. So I started to go again; and says he, but stop, Mister, you didn't pay me for the biscuit. What, says I, do you mean to impose upon me? do you think I am going to pay you for the biscuit and let you keep 'em to? Aint they there now on your shelf, what more do you want? I guess sir, you don't whittle me in that way. So I turned about and marched off, and left the feller staring and thinking and scratching his head, as though he was struck with a dunderment. Howsomever, I didn't want to cheat him, only jest to show 'em it wan't so easy a matter to pull my eye teeth out, so I called in next day and paid him his two cents.

A DOSE OF PAIN KILLER

MARK TWAIN

Tom Sawyer's Aunt Polly was one of those people who are infatuated with patent medicines and all new-fangled methods of producing health or mending it. She was an inveterate experimenter in these things. When something fresh in this line came out she was in a fever, right away, to try it; not on herself, for she was never ailing, but on anybody else that came handy. She was a subscriber for all the "Health" periodicals and phrenological frauds; and the solemn ignorance they were inflated with was breath to her nostrils. All the "rot" they contained about ventilation, and how to go to bed, and how to get up, and what to eat, and what to drink, and how much exercise to take, and what frame of mind to keep one's self in, and what sort of clothing to wear, was all gospel to her, and she never observed that her health-journals of the current month customarily upset everything they had recommended the month before. She was as simple-hearted and honest as the day was long, and so she was an easy victim. She gathered together her quack periodicals and her quack medicines, and thus armed with death, went about on her pale horse, metaphorically speaking, with "hell following after." But she never suspected that she was not an angel of healing, and the balm of Gilead in disguise, to the suffering neighbors.

The water treatment was new, now, and Tom's low condition was a windfall to her. She had him out at daylight every morning, stood him up in the woodshed and drowned him with a deluge of cold water; then she scrubbed him down with a towel like a file, and so brought him to; then she rolled him up in a wet sheet and put him away under blankets till she sweated his soul clean and "the yellow stains of it came through his pores"—as Tom said.

Yet notwithstanding all this, the boy grew more and more melancholy and pale and dejected. She added hot baths, sitz baths, shower baths and plunges. The boy remained as dismal as a hearse. She began to assist the water with a slim oatmeal diet and blister plasters. She calculated his capacity as she would a jug's, and filled him up every day with quack cure-alls.

Tom had become indifferent to persecution by this time. This phase filled the old lady's heart with consternation. This indifference must be broken up at any cost. Now she heard of Pain-killer for the first time. She ordered a lot at once. She tasted it and was filled with gratitude. It was simply fire in a liquid form. She dropped the water treatment and everything else, and pinned her faith to Pain-killer. She gave Tom a teaspoonful, and watched with the deepest anxiety for the result. Her troubles were instantly at rest, her soul at peace again; for the "indifference" was broken up. The boy could not have shown a wilder, heartier interest, if she had built a fire under him.

Tom felt that it was time to wake up; this sort of life might be romantic enough, in his blighted condition, but it was getting to have too little sentiment and too much distracting variety about it.

So he thought over various plans for relief, and finally hit upon that of professing to be fond of Pain-killer. He asked for it so often that he became a nuisance, and his aunt ended by telling him to help himself and quit bothering her. If it had been Sid, she would have had no misgivings to alloy her delight; but since it was Tom, she watched the bottle clandestinely. She found that the medicine did really diminish, but it did not occur to her that the boy was mending the health of a crack in the sitting-room floor with it.

One day Tom was in the act of dosing the crack, when his aunt's yellow cat came along, purring, eyeing the teaspoon avariciously, and begging for a taste. Tom said:

"Don't ask for it unless you want it, Peter."

But Peter signified that he did want it.

"You better make sure."

Peter was sure.

"Now you've asked for it, and I'll give it to you, because there ain't anything mean about *me*; but if you find you don't like it, you mustn't blame anybody but your own self."

Peter was agreeable. So Tom pried his mouth open and poured down the Pain-killer. Peter sprang a couple of yards in the air, and then delivered a war-whoop and set off round and round the room, banging against furniture, upsetting flower-pots and making general havoc. Next he rose on his hind feet and pranced around, in a frenzy of enjoyment, with his head over his shoulder and his voice proclaiming his unappeasable happiness. Then he went tearing around the house again, spreading chaos and destruction in his path. Aunt Polly entered in time to see him throw a few double summersets, deliver a final mighty hurrah, and sail through the open window, carrying the rest of the flower-pots with him. The old lady stood petrified with astonishment, peering over her glasses; Tom lay on the floor expiring with laughter.

"Tom, what on earth ails that cat?"

"*I* don't know, aunt," gasped the boy.

"Why, I never see anything like it. What *did* make him act so?"

" 'Deed I don't know, Aunt Polly: cats always act so when they're having a good time."

"They do, do they?" There was something in the tone that made Tom apprehensive.

"Yes'm. That is, I believe they do."

"You *do*?"

"Yes'm."

The old lady was bending down, Tom watching with interest emphasized by anxiety. Too late he divined her "drift." The handle of the tell-tale teaspoon was visible under the bed-valance. Aunt Polly took it, held it up. Tom winced, and dropped his eyes. Aunt Polly raised him by the usual handle—his ear—and cracked his head soundly with her thimble.

"Now, sir, what do you want to treat that poor dumb beast so, for?"

"I done it out of pity for him—because he hadn't any aunt."

"Hadn't any aunt!—you numscull. What has that got to do with it?"

"Heaps. Because if he'd a had one she'd a burst him out herself! She'd a roasted his bowels out of him 'thout any more feeling than if he was a human!"

"Aunt Polly felt a sudden pang of remorse. This was putting the thing in a new light; what was cruelty to a cat *might* be cruelty to a boy, too. She began to soften; she felt sorry. Her eyes watered a little, and she put her hand on Tom's head and said gently:

"I was meaning for the best, Tom. And, Tom, it *did* do you good."

Tom looked up in her face with just a perceptible twinkle peeping through his gravity:

"I know you was meaning for the best, aunty, and so was I with Peter. It done *him* good, too. I never see him get around so since—"

"O, go 'long with you, Tom, before you aggravate me again. And you try and see if you can't be a good boy, for once, and you needn't take any more medicine."

FABLES OF THE HODJA

SAMUEL S. COX

Narr-ed-din Hodja is an imaginary person. He holds the same rank with the Turks as Æsop with the Greeks. It is a fictitious name, under which a large number of anecdotes have been collected and compiled. Narr-ed-din Hodja, as the title (Hodja) implies, is supposed to be a man learned in religion. He is the representative and exemplar of Turkish humor, pure and simple. He is represented as living at Bagdad. All the surroundings attached to his anecdotes are Turkish. He is not supposed, like Æsop, to have written them himself, but he is simply connected, supposititiously, with humorous sayings and doings.

One day Narr-ed-din Hodja is too lazy to preach his usual sermon at the mosque. He simply addresses himself to his congregation, saying:

"Of course ye know, oh, faithful Mussulmans, what I am going to say to you?"

As the Hodja stops, evidently waiting for an answer, the congregation cry out with one voice:

"No, Hodja Effendi, we do not know."

"Then if you do not know, I have nothing to say to you," replies the Hodja, and immediately leaves the pulpit.

Next day he again addresses his congregation, saying:

"Know ye, oh faithful Mussulmans, what I am going to say to you?"

Fearing that if, as on the previous day, they say "No," the Hodja would leave them again without a sermon, the congregation this time, replies:

"Yes, Hodja, we do know."

"Then if you do know what I am going to say," quietly says the Hodja, "of course there is no need of my saying it." He again steps down from the pulpit, to the consternation of the congregation.

On the third day, the Hodja again puts the question:

"Know ye, oh faithful Mussulmans, what I am going to say to you?"

The congregation, determined not to be disappointed again, take some council among themselves on the question. Accordingly some of them reply:

"No, Hodja, we do not know," while others cry:

"Yes, Hodja we do know."

"Very well, then," says the Hodja, "as there are some of you who do know, and others who do not know, what I was going to say, let those who do know, tell it to those that do not know;" and he quickly descends from the pulpit.

The moral of this story is not always in the mind of the clergy. It is this:

If you can find nothing worth saying, do not trespass on the congregation by trying to say it.

———

Another story is told of the Hodja. He used to teach in the parish school. He had taught his pupils that, whenever he happened to sneeze, they should all stand up, and, clapping their hands together, should cry out:

"God grant you long life, Hodja!"

This the pupils regularly did whenever the Hodja sneezed. One day the bucket gets loose and falls into the well of the schoolhouse. As the pupils are afraid to go down into the well to fetch up the bucket, Narred-din Hodja undertakes the task.

He accordingly strips, and tying a rope round his waist, asks his pupils to lower him carefully into the well, and pull him up again when he gives the signal. The Hodja goes down, and having caught the bucket, shouts out to his pupils to pull him up again. This they do. The Hodja is nearly out of the well, when he suddenly sneezes! Upon this, his pupil immediately let go the rope, begin to knock their hands together, and shout down the well:

"God grant you long life, Hodja!"

But the poor Hodja tumbles down to the bottom of the well with a tremendous crash, breaking his head and several of his bones.

The moral of this story is—*too neat for explication.*

———

A mendicant knocks at the Hodja's door.

"What do you want, my friend?" asks the Hodja, putting his head out of an upper floor window.

"Come down, Hodja Effendi, and I will tell you," replies the mendicant.

The Hodja obeys, and coming down to the door, asks again of the man what is wanted.

"Alms," is the answer.

"Oh! very well," said the Hodja, "come with me up-stairs."

Leading the way, the Hodja conducts the man to the top-most floor of his house. Arrived there, he turns round and remarks:

"I am very much distressed, my good friend, but I have no alms to give you."

"Why did you not say so down below?" inquires the man angrily.

"Why did you not tell me what you wanted when I asked you from the window? Did you not make me come down to the door?" retorts the Hodja.

The moral whereof is:

Be polite and considerate when you beg favors.

The Dog and the Bees

AMBROSE BIERCE

A dog being very much annoyed by bees, ran, quite accidentally, into an empty barrel lying on the ground, and looking out at the bung-hole, addressed his tormenters thus:

"Had you been temperate, stinging me only one at a time, you might have got a good deal of fun out of me. As it is, you have driven me into a secure retreat; for I can snap you up as fast as you come in through the bung-hole. Learn from this the folly of intemperate zeal."

When he had concluded, he awaited a reply. There wasn't any reply; for the bees had never gone near the bung-hole; they went in the same way as he did, and made it very warm for him.

The lesson of this fable is that one cannot stick to his pure reason while quarreling with bees.

Sicily Burns's Wedding

GEORGE W. HARRIS

George Washington Harris was born in Allegheny City, Pa., in 1814, and died in Knoxville, Tenn., in 1869. He spent most of his life in Tennessee, and was at one time a river captain. His "Sut Lovingood Yarns" first appeared in Nashville journals.

"Hey, Ge-orge!" rang among the mountain slopes; and looking up to my left, I saw "Sut" tearing along down a steep point, heading me off, in a long kangaroo lope, holding his flask high above his head, and hat in hand. He brought up near me, banteringly shaking the half-full "tickler," within an inch of my face.

"Whar am yu gwine? take a suck, hoss? This yere truck's *ole*. I kotch hit myse'f, hot this mornin frum the still wum. Nara durn'd bit ove strike-nine in hit—I put that ar piece ove burnt dried peach in myse'f tu gin hit color—better nur ole Bullen's plan: he puts in tan ooze, in what he sells, an' when that haint handy, he uses the red warter outen a pon' jis' below his barn—makes a pow'ful natral color, but don't help the taste much. Then he correcks that wif red pepper; hits an orful mixtry, that whisky ole Bullen makes; no wonder he seed 'Hell-sarpints.' He's pisent ni ontu three-quarters ove the b'levin parts ove his congregashun wif hit, an' tuther quarter he's sot intu ruff stealin' an' cussin'. Ef his still-'ous don't burn down, ur he peg out hisse'f, the neighborhood am ruinated a-pas' salvashun. Haint he the durndes sampil ove a passun yu ever seed enyhow?

"Say, George, du yu see these yere well-poles what I uses fur laigs? Yu sez yu sees em, dus yu?"

"Yes."

"Very well; I passed 'em a-pas' each uther tuther day, right peart. I put one out a-head, jis' so, an' then tuther 'bout nine feet a-head ove hit agin, jis' so, an' then kep on a-duin hit.

"George, yu don't onderstan life yet scarcely at all, got a heap tu larn, a heap. But 'bout my swappin my laigs so fas'—these yere very par ove laigs. I hed got about a fox squirril skin full ove biled co'n juice packed onder my shut, an' onder my hide too, I mout es well add, an' wer aimin fur Bill Carr's on foot. When I got in sight ove ole man Burns's, I seed ni ontu fifty hosses an' muels hitch'd tu the fence. Dur-nashun! I jis' then tho't ove hit—'twer Sicily's wedding day. She married ole Clapshaw, the suckit rider. The very feller hu's faith gin out when he met me sendin sody all over creashun. Suckit-riders am sur-jestif things tu me. They preaches agin me, an' I hes no chance tu preach back at them. Ef I cud I'd make the institushun behave hitsef better nur hit dus. They hes sum wunderful pints, George. Thar am two things nobody never seed: wun am a dead muel, an' tuther is a suckit-rider's grave. Kaze why, the he muels all turn intu old field school-masters, an' the she ones intu strong minded wimen, an' then when thar times cums, they dies sorter like uther folks. An' the suckit-riders ride ontil they marry; ef they marrys money, they turns intu store-keepers, swaps hosses, an' stays away ove colleckshun Sundays. Them what marrys, an' by sum orful mistake *misses the money*, jis turns intu polertishuns, sells ile well stock, an' dies sorter in the human way too.

"But 'bout the wedding. Ole Burns hed a big black an' white bull, wif a ring in his snout, an' the rope tied up roun his ho'ns. They rid 'im tu mill, an' sich like, wif a saddil made outen two dorgwood forks, an' two clapboards, kivered wif a ole piece ove carpet, rope girth, an' rope stirrups wif a loop in hit fur the foot. Ole 'Sock,' es they call'd the bull, hed jis got back frum mill, an' wer turn'd intu the yard, saddil an' all, tu solace hissef a-pickin grass. I wer slungin roun the outside ove the hous', fur they hedn't hed the manners tu ax me in, when they sot down tu dinner. I wer pow'fully hurt 'bout hit, an' happen'd tu think— SODY. So I sot in a-watchin fur a chance tu du sumthin. I fus tho't I'd shave ole Clapshaw's hoss's tail, go tu the stabil an' shave Sicily's mare's tail, an' ketch ole Burns out, an shave his tail too. While I wer a-studyin 'bout this, ole Sock wer a-nosin 'roun, an' cum up ontu a big baskit what hilt a littil shattered co'n; he dipp'd in his head tu git hit, an' I slipp'd up an' jerked the handil over his ho'ns.

"Now, George, ef yu knows the nater ove a cow brute, they is the durndes' fools amung all the beastes ('scept the Lovingoods); when they gits intu tribulashun, they knows nuffin but tu shot thar eyes, beller, an' back, an' keep a-backin'. Well, when ole Sock raised his head an' foun' hissef in darkness, he jis twisted up his tail, snorted the shatter'd co'n outen the baskit, an' made a tremenjus lunge agin the hous'. I learn the picters a-hangin agin the wall on the inside a-fallin'.

He fotch a deep, loud, rusty beller, mout been hearn a mile, an' then sot intu a onendin sistem ove backin'. A big craw-fish wif a hungry coon a-reachin' fur him, wer jis' nowhar. Fust agin one thing, then over anuther, an' at las' agin the bee-bainch, knockin' hit an' a dozen stan' ove bees heads over heels, an' then stompin' back'ards thru the mess. Hit haint much wuf while tu tell what the bees did, ur how soon they sot intu doin' it. They am pow'ful quick-tempered littil critters, eny-how. The air wer dark wif 'em, an' Sock wer kivered all over, frum snout to tail, so clost yu cudent a-sot down a grain ove wheat fur bees, an' they wer a-fitin one another in the air fur a place on the bull. The hous' stood on sidlin' groun', an' the back door were even wif hit. So

Sock happen to hit hit plum, jes' backed intu the hous' onder 'bout two hundred an' fifty poun's of steam, bawlin' orful, an' every snort he fotch he snorted away a quart ove bees ofen his sweaty snout. He wer the leader ove the bigges' an the maddest army ove bees in the world. Thar wer at leas' five solid bushels ove 'em. They hed filled the baskit, an' hed lodgd onto his tail ten deep, ontil hit wer es thick es a waggin tung. He hed hit stuck strait up in the air, an' hit looked adzackly like a dead pine kivered wif ivey. I think he wer the hottes' an' wus hurtin' bull then livin'; his temper, too, seemed to be pow'fully flustrated. Ove *all* the durn'd times an' kerryins on yu *ever* hearn tell on ere thar an' tharabouts. He cum tail fust agin the ole two-story Dutch clock, an' fotch hit, bustin' hits runnin' geer outen hit, the littil wheels a-trundlin' over the floor, an' the bees even chasin' them. Nex' pass, he fotch up agin the foot ove a big dubbil injine bedstead, rarin' hit on aind an' punchin' one ove the posts thru a glass winder. The nex' tail-fus' experdishun wer made aginst the caticorner'd cupboard, outen which he made a perfeck momox. Fus' he upsot hit, smashin' in the glass doors, an' then jis sot in an' stomp'd everything on the shelves intu giblits, a-tryin' tu back furder in that direckshun, an' tu git the bees ofen his laigs.

"Pickil crocks, perserves jars, vinegar jugs, seed bags, yarb bunches, paragorick bottils, aig baskits, an' delf war—all mix'd dam per-miskusly, an' not worth the sortin', by a duller an' a ha'f. Nex', he got a far back acrost the room agin the board pertishun; he went thru hit like hit hed been paper, takin' wif him 'bout six foot squar ove hit in splin-ters an' broken boards intu the nex' room, whar they wer eatin' dinner, an' rite yere the fitin' becum gineral, an' the dancin', squawkin', cussin' an' dodgin' begun.

"Clapshaw's ole mam wer es deaf es a dogiron, an' sot at the aind ove the tabil, nex' to whar ole Sock busted thru the wall; tail fus' he cum agin her cheer, a-histin' her an' hit ontu the tabil. Now, the smashin' ove delf, an' the mixin' ove vittils begun. They hed sot severil tabils tugether tu make hit long enuf. So he jis rolled 'em up a-top ove one anuther, and thar sot ole Missis Clapshaw a-straddil ove the top ove the pile, a-fitin' bees like a mad wind-mill, wif her calliker cap in one han', fur a wepun', an' a cract frame in tuther, an' a-kickin' an' a-spurrin' like she wer ridin' a lazy hoss arter the doctor, an' a-screamin' fire and murder es fas' es she cud name 'em over.

"Taters, cabbige, meat, soup, beans, sop, dumplins', an' the truck what yu wallers 'em in; milk, plates, pies, puddins, an' every durn fixin' yu cud think ove in a week, were thar, mix'd an' mashed, like hid had been thru a thrashin'-meesheen. Ole Sock still kep' a-backin', an' backed the hole pile, ole 'oman an' all, also sum cheers, outen the frunt door, an' down seven steps intu the lane, an' then, by golly, turn'd a fifteen hundred poun' summerset hisself arter 'em, lit a-top ove the mix'd up mess, flat ove his back, an' then kicked hissef ontu his feet agin. About the time he ris, ole man Burns—yu know how fat an' stumpy, an' cross-grained he is, enyhow—made a vigrus mad snatch at the baskit, an' got a savin holt ontu it, but cudent *let go quick enuf;* fur ole Sock jis snorted, bawled, an' histed the ole cuss heels fust up intu the air, an' he lit on the bull's back, an' hed the baskit in his han'.

"Jis' es soon as ole Blackey got the use ove his eyes, he tore off down the lane, tu outrun the bees, so durn'd fast that ole Burns wer feard tu try tu git off. So he jis socked his feet intu the rope loops, an' then cummenc'd the durndes' bull-ride mortal man ever ondertuck. Sock run atwixt the hitched critters an' the rail-fence, ole Burns fust fitin' him over the head wif the baskit to stop him, an' then fitin' the bees wif hit. I'll jis' be durn'd ef I didn't think he hed four or five baskits, hit wer in so meny places at onst. Well, Burns, baskit, an' bull, an' bees skared every durn'd hoss an' muel loose frum that fence—bees ontu all ove 'em; bees, by golly, everywhar. Mos' on 'em, too, tuck a fence-rail along, fas' tu the bridil-reins. A heavy cloud ove dus', like a harycane hed been blowin', hid all the hosses, an' away abuv hit yu cud see tails an' ainds ove fence-rails a-flyin' about; now an' then a par ove bright hine shoes wud flash in the sun like two sparks, an' away ahead were the baskit a-sirklin' roun' an' about at random. Brayin', nickerin', the bellerin' ove the bull, clatterin' ove runnin' hoofs, an' a mons'ous rushin' soun' made up the noise. Lively times in that lane jis' then, warnt thar?

"I swar ole Burns kin beat eny man on top ove the yeath a-fitin bees wif a baskit. Jis' set 'im a-straddil ove a mad bull, an' let thar be bees enuf tu exhite the ole man, an' the man what beats him kin break me. Hosses an' muels were tuck up all over the county, an' sum wer forever los'. Yu cudent go eny course, in a cirkil ove a mile, an' not find buckils, stirrups, straps, saddil-blankits, ur sumthin' belongin' to a saddilhoss. Now don't forgit that about that hous' thar wer a good time bein' had ginerally. Fellers an' gals loped outen windows, they rolled outen the doors in bunches, they clomb the chimleys, they darted onder the house jis tu dart out agin, they tuck tu the thicket, they rolled in the wheat-field lay down in the crick, did everything but stan' still. Sum made a strait run *fur* home, an' sum es strait a run *frum* home; livelyest folks I ever did see."

BALLAD OF THE RHINE

HANS BREITMANN

Charles Godfrey Leland, the author of the "Hans Breitmann Ballads," and the accomplished translator of "Heine," was born at Philadelphia, in 1824, and graduated at New Jersey College in 1845. He afterwards pursued his studies in the Universities of Heidelberg, Munich and Paris; and then returned to Philadelphia, took up the law, but soon relinquished it for a literary life. He is the author of various works, and is a student of many modern literatures; he is especially known for his researches in the language and history of the Gypsies. He has lived chiefly in England during the last ten or fifteen years.

> Der noble Ritter Hugo
>   Von Schwillensaufenstein,
> Rode out mit shpeer and helmet,
>   Und he coom to de panks of de Rhine.
>
> Und oop dere rose a meer maid,
>   Vot hadn't got nodings on,
> Und she say, "Oh, Ritter Hugo,
>   Vhere you goes mit yourself alone?"
>
> Und he says, "I rides in de creenwood
>   Mit helmet und mit shpeer,
> Till I cooms into em Gasthaus,
>   Und dere I trinks some beer."
>
> Und den outshpoke de maiden
>   Vot hadn't got nodings on:
> "I tont dink mooch of beoplesh
>   Dat goes mit demselfs alone.

"You'd petter coom down in de wasser,
    Vere deres heaps of dings to see,
Und have a shplendid tinner
    Und drafel along mit me.

"Dere you sees de fisch a schwimmin,
    Und you catches dem efery one:"—
So sang dis wasser maiden
    Vot hadn't got nodings on.

"Dere ish drunks all full mit money
    In ships dat vent down of old;
Und you helpsh yourself, by dunder!
    To shimmerin crowns of gold.

"Shoost look at dese shpoons und vatches!
    Shoost see dese diamant rings!
Coom down und full your bockets,
    Und I'll giss you like avery dings.

Vot you vantsh mit your schnapps und lager?
    Coom down into der Rhine!
Der ish pottles der Kaiser Charlemagne
    Vonce filled mit gold-red wine!"

Dat fetched him—he shtood all shpell pound;
    She pooled his coat-tails down,
She drawed him oonder der wasser,
    De maiden mit nodings on.

———

THE QUICKEST WAY to take the starch out ov a man who iz allwuss blameing himself, iz to agree with him. This aint what he iz looking for.

JOSH BILLINGS

THE EXPENSIVE TREAT OF COL. MOSES GRICE

RICHARD MALCOLM JOHNSTON

Richard Malcolm Johnston, born in Hancock County, Ga., March 8, 1822, has a literary reputation of many years, originating with the "Dukesborough Tales," and identified with several characteristic works of humor, fancy and imagination.

Besides an incipient ventriloquist who had included it in a limited provincial tour which he was making, in some hope of larger development of his artistic powers, the only show that had visited Dukesborough thus far was the wax figures. The recollection of that had ever remained unsatisfactory. I can just remember that one of the figures was William Pitt, and another the Sleeping Beauty; that the former was the saddest and the yellowest great statesman that I had had opportunity, thus far, to look upon, and the latter—well, it is not pleasant, even now, to recall how dead, how long time dead, she appeared. When Aggy, my nurse, seeing me appalled at the sight, repeatedly asseverated, "De lady is jes a-tired and a-takin' of a nap," I cried the louder, and plucked so at Aggy that she had to take me away. Though not thus demonstrative, yet even elderly country people acknowledged to disappointment, and there was a general complaint that if what had been was the best that could be done by Dukesborough in the way of public entertainment, it might as well take itself away from the great highway of human travel, suspend its school, sell out its two stores at cost, abolish its tavern and post-office, tear down its blacksmith's and shoe shops, and, leaving only its meeting-house, resolve itself into the elements from which it had been aggregated. Not that these were the very words: but surely their full equivalents were employed when William Pitt, the Sleeping Beauty, and their pale associates had silently left the town.

As for a circus, such an institution was not known, except by hearsay, even to Colonel Moses Grice, of the Fourteenth Regiment

Georgia Militia, though he was a man thirty-five years old, over six feet high, of proportional weight, owned a good plantation and at least twenty negroes, and had seen the theatre as many as three times in the city of Augusta. The ideas the Colonel had received there were such, he said, as would last him to the end of his days—a period believed to be remote, barring, of course, all contingencies of future wars. To this theatrical experience he had been desirous, for some time, to add that of the circus, assured in his mind that from what he had heard, it was a good thing. It happened once, while on a visit to Augusta—whither he had accompanied a wagon-load of his cotton, partly on that business, but mainly to see the great world there—that he met at Collier's tavern, where he sojourned, a circus forerunner, who was going the rounds with his advertisements. Getting soon upon terms of intimacy with one who seemed to him the most agreeable, entertaining and intelligent gentleman that he had ever met, Colonel Grice imparted to him such information about Dukesborough that, although that village was not upon the list of appointments—Dukesborough, in point of fact (to his shame the agent confessed it) not having been even heard of—yet a day was set for its visitation, and, when visited, another was set for the appearance there of the Great World-Renowned Circus, which claimed for its native homes London, Paris and New York.

It would be entertaining to a survivor of that period to make even small boys, from families of most limited means in this generation, comprehend the interest excited by those advertisements, in huge black and red letters, that were tacked upon the wall of Spouter's tavern. From across Beaver Dam, Rocky Creek, the Ogeechee, from even the head-waters of streams leading to the Oconee, they came to read over and spell over the mighty words. Colonel Grice, who had been found, upon his own frank admission, to be the main mover, was forced to answer all inquiries concerning its magnitude, its possible influences upon the future of Dukesborough, and kindred subjects. There would have been a slight drawback to the general eager expectation on grounds moral and religious; but the World-Renowned had anticipated and provided against that, as will hereafter appear. Then Colonel Grice had signified his intention of meeting the impending institution on the occasion of at least two of its exhibitions before its arrival, and should take it upon himself to warn it of the kind of people it was coming among.

The Colonel resided five miles south of the village. He had a wife, but no child (a point on which he was, perhaps, a little sore), was not in debt, was hospitable, an encourager, especially in words, of public and private enterprises, and enthusiastically devoted, though without experience in wars, to the military profession, which—if he might use the expression—he would call his second wife. Off the muster-field he habitually practiced that affability which is pleasant because so rare to see in the warrior class. When in full uniform and at the head of the regiment, with girt sword and pistol-holster, he did indeed look like a man not to be fooled with; and the sound of his voice in utterance of military orders was such as to show that he intended those orders to be heard and obeyed. When the regiment was disbanded, the sternness would depart from his mien, and, though yet unstripped of weapons and regalia, he would smile blandly, as if to reassure spectators that, for the present, the danger was over, and friends might approach without apprehension.

The Colonel met the circus even farther away than he at first had intended. He had determined to study it, he said, and he traveled some seventy miles on horseback, attending daily and nightly exhibitions. Several times during this travel, and afterwards, on the forenoon of the great day in Dukesborough, he was heard to say that, if he were limited to one word with which to describe what he had seen, that word would be—*grandeur*. "As for what sort of a people them circus people are," he said, "in a moral and in a religious sense, now—ahem! you know, gentlemen and ladies, especially ladies—ah, ha! I'm not a member, but I'm as great a respecter of religion as can be found in the whole State of Georgia. Bein' raised to that, I pride myself on that. Now, these circus people, they ain't what I should call a highly moral, that is, they ain't a strictly *religious* people. You see, gentlemen, that ain't, not religion ain't, so to speak, their business. They ain't goin' about preachin', and havin' camp-meetin' revivals, and givin' singin'-school lessons. They are—I wish I could explain myself about these circus people. These circus people are a-tryin'—you know, gentlemen, different people makes their livin' in different ways; and these circus people are jes a-tryin' to do exactly the same thing in jes exactly the same way. Well, gentlemen, *grandeur* is the word I should say about their performances. I should not confine myself to the word *religion*. Strictly speakin', that word do not embrace all the warious warieties, so to speak, of a circus. *My* word would be GRANDEUR; and I think that's the word you all will use when that tent is up, that door is open, and you are rushin' into its—its—I don't know whether to use the word *jaws* or *departments*. But, for the sake of decency, I'll say—*departments*. As for moral and religious, gentlemen—*and* 'specially ladies—I tell you, it ain't neither a camp-meetin', a'sociation, a quarterly meetin', nor a singin'-school. I'm not a member, but I'm a respecter; and as to all that, and all them, Dukesborough may go farther and fare worse. That's all I got to say."

On the day before, Colonel Grice, by this time grown intimate with the manager, and as fond of him as if he had been his own brother (some said even fonder), in the fullness of his heart had invited the whole force to breakfast with him on the way to Dukesborough, and the invitation had been accepted. What was consumed was enormous; but he could afford it, and his wife, especially with distinguished visitors, was as hospitable and openhearted as himself.

Other persons besides boys believed in their hearts that they might not have been able to endure another day's delay of the show. For a brief period the anxiety of the school-children amounted to anguish when the master expressed doubts as to a holiday; for holidays then were infrequent, and schoolmasters had to be over-persuaded. But the present incumbent yielded early, with becoming reluctance, to what seemed to be the general desire. The eagerly expected morning came at last. Many who knew that the circus was lingering at Colonel Grice's went forth to meet it, some on foot, some on horseback. Some started even in gigs and other carriages, but, being warned by old people, turned, unhooked their horses, and hitched them to swinging limbs in the very farthest part of the graveyard grove, and then set out on foot. The great show had put foremost its best wagon, but nobody had any sort of idea what things those were which the military gentlemen who rode in it carried in their hands. One person, known generally to carry a cool head, said that one of these things looked to him like a drum, though of a size comparatively enormous, but the idea was generally scorned.

"Where you goin', there, Polly Ann?" said Mrs. Watts to her little daughter, who was opening the gate. "My Lord!" exclaimed the mother instantly afterwards, as the band struck up. Then she rushed out herself and ran over Polly Ann, knocking her down. Polly Ann got up again and followed. "Stay behind there, you, Jack, and you, Susan! You want to git eat up by them camels and varmints? I never see sich children for cur'osity. They've got as much cur'osity as—as—"

"As we have," said Mrs. Thompson, laughing, as she attempted in vain to drive back her own little brood.

The effect of the music in the long, covered wagon, drawn by six gray horses slowly before the long procession, no words can describe. It put all, the aged and the young, into a tremor. Old Mr. Leadbetter, one of the deacons, who had been very "jubous," as he said, about the whole thing, was trying to read a chapter somewhere in Romans, when, at the very first blast, his spectacles jumped off his nose, and he told a few of the brethren afterwards, confidentially, that he never could recollect afterwards, where he had left off. As for Mrs. Bland, she actually danced in her piazza for, probably, as many as a dozen bars, and, when "had up" about it, pleaded in abatement, that she did it entirely unbeknownst to herself, and that she couldn't have holp it if it had been to have saved her life. It might have gone hard with the defendant had not some of her triers been known to march in time to the band, and, besides, they had staid after the close of the animal show, contrary to the special inhibition against the circus. For the World-Renowned had provided against the scruples of the straitest sects by attaching to itself a small menagerie of animals, whose exhibition had been appointed for the opening. There were a camel, a lion, a zebra, a hyena, two leopards, a porcupine, six monkeys, a bald eagle and some parrots. By some means, never fully known, the most scrupulous of the spectators had gotten (late during this first act) to the very loftiest and remotest seats in the amphitheatre, and when the animals were shut from the view, these persons, though anxious, were unable to retire without stepping over the shoulders of those beneath—a thing that no decent person could be expected to do. So Mrs. Bland got off with a mild rebuke.

As the cavalcade proceeded, it was a sight to see those who came in late in vehicles hastily turning in, apprehensive of the effect upon their horses of the music and the smell of the wild animals. For the first and only time in the history of Dukesborough, there was momentary danger of a blockade of wheels in its one street.

"A leetle more," said old Tony to the other negroes at home that night—he was the driver of the Booker carriage—"a leetle more, and I'd a driv' right into the camel's mouth."

For some reason, possibly its vast size and the peculiar dip of its under-lip in the pictures, the camel seemed to be regarded as the most carnivorous of the wild beasts, and especially fond of human flesh.

The place selected for the tent was the area west of Sweep's shoe-shop, at the foot of the hill on which the Basil mansion stood. When the door was opened at last, the crowd surged in. Colonel Grice waited long, in order to see that no one of any condition was excluded for want of the entrance-fee. For at last this was regarded by him rather as a treat of his own to his neighbors, and he wanted it to be complete. Then he walked in with the deliberateness of an owner of the establishment, and contemplated everything with benignant complaisance. Those ladies and gentlemen who were within the sound of his voice, as he went the rounds of the boxes containing the animals, were fortunate.

"Be keerful there, boys—be keerful," he said, kindly but seriously, to some little fellows who were leaning against the rope and studying the porcupine. "Be keerful. That's the cilibrated pockapine. You see them sharp things on him? Well, them's his quills, and which, when he's mad, he shoots 'em like a bow-'narrow, and they goes clean through people."

The boys backed, although the little creature looked as if his quiver had been well nigh exhausted in previous wars.

"That's the hyner," said the Colonel, moving on, "and they say he's the most rhinocerous varmint of 'em all. Of all victuals, he loves folks the best, though he some rather that somebody or something else would kill 'em, and then him come on about a week or sich a matter afterwards. They scratches up graveyards, and in the countries where they raise, people has to bury their kin-folks in stone coffins."

"Oh, goodness gracious, Colonel! Let's go on!"

This exclamation was made by Miss Angeline Spouter, the thinnest of the party, who was locked arm in arm with Miss Georgiana Pea, the thickest.

"No danger, Miss Angeline—no danger at all," answered the Colonel, briskly raising his arm aloft that all might see what was between them and the beast, at which he looked as if it were his own pet hyena and would not think of leaving its lair without his order. "No danger whatsomever. Even if he could git out, he'd have to ride over me, and, besides, it's mostly corpses that he'd be arfter, and—ah—I don't think, anyway, that *you'd* be in the slightest danger."

As he said this, the Colonel looked rather argumentatively, and at Miss Pea more than Miss Spouter.

"Oh," said Miss Pea, gayly, "if the creetur could get out, and then took a notion for live folks, I'd be the one he'd make for, certain sure."

The hyena, though ugly and ferocious, did not look at his spectators once, but continued pacing up and down in his narrow cage, at either end of which, when reaching it, he thrust his snout against the roof, as if his thoughts were tending upwards rather than downwards. I have never forgotten how unhappy seemed that poor beast. To all the other animals there was some relief of captivity in their various degrees of domestication and affiliation with man. The lion evidently loved his keeper; even the leopards seemed rather fond of him. But the hyena, more narrowly caged than all, conquered, not subdued, wholly un-tamed, constantly rolling his fiery gray eyes, appeared to have his thoughts ever upon revenge and escape to his native wilds. I, a young child, could not but pity him; and it occurred to me then that if ever he should become free, and then be tempted, at least, to an appetizer of living human flesh before reaching the graveyard, he most likely would fasten upon the manager of the Great World-Renowned.

Just as the party was about to pass on, the wretched beast, stopping for a moment, his snout pressed to the roof, uttered several short, loud, hoarse, terrific howls. Miss Spouter screamed, Miss Pea laughed hys-terically, and Colonel Grice, before he knew it, was on the outside of his knot of followers. Recovering himself—for he was without his sword and pistol-holster—he stepped quickly back to the front, looked threateningly, and afterwards disdainfully, at the hyena, who had re-sumed his walks, and said:

"You rhinoceros varmint, you! Thinkin' of them graveyards you've robbed, and hungry for some more of 'em, ah! These is live folks, my boy; and they ain't quite ready for you yit, nor won't be for some time, I hope." Then he led on to the monkeys.

"Hello, Bill! I knowed you'd be here; got your boys with you, too, I see."

The person addressed by Colonel Grice was a tall, stout young farmer. Over his other clothes he wore a loosely fitting round jacket, of thick, home-made stuff, with capacious pockets. In each of these were one foot and a considerable portion of a leg of a child about two years old. Their other feet rested easily in the man's hands, which were tucked up for that purpose, while one arm of each was around his neck. The children were exactly alike, except a shade's difference in the color of their eyes. This was Mr. Bill Williams, who, three years before, had been married to Miss Caroline Thigpen. At this double birth, Mr. Williams was proud, and even exultant. Out of the many names suggested for the twins, he early selected those of the renowned offspring of Mars and Rhea Sylvia. Modifying them, however, somewhat for his own reasons, he called and so wrote them in his Bible, "Romerlus" and Remerlus."

"*Remus*, Mr. Bill," urged the friend who had suggested the names. "Remus, *not* Remulus: Romulus and Remus are the names."

"No, Philip," he answered; "its Romerlus and Remerlus. One's jest as old as t'other, or nigh and about; and he's as big, and he's as good-lookin', and his brother's name sha'n't be no bigger'n his'n."

As soon as they were able to stand without harm, he accustomed them to this mode of travel, and he was never so contented as when he and they went out thus together.

"I knowed you'd be here, Bill, and your boys."

"Yes Kurnel, I thought comin' to see the beastesses and varmints might sort o' be a start to 'em in jography. You Rom—you Reme, you needn't squeeze me so tight. They ain't no danger in *them* things."

The children, plucky for their age, and with considerable experience in travel, had gone easily enough thus far; but when they looked upon these creatures, so like, yet so unlike, mankind, they shrank from the view, and clung closely to their father. Colonel Grice, recovered from the embarrassment occasioned by the hyena, was pleased at the apprehension of the twins.

"Natchel, Bill, perfec'ly natchel. You know some folks says monkeys is kin to us, and the boys, mebbe, don't like the looks of their relations."

"They ain't no kin o' mine, Kurnel, nor theirn," answered Mr. Bill. "Ef you think they're humans, supposin' you—as you hain't no children of your own—supposin' you adopt one of 'em?"

Mr. Bill suspected that the Colonel might be alluding to the fabled she-wolf. The Colonel, however, had never heard of the distinguished originals of Roman story. His remark was a mere *jeu d'esprit*, springing naturally from the numerous sources of satisfaction of the occasion.

The wild beasts were finally hidden from view, and all repaired to their seats. Colonel Grice sat high, and near the entrance of the rear tent from which the circus performers were to emerge. Mr. Williams sat on the lowest tier, near the main entrance. He had taken his boys out of his pockets and held them on his knees. The Colonel, when he could get an opportunity, quietly, and in a very pleasant way, called the ring-master's attention to him, who smiled and nodded. Then the curtain was pushed aside from the rear tent, the band struck up, and the piebald horses came marching in with their silent riders, who, at first, looked as if they had just come from the bath, and had had time for only a limited toilet. Old Miss Sally Cash, cousin and close neighbor of Colonel Grice, exclaimed,

"Lor'-a-mercy, Mose! Them ain't folks, is they? Them's wax figgers, ain't they?"

"I assure you, cousin Sally, that they're folks," answered the Colonel, with marked candor. He had great respect for his cousin Sally, and some awe.

"I thought they was wax figgers, sot on springs. They ain't like no folks that I've ever saw, and I've saw a good many people in my time, both here and in Agusty." It was one of Miss Cash's boasts, which few country women of that generation could make, that she had once been to that famous city. After a short interval, she added: "I b'lieve yit they're wax figgers."

At that moment the clown, all spotted and streaked, bringing up the rear, shouted,

"Here we all are, my masters."

"My Lord-a'mighty!" exclaimed Miss Cash and some three hundred other females. Only Colonel Grice, and a very few others, who had been at yesterday's exhibition, could preserve any amount of coolness. The rest abandoned themselves to unlimited wonder.

"I'm sixty-nine year old," said old Mr. Pate, "and I never see sich as that before, and I never 'spected to see sich as that."

As they made their involutions and evolutions, destined apparently to be endless in number and variety, the old man looked on as if in his age he was vouchsafed the witness of the very last and highest achievement of human endeavor.

"Do you think that's decent, Mose?" asked Miss Cash. The performers were then in the act of the "ground and lofty tumbling," turning somersaults forward, backward, over one another, lying on their backs, throwing up their legs, and springing to their feet, etc., until they were panting and blue in the face. Miss Cash was not disposed that her cousin Mose should know how much she was interested in this performance.

"I shouldn't say it was *on*decent, cousin Sally."

"I don't say it is," said Miss Cash.

"You know," said the Colonel, winking slyly to his wife, and other friends of both sexes, "nobody is obleeged to stay and see the show. Anybody can go that wants to. They ain't no law ag'in goin', if anybody's desires is to git away."

"No," answered Miss Cash, downright. "I've paid my half a dollar, and they sha'n't cheat me out of it, nor nary part of it."

The next scene was one which Colonel Grice had eagerly anticipated. A steed rushed into the ring. He was as wild, apparently, as Mazeppa's, and the clown, when the ring-master inquired for the rider, answered, in a pitiful tone, that he was sick, and none other of the *troupe* would dare to take his place. Then followed the usual fun of the master ordering the clown to ride the horse, and the clown after vain remonstrance, trying to catch the horse, and the horse refusing to be caught; and, finally, the giving up the chase, and the master lashing the recusant beast around the ring, and wishing in vain for a rider to set him off properly. In the midst of this, an extremely drunken young man, homely clad, came through the main entrance, after a dispute and a scuffle with the door-keeper, and, staggering to where Mr. Bill Williams sat, looked down upon him.

"Two babies. One *(hic)* yours, s'pose."

"Yes," said Mr. Bill.

"And *(hic)* t'other—"

"My wife's; but that ain't nobody's business but ourn. You pass on."

The stranger declined, and fixing his muddled attention on what was going on in the ring, said:

"I can *(hic)* ride that horse—"

The words were no sooner uttered than the man stumbled upon the track, just after the horse had dashed past. The whole audience, except Colonel Grice and the select few, rose and cried out in horror.

"Take him out, Bill! Take him out!" cried Colonel Grice. Indeed, Mr. Bill had already slid his babies into his wife's lap, and was dragging the man out of the ring. He insisted upon returning.

"Look a-here, my friend," said Mr. Bill, "I don't know you, nor nobody else don't seem to know you; but if I didn't have Rom and Reme—"

The fellow made another rush. Mr. Bill took hold of him, but, receiving a trip, he fell flat, and the stranger fell into the ring, rolling out of the track in lucky time. The ring-master seemed much embarrassed.

"Oh, give him a little ride, captain!" cried out Colonel Grice. "If he falls, he's too drunk to git badly hurt."

"It's a shame, Mose!" remonstrated Miss Cash. "I did't come here and pay my money to see people killed. Notwithstandin' and never o'-the-less the poor creeter's drunk, and not hardly fitten to live, he ought by good rights to have some time to prepar' for the awful change that—"

But by this time Mazeppa was mounted and dashing away; and but that Miss Cash had made up her mind not to be cheated out of any portion of her money, she would have shut her eyes, or veiled her face, as the maddened animal sped along, while the infatuated inebriate clung to his mane. An anxious time it was. Kind-hearted people were sorry they had come. In the struggle between life and death, the stranger seemed to be beginning to sober. Sooner than could have been expected, he raised himself from the horse's neck (Miss Cash twisting her mouth and screwing her neck as he reeled back and forth from side to side), gathered up the reins, shook from his feet the thick shoes he was clad with, flung aside his old hat, brushed up his curly hair, and, before Miss Cash could utter a word, was on his feet. Then began that prolonged metamorphosis which old Mr. Pate was never satisfied with recounting, whether to those who saw it or those who saw it not.

"Coat after coat, breeches after breeches, gallis after gallis, shirt after shirt, ontwell he shucked hisself nigh as clean as a ear o' corn."

When everybody saw that the stranger was one of the showmen, the fun rose to a height that delayed for full five minutes the next scene. As for Colonel Grice, his handkerchief was positively wet with the tears he had shed. Even Mr. Bill forgot his own discomfiture in the universal glee.

"It's a shame, Mose," said Miss Cash, "to put such a trick on Bill Williams, and that right where his wife is. It would be a good thing if he could put it back on you."

Even at this late day, a survivor of that period can scarcely recall without some exaltation of feeling that young girl of eleven (who had been advertised as "Mademoiselle Louise, the Most Celebrated Equestrienne in the world"), as she ran out with the daintiest of frocks, the pinkest of stockings, the goldenest of flounces, the bluest of belts, the curliest of hair, the peachiest of cheeks, kissed her hand to the audience, put one foot into the clown's hand, and flew into the saddle. As she went around, dancing upon that horse in full gallop, hopping over her whip and jumping through rings, and, when seated, smoothed down her skirt and waved her sleeveless arms—well, there was one boy (his name was Seaborn Byne) that declared he "would be dinged if it wasn't enough to melt the hearts clean outen a statchit." Other boys cordially endorsed this speech. As for Jack Watts, just turned of his tenth year, with the example before him of his older brother Tommy (dead in love at thirteen and some upwards, with Miss Wilkins the schoolmistress), he ran away from home the next morning, and followed for three miles the circus, begging to be taken into its employ, stipulating for only board and clothes. When caught, brought back, and properly attended to by his mother, the villain was suspected, and almost as good as confessed, that his purpose was to avail himself of an opportunity to seize upon the person of Mademoiselle Louise and her imagined vast treasures, and bear them to some distant foreign shore—on which one in special, in his exigent haste, he had not yet been able fully to determine.

In the interval before the last, named "The Wonderful Tooth-drawing Coffee-pot Fire-cracker Scene," an incident occurred that was not on the programme—an interlude, as it were, improvised by the exuberant spirits of both spectators and showmen. Colonel Grice, deeply gratified at the success of what, without great stretch, might be called his own treat, was in the mood to receive special attention and compliment from any source. When the pretended inebriate had been lifted upon Mazeppa, the clown took a bottle from his pocket, tasted it when he had gotten behind his master, smacked his lips, set it down by the middle pole, and, being detected in one of his resortings to it, was reproached for not inviting some one to drink with him. They were on the portion of the ring next the main entrance.

"Why don't you invite Colonel Grice?" said Mr. Bill Williams, in a low voice. "He expects it."

The master turned to notice from whom the suggestion proceeded, and, before he could determine, the clown, though with some hesitation, said,

"If Colonel Grice—"

"Stop it!" whispered the master.

But it was too late. The Colonel had already risen, and was carefully descending.

"Is you goin' there, Mose, shore enough?" said Miss Cash. "It do look like Mose is complete carried away with them circus people and hisself."

Having gotten safely over the intervening heads and shoulders, the Colonel stepped with dignity into the ring, at the same time feeling somewhat of the embarrassment which will sometimes befall the very greatest warrior when, without his weapons, he knows himself to be the object of the attention of a large number of civilians, both male and female. This embarrassment hindered his observation of the captain's winks, and the clown's pouring a portion of the liquor upon the ground. He walked up rapidly and extended his hand. The clown, with an effort at mirthfulness, the more eager because he was doubtful of perfect success, withdrew the bottle from his grasp, spread out his legs, squatted his body, and, applying the thumb of his disengaged hand to his nose, wriggled his fingers at the Colonel's face, winking frantically the while, hoping the latter would advance the joke by insistence.

In this he miscalculated. Persons who claimed to have seen Colonel Moses Grice, on previous occasions, what was called *mad*, said that all these were childish fretfulness compared with his present condition of mind, when, after the withdrawal of the bottle, the whole audience, Miss Cash louder than all, broke into uproarious laughter. Fortunately the enraged chieftain had nor sword, nor pistol, nor even walking-cane. His only weapon was his tongue. Stepping back a pace or two, and glaring upon the ludicrous squatter, he shouted:

"You spotted-backed, striped-legged, streaked-faced, speckled-b-breasted, p'inted-hatted son-of-a-gun!"

With each ejaculation of these successive, uncommon appellations, the poor clown lifted himself somewhat, and by the time their climax was reached was upright, and, dressed as he was, seemed most pitiful.

"My dear Colonel Grice—" he began.

"Shet up your old red mouth," broke in the Colonel. "I didn't *want* your whisky. I got better whisky at home than you know anything about. But as you asked me to drink, like, as I thought, one gentleman would ask another gentleman, I didn't feel like refusin' you. I give the whole of you your breakfast, your blasted varmints and all; I put at least twenty into your cussed old show; and after that—"

"My dear-est Colonel Grice!"

"Oh, you p'inted-hatted, streaked-fac-ed, speckled-b-breasted—" beginning, as it were, a back-handed stroke by reversing the order of his epithets.

At this moment the ring-master, who had not been able thus far to get in a single word, said in a loud but calm tone:

"Colonel Grice, don't you see that it was a mere jest, and that the suggestion came from one of your neighbors? The bottle contains nothing but water. We beg your pardon if you are offended; but I can but think that the abusive words you have used already are quite enough."

"Come, Mose! come!" cried Miss Cash, who had just been able to stop her laughter. "Give and take, Mose. You put it onto Bill Williams, and he stood it; and he put it back onto you, and now you can't stand it, eh?" And the old lady again fairly screamed with laughter, while hundreds of others joined.

The Colonel stood for a moment, hesitating. Then he suddenly turned, and, remarking that this was no place for a gentleman, walked towards the entrance.

"You goin' to let 'em cheat you out of the balance of your money that way, Mose?" asked Miss Cash. He turned again. Finding himself wholly without support, and unwilling to lose the great scene of the "Tooth-drawing," etc., he halted and stood until it was over. By that time he was considerably mollified, and the manager, approaching, apologized for himself, the clown, and all his *troupe*, and begged that he would join in a glass of the genuine at Spouter's tavern.

How could the Colonel refuse? He could not, and he did not.

"Go with us, won't you, sir?" said the manager, addressing Mr. Williams. "We had some little fun at your expense also; but I hope you bear us no malice, as we never intend to hurt feelings."

"Sperrits," answered Mr. Bill, "is a thing I seldom teches—that is, I don't tech it reglar; but I'll try a squirrel-load with you—jes a moderate size squirrel-load."

At Spouter's all was cordially made up. Mr. Bill set Rom and Reme on the counter, and the clown gave them a big lump of white sugar apiece.

"They seem to be nice, peaceable little fellows," said he. "Do they ever dispute?"

"Oh, not a great deal," answered Mr. Bill. "Sometimes Rom—that's the bluest-eyed one—he wants to have all his feed before Reme gits any o' his'n, and he claws at the spoon, and Reme's nose. But when he does that, I jes set *him* right down, I does, and I makes him wait ontwell Reme's fed. I tends to raise 'em to be peaceable, and to give and take, and to be friends as well as brothers, which is mighty far from bein' always the case in families."

Mr. Bill knew that Colonel Grice and his younger brother Abram had not spoken together for years.

"Right, Bill," said the Colonel. "Raise 'em right. Take keer o' them boys, Bill. Two at a time comes right hard on a fellow, though, don't it, Bill? Expensive, eh?" and the Colonel winked pleasantly all around.

"Thank ye, Kurnel; I'll do the best I can. I shall raise em to give and take. No, Kurnel, not so very hard. Fact, I wa'n't a-expectin' but one, yit, when Reme come, I thought jest as much o' him as I did o' Rom. No, Kurnel, it wouldn't be my desires to be a married man and have nary ar—to leave what little prop'ty I got to. And now, sence I got two instid o' one, and them o' the same size, I feel like I'd be sort o' awk'ard 'ithout both of 'em. You see, Kurnel, they balances agin one another in my pockets. No, Kurnel, better two than nary one; and in that way you can larn 'em better to give and take. Come, Rom, come, Reme—git in; we must be a-travelin'." He backed up to the counter, and the boys, shifting their sugar-lumps to suit, stepped aboard and away they went.

After that day Dukesborough thought she could see no reason why she might not be named among the leading towns of middle Georgia.

A PARTY were enjoying the evening breeze on board a yacht.

"The wind has made my moustache taste quite salt," remarked a young man who had been for some time occupied in biting the hair that fell over his upper lip. "I know it!" innocently said a pretty girl. And she wondered why all her friends laughed. "People are so childish," she remarked.—*Newspaper.*

One of Mr. Ward's Business

Letters

ARTEMUS WARD

To the Editor of the——:

Sir—I'm movin' along—slowly along—down tords your place. I want you should rite me a letter, saying how is the show bizniss in your place. My show at present consists of three moral Bares, a Kangaroo (a amoozin little Raskal—t'would make you larf yourself to deth to see the little cuss jump up and squeal), wax figgers of G. Washington Gen. Tayler John Bunyan Capt. Kidd and Dr. Webster in the act of killin' Dr. Parkman, besides several miscellanyus moral wax statoots of celebrated piruts & murderers, &c., ekalled by few & exceld by none. Now Mr. Editor, scratch orf a few lines sayin' how is the show bizniss down to your place. I shall hav my hanbills dun at your offiss. Depend upon it. I want you should git my hanbills up in flamin' stile. Also git up a tremenjus excitemunt in yr. paper 'bowt my onparaleld Show. We must fetch the public sumhow. We must wurk on their feelin's. Cum the moral on 'em strong. If it's a temperance community tell 'em I sined the pledge fifteen minits arter Ise born, but on the contery, ef your people take their tods, say Mister Ward is as Jenial a feller as ever we met, full of conwiviality, & the life an' sole of the Soshul Bored. Take, don't you? If you say anythin' abowt my show, say my snaiks is as harmliss as the new born Babe. What a interestin study it is to see a zewological animil like a snake under perfect subjecshun! My kangaroo is the most larfable little cuss I ever saw. All for 15 cents. I am anxyus to skewer your inflooence. I repeet in regard to them hanbills that I shall git em struck orf up to your printin' office. My perliteral sentiments agree with yourn exactly. I know they do, becawz I never saw a man whoos didn't.

Respectively yures,   A. WARD.

P.S.—You scratch my back & Ile scratch your back.

Woman Suffrage

R. J. BURDETTE

The women in Kansas vote at the school elections. At a recent election at Osage City one woman went up to vote, but before she got through telling the judges what a time her Willie had with the scarlet fever when he was only two years old, it was time to close the polls and she had forgotten to deposit her ballot.

On "Forts"

ARTEMUS WARD

Every man has got a Fort. It's sum men's fort to do one thing, and some other men's fort to do another, while there is numeris shiftliss critters goin' round loose whose fort is not to do nothin'.

Shakspeer rote good plase, but he wouldn't hav succeeded as a Washington correspondent of a New York daily paper. He lackt the rekesit fancy and imagginashun.

That's so!

Old George Washington's Fort was not to hev eny public man of the present day resemble him to eny alarmin' extent. Whare bowts can George's ekal be found? I ask, & boldly answer no whares, or any whare else.

Old man Townsin's Fort was to maik Sassyperiller. "Goy to the world! anuther life saived!" (Cotashun from Townsin's advertisemunt.)

Cyrus Field's Fort is to lay a sub-machine tellegraf under the boundin billers of the Oshun, and then have it Bust.

Spaldin's Fort is to maik Prepared Gloo, which mends everything. Wonder ef it will mend a sinner's wickid waze. (Impromptoo goak.)

Zoary's Fort is to be a femaile circus feller.

My Fort is the grate moral show bizniss & ritin choice famerly literatoor for the noospapers. That's what's the matter with *me*.

&., &., &. So I mite go on to a indefnit extent.

Twict Iv'e endevered to do things which thay wasn't my Fort. The fust time was when I undertuk to lick a owdashus cuss who cut a hole in my tent & krawld threw. Sez I, "My jentle Sir, go out or I shall fall onto you putty hevy." Sez he, "Wade in, Old wax figgers," whereupon I went for him, but he cawt me powerful on the hed & knockt me threw the tent into a cow pastur. He pursood the attack & flung me into a mud puddle. As I arose & rung out my drencht garmints I koncluded fitin wasn't my Fort. I'le now rize the kurtin upon Seen 2nd: It is rarely seldum that I seek consolation in the Flowin' Bole. But in a certain town in Injianny in the Faul of 18—, my orgin grinder got sick with the fever & died. I never felt so ashamed in my life, & I thowt I'd hist in a few swallows of suthin strength'nin. Konsequents was I histid in so much I dident zackly know whare bowts I was. I turned my livin wild beasts of Pray loose into the streets and spilt all my wax wurks. I then bet I cood play hoss. So I hitched myself to a Kanawl bote, there bein' two other hosses hitcht on also, one behind and anuther ahead of me. The driver hollerd for us to git up, and we did. But the hosses bein' onused to sich a arrangemunt begun to kick & squeal and rair up. Konsequents was I was kickt vilently in the stummuck & back, and presuntly I fownd myself in the Kanawl with the other hosses, kickin' & yellin' like a tribe of Cusscaroorus savvijis. I was rescood, & as I was bein' carrid to the tavern on a hemlock Bored I sed in a feeble voise, "Boys, playin' hoss isn't my Fort."

MORUL—Never don't do nothin' which isn't your Fort, for ef you do you'll find yourself splashin' round in the Kanawl, figgeratively speakin'.

THE FOX AND THE CROW

GEO. T. LANIGAN

A Crow, having secured a Piece of Cheese, flew with its Prize to a lofty Tree, and was preparing to devour the Luscious Morsel, when a crafty Fox, halting at the foot of the Tree, began to cast about how he might obtain it. "How tasteful," he cried, in well-feigned Ecstasy, "is your

Dress; it cannot surely be that your Musical Education has been neglected. Will you not oblige—?" "I have a horrid Cold," replied the Crow, "and never sing without my Music, but since you press me—. At the same time, I should add that I have read Æsop, and been there before." So saying, she deposited the Cheese in a safe Place on the Limb of the Tree, and favored him with a Song. "Thank you," exclaimed the Fox, and trotted away, with the Remark that Welsh Rabbits never agreed with him, and were far inferior in Quality to the animate Variety.

Moral.—The foregoing Fable is supported by a whole Gatling Battery of Morals. We are taught (1) that it Pays to take the Papers; (2) that Invitation is not Always the Sincerest Flattery; (3) that a Stalled Rabbit with Contentment is better than No Bread, and (4) that the Aim of Art is to Conceal Disappointment.

A WELL-DRESSED negro applied to the judge of probate of this city for a marriage license. Being asked how old his intended was, he answered with great animation, "Just sixteen, judge—sweet sixteen, and de handsomest girl in town." The judge said he could not do it, as the law forbade him to issue license to any one under eighteen. "Well, hold on, judge," exclaimed the man, "I know dat dem girls am deceitful, and lie about deir age. She is nineteen, if a day." "Will you swear to it?" asked the judge. "Yes, sah," he replied, and did. "And how old are you?" said the judge. The chap looked suspicious, and replied cautiously, "Thirty-five," and added, "If dat won't do, judge, I've got more back."—*Newspaper*

EUROPEAN DIET

MARK TWAIN

A man accustomed to American food and American domestic cookery would not starve to death suddenly in Europe; but I think he would gradually waste away, and eventually die.

He would have to do without his accustomed morning meal. That is too formidable a change altogether; he would necessarily suffer from it. He could get the shadow, the sham, the base counterfeit of that meal; but that would do him no good, and money could not buy the reality.

To particularize: the average American's simplest and commonest form of breakfast consists of coffee and beefsteak; well, in Europe, coffee is an unknown beverage. You can get what the European hotel keeper thinks is coffee, but it resembles the real thing as hypocrisy resembles holiness. It is a feeble, characterless, uninspiring sort of stuff, and almost as undrinkable as if it had been made in an American hotel. The milk used for it is what the French call "Christian" milk—milk which has been baptized.

After a few months' acquaintance with European "coffee," one's mind weakens, and his faith with it, and he begins to wonder if the rich beverage of home, with its clotted layer of yellow cream on top of it is not a mere dream, after all, and a thing which never existed.

Next comes the European bread—fair enough, good enough, after a fashion, but cold; cold and tough, and unsympathetic; and never any change, never any variety—always the same tiresome thing.

Next, the butter—the sham and tasteless butter; no salt in it, and made of goodness knows what.

Then there is the beefsteak. They have it in Europe, but they don't know how to cook it. Neither will they cut it right. It comes on the table in a small, round, pewter platter. It lies in the centre of this platter, in a bordering bed of grease-soaked potatoes; it is the size, shape, and thickness of a man's hand with the thumb and fingers cut off. It is a little overdone, is rather dry, it tastes pretty insipidly, it rouses no enthusiasm.

Imagine a poor exile contemplating that inert thing; and imagine an angel suddenly sweeping down out of a better land and setting before him a mighty porter-house steak an inch and a half thick, hot and sputtering from the griddle; dusted with fragrant pepper; enriched with little melting bits of butter of the most unimpeachable freshness and genuineness; the precious juices of the meat trickling out and joining the gravy, archipelagoed with mushrooms; a township or two of tender, yellowish fat gracing an outlying district of this ample county of beefsteak; the long white bone which divides the sirloin from the tenderloin still in its place; and imagine that the angel also adds a great cup of American home-made coffee, with the cream a-froth on top, some real butter, firm and yellow and fresh, some smoking hot biscuits, a plate of hot buckwheat cakes, with transparent syrup—could words describe the gratitude of this exile?

The European dinner is better than the European breakfast, but it has its faults and inferiorities; it does not satisfy. He comes to the table eager and hungry; he swallows his soup—there is an undefinable lack about it somewhere; thinks the fish is going to be the thing he wants—eats it and isn't sure; thinks the next dish is perhaps the one that will hit the hungry place—tries it, and is conscious that there was a something wanting about it also. And thus he goes on, from dish to dish, like a boy after a butterfly, which just misses getting caught, every time it alights, but somehow doesn't get caught after all; and at the end the exile and the boy have fared about alike: the one is full, but grievously unsatisfied, the other has had plenty of exercise, plenty of interest, and a fine lot of hopes, but he hasn't got any butterfly. There is here and there an American who will say he can remember rising from a European table d' hôte perfectly satisfied; but we must not overlook the fact that there is also here and there an American who will lie.

The number of dishes is sufficient; but, then, it is such a monotonous variety of *unstriking* dishes. It is an inane dead level of "fair-to-middling." There is nothing to *accent* it. Perhaps if the roast of mutton or of beef—a big generous one—were brought on the table and carved in full view of the client, that might give the right sense of earnestness and reality to the thing, but they don't do that; they pass the sliced meat around on a dish, and, so you are perfectly calm, it does not stir you in the least. Now a vast roast turkey, stretched on the broad of his back, with his heels in the air and the rich juices oozing from his fat sides . . . But I may as well stop there, for they would not know how to cook him. They can't even cook a chicken respectably; and as for carving it, they do that with a hatchet.

This is about the customary table d' hôte bill in summer:

Soup (characterless).

Fish—sole, salmon or whiting—usually tolerably good.

Roast—mutton or beef—tasteless—and some last year's potatoes.

A pâté, or some other made-dish—usually good—"considering."

One vegetable—brought on in state, and all alone—usually insipid lentils, or string beans, or indifferent asparagus.

Roast chicken, as tasteless as paper.

Lettuce-salad—tolerably good.

Decayed strawberries or cherries.

Sometimes the apricots and figs are fresh, but this is no advantage, as these fruits are of no account anyway.

The grapes are generally good, and sometimes there is a tolerably good peach, by mistake.

The variations of the above bill are trifling. After a fortnight one discovers that the variations are only apparent, not real; in the third week you get what you had the first, and in the fourth week you get what you had the second. Three or four months of this weary sameness will kill the robustest appetite.

It has now been many months, at the present writing, since I have had a nourishing meal, but I shall soon have one—a modest, private affair, all to myself. I have selected a few dishes, and made out a little bill of fare—which will go home in the steamer that precedes me, and be hot when I arrive—as follows:

Radishes.

Baked apples, with cream.

Fried oysters; stewed oysters.

Frogs.

American coffee, with real
    cream.

American butter.

Fried chicken, Southern style.

Porter-house steak.

Saratoga potatoes.

Broiled chicken, American style.

Hot biscuits, Southern style.

Hot wheat-bread, Southern style.

Hot buckwheat cakes.

American toast.

Clear maple syrup.

Virginia bacon, broiled.

Blue-points, on the half shell.

Cherry-stone clams.

San Francisco mussels, steamed.

Oyster soup.

Clam soup.

Philadelphia Terrapin soup.

Oysters roasted in shell—
    Northern style.

Soft-shell crabs.

Connecticut shad.

Baltimore perch.

Brook trout, from Sierra
    Nevadas.

Lake trout, from Tahoe.

Sheep-head and croakers,
    from New Orleans.

Black bass from the Mississippi.

American roast beef.

Roast turkey, Thanksgiving style.

Cranberry sauce.

Celery.

Roast wild turkey.

Woodcock.

Canvas-back duck,
    from Baltimore.

Prairie hens, from Illinois.
Missouri partridges, broiled.
'Possum.
Coon.
Boston bacon and beans.
Bacon and greens, Southern
   style.
Hominy.
Boiled onions.
Turnips.
Pumpkin.
Squash.
Asparagus.
Butter beans.
Sweet potatoes.
Lettuce.
Succotash.
String beans.
Mashed potatoes.
Catsup.
Boiled potatoes, in their skins.
New potatoes, minus the skins.
Early Rose potatoes, roasted in
   the ashes, Southern style,
   served hot.

Sliced tomatoes, with sugar or
   vinegar.
Stewed tomatoes.
Green corn, cut from the ear and
   served with butter and
   pepper.
Green corn, on the ear.
Hot corn-pone, with chitlings,
   Southern style.
Hot hoe-cake, Southern style.
Hot egg-bread, Southern style.
Hot light-bread, Southern style.
Buttermilk.
Iced sweet milk.
Apple dumplings, with real
   cream.
Apple pie.
Apple fritters.
Apple puffs, Southern style.
Peach cobbler, Southern style.
Peach pie.
American mince pie.
Pumpkin pie.
Squash pie.
All sorts of American pastry.

Fresh American fruits of all sorts, including strawberries, which are not to
be doled out as if they were jewelry, but in a more liberal way.
Ice-water—not prepared in the ineffectual goblet, but in the sincere and
capable refrigerator.

Americans intending to spend a year or so in European hotels, will
do well to copy this bill and carry it along. They will find it an excellent thing to get up an appetite with, in the dispiriting presence of the
squalid table d'hôte.

————

WE READ that Esaw sold out hiz birth rite for soup, and menny wonder
at hiz extravegance, but Esaw diskovered arly, what menny a man haz
diskovered since, that it iz hard work tew live on a pedigree.

If i waz starving, I wouldn't hesitate tew swap oph all the pedigree I had, and all mi relashuns had, for a quart of pottage, and throw two grate grandfathers into the bargain.

JOSH BILLINGS

THE VACATION OF MUSTAPHA

R. J. BURDETTE

Now in the sixth month, in the reign of the good Caliph, it was so that Mustapha said, "I am wearied with much work; thought, care and worry have worn me out; I need repose, for the hand of exhaustion is upon me, and death even now lieth at the door."

And he called his physician, who felt of his pulse and looked upon his tongue and said:

"Twodollahs!" (For this was the oath by which all physicians swore.) "Of a verity thou must have rest. Flee unto the valley of quiet, and close thine eyes in dreamful rest; hold back thy brain from thought and thy hand from labor, or you will be a candidate for the asylum in three weeks."

And he heard him, and went out and put the business in the hands of the clerk, and went away to rest in the valley of quiet. And he went to his Uncle Ben's, whom he had not seen for lo! these fourteen years. Now, his Uncle Ben was a farmer, and abode in the valley of rest, and the mountains of repose rose round about him. And he was rich, and well favored, and strong as an ox, and healthy as an onion crop. Ofttimes he boasted to his neighbors that there was not a lazy bone in his body, and he swore that he hated a lazy man.

And Mustapha wist not that it was so.

But when he reached his Uncle Ben's they received him with great joy, and placed before him a supper of homely viands well cooked, and piled up on his plate like the wreck of a box-car. And when he could not eat all, they laughed him to scorn.

And after supper they sat up with him and talked with him about relatives whereof he had never, in all his life, so much as heard. And he answered their questions at random, and lied unto them, professing to know Uncle Ezra and Aunt Bethesda, and once he said that he had a letter from Uncle George last week.

Now they all knew that Uncle George was shot in a neighbor's sheep pen, three years ago, but Mustapha wist not that it was so, and he was sleepy, and only talked to fill up the time. And then they talked politics to him, and he hated politics. So about one o'clock in the morning they sent him to bed.

Now the spare room wherein he slept was right under the roof, and there were ears and bundles of ears of seed corn hung from the rafters, and he bunged his eyes with the same, and he hooked his chin in festoons of dried apples, and shook dried herbs and seeds down his back as he walked along, for it was dark. And when he sat up in bed in the night he ran a scythe in his ear.

And it was so that the four boys slept with him, for the bed was wide. And they were restless, and slumbered crosswise and kicked, so that Mustapha slope not a wink that night, neither closed he his eyes.

And about the fourth hour after midnight his Uncle Ben smote him on the back and spake unto him, saying:

"Awake, arise, rustle out of this and wash your face, for the liver and bacon are fried and the breakfast waiteth. You will find the well down at the other end of the cow-lot. Take a towel with you."

When they had eaten, his Uncle Ben spake unto him, saying: "Come, let us stroll around the farm."

And they walked about eleven miles. And his Uncle Ben sat him upon a wagon and taught him how to load hay. Then they drove into the barn, and he taught him how to unload it. Then they girded up their loins and walked four miles, even into the forest, and his Uncle Ben taught him how to chop wood, and then walked back to supper. And the morning and the evening were the first day, and Mustapha wished that he were dead.

And after supper his Uncle Ben spoke once more, and said: "Come, let us have some fun." And so they hooked up a team and drove nine miles, down to Belcher's Branch, where there was a hop. And they danced until the second hour in the morning.

When the next day was come—which wasn't long, for already the night was far spent—his Uncle Ben took him out and taught him how to make rail fence. And that night there was a wedding, and they danced, and made merry, and drank, and ate, and when they went to bed at three o'clock, Mustapha prayed that death might come to him before breakfast-time. But breakfast had an early start, and got there first. And his Uncle Ben took him down to the creek, and taught him how to wash and shear sheep. And when evening was come they went to spelling-school, and they got home at the first hour after midnight, and Uncle Ben marveled that it was so early. And he lighted his pipe, and sat up for an hour and told Mustapha all about the forty acres he bought last spring of old Mosey Stringer, to finish out that north half, and about the new colt that was foaled last spring.

And when Mustapha went to bed that morning he bethought himself of a dose of strychnine he had with him, and he said his prayers wearily, and he took it.

But the youngest boy was restless that night, and kicked all the poison out of him in less then ten seconds.

And in the morning, while it was yet night, they ate breakfast. And his Uncle Ben took him out and taught him how to dig a ditch.

And when evening was come there was a revival meeting at Ebenezer Methodist church, and they all went. And there were three regular preachers and two exhorters, and a Baptist evangelist. And when midnight was come, they went home and sat up and talked over the meeting until it was bed-time.

Now, when Mustapha was at home, he left his desk at the fifth hour in the afternoon, and he went to bed at the third hour after sunset, and he arose not until the sun was high in the heavens.

So the next day, when his Uncle Ben would take him out into the field and show him how to make a post-and-rail fence, Mustapha would swear at him, and smote him with an axe-helve and fled, and got himself home.

And Mustapha sent for his physician and cursed him. And he said he was tired to death; he turned his face to the wall and died. So Mustapha was gathered to his fathers.

And his physician and his friends mourned and said, "Alas, he did not rest soon enough. He tarried at his desk too long."

But his Uncle Ben, who came in to attend the funeral, and had to do all his weeping out of one eye, because the other was blacked half way down to his chin, said it was a pity, but Mustapha was too awfully lazy to live, and he had no get up about him.

But Mustapha wist not what they said, because he was dead. So they divided his property among them, and said if he wanted a tombstone he might have attended to it himself, while he was yet alive, because they had no time.—*Burlington Hawkeye*

———

WHAT the milkman said when he found a fish in the lacteal fluid: "Good heavens! the brindle cow has been in swimming again."—*Newspaper*

THE FIRST PIANO IN A MINING CAMP

SAM DAVIS

Mr. Samuel Davis was formerly a reporter for the San Francisco *Argonaut*, and is now the editor of the Carson *Appeal*.

In 1858—it might have been five years earlier or later; this is not the history for the public schools—there was a little camp about ten miles from Pioche, occupied by upwards of three hundred miners, every one of whom might have packed his prospecting implements and left for more inviting fields any time before sunset. When the day was over, these men did not rest from their labors, like the honest New England agriculturist, but sang, danced, gambled, and shot each other, as the mood seized them.

One evening the report spread along the main street (which was the only street) that three men had been killed at Silver Reef, and that the bodies were coming in. Presently a lumbering old conveyance labored up the hill, drawn by a couple of horses, well worn out with their pull. The cart contained a good-sized box, and no sooner did its outlines become visible, through the glimmer of a stray light here and there, than it began to affect the idlers. Death always enforces respect, and even though no one had caught sight of the remains, the crowd gradually became subdued, and when the horses came to a stand-still, the cart was immediately surrounded. The driver, however, was not in the least impressed with the solemnity of his commission.

"All there?" asked one.

"Haven't examined. Guess so."

The driver filled his pipe, and lit it as he continued:

"Wish the bones and load had gone over the grade!"

A man who had been looking on stepped up to the man at once.

"I don't know who you have in that box, but if they happen to be any friends of mine, I'll lay you alongside."

"We can mighty soon see," said the teamster, coolly. "Just burst the lid off, and if they happen to be the men you want, I'm here."

The two looked at each other for a moment, and then the crowd gathered a little closer, anticipating trouble.

"I believe that dead men are entitled to good treatment, and when you talk about hoping to see corpses go over a bank, all I have to say is, that it will be better for you if the late lamented ain't my friends."

"We'll open the box. I don't take back what I've said, and if my language don't suit your ways of thinking, I guess I can stand it."

With these words the teamster began to pry up the lid. He got a board off, and then pulled out some old rags. A strip of something dark, like rosewood, presented itself.

"Eastern coffins, by thunder!" said several, and the crowd looked quite astonished.

Some more boards flew up, and the man who was ready to defend his friend's memory shifted his weapon a little. The cool manner of the teamster had so irritated him that he had made up his mind to pull his weapon at the first sight of the dead, even if the deceased was his worst and oldest enemy. Presently the whole of the box cover was off, and the teamster, clearing away the packing revealed to the astonished group the top of something which puzzled all alike.

"Boys," said he, "this is a pianner."

A general shout of laughter went up, and the man who had been so anxious to enforce respect for the dead, muttered something about feeling dry, and the keeper of the nearest bar was several ounces better off by the time the boys had given the joke all the attention it called for.

Had a dozen dead men been in the box, their presence in the camp could not have occasioned half the excitement that the arrival of that lonely piano caused. By the next morning it was known that the instrument was to grace a hurdy-gurdy saloon, owned by Tom Goskin, the leading gambler in the place. It took nearly a week to get this wonder on its legs, and the owner was the proudest individual in the State. It rose gradually from a recumbent to an upright position amid a confusion of tongues, after the manner of the tower of Babel.

Of course everybody knew just how such an instrument should be put up. One knew where the "off hind leg" should go, and another was posted on the "front piece."

Scores of men came to the place every day to assist.

"I'll put the bones in good order."

"If you want the wires tuned up, I'm the boy."

"I've got music to feed it for a month."

Another brought a pair of blankets for a cover, and all took the liveliest interest in it. It was at last in a condition for business.

"It's been showin' its teeth all the week. We'd like to have it spit out something."

Alas! there wasn't a man to be found who could play upon the instrument. Goskin began to realize that he had a losing speculation on his hands. He had a fiddler, and a Mexican who thrummed a guitar. A pianist would have made his orchestra complete. One day a three-card monte player told a friend confidentially that he could "knock any amount of music out of the piano, if he only had it alone a few hours, to get his hand in." This report spread about the camp, but on being questioned he vowed that he didn't know a note of music. It was noted, however, as a suspicious circumstance, that he often hung about the instrument, and looked upon it longingly, like a hungry man gloating over a beefsteak in a restaurant window. There was no doubt but that this man had music in his soul, perhaps in his fingers'-ends, but did not dare to make trial of his strength after the rules of harmony had suffered so many years of neglect. So the fiddler kept on with his jigs, and the greasy Mexican pawed his discordant guitar, but no man had the nerve to touch the piano. There were, doubtless, scores of men in the camp who would have given ten ounces of gold dust to have been half an hour alone with it, but every man's nerve shrank from the jeers which the crowd would shower upon him should his first attempt prove a failure. It got to be generally understood that the hand which first essayed to draw music from the keys must not slouch its work.

It was Christmas Eve, and Goskin, according to his custom, had decorated his gambling hell with sprigs of mountain cedar, and a shrub whose crimson berries did not seem a bad imitation of English holly. The piano was covered with evergreens, and all that was wanting to completely fill the cup of Goskin's contentment was a man to play the instrument.

"Christmas night, and no piano-pounder," he said. "This is a nice country for a Christian to live in."

Getting a piece of paper, he scrawled the words:

$20 Reward
To a compitant Pianer Player.

This he stuck up on the music-rack, and, though the inscription glared at the frequenters of the room until midnight, it failed to draw any musician from his shell.

So the merry-making went on; the hilarity grew apace. Men danced and sang to the music of the squeaky fiddle and worn-out guitar, as the jolly crowd within tried to drown the howling of the storm without. Suddenly they became aware of the presence of a white-haired man, crouching near the fire-place. His garments—such as were left—were wet with melting snow, and he had a half-starved, half-crazed expression. He held his thin, trembling hands toward the fire, and the light of the blazing wood made them almost transparent. He looked about him once in a while, as if in search of something, and his presence cast such a chill over the place that gradually the sound of the revelry was hushed, and it seemed that this waif of the storm had brought in with it all of the gloom and coldness of the warring elements. Goskin, mixing up a cup of hot egg-nogg, advanced and remarked cheerily:

"Here, stranger, brace up! This is the real stuff."

The man drained the cup, smacked his lips, and seemed more at home.

"Been prospecting, eh? Out in the mountains—caught in the storm? Lively night, this!"

"Pretty bad," said the man.

"Must feel pretty dry?"

The man looked at his streaming clothes and laughed, as if Goskin's remark was a sarcasm.

"How long out?"

"Four days."

"Hungry?"

The man rose up, and walking over to the lunch counter, fell to work upon some roast bear, devouring it like any wild animal would have done. As meat and drink and warmth began to permeate the stranger, he seemed to expand and lighten up. His features lost their pallor, and he grew more and more content with the idea that he was not in the grave. As he underwent these changes, the people about him got merrier and happier, and threw off the temporary feeling of depression which he had laid upon them.

"Do you always have your place decorated like this?" he finally asked of Goskin.

"This is Christmas Eve," was the reply.

The stranger was startled.

"December twenty-fourth, sure enough."

"That's the way I put it up, pard."

"When I was in England I always kept Christmas. But I had forgotten that this was the night. I've been wandering about in the mountains until I've lost track of the feasts of the church."

Presently his eye fell upon the piano.

"Where's the player?" he asked.

"Never had any," said Goskin, blushing at the expression.

"I used to play when I was young."

Goskin almost fainted at the admission.

"Stranger, do tackle it, and give us a tune! Nary man in this camp ever had the nerve to wrestle with that music-box." His pulse beat faster, for he feared that the man would refuse.

"I'll do the best I can," he said.

There was no stool, but seizing a candle-box, he drew it up and seated himself before the instrument. It only required a few seconds for a hush to come over the room.

"That old coon is going to give the thing a rattle."

The sight of a man at the piano was something so unusual that even the faro-dealer, who was about to take in a fifty-dollar bet on the trey, paused and did not reach for the money. Men stopped drinking, with the glasses at their lips. Conversation appeared to have been struck with a sort of paralysis, and cards were no longer shuffled.

The old man brushed back his long white locks, looked up to the ceiling, half closed his eyes, and in a mystic sort of reverie passed his fingers over the keys. He touched but a single note, yet the sound thrilled the room. It was the key to his improvisation, and as he wove his chords together the music laid its spell upon every ear and heart. He felt his way along the keys, like a man treading uncertain paths; but he gained confidence as he progressed, and presently bent to his work like a master. The instrument was not in exact tune, but the ears of his audience, through long disuse, did not detect anything radically wrong. They heard a succession of grand chords, a suggestion of paradise, melodies here and there, and it was enough.

"See him counter with his left!" said an old rough, enraptured.

"He calls the turn every time on the upper end of the board," responded a man with a stack of chips in his hand.

The player wandered off into the old ballads they had heard at home. All the sad and melancholy and touching songs, that came up like dreams of childhood, this unknown player drew from the keys. His hands kneaded their hearts like dough, and squeezed out tears as from a wet sponge. As the strains flowed one upon the other, they saw their homes of the long ago reared again; they were playing once more where the apple blossoms sank through the soft air to join the violets on the green turf of the old New England States; they saw the glories of the Wisconsin maples and the haze of the Indian summer blending their hues together; they recalled the heather of Scottish hills, the white cliffs of Britain, and heard the sullen roar of the sea, as it beat upon their memories, vaguely. Then came all the old Christmas carols, such as they had sung in church thirty years before; the subtile music that brings up the glimmer of wax tapers, the solemn shrines, the evergreen, holly, misletoe, and surpliced choirs. Then the remorseless performer planted his final stab in every heart with "Home, Sweet Home."

When the player ceased, the crowd slunk away from him. There was no more revelry and devilment left in his audience. Each man wanted to sneak off to his cabin and write the old folks a letter. The day was breaking as the last man left the place, and the player, laying his head down on the piano, fell asleep.

"I say, pard," said Goskin, "don't you want a little rest?"

"I feel tired," the old man said. "Perhaps you'll let me rest here for the matter of a day or so."

He walked behind the bar, where some old blankets were lying, and stretched himself upon them.

"I feel pretty sick. I guess I won't last long. I've got a brother down in the ravine—his name's Driscoll. He don't know I'm here. Can you get him before morning. I'd like to see his face once before I die."

Goskin started up at the mention of the name. He knew Driscoll well.

"He your brother? I'll have him here in half an hour."

As he dashed out into the storm the musician pressed his hand to his side and groaned. Goskin heard the word "Hurry!" and sped down the ravine to Driscoll's cabin. It was quite light in the room when the two men returned. Driscoll was pale as death.

"My God! I hope he's alive! I wronged him when we lived in England, twenty years ago."

They saw the old man had drawn the blankets over his face, The two stood a moment, awed by the thought that he might be dead. Goskin lifted the blanket, and pulled it down astonished. There was no one there!

"Gone!" cried Driscoll, wildly.

"Gone!" echoed Goskin, pulling out his cash-drawer. "Ten thousand dollars in the sack, and the Lord knows how much loose change in the drawer!"

The next day the boys got out, followed a horse's tracks through the snow, and lost them in the trail leading towards Pioche.

There was a man missing from the camp. It was the three-card monte man, who used to deny point-blank that he could play the scale. One day they found a wig of white hair, and called to mind when the "stranger" had pushed those locks back when he looked toward the ceiling for inspiration, on the night of December 24, 1858.

DARIUS GREEN AND HIS

FLYING-MACHINE

J. T. TROWBRIDGE

J. T. Trowbridge, best known, perhaps, by his stories for boys, but eminent as a poet, novelist and dramatist, was born at Ogden, N. Y., in 1827, and began to write for the New York press while still in his teens. At twenty he went to Boston, in and near which city he has ever since lived.

If ever there lived a Yankee lad,
Wise or otherwise, good or bad,
Who, seeing the birds fly, didn't jump
With flapping arms from stake or stump,
    Or, spreading the tail
    Of his coat for a sail,
Take a soaring leap from post or rail,
    And wonder why
    He couldn't fly,
And flap and flutter, and wish and try—
If ever you knew a country dunce
Who didn't try that as often as once,
All I can say is, that's a sign
He never would do for a hero of mine.

An aspiring genius was D. Green:
The son of a farmer—age fourteen;
His body was long and lank and lean—
Just right for flying, as will be seen;
He had two eyes as bright as a bean,
And a freckled nose that grew between,
A little awry—for I must mention
That he had riveted his attention
Upon his wonderful invention,
Twisting his tongue as he twisted the strings
And working his face as he worked the wings,
And with every turn of gimlet and screw

Turning and screwing his mouth round too,
    Till his nose seemed bent
    To catch the scent,
Around some corner, of new-baked pies,
And his wrinkled cheeks and his squinting eyes,
Grew puckered into a queer grimace,
That made him look very droll in the face,
    And also very wise.
And wise he must have been, to do more
Than ever a genius did before,
Excepting Dædalus of yore
And his son Icarus, who wore
    Upon their backs
    Those wings of wax
He had read of in the old almanacks.
Darius was clearly of the opinion,
That the air was also man's dominion,
And that, with paddle or fin or pinion,
    We soon or late
    Should navigate
The azure as now we sail the sea.
The thing looks simple enough to me;
    And if you doubt it,
Hear how Darius reasoned about it.

    "The birds can fly,
    An' why can't I?
    Must we give in,"
    Says he with a grin,
    " 'T the bluebird an' phœbe
    Are smarter'n we be?
Jest fold our hands an' see the swaller
An' blackbird an' catbird beat us holler?
Doos the leetle chatterin', sassy wren,
No bigger'n my thumb, know more than men?
    Jest show me that!
    Er prove't the bat
Hez got more brains than's in my hat,
An' I'll back down, an' not till then!"

He argued further: "Ner I can't see
What's th' use o' wings to a bumble-bee,
Fer to git a livin' with, more'n to me—
    Ain't my business
    Importanter'n his'n is?
  "That Icarus
  Was a silly cuss—
Him an' his daddy Dædalus.
They might 'a' knowed wings made o' wax
Wouldn't stan' sun-heat an' hard whacks.
    I'll make mine o' luther,
    Er suthin' er other."

And he said to himself, as he tinkered and planned,
"But I ain't goin' to show my hand
To nummies that never can understand
The fust idee that's big an' grand.
    They'd 'a' laft an' made fun
O' Creation itself afore't was done!"
So he kept his secret from all the rest,
Safely buttoned within his vest;
And in the loft above the shed
Himself he locks, with thimble and thread
And wax and hammer and buckles and screws,
And all such things as geniuses use—
Two bats for patterns, curious fellows!
A charcoal-pot and a pair of bellows;
An old hoop-skirt or two, as well as
Some wire, and several old umbrellas;
A carriage-cover, for tail and wings;
A piece of harness; and straps and strings;
    And a big strong box,
    In which he locks
These and a hundred other things.

His grinning brothers, Reuben and Burke
And Nathan and Jotham and Solomon, lurk
Around the corner to see him work—
Sitting cross-legged, like a Turk,
Drawing the waxed-end through with a jerk,

And boring the holes with a comical quirk
Of his wise old head, and a knowing smirk.
But vainly they mounted each other's backs,
And poked through knot-holes and pried through cracks
With wood from the pile and straw from the stacks
He plugged the knot-holes and calked the cracks;
And a bucket of water, which one would think
He had brought up into the loft to drink
  When he chanced to be dry,
  Stood always nigh,
  For Darius was sly!
And whenever at work he happened to spy
At chink or crevice a blinking eye,
He let a dipper of water fly.
"Take that! an' ef ever ye git a peep,
Guess ye'll ketch a weasel asleep!"
  And he sings as he locks
  His big strong box:—

SONG.

"The weasel's head is small an' trim,
An' he is leetle an' long an' slim,
An' quick of motion an' nimble of limb,
  An' ef yeou'll be
  Advised by me,
Keep wide awake when ye're ketchin' him!"

  So day after day
He stitched and tinkered and hammered away,
  Till at last 't was done—
The greatest invention under the sun!
"An' now," says Darius, "hooray fer some fun!"
  'T was the Fourth of July,
  And the weather was dry,
And not a cloud was on all the sky,
Save a few light fleeces, which here and there,
  Half mist, half air,
Like foam on the ocean went floating by:
Just as lovely a morning as ever was seen
For a nice little trip in a flying machine.

Thought cunning Darius: "Now I sha'n't go
Along 'ith the fellows to see the show.
I'll say I've got sich a terrible cough!
An' then, when the folks 'ave all gone off,
    I'll hev full swing
    Fer to try the thing,
An' practyse a leetle on the wing."

"Ain't goin' to see the celebration?"
Says Brother Nate, "No; botheration!
I've got sich a cold—a toothache—I—
My gracious!—feel's though I should fly!"
    Said Jotham, " 'Sho!
    Guess ye better go."
    But Darius said, "No!
Shouldn't wonder 'f yeou might see me, though,
'Long 'bout noon, ef I git red
O' this jumpin', thumpin' pain 'n my head."
For all the while to himself he said:—
    "I tell ye what!
I'll fly a few times around the lot,
To see how't seems; then soon's I've got
The hang o' the thing, ez likely 's not,
    I'll astonish the nation,
    An' all creation,
By flyin' over the celebration!
Over their heads I'll sail like an eagle;
I'll balance myself on my wings like a sea-gull;
I'll dance on the chimbleys; I'll stan' on the steeple;
I'll flop up to winders an' scare the people!
I'll light on the libbe'ty-pole, an' crow;
An' I'll say to the gawpin' fools below,
    'What world's this 'ere
    That I've come near?'
Fer I'll make 'em b'lieve I'm a chap f'm the moon;
An' I'll try a race 'ith their ol' bulloon!"

    He crept from his bed;
And, seeing the others were gone, he said,
"I'm a gittin' over the cold 'n my head."
    And away he sped,

To open the wonderful box in the shed.
His brothers had walked but a little way,
When Jotham to Nathan chanced to say,
"What on airth is he up to, hey?"
"Don'o'—the' 's suthin' er other to pay,
Er he wouldn't 'a' stayed to hum to-day."
Says Burke, "His toothache's all 'n his eye!
He never 'd miss a Fo'th-o'-July,
Ef he hedn't got some machine to try."
Then Sol, the little one, spoke: "By darn!
Le's hurry back an' hide'n the barn,
An' pay him for tellin' us that yarn!"
"Agreed!" Through the orchard they creep,
Along by the fences, behind the stack,
And one by one, through a hole in the wall,
In under the dusty barn they crawl,
Dressed in their Sunday garments all;
And a very astonishing sight was that,
When each in his cobwebbed coat and hat
Came up through the floor like an ancient rat.
          And there they hid;
          And Reuben slid
The fastenings back, and the door undid.
          "Keep dark!" said he,
"While I squint an' see what the' is to see."

As knights of old put on their mail—
          From head to foot
          An iron suit,
Iron jacket and iron boot,
Iron breeches, and on the head
No hat, but an iron pot instead,
          And under the chin the bail—
I believe they called the thing a helm;
And the lid they carried they called a shield;
And, thus accoutred, they took the field,
Sallying forth to overwhelm
The dragons and pagans that plagued the realm—

          So this modern knight
          Prepared for flight,

Put on his wings and strapped them tight;
Jointed and jaunty, strong and light;
Buckled them fast to shoulder and hip—
Ten feet they measured from tip to tip!
And a helm had he, but that he wore,
Not on his head like those of yore,
      But more like the helm of a ship.

   "Hush!" Reuben said,
   "He's up in the shed!
He's opened the winder—I see his head!
    He stretches it out
    And pokes it about,
Lookin' to see 'f the coast is clear,
     An' nobody near—
Guess he don'o' who's hid in here!
He's riggin' a spring-board over the sill!
Stop laffin', Solomon! Burke, keep still!
He's a climbin' out now—Of all the things!
What's he got on? I vow, it's wings!
An' that t'other thing? I vum, it's a tail!
An' there he sets like a hawk on a rail!
Steppin' careful, he travels the length
Of his spring-board, and teeters to try its strength.
Now he stretches his wings, like a monstrous bat;
Peeks over his shoulder this way an' that,
Fer to see 'f the' 's any one passin' by;
But the' 's on'y a ca'f an' a goslin nigh.
They turn up at him a wonderin' eye,
To see—The dragon! he's goin' to fly!
Away he goes! Jimminy! what a jump!
    Flop—flop—an' plump
    To the ground with a thump!
Flutterin' an' flound'rin', all'n a lump!"

As a demon is hurled by an angel's spear,
Heels over head, to his proper sphere—
Heels over head, and head over heels,
Dizzily down the abyss he wheels—
So fell Darius. Upon his crown,
In the midst of the barn-yard, he came down,

In a wonderful whirl of tangled strings,
Broken braces and broken springs,
Broken tail and broken wings,
Shooting-stars, and various things—
Barn-yard litter of straw and chaff,
And much that wasn't so sweet by half.
Away with a bellow fled the calf.
And what was that? Did the gosling laugh?
    'Tis a merry roar
    From the old barn-door,
And he hears the voice of Jotham crying,
"Say, D'rius! how de yeou like flyin'?"

Slowly, ruefully, where he lay,
Darius just turned and looked that way,
As he stanched his sorrowful nose with his cuff.
"Wall, I like flyin' well enough,"
He said; "but the' ain't sich a thunderin' sight
O' fun in't when ye come to light."

MORAL.

I just have room for the moral here:
And this is the moral—Stick to your sphere.
Or, if you insist, as you have the right,
On spreading your wings for a loftier flight,
The moral is—Take care how you light.

PLUMBERS

CHARLES DUDLEY WARNER

Speaking of the philosophical temper, there is no class of men whose society is more to be desired for this quality than that of plumbers. They are the most agreeable men I know; and the boys in the business begin to be agreeable very early. I suspect the secret of it is, that they are agreeable by the hour. In the dryest days my fountain became disabled: the pipe was stopped up. A couple of plumbers, with the implements of their craft, came out to view the situation. There was a good deal of difference of opinion about where the stoppage was. I found the plumbers perfectly willing to sit down and talk about it—talk by the hour. Some of their guesses and remarks were exceedingly ingenious; and their general observations on other subjects were excellent in their way, and could hardly have been better if they had been made by the job. The work dragged a little—as it is apt to do by the hour. The plumbers had occasion to make me several visits. Sometimes they would find, upon arrival, that they had forgotten some indispensable tool, and one would go back to the shop, a mile and a half, after it, and his companion would await his return with the most exemplary patience, and sit down and talk—always by the hour. I do not know but it is a habit to have something wanted at the shop. They seemed to me very good workmen, and always willing to stop and talk about the job, or anything else, when I went near them. Nor had they any of that impetuous hurry that is said to be the bane of our American civilization. To their credit be it said, that I never observed anything of it in them. They can afford to wait. Two of them will sometimes wait nearly half a day while a comrade goes for a tool. They are patient and philosophical. It is a great pleasure to meet such men. One only wishes there was some work he could do for *them* by the hour. There ought to be reciprocity. I think they have very nearly solved the problem of Life: it is to work for other people, never for yourself, and get your pay by the hour. You then have no anxiety, and little work. If you do things by the job you are perpetually driven: the hours are scourges. If you work by the hour, you gently sail on the stream of Time, which is always bearing you on to the haven of Pay, whether you make any effort or not. Working by the hour tends to make one moral. A plumber working by the job, trying to unscrew a rusty, refractory nut in a cramped position, where the tongs continually slipped off, would swear; but I never heard one of them swear, or exhibit the least impatience at such a vexation, working by the hour. Nothing can move a man who is paid by the hour. How sweet the flight of time seems to his calm mind!

———

A MAN with a pot of green paint can stand where he pleases on a ferryboat.—*Newspaper*

The Remarkable Wreck of the "Thomas Hyke"

FRANK R. STOCKTON

Francis Richard Stockton, a master in his peculiar sort of humor, was born at Philadelphia in 1834, and was graduated from the Central High School. He learned wood-engraving, and wrote continuously, with varying success, for many different magazines, achieving somewhat tardily the fame due his unique and beautiful talent.

It was half-past one by the clock in the office of the Registrar of Woes. The room was empty, for it was Wednesday, and the Registrar always went home early on Wednesday afternoons. He had made that arrangement when he accepted the office. He was willing to serve his fellow-citizens in any suitable position to which he might be called, but he had private interests which could not be neglected. He belonged to his country, but there was a house in the country which belonged to him; and there were a great many things appertaining to that house which needed attention, especially in pleasant summer weather. It is true he was often absent on afternoons which did not fall on the Wednesday, but the fact of his having appointed a particular time for the furtherance of his outside interests so emphasized their importance that his associates in the office had no difficulty in understanding that affairs of such moment could not always be attended to in a single afternoon of the week.

But although the large room devoted to the especial use of the Registrar was unoccupied, there were other rooms connected with it which were not in that condition. With the suite of offices to the left we have nothing to do, but will confine our attention to a moderate-sized room to the right of the Registrar's office, and connected by a door, now closed, with that large and handsomely furnished chamber. This was the office of the Clerk of Shipwrecks, and it was at present occupied by five persons. One of these was the clerk himself, a man of goodly appearance, somewhere between twenty-five and forty-five years of age, and of a demeanor such as might be supposed to belong to one who had occupied a high position in state affairs, but who, by the cabals of his enemies, had been forced to resign the great operations of statesmanship which he had been directing, and who now stood, with a quite resigned air, pointing out to the populace the futile and disastrous efforts of the incompetent one who was endeavoring to fill his place. The Clerk of Shipwrecks had never fallen from such a position, having never occupied one, but he had acquired the demeanor referred to without going through the preliminary exercises.

Another occupant was a very young man, the personal clerk of the Registrar of Woes, who always closed all the doors of the office of that functionary on Wednesday afternoons, and at other times when outside interests demanded his principal's absence, after which he betook himself to the room of his friend the Shipwreck Clerk.

Then there was a middle-aged man named Mathers, also a friend of the clerk, and who was one of the eight who had made application for a sub-position in this department, which was now filled by a man who was expected to resign when a friend of his, a gentleman of influence in an interior county, should succeed in procuring the nomination as congressional representative of his district of an influential politician, whose election was considered assured in case certain expected action on the part of the administration should bring his party into power. The person now occupying the sub-position hoped then to get something better, and Mathers, consequently, was very willing, while waiting for the place, to visit the offices of the department and acquaint himself with its duties.

A fourth person was J. George Watts, a juryman by profession, who had brought with him his brother-in-law, a stranger in the city.

The Shipwreck Clerk had taken off his good coat, which he had worn to luncheon, and had replaced it by a lighter garment of linen, much bespattered with ink; and he now produced a cigar-box, containing six cigars.

"Gents," said he, "here is the fag end of a box of cigars. It's not like having the pick of the box, but they are all I have left."

Mr. Mathers, J. George Watts, and the brother-in-law each took a cigar, with that careless yet deferential manner which always distinguishes the treatee from the treator; and then the box was protruded in an off-hand way toward Harry Covare, the personal clerk of the Registrar; but this young man declined, saying that he preferred cigarettes, a package of which he drew from his pocket. He had very often seen that cigar-box with a Havana brand, which he himself had brought from the other room after the Registrar had emptied it, passed around with six cigars, no more nor less, and he was wise enough to know that the Shipwreck Clerk did not expect to supply him with smoking material. If that gentleman had offered to the friends who generally dropped in on him on Wednesday afternoon the paper bag of cigars sold at five cents each when bought singly, but half a dozen for a quarter of a dollar, they would have been quite as thankfully received; but it better pleased his deprecative soul to put them in an empty cigar-box, and thus throw around them the halo of the presumption that ninety-four of their imported companions had been smoked.

The Shipwreck Clerk, having lighted a cigar for himself, sat down in his revolving chair, turned his back to his desk, and threw himself into an easy cross-legged attitude, which showed that he was perfectly at home in that office. Harry Covare mounted a high stool, while the visitors seated themselves in three wooden arm-chairs. But few words had been said, and each man had scarcely tossed his first tobacco ashes on the floor when some one wearing heavy boots was heard opening an outside door and entering the Registrar's room. Harry Covare jumped down from his stool, laid his half-smoked cigarette thereon, and bounced into the next room, closing the door after him. In about a minute he returned, and the Shipwreck Clerk looked at him inquiringly.

"An old cock in a pea-jacket," said Mr. Covare, taking up his cigarette, and mounting his stool. "I told him the Registrar would be here in the morning. He said he had something to report about a shipwreck; and I told him the Registrar would be here in the morning. Had to tell him that three times, and then he went."

"School don't keep Wednesday afternoons," said Mr. J. George Watts, with a knowing smile.

"No, sir," said the Shipwreck Clerk, emphatically, changing the crossing of his legs. "A man can't keep grinding on day in and out without breaking down. Outsiders may say what they please about it, but it can't be done. We've got to let up sometimes. People who do the work need the rest just as much as those who do the looking on."

"And more too, I should say," observed Mr. Mathers.

"Our little let-up on Wednesday afternoons," modestly observed Harry Covare, "is like death; it is sure to come, while the let-ups we get other days are more like the diseases which prevail in certain areas; you can't be sure whether you're going to get them or not."

The Shipwreck Clerk smiled benignantly at this remark, and the rest laughed. Mr. Mathers had heard it before, but he would not impair the pleasantness of his relations with a future colleague by hinting that he remembered it.

"He gets such ideas from his beastly statistics," said the Shipwreck Clerk.

"Which come pretty heavy on him sometimes, I expect," observed Mr. Mathers.

"They needn't," said the Shipwreck Clerk, "if things were managed here as they ought to be. If John J. Laylor," meaning thereby the Registrar, "was the right kind of a man, you'd see things very different here from what they are now. There'd be a larger force."

"That's so," said Mr. Mathers.

"And not only that, but there'd be better buildings, and more accommodations. Were any of you ever up to Anster? Well, take a run up there some day, and see what sort of buildings the department has there. William Q. Green is a very different man from John J. Laylor. You don't see him sitting in his chair and picking his teeth the whole winter, while the representative from his district never says a word about his department from one end of a session of Congress to the other. Now if I had charge of things here, I'd make such changes that you wouldn't know the place. I'd throw two rooms off here, and a corridor and entrance door at that end of the building. I'd close up this door," pointing toward the Registrar's room, "and if John J. Laylor wanted to come in here, he might go round to the end door like other people."

The thought struck Harry Covare that in that case there would be no John J. Laylor, but he would not interrupt.

"And what is more," continued the Shipwreck Clerk, "I'd close up this whole department at twelve o'clock on Saturdays. The way things are managed now, a man has no time to attend to his own private business. Suppose I think of buying a piece of land, and want to go out and look at it, or suppose any one of you gentlemen were here and thought of buying a piece of land, and wanted to go out and look at it, what are you going to do about it? You don't want to go on Sunday, and when are you going to go?"

Not one of the other gentlemen had ever thought of buying a piece of land, nor had they any reason to suppose that they ever would purchase an inch of soil, unless they bought it in a flowerpot; but they all agreed that the way things were managed now, there was no time for a man to attend to his own business.

"But you can't expect John J. Laylor to do anything," said the Shipwreck Clerk.

However, there was one thing which that gentleman always expected John J. Laylor to do. When the clerk was surrounded by a number of persons in hours of business, and when he had succeeded in impressing them with the importance of his functions, and the necessity of paying deferential attention to himself if they wished their business attended to, John J. Laylor would be sure to walk into the office and address the Shipwreck Clerk in such a manner as to let the people present know that he was a clerk and nothing else, and that he, the Registrar, was the head of that department. These humiliations the Shipwreck Clerk never forgot.

There was a little pause here, and then Mr. Mathers remarked:

"I should think you'd be awfully bored with the long stories of shipwrecks that the people come and tell you."

He hoped to change the conversation because, although he wished to remain on good terms with the subordinate officers, it was not desirable that he should be led to say much against John J. Laylor.

"No, sir," said the Shipwreck Clerk, "I am not bored. I did not come here to be bored, and as long as I have charge of this office I don't intend to be. The long-winded old salts who come here to report their wrecks never spin out their prosy yarns to me. The first thing I do is to let them know just what I want of them; and not an inch beyond that does a man of them go, at least while I am managing the business. There are times when John J. Laylor comes in, and puts in his oar, and wants to hear the whole story, which is pure stuff and nonsense, for John J. Laylor doesn't know anything more about a shipwreck than he does about—"

"The endemics in the Lake George area," suggested Harry Covare.

"Yes; or any other part of his business," said the Shipwreck Clerk; "and when he takes it into his head to interfere, all business stops until some second mate of a coal-schooner has told his whole story, from his sighting land on the morning of one day to his getting ashore on it on the afternoon of the next. Now I don't put up with any such nonsense. There's no man living that can tell me anything about shipwrecks. I've never been to sea myself, but that's not necessary; and if I had gone, it's not likely I'd been wrecked. But I've read about every kind of ship-wreck that ever happened. When I first came here I took care to post myself upon these matters, because I knew it would save trouble. I have read 'Robinson Crusoe,' 'The Wreck of the *Grosvenor*,' 'The Sink-ing of the *Royal George*,' and wrecks by water-spouts, tidal waves, and every other thing which would knock a ship into a cocked hat, and I've classified every sort of wreck under its proper head; and when I've found out to what class a wreck belongs, I know all about it. Now, when a man comes here to report a wreck, the first thing he has to do is just to shut down on his story, and to stand up square and answer a few questions that I put to him. In two minutes I know just what kind of shipwreck he's had; and then, when he gives me the name of his ves-sel, and one or two other points, he may go. I know all about that wreck, and I make a much better report of the business than he could have done if he'd stood here talking three days and three nights. The amount of money that's been saved to our tax-payers by the way I've systematized the business of this office is not to be calculated in fig-ures."

The brother-in-law of J. George Watts knocked the ashes from the remnant of his cigar, looked contemplatively at the coal for a moment, and then remarked:

"I think you said there's no kind of shipwreck you don't know about?"

"That's what I said," replied the Shipwreck Clerk.

"I think," said the other, "I could tell you of a shipwreck, in which I was concerned, that wouldn't go into any of your classes."

The Shipwreck Clerk threw away the end of his cigar, put both his hands into his trousers' pockets, stretched out his legs, and looked steadfastly at the man who had made this unwarrantable remark. Then a pitying smile stole over his countenance, and he said: "Well, sir, I'd like to hear your account of it; and before you get a quarter through I can stop you just where you are, and go ahead and tell the rest of the story myself."

"That's so," said Harry Covare. "You'll see him do it just as sure pop as a spread rail bounces the engine."

"Well, then," said the brother-in-law of J. George Watts, "I'll tell it." And he began:

"It was just two years ago, the first of this month, that I sailed for South America in the *Thomas Hyke*."

At this point the Shipwreck Clerk turned and opened a large book at the letter T.

"That wreck wasn't reported here," said the other, "and you won't find it in your book."

"At Anster, perhaps?" said the Shipwreck clerk, closing the volume, and turning round again.

"Can't say about that," replied the other. "I've never been to Anster, and haven't looked over their books."

"Well, you needn't want to," said the clerk. "They've got good accommodations at Anster, and the Registrar has some ideas of the duties of his post, but they have no such system of wreck reports as we have here."

"Very like," said the brother-in-law. And he went on with his story. "The *Thomas Hyke* was a small iron steamer of six hundred tons, and she sailed from Ulford for Valparaiso with a cargo principally of pig-iron."

"Pig-iron for Valparaiso!" remarked the Shipwreck Clerk. And then he knitted his brows thoughtfully, and said, "Go on."

"She was a new vessel," continued the narrator, "and built with water-tight compartments; rather uncommon for a vessel of her class, but so she was. I am not a sailor, and don't know anything about ships. I went as passenger, and there was another one named William Anderson, and his son Sam, a boy about fifteen years old. We were all going to Valparaiso on business. I don't remember just how many days we were out, nor do I know just where we were, but it was somewhere off the coast of South America, when, one dark night—with a fog besides, for aught I know, for I was asleep—we ran into a steamer coming north. How we managed to do this, with room enough on both sides for all the ships in the world to pass, I don't know; but so it was. When I got on deck the other vessel had gone on, and we never saw anything more of her. Whether she sunk or got home is something I can't tell. But we pretty soon found that the *Thomas Hyke* had some of the plates in her bow badly smashed, and she took in water like a thirsty dog. The captain had the forward water-tight bulkhead shut tight, and the pumps set to work, but it was no use. That forward compartment just filled up with water, and the *Thomas Hyke* settled down with her bow clean under. Her deck was slanting forward like the side of a hill, and the propeller was lifted up so that it wouldn't have worked even if the engine had been kept going. The captain had the masts cut away, thinking this might bring her up some, but it didn't help much. There was a pretty heavy sea on, and the waves came rolling up the slant of the deck like the surf on the sea-shore. The captain gave orders to have all the hatches battened down, so that water couldn't get in, and the only way by which any one could go below was by the cabin door, which was aft. This work of stopping up all openings in the deck was a dangerous business, for the decks sloped right down into the water, and if anybody had slipped, away he'd have gone into the ocean, with nothing to stop him; but the men made a line fast to themselves and worked away with a good-will, and soon got the deck and the house over the engine as tight as a bottom. The smoke-stack, which was well forward, had been broken down by a spar when the masts had been cut, and as the waves washed into the hole that it left, the captain had this plugged up with old sails, well fastened down. It was a dreadful thing to see the ship a-lying with her bows clean under water, and her stern sticking up. If it hadn't been for her water-tight compartments that were left uninjured, she would have gone down to the bottom as slick as a whistle. On the afternoon of the day after the collision the wind fell and the sea soon became pretty smooth. The captain was quite sure that there would be no trouble about keeping afloat until some ship came along and took us off. Our flag was flying, upside down, from a pole in the stern; and if anybody saw a ship making such a guy of herself as the *Thomas Hyke* was then doing, they'd be sure to come to see what was the matter with her, even if she had no flag of distress flying. We tried to make ourselves as comfortable as we could, but this wasn't easy with everything on such a dreadful slant. But that night we heard a rumbling and grinding noise down in the hold, and the slant seemed to get worse. Pretty soon the captain roused all hands, and told us that the cargo of pig-iron was shifting and sliding down to the bow, and that it wouldn't be long before it would break through all the bulkheads, and then we'd fill and go to the bottom like a shot. He said we must all take to the boats, and get away as quick as we could. It was an easy matter launching the boats. They didn't lower them outside from the davits, but they just let 'em down on deck and slid 'em along forward into the water, and then held 'em there with a rope till everything was ready to start. They launched three boats, put plenty of provisions and water in 'em, and then everybody began to get aboard. But William Anderson and me, and his son Sam, couldn't make up our minds to get into those boats and row out on the dark, wide ocean. They were the biggest boats we had, but still they were little things enough. The ship seemed to us to be a good deal safer, and more likely to be seen when day broke than those three boats, which might be blown off if the wind rose, nobody knew where. It seemed to us that the cargo had done all the shifting it intended to, and the noise below had stopped; and, altogether, we agreed that we'd rather stick to the ship than go off in those boats. The captain, he tried to make us go, but we wouldn't do it, and he told us if we chose to stay behind and be drowned it was our affair, and he couldn't help it; and then he said there was a small boat aft, and we'd better launch her, and have her ready in case things should get worse, and we should make up our minds to leave the vessel. He and the rest then rowed off so as not to be caught in the vortex if the steamer went down, and we three stayed aboard. We launched the small boat in the way we'd seen the others launched, being careful to have ropes tied to us while we were doing it; and we put things aboard that we thought we should want. Then we went into the cabin, and waited for morning. It was a queer kind of a cabin, with a floor inclined like the roof of a house, but we sat down in the corners, and were glad to be there. The swinging lamp was burning, and it was a good deal more cheerful in there than it was outside. But about daybreak the grinding and rumbling down below began again, and the bow of the *Thomas Hyke* kept going down more and more; and it wasn't long before the forward bulkhead of the cabin, which was what you might call its front wall when everything was all right, was under our feet, as level as a floor, and the lamp was lying close against the ceiling that it was hanging from. You may be sure that we thought it was time to get out of that. There were benches with arms to them fastened to the floor, and by these we climbed up to the foot of the cabin stairs, which, being turned bottom upward, we went down, in order to get out. When we reached the cabin door we saw part of the deck below us, standing up like the side of a house that is built in the water, as they say the houses in Venice are. We had made our boat fast to the cabin door by a long line, and now we saw her floating quietly on the water, which was very smooth, and about twenty feet below us. We drew her up as close under us as we could, and then we let the boy Sam down by a rope, and, after some kicking and swinging, he got into her; and then he took the oars, and kept her right under us while we scrambled down by the ropes which we had used in getting her ready. As soon as we were in the boat we cut the rope and pulled away as hard as we could; and when we got to what we thought was a safe distance, we stopped to look at the *Thomas Hyke.* You never saw such a ship in all your born days. Two-thirds of the hull was sunk in the water, and she was standing straight up and down, with the stern in the air, her rudder up as high as the topsail ought to be, and the screw propeller looking like the wheel on the top of one of these windmills that they have in the country for pumping up water. Her cargo had shifted so far forward that it had turned her right upon end, but she couldn't sink, owing to the air in the compartments that the water hadn't got into; and on the top of the whole thing was the distress flag flying from the pole which stuck out over the stern. It was broad daylight, but not a thing did we see of the other boats. We'd supposed that they wouldn't row very far, but would lay off at a safe distance until daylight; but they must have been scared, and rowed farther than they intended. Well, sir, we stayed in that boat all day, and watched the *Thomas Hyke,* but she just kept as she was, and didn't seem to sink an inch. There was no use of rowing away, for we had no place to row to; and, besides, we thought that passing ships would be much more likely to see that stern sticking high in the air than our little boat. We had enough to eat, and at night two of us slept while the other watched, dividing off the time, and taking turns at this. In the morning, there was the *Thomas Hyke* standing stern up just as before. There was a long swell on the ocean now, and she'd rise and lean over a little on each wave, but she'd come up again just as straight as before. That night passed as the last one had, and in the morning we found we'd drifted a good deal farther from the *Thomas Hyke,* but she was floating just as she had been, like a big buoy that's moored over a sand-bar. We couldn't see a sign of the boats, and we about gave them up. We had our breakfast, which was a pretty poor meal, being nothing but hard-tack and what was left of a piece of boiled beef. After we'd sat for awhile doing nothing, but feeling mighty uncomfortable, William Anderson said: 'Look here, do you know that I think we would be three fools to keep on shivering all night and living on hard-tack in the day-time, when there's plenty on that vessel for us to eat, and to keep us warm. If she's floated that way for two days and two nights, there's no knowing how much longer she'll float, and we might as well go on board and get the things we want as not.' 'All right,' said I, for I was tired doing nothing, and Sam was as willing as anybody. So we rowed up to the steamer, and stopped close to the deck, which, as I said before, was standing straight up out of the water like the wall of a house. The cabin door, which was the only opening into her, was about twenty feet above us, and the ropes which we had tied to the rails of the stairs inside were still hanging down. Sam was an active youngster, and he managed to climb up one of these ropes; but when he got up to the door he drew it up and tied knots in it about a foot apart, and then he let it down to us, for neither William Anderson nor me could go up a rope hand-over-hand without knots or something to hold on to. As it was, we had a lot of bother getting up, but we did it at last; and then we walked up the stairs, treading on the front part of each step instead of the top of it, as we would have done if the stairs had been in their proper position. When we got to the floor of the cabin, which was now perpendicular like a wall, we had to clamber down by means of the furniture, which was screwed fast, until we reached the bulkhead, which was now the floor of the cabin. Close to this bulkhead was a small room, which was the steward's pantry, and here we found lots of things to eat, but all jumbled up in a way that made us laugh. The boxes of biscuits and the tin cans and a lot of bottles in wicker covers were piled up on one end of the room, and everything in the lockers and drawers was jumbled together. William Anderson and me set to work to get out what we thought we'd want, and we told Sam to climb up into some of the staterooms, of which there were four on each side of the cabin, and get some blankets to keep us warm, as well as a few sheets, which we thought we could rig up for an awning to the boat—for the days were just as hot as the nights were cool. When we'd collected what we wanted, William Anderson and me climbed into our own rooms, thinking we'd each pack a valise with what we most wanted to save of our clothes and things; and while we were doing this, Sam called out to us that it was raining.

He was sitting at the cabin door, looking out. I first thought to tell him to shut the door, so's to keep the rain from coming in; but when I thought how things really were, I laughed at the idea. There was a sort of little house built over the entrance to the cabin, and in one end of it was the door; and in the way the ship now was, the open doorway was underneath the little house, and of course no rain could come in. Pretty soon we heard the rain pouring down, beating on the stern of the vessel like hail. We got to the stairs and looked out. The rain was falling in perfect sheets, in a way you never see, except round about the tropics. 'It's a good thing we're inside,' said William Anderson, 'for if we'd been out in this rain we'd been drowned in the boat.' I agreed with him, and we made up our minds to stay where we were until the rain was over. Well, it rained about four hours; and when it stopped and we looked out, we saw our little boat nearly full of water, and sunk so deep that if one of us had stepped on her she'd have gone down, sure. 'Here's a pretty kettle of fish,' said William Anderson; 'there's nothing for us to do now but to stay where we are.' I believe in his heart he was glad of that, for if ever a man was tired of a little boat, William Anderson was tired of that one we'd been in for two days and two nights. At any rate there was no use talking about it, and we set to work to make ourselves comfortable. We got some mattresses and pillows out of the staterooms, and when it began to get dark we lighted the lamp, which we had filled with sweet-oil from a flask in the pantry, not finding any other kind, and we hung it from the railing of the stairs. We had a good night's rest, and the only thing that disturbed me was William Anderson lifting up his head every time he turned over, and saying how much better this was than that blasted little boat. The next morning we had a good breakfast, even making some tea with a spirit lamp we found, using brandy instead of alcohol. William Anderson and I wanted to get into the captain's room, which was near the stern, and pretty high up, so as to see if there was anything there that we ought to get ready to save when a vessel should come along and pick us up; but we were not good at climbing, like Sam, and we didn't see how we could get up there. Sam said he was sure he had once seen a ladder in the compartment just forward of the bulkhead, and as William was very anxious to get up to the captain's room, we let the boy go and look for it. There was a sliding door in the bulkhead under our feet, and we opened this far enough to let Sam get through, and he scrambled down like a monkey into the next compartment, which was light enough, although the lower half of it, which was next to the engine-room, was under the water-line. Sam actually found a ladder with hooks at one end of it, and while he was handing it up to us, which was very hard to do, for he had to climb up on all sorts of things, he let it topple over, and the end with the iron hooks fell against the round glass of one of the port-holes. The glass was very thick and strong, but the ladder came down very heavy and shivered it. As bad luck would have it, this window was below the water-line, and the water came rushing in in a big spout. We chucked blankets down to Sam for him to stop up the hole, but 'twas of no use; for it was hard for him to get at the window, and when he did the water came in with such force that he couldn't get a blanket in the hole. We were afraid he'd be drowned down there, and told him to come out as quick as he could. He put up the ladder again, and hooked it on to the door in the bulkhead, and we held it while he climbed up. Looking down through the doorway, we saw, by the way the water was pouring in at the opening, that it wouldn't be long before that compartment was filled up; so we shoved the door to and made it all tight, and then said William Anderson: 'The ship'll sink deeper and deeper as that fills up, and the water may get up to the cabin door, and we must go and make that as tight as we can.' Sam had pulled the ladder up after him, and this we found of great use in getting to the foot of the cabin stairs. We shut the cabin door, and locked and bolted it; and as it fitted pretty tight, we didn't think it would let in much water if the ship sunk that far. But over the top of the cabin stairs were a couple of folding doors, which shut down hor-izontally when the ship was in its proper position, and which were only used in very bad, cold weather. These we pulled to and fastened tight, thus having a double protection against the water. Well, we didn't get this done any too soon, for the water did come up to the cabin door, and a little trickled in from the outside door, and through the cracks in the inner one. But we went to work and stopped these up with strips from the sheets, which we crammed well in with our pocket-knives. Then we sat down on the steps and waited to see what would happen next. The doors of all the staterooms were open, and we could see through the thick plate-glass windows in them, which were all shut tight, that the ship was sinking more and more as the water came in. Sam climbed up into one of the after staterooms, and said the outside water was nearly up to the stern; and pretty soon we looked up to the two port-holes in the stern, and saw that they were covered with water; and as more and more water could be seen there, and as the light came through less easily, we knew that we were sinking under the surface of the ocean. 'It's a mighty good thing,' said William Anderson, 'that no water can get in here.' William had a hopeful kind of mind, and always looked on the bright side of things; but I must say that I was dreadfully scared when I looked through those stern windows and saw water instead of sky. It began to get duskier and duskier as we sank lower and lower, but still we could see pretty well, for it's astonishing how much light comes down through water. After a little while we noticed that the light remained about the same; and then William Anderson, he sings out, 'Hooray, we've stopped sinking!' 'What difference does that make?' says I, 'we must be thirty or forty feet under water, and more yet for aught I know.' 'Yes, that may be,' said he, 'but it is clear that all the water has got into that compartment that can get in, and we have sunk just as far down as we are going.' 'But that don't help matters,' said I; 'thirty or forty feet under water is just as bad as a thousand is, to a drowning man.' 'Drowning!' said William; 'how are you going to be drowned? No water can get in here.' 'Nor no air, either,' said I; 'and people are drowned for want of air, as I take it.' 'It would be a queer sort of thing,' said William, 'to be drowned in the ocean, and yet stay as dry as a chip. But it's no use being worried about air. We've got enough here to last us for ever so long. This stern compartment is the biggest in the ship, and it's got lots of air in it. Just think of that hold! It must be nearly full of air. The stern compartment of the hold has got nothing in it but sewing-machines. I saw 'em loading her. The pig-iron was mostly amidships, or at least forward of this compartment. Now, there's no kind of a cargo that'll accommodate as much air as sewing-machines. They're packed in wooden frames, not boxes, and don't fill up half the room they take. There's air all through and around 'em. It's a very comforting thing to think the hold isn't filled up solid with bales of cotton or wheat in bulk.' It might be comforting, but I couldn't get much good out of it. And now Sam, who had been scrambling all over the cabin to see how things were going on, sung out that the water was leaking in a little again at the cabin door and around some of the iron frames of the windows. 'It's a lucky thing,' said William Anderson, 'that we didn't sink any deeper, or the pressure of the water would have burst in those heavy glasses. And what we've got to do now is, to stop up all the cracks. The more we work, the livelier we'll feel.' We tore off more strips of sheets, and went all round, stopping up cracks wherever we found them. 'It's fortunate,' said William Anderson, 'that Sam found that ladder, for we would have had hard work getting to the windows of the stern staterooms without it; but by resting it on the bottom step of the stairs, which now happens to be the top one, we can get to any part of the cabin.' I couldn't help thinking that if Sam hadn't found the ladder it would have been a good deal better for us; but I didn't want to damp William's spirits, and I said nothing.

"And now I beg your pardon, sir," said the narrator, addressing the Shipwreck Clerk, "but I forgot that you said you'd finish this story yourself. Perhaps you'd like to take it up just here?"

The Shipwreck Clerk seemed surprised, and had, apparently, forgotten his previous offer. "Oh, no," said he, "tell your own story. This is not a matter of business."

"Very well, then," said the brother-in-law of J. George Watts, "I'll go on. We made everything as tight as we could, and then we got our supper, having forgotten all about dinner, and being very hungry. We didn't make any tea, and we didn't light the lamp, for we knew that would use up air; but we made a better meal than three people sunk out of sight in the ocean had a right to expect. 'What troubles me most,' said William Anderson, as he turned in, 'is the fact that if we are forty feet under water, our flagpole must be covered up. Now, if the flag was sticking out, upside down, a ship sailing by would see it and would know there was something wrong.' 'If that's all that troubles you,' said I, 'I guess you'll sleep easy. And if a ship was to see the flag, I wonder how they'd know we were down here, and how they'd get us out if they did!' 'Oh, they'd manage it,' said William Anderson; 'trust those sea-captains for that.' And then he went to sleep. The next morning the air began to get mighty disagreeable in the part of the cabin where we were, and then William Anderson he says: 'What we've got to do is to climb up into the stern staterooms, where the air is purer. We can come down here to get our meals, and then go up again to breathe comfortable.' 'And what are we going to do when the air up there gets foul?' says I to William, who seemed to be making arrangements for spending the summer in our present quarters. 'Oh, that'll be all right,' said he. 'It don't do to be extravagant with air any more than with anything else. When we've used up all there is in this cabin, we can bore holes through the floor into the hold and let in air from there. If we're economical, there'll be enough to last for dear knows how long.' We passed the night each in a stateroom, sleeping on the end wall instead of the berth, and it wasn't till the afternoon of the next day that the air of the cabin got so bad we thought we'd have some fresh; so we went down on the bulkhead, and with an auger that we found in the pantry we bored three holes, about a yard apart, in the cabin floor, which was now one of the walls of the room, just as the bulkhead was the floor, and the stern end, where the two round windows were, was the ceiling or roof. We each took a hole, and I tell you, it was pleasant to breathe the air which came in from the hold. 'Isn't this jolly?' said William Anderson. 'And we ought to be mighty glad that that hold wasn't loaded with codfish or soap. But there's nothing that smells better than new sewing-machines that haven't ever been used, and this air is pleasant enough for anybody.' By William's advice we made three plugs, by which we stopped up the holes when we thought we'd had air enough for the present. 'And now,' says he, 'we needn't climb up into those awkward staterooms any more. We can just stay down here and be comfortable, and let in air when we want it.' 'And how long do you suppose that air in the hold is going to last?' said I. 'Oh, ever so long,' said he, 'using it so economically as we do; and when it stops coming out lively through these little holes, as I suppose it will after a while, we can saw a big hole in this flooring, and go into the hold and do our breathing, if we want to.' That evening we did saw a hole about a foot square, so as to have plenty of air while we were asleep, but we didn't go into the hold, it being pretty well filled up with machines; though the next day Sam and I sometimes stuck our heads in for a good sniff of air, though William Anderson was opposed to this, being of the opinion that we ought to put ourselves on short rations of breathing, so as to make the supply of air hold out as long as possible. 'But what's the good,' said I to William, 'of trying to make the air hold out if we've got to be suffocated in this place after all?' 'What's the good?' says he. 'Haven't you enough biscuits, and canned meats, and plenty of other things to eat, and a barrel of water in that room opposite the pantry, not to speak of wine and brandy, if you want to cheer yourself up a bit; and haven't we good mattresses to sleep on, and why shouldn't we try to live and be comfortable as long as we can?' 'What I want,' said I, 'is to get out of this box. The idea of being shut up in here down under water is more than I can stand. I'd rather take my chances going up to the surface and swimming about till I found a piece of the wreck, or something to float on.' 'You needn't think of anything of that sort,' said William, 'for if we were to open a door or a window to get out, the water'd rush in and drive us back and fill up this place in no time; and then the whole concern would go to the bottom. And what would you do if you did get to the top of the water? It's not likely you'd find anything there to get on, and if you did you wouldn't live very long floating about with nothing to eat. No, sir,' says he, 'what we've got to do is to be content with the comforts we have around us, and something will turn up to get us out of this; you see if it don't.' There was no use talking against William Anderson, and I didn't say any more about getting out. As for Sam, he spent his time at the windows of the staterooms a-looking out. We could see a good way into the water, further than you would think, and we sometimes saw fishes, especially porpoises, swimming about, most likely trying to find out what a ship was doing hanging bows down under water. What troubled Sam was that a sword-fish might come along and jab his sword through one of the windows. In that case it would be all up, or rather down, with us. Every now and then he'd sing out, 'Here comes one!' And then, just as I'd give a jump, he'd say, 'No, it isn't; it's a porpoise.' I thought from the first, and I think now, that it would have been a great deal better for us if that boy hadn't been along. That night there was a good deal of motion to the ship, and she swung about and rose up and down more than she had done since we'd been left in her. 'There must be a big sea running on top,' said William Anderson, 'and if we were up there we'd be tossed about dreadful. Now the motion down here is just as easy as a cradle, and, what's more, we can't be sunk very deep; for if we were, there wouldn't be any motion at all.' About noon the next day we felt a sudden tremble and shake run through the whole ship, and far down under us we heard a rumbling and grinding, that nearly scared me out of my wits. I first thought we'd struck bottom, but William he said that couldn't be, for it was just as light in the cabin as it had been, and if we'd gone down it would have grown much darker, of course. The rumbling stopped after a little while, and then it seemed to grow lighter instead of darker; and Sam, who was looking up at the stern windows over our heads, he sung out, 'Sky!' And, sure enough, we could see the blue sky, as clear as daylight, through those windows! And then the ship, she turned herself on the slant, pretty much as she had been when her forward compartment first took in water, and we found ourselves standing on the cabin floor instead of the bulkhead. I was near one of the open staterooms, and as I looked in, there was the sunlight coming through the wet glass in the window, and more cheerful than anything I ever saw before in this world. William Anderson he just made one jump, and, unscrewing one of the stateroom windows, he jerked it open. We had thought the air inside was good enough to last some time longer; but when that window was open and the fresh air came rushing in, it was a different sort of thing, I can tell you. William put his head out, and looked up and down and all around. 'She's nearly all out of water!' he shouted, 'and we can open the cabin door.' Then we all three rushed at those stairs, which were nearly right side up now, and we had the cabin door open in no time. When we looked out, we saw that the ship was truly floating pretty much as she had been when the captain and crew left her, though we all agreed that her deck didn't slant as much forward as it did then. 'Do you know what's happened?' sung out William Anderson, after he'd stood still for a minute, to look around and think. 'That bobbing up and down that the vessel got last night shook up and settled down the pig-iron inside of her, and the iron plates in the bow, that were smashed and loosened by the collision, have given way under the weight, and the whole cargo of pig-iron has burst through and gone to the bottom. Then, of course, up we came! Didn't I tell you something would happen to make us all right?'

"Well, I won't make this story any longer than I can help. The next day after that, we were taken off by a sugar-ship bound north, and we were carried safe back to Ulford, where we found our captain and the crew, who had been picked up by a ship after they'd been three or four days in their boats. This ship had sailed our way to find us, which, of course, she couldn't do, as at that time we were under water and out of sight.

"And now, sir," said the brother-in-law of J. George Watts to the Shipwreck Clerk, "to which of your classes does this wreck of mine belong?"

"Gents," said the Shipwreck Clerk, rising from his seat, "it's four o'clock, and at that hour this office closes."

Qu.—How fast duz sound travel?

Ans.—This depends a good deal upon the natur ov the noize yu are talking about. The sound ov a dinner horn, for instance, travels a half a mile in a seckoned, while an invitashun tew git up in the morning I hav known to be 3 quarters ov an hour going up two pair ov stairs, and then not hav strength enuff left tew be heard.

JOSH BILLINGS

EXPERIENCE OF THE McWILLIAMSES
WITH MEMBRANEOUS CROUP

MARK TWAIN

[*As related to the author by Mr. McWilliams, a pleasant New York gentleman whom the said author met by chance on a journey.*]

Well, to go back to where I was before I digressed, to explain to you how that frightful and incurable disease, membraneous croup, was ravaging the town and driving all mothers mad with terror. I called Mrs. McWilliams's attention to little Penelope and said:

"Darling, I wouldn't let that child be chewing that pine stick, if I were you."

"Precious, where is the harm in it?" said she, but at the same time preparing to take away the stick—for women cannot receive even the most palpably judicious suggestion without arguing it; that is, married women.

I replied:

"Love, it is notorious that pine is the least nutritious wood that a child can eat."

My wife's hand paused in the act of taking the stick, and returned itself to her lap. She bridled perceptibly, and said:

"Hubby, you know better than that. You know you do! Doctors *all* say that the turpentine in pine wood is good for weak back and the kidneys."

"Ah—I was under a misapprehension. I did not know that the child's kidneys and spine were affected, and that the family physician had recommended—"

"Who said the child's spine and kidneys were affected?"

"My love, you intimated it."

"The idea! I never intimidated anything of the kind."

"Why, my dear, it hasn't been two minutes since you said—"

"Bother what I said! I don't care what I did say. There isn't any harm in the child's chewing a bit of pine stick if she wants to, and you know it perfectly well. And she *shall* chew it, too. So there, now!"

"Say no more, my dear. I now see the force of your reasoning, and I will go and order two or three cords of the best pine wood to-day. No child of mine shall want while I—"

"O, *please* go along to your office and let me have some peace. A body can never make the simplest remark but you must take it up and go to arguing and arguing and arguing, till you don't know what you are talking about, and you *never* do!"

"Very well, it shall be as you say. But there is a want of logic in your last remark which—"

However, she was gone with a flourish before I could finish, and had taken the child with her. That night at dinner she confronted me with a face as white as a sheet:

"O, Mortimer, there's another! Little Georgie Gordon is taken."

"Membraneous croup?"

"Membraneous croup."

"Is there any hope for him?"

"None in the wide world. O, what is to become of us!"

By and by a nurse brought in our Penelope to say good-night and offer the customary prayer at the mother's knee. In the midst of "Now I lay me down to sleep," she gave a slight cough. My wife fell back like one stricken with death. But the next moment she was up and brimming with the activities which terror inspires.

She commanded that the child's crib be removed from the nursery to our bedroom; and she went along to see the order executed. She took me with her, of course. We got matters arranged with speed. A cot bed was put up in my wife's dressing-room for the nurse. But now Mrs.

McWilliams said we were too far away from the other baby, and what if *he* were to have the symptoms in the night—and she blanched again, poor thing.

We then restored the crib and the nurse to the nursery, and put up a bed for ourselves in a room adjoining.

Presently, however, Mrs. McWilliams said, "Suppose the baby should catch it from Penelope?" This thought struck a new panic to her heart, and the tribe of us could not get the crib out of the nursery again fast enough to satisfy my wife, though she assisted in her own person and wellnigh pulled the crib to pieces in her frantic hurry.

We moved down-stairs; but there was no place there to stow the nurse, and Mrs. McWilliams said the nurse's experience would be an inestimable help. So we returned, bag and baggage, to our own bed-room once more, and felt a great gladness, like storm-buffeted birds that have found their nest again.

Mrs. McWilliams sped to the nursery to see how things were going on there. She was back in a moment with a new dread. She said:

"What *can* make Baby sleep so?"

I said:

"Why, my darling, Baby *always* sleeps like a graven image."

"I know, I know. But there's something peculiar about his sleep, now. He seems to—to—he seems to breathe so *regularly*. O, this is dreadful!"

"But, my dear, he always breathes regularly."

"Oh, I know it, but there's something frightful about it now. His nurse is too young and inexperienced. Maria shall stay there with her, and be on hand if anything happens."

"That is a good idea, but who will help *you*?"

"You can help me all I want. I wouldn't allow anybody to do any-thing but myself, any how, at such a time as this."

I said I would feel mean to lie abed and sleep, and leave her to watch and toil over our little patient all the weary night. But she reconciled me to it. So old Maria departed and took up her ancient quarters in the nursery.

Penelope coughed twice in her sleep.

"Oh, why *don't* that doctor come! Mortimer, this room is too warm. This room is certainly too warm. Turn off the register—quick!"

I shut it off, glancing at the thermometer at the same time, and wondering to myself if 70 *was* too warm for a sick child.

The coachman arrived from down-town now, with the news that our physician was ill and confined to his bed. Mrs. McWilliams turned a dead eye upon me, and said in a dead voice:

"There is a Providence in it. It is foreordained. He never was sick before. Never. We have not been living as we ought to live, Mortimer. Time and time again I have told you so. Now you see the result. Our child will never get well. Be thankful if you can forgive yourself; I never can forgive *my*self."

I said, without intent to hurt, but with heedless choice of words, that I could not see that we had been living such an abandoned life.

"*Mortimer!* Do you want to bring the judgment upon Baby, too!"

Then she began to cry, but suddenly exclaimed:

"The doctor must have sent medicines!"

I said:

"Certainly. They are here. I was only waiting for you to give me a chance."

"Well, do give them to me! Don't you know that every moment is precious now? But what was the use in sending medicines, when he *knows* that the disease is incurable?"

I said that while there was life there was hope.

"Hope! Mortimer, you know no more what you are talking about than the child unborn. If you would—. As I live, the directions say, give one teaspoonful once an hour! Once an hour!—as if we had a whole year before us to save the child in! Mortimer, please hurry. Give the poor perishing thing a tablespoonful, and *try* to be quick!"

"Why, my dear, a tablespoonful might—"

"*Don't* drive me frantic! . . . . There, there, there! my precious, my own; it's nasty bitter stuff, but it's good for Nelly—good for Mother's precious darling; and it will make her well. There, there, there! put the little head on Mamma's breast and go to sleep, and pretty soon—oh, I know she can't live till morning! Mortimer, a tablespoonful every half hour will—. Oh, the child needs belladonna too; I know she does—and aconite. Get them, Mortimer. Now, do let me have my way. You know nothing about these things."

We now went to bed, placing the crib close to my wife's pillow. All this turmoil had worn upon me, and within two minutes I was something more than half asleep. Mrs. McWilliams roused me:

"Darling, is that register turned on?"

"No."

"I thought as much. Please turn it on at once. The room is cold."

I turned it on, and presently fell asleep again. I was aroused once more:

"Dearie, would you mind moving the crib to your side of the bed? It is nearer the register."

I moved it, but had a collision with the rug and woke up the child. I dozed off once more, while my wife quieted the sufferer. But in a little while these words came murmuring remotely through the fog of my drowsiness:

"Mortimer, if we only had some goose-grease—will you ring?"

I climbed dreamily out, and stepped on a cat, which responded with a protest, and would have got a convincing kick for it if a chair had not got it instead.

"Now, Mortimer, why do you want to turn up the gas and wake up the child again?"

"Because I want to see how much I am hurt, Caroline."

"Well, look at the chair, too—I have no doubt it is ruined. Poor cat, suppose you had—"

"Now I am not going to suppose anything about the cat. It never would have occurred if Maria had been allowed to remain here and attend to these duties, which are in her line, and are not in mine."

"Now, Mortimer, I should think you would be ashamed to make a remark like that. It is a pity if you cannot do the few little things I ask of you at such an awful time as this when our child—"

"There, there, I will do anything you want. But I can't raise anybody with this bell. They're all gone to bed. Where is the goose-grease?"

"On the mantel-piece in the nursery. If you'll step there and speak to Maria—"

I fetched the goose-grease and went to sleep again. Once more I was called:

"Mortimer, I so hate to disturb you, but the room is still too cold for me to try to apply this stuff. Would you mind lighting the fire? It is all ready to touch a match to."

I dragged myself out and lit the fire, and then sat down disconsolate.

"Mortimer, don't sit there and catch your death of cold. Come to bed."

As I was stepping in, she said:

"But wait a moment. Please give the child some more of the medicine."

Which I did. It was a medicine which made a child more or less lively; so my wife made use of its waking interval to strip it and grease it all over with the goose-oil. I was soon asleep once more, but once more I had to get up.

"Mortimer, I feel a draft. I feel it distinctly. There is nothing so bad for this disease as a draft. Please move the crib in front of the fire."

I did it; and collided with the rug again, which I threw in the fire. Mrs. McWilliams sprang out of bed and rescued it, and we had some words. I had another trifling interval of sleep, and then got up, by request, and constructed a flax-seed poultice. This was placed upon the child's breast, and left there to do its healing work.

A wood fire is not a permanent thing. I got up every twenty minutes and renewed ours, and this gave Mrs. McWilliams the opportunity to shorten the times of giving the medicines by ten minutes, which was a great satisfaction to her. Now and then, between times, I reorganized the flax-seed poultices, and applied sinapisms and other sorts of blisters where unoccupied places could be found upon the child. Well, toward morning the wood gave out, and my wife wanted me to go down cellar and get some more. I said:

"My dear, it is a laborious job, and the child must be nearly warm enough, with her extra clothing. Now mightn't we put on another layer of poultices and—"

I did not finish, because I was interrupted. I lugged wood up from below for some little time, and then turned in and fell to snoring as only a man can whose strength is all gone and whose soul is worn out. Just at broad daylight I felt a grip on my shoulder that brought me to my senses suddenly. My wife was glaring down upon me and gasping. As soon as she could command her tongue she said:

"It is all over! All over! The child's perspiring! What *shall* we do?"

"Mercy! how you terrify me! *I* don't know what we ought to do. Maybe if we scraped her and put her in the draft again—"

"O, idiot! There is not a moment to lose! Go for the doctor. Go yourself. Tell him he *must* come, dead or alive."

I dragged that poor sick man from his bed and brought him. He looked at the child and said she was not dying. This was joy unspeakable to me, but it made my wife as mad as if he had offered her a personal affront. Then he said the child's cough was only caused by some trifling irritation or other in the throat. At this I thought my wife had a mind to show him the door. Now the doctor said he would make the child cough harder and dislodge the trouble. So he gave her something that sent her into a spasm of coughing, and presently up came a little wood splinter or so.

"This child has no membraneous croup," said he. "She has been chewing a bit of pine shingle or something of the kind, and got some little slivers in her throat. They won't do her any hurt."

"No," said I, "I can well believe that. Indeed, the turpentine that is in them is very good for certain sorts of diseases that are peculiar to children. My wife will tell you so."

But she did not. She turned away in disdain and left the room; and since that time there is one episode in our life which we never refer to. Hence the tide of our days flows by in deep and untroubled serenity.

[Very few married men have such an experience as McWilliams's, and so the author of this book thought that maybe the novelty of it would give it a passing interest to the reader.]

THE HODJA'S DONKEY ON HIS VERACITY

S. S. COX

A friend calls on Narr-ed-din to borrow his donkey.

"Very sorry," says the Hodja, who does not want to lend the animal, "but the donkey is not here; I have hired him out for the day."

Unfortunately, just at that moment the donkey begins to bray loudly, thus giving the direct lie to the Hodja.

"How is this, Hodja?" says his friend; "you say the donkey is away, and here he is braying in the stable!"

The Hodja, nothing daunted, replies in a grave manner:

"My dear sir, please do not demean yourself so low as to believe the donkey rather than myself—a fellow-man and a venerable Hodja with a long gray beard."

The moral of the last fable some people will never perceive. It is this:

An ass will always reveal himself by some inappropriate remark. Asses should be seldom seen, and never heard. The wise man hideth his ass when the borrower cometh around.

LITTLE BREECHES

JOHN HAY

John Hay, born in Salem, Ind., October 8, 1838, and best known as a humorist through his "Pike County Ballads," has had a varied career in politics, war, diplomacy, journalism and literature. Appointed one of Lincoln's private secretaries in 1861, he served with ability in the war, with distinction as Secretary of Legation in Paris, Vienna and Madrid, wrote his signally important book on Spain, "Castilian Days," became connected with the N. Y. *Tribune* on his return, and was afterwards Assistant Secretary of State under President Hayes. He is a graduate of Brown University, and was bred to the law.

I don't go much on religion,
　　I never ain't had no show;
But I've got a middlin' tight grip, sir,
　　On the handful o' things I know.
I don't pan out on the prophets
　　And free-will, and that sort of thing—
But I b'lieve in God and the angels,
　　Ever sence one night last spring.

I come into town with some turnips,
　　And my little Gabe come along—
No four-year-old in the county
　　Could beat him for pretty and strong,
Peart and chipper and sassy,
　　Always ready to swear and fight—

And I'd larnt him to chaw terbacker
    Jest to keep his milk-teeth white.

The snow come down like a blanket
    As I passed by Taggart's store;
I went in for a jug of molasses
    And left the team at the door.
They scared at something and started—
    I heard one little squall,
And hell-to-split over the prairie
    Went team, Little Breeches and all.

Hell-to-split over the prairie!
    I was almost froze with skeer;
But we rousted up some torches,
    And sarched for 'em far and near.
At last we struck horses and wagon.
    Snowed under a soft white mound,
Upsot, dead beat—but of little Gabe
    Nor hide nor hair was found.

And here all hope soured on me,
    Of my fellow-critter's aid—
I jest flopped down on my marrow-bones,
    Crotch-deep in the snow, and prayed.

By this, the torches was played out,
    And me and Isrul Parr
Went off for some wood to a sheepfold
    That he said was somewhar thar.

We found it at last, and a little shed
    Where they shut up the lambs at night.
We looked in and seen them huddled thar,
    So warm and sleepy and white;
And THAR sot Little Breeches, and chirped,
    As peart as ever you see,
"I want a chaw of terbacker,
    And that's what's the matter of me."

How did he git thar? Angels.
    He could never have walked in that storm,

They jest scooped down and toted him
   To what it was safe and warm.
And I think that saving a little child,
   And bringing him to his own,
Is a derned sight better business
   Than loafing around The Throne.

LOVE'S YOUNG DREAM

W. D. HOWELLS

"Our acquaintance has the charm of novelty every time we meet," she said once, when pressed hard by Mrs. Ellison. "We are growing better strangers, Mr. Arbuton and I. By and by, some morning, we shall not know each other by sight. I can barely recognize him now, though I thought I knew him pretty well once. I want you to understand that I speak as an unbiased spectator, Fanny."

"Oh, Kitty! how can you accuse me of trying to pry into your affairs?" cries injured Mrs. Ellison, and settles herself in a more comfortable posture for listening.

"I don't accuse you of anything. I'm sure you've a right to know everything about me. Only, I want you really to know."

"Yes, dear," says the matron, with hypocritical meekness.

"Well," resumes Kitty, "there are things that puzzle me more and more about him—things that used to amuse me at first, because I didn't actually believe that they could be, and that I felt like defying afterwards. But now I can't bear up against them. They frighten me, and seem to deny me the right to be what I believe I am."

"I don't understand you, Kitty."

"Why, you've seen how it is with us at home, and how Uncle Jack has brought us up. We never had a rule for anything, except to do what was right, and to be careful of the rights of others."

"Well!"

"Well, Mr. Arbuton seems to have lived in a world where everything is regulated by some rigid law that it would be death to break. Then, you know, at home we are always talking about people, and discussing them; but we always talk of each person for what he is in himself, and I always thought a person could refine himself if he tried, and was sincere, and not conceited. But *he* seems to judge people according to their origin and locality and calling, and to believe that all refinement must come from just such training and circumstances as his own. Without exactly saying so, he puts everything else quite out of the question. He doesn't appear to dream that there can be any different opinion. He tramples upon all that I have been taught to believe; and though I cling the closer to my idols, I can't help, now and then, trying myself by his criterions; and then I find myself wanting in every civilized trait, and my whole life coarse and poor, and all my associations hopelessly degraded. I think his ideas are hard and narrow, and I believe that even my little experience would prove them false; but then, they are his, and I can't reconcile them with what I see is good in him."

Kitty spoke with half-averted face where she sat beside one of the front windows, looking absently out on the distant line of violet hills beyond Charlesbourg, and now and then lifting her glove from her lap and letting it drop again.

"Kitty," said Mrs. Ellison in reply to her difficulties, "you oughtn't to sit against a light like that. It makes your profile quite black to any one back in the room."

"Oh well, Fanny, I'm not black in reality."

"Yes, but a young lady ought always to think how she is looking. Suppose some one was to come in."

"Dick's the only one likely to come in just now, and he wouldn't mind it. But if you like it better, I'll come and sit by you," said Kitty, and took her place beside the sofa.

Her hat was in her hand, her sacque on her arm; the fatigue of a recent walk gave her a soft pallor, and languor of face and attitude. Mrs. Ellison admired her pretty looks, with a generous regret that they should be wasted on herself, and then asked, "Where were you this afternoon?"

"Oh, we went to the Hotel Dieu, for one thing, and afterwards we looked into the courtyard of the convent; and there another of his pleasant little traits came out—a way he has of always putting you in the wrong, even when it's a matter of no consequence any way, and there needn't be any right or wrong about it. I remembered the place because Mrs. March, you know, showed us a rose that one of the nuns in the hospital gave her, and I tried to tell Mr. Arbuton about it, and he graciously took it as if poor Mrs. March had made an advance towards his acquaintance. I do wish you could see what a lovely place that courtyard is, Fanny. It's so strange that such a thing should be right there, in the heart of this crowded city; but there it was with its peasant cottage on one side, and its long low barns on the other, and those wide-horned Canadian cows munching at the racks of hay outside, and pigeons and chickens all about among their feet"—

"Yes, yes; never mind all that, Kitty. You know I hate nature. Go on about Mr. Arbuton," said Mrs. Ellison, who did not mean a sarcasm.

"It looked like a farmyard in a picture, far out in the country somewhere," resumed Kitty; "and Mr. Arbuton did it the honor to say it was just like Normandy."

"Kitty!"

"He did, indeed, Fanny; and the cows didn't go down on their knees out of gratitude either. Well, off on the right were the hospital buildings climbing up, you know, with their stone walls and steep roofs, and windows dropped about over them, like our convent here; and there was an artist there, sketching it all; he had such a brown, pleasant face, with a little black mustache and imperial, and such gay black eyes, that nobody could help falling in love with him; and he was talking in such a free-and-easy way with the lazy workmen and women overlooking him. He jotted down a little image of the Virgin in a niche on the wall, and one of the people called out—Mr. Arbuton was translating— 'Look there! with one touch he's made our Blessed Lady.' 'Oh,' says the painter, 'that's nothing; with three touches I can make the entire Holy Family.' And they all laughed; and that little joke, you know, won my heart,—I don't hear many jokes from Mr. Arbuton—and so I said what a blessed life a painter's must be, for it would give you a right to be a vagrant, and you could wander through the world, seeing everything that was lovely and funny, and nobody could blame you; and I wondered everybody who had the chance didn't learn to sketch. Mr. Arbuton took it seriously, and said people had to have something more than the chance to learn before they could sketch, and that most of them were an affliction with their sketch-books, and he had seen too much of the sad effects of drawing from casts. And he put me in the wrong, as he always does. Don't you see? I didn't want to learn drawing; I wanted to be a painter, and go about sketching beautiful old convents, and sit on camp-stools on pleasant afternoons, and joke with people. Of course, he couldn't understand that. But I know the artist could. Oh, Fanny, if it had only been the painter whose arm I took that first day on the boat, instead of Mr. Arbuton! But the worst of it is, he is making a hypocrite of me, and a cowardly, unnatural girl. I wanted to go nearer and look at the painter's sketch; but I was ashamed to say I'd never seen a real artist's sketch before, and I'm getting to be ashamed, or to seem ashamed, of a great many innocent things. He has a way of not seeming to think it possible that any one he associates with can differ from him. And I do differ from him. I differ from him as much as my whole past life differs from his; I know I'm just the kind of production he disapproves of, and that I'm altogether irregular and unauthorized and unjustifiable; and though it's funny to have him talking to me as if I must have the sympathy of a rich girl with his ideas, it's provoking, too, and it's very bad for me. Up to the present moment, Fanny, if you want to know, that's the principal effect of Mr. Arbuton on me. I'm being gradually snubbed and scared into treasons, stratagems, and spoils."

Mrs. Ellison did not find all this so very grievous, for she was one of those women who like a snub from the superior sex, if it does not involve a slight to their beauty or their power of pleasing. But she thought it best not to enter into the question, and merely said, "But surely, Kitty, there are a great many things in Mr. Arbuton that you must respect."

"Respect? Oh, yes, indeed! But respect isn't just the thing for one who seems to consider himself sacred. Say *revere*, Fanny; say revere!"

Kitty had risen from her chair, but Mrs. Ellison waved her again to her seat with an imploring gesture. "Don't go, Kitty; I'm not half done with you yet. You *must* tell me something more. You've stirred me up so, now. I know you don't always have such disagreeable times. You've often come home quite happy. What do you generally find to talk about? Do tell me some particulars for once."

"Why, little topics come up, you know. But sometimes we don't talk at all, because I don't like to say what I think or feel, for fear I should be thinking or feeling something vulgar. Mr. Arbuton is rather a blight upon conversation in that way. He makes you doubtful whether there isn't something a little common in breathing, and the circulation of the blood, and whether it wouldn't be true refinement to stop them."

"Stuff, Kitty! He's very cultivated, isn't he? Don't you talk about books? He's read everything, I suppose."

"Oh, yes, he's *read* enough."

"What do you mean?"

"Nothing. Only sometimes it seems to me as if he hadn't read because he loved it, but because he thought it due to himself. But maybe I'm mistaken. I could imagine a delicate poem shutting up half its sweetness from his cold, cold scrutiny,—if you will excuse the floweriness of the idea."

"Why, Kitty! don't you think he's refined? I'm sure, I think he's a *very* refined person."

"He's a very elaborated person. But I don't think it would make much difference to him what our opinion of him was. His own good opinion would be quite enough."

"Is he—is he—always agreeable?"

"I thought we were discussing his mind, Fanny. I don't know that I feel like enlarging upon his manners," said Kitty, slyly.

"But surely, Kitty," said the matron, with an air of argument, "there's some connection between his mind and his manners."

"Yes, I suppose so. I don't think there's much between his heart and his manners. They seem to have been put on him instead of having come out of him. He's very well trained, and nine times out of ten he's so exquisitely polite that it's wonderful; but the tenth time he may say something so rude that you can't believe it."

"Then you like him nine times out of ten."

"I didn't say that. But for the tenth time, it's certain, his training doesn't hold out, and he seems to have nothing natural to fall back upon. But you can believe that, if he knew he'd been disagreeable, he'd be sorry for it."

"Why, then, Kitty, how can you say that there's no connection between his heart and manners? This very thing proves that they come from his heart. Don't be illogical, Kitty," said Mrs. Ellison, and her nerves added, *sotto voce*, "if you *are* so abominably provoking!"

"Oh," responded the young girl, with the kind of laugh that meant it was, after all, not such a laughing matter, "I didn't say he'd be sorry for *you!* Perhaps he would; but he'd be certain to be sorry for himself. It's with his politeness as it is with his reading; he seems to consider it something that's due to himself as a gentleman to treat people well;

and it isn't in the least as if he cared for *them*. He wouldn't like to fail in such a point."

"But, Kitty, isn't that to his credit?"

"Maybe. I don't say. If I knew more about the world, perhaps I should admire it. But now, you see"—and here Kitty's laugh grew more natural, and she gave a subtle caricature of Mr. Arbuton's air and tone as she spoke—"I can't help feeling that it's a little—vulgar."

Mrs. Ellison could not quite make out how much Kitty really meant of what she had said. She gasped once or twice for argument; then she sat up, and beat the sofa-pillows vengefully in composing herself anew, and finally—"Well, Kitty, I'm sure I don't know what to make of it all," she said with a sigh.

"Why, we're not obliged to make anything of it, Fanny, there's that comfort," replied Kitty; and then there was a silence, while she brooded over the whole affair of her acquaintance with Mr. Arbuton, which this talk had failed to set in a more pleasant or hopeful light. It had begun like a romance; she had pleased her fancy, if not her heart, with the poetry of it; but at last she felt exiled and strange in his presence. She had no right to a different result, even through any deep feeling in the matter; but while she owned, with her half-sad, half-comical, consciousness, that she had been tacitly claiming and expecting too much, she softly pitied herself, with a kind of impersonal compassion, as if it were some other girl whose pretty dream had been broken. Its ruin involved the loss of another ideal; for she was aware that there had been gradually rising in her mind an image of Boston, different alike from the holy place of her childhood, the sacred city of the anti-slavery heroes and martyrs, and from the jesting, easy, sympathetic Boston of Mr. and Mrs. March. This new Boston with which Mr. Arbuton inspired her, was a Boston of mysterious prejudices and lofty reservations; a Boston of high and difficult tastes, that found its social ideal in the Old World, and that shrank from contact with the reality of this; a Boston as alien as Europe to her simple experiences, and that seemed to be proud only of the things that were unlike other American things; a Boston that would rather perish by fire and sword than be suspected of vulgarity; a critical, fastidious, and reluctant Boston, dissatisfied with the rest of the hemisphere, and gelidly self-satisifed in so far as it was not in the least the Boston of her fond preconceptions. It was, doubtless, no more the real Boston we know and love, than either of the others; and it perplexed her more than it need, even if it had not been mere phantasm. It made her suspicious of Mr. Arbuton's behavior towards her, and observant of little things that might very well have otherwise escaped her. The bantering humor, the light-hearted trust and self-reliance with which she had once met him, deserted her, and only returned fitfully when some accident called her out of herself, and made her forget the differences that she now too plainly saw in their ways of thinking and feeling. It was a greater and greater effort to place herself in sympathy with him; she relaxed into a languid self-contempt, as if she had been playing a part, when she succeeded. "Sometimes, Fanny," she said, now, after a long pause, speaking in behalf of that other girl she had been thinking of, "it seems to me as if Mr. Arbuton were all gloves and slim umbrella—the mere husk of well-dressed culture and good manners. His looks *do* promise everything; but, oh dear me! I should be sorry for any one that was in love with him. Just imagine some girl meeting with such a man, and taking a fancy to him! I suppose she never would quite believe but that he must somehow be what she first thought him, and she would go down to her grave believing that she had failed to understand him. What a curious story it would make!"

"Then why don't you write it, Kitty?" asked Mrs. Ellison. "No one could do it better."

Kitty flushed quickly; then she smiled: "Oh, I don't think I could do it at all. It wouldn't be a very easy story to work out. Perhaps he might never do anything positively disagreeable enough to make anybody condemn him. The only way you could show his character would be to have her do and say hateful things to him, when she couldn't help it, and then repent of it, while he was impassively perfect through everything. And perhaps, after all, he might be regarded by some stupid people as the injured one. Well, Mr. Arbuton has been very polite to us, I'm sure, Fanny," she said after another pause, as she rose from her chair, "and maybe I'm unjust to him. I beg his pardon of you; and I wish," she added, with a dull disappointment quite her own, and a pang of surprise at words that seemed to utter themselves, "that he would go away."

"Why, Kitty, I'm shocked!" said Mrs. Ellison, rising from her cushions.

"Yes; so am I, Fanny."

"Are you really tired of him, then?"

Kitty did not answer, but turned away her face a little, where she stood beside the chair in which she had been sitting.

Mrs. Ellison put out her hand towards her. "Kitty, come here," she said with imperious tenderness.

"No, I won't, Fanny," answered the young girl, in a trembling voice. She raised the glove that she had been nervously swinging back and forth, and bit hard upon the button of it. "I don't know whether I'm tired of *him*—though he isn't a person to rest one a great deal—but I'm tired of *it*. I'm perplexed and troubled the whole time, and I don't see any end to it. Yes, I wish he would go away! Yes, he *is* tiresome! What is he staying here for? If he thinks himself so much better than all of us, I wonder he troubles himself with our company. It's quite time for him to go. No, Fanny, no," cried Kitty, with a little broken laugh, still rejecting the outstretched hand; "I'll be flat in private, if you please." And dashing her hand across her eyes, she flitted out of the room. At the door, she turned and said, "You needn't think it's what you think it is, Fanny."

"No indeed, dear; you're just overwrought."

"For I really wish he'd go."

THE BELLE OF VALLEJO

W. L. ALDEN

Vallejo, California, possesses a young lady of extraordinary beauty. She is, moreover, as intelligent and bold as she is beautiful, and in grappling with a sudden emergency she is probably unequaled by any one of her sex. Naturally, she is the admiration of every young man in the town. In fact, she is beyond the reach of rivalry. The other young ladies of Vallejo are perfectly well aware that it is hopeless for them to enter the lists with her. They never expect to receive calls from marriageable young men except on the off nights of the Vallejo belle, and though they doubtless murmur secretly against this dispensation, they apparently accept it as a law of nature.

For two years the beauty in question, whom we will call Miss Ecks, received the homage of her multitudinous admirers, and took an evident delight in adding to their number. So far from selecting any particular young man for front-gate or back-piazza duty, she preferred to entertain one or two dozen simultaneous admirers in the full blaze of the brilliantly lighted front parlor. It is only fair to add that she was an earnest young woman, who despised coquetry and never dreamed of showing favor to one young man in order to exasperate the rest.

That so brilliant a girl should have finally selected a meek young minister on whom to lavish her affections was certainly a surprise to all who knew her, and when it was first rumored that she had made such a selection, Vallejo refused to believe it. The minister made his regular nightly calls upon the object of his affections, but an average quantity of eleven other young men never failed to be present. Of course, he could not obtain a single moment of private happiness with his eleven rivals sitting all around the room, unless he made his evening call at a preposterously early hour. He did try this expedient once or twice, but the only result was that the eleven admirers at once followed his example. In these circumstances he began to grow thin with suppressed affection, and the young lady, alarmed at his condition, made up her mind that something must be done without delay.

About three weeks ago the young minister presented himself in his beloved's front parlor at 6:50 P.M., and, in the ten minutes that elapsed before the first of his rivals rang the bell, he painted the misery of courting by battalions in the most harrowing terms. Miss Ecks listened to him with deep sympathy, and promised him that if he would stay until nine o'clock, the last of the objectionable young men would be so thoroughly disposed of that for the rest of the evening he would have the field to himself. Full of confidence in the determination and resources of his betrothed, his spirits returned, and he was about to express his gratitude with his lips, as well as his heart, when the first young man was ushered into the room.

Miss Ecks received her unwelcome guest with great cordiality, and invited him to sit on a chair the back of which was placed close to a door. The door in question opened outward, and upon the top of a flight of stairs leading to the cellar. The latch was old and out of order, and the least pressure would cause it to fly open. In pursuance of a deep-laid plan, Miss Ecks so molded her conversation as to place the visitor at his ease. In a very few moments, he ceased to twist his fingers and writhe his legs, and presently tilted back his chair after the manner of a contented and happy man. No sooner did the back of the chair touch the door than the latter flew open, and the unhappy guest disappeared into the cellar with a tremendous crash. Checking the cry that arose from the astonished clergyman, Miss Ecks quietly reclosed the fatal door, placed a fresh chair in its vicinity, and calmly remarked, "That's one of them."

In five minutes more the second young man entered. Like his predecessor, he seated himself on the appointed chair, tipped back upon its hind-legs, and instantly vanished. "That's two of them," remarked the imperturbable beauty, as she closed the door and once more re-set the trap. From this time until nine o'clock a constant succession of young men went down those cellar stairs. Some of them groaned slightly after reaching the bottom, but not one returned. It was an unusually good night for young men, and Miss Ecks caught no less than fourteen between seven and nine o'clock. As the last one disappeared she turned to her horrified clergyman and said, "That's the last of them! Now for business!" but that mild young man had fainted. His nerves were unable to bear the strain, and when the moment of his wished-for monopoly of his betrothed had arrived he was unable to enjoy it.

Later in the evening he revived sufficiently to seek a railway station and fly forever from his remorseless charmer. The inquest that was subsequently held upon the fourteen young men will long be remembered as a most impressive scene. Miss Ecks was present with her black hair loose, and the tears stood in her magnificent eyes as she testified that she could not imagine what induced the young men to go down cellar. The jury without the slightest hesitation found that they had one and all committed suicide, and the coroner personally thanked the young lady for her lucid testimony. She is now more popular than ever, and, with the loss of her own accepted lover, has renewed her former fondness for society, and nightly entertains all the surviving young men of Vallejo.

This shows what the magnificent climate of California can accomplish in the production of girls, when it really tries.

KITTY ANSWERS

W. D. HOWELLS

It was the dimmest twilight when Kitty entered Mrs. Ellison's room and sank down on the first chair in silence.

"The colonel met a friend at the St. Louis, and forgot about the expedition, Kitty," said Fanny, "and he only came in half an hour ago. But it's just as well; I know you've had a splendid time. Where's Mr. Arbuton?"

Kitty burst into tears.

"Why, has anything happened to him!" cried Mrs. Ellison, springing towards her.

"To him? No! What should happen to *him?*" Kitty demanded with an indignant accent.

"Well, then, has anything happened to *you?*"

"I don't know if you can call it *happening*. But I suppose you'll be satisfied now, Fanny. He's offered himself to me." Kitty uttered the last words with a sort of violence, as if, since the fact must be stated, she wished it to appear in the sharpest relief.

"Oh dear!" said Mrs. Ellison, not so well satisfied as the successful match-maker ought to be. So long as it was a marriage in the abstract, she had never ceased to desire it; but as to the actual union of Kitty and this Mr. Arbuton, of whom, really, they knew so little, and of whom, if she searched her heart, she had as little liking as knowledge, it was another affair. Mrs. Ellison trembled at her triumph, and began to think that failure would have been easier to bear. Were they in the least suited to each other? Would she like to see poor Kitty chained for life to that impassive egotist, whose very merits were repellent, and whose modesty even seemed to convict and snub you? Mrs. Ellison was not able to put the matter to herself with moderation, either way; doubtless she did Mr. Arbuton injustice now. "Did you accept him?" she whispered, feebly.

"Accept him?" repeated Kitty. "No!"

"Oh dear!" again sighed Mrs. Ellison, feeling that this was scarcely better, and not daring to ask further.

"I'm dreadfully perplexed, Fanny," said Kitty, after waiting for the questions which did not come, "and I wish you'd help me think."

"I will, darling. But I don't know that I'll be of much use. I begin to think I'm not very good at thinking."

Kitty, who longed chiefly to get the situation more distinctly before herself, gave no heed to this confession, but went on to rehearse the whole affair. The twilight lent her its veil; and in the kindly obscurity she gathered courage to face all the facts, and even to find what was droll in them.

"It was very solemn, of course, and I was frightened; but I tried to keep my wits about me, and *not* to say yes, simply because that was the easiest thing. I told him that I didn't know—and I don't; and that I must have time to think—and I must. He was very ungenerous, and said he had hoped I had already had time to think; and he couldn't seem to understand, or else I couldn't very well explain, how it had been with me all along."

"He might certainly say you had encouraged him," Mrs. Ellison remarked, thoughtfully.

"Encouraged him, Fanny? How can you accuse me of such indelicacy?"

"Encouraging isn't indelicacy. The gentlemen *have* to be encouraged, or of course they'd never have any courage. They're so timid, naturally."

"I don't think Mr. Arbuton is very timid. He seemed to think that he had only to ask as a matter of form, and I had no business to say anything. What has he ever done for me? And hasn't he often been intensely disagreeable? He oughtn't to have spoken just after overhearing what he did. It was horrid to do so. He was very obtuse, too, not to see that girls can't always be so certain of themselves as men, or, if they are, don't know they are as soon as they're asked."

"Yes," interrupted Mrs. Ellison, "that's the way with girls. I do believe that most of them—when they're young like you, Kitty—never think of marriage as the end of their flirtations. They'd just like the attentions and the romance to go on forever, and never turn into anything more serious; and they're not to blame for that, though they *do* get blamed for it."

"Certainly," assented Kitty, eagerly, "that's it; that's just what I was saying; that's the very reason why girls must have time to make up their minds. *You* had, I suppose."

"Yes, two minutes. Poor Dick was going back to his regiment, and stood with his watch in his hand. I said no, and called after him to correct myself. But, Kitty, if the romance had happened to stop without his saying anything, you wouldn't have liked that either, would you?"

"No," faltered Kitty, "I suppose not."

"Well, then, don't you see? That's a great point in his favor. How much time did you want, or did he give you?"

"I said I should answer before we left Quebec," answered Kitty, with a heavy sigh.

"Don't you know what to say now?"

"I can't tell. That's what I want you to help me think out."

Mrs. Ellison was silent for a moment before she said, "Well, then, I suppose we shall have to go back to the very beginning."

"Yes," assented Kitty, faintly.

"You did have a sort of fancy for him the first time you saw him, didn't you?" asked Mrs. Ellison, coaxingly, while forcing herself to be systematic and coherent, by a mental strain of which no idea can be given.

"Yes," said Kitty, yet more faintly; adding, "but I can't tell just what sort of a fancy it was. I suppose I admired him for being handsome and stylish, and for having such exquisite manners."

"Go on," said Mrs. Ellison. "And after you got acquainted with him?"

"Why, you know we've talked that over once already, Fanny."

"Yes, but we oughtn't to skip anything now," replied Mrs. Ellison, in a tone of judicial accuracy which made Kitty smile.

But she quickly became serious again, and said, "Afterwards I couldn't tell whether to like him or not, or whether he wanted me to. I think he acted very strangely for a person in—love. I used to feel so troubled and oppressed when I was with him. He seemed always to be making himself agreeable under protest."

"Perhaps that was just your imagination, Kitty."

"Perhaps it was; but it troubled me just the same."

"Well, and then?"

"Well, and then after that day of the Montgomery expedition, he seemed to change altogether, and to try always to be pleasant, and to do everything he could to make me like him. I don't know how to account for it. Ever since then he's been extremely careful of me, and behaved—of course without knowing it—as if I belonged to him already. Or may be I've imagined that too. It's very hard to tell what has really happened the last two weeks."

Kitty was silent, and Mrs. Ellison did not speak at once. Presently she asked, "Was his acting as if you belonged to him disagreeable?"

"I can't tell. I think it was rather presuming. I don't know why he did it."

"Do you respect him?" demanded Mrs. Ellison.

"Why, Fanny, I've always told you that I did respect some things in him."

Mrs. Ellison had the facts before her, and it rested upon her to sum them up, and do something with them. She rose to a sitting posture, and confronted her task.

"Well, Kitty, I'll tell you: I don't really know what to think. But I can say this: if you liked him at first, and then didn't like him, and afterwards he made himself more agreeable, and you didn't mind his behaving as if you belonged to him, and you respected him, but after all didn't think him fascinating—"

"He *is* fascinating—in a kind of way. He was, from the beginning. In a story his cold, snubbing, putting-down ways would have been perfectly fascinating."

"Then why didn't you take him?"

"Because," answered Kitty, between laughing and crying, "it isn't a story, and I don't know whether I like him."

"But do you think you might get to like him?"

"I don't know. His asking brings back all the doubts I ever had of him, and that I've been forgetting the past two weeks. I can't tell whether I like him or not. If I did, shouldn't I trust him more?"

"Well, whether you are in love or not, I'll tell you what you *are*, Kitty," cried Mrs. Ellison, provoked with her indecision, and yet relieved that the worst, whatever it was, was postponed thereby for a day or two.

"What?"

"You're—"

But at this important juncture the colonel came lounging in, and Kitty glided out of the room.

"Richard," said Mrs. Ellison, seriously, and in a tone implying that it was the colonel's fault, as usual, "you know what has happened, I suppose."

"No, my dear, I don't; but no matter: I will presently, I dare say."

"Oh, I wish for once you wouldn't be so flippant. Mr. Arbuton has offered himself to Kitty."

Colonel Ellison gave a quick, sharp whistle of amazement, but trusted himself to nothing more articulate.

"Yes," said his wife, responding to the whistle, "and it makes me perfectly wretched."

"Why, I thought you liked him."

"I didn't *like* him; but I thought it would be an excellent thing for Kitty."

"And won't it?"

"She doesn't know."

"No!"

The colonel was silent, while Mrs. Ellison stated the case in full, and its pending uncertainty. Then he exclaimed vehemently, as if his amazement had been growing upon him, "This is the most astonishing thing in the world! Who would ever have dreamt of that young iceberg being in love?"

"Haven't I *told* you all along he was?"

"Oh, yes, certainly; but that might be taken either way, you know. You would discover the tender passion in the eye of a potato."

"Colonel Ellison," said Fanny, with sternness, "why do you suppose he's been hanging about us for the last four weeks? Why should he have stayed in Quebec? Do you think he pitied *me*, or found *you* so agreeable?"

"Well, I thought he found us just tolerable, and was interested in the place."

Mrs. Ellison made no direct reply to this pitiable speech, but looked a scorn which, happily for the colonel, the darkness hid. Presently she said that bats did not express the blindness of men, for any bat could have seen what was going on.

"Why," remarked the colonel, "I did have a momentary suspicion that day of the Montgomery business; they both looked very confused when I saw them at the end of that street, and neither of them had anything to say; but that was accounted for by what you told me afterwards about his adventure. At the time I didn't pay much attention to the matter. The idea of his being in love seemed too ridiculous."

"Was it ridiculous for you to be in love with me?"

"No; and yet I can't praise my condition for its wisdom, Fanny."

"Yes! that's *like* men. As soon as one of them is safely married, he thinks all the love-making in the world has been done forever, and he can't conceive of two young people taking a fancy to each other."

"That's something so, Fanny. But granting—for the sake of argument merely—that Boston has been asking Kitty to marry him, and she doesn't know whether she wants him, what are we to do about it? *I* don't like him well enough to plead his cause; do you? When does Kitty think she'll be able to make up her mind?"

"She's to let him know before we leave."

The colonel laughed. "And so he's to hang about here on uncertainties for two whole days! That *is* rather rough on him. Fanny, what made you so eager for this business?"

"Eager? I *wasn't* eager."

"Well, then—reluctantly acquiescent?"

"Why, she's so literary, and that."

"And what?"

"How insulting! Intellectual, and so on; and I thought she would be just fit to live in a place where everybody is literary and intellectual. That is, I thought that, if I thought anything."

"Well," said the colonel, "you may have been right on the whole, but I don't think Kitty is showing any particular force of mind, just now, that would fit her to live in Boston. My opinion is, that it's ridiculous for her to keep him in suspense. She might as well answer him first as last. She's putting herself under a kind of obligation by her delay. I'll talk to her—"

"If you do, you'll kill her. You don't know how she's wrought up about it."

"Oh, well, I'll be careful of her sensibilities. It's my duty to speak with her. I'm here in the place of a parent. Besides, don't I know Kitty? I've almost brought her up."

"Maybe you're right. You're all so queer that perhaps you're right. Only, do be careful, Richard. You must approach the matter very delicately—indirectly, you know. Girls are different, remember, from young men, and you mustn't be blunt. Do manœuvre a little, for once in your life."

"All right, Fanny; you needn't be afraid of my doing anything awkward or sudden. I'll go to her room pretty soon, after she is quieted down, and have a good, calm old fatherly conversation with her."

The colonel was spared this errand; for Kitty had left some of her things on Fanny's table, and now came back for them with a lamp in her hand. Her averted face showed the marks of weeping; the corners of her firm-set lips were downward bent, as if some resolution which she had taken was very painful. This the anxious Fanny saw; and she made a gesture to the colonel which any woman would have understood to enjoin silence, or, at least, the utmost caution and tenderness of speech. The colonel summoned his *finesse* and said, cheerily, "Well, Kitty, what's Boston been saying to you?"

Mrs. Ellison fell back upon her sofa as if shot, and placed her hand over her face.

Kitty seemed not to hear her cousin. Having gathered up her things, she bent an unmoved face and an unseeing gaze full upon him, and glided from the room without a word.

"Well, upon my soul," cried the colonel, "this is a pleasant, nightmarish, sleep-walking, Lady-Macbethish little transaction. Confound it, Fanny! this comes of your wanting me to manœuvre: if you'd let me come straight *at* the subject—like a *man*—"

"*Please*, Richard, don't say anything more now," pleaded Mrs. Ellison in a broken voice. "You can't help it, I know; and I must do the best I can under the circumstances. Do go away for a little while, darling! Oh, dear!"

As for Kitty, when she had got out of the room in that phantasmal fashion, she dimly recalled, through the mists of her own trouble, the colonel's dismay at her so glooming upon him, and began to think that she had used poor Dick more tragically than she need, and so began to laugh softly to herself; but while she stood there at the entry window a moment, laughing in the moonlight, that made her lamp-flame thin, and painted her face with its pale lustre, Mr. Arbuton came down the attic stairway. He was not a man of quick fancies; but to one of even slower imaginations and of calmer mood, she might very well have seemed unreal, the creature of a dream, fantastic, intangible, insensible, arch, not wholly without some touch of the malign. In his heart he groaned over her beauty as if she were lost to him forever in this elfish transfiguration.

"Miss Ellison!" he scarcely more than whispered.

"You ought not to speak to me now," she answered, gravely.

"I know it; but I could not help it. For heaven's sake, do not let it tell against me. I wished to ask, if I should not see you to-morrow, to beg that all might go on as had been planned, and as if nothing had been said to-day."

"It'll be very strange," said Kitty. "My cousins know everything now. How can we meet before them?"

"I'm not going away without an answer, and we can't remain here without meeting. It will be less strange if we let everything take its course."

"Well."

"Thanks."

He looked strangely humbled, but even more bewildered than humbled.

She listened while he descended the steps, unbolted the street door, and closed it behind him. Then she passed out of the moonlight into her own room, whose close-curtained space the lamp filled with its ruddy glow, and revealed her again, no malicious sprite, but a very puzzled, conscientious, anxious young girl.

FOURTH OF JULY ORATION

Delivered July 4th, at Weathersfield, Connecticut, 1859

ARTEMUS WARD

[I delivered the follerin, about two years ago, to a large and discriminating awjince. I was 95 minits passin' a given pint. I have revised the orashun, and added sum things which makes it approposser to the times than it otherwise would be. I have also corrected the grammars and punktooated it. I do my own punktooatin nowdays. The Printers in *Vanity Fair* offiss can't punktooate worth a cent.]

Feller Citizens: I've been honored with a invite to norate before you to-day; and when I say that I skurcely feel ekal to the task, I'm sure you will believe me.

Weathersfield is justly celebrated for her onyins and patritism the world over, and to be axed to paws and address you on this my fust perfeshernal tower threw New England, causes me to feel—to feel—I may say it causes me to *feel*. (Grate applaws. They thought this was one of my eccentricities, while the fact is I was stuck. This between you and I.)

I'm a plane man. I don't know nothin' about no ded languages and am a little shaky on livin' ones. There4, expect no flowry talk from me. What I shall say will be to the pint, right strate out.

I'm not a politician, and my other habits air good. I've no enemys to reward, nor friends to sponge. But I'm a Union man. I luv the Union—it is a Big thing—and it makes my hart bleed to see a lot of ornery peple a-movin' heaven—no, not heaven, but the other place—and earth, to bust it up. Too much good blud was spilt in courtin' and marryin' that hily respectable female, the Goddess of Liberty, to git a divorce from her now. My own State of Injianny is celebrated for unhitchin' marrid peple with neatness and despatch, but you can't git a divorce from the Goddess up there. Not by no means. The old gal has behaved herself too well to cast her off now. I'm sorry the picters don't give her no shoes or stockins, but the band of stars upon her hed must continner to shine undimd, forever. I'm for the Union as she air, and withered be the arm of every ornery cuss who attempts to bust her up. That's me. I hav sed! [It was a very sweaty day, and at this pint of the orashun a man fell down with sunstroke. I told the awjince that considerin' the large number of putty gals present I was more afraid of a DAWTER STROKE. This was impromptoo, and seemed to amoose them very much.]

Feller Citizens—I hain't got time to notis the growth of Ameriky frum the time when the Mayflowers cum over in the *Pilgrim* and brawt Plymmuth Rock with them, but every skool boy nose our kareer has bin tremenjis. You will excuse me if I don't praise the early settlers of the Kolonies. Peple which hung idiotic old wimin for witches, burnt holes in Quakers' tongues and consined their feller critters to the tredmill and pillery on the slitest provocashun may have bin very nice folks in their way, but I must confess I don't admire their stile, and will pass them by. I spose they ment well, and so, in the novel and techin langwidge of the nusepapers, "peas to their ashis." Thare was no diskount, however, on them brave men who fit, bled and died in the American Revolushun. We needn't be afraid of setting 'em up two steep. Like my show, they will stand any amount of prase. G. Washington was abowt the best man this world ever sot eyes on. He was a clear-heded, warm-harted, and stiddy-goin' man. He never slopt over! The prevalin weakness of most public men is to SLOP OVER! [Put them words in large letters—A. W.] They git filled up and slop. They Rush Things. They travel too much on the high presher principle. They git on to the fust poplar hobbyhoss whitch trots along, not carin' a sent whether the beest is even-goin', clear sited and sound, or spavined, blind and bawky. Of course they git throwed eventooally, if not sooner. When they see the multitood goin' it blind they go Pel Mel with it, instid of exertin' theirselves to set it right. They can't see that the crowd which is now bearin' them triumfantly on its shoulders will soon diskiver its error and cast them into the hoss pond of Oblivyun, without the slitest hesitashun. Washington never slopt over. That wasn't George's stile. He luved his country dearly. He wasn't after the spiles. He was a human angil in a 3 kornered hat and knee britches, and we sha'n't see his like right away. My friends, we can't all be Washington's, but we kin all be patrits & behave ourselves in a human and a Christian manner. When we see a brother goin' down hill to Ruin let us not give him a push, but let us seeze rite hold of his coat-tails and draw him back to Morality.

Imagine G. Washington and P. Henry in the character of seseshers! As well fancy John Bunyan and Dr. Watts in spangled tites, doin the trapeze in a one-horse circus!

I tell you, feller-citizens, it would have been ten dollars in Jeff Davis's pocket if he'd never bin born!

———

Be shure and vote at leest once at all eleckshuns. Buckle on yer armer and go to the Poles. See two it that your naber is there. See that the kripples air provided with carriages. Go to the Poles and stay all day. Bewair of the infamous lies whitch the Opposishun will be sartin to git up fur perlitical effek on the eve of eleckshun. To the Poles! and when you git there vote jest as you darn please. This is a privilege we all persess, and it is 1 of the booties of this grate and free land.

I see mutch to admire in New Englan'. Your gals in particklar air abowt as snug bilt peaces of Calliker as I ever saw. They air fully equal to the corn fed gals of Ohio and Injianny, and will make the bestest kind of wives. It sets my Buzzum on fire to look at 'em.

Be still, my sole, be still,

& you, Hart, stop cuttin up!

I like your school houses, your meetin' houses, your enterprise, gumpshun &c., but your favorite Bevridge I disgust. I allude to New England Rum. It is wuss nor the korn whisky of Injianny, which eats threw stone jugs & will turn the stummuck of the most shiftliss Hog. I seldom seek consolashun in the flowin Bole, but t'other day I wurrid down some of your Rum. The fust glass indused me to swear like a infooriated trooper. On takin' the secund glass I was seezed with a desire to break winders, & arter imbibin' the third glass I knockt a small boy down, pickt his pocket of a *New York Ledger*, and wildly commenced readin' Sylvanus Kobb's last Tail. It's dreadful stuff—a sort of lickwid litenin, gut up under the personal supervishun of the devil—tears men's inards all to peaces and makes their noses blossom as the Lobster. Shun it as you would a wild hyeny with a firebrand tied to his tale, and while you air abowt it you will do a first-rate thing for yourself and everybody abowt you by shunnin all kinds of intoxication lickers. You don't need 'em no more'n a cat needs 2 tales, sayin' nothin' abowt the trubble and sufferin' they cawse. But unless your inards air cast-iron, avoid New Englan's favorite Bevridge.

My friends, I'm dun. I tear myself away from you with tears in my eyes & a pleasant odor of Onyins abowt my close. In the langwidge of Mister Catterline to the Rummuns, I go, but perhaps I shall cum back agin. Adoo, peple of Weathersfield. Be virtuous & you'll be happy

THE PARSON'S HORSE-RACE

HARRIET BEECHER STOWE

Harriet Beecher Stowe, the author of "Uncle Tom's Cabin," the most famous novel ever written, and of other works of world-wide celebrity, was born at Litchfield, Conn., in 1812. She was married in her twenty-first year to Calvin E. Stowe, and removed from Hartford to Cincinnati, where she wrote her first books, and gathered the material for her great work. She has, since 1850, lived in the East, and now divides her year between Hartford and Florida. "Oldtown Fireside Stories" is one of several volumes of New England sketches.

"Wal, now, this 'ere does beat all! I wouldn't 'a' thought it o' the deacon."

So spoke Sam Lawson, drooping in a discouraged, contemplative attitude in front of an equally discouraged looking horse, that had just been brought to him by the Widow Simpkins for medical treatment. Among Sam's many accomplishments, he was reckoned in the neighborhood an oracle in all matters of this kind, especially by women, whose helplessness in meeting such emergencies found unfailing solace under his compassionate willingness to attend to any business that did not strictly belong to him, and from which no pecuniary return was to be expected.

The Widow Simpkins had bought this horse of Deacon Atkins, apparently a fairly well-appointed brute, and capable as he was good-looking. A short, easy drive, when the Deacon held the reins, had shown off his points to advantage; and the widow's small stock of ready savings had come forth freely in payment for what she thought was a bargain. When, soon after coming into possession, she discovered that her horse, if driven with any haste, panted in a fearful manner, and that he appeared to be growing lame, she waxed wroth, and went to the Deacon in anger, to be met only with the smooth reminder that the animal was all right when she took him; that she had seen him tried herself. The widow was of a nature somewhat spicy, and expressed herself warmly: "It's a cheat and a shame, and I'll take the law on ye!"

"What law will you take?" said the unmoved Deacon. "Wasn't it a fair bargain?"

"I'll take the law of God," said the widow, with impotent indignation; and she departed to pour her cares and trials into the ever ready ear of Sam. Having assumed the care of the animal, he now sat contemplating it in a sort of trance of melancholy reflection.

"Why, boys," he broke out, "why didn't she come to me afore she bought this crittur? Why, I knew all about him! That 'ere crittur was jest ruined a year ago last summer, when Tom, the Deacon's boy there, come home from college. Tom driv him over to Sherburn and back that 'ere hot Fourth of July. 'Member it, 'cause I saw the crittur when he come home. I sot up with Tom takin' care of him all night. That 'ere crittur had the thumps all night, and he hain't never been good for nothin' since. I telled the Deacon he was a gone hoss then, and wouldn't never be good for nothin'. The Deacon, he took off his shoes, and let him run to pastur' all summer, and he's ben a-feedin' and nussin' on him up; and now he's put him off on the widder. I wouldn't 'a' thought it o' the Deacon! Why, this hoss'll never be no good to her! That 'ere's a used-up crittur, any fool may see! He'll mabbe do for about a quarter of an hour on a smooth road; but come to drive him as a body wants to drive, why, he blows like my bellowsis; and the Deacon knew it—must 'a' known it!"

"Why, Sam!" we exclaimed, "ain't the Deacon a good man?"

"Wal, now, there's where the shoe pinches! In a gin'al way the Deacon *is* a good man—he's consid'able more than middlin' good; gin'ally he adorns his perfession. On most p'ints I don't hev nothin' agin the Deacon; and this 'ere ain't a bit like him. But there 'tis! Come to hosses, there's where the unsanctified natur' comes out. Folks will cheat about hosses when they won't about 'most nothin' else." And Sam leaned back on his cold forge, now empty of coal, and seemed to deliver himself to a mournful train of general reflection. "Yes, hosses does seem to be sort o' unregenerate critturs," he broke out: "there's suthin about hosses that deceives the very elect. The best o' folks gets tripped up when they come to deal in hosses."

"Why, Sam, is there anything bad in horses?" we interjected timidly.

" 'Tain't the hosses," said Sam with solemnity. "Lordy massy! the hosses is all right enough! Hosses is scriptural animals. Elijah went up to heaven in a chari't with hosses, and then all them lots o' hosses in the Ravelations—black and white and red, and all sorts o' colors. That 'ere shows hosses goes to heaven; but it's more'n the folks that hev 'em is likely to, ef they don't look out.

"Ministers, now," continued Sam, in a soliloquizing vein—"folks allers thinks it's suthin' sort o' shaky in a minister to hev much to do with hosses—sure to get 'em into trouble. There was old Parson Williams of North Billriky got into a dreffful mess about a hoss. Lordy massy! he wern't to blame, neither; but he got into the dreffulest scrape you ever heard on—come nigh to unsettlin' him."

"O Sam, tell us all about it!" we boys shouted, delighted with the prospect of a story.

"Wal, wait now till I get off this crittur's shoes, and we'll take him up to pastur', and then we can kind o' set by the river, and fish. Hepsy wanted a mess o' fish for supper, and I was cal'latin' to git some for her. You boys go and be digging bait, and git yer lines."

And so, as we were sitting tranquilly beside the Charles River, watching our lines, Sam's narrative began:

"Ye see, boys, Parson Williams—he's dead now, but when I was a boy he was one of the gret men round here. He writ books. He writ a tract agin the Armenians, and put 'em down; and he writ a big book on the millennium (I've got that 'ere book now); and he was a smart preacher. Folks said he had invitations to settle in Boston, and there ain't no doubt he might 'a' hed a Boston parish ef he'd 'a' ben a mind ter take it; but he'd got a good settlement and a handsome farm in North Billriky, and didn't care to move; thought, I s'pose, that 'twas better to be number one in a little place than number two in a big un. Anyway, he carried all before him where he was.

"Parson Williams was a tall, straight, personable man; come of good family—father and grand'ther before him all ministers. He was putty up and down, and commandin' in his ways, and things had to go putty much as he said. He was a good deal sot by, Parson Williams was, and his wife was a Derby—one o' them rich Salem Derbys—and brought him a lot o' money; and so they lived putty easy and comfortable so fur as this world's goods goes. Well, now, the parson wa'n't reely what you call worldly-minded; but then he was one o' them folks that *knows what's good* in temporals as well as sperituals, and allers liked to hev the best that there was goin'; and he allers had an eye to a good hoss.

"Now, there was Parson Adams and Parson Scranton, and most of the other ministers: they didn't know and didn't care what hoss they hed; jest jogged round with these 'ere poundin', potbellied, sleepy critturs that ministers mostly hes—good enough to crawl around to funerals and ministers' meetin's and 'sociations and sich; but Parson Williams, he allers would hev a hoss as was a hoss. He looked out for *blood;* and, when these 'ere Vermont fellers would come down with a drove, the parson he hed his eyes open, and knew what was what. Couldn't none of 'em cheat him on hoss flesh! And so one time when Zach Buel was down with a drove, the doctor he bought the best hoss in the lot. Zach said he never see a parson afore that he couldn't cheat;

but he said the doctor reely knew as much as he did, and got the very one he'd meant to 'a' kept for himself.

"This 'ere hoss was a peeler, I'll tell you! They'd called him Tamerlane, from some heathen feller or other: the boys called him Tam, for short. Tam was a great character. All the fellers for miles round knew the doctor's Tam, and used to come clear over from the other parishes to see him.

"Wal, this 'ere sot up Cuff's back high, I tell you! Cuff was the doctor's nigger man, and he was nat'lly a drefful proud crittur. The way he would swell and strut and brag about the doctor and his folks and his things! The doctor used to give Cuff his cast-off clothes: and Cuff would prance round in 'em, and seem to think he was a doctor of divinity himself, and had the charge of all natur'.

"Well, Cuff he reely made an idol o' that 'ere hoss—a reg'lar graven image—and bowed down and worshiped him. He didn't think nothin' was too good for him. He washed and brushed and curried him, and rubbed him down till he shone like a lady's satin dress; and he took pride in ridin' and drivin' him, 'cause it was what the doctor wouldn't let nobody else do but himself. You see, Tam weren't no lady's hoss. Miss Williams was 'fraid as death of him; and the parson he hed to git her a sort o' low-sperited crittur that she could drive herself. But he liked to drive Tam; and he liked to go round the country on his back, and a fine figure of a man he was on him, too. He didn't let nobody else back him or handle the reins but Cuff; and Cuff was drefful set up about it, and he swelled and bragged about that ar hoss all round the country. Nobody couldn't put in a word 'bout any other hoss, without Cuff's feathers would be all up stiff as a tom-turkey's tail; and that's how Cuff got the doctor into trouble.

"Ye see, there nat'lly was others that thought they'd got horses, and didn't want to be crowed over. There was Bill Atkins, out to the west parish, and Ike Sanders, that kep' a stable up to Pequot Holler: they was down a-lookin' at the parson's hoss, and a-bettin' on their'n, and a darin' Cuff to race with 'em.

"Wal, Cuff, he couldn't stan' it, and, when the doctor's back was turned, he'd be off on the sly, and they'd hev their race; and Tam he beat 'em all. Tam, ye see, boys, was a hoss that couldn't and wouldn't hev a hoss ahead of him—he jest *wouldn't!* Ef he dropped down dead in his tracks the next minit, he *would* be ahead; and he allers got ahead.

And so his name got up, and fellers kep' comin to try their horses: and Cuff'd take Tam out to race with fust one and then another till this 'ere got to be a reg'lar thing, and begun to be talked about.

"Folks sort o' wondered if the doctor knew; but Cuff was sly as a weasel, and allers had a story ready for every turn. Cuff was one of them fellers that could talk a bird off a bush—master hand he was to slick things over!

"There was folks as said they believed the doctor was knowin' to it, and that he felt a sort o' carnal pride sech as a minister oughtn't fer to hev, and so shet his eyes to what was a-goin' on. Aunt Sally Nickerson said she was sure on't. 'Twas all talked over down to old Miss Bummiger's funeral, and Aunt Sally she said the church ought to look into't. But everybody knew Aunt Sally: she was allers watchin' for folks' haltin's, and settin' on herself up to jedge her neighbors.

"Wal, I never believed nothin' agin Parson Williams: it was all Cuff's contrivances. But the fact was, the fellers all got their blood up, and there was hoss-racin' in all the parishes; and it got so they'd even race hosses a Sunday.

"Wal, of course they never got the doctor's hoss out a Sunday. Cuff wouldn't 'a' durst to do that, Lordy massy, no! He was allers there in church, settin' up in the doctor's clothes, rollin' up his eyes, and lookin' as pious as ef he never thought o' racin' hosses. He was an awful solemn-lookin' nigger in church, Cuff was.

"But there was a lot o' them fellers up to Pequot Holler—Bill Atkins, and Ike Sanders, and Tom Peters, and them Hokum boys—used to go out arter meetin' Sunday arternoon, and race hosses. Ye see, it was jest close to the State-line, and, if the s'lectmen was to come down on 'em, they could jest whip over the line, and they couldn't take 'em.

"Wal, it got to be a great scandal. The fellers talked about it up to the tavern; and the deacons and the tithingman, they took it up and went to Parson Williams about it; and the parson he told 'em jest to keep still, not let the fellers know that they was bein' watched, and next Sunday he and the tithingman and the constable, they'd ride over, and catch 'em in the very act.

"So next Sunday arternoon Parson Williams and Deacon Popkins and Ben Bradley (he was constable that year), they got on to their hosses, and rode over to Pequot Holler. The doctor's blood was up, and he meant to come down on 'em strong; for that was his way o' doin' in his parish. And they was in a sort o' day-o'-jedgment frame o' mind, and jogged along solemn as a hearse, till, come to rise the hill above the holler, they see three or four fellers with their hosses gittin' ready to race; and the parson says he, 'Let's come on quiet, and get behind these bushes, and we'll see what they're up to, and catch 'em in the act.'

"But the mischief on't was, that Ike Sanders see 'em comin,' and he knowed Tam in a minit—Ike knowed Tam of old—and he jest tipped the wink to the rest. 'Wait, boys,' says he: 'let 'em git close up, and then I'll give the word, and the doctor's hoss will be racin' ahead like thunder.'

"Wal, so the doctor and his folks they drew up behind the bushes, and stood there innocent as could be, and saw 'em gittin' ready to start. Tam, he begun to snuffle and paw, but the doctor never mistrusted what he was up to till Ike sung out, 'Go it, boys!' and the hosses all started, when, sure as you live, boys! Tam give one fly, and was over the bushes, and in among 'em, goin' it like chain-lightnin' ahead of 'em all.

"Deacon Popkins and Ben Bradley jest stood and held their breath to see 'em all goin' it so like thunder; and the doctor, he was took so sudden it was all he could do to jest hold on anyway: so away he went, and trees and bushes and fences streaked by him like ribbins. His hat flew off behind him, and his wig arter, and got catched in a barberry-bush; but Lordy massy! he couldn't stop to think o' them. He jest leaned down, and caught Tam round the neck, and held on for dear life till they come to the stopping-place.

"Wal, Tam was ahead of them all, sure enough, and was snorting and snuffling as if he'd got the very old boy in him, and was up to racing some more on the spot.

"That 'ere Ike Sanders was the impudentest feller that ever you see, and he roared and rawhawed at the doctor. 'Good for you, parson!' says he. 'You beat us all holler,' says he. 'Takes a parson for that, don't it, boys?' he said. And then he and Ike and Tom, and the two Hokum boys, they jest roared, and danced round like wild critturs. Wal, now, only think on't, boys, what a situation that 'ere was for a minister—a man that had come out with the best of motives to put a stop to Sabbath-breakin'! There he was all rumpled up and dusty, and his wig hangin' in the bushes, and these 'ere ungodly fellers gettin' the laugh on him, and all acause o' that 'ere hoss. There's times, boys, when ministers must be tempted to swear, if there ain't preventin' grace, and this was one o' them times to Parson Williams. They say he got red in the face, and looked as if he should bust, but he didn't say nothin': he scorned to answer. The sons o' Zeruiah was too hard for him, and he let 'em hev their say. But when they'd got through, and Ben had brought him his hat and wig, and brushed and settled him ag'in, the parson he says, 'Well, boys, ye've had your say and your laugh; but I warn you now I won't have this thing goin' on here any more,' says he; 'so mind yourselves.'

"Wal, the boys see that the doctor's blood was up, and they rode off pretty quiet; and I believe they never raced no more in that spot.

"But there ain't no tellin' the talk this 'ere thing made. Folks will talk, you know; and there wer'n't a house in all Billriky, nor in the south parish nor centre, where it wer'n't had over and discussed. There was the deacon, and Ben Bradley was there, to witness and show jest how the thing was, and that the doctor was jest in the way of his duty; but folks said it made a great scandal; that a minister hadn't no business to hev that kind o' hoss, and that he'd give the enemy occasion to speak reproachfully. It reely did seem as if Tam's sins was imputed to the doctor; and folks said he ought to sell Tam right away, and get a sober minister's hoss.

"But others said it was Cuff that had got Tam into bad ways; and they do say that Cuff had to catch it pretty lively when the doctor come to settle with him. Cuff thought his time had come, sure enough, and was so scairt that he turned blacker'n ever: he got enough to cure him o' hoss-racin' for one while. But Cuff got over it arter a while, and so did the doctor. Lordy massy! there ain't nothin' lasts forever! Wait long enough, and 'most every thing blows over. So it turned out about the doctor. There was a rumpus and a fuss, and folks talked and talked, and advised; everybody had their say: but the doctor kep' right straight on, and kep' his hoss all the same.

"The ministers, they took it up in the 'sociation; but, come to tell the story, it sot 'em all a-laughin', so they couldn't be very hard on the doctor.

"The doctor felt sort o' streaked at fust when they told the story on him; he didn't jest like it: but he got used to it, and finally, when he was twitted on't, he'd sort o' smile, and say, 'Anyway, Tam beat 'em: that's one comfort.' "

Wrecked in Port

R. J. BURDETTE

As you go to Boston and Hartford by way of the Boston and Albany Railroad, if you take the morning express there are two parlor cars thereunto attached, with all the appurtenances thereunto appertaining, including a porter with a wisp broom in one hand and a place for a quarter in the other. Now these two parlor cars are twins, differing only, as in the case with twins, in their manners. The last time I went out that way, one of these cars was "Governor Hawley," and the other was " 'Tother Gov'nor," I don't remember who.

All went well until we reached Springfield. There the usual halt of five or ten minutes was made, the parlor car for Albany was switched off to its proper train, and we went thundering on to Hartford.

Before we were well out of the depot an old gentleman confronted me. Round faced, well dressed, quick spoken, a little crusty, and a general air of authority about him.

"Young man," he said, sharply, "out of that!"

"Out of which?" I said, in innocent surprise.

"Out of that chair!" snapped the old party. "Come, be lively; I want to sit down."

I was puzzled and annoyed, and stammered something about this being a parlor car and—

"Yes, yes," he said impatiently, "I know all about that; this is a parlor car, and you've got my seat. Get up and get out of it now without any more words. Get a seat of your own somewhere, and don't go around appropriating other people's chairs when they've gone for lunch. Get out, young fellow!"

I am naturally a very meek man, but I did make one more desperate effort to retain my seat. I said I had occupied that seat—"

"Ever since I got out of it at Springfield," snarled the old man. "I rode in that seat all the way from Boston, and the minute I left it you jumped into it. And now you jump out of it, and no more words about it, or I'll make the car full of trouble for you."

It began to dawn upon me then just how matters stood. In fact I knew, but I was nettled. Everybody in the car was laughing at me, and I do hate to be laughed at. I determined to wait for my sure revenge. I said: "You'll be sorry if you take this chair." He snorted fiercely, and I abdicated, without another word, in favor of the testy old jumper of claims who thus summarily evicted me. I arose, gathered up my hat, overcoat, lap-tablet, newspapers, book, big valise, little valise and arctics, and thus burdened walked meekly to the rear of the car and sat down on the meanest, poorest, most uncomfortable seat in the train—the upholstered bench under the big mirror. The wood-box in the smoking-car is an easy-chair in comparison with that bench. By and by the old chair grabber called out:

"Young man, where is that little red hand bag I left here?"

I meekly said, "I hadn't never tetched it," and he roared out that it was there when I took his chair. But just then the conductor came along and glanced at his ticket, while the old party explained how I had made way with his little red hand bag. "That young man back there," he explained, "was in my chair when I returned, and my over-shoes and a little red leather hand bag is—"

The conductor, a brisk, taciturn man, full of his own business, here handed back the old party's ticket.

"Wrong train," he said, brusquely. "Get off at next station. This train for Hartford and New York."

The old gentleman's face was a study.

"For Ha-Ha-wha-what!" he shouted. "I know better! Told me at Boston this car went through to Albany."

"Le'me see parlor car ticket," said the conductor, briefly. "Yes, that's all right, you're on wrong car; this ticket for the other car. Your baggage half way t' Albany by this time. Get off at Hartford."

"Well, when can I get a train back to Springfield?" wailed the jumper of chairs.

"T'-night," said the conductor, and passed on to the next car.

Then I arose. I gathered up in my weak and long-suffering arms my hat, overcoat, lap-tablet, newspapers, book, big valise, little valise and arctics, and walked back to that chair and stood before the most crest-fallen man the immortal gods ever pitied. I didn't say anything; I didn't make a gesture; I just stood up before him, holding my goods, personal effects and railway chattels in my arms and looked at him. He arose

and vamoosed the claim. And as I settled down in my recovered possession I made only one remark. I said to the poor old gentleman:

"I told you you'd be sorry if you took this chair!"

And he marched back and took a seat on the upholstered bench, to
the merry laughter of the happy passengers. And the last time I looked
around, oh crowning woe, the conductor was making him pay a quarter for his seat in the parlor car.

A PLEASURE EXERTION

MARIETTA HOLLEY

Marietta Holley was born in Jefferson County, N.Y., in 1844. She has writ-
ten a number of books, sketches, etc., under the pen name of "Josiah Allen's
Wife," which include "My Opinions and Betsy Bobbett's," "Josiah Allen's
Wife, as P.A. and P.I." (1877), "Sweet Cicely" (1887), and a volume of
"Poems" (1888).

Wal, the very next mornin' Josiah got up with a new idee in his head.
And he broached it to me to the breakfast-table. They have been havin'
sights of pleasure exertions here to Jonesville lately. Every week
a'most they would go off on a exertion after pleasure, and Josiah was
all up on end to go too.

That man is a well-principled man as I ever see, but if he had his
head, he would be worse than any young man I ever see to foller up
picnics and 4th of Julys and camp-meetin's and all pleasure exertions.
But I don't encourage him in it. I have said to him time and again:
"There is a time for everything, Josiah Allen, and after anybody has
lost all their teeth and every mite of hair on the top of their head, it is
time for 'em to stop goin' to pleasure exertions."

But good land! I might jest as well talk to the wind! If that man
should get to be as old as Mr. Methusler, and be goin' on a thousand
years old, he would prick up his ears if he should hear of a exertion.
All summer long that man has beset me to go to 'em, for he wouldn't
go without me. Old Bunker Hill himself hain't any sounder in principle than Josiah Allen, and I have had to work head-work to make ex-

cuses and quell him down. But last week they was goin' to have one out on the lake, on a island, and that man sot his foot down that go he would.

We was to the breakfast-table a talkin' it over, and says I:

"I sha'n't go, for I am afraid of big water, anyway."

Says Josiah: "You are jest as liable to be killed in one place as another."

Says I, with a almost frigid air, as I passed him his coffee, "Mebby I shall be drounded on dry land, Josiah Allen, but I don't believe it."

Says he, in a complainin' tone: "I can't get you started onto a exertion for pleasure any way."

Says I, in a almost eloquent way: "I don't believe in makin' such exertions after pleasure. As I have told you time and agin, I don't believe in chasin' of her up. Let her come of her own free will. You can't ketch her by chasin' after her no more than you can fetch up a shower in a drowth by goin' out doors and runnin' after a cloud up in the heavens above you. Sit down and be patient, and when it gets ready the refreshin' rain-drops will begin to fall without none of your help. And it is jest so with pleasure, Josiah Allen; you may chase her up over all the oceans and big mountains of the earth, and she will keep ahead of you all the time; but set down and not fatigue yourself a thinkin' about her, and like as not she will come right into your house unbeknown to you."

"Wal," says he, "I guess I'll have another griddle-cake, Samantha."

And as he took it, and poured the maple-syrup over it, he added gently, but firmly:

"I shall go, Samantha, to this exertion, and I should be glad to have you present at it, because it seems jest to me as if I should fall overboard durin' the day."

Men are deep. Now that man knew that no amount of religious preachin' could stir me up like that one speech. For though I hain't no hand to coo, and don't encourage him in bein' spoony at all, he knows that I am wrapped almost completely up in him. I went.

Wal, the day before the exertion Kellup Cobb come into our house of a errant, and I asked him if he was goin' to the exertion; and he said he would like to go, but he dassent.

"Dassent!" says I. "Why dassent you?"

"Why," says he, "how would the rest of the wimmin round Jonesville feel if I should pick out one woman and wait on her?" Says he bitterly: "I hain't perfect, but I hain't such a cold-blooded rascal as not to have any regard for wimmin's feelin's. I hain't no heart to spile all the comfort of the day for ten or a dozen wimmen."

"Why," says I, in a dry tone, "one woman would be happy, accordin' to your tell."

"Yes, one woman happy, and ten or fifteen gauled—bruised in the tenderest place."

"On their heads?" says I, inquirin'ly.

"No," says he, "their hearts. All the girls have probable had more or less hopes that I would invite 'em—make a choice of 'em. But when the blow was struck, when I had passed 'em by and invited some other, some happier woman, how would them slighted ones feel? How do you s'pose they would enjoy the day, seein' me with another woman, and they droopin' round without me? That is the reason, Josiah Allen's wife, that I dassent go. It hain't the keepin' of my horse through the day that stops me. For I could carry a quart of oats and a little jag of hay in the bottom of the buggy. If I had concluded to pick out a girl and go, I had got it all fixed out in my mind how I would manage. I had thought it over, while I was ondecided and duty was a strugglin' with me. But I was made to see where the right way for me lay, and I am goin' to foller it. Joe Purday is goin' to have my horse, and give me seven shillin's for the use of it and its keepin'. He come to hire it just before I made up my mind that I hadn't ort to go.

"Of course it is a cross to me. But I am willin' to bear crosses for the fair sect. Why," says he, a comin' out in a open, generous way, "I would be willin', if necessary for the general good of the fair sect—I would be willin' to sacrifice ten cents for 'em, or pretty nigh that, I wish so well to 'em. I *hain't* that enemy to 'em that they think I am. I can't marry 'em all, Heaven knows I can't, but I wish 'em well."

"Wal," says I, "I guess my dish-water is hot; it must be pretty near bilin' by this time."

And he took the hint and started off. I see it wouldn't do no good to argue with him that wimmen didn't worship him. For when a feller once gets it into his head that female wimmen are all after him, you might jest as well dispute the wind as argue with him. You can't convince him nor the wind—neither of 'em—so what's the use of wastin' breath on 'em. And I didn't want to spend a extra breath that day, anyway, knowin' I had such a hard day's work in front of me, a finishin' cookin' up provisions for the exertion, and gettin' things done up in the house so I could leave 'em for all day.

We had got to start about the middle of the night; for the lake was 15 miles from Jonesville, and the old mare bein' so slow, we had got to start an hour or two ahead of the rest. I told Josiah in the first on't, that I had just as lives set up all night, as to be routed out at two o'clock. But he was so animated and happy at the idee of goin' that he looked on the bright side of everything, and he said that we would go to bed before dark, and get as much sleep as we commonly did. So we went to bed the sun an hour high. And I was truly tired enough to lay down, for I had worked dretful hard that day—almost beyond my strength. But we hadn't more'n got settled down into the bed, when we heard a buggy and a single wagon stop at the gate, and I got up and peeked through the window, and I see it was visitors come to spend the evenin'—Elder Bamber and his family, and Deacon Dobbinses' folks.

Josiah vowed that he wouldn't stir one step out of that bed that night. But I argued with him pretty sharp, while I was throwin' on my clothes, and I finally got him started up. I hain't deceitful, but I thought if I got my clothes all on before they came in, I wouldn't tell 'em that I had been to bed that time of day. And I did get all dressed up, even to my handkerchief pin. And I guess they had been there as much as ten minutes before I thought that I hadn't took my night-cap off. They looked dreadful curious at me, and I felt awful meachin'. But I jest ketched it off, and never said nothin'. But when Josiah come out of the bedroom with what little hair he has got standin' out in every direction, no two hairs a layin' the same way, and one of his galluses a hangin' most to the floor under his best coat, I up and told 'em. I thought mebby they wouldn't stay long. But Deacon Dobbinses' folks seemed to be all waked up on the subject of religion, and they proposed we should turn it into a kind of a conference meetin'; so they never went home till after ten o'clock.

It was most eleven when Josiah and me got to bed again. And then jest as I was gettin' into a drowse, I heerd the cat in the buttery, and I got up to let her out. And that roused Josiah up, and he thought he heered the cattle in the garden, and he got up and went out. And there we was a marchin' round most all night.

And if we would get into a nap, Josiah would think it was mornin', and he would start up and go out to look at the clock. He seemed so afraid we would be belated, and not get to that exertion in time. And there we was on our feet most all night. I lost myself once, for I dreampt that Josiah was a-drownin', and Deacon Dobbins was on the shore a-prayin' for him. It started me so, that I jist ketched hold of Josiah and hollered. It skairt him awfully, and says he, "What does ail you, Samantha? I hain't been asleep before, to-night, and now you have rousted me up for good. I wonder what time it is!"

And then he got out of bed again, and went and looked at the clock. It was half-past one, and he said "He didn't believe we had better go to sleep again, for fear we would be too late for the exertion, and he wouldn't miss that for nothin'."

"Exertion!" says I, in a awful cold tone. "I should think we had had exertion enough for one spell."

But as bad and wore out as Josiah felt bodily, he was all animated in his mind about what a good time he was a-goin' to have. He acted foolish, and I told him so. I wanted to wear my brown-and-black gingham and a shaker, but Josiah insisted that I should wear a new lawn dress that he had brought me home as a present, and I had jest got made up. So, jest to please him, I put it on, and my best bonnet.

And that man, all I could do and say, would put on a pair of pantaloons I had been a makin' for Thomas Jefferson. They was gettin' up a military company to Jonesville, and these pantaloons was blue, with a red stripe down the sides—a kind of uniform. Josiah took a awful fancy to 'em, and says he:

"I will wear 'em, Samantha; they look so dressy."

Says I: "They hain't hardly done. I was goin' to stitch that red stripe on the left leg on again. They hain't finished as they ort to be, and I would not wear 'em. It looks vain in you."

Says he: "I will wear 'em, Samantha. I will be dressed up for once."

I didn't contend with him. Thinks I: we are makin' fools of ourselves by goin' at all, and if he wants to make a little bigger fool of himself, by wearin' them blue pantaloons, I won't stand in his light. And then I had got some machine oil onto 'em, so I felt that I had got to wash 'em, anyway, before Thomas J. took 'em to wear. So he put 'em on.

I had good vittles, and a sight of 'em. The basket wouldn't hold 'em all, so Josiah had to put a bottle of red rossberry jell into the pocket of his dress-coat, and lots of other little things, such as spoons and knives and forks, in his pantaloons and breastpockets. He looked like Captain

Kidd armed up to the teeth, and I told him so. But good land! he would have carried a knife in his mouth if I had asked him to, he felt so neat about goin', and boasted so on what a splendid exertion it was goin' to be.

We got to the lake about eight o'clock, for the old mare went slow. We was about the first ones there, but they kep' a comin', and before ten o'clock we all got there.

The young folks made up their minds they would stay and eat their dinner in a grove on the mainland. But the majority of the old folks thought it was best to go and set our tables where we laid out to in the first place. Josiah seemed to be the most rampant of any of the company about goin'. He said he shouldn't eat a mouthful if he didn't eat it on that island. He said, what was the use of goin' to a pleasure exertion at all if you didn't try to take all the pleasure you could. So about twenty old fools of us sot sail for the island.

I had made up my mind from the first on't to face trouble, so it didn't put me out so much when Deacon Dobbins, in gettin' into the boat, stepped onto my new lawn dress and tore a hole in it as big as my two hands, and ripped it half offen the waist. But Josiah havin' felt so animated and tickled about the exertion, it worked him up awfully when, jest after we had got well out onto the lake, the wind took his hat off and blew it away out onto the lake. He had made up his mind to look so pretty that day that it worked him up awfully. And then the sun beat down onto him; and if he had had any hair onto his head it would have seemed more shady.

But I did the best I could by him. I stood by him and pinned on his red bandanna handkerchief onto his head. But as I was a fixin' it on, I see there was suthin' more than mortification ailed him. The lake was rough and the boat rocked, and I see he was beginnin' to be awful sick. He looked deathly. Pretty soon I felt bad, too. Oh! the wretchedness of that time. I have enjoyed poor health considerable in my life, but never did I enjoy so much sickness in so short a time as I did on that pleasure exertion to that island. I s'pose our bein' up all night a'most made it worse. When we reached the island we was both weak as cats.

I sot right down on a stun and held my head for a spell, for it did seem as if it would split open. After a while I staggered up onto my feet, and finally I got so I could walk straight and sense things a little;

though it was tejus work to walk, anyway, for we had landed on a sand-bar, and the sand was so deep it was all we could do to wade through it, and it was as hot as hot ashes ever was.

Then I began to take the things out of my dinner-basket. The butter had all melted, so we had to dip it out with a spoon. And a lot of water had washed over the side of the boat, so my pies and tarts and delicate cake and cookies looked awful mixed up. But no worse than the rest of the company's did.

But we did the best we could, and the chicken and cold meats bein' more solid, had held together quite well, so there was some pieces of it conside'able hull, though it was all very wet and soppy. But we separated 'em out as well as we could, and begun to make preparations to eat. We didn't feel so animated about eatin' as we should if we hadn't been so sick to our stomachs. But we felt as if we must hurry, for the man that owned the boat said he knew it would rain before night, by the way the sun scalded.

There wasn't a man or a woman there but what the presperation and sweat jest poured down their faces. We was a haggard and melancholy lookin' set. There was a piece of woods a little ways off, but it was up quite a rise of ground, and there wasn't one of us but what had the rheumatiz more or less. We made up a fire on the sand, though it seemed as if it was hot enough to steep the tea and coffee as it was.

After we got the fire started, I histed a umberell and sot down under it, and fanned myself hard, for I was afraid of a sunstroke.

Wal, I guess I had set there ten minutes or more, when all of a sudden I thought, Where is Josiah? I hadn't seen him since we had got there. I riz up and asked the company, almost wildly, if they had seen my companion, Josiah.

They said, "No, they hadn't."

But Celestine Wilkin's little girl, who had come with her grandpa and grandma Gowdy, spoke up, and says she:

"I seen him goin' off towards the woods. He acted dretful strange, too; he seemed to be a walkin' off sideways."

"Had the sufferin's he had undergone made him delerious?" says I to myself; and then I started off on the run towards the woods, and old Miss Bobbet, and Miss Gowdy, and Sister Bamber, and Deacon Dobbinses' wife all rushed after me.

Oh, the agony of them two or three minutes! my mind so distracted with fourbodin's, and the presperation and sweat a pourin' down. But all of a sudden, on the edge of the woods, we found him. Miss Gowdy weighin' a little less than me, mebby 100 pounds or so, had got a little ahead of me. He sot backed up against a tree, in a awful cramped position, with his left leg under him. He looked dretful uncomfortable. But when Miss Gowdy hollered out: "Oh, here you be! We have been skairt about you. What is the matter?" he smiled a dretful sick smile, and says he: "Oh, I thought I would come out here and meditate a spell. It was always a real treat to me to meditate."

Just then I come up a pantin' for breath, and as the wimmen all turned to face me, Josiah scowled at me, and shook his fist at them four wimmen, and made the most mysterious motions of his hands towards 'em. But the minute they turned round he smiled in a sickish way, and pretended to go to whistlin'.

Says I, "What is the matter, Josiah Allen? What are you off here for?"

"I am a meditatin', Samantha."

Says I, "Do you come down and jine the company this minute, Josiah Allen. You was in a awful takin' to come with 'em, and what will they think to see you act so?"

The wimmen happened to be a lookin' the other way for a minute, and he looked at me as if he would take my head off, and made the strangest motions towards 'em; but the minute they looked at him he would pretend to smile—that deathly smile.

Says I, "Come, Josiah Allen, we're goin' to get dinner right away, for we are afraid it will rain."

"Oh, wal," says he, "a little rain, more or less, hain't a goin' to hender a man from meditatin'."

I was wore out, and says I, "Do you stop meditatin' this minute, Josiah Allen!"

Says he, "I won't stop, Samantha. I let you have your way a good deal of the time; but when I take it into my head to meditate, you hain't a goin' to break it up."

Jest at that minute they called to me from the shore to come that minute to find some of my dishes. And we had to start off. But oh! the gloom of my mind that was added to the lameness of my body. Them strange motions and looks of Josiah wore on me. Had the sufferin's of the night, added to the trials of the day, made him crazy? I thought more'n as likely as not I had got a luny on my hands for the rest of my days.

And then, oh how the sun did scald down onto me, and the wind took the smoke so into my face that there wasn't hardly a dry eye in my head. And then a perfect swarm of yellow wasps lit down onto our vittles as quick as we laid 'em down, so you couldn't touch a thing without runnin' a chance to be stung. Oh, the agony of that time! the distress of that pleasure exertion! But I kep' to work, and when we had got dinner most ready, I went back to call Josiah again. Old Miss Bobbet said she would go with me, for she thought she see a wild turnip in the woods there, and her Shakespeare had a awful cold, and she would try to dig one to give him. So we started up the hill again. He set in the same position, all huddled up, with his leg under him, as uncomfortable a lookin' creeter as I ever see. But when we both stood in front of him, he pretended to look careless and happy, and smiled that sick smile.

Says I, "Come, Josiah Allen; dinner is ready."

"Oh! I hain't hungry," says he. "The table will probable be full. I had jest as lieves wait."

"Table full!" says I. "You know jest as well as I do that we are eatin' on the ground. Do you come and eat your dinner this minute!"

"Yes, do come," says Miss Bobbet; "we can't get along without you!"

"Oh!" says he, with a ghastly smile, a pretendin' to joke, "I have got plenty to eat here—I can eat muskeeters."

The air was black with 'em, I couldn't deny it.

"The muskeeters will eat you, more likely," says I. "Look at your face and hands; they are all covered with 'em."

"Yes, they have eat considerable of a dinner out of me, but I don't begrech 'em. I hain't small enough, nor mean enough, I hope, to begrech 'em one good meal."

Miss Bobbet started off in search of her wild turnip, and after she had got out of sight Josiah whispered to me with a savage look, and a tone sharp as a sharp axe:

"Can't you bring forty or fifty more wimmen up here? You couldn't come here a minute, could you, without a lot of other wimmen tight to your heels?"

I begun to see daylight, and after Miss Bobbet had got her wild turnip and some spignut, I made some excuse to send her on ahead, and then Josiah told me all about why he had gone off by himself alone, and why he had been a settin' in such a curious position all the time since we had come in sight of him.

It seems he had sot down on that bottle of rossberry jell. That red stripe on the side wasn't hardly finished, as I said, and I hadn't fastened my thread properly, so when he got to pullin' at 'em to try to wipe off the jell, the thread started, and bein' sewed on a machine, that seam jest ripped from top to bottom. That was what he had walked off side-ways towards the woods for. But Josiah Allen's wife hain't one to desert a companion in distress. I pinned 'em up as well as I could, and I didn't say a word to hurt his feelin's, only I jest said this to him, as I was fixin' 'em: I fastened my gray eye firmly, and almost sternly, onto him, and says I:

"Josiah Allen, is this pleasure?" Says I, "You was determined to come."

"Throw that in my face agin, will you? What if I was? There goes a pin into my leg! I should think I had suffered enough without your stabbin' of me with pins."

"Wal, then, stand still, and not be a caperin' round so. How do you s'pose I can do anything with you a tossin' round so?"

"Wal, don't be so aggravatin', then."

I fixed 'em as well as I could, but they looked pretty bad, and there they was all covered with jell, too. What to do I didn't know. But finally I told him I would put my shawl onto him. So I doubled it up corner-ways as big as I could, so it almost touched the ground behind, and he walked back to the table with me. I told him it was best to tell the company all about it, but he just put his foot down that he wouldn't, and I told him, if he wouldn't, that he must make his own excuses to the company about wearin' the shawl. So he told 'em he always loved to wear summer shawls; he thought it made a man look so dressy.

But he looked as if he would sink, all the time he was a sayin' it. They all looked dretful curious at him, and he looked as meachin' as if he had stole sheep—and meachin'er—and he never took a minute's comfort, nor I nuther. He was sick all the way back to the shore, and so was I. And jest as we got into our wagons and started for home, the rain began to pour down. The wind turned our old umberell inside out in no time. My lawn dress was most spilte before, and now I give up my bonnet. And I says to Josiah:

"This bonnet and dress are spilte, Josiah Allen, and I shall have to buy some new ones."

"Wal, wal! who said you wouldn't?" he snapped out.

But it were on him. Oh, how the rain poured down! Josiah, havin' nothin' but a handkerchief on his head, felt it more than I did. I had took a apron to put on a gettin' dinner, and I tried to make him let me pin it on his head. But says he, firmly:

"I hain't proud and haughty, Samantha, but I do feel above ridin' out with a pink apron on for a hat."

"Wal, then," says I, "get as wet as sop, if you had ruther."

I didn't say no more, but there we jest sot and suffered. The rain poured down; the wind howled at us; the old mare went slow; the rheumatiz laid holt of both of us; and the thought of the new bonnet and dress was a wearin' on Josiah, I knew.

There wasn't a house for the first seven miles, and after we got there I thought we wouldn't go in, for we had got to get home to milk, any-way, and we was both as wet as we could be. After I had beset him about the apron, we didn't say hardly a word for as much as thirteen miles or so; but I did speak once, as he leaned forward, with the rain drippin' offen his bandanna handkerchief onto his blue pantaloons. I says to him in stern tones:

"Is this pleasure, Josiah Allen?"

He give the old mare a awful cut, and says he: "I'd like to know what you want to be so aggravatin' for."

I didn't multiply any more words with him, only as we drove up to our doorstep, and he helped me out into a mud puddle, I says to him:

"Mebby you'll hear to me another time, Josiah Allen."

And I'll bet he will. I hain't afraid to bet a ten-cent bill that that man won't never open his mouth to me again about a pleasure exertion.

THE ANT AND THE GRAIN OF CORN

AMBROSE BIERCE

An ant laden with a grain of corn, which he had acquired with infinite toil, was breasting a current of his fellows, each of whom, as is their

THE ANT AND THE GRAIN OF CORN.

etiquette, insisted upon stopping him, feeling him all over, and shaking hands. It occurred to him that an excess of ceremony is an abuse of courtesy. So he laid down his burden, sat upon it, folded all his legs tight to his body, and smiled a smile of great grimness.

"Hullo! what's the matter with *you?*" exclaimed the first insect whose overtures were declined.

"Sick of the hollow conventionalities of a rotten civilization," was the rasping reply. "Relapsed into the honest simplicity of primitive observances. Go to grass!"

"Ah! then we must trouble you for that corn. In a condition of primitive simplicity there are no rights of property, you know. These are 'hollow conventionalities.' "

A light dawned upon the intellect of that pismire. He shook the reefs out of his legs; he scratched the reverse of his ear; he grappled that cereal, and trotted away like a giant refreshed. It was observed that he submitted with a wealth of patience to manipulation by his friends and neighbors, and went some distance out of his way to shake hands with strangers on competing lines of traffic.

————

"What makes that noise?" asked a little boy on the train, the other day. "The cars," answered his mother. "What for?" "Because they are moving." "What are they moving for?" "The engine makes them." "What engine?" "The engine in front." "What's it in front for?" "To pull the train." "What train?" "This one." "This car?" repeated the youngster, pointing to the one in which they sat. "Yes." "What does it pull for?" "The engineer makes it." "What engineer?" "The man on the engine." "What engine?" "The one in front." "What is that in front for?" "I told you that before." "Told who what?" "Told you." "What for?" "Oh, be still; you are a nuisance." "What's a nuisance?" "A boy who asks too many questions." "Whose boy? My boy." "What questions?" The conductor came through just then and took up the tickets, and the train pulled up to the station before we could get all the conversation. The last we heard, as the lady jerked the youngster off the platform, was, "What conductor?"—*Newspaper*

The Man and the Goose

AMBROSE BIERCE

A man was plucking a living goose, when his victim addressed him thus:

"Suppose *you* were a goose; do you think you would relish this sort of thing?"

"Well, suppose I were," answered the man; "do you think *you* would like to pluck me?"

"Indeed I would!" was the emphatic, natural, but injudicious reply.

"Just so," concluded her tormentor; "that's the way *I* feel about the matter."

Nevada Nabobs in New York

MARK TWAIN

In Nevada there used to be current the story of an adventure of two of her nabobs, which may or may not have occurred. I give it for what it is worth:

Col. Jim had seen somewhat of the world, and knew more or less of its ways; but Col. Jack was from the back settlements of the States, had led a life of arduous toil, and had never seen a city. These two, blessed with sudden wealth, projected a visit to New York—Col. Jack to see the sights, and Col. Jim to guard his unsophistication from misfortune. They reached San Francisco in the night, and sailed in the morning. Arrived in New York, Col. Jack said:

"I've heard tell of carriages all my life, and now I mean to have a ride in one; I don't care what it costs. Come along."

They stepped out on the sidewalk, and Col. Jim called a stylish barouche. But Col. Jack said:

"*No*, sir! None of your cheap-John turn-outs for me. I'm here to have a good time, and money ain't any object. I mean to have the nobbiest rig that's going. Now here comes the very trick. Stop that yaller one with the pictures on it—don't you fret—I'll stand all the expenses myself."

So Col. Jim stopped an empty omnibus, and they got in. Said Col. Jack:

"Ain't it gay, though? Oh, no, I reckon not! Cushions and windows and pictures, till you can't rest. What would the boys say if they could see us cutting a swell like this in New York? By George, I wish they *could* see us!"

Then he put his head out of the window, and shouted to the driver:

"Say, Johnny, this suits *me!*—suits yours truly, you bet, you! I want this shebang all day. I'm *on* it, old man! Let 'em out! Make 'em go! We'll make it all right with *you*, Johnny!"

The driver passed his hand through the strap-hole, and tapped for his fare—it was before the gongs came into common use. Col. Jack took the hand, and shook it cordially. He said:

"You twig me, old pard! All right between gents. Smell of *that*, and see how you like it!"

And he put a twenty-dollar gold piece in the driver's hand. After a moment the driver said he could not make change.

"Bother the change! Ride it out. Put it in your pocket."

Then to Col. Jim, with a sounding slap on his thigh:

"*Ain't* it style, though? Hanged if I don't hire this thing every day for a week."

The omnibus stopped, and a young lady got in. Col. Jack stared a moment, then nudged Col. Jim with his elbow:

"Don't say a word," he whispered. "Let her ride, if she wants to. Gracious, there's room enough!"

The young lady got out her porte-monnaie, and handed her fare to Col. Jack.

"What's this for?" said he.

"Give it to the driver, please."

"Take back your money, madam. We can't allow it. You're welcome to ride here as long as you please, but this shebang's chartered, and we can't let you pay a cent."

The girl shrunk into a corner, bewildered. An old lady with a basket climbed in, and proffered her fare.

"Excuse me," said Col. Jack. "You're perfectly welcome here, madam, but we can't allow you to pay. Set right down there, mum, and don't you be the least uneasy. Make yourself just as free as if you was in your own turn-out."

Within two minutes, three gentlemen, two fat women, and a couple of children entered.

"Come right along, friends," said Col. Jack; "don't mind *us*. This is a free blow-out." Then he whispered to Col. Jim, "New York ain't no sociable place, I don't reckon—it ain't no *name* for it!"

He resisted every effort to pass fares to the driver, and made everybody cordially welcome. The situation dawned on the people, and they pocketed their money, and delivered themselves up to covert enjoyment of the episode. Half a dozen more passengers entered.

"Oh, there's *plenty* of room," said Col. Jack. "Walk right in, and make yourselves at home. A blow-out ain't worth anything *as* a blow-out, unless a body has company." Then in a whisper to Col. Jim: "But *ain't* these New Yorkers friendly? And ain't they cool about it, too? Icebergs ain't anywhere. I reckon they'd tackle a hearse, if it was going their way."

More passengers got in; more yet, and still more. Both seats were filled, and a file of men were standing up, holding on to the cleats overhead. Parties with baskets and bundles were climbing up on the roof. Half-suppressed laughter rippled up from all sides.

"Well, for clean, cool, out-and-out cheek, if this don't bang anything that ever I saw, I'm an Injun!" whispered Col. Jack.

A Chinaman crowded his way in:

"I weaken!" said Col. Jack. "Hold on, driver! Keep your seats, ladies and gents. Just make yourselves free—everything's paid for. Driver, rustle these folks around as long as they're a mind to go—friends of ours, you know. Take them everywheres—and if you want more money, come to the St. Nicholas, and we'll make it all right. Pleasant journey to you, ladies and gents—go it just as long as you please—it sha'n't cost you a cent!"

The two comrades got out, and Col. Jack said:

"Jimmy, it's the sociablest place *I* ever saw. The Chinaman waltzed in as comfortable as anybody. If we'd stayed awhile, I reckon we'd had some niggers. B' George! we'll have to barricade our doors to-night, or some of these ducks will be trying to sleep with us."

A JERSEY CENTENARIAN

BRET HARTE

Francis Bret Harte is a native of Albany, N. Y., where he was born in 1837. At the age of seventeen he went to California, where he remained till his thirty-fourth year, and where he was miner, printer, express agent, school teacher, U. S. Marshal's clerk and clerk of the Surveyor-General. He also held a position in the mint. He was a journalist, and at the time he achieved his sudden and extraordinary popularity, he was editor of the *Overland Monthly*, which he had managed from the beginning. He had already achieved distinction on the Pacific coast as a poet and humorist when he returned to the East in 1871. After lecturing throughout the country, he made New York his home until appointed Commercial Agent at Crefeldt, in Germany, by President Hayes. He was afterwards promoted to the Consulate at Glasgow. He has contributed to the leading periodicals in England and America, and is widely known by translations in every language of Europe.

I have seen her at last. She is a hundred and seven years old, and remembers George Washington quite distinctly. It is somewhat confusing, however, that she also remembers a contemporaneous Josiah W. Perkins, of Basking Ridge, N.J., and, I think, has the impression that Perkins, was the better man. Perkins, at the close of the last century, paid her some little attention. There are a few things that a really noble woman of a hundred and seven never forgets.

It was Perkins, who said to her in 1795, in the streets of Philadelphia, "Shall I show thee General Washington?" Then she said, carelesslike (for you know, child, at that time it wasn't what it is now to see General Washington)—she said, "So do, Josiah, so do!" Then he pointed to a tall man who got out of a carriage, and went into a large house. He was larger than you be. He wore his own hair—not powdered; had a flowered chintz vest, with yellow breeches and blue stockings, and a broad-brimmed hat. In summer he wore a white straw hat, and at his farm at Basking Ridge he always wore it. At this point, it became too evident that she was describing the clothes of the all-fascinating Perkins: so I gently but firmly led her back to Washington.

Then it appeared that she did not remember exactly what he wore. To assist her, I sketched the general historic dress of that period. She said she thought he was dressed like that. Emboldened by my success, I added a hat of Charles II, and pointed shoes of the eleventh century. She indorsed these with such cheerful alacrity that I dropped the subject.

The house upon which I had stumbled, or, rather, to which my horse—a Jersey hack, accustomed to historic research—had brought me, was low and quaint. Like most old houses, it had the appearance of being encroached upon by the surrounding glebe, as if it were already half in the grave, with a sod or two, in the shape of moss, thrown on it, like ashes on ashes, and dust on dust. A wooden house, instead of acquiring dignity with age, is apt to lose its youth and respectability together. A porch, with scant, sloping seats, from which even the winter's snow must have slid uncomfortably, projected from a doorway that opened most unjustifiably into a small sitting-room. There was no vestibule, or *locus pœnitentiæ*, for the embarrassed or bashful visitor: he passed at once from the security of the public road into shameful privacy. And here, in the mellow autumnal sunlight, that, streaming through the maples and sumach on the opposite bank, flickered and danced upon the floor, she sat and discoursed of George Washington, and thought of Perkins. She was quite in keeping with the house and the season, albeit a little in advance of both; her skin being of a faded russet, and her hands so like dead November leaves, that I fancied they even rustled when she moved them.

For all that, she was quite bright and cheery; her faculties still quite vigorous, although performing irregularly and spasmodically. It was somewhat discomposing, I confess, to observe that at times her lower jaw would drop, leaving her speechless, until one of the family would notice it, and raise it smartly into place with a slight snap—an operation always performed in such an habitual, perfunctory manner, generally in passing to and fro in their household duties, that it was very trying to the spectator. It was still more embarrassing to observe that the dear old lady had evidently no knowledge of this, but believed she was still talking, and that, on resuming her actual vocal utterance, she was often abrupt and incoherent, beginning always in the middle of a sentence, and often in the middle of a word. "Sometimes," said her daughter, a giddy, thoughtless young thing of eighty-five—"sometimes just moving her head sort of unhitches her jaw; and, if we don't happen to see it, she'll go on talking for hours without ever making a sound." Although I was convinced, after this, that during my interview I had lost several important revelations regarding George Washington through these peculiar lapses, I could not help reflecting how beneficent were these provisions of the Creator—how, if properly studied and applied, they might be fraught with happiness to mankind—how a slight jostle or jar at a dinner-party might make the post-prandial eloquence of garrulous senility satisfactory to itself, yet harmless to others—how a more intimate knowledge of anatomy, introduced into the domestic circle, might make a home tolerable at least, if not happy—how a long-suffering husband, under the pretense of a conjugal caress, might so unhook his wife's condyloid process as to allow the flow of expostulation, criticism or denunciation to go on with gratification to her, and perfect immunity to himself.

But this was not getting back to George Washington and the early struggles of the Republic. So I returned to the commander-in-chief, but found, after one or two leading questions, that she was rather inclined to resent his re-appearance on the stage. Her reminiscences here were chiefly social and local, and more or less flavored with Perkins. We got back as far as the Revolutionary epoch, or, rather, her impressions of that epoch, when it was still fresh in the public mind. And here I came upon an incident, purely personal and local, but, withal, so novel, weird and uncanny, that for a while I fear it quite displaced George Washington in my mind, and tinged the autumnal fields beyond with a red that was not of the sumach. I do not remember to have read of it in the books. I do not know that it is entirely authentic. It was attested to me by mother and daughter, as an uncontradicted tradition.

In the little field beyond, where the plough still turns up musket-balls and cartridge-boxes, took place one of those irregular skirmishes between the militiamen and Knyphausen's stragglers, that made the retreat historical. A Hessian soldier, wounded in both legs and utterly helpless, dragged himself to the cover of a hazel-copse, and lay there hidden for two days. On the third day, maddened by thirst, he managed to creep to the rail-fence of an adjoining farm-house, but found himself unable to mount it or pass through. There was no one in the house but a little girl of six or seven years. He called to her, and in a faint voice asked for water. She returned to the house, as if to comply with his request, but, mounting a chair, took from the chimney a heavily loaded Queen Anne musket, and, going to the door, took deliberate aim at the helpless intruder, and fired. The man fell back dead, without a groan. She replaced the musket, and, returning to the fence, covered the body with boughs and leaves, until it was hidden. Two or three days after, she related the occurrence in a careless, casual way, and leading the way to the fence, with a piece of bread and butter in her guileless little fingers, pointed out the result of her simple, unsophisticated effort. The Hessian was decently buried, but I could not find out what became of the little girl. Nobody seemed to remember. I trust that, in after years, she was happily married; that no Jersey Lovelace attempted to trifle with a heart whose impulses were so prompt, and whose purposes were so sincere. They did not seem to know if she had married or not. Yet it does not seem probable that such simplicity of conception, frankness of expression, and deftness of execution, were lost to posterity, or that they failed, in their time and season, to give flavor to the domestic felicity of the period. Beyond this, the story perhaps has little value, except as an offset to the usual anecdotes of Hessian atrocity.

They had their financial panics even in Jersey, in the old days. She remembered when Dr. White married your cousin Mary—or was it Susan?—yes, it was Susan. She remembers that your Uncle Harry brought in an armful of bank-notes—paper money, you know—and threw them in the corner, saying they were no good to anybody. She remembered playing with them, and giving them to your Aunt Anna—no, child, it was your own mother, bless your heart! Some of them was marked as high as a hundred dollars. Everybody kept gold and silver in a stocking, or in a "chaney" vase, like that. You never used money to buy anything. When Josiah went to Springfield to buy anything, he took a cartload of things with him to exchange. That yaller picture-frame was paid for in greenings. But then people knew jest what they had. They didn't fritter their substance away in unchristian trifles, like your father, Eliza Jane, who doesn't know that there is a God who will smite him hip and thigh; for vengeance is mine, and those that believe in me. But here, singularly enough, the inferior maxillaries gave out, and her jaw dropped. (I noticed that her giddy daughter of eighty-five was sitting near her, but I do not pretend to connect this fact with the arrested flow of personal disclosure.) Howbeit, when she recovered her speech again, it appeared that she was complaining of the weather.

The seasons had changed very much since your father went to sea. The winters used to be terrible in those days. When she went over to Springfield, in June, she saw the snow still on Watson's Ridge. There were whole days when you couldn't get over to William Henry's, their next neighbor, a quarter of a mile away. It was that drefful winter that the Spanish sailor was found. You don't remember the Spanish sailor, Eliza Jane—it was before your time. There was a little personal skirmishing here, which I feared, at first, might end in a suspension of maxillary functions, and the loss of the story: but here it is. Ah, me! it is a pure white winter idyl: how shall I sing it this bright, gay autumnal day?

It was a terrible night, that winter's night, when she and the century were young together. The sun was lost at three o'clock: the snowy night came down like a white sheet, that flapped around the house, beat at the windows with its edges, and at last wrapped it in a close embrace. In the middle of the night, they thought they heard above the wind a voice crying, "Christus, Christus!" in a foreign tongue. They opened the door—no easy task in the north wind that pressed its strong shoulders against it—but nothing was to be seen but the drifting snow. The next morning dawned on fences hidden, and a landscape changed and obliterated with drift. During the day, they again heard the cry of "Christus!" this time faint and hidden, like a child's voice. They searched in vain: the drifted snow hid its secret. On the third day they broke a path to the fence, and then they heard the cry distinctly. Digging down, they found the body of a man—a Spanish sailor, dark and bearded, with ear-rings in his ears. As they stood gazing down at his cold and pulseless figure, the cry of "Christus!" again rose upon the wintry air; and they turned and fled in superstitious terror to the house. And then one of the children, bolder than the rest, knelt down, and opened the dead man's rough pea-jacket, and found—what think you!—a little blue-and-green parrot, nestling against his breast. It was the bird that had echoed mechanically the last despairing cry of the life that was given to save it. It was the bird, that ever after, amid outlandish oaths and wilder sailor-songs, that I fear often shocked the pure ears of its gentle mistress, and brought scandal into the Jerseys, still retained that one weird and mournful cry.

The sun meanwhile was sinking behind the steadfast range beyond, and I could not help feeling that I must depart with my wants unsatisfied. I had brought away no historic fragment: I absolutely knew little or nothing new regarding George Washington. I had been addressed variously by the names of different members of the family who were dead and forgotten; I had stood for an hour in the past: yet I had not added to my historical knowledge, nor the practical benefit of your readers. I spoke once more of Washington, and she replied with a reminiscence of Perkins.

Stand forth, O Josiah W. Perkins, of Basking Ridge, N.J.! Thou wast of little account in thy life, I warrant; thou didst not even feel the greatness of thy day and time; thou didst criticise thy superiors; thou wast small and narrow in thy ways; thy very name and grave are unknown and uncared for: but thou wast once kind to a woman who survived thee, and, lo! thy name is again spoken of men, and for a moment lifted up above thy betters.

PHŒNIX AT SEA

JOHN PHŒNIX

Bright and beautiful rose the sun, from out the calm blue sea, its early rays gleaming on the snow-white decks of the *Northerner*, and "gilding refined gold" as they penetrated the stateroom "A," and lingering, played among the tresses of the slumbering McAuburn. It was a lovely morning; "the winds were all hushed, and the waters at rest," and no sound was heard but the throbbing of the engine and the splash of the paddle-wheels as the gallant old *Northerner* sped on her way, "tracking the trackless sea." Two sailors, engaged in their morning devotions with the holy-stones near my room, amused me not a little. One of them, either accidentally or with "malice prepense," threw a bucket of water against the bulwark, which, *ricocheting*, struck the other on his dorsal extremity, as he leaned to his work, making that portion of his frame exceedingly damp and him exceedingly angry. "You just try that again, —— your soul," exclaimed the offended one, "and I'll slap your chops for you." "Oh, yes, you will," sarcastically rejoined he of the water bucket. I've heerd of you afore! *You're old chop-slapper's son, aint you? Father went round slapping people's chops, didn't he?*" Then followed a short fight, in which, as might have been expected, "Old chop-slapper's son" got rather the worst of it.

There was no excuse for being sick that morning, so our passengers, still pale, but with cheerful hope depicted in their countenances, soon began to throng the deck; segars were again brought into requisition, and we had an opportunity of ascertaining "whether there was any Bourbon among us." A capital set of fellows they were. There was Moore, and Parker, and Bowers (one of Joe Bowers's boys), and Sarsaparilla Meade, and Freeman, which last mentioned gentlemen, so amusing were they, appeared to be travelling *expressly* to entertain us. And there were no ladies, which to me was a blessed dispensation.

> "Oh, woman! in our hours of ease
> Uncertain, coy, and hard to please;
> When pain and anguish wring the brow,
> A ministering angel thou."

Certainly: but at sea, Woman, you are decidedly disagreeable. In the first place, you generally bring babies with you, which are a crying evil, and then you have to have the best stateroom and the finest seat at the table, and monopolize the captain's attention and his room, and you make remarks to one another about us, and our segars and profanity, and accuse us of singing rowdy songs nights; and you generally wind up by doing some scandalous thing yourself, when half of us take your part and the other half don't, and we get all together by the ears, and a pretty state of affairs ensues. No, woman! you are agreeable enough on shore, if taken homeopathically, but on a steamer, you are a decided nuisance.

We had a glorious day aboard the old *Northerner*; we played whist, and sang songs, and told stories, many of which were coeval with our ancient school-lessons, and, like them, came very easy, going over the second time, and many drank strong waters, and becoming mopsed thereon, toasted "the girls we'd left behind us," whereat one, who, being a temperance man, had guzzled soda-water until his eyes seemed about to *pop* from his head, pondered deeply, sighed, and said nothing. And so we laughed and sang and played and whiskied and soda-watered through the day. And fast the old *Northerner* rolled on. And at night the Captain gave us a grand game supper in his room, at which game we played not, but went at it in sober earnest; and then there were more songs (the same ones, though, and the same stories too, over again), and some speechifying, and much fun, until at eight bells we separated, some shouting, some laughing, some crying (but not with sorrow), but all extremely happy, and so we turned in. But before I sought stateroom A that night, I executed a small scheme, for insuring undisturbed repose, which I had revolved in my mind during the day, and which met with the most brilliant success, as you shall hear.

You remember the two snobs that every night, in the pursuit of exercise under difficulties, walk up and down on the deck, arm in arm, right over your stateroom. You remember how, when just as you are getting into your first doze, they commence, tramp! tramp! tramp! right over your head; then you "hear them fainter, fainter still;" you listen in horrible dread of their return, nourishing the while a feeble-minded hope that they may have gone below—when, horror! here they come, louder, louder, till tramp! tramp! tramp! they go over your head again, and with rage in your heart, at the conviction that sleep is impossible, you sit up in bed and despairingly light an unnecessary segar. They were on board the *Northerner*, and the night before had aroused my indignation to that strong pitch that I had determined on their downfall. So, before retiring, I proceeded to the upper deck, and there did I quietly attach a small cord to the stanchions which, stretching across about six inches from the planking, formed what in maritime matters is known as a "booby trap." This done, I repaired to my room, turned in, and calmly awaited the result. In ten minutes they came; I heard them laughing together as they mounted the ladder. Then commenced the exercise, louder, louder, tramp! tramp!—thump! (a double-barreled thump) down they came together, "Oh, what a fall was there, my countrymen!" Two deep groans were elicited, and then followed what, if published, would make two closely printed royal octavo pages of profanity. I heard them d—n the soul of the man that did it. It was *my* soul that they alluded to, but I cared not, I lay there chuckling;

"they called, but I answered not again," and when at length they limped away, their loud profanity subdued to a blasphemous growl, I turned over in a sweet frame of mind, and, falling instantaneously asleep, dreamed a dream, a happy dream of "home and thee"—Susan Ann Jane!

A VICTIM OF HOSPITALITY

REV. F. W. SHELTON

F. W. Shelton was born at Jamaica, L. I., in 1814. He studied Divinity, and was ordained in 1847. His "Up the River Letters" were written at Fishkill-on-the-Hudson, and published first in the *Knickerbocker Magazine,* of which he was a favorite contributor. He was the author of "The Trollopiad," a satire on English travelers in America, "The Rector of St. Bardolph's," "Peeps from the Belfry," and other bright and spirited volumes, characterized by humor of a quiet and refined sort.

"M——," I said, "I have brought you to a cold, dreary house!" I must tell you that I had been fool enough to bring a friend to my house, and he an invalid man. Sitting in the cars, I espied him, and with a devilish selfishness said, "I will have that man to share with me the dreariness of this cold and misty night." I walked up to him, and tapped him on the shoulder. "Ah!" said he. "Come," said I, in a chirping tone of concealed hypocrisy, "and make my house your home. There is nobody there, but we will have a good time of it. You are going to the Point. Never mind, come with me." In a moment of delusion the infatuated man agreed. After we had conversed for a few minutes in the study we began to feel cold. "Now," said I, "we must have a rousing fire, and a cup of hot tea: that will make us feel better. Excuse me for a moment: amuse yourself till I return. I will step over and ask PALMER to come and kindle a good fire, and help me along. All will be right." "Well," said he. Palmer is my right-hand man. There is an old farm-house about fifty yards off. It used to be a tavern in the Revolutionary War. It has settled a good deal within the last hundred years; that is to say, the walls, the floors, and the beams are sunken very much from the horizontal line observable in the floor of a bowling-alley; and the chimneys

302 · *Mark Twain's Library of Humor*

look weather-beaten. Still, it is a stout and substantial old house, and there is no doubt that it would last, with a little more patching, another hundred years. There is a long piazza in front of it, which is much sunken, and in the yard an old-fashioned well, which has afforded drink to cattle and to men for a century and more. The waters are still transcendently sweet and lucid. When the summer-heats raged in the past August, I used to stop and imbibe, taking my turn out of the tin cup with the itinerating pedler, who had unburdened his back of the wearisome load and placed it beside the trough. Your wine of a good vintage may make the eyes glisten a little at the tables of luxury, but depend upon it, a well of water, pure water, gushing up by the way-side, to the weary and heavy-laden is drink indeed. As I ascended the steps of the piazza, I observed that there was a single-mold candle burning within, and knocked confidently at the door of the house. It was opened. "Is PALMER within?" "No, JOHN is absent. He will be gone over Sunday." Alas! alas! I turned on my heel, opened the garden-gate, and finding the path through the peach-trees with some difficulty on the misty night, went back to the forlorn study.

My invalid friend looked dismal enough. "Come," said I, slapping him on the back very gently (to have done it roughly on the present emergency would have been to insult him), "we have to take care of ourselves. What is more easy? We must flare up. We must have a little light, a little fire. My next-door neighbor is away. That makes not the least difference." With that, I lighted the astral lamp—no, the globe-lamp—a contemptible affair, which is a disgrace to the inventor. You raise the wick as high as possible before it will shed any light at all. In a moment it glares out, and presently becomes dim, filling your apart-ment with suffocating smoke and soot. Confound the lamp, with its brazen shaft and marble pedestal! I could with a good will dash it on the floor.

I remembered that there was an abundance of shavings under the shed. Going out, I collected an arm-full and rammed them into the kitchen stove, put in a few chips, and a stick or two of wood, and ap-plied a match. Then I took the tea-kettle, and tramping to the well, filled it with water, placed it upon the stove, and it presently bubbled. Took down a caddy of black tea. After a while I found a loaf of stale bread, which makes excellent toast. In three-quarters of an hour, dur-ing which I spent the time in purgatory, I returned to the study and said, touching my friend on the shoulder, "Tea is ready." We went into the kitchen and sat down. I said grace. The lamp smoked, the fire burned poorly, the tea was cold, my friend shivered, and I afterward heard that he said that I seemed to think that the globe-lamp was both light and warmth. The ungrateful wretch! After tea, the first natural impulse was to get warm, and still keep ourselves alive. My friend behaved extremely well, all things considered; and as the stove wanted replenishing with shavings every five minutes, he acted once or twice as a volunteer on this mission. He tried to be cheerful, but his visage looked sad. "How stern of lineament, how grim!" For my part I could not but enjoy an inward chuckle, like one who has the best of a bargain in the purchase of a horse. People come to your house to be entertained. In the hands of your hospitality they are like dough, to be molded into any shape of comfort. They fairly lay themselves out to be fêted and feasted and flattered and soothed and comforted, and tucked in at night. They enjoy for the time-being a luxurious irresponsibility. With what composure do they lounge in your arm-chair, and lazily troll their eyes over the pictures in your show-books! How swingingly they saunter on your porch or in your garden, with their minds buoyant as thistledown, lightly inhaling the aromatic breeze, fostered by all whom they meet, and addressing all in lady-tones. Bless their dear hearts, how they do grind their teeth for dinner! Dinner! Sometimes it is no easy matter to get up a dinner. While they are in this opiate state, the man of the house is in cruel perplexity, and beef-steaks are rare. Oh! it is a rich treat and triumph, now and then, to have these fellows on the hip; to see them put to some little exertion to conceal their feelings, when they have expected all exertion to be made on the other part; to scan their physiognomy, and to read their thoughts as plainly as if printed in the clearest and most open type: "This does not pay. You will not catch me in this scrape again. I will go where I can be entertained better." I say that I enjoy their discomfiture, and consider it (if it happens rarely) a rich practical joke. It is entirely natural, and in accordance with correct principles, that they should feel exactly as they do. Does it not agree with what I have already said! Constituted as we are, there must be the outward and visible sign to stir up the devotion of the heart. Your grace of warm welcome will not do. Give your friend a good dinner, or a glass of wine; let the fire be warm and bright. Then he will come again. Otherwise not. It is human nature. At any rate, it is *my* nature. Here, however, we draw the fine hair-line of distinction. If your friend thinks *more* of the animal than of the spiritual; if he neglects any duty, undervalues any friendship, because the outward is poor, meagre, of necessity wanting—call him your friend no more!

"Let us go to bed," said I. "Done," said he. "No, not done. The beds are to be made. There is no chambermaid in the house. What of that? Excuse me for a moment, while you ram a few more shavings into the stove." I go up-stairs into the spare chamber. I can find nothing. After a half-hour's work, I manage, however, to procure pillow-cases, sheets, blankets. I go down-stairs and tap my shivering friend on the shoulder, and say, chirpingly, "Come, you must go to your snuggery, your nest. You will sleep like a top, and feel better in the morning."

I get him into bed, and after his nightcap is on, and his head upon the pillow, I say, "Good night; pleasant dreams to you."

"Good night," he responded, with a feeble smile.

Then I tumbled into my own bed, which was made up anyhow, looking out first on the moon just rising above the fog. Oh! thou cold, dry, brassy Moon! do not shine into my chamber when I want repose. PHŒBE, DIANA, LUNA, call thee by whatever name, let not thy pale smile be cast upon my eyes! If so, sweet sleep is gone, and pleasant dreams. Out, out, OUT with thy skeleton face, O volcanic, brassy Moon!

When the morrow came, I went into my friend's chamber, and, as if he had been a king or a prince, asked him how he had rested during the night, and if the coverlets had kept him warm. He was compelled to say, as he was a man of strict veracity, that he had been a little cold. The undiscriminating varlet! I had given him all the blankets in the house.

It was Sunday morning. A Sunday in the country is a theme on which my invalid friend, who is an author, had expatiated with wonderful effect in one of his books. When he came downstairs, as the shavings were not yet lighted, I took him by the arm and proposed a walk on the grass. But the grass was wettened by copious dews. He returned chilled, and hovered over the cold stove. It was nearly time for breakfast, but I had not given him a word of encouragement on that point. Breakfast was a puzzler. All of a sudden, striking my hand on my forehead, as if in the elicitment of a bright idea, I rushed out of the kitchen, crossed the little garden, and knocked at the door of the old farm-house.

The face of the good landlady was forthwith visible. "Madame," I said, "I am in a little quandary. I have a friend with me; besides ourselves, there is nobody and nothing in the house. Will you have the kindness to provide us breakfast, dinner and tea to-day?"

She most obligingly consented. In half an hour I conducted the author triumphantly to the old mansion. The clean white table-cloth was spread; the room was "as warm as toast," and my friend's spirits revived. We went to church. His responses were heart-felt and audible. On returning, the walk made his blood circulate a little, and as he sat in the rocking-chair in the old farm-house waiting for the broiled chicken and looking up at the white-washed beams, he was the picture of contentment. I was almost provoked with myself for getting him into such a comfortable fix.

THE DONATION PARTY

R. J. BURDETTE

There was a sound of revelry by night.

The flickering rays of the street lamps fell upon the joyful ones as they gathered themselves unto the feast, for lo, they reasoned one with another, Hath not the preacher said, "There is nothing better for a man than that he should eat and drink, and that he should make his soul enjoy good in his labor." So they got themselves up unto the house of feasting and bore their countenances merrily. And it was so that the Painted Pine Pail called aloud unto the Cheap Hearth Broom and said:

"Lo, here, thou fair one with the broom-corn bang, whither goest thou?"

And the Cheap Hearth Broom answered and said:

"Thou knowest."

Therefore said the Painted Pine Pail:

"You bet your blue handle."

And then came unto them the Tin Dipper and the Jar of the Tomato Preserves and the Peck of Beans. And they cried unto them, saying:

"Tarry a little, for we also journey your way."

And they greatly were rejoiced and went their way, and they sang and lifted up the voice and shouted with an exceeding great shout, for their hearts were light as a pay-roll.

And there met them in the way the Hideous Dressing Gown, and the dozen Tin Spoons, and the Odd Slippers, and the square of Oil Cloth, and the Three Old Books, and the Kitchen Chair, and the Yard of Flannel, and the Cotton Tidy, and the Bag of Crackers, and the Awful Pen Wiper, and the Button Hook, and the Bar of Soap, and all the Things. And when they saw them they raised a mighty shout, insomuch that the watchmen of the city were awaked, and one said to another:

"Lo! a noise; let us hasten away, lest we be called in."

For the watchmen of the city wist not what the racket was, and they were afraid, which of a verity was their normal condition.

And the Painted Pine Pail called unto the others and said:

"Journey with our band, for we also go upon thine errand. Moreover, we likewise are going to the donation party."

And they joined the band.

And the Kitchen Chair said: "Of a surety there will be much good-cheer, for the matter is not a surprise, but the birds of the air carried the matter to the parsonage, and the parson's wife hath boiled and baked and brewed all day, that there might be an abundance of provisions and cakes of fine meal and of barley, and oil and wine, and ice cream and grapes, and White Mountain cake and Lady Jane Washington pie, and all that is good and expensive, for after this manner doth always the parson's wife do when she heareth of a donation party."

"It will be the swell feed of all swell feeds," said the Odd Slipper. And he was right.

"It will be the boss lay-out," said also the other Odd Slipper. And he likewise was right. They were both rights.

And they began to make merry.

And when they were come into the parsonage, they made as though they would enter in at the gates, but the gates were locked, as with a skein of telegraph wire. Now the same was barbed.

And there came to the doors of the parsonage an holely Old Rag Carpet, and he rolled himself up and leaned against the door jamb. Now he was old and stricken in years. Often had he been beaten with rods, forty stripes plus a thousand and ten, and many times had he been put down, but as oft he got up and dusted the next spring. Nei-

The Peterkins Decide to Learn the Languages · 307

ther was his natural force abated. Moreover, he carried a stair-rod in his hand, and spoke as one who meant business. And he said:

"Slide! Stay not upon the order of your going, but scatter. Vamoose! Climb out of this. Verily, I was beaten but one day ago, and I am to be pasted down to-night, if peradventure I may hold on to the boards until next spring. It's bad enough that a salary of $500 a year compels me to be tacked down with mucilage; may the beasts of the field rant over me if I lie down to have this howling mob shuffle around on me and grind cake and bread crumbs into my long suffering pores. Stampede, or, by the doom of Jericho, I'll pass around the hat!"

And presently they began to fade down the dusky highway. And the Things sat down by the roadside and cast dust upon their heads. And the Odd Slipper said:

"It seems that we are left."

And he was right. And the other Odd Slipper said:

"I should say left. Verily, we are distanced."

And he also was right. They were all left.

The fust thing a man duz in the morning, iz to feel for hiz pocket-book, and the fust thing a woman duz, iz to see if the looking-glass iz all right.

JOSH BILLINGS

THE PETERKINS DECIDE TO LEARN
THE LANGUAGES

BY LUCRETIA PEABODY HALE

Lucretia Peabody Hale is a well-known author, and the contributor of many ingenious tales for young and old in the leading magazines. She was born at Boston in 1820, and is the sister of Rev. Edward Everett Hale.

Certainly now was the time to study the languages. The Peterkins had moved into a new house, far more convenient than their old one, where they would have a place for everything, and everything in its place. Of course they would then have more time.

Elizabeth Eliza recalled the troubles of the old house; how for a long time she was obliged to sit outside of the window upon the piazza, when she wanted to play on her piano.

Mrs. Peterkin reminded them of the difficulty about the table-cloths. The upper table-cloth was kept in a trunk that had to stand in front of the door to the closet under the stairs. But the under table-cloth was kept in a drawer in the closet. So, whenever the cloths were changed, the trunk had to be pushed away under some projecting shelves to make room for opening the closet door (as the under table-cloth must be taken out first), then the trunk was pushed back to make room for it to be opened for the upper table-cloth, and, after all, it was necessary to push the trunk away again to open the closet-door for the knife-tray. This always consumed a great deal of time.

Now that the china-closet was large enough, everything could find a place in it.

Agamemnon especially enjoyed the new library. In the old house there was no separate room for books. The dictionaries were kept up-stairs, which was very inconvenient, and the volumes of the Encyclopædia could not be together. There was not room for all in one place. So from A to P were to be found down-stairs, and from Q to Z were scattered in different rooms up-stairs. And the worst of it was, you could never remember whether from A to P included P. "I always went up-stairs after P," said Agamemnon, "and then always found it down-stairs, or else it was the other way."

Of course, now there were more conveniences for study. With the books all in one room there would be no time wasted in looking for them.

Mr. Peterkin suggested they should each take a separate language. If they went abroad, this would prove a great convenience. Elizabeth Eliza could talk French with the Parisians; Agamemnon, German with the Germans; Solomon John, Italian with the Italians; Mrs. Peterkin, Spanish in Spain; and perhaps he could himself master all the Eastern languages and Russian.

Mrs. Peterkin was uncertain about undertaking the Spanish; but all the family felt very sure they should not go to Spain (as Elizabeth Eliza dreaded the Inquisition), and Mrs. Peterkin felt more willing.

Still she had quite an objection to going abroad. She had always said she would not go till a bridge was made across the Atlantic, and she was sure it did not look like it now.

Agamemnon said there was no knowing. There was something new every day, and a bridge was surely not harder to invent than a telephone, for they had bridges in the very earliest days.

Then came up the question of the teachers. Probably these could be found in Boston. If they could all come the same day, three could be brought out in the carryall. Agamemnon could go in for them, and could learn a little on the way out and in.

Mr. Peterkin made some inquiries about the Oriental languages. He was told that Sanscrit was at the root of all. So he proposed they should all begin with Sanscrit. They would thus require but one teacher, and could branch out into the other languages afterward.

But the family preferred learning the separate languages. Elizabeth Eliza already knew something of the French. She had tried to talk it, without much success, at the Centennial Exhibition, at one of the side stands. But she found she had been talking with a Moorish gentleman who did not understand French. Mr. Peterkin feared they might need more libraries if all the teachers came at the same hour; but Agamemnon reminded him that they would be using different dictionaries. And Mr. Peterkin thought something might be learned by having them all at once. Each one might pick up something besides the language he was studying, and it was a great thing to learn to talk a foreign language while others were talking about you. Mrs. Peterkin was afraid it would be like the Tower of Babel, and hoped it was all right.

Agamemnon brought forward another difficulty. Of course, they ought to have foreign teachers who spoke only their native languages. But, in this case, how could they engage them to come, or explain to them about the carryall, or arrange the proposed hours? He did not understand how anybody ever began with a foreigner, because he could not even tell him what he wanted.

Elizabeth Eliza thought a great deal might be done by signs and pantomime. Solomon John and the little boys began to show how it might be done. Elizabeth Eliza explained how "*langues*" meant both "languages" and "tongues," and they could point to their tongues. For practice, the little boys represented the foreign teachers talking in their different languages, and Agamemnon and Solomon John went to invite them to come out and teach the family by a series of signs.

Mr. Peterkin thought their success was admirable, and that they might almost go abroad without any study of the languages, and trust to explaining themselves by signs. Still, as the bridge was not yet made, it might be as well to wait and cultivate the languages.

Mrs. Peterkin was afraid the foreign teachers might imagine they were invited out to lunch. Solomon John had constantly pointed to his mouth as he opened it and shut it, putting out his tongue, and it looked a great deal more as if he were inviting them to eat than asking them to teach. Agamemnon suggested that they might carry the separate dictionaries when they went to see the teachers, and that would show that they meant lessons, and not lunch.

Mrs. Peterkin was not sure but she ought to prepare a lunch for them, if they had come all that way; but she certainly did not know what they were accustomed to eat.

Mr. Peterkin thought this would be a good thing to learn of the foreigners. It would be a good preparation for going abroad, and they might get used to the dishes before starting. The little boys were delighted at the idea of having new things cooked. Agamemnon had heard that beer-soup was a favorite dish with the Germans, and he would inquire how it was made in the first lesson. Solomon John had heard they were all very fond of garlic, and thought it would be a pretty attention to have some in the house the first day, that they might be cheered by the odor.

Elizabeth Eliza wanted to surprise the lady from Philadelphia by her knowledge of French, and hoped to begin on her lessons before the Philadelphia family arrived for their annual visit.

There were still some delays. Mr. Peterkin was very anxious to obtain teachers who had been but a short time in this country. He did not want to be tempted to talk any English with them. He wanted the latest and freshest languages, and at last came home one day with a list of "brand-new foreigners."

They decided to borrow the Bromwicks' carryall to use, besides their own, for the first day, and Mr. Peterkin and Agamemnon drove into town to bring all the teachers out. One was a Russian gentleman, traveling, who came with no idea of giving lessons, but perhaps would consent to do so. He could not yet speak English.

Mr. Peterkin had his card-case and the cards of the several gentlemen who had recommended the different teachers, and he went with Agamemnon from hotel to hotel collecting them. He found them all very polite and ready to come, after the explanation by signs agreed upon. The dictionaries had been forgotten, but Agamemnon had a directory, which looked the same and seemed to satisfy the foreigners.

Mr. Peterkin was obliged to content himself with the Russian instead of one who could teach Sanscrit, as there was no new teacher of that language lately arrived.

But there was an unexpected difficulty in getting the Russian gentleman into the same carriage with the teacher of Arabic, for he was a Turk, sitting with a fez on his head, on the back seat! They glared at each other, and began to assail each other in every language they knew, none of which Mr. Peterkin could understand. It might be Russian; it might have been Arabic. It was easy to understand that they would never consent to sit in the same carriage. Mr. Peterkin was in despair; he had forgotten about the Russian war! What a mistake to have invited the Turk!

Quite a crowd collected on the sidewalk in front of the hotel. But the French gentleman politely, but stiffly, invited the Russian to go with him in the first carryall. Here was another difficulty. For the German professor was quietly ensconced on the back seat!

As soon as the French gentleman put his foot on the step and saw him, he addressed him in such forcible language that the German professor got out of the door the other side, and came round on the sidewalk and took him by the collar. Certainly the German and French gentlemen could not be put together, and more crowd collected!

Agamemnon, however, had happily studied up the German word "Herr," and he applied it to the German, inviting him by signs to take a seat in the other carryall. The German consented to sit by the Turk, as they neither of them could understand the other; and at last they started, Mr. Peterkin with the Italian by his side, and the French and Russian teachers behind, vociferating to each other in languages unknown to Mr. Peterkin, while he feared they were not perfectly in harmony; so he drove home as fast as possible. Agamemnon had a silent party. The Spaniard at his side was a little moody, while the Turk and the German behind did not utter a word.

At last they reached the house, and were greeted by Mrs. Peterkin and Elizabeth Eliza, Mrs. Peterkin with her llama lace shawl over her shoulders, as a tribute to the Spanish teacher. Mr. Peterkin was careful to take his party in first, and deposit them in a distant part of the library, far from the Turk or the German, even putting the Frenchman and Russian apart.

Solomon John found the Italian dictionary, and seated himself by his Italian; Agamemnon, with the German dictionary, by the German. The little boys took their copy of the "Arabian Nights" to the Turk. Mr. Peterkin attempted to explain to the Russian that he had no Russian dictionary, as he had hoped to learn Sanscrit of him, while Mrs. Peterkin was trying to inform her teacher that she had no books in Spanish. She got over all fears of the Inquisition, he looked so sad, and she tried to talk a little, using English words, but very slowly, and altering the accent as far as she knew how. The Spaniard bowed, looked gravely interested, and was very polite.

Elizabeth Eliza, meanwhile, was trying her grammar phrases with the Parisian. She found it easier to talk French than to understand him. But he understood perfectly her sentences. She repeated one of her vocabularies, and went on with, "J'ai le livre." "As-tu le pain?" "L'enfant a une poire." He listened with great attention, and replied slowly. Suddenly she started, after making out one of his sentences, and went to her mother to whisper, "They have made the mistake you feared. They think they are invited to lunch! *He* has just been thanking me for our politeness in inviting them to *déjeûner*—that means breakfast!"

"They have not had their breakfast!" exclaimed Mrs. Peterkin, looking at her Spaniard; "he does look hungry! What shall we do?"

Elizabeth Eliza was consulting her father. What should they do? How should they make them understand that they invited them to teach, not lunch. Elizabeth Eliza begged Agamemnon to look out "*apprendre*" in the dictionary. It must mean to teach. Alas, they found it means both to teach and to learn! What should they do? The foreigners were now sitting silent in their different corners. The Spaniard grew more and more sallow. What if he should faint? The Frenchman was rolling up each of his mustaches to a point as he gazed at the German. What if the Russian should fight the Turk? What if the German should be exasperated by the airs of the Parisian?

"We must give them something to eat," said Mr. Peterkin, in a low tone. "It would calm them."

"If I only knew what they were used to eating!" said Mrs. Peterkin.

Solomon John suggested that none of them knew what the others were used to eating, and they might bring in anything.

Mrs. Peterkin hastened out with hospitable intents. Amanda could make good coffee. Mr. Peterkin had suggested some American dish. Solomon John sent a little boy for some olives.

It was not long before the coffee came in, and a dish of baked beans. Next, some olives and a loaf of bread, and some boiled eggs, and some bottles of beer. The effect was astonishing. Every man spoke his own tongue, and fluently. Mrs. Peterkin poured out coffee for the Spaniard, while he bowed to her. They all liked beer; they all liked olives. The Frenchman was fluent about "*les mœurs Americaines.*" Elizabeth Eliza supposed he alluded to their not having set any table. The Turk smiled; the Russian was voluble. In the midst of the clang of the different languages, just as Mr. Peterkin was again repeating, under cover of the noise of many tongues, "How shall we make them understand that we want them to teach?"—at this moment the door was flung open, and there came in the lady from Philadelphia, that day arrived, her first call of the season.

She started back in terror at the tumult of so many different languages. The family, with joy, rushed to meet her. All together they called upon her to explain for them Could she help them? Could she tell the foreigners that they wanted to take lessons? Lessons? They had no sooner uttered the word than their guests all started up with faces beaming with joy. It was the one English word they all knew! They had come to Boston to give lessons! The Russian traveler had hoped to learn English in this way. The thought pleased them more than the *déjéuner*. Yes, gladly would they give lessons. The Turk smiled at the idea. The first step was taken. The teachers knew they were expected to teach.

———

"FATHER," she said, burying her face upon the old man's shoulder, "if I can win the pure, earnest love of an honest, upright man, my life will be full indeed. I ask not for mere wealth. I would love and honor such a man, dear father, if even one hundred thousand dollars were all that he could rightly call his own."

"Noble girl," responded the old man, deeply affected, "I hope you may find him."—*Newspaper*

A Fatal Thirst

BILL NYE

Edgar Wilson Nye was born August 21, 1850, in Penobscot County, Maine, but went early to the West, with which section his humor and his fortunes were long identified. His contributions to the press have given him a reputation commensurate with the country.

From the London *Lancet* we learn that "many years ago a case was recorded by Dr. Otto, of Copenhagen, in which 495 needles passed through the skin of a hysterical girl, who had probably swallowed them during a hysterical paroxysm, but these all emerged from the regions below the diaphragm, and were collected in groups, which gave rise to inflammatory swellings of some size. One of these contained 100 needles. Quite recently Dr. Bigger described before the Society of Surgery, of Dublin, a case in which more than 300 needles were removed from the body of a woman. It is very remarkable in how few cases the needles were the cause of death, and how slight an interference with function their presence and movement cause."

It would seem, from the cases on record, that needles in the system rather assist in the digestion and promote longevity.

For instance, we will suppose that the hysterical girl above alluded to, with 495 needles in her stomach, should absorb the midsummer cucumber. Think how interesting those needles would make it for the great colic promoter!

We can imagine the cheerful smile of the cucumber as it enters the stomach, and, bowing cheerfully to the follicles standing around, hangs its hat upon the walls of the stomach, stands its umbrella in a corner, and proceeds to get in its work.

All at once the cucumber looks surprised and grieved about something. It stops in its heaven-born colic generation, and pulls a rusty needle out of its person. Maddened by the pain, it once more attacks the digestive apparatus, and once more accumulates a choice job lot of needles.

Again and again it enters into the unequal contest, each time losing ground and gaining ground, till the poor cucumber, with assorted hardware sticking out in all directions, like the hair on a cat's tail, at last curls up like a caterpillar, and yields up the victory.

Still, this needle business will be expensive to husbands, if wives once acquire the habit and allow it to obtain the mastery over them.

If a wife once permits this demon appetite for cambric needles to get control of the house, it will soon secure a majority in the senate, and then there will be trouble.

The woman who once begins to tamper with cambric needles is not safe. She may think that she has power to control her appetite, but it is only a step to the maddening thirst for the soul-destroying darning-needle, and perhaps to the button-hook and carpet-stretcher.

It is safer and better to crush the first desire for needles, than, when it is too late, to undertake reformation from the abject slavery to this hellish thirst.

We once knew a sweet young creature, with dewy eye and breath like timothy hay. Her merry laugh rippled out upon the summer air like the joyful music of bald-headed bobolinks.

Everybody loved her, and she loved everybody too. But in a thoughtless moment she swallowed a cambric needle. This did not satisfy her. The cruel thraldom had begun. Whenever she felt depressed and gloomy, there was nothing that would kill her *ennui* and melancholy but the fatal needle-cushion.

From this she rapidly became more reckless, till there was hardly an hour that she was not under the influence of needles.

If she couldn't get needles to assuage her mad thirst, she would take hair-pins or door-keys. She gradually pined away to a mere skeleton. She could no longer sit on one foot and be happy.

Life for her was filled with opaque gloom and sadness. At last she took an overdose of sheep-shears and monkey-wrenches one day, and on the following morning her soul had lit out for the land of eternal summer.

We should learn from this to shun the maddening needle-cushion as we would a viper, and never tell a lie.

Mrs. Brown's Fate

Old Mrs. Bently—Have ye heerd anything about Mrs. Brown, lately, Obadiah?

Old Mr. Bently—She died several days ago. I thought ye knew that?

Old Mrs. Bently—I never heard of it. Poor soul; an' so she's dead!

Old Mr. Bently—Yes, dead an' buried.

Old Mrs. Bently—And buried, too! Oh, my; wuss an' wuss!

—*Newspaper*

Captain Ben's Choice

MRS. FRANCIS LEE PRATT

An old red house on a rocky shore, with a fisherman's bluc boat rocking on the bay, and two white sails glistening far away over the water. Above, the blue, shining sky; and below, the blue, shining sea.

"It seems clever to have a pleasant day," said Mrs. Davids, sighing.

Mrs. Davids said everything with a sigh, and now she wiped her eyes also on her calico apron. She was a woman with a complexion like faded seaweed, who seemed always pitying herself.

"I tell them," said she, "I have had real hard luck. My husband is buried away off in California, and my son died in the army, and he is buried away down South. Neither one of them is buried together."

Then she sighed again. Twice, this time.

"And so," she continued, taking out a pinch of bayberry snuff, "I am left alone in the world. *Alone*, I say! why, I've got a daughter, but she is away out West. She is married to an engineerman. And I've got two grandchildren."

Mrs. Davids took the pinch of bayberry and shook her head, looking as though that was the "hardest luck" of all.

"Well, everybody has to have their pesters, and you'll have to have yours," rejoined Miss Persis Tame, taking a pinch of snuff—the real Maccaboy—twice as large, with twice as fierce an action. "I don't know what it is to bury children, nor to lose a husband; I s'pose I don't; but I know what it is to be jammed round the world and not have a ruff to stick my head under. I wish I had all the money I ever spent traveling—and *that's* twelve dollars!" she continued, regretfully.

"Why in the world don't you marry, and have a home of your own?" sighed Mrs. Davids.

"Well, I don't *expect* to marry. I don't know as I do, at my time of life," responded the spinster. "I rather guess my day for chances is gone by."

"You ain't such a dreadful sight older than I am, though," replied Mrs. Davids, reflectively.

"Not so old by two full years," returned Miss Tame, taking another smart pinch of snuff, as though it touched the empty spot in her heart and did it good. "But *you* ain't looking out for opportunities yet, I suppose?"

Mrs. Davids sighed evasively. "We can't tell what is before us. There is more than one man in want of a wife."

As though to point her words, Captain Ben Lundy came in sight on the beach, his head a long way forward and his shambling feet trying in vain to keep up.

"Thirteen months and a half since Lyddy was buried," continued Mrs. Davids, accepting this application to her words, "and there is Captain Ben taking up with just what housekeeper he can get, and *no* housekeeper at all. It would be an excellent home for you, Persis. Captain Ben always had the name of making a kind husband."

She sighed again, whether from regret for the bereaved man, or for the multitude of women bereft of such a husband.

By this time Captain Ben's head was at the door.

"Morning!" said he, while his feet were coming up. "Quite an accident down here below the lighthouse last night. Schooner ran ashore in the blow, and broke all up into kindling-wood in less than no time. Captain Tisdale's been out looking for dead bodies ever since daylight."

"I knowed it!" sighed Mrs. Davids. "I heard a rushing sound some time about the break of day, that waked me out of a sound sleep, and I knowed then there was a spirit leaving its body. I heard it the night Davids went, or I expect I did. It must have been very nearly at that time."

"Well, I guess it wasn't a spirit, last night," said Captain Ben, "for, as I was going on to say, after searching back and forth, Captain Tisdale came upon the folks, a man and a boy, rolled up in their wet blankets, asleep behind the lifeboat house. He said he felt like he could shake them for staying out in the wet. Wrecks always make for the light-house, so he s'posed those ones were drowned to death, sure enough."

"O, then it couldn't have been them I was warned of!" returned Mrs. Davids, looking as though she regretted it. "It was right over my head, and I waked up just as the thing was rushing past. You haven't heard, have you," she continued, "whether or no there was any other damage done by the gale?"

"I don't know whether you would call it *damage* exactly," returned Captain Ben; "but Loizah Mullers got so scared she left me and went home. She said she couldn't stay and run the chance of another of our coast blows, and off she trapsed."

Mrs. Davids sighed like November. "So you have some hard luck, as well as myself. I don't suppose you can *get* a housekeeper, to keep her long," said she, dismally.

"Abel Grimes tells me it is enough sight easier getting wives than housekeepers, and I'm some of a mind to try that tack," replied Captain Ben, smiling grimly.

Mrs. Davids put up her hand to feel of her back hair, and smoothed down her apron; while Miss Persis Tame blushed like a withered rose, and turned her eyes modestly out of the window.

"I am *so!* But the difficulty is, who will it be? There are so many to select from, it is fairly bothersome," continued Captain Ben, winking fast, and looking as though he was made of dry corn-cobs and hay.

Miss Persis Tame turned about abruptly. "The land alive!" she ejaculated, with such sudden emphasis that the dishes shook on their shelves and Captain Ben in his chair. "It makes me as mad as a March hare to hear men go on as though all they'd got to do was to throw down their handkerchers to a woman, and, no matter who, she'd spring and run to pick it up. It is always, 'Who will I marry?' and not, 'Who will marry me?' "

"Why, there is twice the number of widders that there is of widder-ers here at the P'int. That was what was in my mind," said Captain Ben, in a tone of meek apology. "There is the Widow Keens, she that was

Azubah Muchmore. I don't know but what she would do; Lyddy used to think everything of her, and she is a first-rate of a housekeeper."

"Perhaps so," assented Mrs. Davids, dubiously. "But she is troubled a sight with the head complaint; I suppose you know she is. That is against her."

"Yes," assented Miss Tame. "The Muchmores all have weak heads. And, too, the Widow Keens, she's had a fall lately. She was up in a chair cleaning her top buttery shelf, and somehow one of the chair legs give way—it was loose or something, I expect—and down she went her whole heft. She keeps about, but she goes with two staves."

"I want to know if that is so!" said Captain Ben, his honest soul warming with sudden sympathy. "The widder has seen a sight of trouble."

"Yes, she has lived through a good deal, that woman has. I couldn't live through so much, 'pears to me; but we don't know what we can live through," rejoined Miss Tame.

Captain Ben did not reply, but his ready feet began to move to and fro restlessly; for his heart, more ready yet, had already gone out toward the unfortunate widow.

"It is so bad for a woman to be alone," said he to himself, shambling along the shingly beach a moment after. "Nobody to mend her chairs, or split up her kindlings, or do a chore for her; and she lame into the bargain! It is *too* bad!"

"He has steered straight for the widow Keens's, as sure as A is apple-dumpling," remarked Miss Persis, peering after him from the window.

"Well, I must admit I wouldn't have thought of Captain Ben's being en-a-mored after such a sickly piece of business. But men never know what they want. Won't you just hand me that gum-camphyer bottle, now you are up? It is on that chest of drawers behind you."

"No more they don't," returned Miss Tame, with a plaintive cadence, taking a sniff from the camphor-bottle on the way. "However, I don't begrutch him to her—I don't know as I do. It will make her a good hum, though, if she concludes to make arrangements."

Meantime, Captain Ben Lundy's head was wellnigh at Mrs. Keens's door, for it was situated only around the first sand-hill. She lived in a little bit of a house that looked as though it had been knocked together for a crockery-crate in the first place, with two windows and a rude door thrown in as after-thoughts. In the rear of this house was another tiny building, something like a grown-up hen-coop; and this was where Mrs. Keens carried on the business bequeathed to her by her deceased husband, along with five small children, and one not so small. But, worse than that, one who was "not altogether there," as the English say.

She was about this business now, dressed in a primitive sort of bloomer, with a washtub and clothes-wringer before her, and an army of bathing-suits of every kind and color flapping wildly in the fresh sea air at one side.

From a little farther on, mingling with the sound of the beating surf, came the merry voices of bathers—boarders at the great hotels on the hill.

"Here you be! Hard at it!" said Captain Ben, puffing around the corner like a portable west wind. "I've understood you've had a hurt. Is that so?"

"Oh, no! Nothing to mention," returned Mrs. Keens, turning about a face bright and cheerful as the full moon; and throwing, as by accident, a red bathing-suit over the two broomsticks that leaned against her tub.

Unlike Mrs. Davids, Mrs. Keens neither pitied herself nor would allow anybody else to do so.

"Sho!" remarked Captain Ben, feeling defrauded. He had counted on sacrificing himself to his sympathies, but he didn't give up yet. "You must see some pretty tough times, 'pears to me, with such a parcel of little ones, and only yourself to look to," said he, proceeding awkwardly enough to hang the pile of wrung-out clothes upon an empty line.

"I don't complain," returned the widow, bravely. "My children are not *teusome*; and Jack, why, you would be surprised to see how many things Jack can do, for all he isn't quite right."

As she spoke thus with affectionate pride, Jack came up wheeling a roughly made cart, filled with wet bathing-clothes, from the beach. He looked up at the sound of his mother's voice with something of the dumb tenderness of an intelligent dog. "Jack helps, Jack good boy," said he, nodding with a happy smile.

"Yes, Jack helps. We don't complain," repeated the mother.

"It would come handy, though, to have a man around to see to things and kind o' provide, wouldn't it, though?" persisted Captain Ben.

"Some might think so," replied Mrs. Keens, stopping her wringer to reflect a little. "But I haven't any wish to change my situation," she added, decidedly, going on again with her work.

"Sure on't?" persisted the Captain.

"Certain," replied the widow.

Captain Ben sighed. "I thought ma'be you was having a hard row to hoe, and I thoughts like enough—"

What, he never said, excepting by a beseeching glance at the cheerful widow, for just then an interruption came from some people after bathing-suits.

So Captain Ben moved off with a dismal countenance. But before he had gone far it suddenly brightened. "It might not be for the best," quoth he to himself. "Like enough not. I was very careful not to commit myself, and I am very glad I didn't." He smiled as he reflected on his judicious wariness. "But, however," he continued, "I might as well finish up this business now. There is Rachel Doolittle. Who knows but she'd make a likely wife! Lyddy sot a good deal by her. She never had a quilting or a sewing-bee but what nothing would do but she must give Rachel Doolittle an invite. Yes; I wonder I never decided on her before! She will be glad of a home, sure enough, for she haves to live around, as it were, upon her brothers."

Captain Ben's feet quickened themselves at these thoughts, and had almost overtaken his head, when behold! at a sudden turn in the road there stood Miss Rachel Doolittle, picking barberries from a wayside bush. "My sakes! If she ain't right here, like Rachel in the Bible!" ejaculated Captain Ben, taking heart at the omen.

Miss Doolittle looked up from under her tied-down brown hat in surprise at such a salutation. But her surprise was increased by Captain Ben's next remark.

"It just came into my mind," said he, "that you was the right one to take Lyddy's place. You two used to be such great knit-ups that it will seem 'most like having Lyddy back again. No," he continued, after a little reflection, "I don't know of anybody I had rather see sitting in Lyddy's chair and wearing Lyddy's things than yourself."

"Dear me, Captain Lundy, I couldn't think of it. Paul's folks expect me to stay with them while the boarder-season lasts, and I've as good as promised Jacob's wife I'll spend the winter with her."

"Ain't that a hard life you are laying out for yourself? And then, bum by you will get old or sick, ma'be, and who is going to want you around then? Every woman needs a husband of her own to take care of her."

"I'm able to take care of myself as yet, thanks to goodness! And I am not afraid my brothers will see me suffer in case of sickness," returned Miss Doolittle, her cheeks flaming up like a sumach in October.

"But hadn't you better take a little time to think it over? Ma'be it come sudden to you," pleaded Captain Ben.

"No, I thank you; some things don't need thinking over," answered Miss Doolittle, plucking at the barberries more diligently than ever.

"I wish Lyddy was here. She would convince you you are standing in your own light," returned Lyddy's widower in a perplexed tone.

"I don't need one to come from the dead to show me my own mind," retorted Miss Doolittle, firmly.

"Well, like enough you are right," said Captain Ben, mildly, putting a few stems of barberries in her pail; "ma'be 'twouldn't be best. I don't want to be rash."

And with that he moved off, on the whole congratulating himself he had not decided to marry Miss Doolittle.

"I thought, after she commenced her miserable gift of the gab, that Lyddy used to be free to admit she had a fiery tongue, for all they were such friends. And I'm all for peace myself. I guess, on the whole, ma'be she ain't the one for me, perhaps, and it is as well to look further. *Why*, what in *the* world! Well, there, what have I been thinking of! There is Mrs. Davids, as neat as a new cent, and the master hand to save. She is always taking on; and she will be glad enough to have somebody to look out for her—why, sure enough! And there I was, right at her house this very day, and never once thought of her! What an old dunce!"

But, fortunately, this not being a sin of *com*mission, it could easily be rectified; and directly Captain Ben had turned about and was trotting again toward the red house on the beach.

"Pound for pound of the best white sugar," he heard Miss Tame say as he neared the door.

"White sugar!" repeated Mrs. Davids, her usual sigh drawn out into

Captain Ben's Choice · 323

a little groan. "*White* sugar for *cram*berries! Who ever heard of such a thing! I've always considered I did well when I had plenty of brown."

"Poor creeter!" thought Captain Ben. "How she will enjoy getting into my pantry. Lyddy never complained that she didn't have enough of everything to do *with*."

And in the full ardor of his intended benevolence, he went right in and opened the subject at once. But, to his astonishment, Mrs. Davids refused him. She sighed, but she refused him.

"I've seen trouble enough a'ready, without my rushing into more with my eyes wide open," sighed she.

"Trouble? Why, that is just what I was meaning to save you!" exclaimed the bewildered widower. "Pump right in the house, and stove e'enamost new. And Lyddy never knew what it was to want for a spoonful of sugar or a pound of flour. And such a *handy* buttery and sink! Lyddy used to say she felt the worst about leaving her buttery of anything."

"Should thought she would," answered Mrs. Davids, forgetting to sigh. "However, I can't say that I feel any hankering after marrying a buttery. I've got buttery-room enough here, without the trouble of getting set up in a new place."

"Just as you say," returned the rejected. "I ain't sure as you'd be exactly the one. I *was* a thinking of looking for somebody a little younger."

"Well, here is Persis Tame. Why don't you bespeak her? *She* is younger, and she is in need of a good home. I can recommend her, too, as the first-rate of a cook," remarked Mrs. Davids, benevolently.

Miss Tame had been sitting a little apart by the open window, smiling to herself.

But now she turned about at once. "H'm!" said she, with contempt. "I should rather live under an umbrella tied to a stake, than marry for a *hum*."

So Captain Ben went home without engaging either wife or housekeeper.

And the first thing he saw was Captain Jacob Doolittle's old one-eyed horse eating the apples Loizah Mullers had strung and festooned from nails against the house, to dry.

The next thing he saw was, that, having left a window open, the hens had flown in and gone to housekeeping on their own account. But they were not, like Mrs. Davids, as neat as a new cent, and *not*, also, such master hands to save.

"Shoo! shoo! Get out! Go 'long there with you!" cried Captain Ben, waving the dish-cloth and the poker. "I declare for 't! I most hadn't ought to have left that bread out on the table. They've made a pretty mess of it, and it is every spec there is in the house too. Well, I must make a do of potatoes for supper, with a bit of pie and a mouthful of cake."

Accordingly he went to work building a fire that wouldn't burn. Then, forgetting the simple matter of dampers, the potatoes wouldn't bake. The tea-kettle boiled over and cracked the stove, and after that, boiled dry and cracked itself. Finally the potatoes fell to baking with so much ardor they overdid it and burnt up. And, last of all, the cake-jar and pie-cupboard proved to be entirely empty. Loizah had left on the eve of baking-day.

"The old cat! Well, I'd just as soon live on slapjacks a spell." said Captain Ben, when he made this discovery.

But even slapjacks palled on his palate, especially when he had them always to cook for himself.

" 'Tain't no way to live, this ain't," said he at last. "I'm a good mind to marry as ever I had to eat."

So he put on his hat and walked out. The first person he met was Miss Persis Tame, who turned her back and fell to picking thorough-wort blossoms as he came up.

"Look a here," said he, stopping short, "I'm dreadful put to 't! I can't get ne'er a wife nor ne'er a housekeeper, and I am e'enamost starved to death. I wish you *would* consent to marry with me, if you feel as if you could bring your mind to it. I am sure it would have been Lyddy's wish."

Miss Tame smelt of the thoroughwort blossoms.

"It comes pretty sudden on me," she replied. "I hadn't given the subject any thought. But you *are* to be pitied in your situation."

"Yes. And I'm dreadful lonesome. I've always been used to having Lyddy to talk over things with, and I miss her a sight. And I don't know anybody that has her ways more than you have. You are a good deal such a built woman, and you have the same hitch to your shoulders when you walk. You've got something the same look to your eyes, too;

I noticed it last Sunday in meeting-time," continued the widower, anxiously.

"I do feel for you. A man alone is in a deplorable situation," replied Miss Tame. "I'm sure I'd do anything in my power to help you."

"Well, marry with me then! That is what I want. We could be real comfortable together. I'll go for the license this minute, and we'll be married right away," returned the impatient suitor. "You go up to Elder Crane's, and I'll meet you there as soon as I can fetch around."

Then he hurried away, "without giving me a chance to say 'no,' " said "she that was" Persis Tame, afterward. "So I *had* to marry with him, as you might say. But I've never seen cause to regret it. I've got a first-rate of a hum, and Captain Ben makes a first-rate of a husband. And no hain't he, I hope, found cause to regret it," she added, with a touch of wifely pride; "though I do expect he might have had his pick among all the single women at the Point; but out of them all he chose *me*."

THE MACKREL

JOSH BILLINGS

The mackrel iz a game fish. They ought tew be well edukated, for they are always in schools.

They are very eazy to bite, and are caught with a piece ov old red flannel pettycoat tied onto a hook.

They ain't the only kind ov fish that are caught by the same kind ov bait.

Mackrel inhabit the sea, but those which inhabit the grocerys alwus taste to me az tho they had been born and fatted on salt.

They want a good deal ov freshning before they are eaten, and want a good deal ov freshning afterward.

If I can hav plenty ov mackrel for brekfasst i can generally make the other two meals out ov cold water.

Mackrel are considered by menny folks the best fish that swims, and are called "the salt of the earth."

A Quick Eye for Business

As one of the most prominent young burglars of San Francisco was walking out of court the other day, just after having secured an acquittal regarding his latest job by a prompt and businesslike "divvy" with the powers that be, at the usual rates, a well-to do but anxious-looking stranger touched his arm and beckoned him into a doorway.

"You are 'Teddy, the Ferret,' aren't you," asked the gentleman; "the man who was tried to-day for safe-cracking?"

"Well, wot of it?" replied the housebreaker.

"Why, just this—you'll excuse my speaking so low—but the fact is, I've come all the way from the San Joaquin to look up a party in your line of business."

"Have, eh!"

"Yes—I—well, I've a little proposition to make to you."

"Exactly," said the Ferret calmly; "you're a bank cashier down in the foot-hills."

"How did you know that?" stammered the gentleman, much amazed.

"And your cash and accounts are to be gone over by the directors on the first, and as you can't realize on your stocks, you want me to gag you some time next week, shoot your hat full of holes, find the combination in your breast pocket, and go through the safe in the regular way."

"Great heavens, man! how did you find all that out?"

"Why, I guessed it. It's the regular thing, you know. Got three orders to attend to ahead of yours now. Lemme see! Can't do anything for you next week, but might give you Wednesday and Thursday of the week after. How'll that suit you?"

The cashier said he thought he could make that do, and in less than five minutes they had struck a bargain and arranged the whole affair.

Even New York isn't much ahead of San Francisco in regard to modern conveniences.—*N. Y. World*

THE OWL-CRITIC

A Lesson to Fault-Finders

JAS. T. FIELDS

Jas. T. Fields, the well-known publisher, of the house of Ticknor & Fields, was born at Portsmouth, N. H., in 1817. He went to Boston while still a boy, and was, almost to the day of his death, 1881, identified with its literary history. He was the author of several volumes of verse and prose, and the editor of various posthumous collections—conspicuously those of De Quincey. From 1861 to 1872 he was the editor of *The Atlantic Monthly*.

"Who stuffed that white owl?" No one spoke in the shop:
  The barber was busy, and he couldn't stop;
  The customers, waiting their turns, were all reading
  The *Daily*, the *Herald*, the *Post*, little heeding
  The young man who blurted out such a blunt question;
  Not one raised a head, or even made a suggestion;
            And the barber kept on shaving.

"Don't you see, Mister Brown,"
  Cried the youth, with a frown,
"How wrong the whole thing is,
  How preposterous each wing is,
  How flattened the head is, how jammed down the neck is—
  In short, the whole owl, what an ignorant wreck 't is!
  I make no apology;
  I've learned owl-eology.
  I've passed days and nights in a hundred collections,
  And cannot be blinded to any deflections
  Arising from unskillful fingers that fail
  To stuff a bird right, from his beak to his tail.
  Mister Brown! Mister Brown!
  Do take that bird down,
  Or you'll soon be the laughing-stock all over town!"
            And the barber kept on shaving.

"I've *studied* owls,
 And other night fowls,
 And I tell you
 What I know to be true:
 An owl cannot roost
 With his limbs so unloosed;
 No owl in this world
 Ever had his claws curled,
 Ever had his legs slanted,
 Ever had his bill canted,
 Ever had his neck screwed
 Into that attitude.
 He can't *do* it, because
 'T is against all bird-laws.
 Anatomy teaches,
 Ornithology preaches
 An owl has a toe
 That *can't* turn out so!
 I've made the white owl my study for years,
 And to see such a job almost moves me to tears!
 Mister Brown, I'm amazed
 You should be so gone crazed
 As to put up a bird
 In that posture absurd!
 To *look* at that owl really brings on a dizziness;
 The man who stuffed *him* don't half know his business!"
                                        And the barber kept on shaving.

"Examine those eyes.
 I'm filled with surprise
 Taxidermists should pass
 Off on you such poor glass;
 So unnatural they seem
 They'd make Audubon scream,
 And John Burroughs laugh
 To encounter such chaff.
 Do take that bird down;
 Have him stuffed again, Brown!"
                                        And the barber kept on shaving.

"With some sawdust and bark
  I would stuff in the dark
  An owl better than that,
  I could make an old hat
  Look more like an owl
  Than that horrid fowl,
  Stuck up there so stiff like a side of coarse leather.
  In fact, about *him* there's not one natural feather."

Just then, with a wink and a sly normal lurch,
  The owl, very gravely, got down from his perch,
  Walked round, and regarded his fault-finding critic
  (Who thought he was stuffed) with a glance analytic,
  And then fairly hooted, as if he should say:
"Your learning's at fault *this* time, any way;
  Don't waste it again on a live bird, I pray.
  I'm an owl; you're another. Sir Critic, good-day!"
                              And the barber kept on shaving.

THE KIND-HEARTED SHE-ELEPHANT

GEO. T. LANIGAN

A kind-hearted She-Elephant, while walking through the Jungle where the Spicy Breezes blow soft o'er Ceylon's Isle, heedlessly set foot upon a Partridge, which she crushed to death within a few inches of the Nest containing its Callow Brood. "Poor little things!" said the generous Mammoth. "I have been a Mother myself, and my affection shall atone for the Fatal Consequences of my Neglect." So saying, she sat down upon the Orphaned Birds.

Moral.—The above Teaches us What Home is Without a Mother; also, that it is not every Person who should be intrusted with the Care of an Orphan Asylum.

A Dog in Church

MARK TWAIN

After the hymn had been sung, the Rev. Mr. Sprague turned himself into a bulletin board, and read off "notices" of meetings and societies and things, till it seemed that the list would stretch out to the crack of doom—a queer custom which is still kept up in America, even in cities, away here in this age of abundant newspapers. Often, the less there is to justify a traditional custom, the harder it is to get rid of it.

And now the minister prayed. A good, generous prayer, it was, and went into details: it pleaded for the church, and the little children of the church; for the other churches of the village; for the village itself; for the county; for the State; for the State officers; for the United States; for the churches of the United States; for Congress; for the President; for the officers of the Government; for poor sailors tossed by stormy seas; for the oppressed millions groaning under the heel of European monarchs and Oriental despotisms; for such as have the light and the good tidings, and yet have not eyes to see nor ears to hear withal; for the heathen in the far islands of the sea; and closed with a supplication that the words he was about to speak might find grace and favor, and be as seed sown in fertile ground, yielding in time a grateful harvest of good. Amen.

There was a rustling of dresses, and the standing congregation sat down. The boy whose history this book relates did not enjoy the prayer, he only endured it—if he even did that much. He was restive all through it; he kept tally of the details of the prayer, uncon-sciously—for he was not listening, but he knew the ground of old, and the clergyman's regular route over it—and when a little trifle of new matter was interlarded, his ear detected it and his whole nature re-sented it; he considered additions unfair and scoundrelly. In the midst of the prayer a fly had lit on the back of the pew in front of him, and tortured his spirit by calmly rubbing its hands together, embracing its head with its arms, and polishing it so vigorously that it seemed to al-most part company with the body, and the slender thread of a neck was exposed to view; scraping its wings with its hind legs and smoothing them to its body as if they had been coat tails; going through its whole toilet as tranquilly as if it knew it was perfectly safe. As indeed it was; for as sorely as Tom's hands itched to grab for it, they did not dare— he believed his soul would be instantly destroyed if he did such a thing while the prayer was going on. But with the closing sentence his hand began to curve and steal forward; and the instant the "Amen" was out, the fly was a prisoner of war. His aunt detected the act, and made him let it go.

The minister gave out his text and droned along monotonously through an argument that was so prosy that many a head by and by began to nod—and yet it was an argument that dealt in limitless fire and brimstone, and thinned the predestined elect down to a company so small as to be hardly worth the saving. Tom counted the pages of the sermon; after church he always knew how many pages there had been, but he seldom knew anything else about the discourses. How- ever, this time he was really interested for a little while. The minister made a grand and moving picture of the assembling together of the world's host at the millennium, when the lion and the lamb should lie down together, and a little child should lead them. But the pathos, the lesson, the moral, of the great spectacle were lost upon the boy; he only thought of the conspicuousness of the principal character before the on-looking nations; his face lit with the thought, and he said to himself that he wished he could be that child, if it was a tame lion.

Now he lapsed into suffering again, as the dry argument was re- sumed. Presently he bethought him of a treasure he had, and got it out. It was a large black beetle with formidable jaws—a "pinch-bug," he called it. It was in a percussion-cap box. The first thing the beetle did was to take him by the finger. A natural fillip followed, the beetle went floundering into the aisle and lit on its back, and the hurt finger went into the boy's mouth. The beetle lay there working its helpless legs, unable to turn over. Tom eyed it, and longed for it; but it was safe out of his reach. Other people uninterested in the sermon found relief in the beetle, and they eyed it too. Presently a vagrant poodle dog came idling along, sad at heart, lazy with the summer softness and the quiet, weary of captivity, sighing for change. He spied the beetle; the droop- ing tail lifted and wagged. He surveyed the prize; walked around it; smelt at it from a safe distance; walked around it again; grew bolder, and took a closer smell; then lifted his lip and made a gingerly snatch at it, just missing it; made another, and another; began to enjoy the diversion; subsided to his stomach with the beetle between his paws, and continued his experiments; grew weary at last, and then indifferent and absentminded. His head nodded, and little by little his chin descended and touched the enemy, who seized it. There was a sharp yelp, a flirt of the poodle's head, and the beetle fell a couple of yards away, and lit on its back once more. The neighboring spectators shook with a gentle inward joy, several faces went behind fans and handkerchiefs, and Tom was entirely happy. The dog looked foolish, and probably felt so; but there was resentment in his heart, too, and a craving for revenge. So he went to the beetle and began a wary attack on it again; jumping at it from every point of a circle, lighting with his fore paws within an inch of the creature, making even closer snatches at it with his teeth, and jerking his head till his ears flapped again. But he grew tired once more, after a while; tried to amuse himself with a fly, but found no relief; followed an ant around, with his nose close to the floor, and quickly wearied of that; yawned, sighed, forgot the beetle entirely, and sat down on it! Then there was a wild yelp of agony, and the poodle went sailing up the aisle; the yelps continued, and so did the dog; he crossed the house in front of the altar; he flew down the other aisle; he crossed before the doors; he clamored up the home-stretch; his anguish grew with his progress, till presently he was but a woolly comet moving in its orbit with the gleam and the speed of light. At last the frantic sufferer sheered from its course, and sprang into its master's lap; he flung it out of the window, and the voice of distress quickly thinned away and died in the distance.

By this time the whole church was red-faced and suffocating with suppressed laughter, and the sermon had come to a dead standstill. The discourse was resumed presently, but it went lame and halting, all possibility of impressiveness being at an end; for even the gravest sentiments were constantly being received with a smothered burst of unholy mirth, under cover of some remote pew-back, as if the poor parson had said a rarely facetious thing. It was a genuine relief to the whole congregation when the ordeal was over and the benediction pronounced.

Tom Sawyer went home quite cheerful, thinking to himself that there was some satisfaction about divine service when there was a bit of variety in it. He had but one marring thought; he was willing that the dog should play with his pinch-bug, but he did not think it was up-right in him to carry it off.

A Visit to the Asylum for Aged and Decayed Punsters

OLIVER WENDELL HOLMES

Oliver Wendell Holmes was born in Cambridge, Mass., in 1809, and was graduated at Harvard in 1829. He first studied law, but afterwards took up medicine in the schools of Paris, and, on his return home, became Professor of Anatomy and Physiology at Dartmouth in 1838. From 1847 to 1883 he filled the same chair in Harvard. He is the author of many volumes of poetry and prose, which have all a wide fame, but of which "The Autocrat of the Breakfast Table" is perhaps the best known. He is easily the first of our more literary humorists.

Having just returned from a visit to this admirable institution, in company with a friend who is one of the Directors, we propose giving a short account of what we saw and heard. The great success of the Asylum for Idiots and Feeble-minded Youth, several of the scholars from which have reached considerable distinction, one of them being connected with a leading Daily Paper in this city, and others having served in the State and National Legislatures, was the motive which led to the foundation of this excellent charity. Our late distinguished townsman, Noah Dow, Esquire, as is well known, bequeathed a large portion of his fortune to this establishment—"being thereto moved," as his will expressed it, "by the desire of *N. Dowing* some publick Institution for the benefit of Mankind." Being consulted as to the Rules of the Institution and the selection of a Superintendent, he replied, that "all Boards must construct their own Platforms of operation. Let them select *anyhow*, and he should be pleased." N. E. Howe, Esq., was chosen in compliance with this delicate suggestion.

The charter provides for the support of "One hundred aged and decayed Gentlemen-Punsters." On inquiry if there was no provision for *females*, my friend called my attention to this remarkable psychological fact, namely:

THERE IS NO SUCH THING AS A FEMALE PUNSTER.

This remark struck me forcibly, and, on reflection, I found that *I never knew nor heard of one*, though I have once or twice heard a woman make *a single detached* pun, as I have known a hen to crow.

On arriving at the south gate of the Asylum grounds, I was about to ring, but my friend held my arm and begged me to rap with my stick, which I did. An old man, with a very comical face, presently opened the gate and put out his head.

"So you prefer *Cane* to *A Bell*, do you?" he said, and began chuckling and coughing at a great rate.

My friend winked at me.

"You're here still, Old Joe, I see," he said to the old man.

"Yes, yes; and it's very odd, considering how often I've *bolted*, nights."

He then threw open the double gates for us to ride through.

"Now," said the old man, as he pulled the gates after us, "you've had a long journey."

"Why, how is that, Old Joe?" said my friend.

"Don't you see?" he answered; "there's the *East hinges* on one side of the gate, and there's the *West hinges* on t'other side—haw! haw! haw!"

We had no sooner got into the yard than a feeble little gentleman, with a remarkably bright eye, came up to us, looking very serious, as if something had happened.

"The town has entered a complaint against the asylum as a gambling establishment," he said to my friend the Director.

"What do you mean?" said my friend.

"Why, they complain that there's a *lot o' rye* on the premises," he answered, pointing to a field of that grain, and hobbled away, his shoulders shaking with laughter as he went.

On entering the main building we saw the Rules and Regulations for the Asylum conspicuously posted up. I made a few extracts, which may be interesting.

SECT. 1. OF VERBAL EXERCISES.

5.   Each Inmate shall be permitted to make Puns freely, from eight in the morning until ten at night, except during Service in the Chapel and Grace before Meals.

6.   At ten o'clock the gas will be turned off, and no further Puns, Conundrums, or other play on words will be allowed to be uttered, or to be uttered aloud.

9.   Inmates who have lost their faculties, and cannot any longer make Puns, shall be permitted to repeat such as may be selected for them by the Chaplain out of the work of Mr. *Joseph Miller.*

10.   Violent and unmanageable Punsters who interrupt others, when engaged in conversation, with Puns, or attempts at the same, shall be deprived of their *Joseph Millers*, and, if necessary, placed in solitary confinement.

SECT. III. OF DEPORTMENT AT MEALS.

4.   No inmate shall make any Pun, or attempt at the same, until the Blessing has been asked and the company are decently seated.

7.   Certain Puns having been placed on the *Index Expurgatorius* of the Institution, no Inmate shall be allowed to utter them, on pain of being debarred the perusal of *Punch* and *Vanity Fair*, and, if repeated, deprived of his *Joseph Miller.*

Among these are the following:

Allusions to *Attic salt*, when asked to pass the salt-cellar.

Remarks on the Inmates being *mustered*, etc., etc.

Personal allusions in connection with *carrots* and *turnips.*

Attempts upon the word *tomato*, etc., etc.

The following are also prohibited, excepting to such Inmates as may have lost their faculties, and cannot any longer make Puns of their own:

"——your own *hair* or a wig;" "it will be *long enough*, etc., etc.; "little of its age," etc., etc.; also playing upon the following words: *hospital, mayor, pun, pitied, bread, sauce, sole*, etc., etc., etc. *See* INDEX EXPURGATO-RIUS, *printed for use of Inmates.*

The Superintendent, who went round with us, had been a noted punster in his time, and well known in the business world, but lost his customers by making too free with their names—as in the famous story he set afloat in '29, of *forgeries* attaching to the names of a noted Judge, an eminent lawyer, the Secretary of the Board of Foreign Missions, and the well-known Landlord at Springfield. One of the *four Jerries*, he added, was of gigantic magnitude.

The Superintendent showed some of his old tendencies as he went round with us.

"Do you know"—he broke out all at once—"why they don't take steppes in Tartary for establishing Insane Hospitals?"

We both confessed ignorance.

"Because there are *nomad* people to be found there," he said, with a dignified smile.

He proceeded to introduce us to different Inmates. The first was a middle-aged, scholarly man, who was seated at a table with a Webster's Dictionary and a sheet of paper before him.

"Well, what luck to-day, Mr. Mowzer?" said the Superintendent.

He turned to his notes and read:

"Don't you see Webster *ers* in the words cent*er* and theat*er*?

"If he spells leather *lether*, and feather *fether*, isn't there danger that he'll give us a *bad spell of weather*?

"Besides, Webster is a resurrectionist; he does not allow *u* to rest quietly in the *mould*.

"And again, because Mr. Worcester inserts an illustration in his text, is that any reason why Mr. Webster's publishers should hitch one on in their appendix? It's what I call a *Connect-a-cut* trick.

"Why is his way of spelling like the floor of an oven? Because it is *under bread*."

"Mowzer!" said the Superintendent—"that word is on the Index!"

"I forgot," said Mr. Mowzer—"please don't deprive me of *Vanity Fair*, this one time, Sir."

"These are all, this morning. Good day, Gentlemen. Then to the Superintendent—Add you, Sir!"

The next Inmate was a semi-idiotic-looking old man. He had a heap of block-letters before him, and, as we came up, he pointed, without saying a word, to the arrangements he had made with them on the table. They were evidently anagrams, and had the merit of transposing the letters of the words employed without addition or subtraction. Here are a few of them:

TIMES.	SMITE!
POST.	STOP!
TRIBUNE.	TRUE NIB.
WORLD.	DR. OWL.

ADVERTISER.	RES VERI DAT.
	IS TRUE. READ!
ALLOPATHY.	ALL O' TH' PAY.
HOMŒPATHY.	O, THE ——! O! O, MY! PAH!

The mention of several New York papers led to two or three questions. Thus: Whether the Editor of the Tribune was *H. G. really*? If the complexion of his politics were not accounted for by his being *an eager* person himself? Whether Wendell *Fillips* were not a reduced copy of John *Knocks*? Whether a New York *Feuille toniste* is not the same thing as a *Fellow down East*?

At this time a plausible-looking, bald-headed man joined us, evidently waiting to take a part in the conversation.

"Good morning, Mr. Riggles," said the Superintendent. "Anything fresh this morning? Any Conundrum?"

"Nothing of any account," he answered. "We had hasty-pudding yesterday."

"What has that got to do with conundrums?" asked the Superintendent.

"I asked the Inmates why it was like the Prince."

"Oh! because it comes attended by its *sweet*," said the Superintendent.

"No," said Mr. Riggles, "it is because the 'lasses runs after it."

"Riggles is failing," said the Superintendent, as we moved on.

The next Inmate looked as if he might have been a sailor formerly.

"Ask him what his calling was," said the Superintendent.

"Followed the sea," he replied to the question put by one of us. "Went as mate in a fishing-schooner."

"Why did you give it up?"

"Because I didn't like working for *two-masters*," he replied.

Presently we came upon a group of elderly persons gathered about a venerable gentleman with flowing locks, who was propounding questions to a row of Inmates.

"Can any Inmate give me a motto for M. Berger?" he said.

Nobody responded for two or three minutes. At last one old man, whom I at once recognized as a Graduate of our University (Anno 1800), held up his hand.

"Rem a *cue* tetigit."

"Go to the head of the Class, Josselyn," said the venerable Patriarch.

The successful Inmate did as he was told, but in a very rough way, pushing against two or three of the Class.

"How is this?" said the Patriarch.

"You told me to go up *jostlin'*," he replied.

The old gentlemen who had been shoved about enjoyed the Pun too much to be angry.

Presently the Patriarch asked again—

"Why was M. Berger authorized to go to the dances given to the Prince?"

The Class had to give up this, and he answered it himself:

"Because every one of his carroms was a *tick-it* to the *ball.*"

"Who collects the money to defray the expenses of the last campaign in Italy?" asked the Patriarch.

Here again the Class failed.

"The war-cloud's rolling *Dun*," he answered.

"And what is mulled wine made with?"

Three or four voices exclaimed at once:

"*Sizzle-y* Madeira!"

Here a servant entered, and said, "Luncheon-time." The old gentlemen, who have excellent appetites, dispersed at once, one of them politely asking us if we would not stop and have a bit of bread and a little mite of cheese.

"There is one thing I have forgotten to show you," said the Superintendent—"the cell for the confinement of violent and unmanageable Punsters."

We were very curious to see it, particularly with reference to the alleged absence of every object upon which a play of words could possibly be made.

The Superintendent led us up some dark stairs to a corridor, then along a narrow passage, then down a broad flight of steps into another passage-way, and opened a large door which looked out on the main entrance.

"We have not seen the cell for the confinement of 'violent and unmanageable' Punsters," we both exclaimed.

"This is the *sell!*" he exclaimed, pointing to the outside prospect.

My friend, the Director, looked me in the face so good-naturedly that I had to laugh.

"We like to humor the Inmates," he said. "It has a bad effect, we find, on their health and spirits, to disappoint them of their little pleasantries. Some of the jests to which we have listened are not new to me, though I dare say you may not have heard them often before. The same thing happens in general society, with this additional disadvantage, that there is no punishment provided for 'violent and unmanageable' Punsters, as in our Institution."

We made our bow to the Superintendent, and walked to the place where our carriage was waiting for us. On our way, an exceedingly decrepit old man moved slowly towards us, with a perfectly blank look on his face, but still appearing as if he wished to speak.

"Look!" said the Director—"that is our Centenarian."

The ancient man crawled towards us, cocked one eye, with which he seemed to see a little, up at us, and said:

"Sarvant, young Gentlemen. Why is a—a—a—like a—a—a—? Give it up? Because it's a—a—a—a—."

He smiled a pleasant smile, as if it were all plain enough.

"One hundred and seven last Christmas," said the Director.

"He lost his answers about the age of ninety-eight. Of late years he puts his whole Conundrums in blank—but they please him just as well."

We took our departure, much gratified and instructed by our visit, hoping to have some future opportunity of inspecting the Records of this excellent Charity, and making extracts for the benefit of our Readers.

MINNESOTA WHEAT

"Let's see: they raise some wheat in Minnesota, don't they?" asked a Schoharie granger of a Michigander.

"Raise wheat! Who raises wheat? No, sir; decidedly no, sir. It raises itself. Why, if we undertook to cultivate wheat in that State it would run us out. There wouldn't be any place to put our house."

"But I've been told that grasshoppers take a good deal of it."

"Of course they do. If they didn't, I don't know what we would do. The cussed stuff would run all over the State and drive us out—choke us up. Those grasshoppers are a Godsend, only there ain't half enough of em."

"Is the wheat nice and plump!"

"Plump! Why, I don't know what you call plump wheat, but there are seventeen in our family, including ten servants, and when we want bread we just go out and fetch in a kernal of wheat and bake it."

"Do you ever soak it in water first?"

"Oh, no; that wouldn't do. It would swell a little, and then we couldn't get it in our range oven."—*Newspaper*

GETTING A GLASS OF WATER

F. W. COZZENS

One evening Mrs. S. had retired, and I was busy writing, when it struck me a glass of ice-water would be palatable. So I took the candle and a pitcher, and went down to the pump. Our pump is in the kitchen. A country pump in the kitchen is more convenient; but a well with buckets is certainly most picturesque. Unfortunately, our well-water has not been sweet since it was cleaned out. First I had to open a bolted door that lets you into the basement-hall, and then I went to the kitchen-door, which proved to be locked. Then I remembered that our girl always carried the key to bed with her, and slept with it under her pillow. Then I retraced my steps, bolted the basement-door, and went up in the dining-room. As is always the case, I found, when I could not get any water, I was thirstier than I supposed I was. Then I thought I would wake our girl up. Then I concluded not to do it. Then I thought of the well, but I gave that up on account of its flavor. Then I opened the closet doors; there was no water there; and then I thought of the dumb-waiter! The novelty of the idea made me smile; I took out two of the movable shelves, stood the pitcher on the bottom of the dumb-waiter, got in myself with the lamp; let myself down, until I supposed I was within a foot of the floor below, and then let go!

We came down so suddenly, that I was shot out of the apparatus as if it had been a catapult; it broke the pitcher, extinguished the lamp, and landed me in the middle of the kitchen at midnight, with no fire, and the air not much above the zero point. The truth is, I had miscalculated the distance of the descent—instead of falling one foot, I had fallen five. My first impulse was, to ascend by the way I came down, but I found that impracticable. Then I tried the kitchen door; it was locked. I tried to force it open; it was made of two-inch stuff, and held its own. Then I hoisted a window, and there were the rigid iron bars. If ever I felt angry at anybody it was at myself, for putting up those bars to please Mrs. Sparrowgrass. I put them up, not to keep people in, but to keep people out.

I laid my cheek against the ice-cold barriers and looked out at the sky; not a star was visible; it was as black as ink overhead. Then I thought of Baron Trenck, and the prisoner of Chillon. Then I made a noise! I shouted until I was hoarse, and ruined our preserving-kettle with the poker. That brought our dogs out in full bark, and between us we made night hideous. Then I thought I heard a voice, and listened—it was Mrs. Sparrowgrass calling to me from the top of the stair-case. I tried to make her hear me, but the infernal dogs united with howl and growl and bark, so as to drown my voice, which is naturally plaintive and tender. Besides, there were two bolted doors and double deafened floors between us; how could she recognize my voice, even if she did hear it? Mrs. Sparrowgrass called once or twice, and then got frightened; the next thing I heard was a sound as if the roof had fallen in, by which I understood that Mrs. Sparrowgrass was springing the rattle! That called out our neighbor, already wide awake; he came to the rescue with a bull-terrier, a Newfoundland pup, a lantern and a revolver. The moment he saw me at the window, he shot at me, but fortunately just missed me. I threw myself under the kitchen table and ventured to expostulate with him, but he would not listen to reason. In the excitement I had forgotten his name, and that made matters worse. It was not until he had roused up everybody around, broken in the basement door with an axe, gotten into the kitchen with his cursed savage dogs and shooting-iron, and seized me by the collar, that he recognized me—and then, he wanted me to explain it! But what kind of an explanation could I make to him? I told him he would have to wait until my mind was composed, and then I would let him understand the whole matter fully. But he never would have had the particulars from me, for

I do not approve of neighbors that shoot at you, break in your door, and treat you, in your own house, as if you were a jail-bird. He knows all about it, however—somebody has told him—*somebody* tells every-body everything in our village.

THE HODJA AS A PROPHET

S. S. COX

The Hodja was considered the most learned man in his town. Every one called on him for information and advice. One day a number of people called, and demanded of him a reply to this question:

"When, O Hodja! will be the end of the world?"

"Oh!" says he, "ask me something difficult. That is very easy to an-swer. When my wife dies, it will be the end of half of the world; when I die, then the whole world will end."

Moral by Sir Boyle Roche: *Single misfortunes never come alone, and the greatest possible misfortune is followed by one greater.*

BLUE-JAYS

MARK TWAIN

Animals talk to each other, of course. There can be no question about that; but I suppose there are very few people who can understand them. I never knew but one man who could. I knew he could, however, because he told me so himself. He was a middle-aged, simple-hearted miner, who had lived in a lonely corner of California, among the woods and mountains, a good many years, and had studied the ways of his only neighbors, the beasts and the birds, until he believed he could accurately translate any remark which they made. This was Jim Baker. According to Jim Baker, some animals have only a limited education and use only very simple words, and scarcely ever a comparison or a flowery figure; whereas, certain other animals have a large vocabulary, a fine command of language and a ready and fluent delivery; consequently this latter talk a great deal; they like it; they are conscious of their talent, and they enjoy "showing off." Baker said that, after long and careful observation, he had come to the conclusion that the blue-jays were the best talkers he had found among birds and beasts. Said he:

"There's more *to* a blue-jay than any other creature. He has got more moods and more different kinds of feelings than other creatures; and, mind you, whatever a blue-jay feels, he can put into language. And no mere commonplace language, either, but rattling, out-and-out book-talk—and bristling with metaphor too—just bristling! And as for command of language—why, *you* never see a blue-jay get stuck for a word. No man ever did. They just boil out of him! And another thing: I've noticed a good deal, and there's no bird, or cow, or anything that uses as good grammar as a blue-jay. You may say a cat uses good grammar. Well, a cat does—but you let a cat get excited, once; you let a cat get to pulling fur with another cat on a shed, nights, and you'll hear grammar that will give you the lockjaw. Ignorant people think it's the *noise* which fighting cats make that is so aggravating, but it ain't so; it's the sickening grammar they use. Now I've never heard a jay use bad grammar but very seldom; and when they do, they are as ashamed as a human; they shut right down and leave.

"You may call a jay a bird. Well, so he is, in a measure—because he's got feathers on him, and don't belong to no church, perhaps; but otherwise he is just as much a human as you be. And I'll tell you for why. A jay's gifts, and instincts, and feelings, and interests cover the whole ground. A jay hasn't got any more principle than a Congressman. A jay will lie, a jay will steal, a jay will deceive, a jay will betray; and, four times out of five, a jay will go back on his solemnest promise. The sacredness of an obligation is a thing which you can't cram into no blue-jay's head. Now, on top of all this, there's another thing: a jay can out-swear any gentleman in the mines. You think a cat can swear. Well, a cat can; but you give a blue-jay a subject that calls for his reserve powers, and where is your cat? Don't talk to *me*—I know too much about this thing. And there's yet another thing: in the one little particular of scolding—just good, clean, out-and-out scolding—a blue jay can lay over anything, human or divine. Yes, sir, a jay is everything that a man is. A jay can cry, a jay can laugh, a jay can feel shame, a jay can reason and plan and discuss, a jay likes gossip and scandal, a jay has got a sense of humor, a jay knows when he is an ass just as well as you do—maybe better. If a jay ain't human, he better take in his sign, that's all. Now I am going to tell you a perfectly true fact about some blue-jays.

"When I first begun to understand jay language correctly, there was a little incident happened here. Seven years ago, the last man in this region but me moved away. There stands his house—been empty ever since; a log house, with a plank roof—just one big room, and no more; no ceiling—nothing between the rafters and the floor. Well, one Sunday morning I was sitting out here in front of my cabin with my cat, taking the sun, and looking at the blue hills, and listening to the leaves rustling so lonely in the trees, and thinking of the home away yonder in the States, that I hadn't heard from in thirteen years, when a bluejay lit on that house, with an acorn in his mouth, and says, 'Hello, I reckon I've struck something!' When he spoke, the acorn fell out of his mouth and rolled down the roof, of course, but he didn't care; his mind was all on the thing he had struck. It was a knot-hole in the roof. He cocked his head to one side, shut one eye and put the other one to the hole, like a 'possum looking down a jug; then he glanced up with his bright eyes, gave a wink or two with his wings—which signifies gratification, you understand—and says, 'It looks like a hole, it's located like a hole—blamed if I don't believe it *is* a hole!

"Then he cocked his head down and took another look; he glances up perfectly joyful this time; winks his wings and his tail both, and says, 'Oh, no, this ain't no fat thing, I reckon! If I ain't in luck!—why, it's a perfectly elegant hole!' So he flew down and got that acorn, and fetched it up and dropped it in, and was just tilting his head back with the heavenliest smile on his face, when all of a sudden he was paralyzed into a listening attitude, and that smile faded gradually out of his countenance like breath off'n a razor, and the queerest look of surprise took its place. Then he says, 'Why, I didn't hear it fall!' He cocked his eye at the hole again and took a long look; raised up and shook his head; stepped around to the other side of the hole, and took another look from that side; shook his head again. He studied a while, then he just went into the *de*tails—walked round and round the hole, and spied into it from every point of the compass. No use. Now he took a thinking attitude on the comb of the roof, and scratched the back of his head with his right foot a minute, and finally says, 'Well, it's too many for *me*, that's certain; must be a mighty long hole; however, I ain't got no time to fool around here; I got to 'tend to business; I reckon it's all right—chance it, anyway!'

"So he flew off and fetched another acorn and dropped it in, and tried to flirt his eye to the hole quick enough to see what become of it, but he was too late. He held his eye there as much as a minute; then he raised up and sighed, and says, 'Consound it, I don't seem to understand this thing, no way; however, I'll tackle her again.' He fetched another acorn, and done his level best to see what become of it, but he couldn't. He says, 'Well, *I* never struck no such a hole as this before; I'm of the opinion it's a totally new kind of a hole.' Then he begun to get mad. He held in for a spell, walking up and down the comb of the roof, and shaking his head and muttering to himself; but his feelings got the upper hand of him presently, and he broke loose and cussed himself black in the face. I never see a bird take on so about a little thing. When he got through, he walks to the hole and looks in again for a half a minute; then he says, 'Well, you're a long hole, and a deep hole, and a mighty singular hole altogether—but I've started in to fill you, and I'm d—d if I *don't* fill you, if it takes a hundred years!'

"And with that, away he went. You never see a bird work so since you was born. He laid into his work like a nigger, and the way he hove acorns into that hole for about two hours and a half was one of the most exciting and astonishing spectacles I ever struck. He never stopped to take a look any more—he just hove 'em in, and went for more. Well, at last he could hardly flop his wings, he was so tuckered out. He comes a-drooping down, once more, sweating like a nice-pitcher, drops his acorn in and says, '*Now* I guess I've got the bulge on you by this time!' So he bent down for a look. If you'll believe me, when his head come up again he was just pale with rage. He says, 'I've shoveled acorns enough in there to keep the family thirty years, and if I can see a sign of one of 'em, I wish I may land in a museum with a belly full of sawdust in two minutes!'

"He just had strength enough to crawl up on to the comb and lean his back agin the chimbly, and then he collected his impressions and begun to free his mind. I see in a second that what I had mistook for profanity in the mines was only just the rudiments, as you may say.

"Another jay was going by, and heard him doing his devotions, and stops to inquire what was up. The sufferer told him the whole circumstance, and says, 'Now yonder's the hole, and if you don't believe me, go and look for yourself.' So this fellow went and looked, and comes back and says, 'How many did you say you put in there?' 'Not any less than two tons,' says the sufferer. The other jay went and looked again. He couldn't seem to make it out, so he raised a yell, and three more jays come. They all examined the hole, they all made the sufferer tell it over again, then they all discussed it, and got off as many leather-headed opinions about it as an average crowd of humans could have done.

"They did call in more jays; then more and more, till pretty soon this whole region 'peared to have a blue flush about it. There must have been five thousand of them; and such another jawing and disputing and ripping and cussing, you never heard. Every jay in the whole lot put his eye to the hole, and delivered a more chuckle-headed opinion about the mystery than the jay that went there before him. They examined the house all over, too. The door was standing half-open, and at last one old jay happened to go and light on it and look in. Of course, that knocked the mystery galley-west in a second. There lay the acorns, scattered all over the floor. He flopped his wings and raised a whoop. 'Come here!' he says, 'Come here, everybody; hang'd if this fool hasn't been trying to fill up a house with acorns!' They all came a-swooping down like a blue cloud, and as each fellow lit on the door and took a glance, the whole absurdity of the contract that that first jay had tackled hit him home, and he fell over backwards suffocating with laughter, and the next jay took his place and done the same.

"Well, sir, they roosted around here on the house-top and the trees for an hour, and guffawed over that thing like human beings. It ain't no use to tell me a blue-jay hasn't got a sense of humor, because I know better. And memory too. They brought jays here from all over the United States to look down that hole, every summer for three years. Other birds too. And they could all see the point, except an owl that come from Nova Scotia to visit the Yo Semite, and he took this thing in on his way back. He said he couldn't see anything funny in it. But then, he was a good deal disappointed about Yo Semite, too."

An Italian's View of a New England Winter

J. M. Bailey

There was a burst in a tin conductor leading from the roof of the
house on the corner of Rose and Myrtle streets the other afternoon,
and the water thus escaping ran across the walk. Toward night the
weather stiffened up, and the loose water became a sheet of ice. About
four o'clock the next morning there was a slight fall of snow. In the
basement of the building an Italian gentleman has a fruit store. Shortly
after six o'clock this morning he had his outside wares in a line of display. Peanuts being a specialty with him, two or three bushels of that
article made a tempting pile on a large stand. While he was making
this arrangement, a carpenter with a tool-box on his shoulder came
around the corner, and, stepping on the concealed ice, immediately
threw his tool-box into the street, got up himself, looked around to see
what had happened, and then picked up his tools. This so amused the
Italian that he felt obliged to rush into the shelter of the basement to
conceal his delight. Had he been a native of this country, it might have
suggested itself to him to sweep the thin guise of snow from the ice
and to sprinkle salt or ashes upon it, but being a foreigner, and not very
well acquainted with our language, he did not think of this, but, instead, he posted himself in a position to give him a good view of the
corner, and patiently waited for developments. He saw them. If his object was to get an idea of the fullness and flexibility of the English language, he could not have possibly adopted a better course.

Scarcely had the carpenter gathered up his things and limped off,
when a man smoking came hurrying along. When he reached the ice
he suddenly turned part way around, bit a brier-wood pipe completely
in twain, and slid on his breast off from the walk into the gutter. He got
up, cautiously recovered his pipe, and melted away. The Italian shook
all over.

Following closely after this mishap was a laborer with a dinner-
kettle. When he touched the ice it was difficult for the fruit merchant

to determine whether it was his feet or another part of his person—it was done so quick. The new-comer appeared to suddenly come apart and shut up at the middle, and in the same flash the tin pail described a circle of lightning rapidity, and was then slapped against the pavement with terrific force. At the same instant the Italian saw a piece of pie, several half-slices of buttered bread, two hard-boiled eggs, a piece of cold beef, and a fork and spoon fly off in different directions, while a pint tin of coffee made its appearance, and emptied its contents in the prostrate man's lap. While this individual was getting up to his feet, and securing his pail and cutlery, the Italian managed to blend considerable instruction with the amusement.

Then there came a man with a board on his shoulder. He laid down on the board, with one of his hands under the board. Then he got up, and put the injured hand between his knees, where he pressed it tightly, while he used the most dreadful language the Italian ever heard; and he didn't hear it all either, being so convulsed with laughter as to necessarily divide his attention.

And thus the performance went on until after eight o'clock. Scarcely ten minutes elapsed between the acts. Sometimes a boy would be the hero, then again a couple of merchants, or perhaps somebody connected with a bank. Whoever it might be, he went down, and went down hard, and the Italian watched and improved his mind, and began to think that this country had its advantages as well as its disadvantages. It was eleven minutes past eight when the final catastrophe occurred. This was consummated in the person of a long slim man with a picture under his arm, and a very large woman carrying a basket. The long slim man was somewhat in advance. The Italian, being impressed with the conviction that something of an extraordinary nature was about to transpire, stared with fairly bulging eyes at the coming figure. No sooner did the tall slim man touch the treacherous spot, than the venturing foot kicked out most savagely at the atmosphere, and his body shot around like fireworks. The picture flew from his possession at the same moment, and being thus freed he made a spasmodic clutch with all his limbs at once for a place of refuge, and in a flash his legs whipped about a corner leg of the inoffensive peanut stand, and the great shining yellow pyramid followed him to the pavement. The horrified Italian, stunned for an instant by the enormity of the catastrophe, sought to plunge out to the rescue of his goods, but was too late. The fleshy woman, having rushed to the aid of the tall slim man, who was her husband, was caught herself by the subtle foe, and in her descent, which was by far the most vigorous of the series, she took in two-thirds of the peanuts; and the crash of the demolished fruit, as she pinned it to the walk, might have been heard four squares away.

The unhappy vender reached the place in time to be taken in himself, and the addition of one hundred and thirty pounds of macaroni-fed Italian added to the dismal proportions of the scene. How they got disentangled and on their feet, no one seems able to explain, but the result was reached amid an appalling uproar of Italian, English and feminine noises.

What a great matter a little fire kindleth! Ten cents' worth of salt would have saved all the misery and distress. As it is, Danbury has some twenty persons with damaged backs or legs, the owner of the building has four suits on hand for damages, the tall slim man and his wife are confined to their beds, and on Saturday last the Italian was morosely squatted alongside of the funnel of a steamer bound for Italy.

The Nobleman and the Oyster

AMBROSE BIERCE

A certain Persian nobleman obtained from a cow gipsy a small Oyster. Holding him up by the beard, he addressed him thus:

"You must try to forgive me for what I am about to do; and you might as well set about it at once, for you haven't much time. I should never think of swallowing you if it were not so easy; but opportunity is the strongest of all temptations. Besides, I am an orphan, and very hungry."

"Very well," replied the Oyster; "it affords me genuine pleasure to comfort the parentless and the starving. I have already done my best for our friend here, of whom you purchased me; but although she has an amiable and accommodating stomach, *we couldn't agree.* For this trifling incompatibility—would you believe it?—she was about to stew me! Savior, benefactor, proceed!"

"I think," said the nobleman, rising and laying down the Oyster, "I ought to know something more definite about your antecedents before succoring you. If you couldn't agree with your mistress, you are probably no better than you should be."

People who begin doing something from a selfish motive, frequently drop it when they learn that it is a real benevolence.

CUSTOM HOUSE MORALS

W. D. HOWELLS

The travelers all met at breakfast and duly discussed the adventures of the night; and for the rest, the forenoon passed rapidly and slowly with Basil and Isabel, as regret to leave Quebec, or the natural impatience of travelers to be off, overcame them. Isabel spent part of it in shopping, for she had found some small sums of money and certain odd corners in her trunks still unappropriated, and the handsome stores on the Rue Fabrique were very tempting. She said she would just go in and look; and the wise reader imagines the result. As she knelt over her boxes, trying so to distribute her purchases as to make them look as if they were old—old things of hers, which she had brought all the way round from Boston with her—a fleeting touch of conscience stayed her hand.

"Basil," she said, "perhaps we'd better declare *some* of these things. What's the duty on those?" she asked, pointing to certain articles.

"I don't know. About a hundred per cent. *ad valorem.*"

"*C'est à dire—?*"

"As much as they cost."

"O *then*, dearest," responded Isabel indignantly, "it *can't* be wrong to smuggle! I won't declare a thread!"

"That's very well for you, whom they won't ask. But what if they ask *me* whether there's anything to declare?"

Isabel looked at her husband and hesitated. Then she replied, in terms that I am proud to record in honor of American womanhood: "You mustn't fib about it, Basil" (heroically); "I couldn't respect you if you did" (tenderly); "but" (with decision) "*you must slip out of it some way!*"

A Western Reminiscence

Years ago, when Rock Island was a small village, and its people had lots of fun all to themselves, one of our very sober and dignified citizens put his own head under one end of a yoke and a little bull's under the other, to teach the animal how to be useful and work. When he found the bull was running away with him down a dirt road towards a crowd around the country store on Illinois Street, he measured sixteen feet at a jump, kept up with the bull, and yelled at the top of his voice: "Look out! Here we come, darn our fool souls! Head us, somebody!" and when halted and the yoke was being lifted from his neck, he yelled, "Unyoke the bull; never mind me. I will stand!"—*Newspaper*

—

The Total Depravity of Inanimate Things

KATHERINE KENT CHILD WALKER

Katherine Kent Child Walker was born in Pittsfield, Vt., in 1842. She is a daughter of the Rev. Willard Child. She married the Rev. Edward Ashley Walker in 1856, and has published several juveniles anonymously, edited two compilations of sacred poetry, "The Cross Bearer," and "Songs of Prayer and Praise," translated from the German "Climbing the Glacier," and is best known by an article in *The Atlantic*, entitled "The Total Depravity of Inanimate Things" (September, 1864).

I am confident that, at the annunciation of my theme, Andover, Princeton and Cambridge will skip like rams, and the little hills of East Windsor, Meadville and Fairfax like lambs. However divinity schools may refuse to "skip" in unison, and may butt and batter each other about the doctrine and origin of *human* depravity, all will join devoutly in the *credo*, I believe in the total depravity of inanimate things.

The whole subject lies in a nutshell, or, rather, an apple-skin. We have clerical authority for affirming that all its miseries were let loose upon the human race by "them greenin's" tempting our mother to curious pomological speculations; and from that time till now—Longfellow, thou reasonest well!—"things are not what they seem," but are diabolically otherwise—masked-batteries, nets, gins, and snares of evil.

(In this connection I am reminded of—can I ever cease to remember?—the unlucky lecturer at our lyceum a few winters ago, who, on rising to address his audience, applauding him all the while most vehemently, pulled out his handkerchief, for oratorical purposes only, and inadvertently flung from his pocket three "Baldwins," that a friend had given to him on his way to the hall, straight into the front row of giggling girls.)

My zeal on this subject received new impetus recently from an exclamation which pierced the thin partitions of the country-parsonage, once my home, where I chanced to be a guest.

From the adjoining dressing-room issued a prolonged "Y-ah!"—not the howl of a spoiled child, nor the protest of a captive gorilla, but the whole-souled utterance of a mighty son of Anak, whose amiability is invulnerable to weapons of human aggravation.

I paused in the midst of toilet-exigencies, and listened sympathetically, for I recognized the probable presence of the old enemy to whom the bravest and sweetest succumb.

Confirmation and explanation followed speedily in the half apologetic, wholly wrathful declaration—"The pitcher was made foolish in the first place." I dare affirm that, if the spirit of Lindley Murray himself were at that moment hovering over that scene of trial, he dropped a tear, or, better still, an adverbial *ly* upon the false grammar, and blotted it out forever.

I comprehended the scene at once. I had been there. I felt again the remorseless swash of the water over neat boots and immaculate hose; I saw the perverse intricacies of its meanderings over the carpet, upon which the "foolish" pitcher had been confidingly deposited; I knew, beyond the necessity of ocular demonstration, that, as sure as there were "pipe-hole" or crack in the ceiling of the study below, those inanimate things would inevitably put their evil heads together, and bring to grief the long-suffering Dominie, with whom, during my day, such inundations had been of at least bi-weekly occurrence, instigated by crinoline. The inherent wickedness of that "thing of beauty" will be acknowledged by all mankind, and by every female not reduced to the deplorable poverty of the heroine of the following veracious anecdote.

A certain good bishop, on making a tour of inspection through a mission-school of his diocese, was so impressed by the aspect of all its beneficiaries that his heart overflowed with joy, and he exclaimed to a little maiden whose appearance was particularly suggestive of creature-comforts—"Why, my little girl! you have everything that heart can wish, haven't you?" Imagine the bewilderment and horror of the prelate, when the miniature Flora McFlimsey drew down the corners of her mouth lugubriously, and sought to accommodate the puffs and dimples of her fat little body to an expression of abject misery, as she replied, "No, indeed, sir! I haven't got any—skeleton!"

We who have suffered know the disposition of graceless "skeletons" to hang themselves on "foolish" pitchers, bureau-knobs, rockers, cobble-stones, splinters, nails, and, indeed, any projection a tenth of a line beyond a dead level.

The mention of nails is suggestive of voluminous distresses. Country-parsonages, from some inexplicable reason, are wont to bristle all over with these impish assailants of human comfort.

I never ventured to leave my masculine relatives to their own devices for more than twenty-four consecutive hours, that I did not return to find that they had seemingly manifested their grief at my absence after the old Hebraic method ("more honored in the breach than the observance"), by rending their garments. When summoned to their account, the invariable defense has been a vehement denunciation of some particular *nail* as the guilty cause of my woes.

By the way, O Christian woman of the nineteenth century, did it ever enter your heart to give devout thanks that you did not share the woe of those whose fate it was to "sojourn in Mesech and dwell in the tents of Kedar"? that it did not fall to your lot to do the plain sewing and mending for some Jewish patriarch, or prophet of yore?

Realize, if you can, the masculine aggravation and the feminine long-suffering of a period when the head of a family could neither go down-town, nor even sit at his tent-door, without descrying some wickedness in high places, some insulting placard, some exasperating war-bulletin, some offensive order from headquarters, which caused him to transform himself instantly into an animated ragbag. Whereas, in these women-saving days, similar grievances send President Abraham into his cabinet to issue a proclamation, the Reverend Jeremiah into his pulpit with a scathing homily, Poet-Laureate David to the *Atlantic* with a burning lyric, and Major-General Joab to the privacy of his tent, there to calm his perturbed spirit with Drake's Plantation Bitters. In humble imitation of another, I would state that this indorsement of the potency of a specific is entirely gratuitous, and that I am stimulated thereto by no remuneration, fluid or otherwise.

Blessed be this day of sewing-machines for women, and of safety-valves and innocent explosives for their lords!

But this is a digression.

I awoke very early in life to the consciousness that I held the doctrine which we are considering.

On a hapless day, when I was perhaps five years old, I was, in my own estimation, intrusted with the family dignity, when I was deposited for the day at the house of a lordly Pharisee of the parish, with solemnly repeated instructions in table-manners and the like.

One who never analyzed the mysteries of a sensitive child's heart cannot appreciate the sense of awful responsibility which oppressed me during that visit. But all went faultlessly for a time. I corrected myself instantly each time I said, "Yes, Ma'am," to Mr. Simon, and "No, Sir," to Madam, which was as often as I addressed them; I clenched little fists and lips resolutely, that they might not touch, taste, handle tempting *bijouterie*. I even held in check the spirit of inquiry rampant within me, and indulged myself with only one question to every three minutes of time.

At last I found myself at the handsome dinner-table, triumphantly mounted upon two "Comprehensive Commentaries" and a dictionary, fearing no evil from the viands before me. Least of all did I suspect the vegetables of guile. But deep in the heart of a bland, mealy mouthed potato lurked cruel designs upon my fair reputation.

No sooner had I, in the most approved style of nursery good-breeding, applied my fork to its surface, than the hard-hearted thing executed a wild *pirouette* before my astonished eyes, and then flew on impish wings across the room, dashing out its malicious brains, I am happy to say, against the parlor door, but leaving me in a half-comatose state, stirred only by vague longings for a lodge with "proud Korah's troop," whose destination is unmistakably set forth in the "Shorter Catechism."

There is a possibility that I received my innate distrust of things by inheritance from my maternal grandmother, whose holy horror at the profanity they once provoked from a bosom friend in her childhood was still vivid in her old age.

It was on this wise: When still a pretty Puritan maiden, my grandame was tempted irresistibly by the spring sunshine to the tabooed indulgence of a Sunday-walk. The temptation was probably intensified by the presence of the British troops, giving unwonted fascination to village promenades. Her confederate in this guilty pleasure was a like-minded little saint; so there was a tacit agreement between them that their transgression should be sanctified by a strict adherence to religious topics of conversation. Accordingly they launched boldly upon the great subject which was just then agitating church circles in New England.

Fortune smiled upon these criminals against the Blue Laws, until they encountered a wall surmounted by hickory rails. Without intermitting the discussion, Susannah sprang agilely up. Quoth she, balancing herself for one moment upon the summit—"No, no, Betsey, *I* believe God is the author of sin!" The next, she sprang toward the ground; but a salient splinter, a chip of depravity, clutched her Sunday gown, and converted her, incontinently, it seems, into a confessor of the opposing faith; for history records that, following the above-mentioned dogma, there came from hitherto unstained lips—"The Devil!"

Time and space would, of course, be inadequate to the enumeration of all the demonstrations of the truth of the doctrine of the absolute depravity of things. A few examples only can be cited.

There is melancholy pleasure in the knowledge that a great soul has gone mourning before me in the path I am now pursuing. It was only to-day that, in glancing over the pages of Victor Hugo's greatest work, I chanced upon the following: "Every one will have noticed with what skill a coin let fall upon the ground runs to hide itself, and what art it has in rendering itself invisible; there are thoughts which play us the same trick," etc., etc.

The similar tendency of pins and needles is universally understood and execrated—their base secretiveness when searched for, and their incensing intrusion when one is off guard.

I know a man whose sense of their malignity is so keen that, whenever he catches a gleam of their treacherous lustre on the carpet, he instantly draws his two and a quarter yards of length into the smallest possible compass, and shrieks until the domestic police come to the rescue, and apprehend the sharp little villains. Do not laugh at this. Years ago he lost his choicest friend by the stab of just such a little dastard lying in ambush.

So, also, every wielder of the needle is familiar with the propensity of the several parts of a garment in the process of manufacture to turn themselves wrong side out, and down side up; and the same viciousness cleaves like leprosy to the completed garment so long as a thread remains.

My blood still tingles with a horrible memory illustrative of this truth.

Dressing hurriedly and in darkness for a concert one evening, I appealed to the Dominie, as we passed under the hall-lamp, for a toilet inspection.

"How do I look, father?"

After a sweeping glance came the candid statement— "Beau-tifully!"

Oh, the blessed glamor which invests a child whose father views her "with a critic's eye"!

"Yes, *of course*; but look carefully, please; how is my dress?"

Another examination of apparently severest scrutiny.

"All right, dear! That's the new cloak, is it? Never saw you look better. Come, we shall be late."

Confidingly I went to the hall; confidingly I entered; since the concert-room was crowded with rapt listeners to the Fifth Symphony, I, gingerly, but still confidingly, followed the author of my days, and the critic of my toilet, to the very uppermost seat, which I entered, barely nodding to my finically fastidious friend, Guy Livingston, who was seated near us with a stylish-looking stranger, who bent eyebrows and glass upon me superciliously.

Seated, the Dominie was at once lifted into the midst of the massive harmonies of the Adagio; I lingered outside a moment in order to settle my garments and—that woman's look. What! was that a partially suppressed titter near me? Ah! she has no soul for music! How such ill-timed merriment will jar upon my friend's exquisite sensibilities!

Shade of Beethoven! A hybrid cough and laugh, smothered decorously, but still recognizable, from the courtly Guy himself! What can it mean?

In my perturbation my eyes fell, and rested upon the sack, whose newness and glorifying effect had been already noticed by my lynx-eyed parent.

I here pause to remark, that I had intended to request the compositor to "set up" the coming sentence in explosive capitals, by way of emphasis, but forbear, realizing that it already staggers under the weight of its own significance.

That sack was wrong side out!

Stern necessity, proverbially known as "the mother of invention," and practically the step-mother of ministers' daughters, had made me eke out the silken facings of the front with cambric linings for the back and sleeves. Accordingly, in the full blaze of the concert-room, there sat I, "accoutred as I was," in motley attire—my homely little economies patent to admiring spectators: on either shoulder, budding wings composed of unequal parts of sarcenet-cambric and cotton-batting; and in my heart—*parricide* I had almost said, but it was rather the more filial sentiment of desire to operate for cataract upon my father's eyes. But a moment's reflection sufficed to transfer my indignation to its proper object, the sinful sack itself, which, concerting with its kindred darkness, had planned this cruel assault upon my innocent pride.

A constitutional obtuseness renders me delightfully insensible to one fruitful source of provocation among inanimate things. I am so dull as to regard all distinctions between "rights" and "lefts" as invidious; but I have witnessed the agonized struggles of many a victim of fractious boots, and been thankful that "I am not as other men are," in ability to comprehend the difference between my right and left foot. Still, as already intimated, I have seen wise men driven mad by a thing of leather and waxed-ends.

A little innocent of three years, in all the pride of his first boots, was aggravated, by the perversity of the right to thrust itself on to the left leg, to the utterance of a contraband expletive.

When reproved by his horror-stricken mamma, he maintained a dogged silence.

In order to pierce his apparently indurated conscience, his censor finally said, solemnly:

"Dugald! God knows that you said that wicked word."

"Does He?" cried the baby-victim of reral depravity, in a tone of relief; "then *He* knows it was a doke" (*Anglicè*, joke).

But, mind you, the sin-tempting boot intended no "doke."

The toilet, with its multiform details and complicated machinery, is a demon whose surname is Legion.

Time would fail me to speak of the elusiveness of soap, the knottiness of strings, the transitory nature of buttons, the inclination of suspenders to twist, and of hooks to forsake their lawful eyes, and cleave only unto the hairs of their hapless owner's head. (It occurs to me as barely possible that, in the last case, the hooks may be innocent, and the sinfulness may lie in *capillary* attraction.)

And, O my brother or sister in sorrow, has it never befallen you, when bending all your energies to the mighty task of "doing" your back-hair, to find yourself gazing inanely at the opaque back of your brush, while the hand-mirror, which had maliciously insinuated itself into your right hand for this express purpose, came down upon your devoted head with a resonant whack?

I have alluded, parenthetically, to the possible guilt of capillary attraction, but I am prepared to maintain against the attraction of gravitation the charge of total depravity. Indeed, I should say of it, as did the worthy exhorter of the Dominie's old parish in regard to slavery, "It's the wickedest thing in the world, except sin!"

It was only the other day that I saw depicted upon the young divine's countenance, from this cause, thoughts "too deep for tears," and, perchance, too earthly for clerical utterance.

From a mingling of sanitary and economic considerations, he had cleared his own sidewalk after a heavy snow-storm. As he stood, leaning upon his shovel, surveying with smiling complacency his accomplished task, the spite of the arch-fiend Gravitation was raised against him, and, finding the impish slates (hadn't Luther something to say about "*as many devils as tiles*"?) ready to co-operate, an avalanche was the result, making the last state of that sidewalk worse than the first, and sending the divine into the house with a battered hat, and an article of faith supplementary to the orthodox thirty-nine.

Prolonged reflection upon a certain class of grievances has convinced me that mankind has generally ascribed them to a guiltless source. I refer to the unspeakable aggravation of "typographical errors," rightly so-called—for, in nine cases out of ten, I opine it is the types themselves which err.

I appeal to fellow-sufferers, if the substitutions and interpolations and false combinations of letters are not often altogether too absurd for humanity.

Take as one instance, the experience of a friend who, in writing in all innocency of a session of the Historical Society, affirmed mildly in manuscript, "All went smoothly," but weeks after was made to declare in blatant print, "All went *snoringly!*"

As among men, so in the alphabet, one sinner destroyeth much good.

The genial Senator from the Granite Hills told me of an early aspiration of his own for literary distinction, which was beheaded remorselessly by a villain of this type. By way of majestic peroration to a pathetic article, he had exclaimed, "For what would we exchange the fame of Washington?"—referring, I scarcely need say, to the man of fragrant memory, and not to the odorous capital. The black-hearted little dies, left to their own devices one night, struck dismay to the heart of the aspirant author by propounding in black and white a prosaic inquiry as to what would be considered a fair equivalent for the *farm* of the Father of his Country!

Among frequent instances of this depravity in my own experience, a flagrant example still shows its ugly front on a page of a child's book. In the latest edition of "Our Little Girls" (good Mr. Randolph, pray read, mark, learn and inwardly digest), there occurs a description of a christening, wherein a venerable divine is made to dip "his *head*" into the consecrating water, and lay it upon the child.

Disembodied words are also sinners and the occasions of sin. Who has not broken the Commandments in consequence of the provocation of some miserable little monosyllable eluding his grasp in the moment of his direst need, or of some impertinent interloper thrusting itself in, to the utter demoralization of his well-organized sentences? Who has not been covered with shame at tripping over the pronunciation of some perfectly simple word like "statistics," "inalienable," "inextricable," etc., etc.?

Whose experience will not empower him to sympathize with that unfortunate invalid who, on being interrogated by a pious visitor in regard to her enjoyment of means of grace, informed the horror-stricken inquisitor: "I have not been to church for years, I have been such an *infidel;*" and then, moved by a dim impression of wrong somewhere, as well as by the evident shock inflicted upon her worthy visitor, but conscious of her own integrity, repeated still more emphatically: "No; I have been a confirmed infidel for years."

But a peremptory summons from an animated nursery forbids my lingering longer in this fruitful field. I can only add an instance of corroborating testimony from each member of the circle originating this essay.

The Dominie *loq.*—"Sha'n't have anything to do with it! It's a wicked thing! To be sure, I do remember, when I was a little boy, I used to throw stones at the chip-basket when it upset the cargo I had just laded, and it was a great relief to my feelings too. Besides, you've told stories about me which were anything but true. I don't remember anything about that sack."

Lady-visitor *loq.*—"The first time I was invited to Mr. ——'s (the Hon. ——'s, you know), I was somewhat anxious, but went home flattering myself I had made a creditable impression. Imagine my consternation, when I came to relieve the pocket of my gala gown, donned for the occasion, at discovering among its treasures a tea-napkin, marked gorgeously with the Hon. ——'s family-crest, which had maliciously crept into its depths in order to bring me into disgrace! I have never been able to bring myself to the point of confession, in spite of my subsequent intimacy with the family. If it were not for Joseph's positive assertion to the contrary, I should be of the opinion that his cup of divination conjured itself deliberately and sinfully into innocent Benjamin's sack."

Student *loq.* (Testimony open to criticism.)—"Met pretty girl on the street yesterday. Sure I had on my 'Armstrong' hat when I left home—sure as fate; but when I went to pull it off—by the crown, of course—to bow to pretty girl, I smashed in my beaver! How it got there, don't know. Knocked it off. Pretty girl picked it up and handed it to me. Confounded things, any way!"

Young divine *loq.*—"While I was in the army, I was in Washington on 'leave' for two or three days. One night, at a party, I became utterly bewildered in an attempt to converse, after long desuetude, with a fascinating woman. I went stumbling on, amazing her more and more, until finally I covered myself with glory by the categorical statement that in my opinion General McClellan could 'never get across the Peninsula without a *fattle*, I beg pardon, Madam! what I mean to say is, without a *bight*.' "

School-girl *loq.*—"When Uncle —— was President, I was at the White House at a state-dinner one evening. Senator —— came rushing in frantically after we had been at table some time. No sooner was he seated than he turned to Aunt to apologize for his delay; and, being very much heated, and very much embarrassed, he tugged away desperately at his pocket, and finally succeeded in extracting a huge blue stocking, evidently of home manufacture, with which he proceeded to wipe his forehead very energetically and very conspicuously. I suppose the truth was that the poor man's handkerchiefs were 'on a strike,' and thrust forward this homespun stocking to bring him to terms."

School-girl, No. 2, *loq.*—"My last term at F., I was expecting a box of 'goodies' from home. So when the message came, 'An express-package for you, Miss Fanny!' I invited all my specials to come and assist at the opening. Instead of the expected box, there appeared a misshapen bundle, done up in yellow wrapping-paper. Four such dejected-looking damsels were never seen before as we, standing around the ugly old thing. Finally, Alice suggested:

" 'Open it!'

" 'Oh, I know what it is,' I said; 'it is my old Thibet, that mother has had made over for me.'

" 'Let's see,' persisted Alice.

"So I opened the package. The first thing I drew out was too much for me.

" 'What a funny-looking basque!' exclaimed Alice. All the rest were struck dumb with disappointment.

"No! not a basque at all, but a man's black satin waistcoat! and next came objects about which there could be no doubt—a pair of dingy old trousers, and a swallow-tailed coat! Imagine the chorus of damsels!

"The secret was, that two packages lay in father's office—one for me, the other for those everlasting freedmen. John was to forward mine. He had taken up the box to write my address on it, when the yellow bundle tumbled off the desk at his feet and scared the wits out of his head. So I came in for father's second-hand clothes, and the Ethiopians had the 'goodies'!"

Repentant Dominie *loq.*—"I don't approve of it at all; but then, if you must write the wicked thing, I heard a good story for you to day. Dr. —— found himself in the pulpit of a Dutch Reformed Church the other Sunday. You know he is one who prides himself on his adaptation to places and times. Just at the close of the introductory service, a black gown lying over the arm of the sofa caught his eye. He was rising to deliver his sermon, when it forced itself on his attention again.

" 'Sure enough,' thought he, 'Dutch Reformed clergymen do wear gowns. I might as well put it on.'

"So he solemnly thrust himself into the malicious (as you would say) garment, and went through the services as well as he could, considering that his audience seemed singularly agitated, and indeed on the point of bursting out into a general laugh, throughout the entire service. And no wonder! The good Doctor, in his zeal for conformity, had attired himself in the black cambric duster in which the pulpit was shrouded during week-days, and had been gesticulating his eloquent homily with his arms thrust through the holes left for the pulpit-lamps!"

Oon Criteek de Bernhardt

EUGENE FIELD

The reappearance of Sara Bernhardt in the midst of us has, of course, set our best society circles into a flutter of excitement; and we have been highly edified by the various criticisms which we have heard passed upon that gifted woman's performance of "Fedora" night before last. All these criticisms have flavored of that directness, that frankness, and that rugged discrimination which are so characteristic of true Western culture. Col. J. M. Hill, the esteemed lessee of the Columbia Theatre, told us some weeks ago that his object in securing a season of Bernhardt was to give a series of entertainments which would appeal for appreciation and for patronage to the intellectuality of our *crème de la crème*, and which would be several degrees above the comprehension of the *hoi polloi*. We noticed last Monday evening that the *hoi polloi* were not on hand to welcome the French *artiste*; and we were ineffably pained to notice, too, that the *crème de la crème* was very meagrely represented. This amazed as well as pained us: if Sara Bernhardt cannot pack the Columbia at Col. Hill's popular prices, who, by the memory of Racine and Molière! who—we ask in all solemnity—who can? And what amazed us, furthermore—perhaps we should say what *shocked* us—was the exceeding frigidity with which the select few of our *crème de la crème* received the superb bits of art which Sara Bernhardt threw out, much as an emery wheel emits beauteous varicolored sparks.

"Zis eez awful!" exclaimed Sara to her stage-manager, as she came off the stage after the first act of "Fedora." "Ze play eez in Russia, but ze audiongce eez in ze circle polaire!"

It strikes us that Sara was pretty nearly correct: but for the date on the play-bill, we might have surmised that our French friends were performing amid the surroundings of the glacial period.

"Ze play eez 'Fedora,' " said Sara to M. le Général Carson, *entre acte*, "ze artiste eez Bernhardt, and ze audiongce eez 'Les Miserables!' "

M. le Général came right out and told this to distinguished friends in the lobby. He said it was a bong mo; but young Horace McVicker, who once conducted a Paris-green manufactory in California, and therefore is an accomplished French scholar, corrected M. le Général by alleging that Sara's witticism was not a bong mo, but a judy spree.

The Markeesy di Pullman applauded the famous actress a great deal after he had once located her. In order to make sure of doing the proper thing, he applauded every woman that appeared on the stage; and by the time the second act was fairly under way, he was able to identify the "cantatreese" (as he called her) by the color of her hair. "But," he remarked to his friend, M. le Colonnel Potter Palmer, later in the evening, "I don't mind telling you that I don't like her as well as I do Patti; and as for this man, Sardoo"—

"Sardoo? Who's he?" interrupted M. le Colonnel Palmer.

"Why, he's the man who wrote this piece!" said the Markeesy; "and he doesn't hold a candle to our Italian poets, Danty and Bockashyo."

"I don't know anything about such things," said M. le Colonnel Palmer, meekly. "As for myself, I like to be amused when I go to a show; and I presume I'd like this woman very much if I could see her in one of the fine old English comedies, such as the 'Bunch of Keys,' or the 'Rag Baby.' "

Now, while these two distinguished personages were aware that the play was "Fedora," there were many in the auditorium who had not very clear convictions on this point. M. Thomas J. Hooper, the prominent linseed-oil manufacturer (whose palatial residence on Prairie Avenue is the Mecca of our most cultured society)—M. Hooper, we say, sat through three acts without dreaming that the play was "Fedora."

"I like Clara Morris better in this *rôle*," said he to M. T. Desplaines Wiggins, one of the vice-presidents of the Chicago Literary Club.

"But, my dear fellow," said M. Wiggins, in a tone of expostulation, "Clara Morris never played that part!"

"Never played 'Cameel?'" cried M. Hooper. "Why, bless you, man, I seen her do it right here in this theatre!"

"But this isn't 'Cameel,'" said M. Wiggins, "it's 'Feedorer.'"

"Well, now, I'll bet you fifty it's 'Cameel,'" said M. Hooper, calmly but firmly.

M. Wiggins covered the wager, and M. Billy Lyon decided in favor of Wiggins and "Fedora."

"I knew I was right," exclaimed M. Wiggins, triumphantly, "for I saw it on the programme."

M. Hooper was very much put out. "You don't pronounce that word right, anyway," he muttered, sulkily.

"What word?" demanded M. Wiggins, hotly.

"That word programmay," said M. Hooper. "It's French; and it isn't program, but programmay."

They wagered fifty dollars on it between them, and referred it to M. Jean McConnell.

"At popular prices it's program," said M. McConnell; "but during this engagement it's programmay, sure."

So M. Hooper squared himself financially; and M. Wiggins went down to his seat in the parquettay, muttering something that sounded very like a profane and inexcusable rhyme for program.

But, as we have hinted above, M. Hooper was not the only one in the audience who was unsettled as to what the play was, and what it was all about. Throughout the auditorium, messieurs, mesdames and mademoiselles were sadly bothered to know whether it was "Cameel" or "Faydorah" or "Tayodorah" or "Fru-Fru" or some other morso from the Bernhardt repertevoi. M. James M. Billings, the prominent restaurateur, told his family that the bill had been changed, and that the piece was "Jennie Saper."

"Why, no, 'tain't, pa," protested Mdlle. Billings, "it's 'Faydorah.' "

"Now, look here, Birdie," said M. Billings, sternly, "I know what I'm talking about. As we were comin' in, I asked one of the men in the entry what the piece was, and he said, 'Jennie Saper;' and he knew, for he was a Frenchman."

"Our seats," said M. T. Frelinghuysen Boothby, "were so far back that we had difficulty in making out what Burnhart said; but from what I *did* hear, I would judge that she spoke better English than Rhea—at any rate, I could understand her better than I ever could Rhea."

M. le Colonnel Fitzgerald confessed to being disappointed. "It may be my fault, however," said he, "for I am very rusty in my French, having paid no attention to it since I visited Montreal in the summer of 1880. I brought my 'French Conversations' along with me to-night, but it was of no assistance to me. I hadn't got half through the first scene in the first act when *Fedora* was dying in the last act. This was slow business. Of course there were a good many words and phrases that were familiar, such as 'voyla,' 'toot sweet,' 'tray be-yen,' 'mercee,' 'pardong,' 'bong zhour,' and 'wee wee,' You can depend upon it, that whenever I heard these old friends, I applauded with the nicest and the heartiest discrimination."

Now, all these criticisms and features (and there were many, many more such) interested us—or, at least, they entertained us. But we were grieved to discover a disposition (shall we say a pong-shong?) on the part of the audience, to compare Bernhardt's *Fedora* with Fanny Davenport's. To institute any such comparison would be a sore injustice to both ladies. Bernhardt and Davenport represent two very different dramatic schools: one is the school of avoirdupois, and the other is essentially so different that it must be estimated only under the accepted rules of troy weight. To be more explicit, we will say that, while you would properly weigh Miss Davenport's art on a hay-scales, you must use a more delicate machine if you would seek to learn the true magnitude and concinnity of Bernhardt's art. It is quite true that to both *Fedoras* the same amount of practical appreciation is paid her in Chicago. When Miss Davenport played "Fedora" at the Columbia Theatre last January, she was applauded rapturously by 2,000 delighted tradesfolk at 50 cents a piece: now Bernhardt comes along with her subtle impersonation, and does business to 333 1/3 of the *crème de la crème* of our pork-packers at $3 per head. You see that the box-office receipts are the same in both instances: it would be impossible, therefore, to compare the merits of each actress by the amount of money derived from the performance of each.

It is far from our purpose to institute any invidious comparisons between these two gifted women: each excels in her way; and the way of the one is as far from the way of the other as the beauties of a fat-stock show are removed from the beauties of a floral display. If there is in Fanny's art a breadth and a weight that remind us of the ponderous thud of a meat-axe, there is (it must also be confessed) in Sara's art a daintiness and an insinuation that remind us of the covert swish of a Japanese paper-knife. Horace has explained this very difference in that charming ode wherein he tells of Næera, who, "with ruddy, glowing arm, holds out an earthen cup of goat's milk," while, on the other hand, Lydia extends to the parched poet a silver flagon, "filled to the brim with old Falernian chilled with snow." Now, there is no doubt in our mind that Horace chose the Falernian; but we are not all Horaces; and we presume to say that, as between goat's milk at popular prices, and Falernian at war-rates, a vast majority of Chicagoans would choose the former.

"The last act was a great disappointment," said one of our most cultured beef-canners. "It is there that Davenport gets away with this French woman. Why, Davenport's tussle with that young Rooshan is the grandest piece of art I ever saw! she just tears around and horns the furniture like a Texas steer in a box-car."

George Bowron, leader of the orchestra at the Columbia, says that he knew, just as soon as he saw the score of the incidental music, that Bernhardt's *Fedora* was very unlike Davenport's.

"Bernhardt's score," says he, "is interspersed throughout with 'pianissimo,' 'con moto,' and 'andante.' On the other hand, the music of Davenport's *Fedora* is in big black type, and every other bar is labelled 'forte' or 'fortissimo;' and our trombone-player blew himself into a hemorrhage last January, trying to keep up with the rest of the orchestra in the death-struggle in the last act."

We can see that Bernhardt labors under one serious disadvantage, and that is the fact that her plays are couched in a foreign language. We asked Col. J. M. Hill why Sardoo did not write his plays in English, and he said he supposed it was because Sardoo was a Frenchman. This may be all very well for Paris, but we opine that it will not do in Chicago. What protection has a Chicago audience in a case of this kind? What assurance have we that, while we are admiring this woman's art, the woman herself is not brazenly guying and blackguarding us in her absurd foreign language?

Now, we would not seek to create the impression that Sardoo's work is not meritorious: on the contrary, we are free to say, and we say it boldly, that we recognize considerable merit in it. We fancy, however, that Sardoo is not always original: we find him making use of a good many lines that certainly were not born of his creative genius. As we remember now, Sardoo introduces into his dialogue the very "pardonnez-moy," the very "mongdu," and the very "too zhoors," which we hear every day in our best society; and will he have the effrontery to deny that he has stolen from us—ay, brazenly stolen from us—the very "wee-wee" which is the grand commercial basis upon which Chicago culture stands and defies all competition?

Oh, how glad—how proud—Chicago is that Bronson Howard, and William Shakespeare, and Charley Hoyt, and her other favorite dramatists, have been content to put their plays in honest but ennobling Anglo-Saxon!

LECTURES ON ASTRONOMY

JOHN PHŒNIX

INTRODUCTORY

The following pages were originally prepared in the form of a course of Lectures to be delivered before the Lowell Institute, of Boston, Mass., but, owing to the unexpected circumstance of the author's receiving no invitation to lecture before that institution, they were laid aside shortly after their completion.

Receiving an invitation from the trustees of the Vallecetos Literary and Scientific Institute, during the present summer, to deliver a course of Lectures on any popular subject, the author withdrew his manuscript from the dusty shelf on which it had long lain neglected, and, having somewhat revised and enlarged it, to suit the capacity of the eminent scholars before whom it was to be displayed, repaired to Vallecetos. But, on arriving at that place, he learned, with deep regret, that the only inhabitant had left a few days previous, having availed himself of the opportunity presented by a passing emigrant's horse—and that, in consequence, the opening of the Institute was indefinitely postponed. Under these circumstances, and yielding with reluctance to the earnest solicitations of many eminent scientific friends, he has been induced to place the Lectures before the public in their present form. Should they meet with that success which his sanguine friends prognosticate, the author may be induced subsequently to publish them in the form of a text-book, for the use of the higher schools and universities; it being his greatest ambition to render himself useful in his day and generation, by widely disseminating the information he has acquired among those who, less fortunate, are yet willing to receive instruction.

SAN DIEGO OBSERVATORY, September 1, 1854.

PART I.

CHAPTER I.

The term Astronomy is derived from two Latin words—*Astra*, a star, and *onomy*, a science; and literally means the science of stars. "It is a science," to quote our friend Dick (who was no relation at all of Big Dick, though the latter occasionally caused individuals to see stars), "which has, in all ages, engaged the attention of the poet, the philosopher, and the divine, and been the subject of their study and admiration."

By the wondrous discoveries of the improved telescopes of modern times, we ascertain that upwards of several hundred millions of stars exist, that are invisible to the naked eye—the nearest of which is millions of millions of miles from the Earth; and as we have every reason to suppose that every one of this inconceivable number of worlds is peopled like our own, a consideration of this fact—and that we are undoubtedly as superior to these beings as we are to the rest of mankind—is calculated to fill the mind of the American with a due sense of his own importance in the scale of animated creation.

It is supposed that each of the stars we see in the Heavens in a cloudless night is a sun shining upon its own curvilinear, with light of its own manufacture; and as it would be absurd to suppose its light and heat were made to be diffused for nothing, it is presumed farther, that each sun, like an old hen, is provided with a parcel of little chickens, in the way of planets, which, shining but feebly by its reflected light, are to us invisible. To this opinion we are led, also, by reasoning from analogy, on considering our own Solar System.

THE SOLAR SYSTEM is so called, not because we believe it to be the sole system of the kind in existence, but from its principal body the Sun; the Latin name of which is *Sol.* (Thus we read of Sol Smith, literally meaning the *son* of Old Smith.) On a close examination of the Heavens, we perceive numerous brilliant stars which shine with a steady light (differing from those which surround them, which are always twinkling like a dew-drop on a cucumber-vine), and which, moreover, do not preserve constantly the same relative distance from the stars near which they are first discovered. These are the planets of the SOLAR SYSTEM, which have no light of their own—of which the Earth, on which we reside, is one—which shine by light reflected from the Sun—and which regularly move around that body at different intervals of time and through different ranges in space. Up to the time of a gentleman named Copernicus, who flourished about the middle of the Fifteenth Century, it was supposed by our stupid ancestors that the Earth was the centre of all creation, being a large flat body, resting on a rock which rested on another rock, and so on "all the way down," and that the Sun, planets and immovable stars all revolved about it once in twenty-four hours.

This reminds us of the simplicity of a child we once saw in a railroad-car, who fancied itself perfectly stationary, and thought the fences, houses and fields were tearing past it at the rate of thirty miles an hour; and poking out its head, to see where on earth they went to, had its hat—a very nice one with pink ribbons—knocked off and irrecoverably lost. But Copernicus (who was a son of Daniel Pernicus, of the firm of Pernicus & Co., wool dealers, and who was named Co. Pernicus, out of respect to his father's partners) soon set this matter to rights, and started the idea of the present Solar System, which, greatly improved since his day, is occasionally called the Copernican system. By this system we learn that the Sun is stationed at one *focus* (not hocus, as it is rendered, without authority, by the philosopher Partington) of an ellipse, where it slowly grinds on for ever about its own axis, while the planets, turning about their axes, revolve in elliptical orbits of various dimensions and different planes of inclination around it.

The demonstration of this system in all its perfection was left to Isaac Newton, an English Philosopher, who, seeing an apple tumble down from a tree, was led to think thereon with such gravity, that he finally discovered the attraction of gravitation, which proved to be the great law of Nature that keeps every thing in its place. Thus we see that as an apple originally brought sin and ignorance into the world, the same fruit proved thereafter the cause of vast knowledge and enlightenment—and, indeed, we may doubt whether any other fruit but an apple, and a sour one at that, would have produced these great results—for, had the fallen fruit been a pear, an orange, or a peach, there is little doubt that Newton would have eaten it up and thought no more on the subject.

As in this world you will hardly ever find a man so small but that he has some one else smaller than he to look up to and revolve around him, so in the Solar System we find that the majority of the planets have one or more smaller planets revolving about them. These small bodies are termed secondaries, moons or satellites—the planets themselves being called primaries.

We know at present of eighteen primaries; viz., Mercury, Venus, the Earth, Mars, Flora, Vesta, Iris, Metis, Hebe, Astrea, Juno, Ceres, Pallas, Hygeia, Jupiter, Saturn, Herschel, Neptune, and another unnamed. There are distributed among these, nineteen secondaries, all of which, except our Moon, are invisible to the naked eye.

We shall now proceed to consider, separately, the different bodies composing the Solar System, and to make known what little information, comparatively speaking, science has collected regarding them. And first in order, as in place, we come to

The Sun

This glorious orb may be seen almost any clear day, by looking intently in its direction, through a piece of smoked glass. Through this medium it appears about the size of a large orange, and of much the same color. It is, however, somewhat larger, being, in fact, 887,000 miles in diameter, and containing a volume of matter equal to fourteen hundred thousand globes of the size of the Earth, which is certainly a matter of no small importance. Through the telescope it appears like an enormous globe of fire, with many spots upon its surface, which, unlike those of the leopard, are continually changing.

These spots were first discovered by a gentleman named Galileo, in the year 1611. Though the Sun is usually termed and considered the luminary of day, it may not be uninteresting to our readers to know that it certainly has been seen in the night. A scientific friend of ours from New England (Mr. R. W. Emerson) while traveling through the northern part of Norway, with a cargo of tinware, on the 21st of June, 1836, distinctly saw the Sun in all its majesty, shining at midnight!—in fact, shining *all* night! Emerson is not what you would call a superstitious man, by any means—but he left! Since that time many persons have observed its nocturnal appearance in that part of the country, at the same time of the year. This phenomenon has never been witnessed in the latitude of San Diego, however, and it is very improbable that it ever will be. Sacred history informs us that a distinguished military man named Joshua once caused the Sun to "stand still;" how he did it, is not mentioned. There can, of course. be no doubt of the fact that he arrested its progress, and possibly caused it to "stand *still*"—but translators are not always perfectly accurate, and we are inclined to the opinion that it might have wiggled a very little, when Joshua was not looking directly at it. The statement, however, does not appear so very incredible, when we reflect that seafaring men are in the habit of actually *bringing the Sun down* to the horizon every day at 12 Meridian. This they effect by means of a tool made of brass, glass and silver, called a sextant. The composition of the Sun has long been a matter of dispute.

By close and accurate observation with an excellent opera-glass, we have arrived at the conclusion that its entire surface is covered with water to a great depth; which water, being composed by a process known at the present only to the Creator of the Universe and Mr. Paine, of Worcester, Massachusetts, generates carbureted hydrogen gas, which, being inflamed, surrounds the entire body with an ocean of fire, from which we and the other planets receive our light and heat. The spots upon its surface are glimpses of water obtained through the fire; and we call the attention of our old friend and former schoolmate, Mr. Agassiz, to this fact; as by closely observing one of these spots with a strong refracting telescope, he may discover a new species of fish, with little fishes inside of them. It is possible that the Sun may burn out after awhile, which would leave this world in a state of darkness quite uncomfortable to contemplate; but even under these circumstances it is pleasant to reflect that courting and love-making would probably increase to an indefinite extent, and that many persons would make large fortunes by the sudden rise in value of coal, wood, candles and gas, which would go to illustrate the truth of the old proverb, "It's an ill wind that blows nobody any good."

Upon the whole, the Sun is a glorious creation; pleasing to gaze upon (through smoked glass), elevating to think upon, and exceedingly comfortable to every created being on a cold day; it is the largest, the brightest, and may be considered by far the most magnificent object in the celestial sphere; though with all these attributes it must be confessed that it is occasionally entirely eclipsed by the moon.

CHAPTER II.

We shall now proceed to the consideration of the several planets.

Mercury

This planet, with the exception of the asteroids, is the smallest of the system. It is the nearest to the Sun, and, in consequence, cannot be seen (on account of the Sun's superior light) except at its greatest eastern and western elongations, which occur in March and April, August and September, when it may be seen for a short time immediately after sunset and shortly before sunrise. It then appears like a star of the first magnitude, having a white twinkling light, and resembling somewhat the star Regulus in the constellation Leo. The day in Mercury is about ten minutes longer than ours, its year is about equal to three of our months. It receives six and a half times as much heat from the Sun as we do; from which we conclude that the climate must be very similar to that of Fort Yuma, on the Colorado River. The difficulty of communication with Mercury will probably prevent its ever being selected as a military post; though it possesses many advantages for that purpose, being extremely inaccessible, inconvenient, and, doubtless, singularly uncomfortable. It receives its name from the God, Mercury, in the Heathen Mythology, who is the patron and tutelary Divinity of San Diego County.

Venus

This beautiful planet may be seen either a little after sunset, or shortly before sunrise, according as it becomes the morning or evening star, but never departing quite 48° from the Sun. Its day is about twenty-five minutes shorter than ours; its year seven and a half months, or thirty-two weeks. The diameter of Venus is 7,700 miles, and she receives from the Sun thrice as much light and heat as the Earth.

An old Dutchman named Schroeter spent more than ten years in observations on this planet, and finally discovered a mountain on it twenty-two miles in height, but he never could discover any thing on the mountain, not even a mouse, and finally died about as wise as when he commenced his studies.

Venus, in Mythology, was a Goddess of singular beauty, who became the wife of Vulcan, the blacksmith, and, we regret to add, behaved in the most immoral manner after her marriage. The celebrated case of Vulcan *vs.* Mars, and the consequent scandal, is probably still fresh in the minds of our readers. By a large portion of society, however, she was considered an ill-used and persecuted lady, against whose high tone of morals and strictly virtuous conduct not a shadow of suspicion could be cast; Vulcan, by the same parties, was considered a horrid brute, and they all agreed that it served him right when he lost his case and had to pay the costs of court. Venus still remains the Goddess of Beauty, and not a few of her *protégés* may be found in California.

The Earth

The Earth, or as the Latins called it, Tellus (from which originated the expression, "do tell us,") is the third planet in the Solar System, and the one on which we subsist, with all our important joys and sorrows. The *San Diego Herald* is published weekly on this planet, for five dollars per annum, payable invariably in advance. As the Earth is by no means the most important planet in the system, there is no reason to suppose that it is particularly distinguished from the others by being inhabited. It is reasonable, therefore, to conclude, that all the other planets of the system are filled with living, moving and sentient beings; and as some of them are superior to the Earth in size and position, it is not improbable that their inhabitants may be superior to us in physical and mental organization.

But if this were a demonstrable fact, instead of a mere hypothesis, it would be found a very difficult matter to persuade us of its truth. To the inhabitants of Venus, the Earth appears like a brilliant star, very much, in fact, as Venus appears to us; and, reasoning from analogy, we

MARS AND VENUS.

are led to believe that the election of Mr. Pierce, the European war, or the split in the great Democratic party produced but very little excitement among them.

To the inhabitants of Jupiter, our important globe appears like a small star of the fourth or fifth magnitude. We recollect some years ago gazing with astonishment upon the inhabitants of a drop of water, developed by the Solar Microscope, and secretly wondering whether they were or not reasoning beings, with souls to be saved. It is not altogether a pleasant reflection that a highly scientific inhabitant of Jupiter, armed with a telescope of (to us) inconceivable form, may be pursuing a similar course of inquiry, and indulging in similar speculations regarding our Earth and its inhabitants. Gazing with curious eye, his attention is suddenly attracted by the movements of a grand celebration of Fourth of July in New York, or a mighty convention in Baltimore. "God bless my soul!" he exclaims; "I declare, they're alive, these little creatures; do see them wriggle!" To an inhabitant of the Sun, however, he of Jupiter is probably quite as insignificant, and the Sun man is possibly a mere atom in the opinion of a dweller in Sirius. A little reflection on these subjects leads to the opinion, that the death of an individual man on this Earth, though perhaps as important an event as can occur to himself, is calculated to cause no great convulsion of Nature, or disturb particularly the great aggregate of created beings.

The earth moves round the sun from west to east in a year, and turns on its axis in a day; thus moving at the rate of 68,000 miles an hour in its orbit, and rolling around at the tolerably rapid rate of 1,040 miles per hour. As our readers may have seen that when a man is galloping a horse violently over a smooth road, if the horse, from viciousness or other cause, suddenly stops, the man keeps on at the same rate over the animal's head; so we, supposing the Earth to be suddenly arrested on its axis—men, women, children, horses, cattle and sheep, donkeys, editors and members of Congress, with all our goods and chattels—would be thrown off into the air at the speed of 173 miles a minute, every mother's son of us describing the arc of a parabola, which is probably the only description we should ever be able to give of the affair.

The catastrophe, to one sufficiently collected to enjoy it, would doubtless be exceedingly amusing; but as there would probably be no time for laughing, we pray that it may not occur until after our demise;

when, should it take place, our monument will probably accompany the movement. It is a singular fact, that if a man travel round the Earth in an eastwardly direction, he will find, on returning to the place of departure, he has gained one whole day; the reverse of this proposition being true also, it follows that the Yankees, who are constantly traveling to the West, do not live as long by a day or two as they would if they had staid at home; and supposing each Yankee's time to be worth $1.50 per day, it may be easily shown that a considerable amount of money is annually lost by their roving dispositions.

Science is yet but in its infancy; with its growth, new discoveries of an astounding nature will doubtless be made, among which, probably, will be some method by which the course of the Earth may be altered, and it be steered with the same ease and regularity through space and among the stars as a steamboat is now directed in the water. It will be a very interesting spectacle to see the Earth "rounding to," with her head to the air, off Jupiter, while the moon is sent off laden with mails and passengers for that planet, to bring back the return mails and a large party of rowdy Jupiterians going to attend a grand prize fight in the ring of Saturn.

Well, Christopher Columbus would have been just as much astonished at a revelation of the steamboat and the locomotive engine as we should be to witness the above performance, which our intelligent posterity during the ensuing year, A.D. 2,000, will possibly look upon as a very ordinary and commonplace affair.

Only three days ago we asked a medium where Sir John Franklin was at that time; to which he replied he was cruising about (officers and crew all well) on the interior of the Earth, to which he had obtained entrance through SYMMES HOLE!

With a few remarks upon the Earth's satellite, we conclude the first Lecture on Astronomy; the remainder of the course being contained in a second Lecture, treating of the planets Mars, Jupiter, Saturn and Neptune, the Asteroids, and the fixed stars, which last, being "fixings," are, according to Mr. Charles Dickens, American property.

The Moon

This resplendent luminary, like a youth on the 4th of July, has its first quarter; like a ruined spendthrift, its last quarter; and, like an omnibus, is occasionally full and new. The evenings on which it appears between these last stages are beautifully illumined by its clear, mellow light.

The Moon revolves in an elliptical orbit about the Earth in twenty-nine days, twelve hours, forty-four minutes and three seconds—the time which elapses between one new Moon and another. It was supposed by the ancient philosophers that the Moon was made of green cheese, an opinion still entertained by the credulous and ignorant. Kepler and Tycho Brahe, however, held to the opinion that it was composed of Charlotte Russe, the dark portions of its surface being sponge cake, the light *blanc mange*. Modern advances in science, and the use of Lord Rosse's famous telescope, have demonstrated the absurdity of all these speculations by proving conclusively that the Moon is mainly composed of the *Ferro—sesqui—cyanuret, of the cyanide of potassium!* Up to the latest dates from the Atlantic States, no one has succeeded in reaching the Moon. Should any one do so hereafter, it will probably be a woman, as the sex will never cease making an exertion for that purpose as long as there is a man in it.

Upon the whole, we may consider the moon an excellent institution, among the many we enjoy under a free, republican form of government, and it is a blessed thing to reflect that the President of the United States cannot *veto* it, no matter how strong an inclination he may feel, from principle or habit, to do so.

It has been ascertained beyond a doubt that the Moon has no air. Consequently, the common expressions, "the Moon was gazing down with an air of benevolence," or with "an air of complacency," or with "an air of calm superiority," are incorrect and objectionable, the fact being that the moon has no air at all.

The existence of the celebrated "Man in the Moon" has been frequently questioned by modern philosophers. The whole subject is involved in doubt and obscurity. The only authority we have for believing that such an individual exists, and has been seen and spoken with, is a fragment of an old poem composed by an ancient Astronomer by the name of Goose, which has been handed down to us as follows:

> "The man in the Moon, came down too soon
>   To inquire the way to Norwich;
> The man in the South, he burned his mouth,
>   Eating cold, hot porridge."

The evidence conveyed in this distich is, however, rejected by the skeptical among modern Astronomers, who consider the passage an allegory—"The man in the South" being supposed typical of the late John C. Calhoun, and the "cold, hot porridge" alluded to the project of nullification.

END OF LECTURE FIRST

NOTE BY THE AUTHOR.—Itinerant Lecturers are cautioned against making use of the above production, without obtaining the necessary authority from the proprietors of the *Pioneer Magazine*. To those who may obtain such authority, it may be well to state that at the close of the Lecture it was the intention of the author to exhibit and explain to the audience an orrery, accompanying and interspersing his remarks by a choice selection of popular airs on the hand-organ.

An economical orrery may be constructed by attaching eighteen wires of graduated lengths to the shaft of a candlestick, apples of different sizes being placed at their extremities to represent the Planets, and a central orange, resting on the candlestick, representing the Sun.

An orrery of this description is, however, liable to the objection that, if handed around among the audience for examination, it is seldom returned uninjured. The author has known an instance in which a child four years of age, on an occasion of this kind, devoured in succession the planets Jupiter and Herschel, and bit a large spot out of the Sun, before he could be arrested.

LITTLE CHARLES AND THE FRUIT

One day when little Charles, the good boy of whom I have told you, was on his way to school, he passed by a large orchard in which there were a great many kinds of fruit, and as the sunshine came streaming through the branches of the trees and fell upon the rosy-cheeked apples, the sweet, mellow peaches, and the red cherries, Charles thought they looked very beautiful indeed, and would go down nicely with the lunch which his kind mother had wrapped up in a white napkin for him, and placed in the little basket he carried in his hand.

Some of the fruit hung very near the fence, and as Charles looked at it wishfully he said to himself: "How easily I could climb over there and pluck several of the apples and pears without being discovered, for there is no one in the orchard now. But that would be wrong, and if I did it I should always be sorry, and suffer dreadfully from the pangs of conscience."

So he stood there a little longer. The little birds in the trees were singing their merriest lays, the soft and balmy zephyrs of early summer were kissing the flowers as they nodded their pretty heads in the grass by the roadside, and all nature seemed rejoicing in its strength.

Many times Charles looked up at the fruit, and thought how easy it would be to take it, but every time he did this the small voice would say: "That would be wrong, Charles," and he would resolve not to make any such break.

But pretty soon a bright thought struck him, and his pure young face lighted up with a sunny smile. "I will go to the owner of the orchard," he said, "who lives in yonder house, and tell him how I have conquered temptation. Then he will give me all the fruit I want, because that is the way sturdy farmers always do in the little books I get at Sunday-school."

So he went boldly up to the farm-house, but just as he entered the gate a fierce dog grabbed him by the seat of his panties and wiped the ground with him for a few moments. The nice lunch that his mother had put up for him was distributed all over the yard, and his new jacket looked as if it had been out with the boys. When the farmer heard the noise he came running out of the house and called off the dog.

"What do you want, my little man?" he said to Charles.

So Charles told him he had been tempted to take the fruit, but would not do so because it was wrong. And then he asked the man for some fruit.

The farmer looked at him for a moment, and then he said: "I have two more dogs, both larger than the one you tackled, and unless you are out of here in three jerks of a lamb's tail, they will be lunching, and you will be quite conspicuous in the bill-of-fare."

So Charles ran quickly away, not even stopping to get his basket. A little way down the road he overtook Thomas Tough, who was eating a delicious peach.

"Where did you get that peach, Thomas?" asked Charles.

"Over in that orchard," replied Thomas. "I waited until the Old

Crank who owns the place had gone to breakfast, and then appointed myself receiver of the orchard."

"You are a very wicked boy," said Charles.

"Yes," replied Thomas, "I am a trifle wicked, but I keep Getting to the Front all the time, and my clothes don't seem quite so much Disarranged as yours. You will also notice that my Lunch Basket is with me, and that my piece of Pie for the Noonday Meal is not lying in Farmer Brown's Garden."

When Charles went home that evening he told his Papa what he had done. "You know, Papa," he said, "that I would sooner be right than President."

"Yes," replied his Papa, "but I am not seriously alarmed about your being President either."

—*Chicago Tribune*

Thare iz nothing that yu and I make so menny blunders about, and the world so few, az the aktual amount ov our importance.

Josh Billings

Our Italian Guide

MARK TWAIN

In this connection I wish to say one word about Michael Angelo Buonarotti—I used to worship the mighty genius of Michael Angelo—that man who was great in poetry, painting, sculpture, architecture—great in every thing he undertook. But I do not want Michael Angelo for breakfast—for luncheon—for dinner—for tea—for supper—for between meals. I like a change, occasionally. In Genoa, he designed every thing; in Milan, he or his pupils designed every thing; he designed the Lake of Como; in Padua, Verona, Venice, Bologna, who did we ever hear of, from guides, but Michael Angelo? In Florence, he painted every thing, designed every thing, nearly, and what he did not design he used to sit on a favorite stone and look at, and they showed us the stone. In Pisa, he designed every thing but the old shot-tower, and they would have attributed that to him if it had not been so awfully out of the perpendicular. He designed the piers of Leghorn and the custom-house regulations of Civita Vecchia. But here—here it is frightful. He designed St. Peter's; he designed the Pope; he designed the Pantheon, the uniform of the Pope's soldiers, the Tiber, the Vatican, the Coliseum, the Capitol, the Tarpeian Rock, the Barberini Palace, St. John Lateran, the Campagna, the Appian Way, the Seven Hills, the Baths of Caracalla, the Claudian Aqueduct, the Cloaca Maxima—the eternal bore designed the Eternal City, and unless all men and books do lie, he painted every thing in it! Dan said the other day to the guide, "Enough, enough, enough! Say no more! Lump the whole thing! say that the Creator made Italy from designs by Michael Angelo!"

I never felt so fervently thankful, so soothed, so tranquil, so filled with a blessed peace, as I did yesterday when I learned that Michael Angelo was dead.

But we have taken it out of this guide. He has marched us through miles of pictures and sculpture in the vast corridors of the Vatican; and through miles of pictures and sculpture in twenty other palaces; he has shown us the great picture in the Sistine Chapel, and frescoes enough to fresco the heavens—pretty much all done by Michael Angelo. So with him we have played that game which has vanquished so many guides for us—imbecility and idiotic questions. These creatures never suspect—they have no idea of a sarcasm.

He shows us a figure and says: "Statoo brunzo." (Bronze statue.)

We look at it indifferently, and the doctor asks: "By Michael Angelo?"

"No—not know who."

Then he shows us the ancient Roman Forum. The doctor asks: "Michael Angelo?"

A stare from the guide. "No—thousan' year before he is born."

Then an Egyptian obelisk. Again: "Michael Angelo?"

"Oh, *mon dieu*, genteelmen! Zis is *two* thousan' year before he is born!"

He grows so tired of that unceasing question, sometimes, that he dreads to show us anything at all. The wretch has tried all the ways he can think of to make us comprehend that Michael Angelo is only responsible for the creation of a *part* of the world, but somehow he has not succeeded yet. Relief for overtasked eyes and brain from study and sight-seeing is necessary, or we shall become idiotic sure enough. Therefore this guide must continue to suffer. If he does not enjoy it, so much the worse for him. We do.

In this place I may as well jot down a chapter concerning those necessary nuisances, European guides. Many a man has wished in his heart he could do without his guide; but knowing he could not, has wished he could get some amusement out of him as a remuneration for the affliction of his society. We accomplished this latter matter, and if our experience can be made useful to others, they are welcome to it.

The guides in Genoa are delighted to secure an American party, because Americans so much wonder, and deal so much in sentiment and emotion, before any relic of Columbus. Our guide there fidgeted about as if he had swallowed a spring mattress. He was full of animation—full of impatience. He said:

"Come wis me genteelmen!—come! I show you ze letter writing by Christopher Colombo!—write it himself!—write it wis his own hand!—come!"

He took us to the municipal palace. After much impressive fumbling of keys and opening of locks, the stained and aged document was spread before us. The guide's eyes sparkled. He danced about us and tapped the parchment with his finger:

"What I tell you, genteelmen! Is it not so? See! handwriting Christopher Colombo!—write it himself!"

We looked indifferent—unconcerned. The doctor examined the document very deliberately, during a painful pause. Then he said, without any show of interest:

"Ah—Ferguson—what—what did you say was the name of the party who wrote this?"

"Christopher Colombo! ze great Christopher Colombo!"

Another deliberate examination.

"Ah—did he write it himself, or—or how?"

"He write it himself!—Christopher Colombo! he's own handwriting, write by himself!"

Then the doctor laid the document down and said:

"Why, I have seen boys in America only fourteen years old that could write better than that."

"But zis is ze great Christo—"

"I don't care who it is! It's the worst writing I ever saw. Now you musn't think you can impose on us because we are strangers. We are not fools, by a good deal. If you have got any specimens of penmanship of real merit, trot them out!—and if you haven't, drive on!"

We drove on. The guide was considerably shaken up, but he made one more venture. He had something which he thought would overcome us. He said:

"Ah, genteelmen, you come wis me! I show you beautiful, O, magnificent bust Christopher Colombo!—splendid, grand, magnificent!"

He brought us before the beautiful bust—for it *was* beautiful—and sprang back and struck an attitude:

"Ah, look, genteelmen!—beautiful, grand—bust Christopher Colombo!—beautiful bust, beautiful pedestal!"

The doctor put up his eye-glass—procured for such occasions:

"Ah—what did you say this gentleman's name was?"

"Christopher Colombo!—ze great Christopher Colombo!"

"Christopher Colombo—the great Christopher Colombo. Well, what did *he* do?"

"Discover America!—discover America. Oh, ze devil!"

"Discover America! No—that statement will hardly wash. We are just from America ourselves. We heard nothing about it. Christopher Colombo—pleasant name—is—is he dead?"

"Oh, corpo di Baccho!—three hundred year!"

"What did he die of?"

"I do not know!—I can not tell."

"Small-pox, think?"

"I do not know, genteelmen!—I do not know *what* he die of!"

"Measles, likely?"

"May be—may be—I do *not* know—I think he die of somethings."

"Parents living?"

"Im-posseeble!"

"Ah—which is the bust and which is the pedestal?"

"Santa Maria!—*zis* ze bust!—*zis* ze pedestal!"

"Ah, I see, I see—happy combination—very happy combination, indeed. Is—is this the first time this gentleman was ever on a bust?"

That joke was lost on the foreigner—guides cannot master the subtleties of the American joke.

We have made it interesting for this Roman guide. Yesterday we spent three or four hours in the Vatican again, that wonderful world of curiosities. We came very near expressing interest, sometimes—even admiration—it was very hard to keep from it. We succeeded, though. Nobody else ever did, in the Vatican museums. The guide was bewildered—nonplussed. He walked his legs off, nearly, hunting up extraordinary things, and exhausted all his ingenuity on us, but it was a failure; we never showed any interest in anything. He had reserved what he considered to be his greatest wonder till the last—a royal Egyptian mummy, the best preserved in the world, perhaps. He took us there. He felt so sure, this time, that some of his old enthusiasm came back to him:

"See, genteelmen!—Mummy! Mummy!"

The eye-glass came up as calmly, as deliberately as ever.

"Ah—Ferguson—what did I understand you to say the gentleman's name was?"

"Name?—he got no name!—Mummy!—'Gyptian mummy!"

"Yes, yes. Born here?"

"No! *'Gyptian* mummy!"

"Ah, just so. Frenchman, I presume?"

"No!—*not* Frenchman, not Roman!—born in Egypt!"

"Born in Egypt. Never heard of Egypta before. Foreign locality, likely. Mummy—mummy. How calm he is—how self-possessed. Is, ah—is he dead?"

"Oh, *sacre bleu*, been dead three thousan' year!"

The doctor turned on him savagely:

"Here, now, what do you mean by such conduct as this! Playing us for Chinamen because we are strangers, and trying to learn! Trying to impose your vile second-hand carcasses on *us!*—thunder and lightning, I've a notion to—to—if you've got a nice *fresh* corpse, fetch him out!—or, by George, we'll *brain* you!"

LASTING reputashuns are ov a slo growth: the man who wakes up famus sum morning, iz very apt to go to bed sum night and sleep it all off.

JOSH BILLINGS

SHE HAD TO TAKE HER THINGS ALONG

ROBERT J. BURDETTE

Erasmus T. Ruggleson, a young man of Saxon lineage, worked on a farm out here in Yellow Spring township. He was not rich, but he was industrious, and just too pretty for anything. So was the daughter of the farmer for whom he worked. She was wealthier than Erasmus, but she was not proud. When the chores were done in the winter evenings, she went with him to the singing school, and she walked by his side to church. She loved him; she had rather sit at her casement in the gloaming, and hear him holler "poo-oo-sy!" in long-drawn, mellow cadences, at the hour of the feeding of the swine, than hear Campanini sing "Macaroni del Vermicelli" from "Handorgzanhandi in Venezuela." And he—he was clean gone on her. Mashed past all surgery. When they foolishly let the old man into their plans for each other's happiness and half the farm, the wrathful agriculturist said if he heard one more word of such nonsense, just another word, he would lay that farm waste with physical havoc, and blight its winter wheat with the salt tears of his only child, and that was the kind of father-in-law he was inclined to be.

Naturally, the young people determined to fly. Their plans were laid; the night was set. So was the ladder. At its foot waited the ardent Erasmus Ruggleson, gazing at the window for the appearance of his love. Presently the window opened softly, and a face he loved appeared.

" 'Rasmus!"

"Florence!"

"Yes, dearest. Shall I drop my things right down?"

"Yes, love; I will catch them. Let the bundles fall."

The glittering starlight of the clear March night fell on Erasmus's glad and upturned face. So did a trunk, four feet high, four feet wide, and about eight feet long. It weighed about 2,700 pounds. It contained a few "things" that no woman could be expected to travel without, and Florence had spent three weeks packing that trunk for her elopement.

Erasmus Ruggleson did not scream. He did not moan. He couldn't.

He had no show. Florence came down the ladder, having first, with a maidenly sense of propriety, requested her lover to turn his back and look at the barn. He was busily engaged in looking at the bottom of that trunk, and thinking how like all creation he would yell if he ever got his mouth outdoors again.

Florence reached the foot of the ladder. "Did you get my trunk, Erasmus?" she said, looking around for him.

"Oh, yes!" said a hoarse mocking voice at her elbow. "Oh, yes, he got it! Got it bad, too!"

She turned, knew her papa, shrieked once, twice, again, and once more for the boys, and fainted away.

"I never worried about it a minute," the heartless old man told his neighbors the next day, "though I knowed well enough what was goin' on all the time. I've been married twice, an' I've married off four daughters and two sons, an' if I don't know what baggage a woman carries when she travels, by this time, I'm too old to learn."

And Erasmus Ruggleson! The jury brought in a verdict that he came to his death by habitual drunkenness, and the temperance papers didn't talk about anything else for the next six weeks.

THE GARDEN AND ITS ENEMIES

CHARLES DUDLEY WARNER

I left my garden for a week, just at the close of the dry spell. A season of rain immediately set in, and when I returned, the transformation was wonderful. In one week, every vegetable had fairly jumped forward. The tomatoes which I left slender plants, eaten of bugs and debating whether they would go backward or forward, had become stout and lusty, with thick stems and dark leaves, and some of them had blossomed. The corn waved like that which grows so rank out of the French-English mixture at Waterloo. The squashes—I will not speak of the squashes! The most remarkable growth was the asparagus. There was not a spear above-ground when I went away; and now it had sprung up and gone to seed, and there were stalks higher than my head. I am entirely aware of the value of words, and of moral obligations. When I say that the asparagus had grown six feet in seven days, I expect and wish to be believed. I am a little particular about the statement, for, if there is any prize offered for asparagus at the next agricultural fair, I wish to compete—speed to govern. What I claim is the fastest asparagus. As for eating purposes, I have seen better. A neighbor of mine, who looked in at the growth of the bed, said, "Well, he'd be d——:" but I told him there was no use of affirming now; he might keep his oath till I wanted it on the asparagus affidavit. In order to have this sort of asparagus, you want to manure heavily in the early spring, fork it in, and top-dress (that sounds technical) with a thick layer of chloride of sodium: if you cannot get that, common salt will do, and the neighbors will never notice whether it is the orthodox Na. Cl. 58.5 or not.

I scarcely dare trust myself to speak of the weeds. They grow as if the devil was in them. I know a lady, a member of the Church and a very good sort of woman, considering the subject condition of that class, who says that the weeds work on her to that extent that, in going through her garden, she has the greatest difficulty in keeping the ten commandments in anything like an unfractured condition. I asked her which one? but she said all of them: one felt like breaking the whole lot. The sort of weed which I most hate (if I can be said to hate anything which grows in my garden) is the "pusley," a fat, ground-clinging, spreading, greasy thing, and the most propagatious (it is not my fault if the word is not in the dictionary) plant I know. I saw a Chinaman who came over with a returned missionary, and pretended to be converted, boil a lot of it in a pot, stir in eggs, and mix and eat it with relish—"Me likee he." It will be a good thing to keep the Chinamen on when they come to do our gardening. I only fear they will cultivate it at the expense of the strawberries and melons. Who can say that other weeds which we despise may not be the favorite food of some remote people or tribe. We ought to abate our conceit. It is possible that we destroy in our gardens that which is really of most value in some other place. Perhaps, in like manner, our faults and vices are virtues in some remote planet. I cannot see, however, that this thought is of the slightest value to us here, any more than weeds are.

There is another subject which is forced upon my notice. I like neighbors, and I like chickens; but I do not think they ought to be united near a garden. Neighbors' hens in your garden are an annoyance. Even if they did not scratch up the corn, and peck the strawberries, and eat the tomatoes, it is not pleasant to see them straddling about in their jerky, high-stepping, speculative manner, picking inquisitively here and there. It is of no use to tell the neighbor that his hens eat your tomatoes: it makes no impression on him, for the tomatoes are not his. The best way is to casually remark to him that he has a fine lot of chickens, pretty well grown, and that you like spring chickens broiled. He will take them away at once. The neighbors' small children are also out of place in your garden in strawberry and currant time. I hope I appreciate the value of children. We should soon come to nothing without them, though the Shakers have the best gardens in the world. Without them the common school would languish. But the problem is, what to do with them in a garden. For they are not good to eat, and there is a law against making away with them. The law is not very well enforced, it is true; for people do thin them out with constant dosing, paregoric and soothing-syrups, and scanty clothing. But I, for one, feel that it would not be right, aside from the law, to take the life, even of the smallest child, for the sake of a little fruit, more or less, in the garden. I may be wrong; but these are my sentiments, and I am not ashamed of them. When we come, as Bryant says in his "Iliad," to leave the circus of this life and join that innumerable caravan which moves, it will be some satisfaction to us that we have never, in the way of gardening, disposed of even the humblest child unnecessarily. My plan would be to put them into Sunday-schools more thoroughly, and to give the Sunday-schools an agricultural turn; teaching the children the sacredness of neighbors' vegetables. I think that our Sunday-schools do not sufficiently impress upon children the danger, from snakes and otherwise, of going into the neighbors' gardens.

The Hodja Makes Up His Mind to Marry

S. S. COX

When the Hodja made up his mind to marry, his neighbors came to him and told him that if he married, his "wife would turn his house upside down."

"Very well," says he, "I will take care of that."

A few days after, he began building his house. Instead of beginning at the foundation, he surprises his neighbors by preparing the tiles for the roof. The neighbors come again and inquire of the Hodja:

"What are you doing?"

"I am building my house," he responds.

"But," they reply, "you cannot build a house, starting from the roof."

"Yes," says the Hodja, "but did I not tell you I am going to marry?"

"What then?" say the anxious neighbors, fearing he had gone clean daft.

"What then? Did you not tell me that if I married, my wife would turn my house upside down? Now, I build it so that when she turns it upside down, it will be right-side up. If what you say to me be true, I advise you to follow my plan toward your wives. As they never agree with you, give them the opposite of what you wish, and you will always have your own will."

The moral whereof is: *that often by indirection and tacking, we bring the ship into port.*

The Old Settler

*His Reasons for Thinking There Is Natural Gas in
Deep Rock Gulley*

EDWARD HAROLD MOTT

Edward Harold Mott is a native of Milford, Pike Co., Pa., and is a printer by
trade and journalist by profession. He is a contributor to *Puck*, *The Fudge*,
and other comic papers. He was born January 17, 1845.

"I see by the papers, 'Squire," said the Old Settler, "that they're a finding signs o' coal ile an' nat'ral gas like sixty here an' thar in deestric's
not so terrible fur from here, an' th't konsekently land they usety beg
folks to come an' take offen their hands at any price at all is wuth a dollar now, jist for a peep over the stun wall at it. The minute a feller finds
signs o' ile or nat'ral gas on his plantation he needn't lug home his supplies in a quart jug no more, but kin roll 'em in by the bar'l, fer signs o'
them kind is wuth more an inch th'n a sartin-per-sure grass an' 'tater
farm is wuth an acre."

"Guess yer huggin' the truth pooty clus fer wunst, Major," replied
the 'Squire, "but th' hain't none o' them signs ez likely to strike any-
whar in our bailiwick ez lightnin' is to kill a crow roostin' on the North
Pole. Thuz one thing I've alluz wanted to see," continued the 'Squire,
"but natur' has ben agin me, an' I hain't never seen it, an' that thing is
the h'istin' of a balloon. Th' can't be no balloon h'isted nowhar, I'm
told, 'nless thuz gas to h'ist it with. I s'pose if we'd ha' had gas here, a
good many fellers with balloons 'd ha' kim 'round this way an' showed
us a balloon raisin' ev'ry now an' then. Them must be lucky deestric's
that's got gas, an' I'd like to hev somebody strike it 'round here some'rs,
jist fer the sake o' havin' the chance to see a balloon h'istin' 'fore I turn
my toes up. But that's 'bout es liable to happen ez it is fer me to go out
an' find a silver dollar rollin' up hill, an' my name gouged in it."

"Don't ye be so consarned sure o' that, 'Squire," said the Old Settler,
mysteriously, and with a knowing shake of his head. "Ive been a

thinkin' a leetle sence readin' 'bout them signs o' gas, b'gosh! I hain't been only thinkin', but I've been a recollectin', an' the chances is th't me an' you'll see wonders yet afore we paddle over Jurdan. I'm agoin-ter tell ye fer w'y, but I hadn't orter, 'Squire, an' if it wa'n't fer makin' ye shamed o' yerself, an' showin' th't truth squashed in the mud is bound to git up again if ye give her time, I wouldn't do it. Ye mowt re-member th't jist ten years ago this month I kim in from a leetle b'ar hunt. I didn't bring in no b'ar, but I fotched back an up-an'-up account o' how I had shot one, an' how th' were sumpin fearful an' queer an' amazin' in the p'formances o' that b'ar arter bein' shot. Mebby ye 'member me a tellin' ye that story, 'Squire, an' you a tellin' me right in my teeth th't ye know'd th't some o' yer friends had took to lyin', but th't ye didn't think any of 'em had it so bad ez that. But I hain't a holdin' no gredge, an' now I'll tell ye sumpin' that'll s'prise ye.

"Ez I tol' ye at the time, 'Squire, I got the tip ten year ago this month, th't unless somebody went up to Steve Groner's hill place an' poured a pound or two o' lead inter a big b'ar th't had squatted on tha' farm, th't Steve wouldn't hev no live-stock left to pervide pork an' beef fer his winterin' over, even if he managed to keep hisself an' fam'ly theirselfs from linin' the b'ar's innards. I shouldered my gun an' went up to Steve's to hev some fun with bruin, an' to save Steve's stock and resky him an' his folks from the rampagin' b'ar.

" 'He's a rip-snorter,' Steve says to me, w'en I got thar. 'He don't think nuthin' o' luggin' off a cow,' he says, 'an' ye don't wanter hev yer weather eye shet w'en you an' him comes together,' he says.

" 'B'ars,' I says to Steve, 'b'ars is nuts fer me, an' the bigger an' sassier they be,' I says, 'the more I inj'y 'em,' I says, an' with that I clim' inter the woods to show bruin th't th' wa'n't room enough here below fer me an' him both. 'Tain't necessary fer me to tell o' the half-dozen or more lively skrimmages me an' that b'ar had ez we follered an' chased one another round an' round them woods—how he'd hide ahind some big tree or stump, an' ez I went by, climb on to me with all four o' his feet an' yank an' bite an' claw an' dig meat an' clothes offen me till I slung him off an' made him skin away to save his bacon; an' how I'd lay the same way fer him, an' w'en he come sneakin' 'long arter me agin, pitch arter him like a mad painter, an' swat an' pound an' choke an' rassel him till his tongue hung out, till I were sorry for him, an' let him git away inter the brush agin to recooperate fer the next round. 'Taint wuth w'ile fer me to say anything 'bout them little skrimmages 'cept the last un, an' that un wa'n't a skrimmage, but sumpin' that'd 'a' skeert some folks dead in their tracks.

"Arter havin' a half a dozen or so o' rassels with this big b'ar, jist fer fun, I made up my mind, ez 'twere gettin' late, an' ez Steve Groner's folks was mebby feelin' anxious to hear which was gointer run the farm, them or the b'ar, th't the next heat with bruin would be for keeps. I guess the ol' feller had made up his mind the same way, fer w'en I run agin him the las' time, he were riz up on his hind legs right on the edge o' Deep Rock Gulley, and were waitin' fer me with his jaws wide open. I unslung my gun, an' takin' aim at one o' the b'ar's fore paws, thought I'd wing him an' make him come away from the edge o' the gulley 'fore I tackled him. The ball hit the paw, an' the b'ar throw'd 'em both up. But he throw'd 'em up too fur, an' he fell over back'rds, an' went head foremost inter the gulley. Deep Rock Gulley ain't an inch less'n fifty foot from top to bottom, an' the walls is ez steep as the side of a house. I went up to the edge an' looked over. Ther' were the b'ar layin' on his face at the bottom, whar them queer cracks is in the ground, an' he were a howlin' like a hurricane and kickin' like a mule. Ther' he laid, and he wa'n't able to raise up. Th' wa'n't no way o' gettin' down to him, 'cept by tumblin' down ez he had; an' if ever anybody were poppin' mad, I were, ez I see my meat a layin' at the bottom o' that gulley, an' the crows a getherin' to hev a picnic with it. The more I kep' my eyes on that b'ar the madder I got, an' I were jist about to roll and tumble an' slide down the side o' that gulley ruther than go back home an' say th't I'd let the crows steal a b'ar away from me, w'en I see a funny change comin' over the b'ar. He didn't howl so much, and his kicks wa'n't so vicious. Then his hind parts began to lift themse'fs up offen the ground in a cur'ous sort o' way, and swung an' bobbed in the air. They kep' raisin' higher an' higher, till the b'ar were act'ally standin' on his head, an' swayin' to and fro ez if a wind were blowin' him an' he couldn't help it. The sight was so oncommon out o' the reg'lar way b'ars has o' actin' that it seemed skeery, an' I felt ez if I'd ruther be home diggin' my 'taters. But I kep' on gazin' at the b'ar a circusin' at the bottom o' the gulley, and 't wa'n't long 'fore the hull big carcase begun to raise right up offen the ground an' come a-floatin' up outen that gulley, fer all the world ez if 't wa'n't more'n a feather. The b'ar come up'ards tail foremost, an' I noticed th't he looked consid'able puffed out like, makin' him seem lik' a bar'l sailin' in the air. Ez the b'ar kim a-floatin' out o' the dep's, I could feel my eyes begin to bulge, an' my knees to shake like a jumpin' jack's. But I couldn't move no more'n a stun wall kin, an' thar I stood on the edge o' the gulley, starin' at the b'ar ez it sailed on up t'ords me. The b'ar were making a desper't effort to git itself back to its nat'ral p'sition on all fours, but th' wa'n't no use, an' up he sailed, tail foremost, an' looking ez if he were gointer bust the next minute, he were swelled out so. Ez the b'ar bobbed up and passed by me I could ha' reached out an' grabbed him by the paw, an' I think he wanted me to, the way he acted, but I couldn't ha' made a move to stop him, not if he'd ha' ben my gran'mother. The b'ar sailed on above me, an' th' were a look in his eyes th't I won't never fergit. It was a skeert look, an' a look that seemed to say th't it were all my fault, an' th't I'd be sorry fer it some time. The b'ar squirmed an' struggled agin comin' to setch an' onheerdon end, but up'ards he went, tail foremost, to'ards the clouds.

"I stood thar par'lyzed w'ile the b'ar went up'ard. The crows that had been settlin' round in the trees, 'spectin' to hev a bully meal, went to flyin' an' scootin' around the onfortnit b'ar, an' yelled till I were durn nigh deef. It wa'n't until the b'ar had floated up nigh onto a hundred yards in the air, an' begun to look like a flyin' cub, that my senses kim back to me. Quick ez a flash I rammed a load inter my rifle, wrappin' the ball with a big piece o' dry linen, not havin' time to tear it to the right size. Then I took aim an' let her go. Fast ez that ball went, I could see that the linen round it had been sot on fire by the powder. The ball overtook the b'ar and bored a hole in his side. Then the funniest thing of all happened. A streak o' fire a yard long shot out o' the b'ar's side where the bullet had gone in, an' ez long as that poor bewitched b'ar were in sight—fer o' course I thort at the time th't the b'ar were bewitched—I could see that streak o' fire sailin' along in the sky till it went out at last like a shootin' star. I never knowed w'at become o' the b'ar, an' the hull thing were a startlin' myst'ry to me, but I kim home, 'Squire, an' tol' ye the story, jest ez I've tol' it to ye now, an' ye were so durn polite th't ye said I were a liar. But sence, I've been a thinkin' an' recollectin'. 'Squire, I don't hold no gredge. The myst'ry's plain ez day, now. We don't want no better signs o' gas th'n that, do we, 'Squire?"

"Than what?" said the 'Squire.

"Than what." exclaimed the Old Settler.

"Than that bar, o' course! That's w'at ailed him. It's plain enough th't thuz nat'ral gas on the Groner place, an' th't it leaks outen the ground in Deep Rock Gulley. W'en that b'ar tumbled to the bottom that day, he fell on his face. He were hurt so th't he couldn't get up. O' course the gas didn't shut itself off, but kep' on a leakin', an' shot up inter the b'ar's mouth and down his throat. The onfortnit b'ar couldn't help hisself, an' bimby he were filled with gas like a balloon, till he had to float, an' away he sailed, up an' up an' up. W'en I fired at the b'ar, ez he was floatin' to'ards the clouds, the linen on the bullet carried fire with it, and w'en the bullet tapped the b'ar's side the burnin' linen sot it on fire, showin' th't th' can't be no doubt 'bout it bein' gas th't the b'ar swallered in Deep Rock Gulley. So ye see, 'Squire, I wan't no liar, an' the chances is all in favor o' your seein' a balloon h'isted from gas right in yer own bailiwick afore ye turn up yer toes."

The 'Squire gazed at the Old Settler in silent amazement for a minute or more. Then he threw up his hands and said:

"Wal—I'll—be—durned!"

BOY THE DESTROYER

CHARLES DUDLEY WARNER

The power of a boy is, to me, something fearful. Consider what he can do! You buy and set out a choice pear-tree; you enrich the earth for it, you train and trim it, and vanquish the borer, and watch its slow growth. At length it rewards your care by producing two or three pears, which you cut up and divide in the family, declaring the flavor of the bit you eat to be something extraordinary. The next year, the little tree blossoms full, and sets well; and in the autumn has on its slender, drooping limbs half a bushel of fruit, daily growing more delicious in the sun. You show it to your friends, reading to them the French name, which you can never remember, on the label; and you take an honest pride in the successful fruit of long care. That night your pears shall be required of you by a boy! Along comes an irresponsible urchin, who has not been growing much longer than the tree, with not twenty-five cents' worth of clothing on him, and in five minutes takes off every pear, and retires into safe obscurity. In five minutes the remorseless boy has undone your work of years, and with the easy *nonchalance*, I doubt not, of any agent of fate, in whose path nothing is sacred or safe.

And it is not of much consequence. The boy goes on his way,—to Congress, or to State-prison: in either place he will be accused of stealing, perhaps wrongfully. You learn, in time, that it is better to have had pears and lost them, than not to have had pears at all. You come to know that the least (and rarest) part of the pleasure of raising fruit is the vulgar eating it. You recall your delight in conversing with the nurseryman, and looking at his illustrated catalogues, where all the pears are drawn perfect in form, and of extra size, and at that exact moment between ripeness and decay which it is so impossible to hit in practice. Fruit cannot be raised on this earth to taste as you imagine those pears would taste. For years you have this pleasure, unalloyed by any disenchanting reality. How you watch the tender twigs in spring, and the freshly forming bark, hovering about the healthy growing tree with your pruning-knife many a sunny morning! That is happiness. Then, if you know it, you are drinking the very wine of life; and when the sweet juices of the earth mount the limbs, and flow down the tender stem, ripening and reddening the pendent fruit, you feel that you somehow stand at the source of things, and have no unimportant share in the processes of Nature. Enter, at this moment, boy the destroyer, whose office is that of preserver as well; for, though he removes the fruit from your sight, it remains in your memory immortally ripe and desirable. The gardener needs all these consolations of a high philosophy.

———

MAN waz kreated a little lower than the angells, and he haz been a gitting a little lower ever since.

JOSH BILLINGS

THE TYPE-WRITER

ROBERT J. BURDETTE

CARDINAL—
    "Beneath the sliding rule of men entirely great
    The type-writer is greater than the sword."
OLDGOLD—
    "Who swored, my lord?"
CARDINAL—
    "The man who received the type-writer letter;
    The printers who set up the copy;
    Whole words spelled in the space of one small m,
    With all the letters piled on top of one another,
    Like to a Chinese sentence standing on its head.
    What sense is there in this?—"Rgw? GHops ffl dww d¶"
    And yet I know it means "the horse fell dead."
    In all the lexicons we use there's no such word
    As "kbfitMa)I$n¶;" yet full well I know
    It stands in this man's note for "information;"
    I have so learned the tangled language of the thing.
    That all its jargon is writ plain for me;
    But solely do I fear that learning it,
    I have made a hopeless wreck of temperate speech,
    And lost my front-pew standing in the synagogue.
    See, all around this line of consonants
    Scarred with lost capitals, the proof-reader has drawn
    His awful circle with the pencil blue;
    Stand off: while on this correspondent's head
    I launch the cuss of our Composing Room.
                (The cuss.)
    Dog gone the billy be dog goned man of thumbs,
    The diddledy dag goned chalky fingered loon
    Y gum; 'gaul; od rabbit; jeeminy pelt!
    Gad zooks; odd beddikins; by Venus' glove;

By Mars his gauntlet; by the river side;
Sweet by and by, and bo oh, baby by—"

(At this point the caitiff slowly withers away.)

High-Handed Outrage at Utica

ARTEMUS WARD

In the Faul of 1856 I showed my show in Utiky, a trooly grate sitty in the State of New York.

The people gave me a cordyal recepshun. The press was loud in her prases.

1 day, as I was givin' a descripshun of my Beests and Snaiks in my usual flowry stile, what was my skorn & disgust to see a big burly feller walk up to the cage containin my wax figgers of the Lord's Last Supper, and cease Judas Iscarrot by the feet and drag him out on the ground. He then commenced fur to pound him as hard as he cood.

"What under the son are you abowt?" cried I.

Sez he, "What did you bring this pussylanermus cuss here fur?" & he hit the wax figger another tremenjis blow on the hed.

Sez I, "You egrejus ass, that air's a wax figger—a representashun of the false 'Postle."

Sez he, "That's all very well fur you to say, but I tell you, old man, that Judas Iscarrot can't show hisself in Utiky with impunerty by a darn site!" with which observashun he kaved in Judassis' hed. The young man belonged to 1 of the first famerlies in Utiky. I sood him, and the Joory brawt in a verdick of Arson in the 3d degree.

At Niagara

W. D. HOWELLS

Our friends returned by the shore of the Canadian rapids, having traversed the island by a path through the heart of the woods, and now drew slowly near the Falls again. All parts of the prodigious pageant have an eternal novelty, and they beheld the ever-varying effect of that constant sublimity with the sense of discoverers, or, rather, of people whose great fortune it is to see the marvel in its beginning, and new from the creating Hand. The morning hour lent its sunny charm to this illusion, while in the cavernous precipices of the shores, dark with evergreens, a mystery as of primeval night seemed to linger. There was a wild fluttering of their nerves, a rapture with an under-consciousness of pain, the exaltation of peril and escape, when they came to the three little isles that extend from Goat Island, one beyond another, far into the furious channel. Three pretty suspension-bridges connect them now with the larger island, and under each of these flounders a huge rapid, and hurls itself away to mingle with the ruin of the fall. The Three Sisters are mere fragments of wilderness, clumps of vine-tangled woods, planted upon masses of rock; but they are part of the fascination of Niagara which no one resists; nor could Isabel have been persuaded from exploring them. It wants no courage to do this, but merely submission to the local sorcery; and the adventurer has no other reward than the consciousness of having been where but a few years before no human being had perhaps set foot. She crossed from bridge to bridge with a quaking heart, and at last stood upon the outermost isle, whence, through the screen of vines and boughs, she gave fearful glances at the heaving and tossing flood beyond, from every wave of which at every instant she rescued herself with a desperate struggle. The exertion told heavily upon her strength unawares, and she suddenly made Basil another revelation of character. Without the slightest warning she sank down at the root of a tree, and said, with serious composure, that she could never go back on those bridges; they were not safe. He stared at her cowering form in blank amaze, and put his hands in his pockets. Then it occurred to his dull masculine sense that it must be a joke; and he said, "Well, I'll have you taken off in a boat."

"O *do*, Basil, *do* have me taken off in a boat!" implored Isabel. "You see yourself the bridges are not safe. *Do* get a boat!"

"Or a balloon," he suggested, humoring the pleasantry.

Isabel burst into tears; and now he went on his knees at her side, and took her hands in his. "Isabel! Isabel! Are you crazy?" he cried, as if he meant to go mad himself. She moaned and shuddered in reply; he said, to mend matters, that it was a jest, about the boat; and he was driven to despair when Isabel repeated, "I never can go back by the bridges, never!"

"But what do you propose to do?"

"I don't know; I don't know!"

He would try sarcasm. "Do you intend to set up a hermitage here, and have your meals sent out from the hotel? It's a charming spot, and visited pretty constantly; but it's small, even for a hermitage."

Isabel moaned again, with her hands still on her eyes, and wondered that he was not ashamed to make fun of her.

He would try kindness. "Perhaps, darling, you'll let me carry you ashore?"

"No; that will bring double the weight on the bridge at once."

"Couldn't you shut your eyes, and let me lead you?"

"Why, it isn't the *sight* of the rapids," she said, looking up fiercely. "*The bridges are not safe.* I'm not a *child*, Basil! O, *what* shall we do?"

"I don't know," said Basil, gloomily. "It's an exigency for which I wasn't prepared." Then he silently gave himself to the Evil One, for having probably overwrought Isabel's nerves by repeating that poem about Avery, and by the ensuing talk about Niagara, which she had seemed to enjoy so much. He asked her if that was it; and she answered, "O no, it's nothing but the bridges." He proved to her that the bridges, upon all known principles, were perfectly safe, and that they could not give way. She shook her head, but made no answer, and he lost his patience.

"Isabel," he cried, "I'm ashamed of you!"

"Don't say anything you'll be sorry for afterwards, Basil," she replied, with the forbearance of those who have reason and justice on their side.

The rapids beat and shouted round their little prison-isle, each billow leaping as if possessed by a separate demon. The absurd horror of the situation overwhelmed him. He dared not attempt to carry her ashore, for she might spring from his grasp into the flood. He could not leave her to call for help; and what if nobody came till she lost her mind from terror! Or, what if somebody should come and find them in that ridiculous affliction!

Somebody *was* coming!

"Isabel!" he shouted in her ear, "here come those people we saw in the parlor last night."

Isabel dashed her veil over her face, clutched Basil's with her icy hand, rose, drew her arm convulsively through his, and walked ashore without a word.

In a sheltered nook they sat down, and she quickly "repaired her drooping head and tricked her beams" again. He could see her tearfully smiling through her veil. "My dear," he said, "I don't ask an explanation of your fright, for I don't suppose you could give it. But should you mind telling me why those people were so sovereign against it?"

"Why, dearest! Don't you understand? That Mrs. Richard—whoever she is—is so much like *me!*"

She looked at him as if she had made the most satisfying statement, and he thought he had better not ask further then, but wait in hope that the meaning would come to him.

A New System of English Grammar

JOHN PHŒNIX

I have often thought that the adjectives of the English language were not sufficiently definite for the purposes of description. They have but three degrees of comparison—a very insufficient number, certainly, when we consider that they are to be applied to a thousand objects, which, though of the same general class or quality, differ from each other by a thousand different shades or degrees of the same peculiarity. Thus, though there are three hundred and sixty-five days in a year, all of which must, from the nature of things, differ from each other in the matter of climate—we have but half a dozen expressions to convey to one another our ideas of this inequality. We say—"It is a fine day;" "It is a *very* fine day;" "It is the *finest* day we have seen;" or, "It is an unpleasant day;" "A *very* unpleasant day;" "The *most* unpleasant day we ever saw." But it is plain that none of these expressions give an *exact* idea of the nature of the day, and the two superlative expressions are generally untrue. I once heard a gentleman remark, on a rainy, snowy, windy and (in the ordinary English language) indescribable day, that it was "most preposterous weather." He came nearer to giving a correct idea of it than he could have done by any ordinary mode of expression; but his description was not sufficiently definite.

Again—we say of a lady—"She is beautiful;" "She is *very* beautiful," or "She is *perfectly* beautiful"—descriptions which, to one who never saw her, are no descriptions at all, for among thousands of women he has seen, probably no two are equally beautiful; and as to a *perfectly* beautiful woman, he knows that no such being was ever created—unless by G. P. R. James, for one of the two horsemen to fall in love with, and marry at the end of the second volume.

If I meet Smith in the street, and ask him—as I am pretty sure to do—"How he does?" he infallibly replies—"*Tolerable*, thank you"—which gives me no *exact* idea of Smith's health—for he has made the same reply to me on a hundred different occasions—on every one of which there *must* have been some slight shade of difference in his physical economy, and, of course, a corresponding change in his feelings.

To a man of a mathematical turn of mind—to a student and lover of the exact sciences—these inaccuracies of expression, this inability to understand *exactly* how things are, must be a constant source of annoyance; and to one who, like myself, unites this turn of mind to an ardent love of truth, for its own sake, the reflection that the English language does not enable us to speak the truth with exactness, is peculiarly painful. For this reason I have, with some trouble, made myself thoroughly acquainted with every ancient and modern language, in the hope that I might find some one of them that would enable me to express precisely my ideas; but the same insufficiency of adjectives exists in all except that of the Flathead Indians of Puget Sound, which consists of but forty-six words, mostly nouns; but to the constant use of which exists the objection that nobody but that tribe can understand it. And as their literary and scientific advancement is not such as to make a residence among them, for a man of my disposition, desirable, I have abandoned the use of their language in the belief that for me it is *hyas. cultus.*, or as the Spaniard hath it, *no me vale nada.*

Despairing, therefore, of making new discoveries in foreign languages, I have set myself seriously to work to reform our own; and have, I think, made an important discovery, which, when developed into a system and universally adopted, will give a precision of expression, and a consequent clearness of idea, that will leave little to be desired, and will, I modestly hope, immortalize my humble name as the promulgator of the truth and the benefactor of the human race.

Before entering upon my system I will give you an account of its discovery, which, perhaps, I might with more modesty term an adaptation and enlargement of the idea of another, which will surprise you by its simplicity, and, like the method of standing eggs on end, of Columbus, the inventions of printing, gunpowder and the mariner's compass, prove another exemplification of the truth of Hannah More's beautifully expressed sentiment:

> "Large streams from little fountains flow,
> Large aches from little toe-corns grow."

During the past week my attention was attracted by a large placard embellishing the corners of our streets, headed in mighty capitals, with the word "PHRENOLOGY," and illustrated by a map of a man's head, closely shaven, and laid off in lots, duly numbered from one to forty-seven. Beneath this edifying illustration appeared a legend, informing the inhabitants of San Diego and vicinity that Professor Dodge had arrived, and taken rooms (which was inaccurate, as he had but one room) at the Gyascutus House, where he would be happy to examine and furnish them with a chart of their heads, showing the moral and intellectual endowments, at the low price of three dollars each.

Always gratified with an opportunity of spending my money and making scientific researches, I immediately had my hair cut and carefully combed, and hastened to present myself and my head to the Professor's notice. I found him a tall and thin Professor, in a suit of rusty, not to say seedy, black, with a closely buttoned vest, and no perceptible shirt-collar or wristbands. His nose was red, his spectacles were blue, and he wore a brown wig, beneath which, as I subsequently ascertained, his bald head was laid off in lots, marked and numbered with Indian ink, after the manner of the diagram upon his advertisement. Upon a small table lay many little books with yellow covers, several of the placards, pen and ink, a pair of iron callipers with brass knobs, and six dollars in silver. Having explained the object of my visit, and increased the pile of silver by six half-dollars from my pocket—whereat he smiled, and I observed he wore false teeth (scientific men always do; they love to encourage art)—the Professor placed me in a chair, and rapidly manipulating my head, after the manner of a *sham pooh* (I am not certain as to the orthography of this expression), said that my temperament was "lymphatic, nervous, bilious." I remarked that "I thought myself dyspeptic," but he made no reply. Then seizing on the callipers, he embraced with them my head in various places, and made notes upon a small card that lay near him on the table. He then stated that my "hair was getting very thin on the top," placed in my hand one of the yellow-covered books, which I found to be an almanac containing anecdotes about the virtues of Dodge's Hair Invigorator, and recommending it to my perusal, he remarked that he was agent for the sale of this wonderful fluid, and urged me to purchase a bottle—price two dollars. Stating my willingness to do so, the Professor produced it from a hair trunk that stood in a corner of the room, which he stated, by the way, was originally an ordinary pine box, on which the hair had grown since "the Invigorator" had been placed in it—(a singular fact) and recommended me to be cautious in wearing gloves while rubbing it upon my head, as unhappy accidents had occurred—the hair growing freely from the ends of the fingers, if used with the bare hand. He then seated himself at the table, and rapidly filling up what appeared to me a blank certificate, he soon handed over the following singular document.

PHRENOLOGICAL CHART OF THE HEAD OF M. JOHN PHŒNIX, by FLAT-BROKE B. DODGE, Professor of Phrenology, and inventor and proprietor of Dodge's celebrated Hair Invigorator, Stimulator of the Conscience, and Arouser of the Mental Faculties:

Temperament—*Lymphatic, Nervous, Bilious*

Size of Head, 11	Imitation, 11
Amativeness, 11½	Self-Esteem, ½
Caution, 3	Benevolence, 12
Combativeness, 2½	Mirth, 1
Credulity, 1	Language, 12
Causality, 12	Firmness, 2
Conscientiousness, 12	Veneration, 12
Destructiveness, 9	Philoprogenitiveness, 0

Hope, 10

Having gazed on this for a few moments in mute astonishment—during which the Professor took a glass of brandy and water, and afterwards a mouthful of tobacco—I turned to him and requested an explanation.

"Why," said he, "it's very simple; the number 12 is the maximum, 1 the minimum; for instance, you are as benevolent as a man can be—therefore I mark you, Benevolence, 12. You have little or no self-esteem—hence I place you, Self-esteem, ½. You've scarcely any credulity—don't you see?"

I did see! This was my discovery. I saw at a flash how the English language was susceptible of improvement, and, fired with the glorious idea, I rushed from the room and the house. Heedless of the Professor's request that I would buy more of his Invigorator; heedless of his alarmed cry that I would pay for the bottle I'd got; heedless that I tripped on the last step of the Gyascutus House, and smashed there the precious fluid (the step has now a growth of four inches of hair on it, and the people use it as a door-mat)—I rushed home, and never grew calm till, with pen, ink and paper before me, I commenced the development of my system.

This system—shall I say this great system?—is exceedingly simple, and easily explained in a few words. In the first place, "*figures won't lie.*" Let us, then, represent by the number 100 the maximum, the *ne plus ultra*, of every human quality: grace, beauty, courage, strength, wisdom, learning—everything. Let *perfection*, I say, be represented by 100, and an absolute minimum of all qualities by the number 1. Then, by applying the numbers between, to the adjectives used in conversation, we shall be able to arrive at a very close approximation to the idea we wish to convey; in other words, we shall be enabled to speak the truth. Glorious, soul-inspiring idea! For instance, the most ordinary question asked of you is, "How do you do?" To this, instead of replying, "Pretty well," "Very well," "Quite well," or the like absurdities—after running through your mind that *perfection* of health is 100; no health at all, 1—you say, with a graceful bow, "Thank you, I'm 52 to-day;" or, feeling poorly, "I'm 13, I'm obliged to you;" or, "I'm 68," or "75," or "87½," as the case may be! Do you see how very close, in this way, you may approximate to the truth, and how clearly your questioner will understand what he so anxiously wishes to arrive at—your *exact* state of health?

Let this system be adopted into our elements of grammar, our conversation, our literature, and we become at once an exact, precise, mathematical, truth-telling people. It will apply to everything but politics; there, truth being of no account, the system is useless. But in literature, how admirable! Take an example:

As a 19 young and 76 beautiful lady was 52 gaily tripping down the sidewalk of our 84 frequented street, she accidentally came in contact—100 (this shows that she came in close contact) with a 73 fat but 87 good-humored-looking gentleman, who was 93 (i. e., intently) gazing into the window of a toy-shop. Gracefully 56 extricating herself, she received the excuses of the 96 embarrassed Falstaff with a 68 bland smile, and continued on her way. But hardly—7—had she reached the corner of the block, ere she was overtaken by a 24 young man, 32 poorly dressed, but of an 85 expression of countenance; 91 hastily touching her 54 beautifully rounded arm, he said, to her 67 surprise:

"Madam, at the window of the toy-shop yonder you dropped this bracelet, which I had the 71 good fortune to observe, and now have the 94 happiness to hand to you." (Of course, the expression "94 happiness" is merely the poor man's polite hyperbole.)

Blushing with 76 modesty, the lovely (76, as before, of course) lady took the bracelet—which was a 24 magnificent diamond clasp (24 *magnificent*, playfully sarcastic; it was probably *not* one of Tucker's)—from the young man's hand, and 84 hesitatingly drew from her beautifully 38 embroidered reticule a 67 port-monnaie. The young man noticed the action, and 73 proudly drawing back, added:

"Do not thank me; the pleasure of gazing for an instant at those 100 eyes (perhaps too exaggerated a compliment) has already more than compensated me for any trouble that I might have had."

She thanked him, however, and with a 67 deep blush and a 48 pensive air, turned from him, and pursued with a 33 slow step her promenade.

Of course, you see that this is but the commencement of a pretty little tale, which I might throw off, if I had a mind to, showing, in two volumes, or forty-eight chapters of thrilling interest, how the young man sought the girl's acquaintance, how the interest first excited deepened into love, how they suffered much from the opposition of parents (her parents, of course), and how, after much trouble, annoyance, and many perilous adventures, they were finally married—their happiness, of course, being represented by 100. But I trust that I have said enough to recommend my system to the good and truthful of the literary world; and besides, just at present I have something of more immediate importance to attend to.

You would hardly believe it, but that everlasting (100) scamp of a Professor has brought a suit against me for stealing a bottle of his disgusting Invigorator; and as the suit comes off before a Justice of the Peace whose only principle of law is to find guilty and fine any accused person who he thinks has any money (because if he doesn't he has to take his costs in County Scrip), it behooves me to "take time by the fore-lock." So, for the present, adieu. Should my system succeed to the extent of my hopes and expectations, I shall publish my new grammar early in the ensuing month, with suitable dedication and preface; and should you, with your well-known liberality, publish my prospectus, and give me a handsome literary notice, I shall be pleased to furnish a presentation copy to each of the little Pioneer children.

P. S.—I regret to add, that having just read this article to Mrs. Phœnix, and asked her opinion thereon, she replied, that "if a first-rate magazine article were represented by 100, she should judge this to be about 13; or if the quintessence of stupidity were 100, she should take this to be in the neighborhood of 96." This, as a criticism, is perhaps a little discouraging, but as an exemplification of the merits of my system it is exceedingly flattering. How could she, I should like to know, in ordinary language, have given so *exact* and truthful an idea—how expressed so forcibly her opinion (which, of course, differs from mine) on the subject?

As Dr. Samuel Johnson learnedly remarked to James Boswell, Laird of Auchinleck, on a certain occasion:

"Sir, the proof of the pudding is in the eating thereof."

In Sis's Interest

Omaha Man—"You naughty boy, Dick, don't you know better than to ask people how much money they have? I hope you will excuse the child, Mr. Nicefellow"—"Of course, of course! The little fellow didn't know what he was talking about." Little Dick—"Yes I did, too. Sis said she wished she knew, and I wanted to tell her."—*Newspaper*

THE DEACON'S MASTERPIECE;

or, The Wonderful "One-Hoss Shay"
A Logical Story

O. W. HOLMES

Have you heard of the wonderful one-hoss shay,
That was built in such a logical way
It ran a hundred years to a day,
And then, of a sudden, it—ah, but stay,
I'll tell you what happened without delay,
Scaring the parson into fits,
Frightening people out of their wits—
Have you ever heard of that, I say?

Seventeen hundred and fifty-five.
Georgius Secundus was then alive—
Snuffy old drone from the German hive.
That was the year when Lisbon-town
Saw the earth open and gulp her down,
And Braddock's army was done so brown,
Left without a scalp to its crown.
It was on the terrible Earthquake-day
That the Deacon finished the one-hoss shay.

Now in building of chaises, I tell you what,
There is always *somewhere* a weakest spot—
In hub, tire, felloe, in spring or thill,
In panel, or crossbar, or floor, or sill,
In screw, bolt, thoroughbrace—lurking still,
Find it somewhere you must and will—
Above or below, or within or without—
And that's the reason, beyond a doubt,
That a chaise *breaks down*, but doesn't *wear out*.

But the Deacon swore (as Deacons do,
With an "I dew vum," or an "I tell *yeou*")
He would build one shay to beat the taown,
'n' the keounty, 'n' all the kentry raoun';
It should be so built that it *couldn'* break daown:
—"Fur," said the Deacon, " 't's mighty plain
Thut the weakes' place mus' stan' the strain;
'n' the way t' fix it, uz I maintain,
Is only jest
T' make that place uz strong uz the rest."

So the Deacon inquired of the village folk
Where he could find the strongest oak,
That couldn't be split nor bent nor broke—
That was for spokes and floor and sills;
He sent for lancewood to make the thills;
The crossbars were ash, from the straightest trees,
The panels of white-wood, that cuts like cheese,
But lasts like iron for things like these;
The hubs of logs from the "Settler's ellum"—
Last of its timber—they couldn't sell 'em,
Never an axe had seen their chips,
And the wedges flew from between their lips,
Their blunt ends frizzled like celery-tips;
Step and prop-iron, bolt and screw,
Spring, tire, axle, and linchpin too,
Steel of the finest, bright and blue;
Thoroughbrace bison-skin, thick and wide;
Boot, top, dasher, from tough old hide
Found in the pit when the tanner died.
That was the way he "put her through."—
"There!" said the Deacon, "naow she'll dew!"

Do! I tell you, I rather guess
She was a wonder and nothing less!
Colts grew horses, beards turned gray,
Deacon and Deaconess dropped away,
Children and grandchildren—where were they?
But there stood the stout old one-hoss shay
As fresh as on Lisbon-earthquake-day!

EIGHTEEN HUNDRED—it came and found
The Deacon's masterpiece strong and sound.
Eighteen hundred increased by ten—
"Hahnsum kerridge" they called it then.
Eighteen hundred and twenty came—
Running as usual; much the same.
Thirty and forty at last arrive,
And then come fifty, and FIFTY-FIVE.

Little of all we value here
Wakes on the morn of its hundredth year
Without both feeling and looking queer.
In fact, there's nothing that keeps its youth,
So far as I know, but a tree and truth.
(This is a moral that runs at large;
Take it.—You're welcome.—No extra charge.)

FIRST OF NOVEMBER—the Earthquake-day—
There are traces of age in the one-hoss shay,
A general flavor of mild decay,
But nothing local, as one may say.
There couldn't be—for the Deacon's art
Had made it so like in every part
That there wasn't a chance for one to start.
For the wheels were just as strong as the thills,
And the floor was just as strong as the sills,
And the panels just as strong as the floor,
And the whipple-tree neither less nor more,
And the back-crossbar as strong as the fore,
And spring and axle and hub *encore.*
And yet, *as a whole*, it is past a doubt
In an another hour it will be *worn out!*

First of November, 'Fifty-five!
This morning the parson takes a drive.
Now, small boys, get out of the way!
Here comes the wonderful one-hoss shay,
Drawn by a rat-tailed, ewe-necked bay.
"Huddup!" said the parson.—Off went they.
The parson was working his Sunday's text—
Had got to *fifthly*, and stopped perplexed

At what the—Moses—was coming next.
All at once the horse stood still,
Close by the meet'n'-house on the hill.
—First a shiver, and then a thrill,
Then something decidedly like a spill—
And the parson was sitting upon a rock,
At half past nine by the meet'n'-house clock—
Just the hour of the Earthquake shock!

—What do you think the parson found,
When he got up and stared around?
The poor old chaise in a heap or mound,
As if it had been to the mill and ground!
You see, of course, if you're not a dunce,
How it went to pieces all at once—
All at once, and nothing first—
Just as bubbles do when they burst.

End of the wonderful one-hoss shay.
Logic is logic. That's all I say.

"Not Like in Like, but Like in Difference"

R. J. BURDETTE

"Darling," he said, lovingly, as no other man in the world could say it, "I don't like you to destroy your own beautiful complexion with paint and powder. And if you paint your face, I will paint mine." "Why?" she asked, with pouting lips. "Because," he said, more tenderly than ever, "you are mine. We belong to each other, and what is good for one, is good for the other. We love each other, and must be like each other, and if you put paint on your cheeks this evening, I will paint mine before we go to the theatre." "My own true love," she said, kissing him, "you are right; we must be like each other. I will not paint nor powder my face. And you just sit here by the fire a couple of minutes, and I will run around to Dutch Jake's and spice my breath up with a dish of beer and a Chinese cigarette, and we will be ready to go to the theatre like a pair of engaged Siamese twins with American breaths." And William thought it all over, and told her to go and put on all the feminine fol-de-rols and crinkles she could find in the illustrated advertisements.

LOST IN THE SNOW

MARK TWAIN

We mounted and started. The snow lay so deep on the ground that there was no sign of a road perceptible, and the snow-fall was so thick that we could not see more than a hundred yards ahead, else we could have guided our course by the mountain ranges. The case looked dubious, but Ollendorff said his instinct was as sensitive as any compass, and that he could "strike a bee-line" for Carson City and never diverge from it. He said that if he were to straggle a single point out of the true line, his instinct would assail him like an outraged conscience. Consequently we dropped into his wake happy and content. For half an hour we poked along warily enough, but at the end of that time we came upon a fresh trail, and Ollendorff shouted proudly:

"I knew I was as dead certain as a compass, boys! Here we are, right in somebody's tracks that will hunt the way for us without any trouble. Let's hurry up and join company with the party."

So we put the horses into as much of a trot as the deep snow would allow, and before long it was evident that we were gaining on our predecessors, for the tracks grew more distinct. We hurried along, and at the end of an hour the tracks looked still newer and fresher—but what surprised us was, that the *number* of travelers in advance of us seemed to steadily increase. We wondered how so large a party came to be traveling at such a time and in such a solitude. Somebody suggested that it must be a company of soldiers from the fort, and so we accepted that solution and jogged along a little faster still, for they could not be far off now. But the tracks still multiplied, and we began to think the platoon of soldiers was miraculously expanding into a regiment—Ballou said they had already increased to five hundred! Presently he stopped his horse and said:

"Boys, these are our own tracks, and we've actually been circussing round and round in a circle for more than two hours, out here in this blind desert! By George, this is perfectly hydraulic!"

Then the old man waxed wroth and abusive. He called Ollendorff all manner of hard names—said he never saw such a lurid fool as he was, and ended with the peculiarly venomous opinion that he "did not know as much as a logarythm!"

We certainly had been following our own tracks. Ollendorff and his "mental compass" were in disgrace from that moment. After all our hard travel, here we were on the bank of the stream again, with the inn beyond dimly outlined through the driving snow-fall. While we were considering what to do, the young Swede landed from the canoe and took his pedestrian way Carson-wards, singing his same tiresome song about his "sister and his brother" and "the child in the grave with its mother," and in a short minute faded and disappeared in the white oblivion. He was never heard of again. He no doubt got bewildered and lost, and Fatigue delivered him over to Sleep, and Sleep betrayed him to Death. Possibly he followed our treacherous tracks till he became exhausted and dropped.

Presently the Overland stage forded the now fast receding stream, and started toward Carson on its first trip since the flood came. We hesitated no longer, now, but took up our march in its wake, and trotted merrily along, for we had good confidence in the driver's bump of locality. But our horses were no match for the fresh stage team. We were soon left out of sight; but it was no matter, for we had the deep ruts the wheels made for a guide. By this time it was three in the afternoon, and consequently it was not very long before night came—and not with a lingering twilight, but with a sudden shutting down like a cellar door, as is its habit in that country. The snow-fall was still as thick as ever, and of course we could not see fifteen steps before us; but all about us the white glare of the snow-bed enabled us to discern the smooth sugar-loaf mounds made by the covered sage-bushes, and just in front of us the two faint grooves which we knew were the steadily filling and slowly disappearing wheel-tracks.

Now those sage-bushes were all about the same height—three or four feet; they stood just about seven feet apart, all over the vast desert; each of them was a mere snow-mound, now; in *any* direction that you proceeded (the same as in a well-laid-out orchard) you would find yourself moving down a distinctly defined avenue, with a row of these snow-mounds on either side of it—an avenue the customary width of a road, nice and level in its breadth, and rising at the sides in the most natural way, by reason of the mounds. But we had not thought of this. Then imagine the chilly thrill that shot through us when it finally occurred to us, far in the night, that since the last faint trace of the wheel-tracks had long ago been buried from sight, we might now be wandering down a mere sage-brush avenue, miles away from the road and diverging further and further away from it all the time. Having a cake of ice slipped down one's back is placid comfort compared to it. There was a sudden leap and stir of blood that had been asleep for an hour, and as sudden a rousing of all the drowsing activities in our minds and bodies. We were alive and awake at once—and shaking and quaking with consternation, too. There was an instant halting and dismounting, a bending low and an anxious scanning of the road-bed. Useless, of course; for if a faint depression could not be discerned from an altitude of four or five feet above it, it certainly could not with one's nose nearly against it. We seemed to be in a road, but that was no proof. We tested this by walking off in various directions—the regular snow-mounds and the regular avenues between them convinced each man that *he* had found the true road, and that the others had found only false ones. Plainly, the situation was desperate. We were cold and stiff, and the horses were tired. We decided to build a sage-brush fire and camp out till morning. This was wise, because if we were wandering from the right road, and the snow-storm continued another day, our case would be the next thing to hopeless if we kept on.

All agreed that a camp fire was what would come nearest to saving us, now, and so we set about building it. We could find no matches, and so we tried to make shift with the pistols. Not a man in the party had ever tried to do such a thing before, but not a man in the party doubted that it *could* be done, and without any trouble—because every man in the party had read about it in books many a time, and had naturally come to believe it, with trusting simplicity, just as he had long ago accepted and believed *that other* common book-fraud about Indians and lost hunters making a fire by rubbing two dry sticks together.

We huddled together on our knees in the deep snow, and the horses put their noses together and bowed their patient heads over us; and while the feathery flakes eddied down and turned us into a group of white statuary, we proceeded with the momentous experiment. We broke twigs from a sage-bush and piled them on a little cleared place in the shelter of our bodies. In the course of ten or fifteen minutes all was ready, and then, while conversation ceased and our pulses beat low with anxious suspense, Ollendorff applied his revolver, pulled the trigger, and blew the pile clear out of the county! It was the flattest failure that ever was.

This was distressing, but it paled before a greater horror—the horses were gone! I had been appointed to hold the bridles, but in my absorbing anxiety over the pistol experiment I had unconsciously dropped them, and the released animals had walked off in the storm. It was useless to try to follow them, for their footfalls could make no sound, and one could pass within two yards of the creatures and never see them. We gave them up without an effort at recovering them, and cursed the lying books that said horses would stay by their masters for protection and companionship in a distressful time like ours.

We were miserable enough, before; we felt still more forlorn now. Patiently, but with blighted hope, we broke more sticks and piled them, and once more the Prussian shot them into annihilation. Plainly, to light a fire with a pistol was an art requiring practice and experience, and the middle of a desert at midnight in a snow-storm was not a good place or time for the acquiring of the accomplishment. We gave it up and tried the other. Each man took a couple of sticks and fell to chafing them together. At the end of half an hour we were thoroughly chilled, and so were the sticks. We bitterly execrated the Indians, the hunters, and the books that had betrayed us with the silly device, and wondered dismally what was next to be done. At this critical moment Mr. Ballou fished out four matches from the rubbish of an overlooked pocket. To have found four gold bars would have seemed poor and cheap good luck compared to this. One cannot think how good a match looks under such circumstances—or how lovable and precious, and sacredly beautiful to the eye. This time we gathered sticks with high hopes; and when Mr. Ballou prepared to light the first match, there was an amount of interest centred upon him that pages of writing could not describe. The match burnt hopefully a moment, and then went out. It could not have carried more regret with it if it had been a human life. The next match simply flashed and died. The wind puffed the third one out just as it was on the imminent verge of success. We gathered together closer than ever, and developed a solicitude that was rapt and painful, as Mr. Ballou scratched our last hope on his leg. It lit, burned blue and sickly, and then budded into a robust flame. Shading it with his hands, the old gentleman bent gradually down, and every heart went with him—everybody, too, for that matter—and blood and breath stood still. The flame touched the sticks at last, took gradual hold upon them—hesitated—took a stronger hold—hesitated again—held its breath five heart-breaking seconds, then gave a sort of human gasp and went out.

Nobody said a word for several minutes. It was a solemn sort of silence; even the wind put on a stealthy, sinister quiet, and made no more noise than the falling flakes of snow. Finally a sad-voiced conversation began, and it was soon apparent that in each of our hearts lay the conviction that this was our last night with the living. I had so hoped that I was the only one who felt so! When the others calmly acknowledged their conviction, it sounded like the summons itself. Ollendorff said:

"Brothers, let us die together. And let us go without one hard feeling towards each other. Let us forget and forgive by gones. I know that you have felt hard towards me for turning over the canoe, and for knowing too much, and leading you round and round in the snow—but I meant well; forgive me! I acknowledge freely that I have had hard feelings against Mr. Ballou for abusing me and calling me a logarythm, which is a thing I do not know what, but no doubt a thing considered disgraceful and unbecoming in America, and it has scarcely been out of my mind, and has hurt me a great deal—but let it go; I forgive Mr. Ballou with all my heart, and—"

Poor Ollendorff broke down, and the tears came. He was not alone, for I was crying too, and so was Mr. Ballou. Ollendorff got his voice again, and forgave me for things I had done and said. Then he got out his bottle of whisky, and said that whether he lived or died he would never touch another drop. He said he had given up all hope of life, and although ill-prepared, was ready to submit humbly to his fate; that he wished he could be spared a little longer, not for any selfish reason, but to make a thorough reform in his character, and by devoting himself to helping the poor, nursing the sick, and pleading with the people to guard themselves against the evils of intemperance, make his life a beneficent example to the young, and lay it down at last with the precious reflection that it had not been lived in vain. He ended by saying that his reform should begin at this moment, even here in the presence of death, since no longer time was to be vouchsafed wherein to prosecute it to men's help and benefit—and with that he threw away the bottle of whisky.

Mr. Ballou made remarks of similar purport, and began the reform he could not live to continue, by throwing away the ancient pack of cards that had solaced our captivity during the flood and made it bearable. He said he never gambled, but still was satisfied that the meddling with cards in any way was immoral and injurious, and no man could be wholly pure and blemishless without eschewing them. "And therefore," continued he, "in doing this act, I already feel more in sympathy with that spiritual saturnalia necessary to entire and obsolete reform." These rolling syllables touched him as no intelligible eloquence could have done, and the old man sobbed with a mournfulness not unmingled with satisfaction.

My own remarks were of the same tenor as those of my comrades, and I know that the feelings that prompted them were heartfelt and sincere. We were all sincere, and all deeply moved and earnest, for we were in the presence of death and without hope. I threw away my pipe, and in doing it felt that at last I was free of a hated vice, and one that had ridden me like a tyrant all my days. While I yet talked, the thought of the good I might have done in the world, and the still greater good I might *now* do, with these new incentives and higher and better aims to guide me, if I could only be spared a few years longer, overcame me, and the tears came again. We put our arms about each other's necks and awaited the warning drowsiness that precedes death by freezing.

It came stealing over us presently, and then we bade each other a last farewell. A delicious dreaminess wrought its web about my yielding senses, while the snow-flakes wove a winding-sheet about my conquered body. Oblivion came. The battle of life was done.

I do not know how long I was in a state of forgetfulness, but it seemed an age. A vague consciousness grew upon me by degrees, and then came a gathering anguish of pain in my limbs and through all my body. I shuddered. The thought flitted through my brain, "This is death—this is the hereafter."

Then came a white upheaval at my side, and a voice said with bitterness:

"Will some gentleman be so good as to kick me behind?"

It was Ballou—at least it was a towzled snow image in a sitting posture, with Ballou's voice.

I rose up, and there in the gray dawn, not fifteen steps from us, were the frame buildings of a stage station, and under a shed stood our still saddled and bridled horses!

An arched snow-drift broke up, now, and Ollendorff emerged from it, and the three of us sat and stared at the houses without speaking a word. We really had nothing to say. We were like the profane man who could not "do the subject justice;" the whole situation was so painfully ridiculous and humiliating that words were tame, and we did not know where to commence, anyhow.

The joy in our hearts at our deliverance was poisoned; well-nigh dissipated, indeed. We presently began to grow pettish by degrees, and sullen; and then, angry at each other, angry at ourselves, angry at everything in general, we moodily dusted the snow from our clothing and in unsociable single file plowed our way to the horses, unsaddled them, and sought shelter in the station.

I have scarcely exaggerated a detail of this curious and absurd adventure. It occurred almost exactly as I have stated it. We actually went into camp in a snow-drift in a desert, at midnight, in a storm, forlorn and hopeless, within fifteen steps of a comfortable inn.

For two hours we sat apart in the station and ruminated in disgust. The mystery was gone now, and it was plain enough why the horses had deserted us. Without a doubt, they were under that shed a quarter of a minute after they had left us, and they must have overheard and enjoyed all our confessions and lamentations.

After breakfast we felt better, and the zest of life soon came back. The world looked bright again, and existence was as dear to us as ever. Presently an uneasiness came over me—grew upon me—assailed me without ceasing. Alas, my regeneration was not complete—I wanted to smoke! I resisted with all my strength, but the flesh was weak. I wandered away alone, and wrestled with myself an hour. I recalled my promise of reform, and preached to myself persuasively, upbraidingly, exhaustively. But it was all in vain. I shortly found myself sneaking among the snow-drifts hunting for my pipe. I discovered it after a considerable search, and crept away to hide myself and enjoy it. I remained behind the barn a good while, asking myself how I would feel if my braver, stronger, truer comrades should catch me in my degradation. At last I lit the pipe, and no human being can feel meaner and baser than I did then. I was ashamed of being in my own pitiful company. Still dreading discovery, I felt that perhaps the further side of the barn would be somewhat safer, and so I turned the corner. As I turned the one corner, smoking, Ollendorff turned the other with his bottle to his lips, and between us sat unconscious Ballou deep in a game of "solitaire" with the old greasy cards!

———

NEVER take the Bull bi the horns, Young Man, but take him bi the tail, then yu kan let go when yu want to.

YURE WARM FRIEND,
JOSH BILLINGS

UNCLE JOSHUA DOWNING IN BOSTON

Letter from Joshua Downing, in Boston, to His Nephew, Jack Downing, in Portland

SEBA SMITH

Dear Nephew—I guess you won't be a little struck up when you find out that I'm in Boston—but I had best begin at the beginning, and then I shall get thro' quicker.

After seeing your letter to Ephraim, as I said before, I concluded it wouldn't be a bad scheme to tackle up and take a load of turkies, some apple-sauce, and other notions that the neighbors wanted to get to market, and as your uncle Nat would be in Boston with the ax-handles, we all thought best to try our luck there. Nothing happened worth mentioning on the road, nor till next morning, after I got here and put up in Elm Street. I then got off my watch pretty curiously, as you shall be informed. I was down in the bar-room, and tho't it well enough to look pretty considerable smart, and now and then compared my watch with the clock in the bar, and found it as near right as ever it was—

when a feller stept up to me and ask'd how I'd trade? and says I, for what? and says he, for your watch—and says I, any way that will be a fair shake—upon that says he, I'll give you *my* watch and five dollars. Says I, it's done! He gave me the five dollars, and I gave him my watch. Now, says I, give me *your* watch—and, says he, with a loud laugh, I ha'n't got none—and that kind a turn'd the laugh on me. Thinks I, let them laugh that lose. Soon as the laugh was over, the feller thought he'd try the watch to his ear—why, says he, it don't go—no, says I, not without it's carried—then I began to laugh—he tried to open it, and couldn't start it a hair, and broke his thumb-nail into the bargain. Won't she open? says he. Not's I know on, says I—and then the laugh seemed to take another turn.

Don't you think I got off the old Brittania pretty well, considrin'? And then I thought I'd go and see about my load of turkies and other notions. I expected to have gone all over town to sell my load, but Mr. Doolittle told me if I'd go down to the new market, I should find folks enough to buy all I had at once. So down I goes, and a likely kind of a feller, with an eye like a hawk and quick as a steel-trap for a trade (they called him a 4th staller), came up to the wagon, and before you could say Jack Robinson, we struck a bargain for the whole cargo—and come to weigh and reckon up, I found I should get as much as 10*s.* 6*d.* more than any of us calculated before I left home, and had the apple-sauce left, besides. So I thought I'd jist see how this 4th staller worked his card, to be able to give us so good a price for the turkies, and I went inside the market-house, and a grander sight I never expect to see? But it was the 3d staller instead of the 4th had my turkies all sorted and hung up, and looking so much better that I hardly should known 'em. Pretty soon, a gentleman asked the 3d staller what he asked for turkies? Why, says he, if you want something better than you ever saw before, there's some 't was killed last night, purpose for you. You may take 'em at 9*d*, being it's you. I'll give you 12 cents, said the gentleman, as I've got some of the General Court to dine with me, and must treat well. I sha'n't stand for half a cent with an old customer, says he. And so they traded; and in about the space of half an hour or more, all my turkies went into baskets at that rate. The 4th staller gave me 6*d.* a pound, and I began to think I'd been a little too much in a hurry for trade—but's no use to cry for spilt milk. Then I went up to the State House, to see what was going on there; but I thought I'd get off my apple-sauce on my way—and seeing a sign of old clothes bartered, I stepped in and made a trade, and got a whole suit of superfine black broadcloth from top to toe, for a firkin of applesauce (which didn't cost much, I guess, at home).

Accordingly, I rigged myself up in the new suit, and you'd hardly known me. I didn't like the set of the shoulders, they were so dreadful puckery; but the man said that was all right. I guess he'll find the applesauce full as puckery when he gets down into it—but that's between ourselves. Well, when I got up to the State House I found them to work at the rail road—busy enough, I can tell you—they got a part of it made already. I found most all the folks kept their hats on, except the man who was talking out loud and the man he was talking to—all the rest seemed to be busy about their own consarns. As I didn't see anybody to talk to, I kept my hat on and took a seat, and look'd round to see what was going on. I hadn't been setting long before I saw a slick-headed, sharp-eyed little man, who seemed to have the principal management of the folks, looking at me pretty sharp, as much as to say, who are you? but I said nothing. and looked t'other way—at last he touched me on the shoulder—I thought he was feeling of the puckers. Are you a member? says he—sartin, says I—how long have you taken your seat? says he—about ten minutes, says I. Are you qualified? says he—I guess not, says I. And then he left me. I didn't know exactly what this old gentleman was after—but soon he returned, and said it was proper for me to be qualified before I took a seat, and I must go before the governor! By Jing! I never felt so before in all my born days. As good luck would have it, he was beckoned to come to a man at the desk, and as soon as his back was turned, I give him the slip. Jest as I was going off, the gentleman who bought my turkies of the 4th staller took hold of my arm, and I was afraid at first he was going to carry me to the governor—but he began to talk as sociable as if we had been old acquaintances. How long have you been in the house, Mr. Smith, says he. My name is Downing, says I. I beg your pardon, says he—I mean Downing. It's no offense, says I, I haven't been here long. Then, says he, in a very pleasant way, a few of your brother members are to take pot-luck with me to-day, and I should be happy to have you join them. What's pot-luck? says I. O, a family dinner, says he—no ceremony. I thought by this time I was well qualified for that without going to the Governor. So, says I, yes, and thank ye, too. How long before you'll want me? says I. At 3 o'clock, says he, and gave me a piece of paste board with his name on it, and the name of the street, and the number of his house, and said that would show me the way. Well, says I, I don't know of nothing that will keep me away. And then we parted. I took a considerable liking to him.

After strolling round, and seeing a great many things about the State House and the marble immage of Gin. Washington, standing on a stump in the Porch, I went out into the street they call Bacon street; and my stars! what swarms of women folks I saw all drest up as if they were going to meeting. You can tell Cousin Polly Sandburn, who you know is no slimster, that she needn't take on so about being genteel in her shapes—for the genteelest ladies here beat her as to size all hollow. I don't believe one of 'em could get into our fore dore—and as for their arms—I shouldn't want better measure for a bushel of meal than one of their sleeves could hold. I sha'n't shell out the bushel of corn you say I've lost on Speaker Ruggles at that rate. But this puts me in mind of the dinner which Mr. —— wants I should help the Gineral Court eat. So I took out the piece of paste board and began to inquire my way, and got along completely, and found the number the first time—but the door was locked, and there was no knocker, and I thumpt with my whip handle, but nobody come. And says I to a man going by, don't nobody live here? and says he yes. Well, how do you get in? Why, says he, ring; and says I, ring what? And says he, the bell. And says I, where's the rope? And he says, pull that little brass nub; and so I gave it a twitch, and I'm sure a bell did ring; and who do you think opened the door, with a white apron afore him? You couldn't guess for a week a Sundays—so I'll tell you. It was Stephen Furlong, who kept our district school last winter for 5 dollars a month, and kept bachelor's hall, and helped tend for Gineral Coombs a training days, and make out muster rolls. We was considerably struck up at first, both of us; and when he found I was going to eat dinner with Mr. —— and Gineral Court, he thought it queer kind of doings—but says he, I guess it will be as well for both of us not to know each other a bit more than we can help. And says I, with a wink, you're half right, and in I went. There was nobody in the room but Mr. —— and his wife, and not a sign of any dinner to be seen any where—though I thought now and then, when a side door opened, I could smell cupboard, as they say.

I thought I should be puzzled enough to know what to say, but I hadn't my thoughts long to myself. Mr. —— has about as nimble a tongue as you ever heard, and could say ten words to my one, and I had nothing to do in the way of making talk. Just then I heard a ringing, and Stephen was busy opening the door and letting in the Gineral Court, who all had their hats off, and looking pretty scrumptious, you may depend. I didn't see but I could stand along side of 'em without disparagement, except to my boots, which had just got a lick of beeswax and tallow—not a mite of dinner yet, and I began to feel as if 'twas nearer supper-time than dinner-time—when all at once two doors flew away from each other right into the wall, and what did I see but one of the grandest thanksgiving dinners you ever laid your eyes on—and lights on the table, and silver candlesticks and gold lamps over head—the window shutters closed—I guess more than one of us stared at first, but we soon found the way to our mouths—I made Stephen tend out for me pretty sharp, and he got my plate filled three or four times with soup, which beat all I ever tasted. I sha'n't go through the whole dinner again to you—but I am mistaken if it cost me much for victuals this week, if I pay by the meal at Mr. Doolittle's, who comes pretty near up to a thanksgiving every day. There was considerable talk about stock and manufactories and lier bilities and rimidies and a great loss on stock. I thought this a good chance for me to put in a word—for I calculated I knew as much about raising stock and keeping over as any of 'em. Says I to Mr. ——, there's one thing I've always observed in my experience in stock—just as sure as you try to keep over more stock than you have fodder to carry them well into April, one half will die on your hands, to a sartinty—and there's no remedy for it—I've tried it out and out, and there's no law that can make a ton of hay keep over ten cows, unless you have more carrots and potatoes that you can throw a stick at. This made some of the folks stare who didn't know much about stock—and Steve give me a jog, as much as to say, keep quiet. He thought I was getting into a quog-mire, and soon after, giving me a wink, opened the door and got me out of the room into the entry.

After we had got out of hearing, says I to Steve, how are you getting on in the world—should you like to come back to keep our school if I could get a vote for you?—not by two chalks, says Steve—I know which side my bread is buttered better than all that—I get 12 dollars a month and found, and now and then some old clothes, which is better than keeping a school at 5 dollars and find myself and work out my highway tax besides—then turning up the cape of my *new coat*, says he, I guess I've dusted that before now—most likely, says I, but not in our district school.

Your respectful uncle,
JOSHUA DOWNING

I am a poor man, but i hav this consolashun: i am poor by acksident, not desighn.

JOSH BILLINGS

JOHN PHŒNIX RENDERS THE EDITOR OF THE "SAN DIEGO HERALD" AN ACCOUNT OF HIS STEWARDSHIP

JOHN PHŒNIX

"*Te Deum Laudamus.*"—Judge Ames has returned. With the completion of this article my labors are ended; and wiping my pen on my coat-tail, and placing it behind my sinister ear, with a graceful bow and bland smile for my honored admirers, and a wink of intense meaning for my enemies, I shall abdicate, with dignity, the "Arm-Chair" in favor of its legitimate proprietor.

By the way, this "Arm-Chair" is but a pleasant fiction of "the Judge's"—the only seat in the *Herald* office being the empty nail keg, which I have occupied while writing my leaders upon the inverted sugar box that answers the purpose of a table. But such is life. Divested of its poetry and romance, the objects of our highest admiration become mere commonplaces, like the *Herald's* chair and table. Many ideas which we have learned to love and reverence, from the poetry of imagination, as tables, become old sugar boxes on close inspection and more intimate acquaintance. 'Sic'—but I forbear that sickening and hackneyed quotation.

During the period in which I have had control over the *Herald* I have endeavored, to the best of my ability, to amuse and interest its readers, and I cannot but hope that my good-humored efforts have proved successful. If I have given offense to any by the tone of my remarks, I assure them that it has been quite unintentional, and to prove that I bear no malice, I hereby accept their apologies. Certainly no one can complain of a lack of versatility in the last six numbers. Commencing as an Independent Journal, I have gradually passed through all the stages of incipient Whiggery, decided Conservatism, dignified Recantation, budding Democracy, and rampant Radicalism, and I now close the series with an entirely literary number, in which I have carefully abstained from the mention of Baldo and Wigler—I mean, Wagler and Bildo; no, never mind—as Toodles says, I haven't mentioned *any of 'em*, but been careful to preserve a perfect armed neutrality.

The paper this week will be found particularly stupid. This is the result of deep design on my part; had I attempted anything remarkably brilliant, you would all have detected it, and said, probably with truth: Ah, this is Phœnix's last appearance; he has tried to be very funny, and has made a miserable failure of it. Hee! hee! hee! Oh, no, my Public, an ancient weasel may not be detected in the act of slumber, in that manner! I was well aware of all this, and have been as dull and prosy as possible, to avoid it. Very little news will be found in the *Herald* this week: the fact is, there never is much news in it, and it is very well that it is so; the climate here is so delightful, that residents, in the enjoyment of their *dolce far niente*, care very little about what is going on elsewhere, and residents in other places care very little about what is going on in San Diego, so all parties are likely to be gratified with the little paper, "and long may it wave."

In conclusion, I am gratified to be able to state that Johnny's office (the fighting department), for the last six weeks, has been a sinecure, and with the exception of the atrocious conduct of one miscreant, who was detected very early one morning in the act of chalking A S S on our office door, and who was dismissed with a harmless kick, and a gentle admonition that he should not write his name on other persons' property, our course has been peaceful, and undisturbed by any expression of an unpleasant nature.

So, farewell Public: I hope you will do well; I do, upon my soul. This leader is ended, and if there be any man among you who thinks he could write a better one, let him try it, and if he succeeds, I shall merely remark, that I could have done it myself if I had tried. Adios!

Respectfully Yours.

INTERVIEW BETWEEN THE EDITOR AND PHŒNIX

The *Thomas Hunt* had arrived; she lay at the wharf at New Town, and a rumor had reached our ears that "the Judge" was on board. Public anxiety had been excited to the highest pitch to witness the result of the meeting between us. It had been stated publicly that "the Judge" would whip us the moment he arrived; but though we thought a conflict probable, we had never been very sanguine as to its terminating in this manner. Coolly we gazed from the window of the Office upon the New Town road; we descried a cloud of dust in the distance; high above it waved a whip lash, and we said, "the Judge" cometh, and "his driving is like Jehu the son of Nimshi, for he driveth furiously."

Calmly we seated ourselves in the "arm-chair," and continued our labors upon our magnificent Pictorial. Anon, a step, a heavy step, was heard upon the stairs, and "the Judge" stood before us.

"In shape and gesture proudly eminent, stood like a tower: . . . . but his face deep scars of thunder had intrenched, and care sat on his faded cheek; but under brows of dauntless courage and considerable pride, waiting revenge."

We rose, and with an unfaltering voice said: "Well, Judge, how do you do?" He made no reply, but commenced taking off his coat.

We removed ours, also our cravat.

———

The sixth and last round is described by the pressman and compositors as having been fearfully scientific. We held "the Judge" down over the Press by our nose (which we had inserted between his teeth for that purpose), and while our hair was employed in holding one of his hands, we held the other in our left, and with the "sheep's-foot" brandished above our head, shouted to him, "Say Waldo." "Never!" he gasped:

"Oh! my Bigler he would have muttered,
  But that he 'dried up' ere the word was uttered."

At this moment, we discovered that we had been laboring under a "misunderstanding," and through the amicable intervention of the pressman, who thrust a roller between our faces (which gave the whole affair a very different complexion), the *matter* was finally settled on the most friendly terms—"and without prejudice to the honor of either party." We write this while sitting without any clothing, except our left stocking, and the rim of our hat encircling our neck like a "ruff" of the Elizabethan era—that article of dress having been knocked over our head at an early stage of the proceedings, and the crown subsequently torn off; while the Judge is sopping his eye with cold water in the next room, a small boy standing beside the sufferer with a basin, and glancing with interest over the advertisements on the second page of the *San Diego Herald*, a fair copy of which was struck off upon the back of his shirt, at the time we held him over the Press. Thus ends our description of this long anticipated personal collision, of which the public can believe precisely as much as they please. If they disbelieve the whole of it, we shall not be at all offended, but can simply quote, as much to the point, what might have been the commencement of our epitaph, had we fallen in the conflict—

"HERE LIES PHŒNIX"

ECONOMICAL INDEED

"Economy is wealth," but the most economical person yet heard of is a shoe dealer in a small town in M——, who stops his clock when he closes his store at night, in order to save time.—*Newspaper*

Hans Breitmann's Party

HANS BREITMANN

Hans Breitmann gife a barty,
  Dey had biano-blayin';
I felled in lofe mit a 'Merican frau,
  Her name vas Madilda Yane.
She hat haar as prown ash a pretzel,
  Her eyes vas himmel-plue,
Und ven dey looket indo mine,
  Dey shplit mine heart in two.

Hans Breitmann gife a barty,
  I vent dere, you'll pe pound.
I valtzet mit Madilda Yane
  Und vent shpinnen round und round.
De pootiest Fraulein in de House,
  She vayed 'pout dwo hoondred pound,
Und efery dime she gife a shoomp
  She make de vindows sound.

Hans Breitmann gife a barty,
  I dells you, it cost him dear.
Dey rolled in more ash sefen kecks
  Of foost-rate Lager Beer.
Und venefer dey knocks de shpicket in
  De Deutschers gifes a cheer.
I dinks dat so vine a barty
  Nefer coom to a het dis year.

Hans Breitmann gife a barty;
  Dere all vas Souse und Brouse,
Ven de sooper comed in, de gompany
  Did make demselfs to house;
Dey ate das Brot und Gensy broost,
  De Bratwurst and Braten fine,
Und vash der Abendessen down
  Mit four parrels of Neckarwein.

Hans Breitman gife a barty
  We all cot troonk ash bigs.
I poot mine mout to a parrel of bier
  Und emptied it oop mit a schwigs.
Und den I gissed Madilda Yane
  Und she shlog me on de kop,
Und de gompany fited mit daple-lecks
  Dill de coonshtable made oos shtop

Hans Breitmann gife a barty—
  Where ish dat barty now!
Where ish de lofely golden cloud
  Dat float on de moundain's prow?
Where ish de himmelstrahlende Stern—
  De shtar of de shpirit's light?
All goned afay mit de Lager Beer—
  Afay in de ewigkeit!

A New Patent Medicine Operation

Q. K. PHILANDER DOESTICKS

Mortimer N. Thompson, once so widely known as Q. K. Philander Doesticks, was born in Michigan in 1830, and found his way to New York as a
journalist, where his dashing and extravagant drolleries soon attracted attention. He had long survived their popularity when he died, in 1875.

As I too desired to have a mansion on the Fifth Avenue, like the Medical Worthy of Sarsaparilla memory, and wished, like him, to be able to
build a patent medicine palace, with a private chapel under the back-
stairs, and a conservatory down cellar, I cast about me for some means
whereby the requisite cash might be reputably accumulated.

I feared that the Panacea and Cure-Everything trick had been
played too often, but I determined to make one big try, and I think that
at last my fortune is made.

Congratulate me—I am immortalized, and I've done it myself. My
name will be handed down to posterity as that of a universal benefactor. The hand which hereafter writes on the record of Fame the names

of Ayer, Sands, Townsend, Moffat, Morrison and Brandreth must also inscribe, side by side with these distinguished appellations, the no less brilliant cognomen of the undying Doesticks.

Emulous of the deathly notoriety which has been acquired by the medicinal worthies just mentioned, *I* also resolved to achieve a name and a fortune in the same reputable and honest manner.

Bought a gallon of tar, a cake of beeswax, and a firkin of lard, and in twenty-one hours I presented to the world the first batch of *"Doesticks' Patent, Self-Acting, Four Horse-Power Balsam,"* designed to cure all diseases of mind, body or estate, to give strength to the weak, money to the poor, bread and butter to the hungry, boots to the barefoot, decency to blackguards, and common sense to the Know-Nothings. It acts physically, morally, mentally, psychologically, physiologically and geologically, and it is intended to make our sublunary sphere a blissful paradise, to which Heaven itself shall be but a side-show.

I have not yet brought it to absolute perfection, but even now it acts with immense force, as you will perceive by the accompanying testimonials and records of my own individual experience. You will observe that I have not resorted to the usual manner of preparing certificates: which is, to be certain that all those intended for Eastern circulation shall seem to come from some formerly unheard-of place in the West, while those sent to the West shall be dated at some place forty miles east of sunrise. But I send to *you*, as representing the western country, a certificate from an Oregon farmer.

"DEAR SIR: The land composing my farm has hitherto been so poor that a Scotchman couldn't get his living off it; and so stony that we had to slice our potatoes and plant them edgeways; but, hearing of your balsam, I put some on the corner of a ten-acre lot surrounded by a rail-fence, and in the morning I found the rocks had entirely disappeared—a neat stone wall encircled the field, and the rails were split into ovenwood and piled up symmetrically in my back yard.

"Put half an ounce into the middle of a huckleberry swamp—in two days it was cleared off, planted with corn and pumpkins, and had a row of peach-trees in full bloom through the middle.

"As an evidence of its tremendous strength, I would state that it drew a striking likeness of my eldest daughter—drew my youngest boy out of the mill-pond—drew a blister all over his stomach—drew a load of potatoes four miles to market, and eventually drew a prize of ninety-seven dollars in the State Lottery.

"And the effect upon the inhabitants hereabout has been so wonderful that they have opened their eyes to the good of the country, and are determined to vote for a Governor who is opposed to frosts in the middle of June, and who will make a positive law against freshets, hailstorms and the seventeen-year locusts."

There, isn't that *some*?

But I give one more, from a member of the senior class in a Western college, who, although misguided, neglected and ignorant, is undoubtedly as honest and sincere as his Prussianized education will admit of.

I have corrected the orthography, and revised some grammatical inaccuracies; but, besides attending to these trifles, inserting marks of punctuation, and putting the capitals in the right places, I assure you I have made no alteration.

"SALL HARBOR, *June 31, 1854.*

"MY DEAR DOCTOR. [You know I attended medical lectures half a winter, and once assisted in getting a crooked needle out of a baby's leg; so I understand perfectly well the theory and practice of medicine, and the *Doctor* is perfectly legitimate under the Prussian system.] By the incessant study required in this establishment, I had become worn down so thin that I was obliged to put on an overcoat to cast a shadow—but accidentally hearing of your Balsam, I obtained a quantity, and, in obedience to the Homœopathic principles of this Institution, took an *infinitesimal* dose only; in four days I measured one hundred and eighty-two inches round the waist; could chop eleven cords of hickory wood in two hours and a half; and, on a bet, carried a yoke of oxen two miles and a quarter in my left hand, my right being tied behind me, and if any one doubts the fact, the oxen are still to be seen.

"About two weeks after this, I had the pleasure of participating in a gunpowder explosion, on which occasion my arms and legs were scattered over the village, and my mangled remains pretty equally distributed throughout the entire county.

"Under these circumstances my life was despaired of, and my classmates had bought a pine coffin, and borrowed whole shirts to attend the funeral in; when the invincible power of your four horse-power balsam (which I happened to have in my vest pocket) suddenly brought together the scattered pieces of my body—collected my limbs from the rural districts—put new life into my shattered frame, and I was restored uninjured to my friends, with a new set of double teeth.

"I have preserved the label which enveloped the bottle, and have sewed it into the seat of my pantaloons, and now I bid grim death defiance, for I feel that I am henceforth unkillable, and in fact I am even now generally designated the '*Great Western Achilles*.'

"Yours entirely,
Ski Hy."

I feel that, after this, I need give you no more reports of third persons, but will detail some of my own personal experience of the article.

I caused some to be applied to the Washtenaw Bank after its failure, and while the Balsam lasted the Bank redeemed its notes with specie.

The cork of one of the bottles dropped upon the head of a childless widow, and in six weeks she had a young and blooming husband.

Administered some to a hack-driver in a glass of gin and sugar, and that day he swindled but seven people, and only gave two of them bad money in change.

Gave a few drops gratis to a poor woman who was earning a precarious subsistence by making calico shirts with a one-eyed needle, and the next day she was discovered to be heir to a large fortune.

Gave some to an up-town actor, and that night he said "damned" only twenty-one times.

One of the daily papers got the next dose, and in the next edition but one there were but four editorial falsehoods, seven indecent advertisements, and two columns and a half of homemade "Foreign Correspondence."

Caused fifteen drops to be given to the low comedian of a Broadway Theatre, and that night he was positively dressed more like a man than a monkey, actually spoke some lines of the author, made only three inane attempts at puerile witticisms—only twice went out of his way to introduce some grossly indelicate line into his part, and, for a wonder, lost so much of his self-conceit that for a full half hour he did not believe himself the greatest comedian in the world.

Gave some to a newsboy, and he manufactured but three fires, a couple of murders, and one horrible railroad accident, in the next thirty minutes.

Put some on the outside of the Crystal Palace, and the same day the stock went from twenty-two up to forty-four.

Our whole Empire City is entirely changed by the miraculous power of "Doesticks' Patent Self-acting Four Horse-Power Balsam." The gas is lighted on the dark nights, instead of on the moonlight evenings—there are no more highway robberies in the streets, or, if there are, the offenders, when arrested, are instantly discharged by the police magistrate. No more building materials on the sidewalks; no more midnight murders; no more Sunday rows; no more dirty streets; no more duels in Hoboken; and no more lies in the newspapers.

Broadway is swept and garnished: the M. P.'s are civil, and the boys don't steal any more dogs. In fact, so well content are we now with our City, that we feel, as the Hibernian poet so beautifully says:

> "O, if there be an Elysium on earth,
> It is this—it is this!"

It iz a wize man who proffits bi hiz own experience—but it iz a good deal wizer one, who lets the rattlesnaik bite the other phellow.

JOSH BILLINGS

THE CENTIPEDE AND
THE BARBARIC YAK

G. T. LANIGAN

While a Centipede was painfully toiling over the Libyan Desert he was encountered by a barbaric Yak, who scornfully asked him how were his poor Feet. The humble Creature made no reply at the time, but some days later found the barbaric Yak taken in the nets of the Hunter and almost devoured by Insects, which fled at the approach of the Centipede. "Help, help, my good friend!" exclaimed the unfortunate Beast; "I cannot move a muscle in these cruel Toils, and the ravenous Insects have devoured my delicate Flesh." "Say you so?" responded the Centipede. "Can you really not defend yourself?" "Alas! how can I?" replied the Yak. "See you not how straitly I am bound?" "And is your Flesh then so delicate?" "It is, though I say it who should not." "Then," said the Centipede, "I guess I'll take a bite myself."

Moral.—The other man's Extremity is often our Opportunity.

THE CAYOTE

MARK TWAIN

Along about an hour after breakfast we saw the first prairie-dog villages, the first antelope and the first wolf. If I remember rightly, this latter was the regular *cayote* (pronounced ky-*o*-te) of the farther deserts. And if it *was*, he was not a pretty creature, or respectable either, for I got well acquainted with his race afterward, and can speak with confidence. The cayote is a long, slim, sick and sorry-looking skeleton, with a gray wolf-skin stretched over it, a tolerably bushy tail that forever sags down with a despairing expression of forsakenness and misery, a furtive and evil eye, and a long, sharp face, with slightly lifted lip and exposed teeth. He has a general slinking expression all over. The cayote is a living, breathing allegory of Want. He is *always* hungry. He is always poor, out of luck and friendless. The meanest creatures despise him, and even the fleas would desert him for a velocipede. He is so spiritless and cowardly that even while his exposed teeth are pretending a threat, the rest of his face is apologizing for it. And he is *so* homely!—so scrawny and ribby and coarse-haired and pitiful. When he sees you, he lifts his lip and lets a flash of his teeth out, and then turns a little out of the course he was pursuing, depresses his head a bit, and strikes a long, soft-footed trot through the sage-brush, glancing over his shoulder at you from time to time, till he is about out of easy pistol range, and then he stops and takes a deliberate survey of you; he will trot fifty yards and stop again, another fifty, and stop again;

and finally the gray of his gliding body blends with the gray of the sage-brush, and he disappears. All this is when you make no demonstration against him; but if you do, he develops a livelier interest in his journey, and instantly electrifies his heels, and puts such a deal of real estate between himself and your weapon that by the time you have raised the hammer you see that you need a Minie rifle, and by the time you have got him in line you need a rifled cannon, and by the time you have "drawn a bead" on him you see well enough that nothing but an unusually long-winded streak of lightning could reach him where he is now. But if you start a swift-footed dog after him, you will enjoy it ever so much—especially if it is a dog that has a good opinion of himself and has been brought up to think he knows something about speed. The cayote will go swinging gently off on that deceitful trot of his, and every little while he will smile a fraudful smile over his shoulder, that will fill that dog entirely full of encouragement and worldly ambition, and make him lay his head still lower to the ground, and stretch his neck further to the front, and pant more fiercely, and stick his tail out straighter behind, and move his furious legs with a yet wilder frenzy, and leave a broader and broader, and higher and denser cloud of desert sand smoking behind, and marking his long wake across the level plain! And all this time the dog is only a short twenty feet behind the cayote, and to save the soul of him he cannot understand why it is that he cannot get perceptibly closer; and he begins to get aggravated, and it makes him madder and madder to see how gently the cayote glides along and never pants or sweats or ceases to smile; and he grows still more and more incensed to see how shamefully he has been taken in by an entire stranger, and what an ignoble swindle that long, calm, soft-footed trot is; and next he notices that he is getting fagged, and that the cayote actually has to slacken speed a little to keep from running away from him—and *then* that town-dog is mad in earnest, and he begins to strain and weep and swear, and paw the sand higher than ever, and reach for the cayote with concentrated and desperate energy. This "spurt" finds him six feet behind the gliding enemy, and two miles from his friends. And then, in the instant that a wild new hope is lighting up his face, the cayote turns and smiles blandly upon him once more, and with a something about it which seems to say: "Well, I shall have to tear myself away from you, bub— business is business, and it will not do for me to be fooling along this way all day"—and forthwith there is a rushing sound, and the sudden splitting of a long crack through the atmosphere, and behold, that dog is solitary and alone in the midst of a vast solitude!

It makes his head swim. He stops, and looks all around; climbs the nearest sand-mound and gazes into the distance; shakes his head reflectively, and then, without a word, he turns and jogs along back to his train, and takes up a humble position under the hindmost wagon, and feels unspeakably mean, and looks ashamed, and hangs his tail at half-mast for a week. And for as much as a year after that, whenever there is a great hue and cry after a cayote, that dog will merely glance in that direction without emotion, and apparently observe to himself, "I believe I do not wish any of the pie."

The cayote lives chiefly in the most desolate and forbidding deserts, along with the lizard, the jackass-rabbit and the raven, and gets an uncertain and precarious living, and earns it. He seems to subsist almost wholly on the carcases of oxen, mules and horses that have dropped out of emigrant trains and died, and upon windfalls of carrion, and occasional legacies of offal bequeathed to him by white men who have been opulent enough to have something better to butcher than condemned army bacon. He will eat anything in the world that his first cousins, the desert-frequenting tribes of Indians, will, and they will eat anything they can bite. It is a curious fact that these latter are the only creatures known to history who will eat nitro-glycerine, and ask for more—if they survive.

The cayote of the deserts beyond the Rocky Mountains has a peculiarly hard time of it, owing to the fact that his relations, the Indians, are just as apt to be the first to detect a seductive scent on the desert breeze, and follow the fragrance to the late ox it emanated from, as he is himself; and when this occurs, he has to content himself with sitting off at a little distance, watching those people strip off and dig out everything edible, and walk off with it. Then he and the waiting ravens explore the skeleton and polish the bones. It is considered that the cayote, and the obscene bird, and the Indian of the desert, testify their blood kinship with each other in that they live together in the waste places of the earth on terms of perfect confidence and friendship, while hating all other creatures and yearning to assist at their funerals. He does not mind going a hundred miles to breakfast, and a hundred and fifty to dinner, because he is sure to have three or four days between meals, and he can just as well be traveling and looking at the scenery, as lying around doing nothing and adding to the burdens of his parents.

THE HODJA'S HOUSE

S. S. COX

The Hodja having built his house to his own satisfaction and that of everybody else—offers it for sale. He makes a bargain, but asks of the purchaser, as a favor, to be allowed to drive a nail on the wall of one of the rooms; the nail to be his own property. This is granted.

The buyer is soon established in the house. Shortly after midnight, the owner hears a knock at his outer door. He descends to inquire:

"Who is there?"

"It is I," says the Hodja; "I wish to tie a string on my nail." Two or three days pass, when again the knock is heard about the same hour. Again the demand is made:

"What is wanting?"

The answer comes: "I pray you, good friend, I should like to untie that string from my property." This performance being repeated several times, compels the purchaser to abandon his purchase for a song.

The moral of which is: *to make sure of the character of the vender, when you become the vendee.*

THE BOY AND THE TORTOISE

AMBROSE BIERCE

"Permit me to help you on in the world, sir," said a boy to a traveling tortoise, placing a glowing coal upon the animal's back.

"Thank you," replied the unconscious beast; "I alone am responsible for the time of my arrival, and I alone will determine the degree of celerity required. The gait I am going will enable me to keep all my present appointments."

A genial warmth began about this time to pervade his upper crust, and a moment after he was dashing away at a pace comparatively tremendous.

"How about those engagements?" sneered the grinning urchin.

"I've recollected another one," was the hasty reply.

THE FRIEND OF MY YOUTH

T. B. ALDRICH

In one of the episodes in his entertaining volume of "Vagabond Adventures," Mr. Keeler takes the reader with him on a professional cruise in Dr. Spaulding's Floating Palace. This Floating Palace—a sort of Barnum's Museum with a keel—was designed for navigation on Southern and Western rivers, and carried a cargo of complex delights that must have much amazed the simple dwellers on the banks of the Ohio and Mississippi. Here, on board of this dramatical Noah's Ark, the reader finds himself on the pleasantest terms conceivable with negro minstrels, danseuses, apostolic wax-works, moral acrobats, stuffed animals, vocalists, and a certain Governor Dorr.

It was with a thrill of honest pleasure that I came upon this picturesque outcast unexpectedly embalmed, like a fly in amber, in Mr. Keeler's autobiography. There was a time when I was proud to know this Governor Dorr; when I hung upon the rotund music of his lips, listened to his marvelous stories of moving accidents by flood and field, and was melted to the very heart at those rare moments when, in a three-cornered room in the rear of Wall's Drug Store, he would favor me with some of the most lachrymose and sentimental poems that ever came of a despondent poet. At this epoch of my existence, Governor Dorr, with his sarcastic winks, his comic melancholy, his quotations from Shakespeare, and his fearful knowledge of the outside world, was in my eyes the personification of all that was learned, lyrical, romantic and daring. A little later, my boyish admiration was shattered by the discovery that my Admirable Crichton was—well, it is of no use now to mince words—an adventurer and a gambler. With a kind of sigh that is at present a lost art to me, I put him aside with those dethroned idols and collapsed dreams which accumulate on one's hands as one advances in life, and of which I already had a promising collection when I was about twenty. I cast off Governor Dorr, I repeat; but, oddly enough, Governor Dorr never cast *me* off, but persisted in turning up at intervals of four or five years, in the tender and pathetic character of "the friend of my youth."

As Governor Dorr is the only gentleman in his line of business who ever evinced any interest in me, I intend to make the most of him; and, indeed, among my reputable acquaintances, there is none who deserves to fare better at my hands. My reputable acquaintances have sometimes bored me, and taught me nothing. Now Governor Dorr, in the ethereal shape of a reminiscence, has not only been a source of great amusement to me at various times, but has taught me by his own funest example that whatever gifts a man may possess, if he have no moral principle he is a failure. Wanting the gift of honesty, Governor Dorr was a gambler and a sharper, and is dead.

———

I was a schoolboy at Rivermouth, when Governor Dorr swept like a brilliant comet into the narrow arc of my observation.* One day in the summer of 18—, I was going home from school, when I saw, standing in front of Wall's Drug Store a showily dressed person, who seemed to me well advanced in years—that is to say, twenty-five or thirty. He was the centre of a small circle of idle fellows about town, who were drinking in with obvious relish one of those pre-Raphaelite narratives which I was afterwards destined to swallow with open-mouthed wonder. The genial twinkle of the man's blue eyes, the glow of his half-smoked cigar, and the blaze of the diamond on his little finger, all seemed the members of one radiant family. To this day I cannot disassociate a sort of glitter with the memory of my first glimpse of Governor Dorr. He had finished speaking as I joined the group; I had caught only the words, "and that was the last of gallant Jack Martin-

———

*"Governor Dorr," I should explain, was a sobriquet, but when or how it attached itself to him, I never knew. His real name I suppress for the sake of some that may bear it, if there are any so unfortunate.

way," delivered in a singularly mellow barytone voice, when he turned abruptly and disappeared behind the orange and purple jars in Dr. Wall's shop-window.

Who is gallant Jack Martinway, I wondered, and who is this dazzling person that wears his best clothes on a week-day? I took him for some distinguished military hero, and, with a fine feeling for anachronism, immediately connected him with the portrait of Sir Walter Raleigh in Mitchell's Geography—a work I was at that time neglecting with considerable perseverance.

The apparition of so bewildering a figure in our staid, slow-going little town was likely to cause a sensation. The next day in school I learned all about him. He was Governor Dorr; he had once been a boy in Rivermouth, like us, but had gone off years ago to seek his fortune, and now he had come back immensely wealthy from somewhere— South America or the Chincha Islands, where he was governor—and was going to settle down in his native town and buy the "Janvrin Place"—an estate which the heirs were too poor to keep, and nobody else rich enough to purchase.

This was appetizing, and after school I wandered up to Wall's Drug Store to take a look at my gilded townsman, of whom I was not a little proud.

I was so dazed at the time, that I do not recollect how it all came about; but Governor Dorr was in the shop, holding a glass of soda-water in one hand and leaning elegantly on the Gothic fountain; I entered with the weak pretence of buying a slate-pencil; the Governor spoke to me, and then—I can recall nothing except that, when I recovered from my embarrassment and confusion, I was drinking soda-water with the Great Mogul, strangling myself with the lively beverage, and eliciting from him the laughing advice that I shouldn't drink it while it was boiling.

It was an aggravated case of friendship at first sight. In less than a week my admiration for Governor Dorr was so pure, unselfish and unquestioning that it saddens me now to remember it, knowing that the stock is exhausted. Every Wednesday and Saturday afternoon—our half-holidays—I hurried to Wall's Drug Store to meet my friend. Here were his headquarters, and a most profitable customer he must have been, for when he was not drinking soda-water he was smoking the Doctor's cigars.

In the rear of the shop was a small triangular room where Dr. Wall manufactured a patent eclectic cough syrup, and where he allowed us to sit rainy afternoons. Nothing about me, as I write, is so real as a vision of that musty, penny-royal-smelling little room, with Governor Dorr sitting on a reversed mortar and accenting the spirited parts of some Homeric story with a circumflex flourish of the Doctor's iron pestle, on the end of which was always a thin crust of the prescription last put up. Rows of croupy square bottles filled with a dark-colored mixture and labeled "Cough Syrup" look down on me from their dusty shelves, and I am listening again as of old.

In pleasant weather we sauntered about town, or strolled off into those pretty lanes which make Rivermouth, and rural places like Rivermouth, a paradise for lovers. In all these hours with Governor Dorr, I never knew him to let fall a word that a child should not hear. Perhaps my innocence and my unconcealed reverence for him touched and drew the better part of his heart to me, for it had a better part—one uncontaminated little piece for children.

Our conversations turned chiefly on his travels, literature, literary men and actors. His talk, I may remark, was very full on literary men; he knew them well, and was on astonishingly familiar personal terms with all the American authors quoted in my Third Reader, especially with Joel Barlow, who, I subsequently learned, had quitted this planet about a half a century previous to the birth of my friend. He called him "Joel," quite familiarly, and sometimes his "dear old friend Joe Barlow, the Hasty-pudding Man!"

Shakespeare, however, was the weakness, or the strength, of Governor Dorr. I am glad he did not have the effrontery to claim *his* acquaintance *in propria persona*. I am afraid that would have shaken my faith and spoiled me for enjoying my comrade's constant quotations. I am not sure, though, for I trusted so implicitly in the superior knowledge of Governor Dorr that on one occasion he convinced me that Herrick was a contemporary American author, and not an old English poet, as I had read somewhere. "Why, my dear boy," he exclaimed, "I know him well. He is a fellow of infinite jest, and his father edits the New York *Sunday Atlas!*" And the Governor drew forth a copy of the journal, and showed me the name of ANSON HERRICK in large capitals at the head of the paper. After that, I was entirely adrift on what is called "the sea of English literature."

To return to the Bard of Avon, "the immortal Bill," as my friend apostrophized him in moments of enthusiasm. The daily talk of the Governor would have come to a dead-lock, if he had been debarred the privilege of drawing at sight on his favorite poet. Take Shakespeare from Dorr, and naught remains. It was remarkable how the plays helped him out; now it was *Othello*, and now it was *Touchstone*, and now it was *Prospero*, who flew to his assistance with words and phrases so pat that they seemed created for the occasion. His voice, at that time rich, strong, and varied as the lines themselves, made it a delight to hear him repeat a long passage. I was not often able to follow the sense of the text, but the music bore me on with it. I can hear him now, saying:

> "In such a night
> Troilus, methinks, mounted the Trojan walls,
> And sighed his soul toward the Grecian tents,
> Where Cressid lay that night.
>
> "In such a night,
> Stood Dido with a willow in her hand
> Upon the wild sea-banks, and waved her love
> To come again to Carthage."

I never read the lines but I feel his hand laid suddenly upon my shoulder, and fancy myself standing on the old Mill-Dam Bridge at Rivermouth, with the water rushing through the sluices, and the rest of the pond lying like a sheet of crinkled silver in the moonlight.

My intercourse with Governor Dorr was not carried on without the cognizance of my family. They raised no objections. The Governor was then in his best style, and, by his good-nature and free-and-easy ways, more or less won everybody. The leading men of the town touched their hats to him on the street, and chatted with him at the post-office. It must be confessed, though, that the Governor was a sore puzzle to those worthy people. His fluency of money and language was not a local characteristic. He had left the place about ten years before, a poor boy, and now he had dropped down from nobody knew where, like an aerolite, mysteriously gay and possibly valuable.

The fact is, he must have been merely a gambler at this period, and had not entered upon that more aggressive career which afterwards made him well known to the police of Boston, New York and New Orleans. At all events, his fame had not reached Rivermouth; and though my family wondered what I saw in him or he in me to build a friendship on—the disparity in our ages being so great—they by no means objected to the intimacy, and it continued.

What impressed me most in Governor Dorr, next to his literary endowments, was his generous nature, his ready and practical sympathy for all sorts of unfortunate people. I have known him to go about the town half the morning with a blind man, selling his brooms for him at extortionate prices. I have seen the tears spring to his eyes at the recital of some story of suffering among the factory hands, many of whom were children. His love for these pale little men and women, as I think of it, is very touching; and it seems one of the finest things in the world to me now, and at the time it struck me as an epical exhibition of human sympathy, that he once purchased an expensive pair of skates for a little boy who had been born a cripple.

No doubt these facile sympathies were as superficial as letter-paper, as short-lived as those midges which are born and become great-grandfathers and die in the course of a single hour; but they endeared the Governor to me, and maybe, when the final reckoning comes, all those good impulses will add up to something handsome; who can tell?

Nearly six months had passed since the beginning of our acquaintance, when one morning my noble friend and my copy of Shakespeare—an illegibly printed volume bound in seedy law-calf, but the most precious of my earthly treasures—disappeared from the town simultaneously. Governor Dorr had gone, as he had come, without a word of warning, leaving his "ancient," as he was pleased to call me, the victim of abject despair.

What complicated events caused the abrupt departure of my friend and my calf-skin Shakespeare from Rivermouth never transpired. Perhaps he had spent all his money; perhaps he was wanted by a pal in New York, for some fresh piece of deviltry; or, what is more probable, the pastoral sweetness of life at Rivermouth had begun to cloy on his metropolitan palate.

It may have been five or it may have been ten months after his exodus that my late companion became known to the town in his true colors. He had been tripped up in some disreputable transaction or another, and had played a rather unenviable *rôle* in the New York police reports. I had been entertaining, not an angel, but a gambler unawares. My mortification was unassumed, and I banished the fascinating Governor Dorr from my affections forever.

A few years afterwards I left Rivermouth myself. The friend of my youth had become a faded memory. I had neither seen nor heard of him in the meanwhile; and the summer when I planned to pass the whole of a long vacation at my boyhood's home, the Governor assumed but a subordinate part in the associations naturally evoked by the proposed visit.

In my first walk through the town after my arrival, it was with a sort of comical consternation that I beheld Governor Dorr standing in front of Wall's Drug Store, smoking the very same cigar, it seemed, and skillfully catching the sunlight on the facets of that identical diamond ring.

The same, and not the same. He looked older, and was not so well groomed as he used to be; his lower jaw had grown heavier and his figure not improved. There was a hard expression in his face, and that inexplicable something all over him which says as plainly as a whisper to the ear, "This is a Black Sheep."

At the crossing our eyes met. Would he recognize his quondam chum and dupe, after all these years? The Governor gazed at me earnestly for ten seconds, then slowly drew back, and lifting his hat with a magnificent, grand air quite his own, made me an obeisance so involved and elaborate that it would be mere rashness to attempt to describe it.

The lady at my side gave my arm a convulsive grasp, and whispered, "Who is that dreadful man?"

"O, that?—that is the friend of my youth!"

Though I made light of the meeting, I was by no means amused by it. I saw that if Governor Dorr insisted on presuming on his old acquaintance, he might render it very disagreeable for me; I might have to snub him, perhaps quarrel with him. His presence was altogether annoying and depressing.

It appears that the man had been lying about Rivermouth for the last twelvemonth. When he was there before he had mystified the town, but now he terrified it. The people were afraid of him, and Governor Dorr knew it, and was having what he would have described as "a very soft thing." He touched his hat to all the pretty girls in the place, talked to everybody, and ministered to the spiritual part of his nature, now and then, by walking down the street familiarly with an eminent divine, who did not deem it prudent to resent the impertinence. For it was noticed by careful observers, that when any person repelled Governor Dorr, that person's wood-house caught on fire mysteriously, or a successful raid was undertaken in the direction of that person's family plate.

These trifling mishaps could never be traced to the Governor's agency, but the remarkable precision with which a catastrophe followed any slight offered to him made the townspeople rather civil than otherwise to their lively guest.

The authorities, however, were on the alert, and one night, a week after my arrival, the Governor was caught *flagrante delicto*, and lodged by Sheriff Adams in the Stone Jail, to my great relief, be it said; for the dread of meeting the man in my walks to the post-office and the reading-room had given me the air of a person seeking to elude the vigilance of justice.

I forget which of the laws the Governor had offended—he was quite impartial in his transgressions, by the way—but it was one that insured him a stationary residence for several months, and I considered myself well rid of the gentleman. But I little knew of the resources of Governor Dorr.

He had been in the habit of contributing poems and sketches of a lurid nature to one of the local newspapers, and now, finding the time to hang heavily on his hands in the solitude of his cell, the window of which overlooked the main street of the town, he began a series of letters to the editor of the journal in question.

These letters were dated from the Hôtel d'Adams (a graceful tribute to the sheriff of the county), and consisted of descriptions of what he saw from his cell-window, with sharp, shrewd and witty hits at the peculiarities of certain notable persons of the town, together with some attempts at fine writing not so successful. His observations on the townspeople were delicious. He had a neat, humorous touch, which, with training and under happier stars, might have won him reputation.

How I enjoyed those letters! How impatiently I awaited the semi-weekly appearance of the squalid journal containing them; with what eager fingers I unfolded the damp sheet, until, alas! one luckless morning there came a letter devoted wholly to myself. The "Leaves from the Diary of a Gentleman of Elegant Leisure" no longer seemed witty to me. And in truth, this leaf was not intended to be witty. It was in the Governor's best sentimental vein. He informed me that he had "from afar" watched over my budding career with the fondness of an elder brother, and that his heart, otherwise humble and unassuming, owned to a throb of honest pride and exultation when he remembered that it was he who had first guided my "nursling feet" over the flowery fields of English poesy, and bathed with me up to the chin in that "Pierian flood" which I had since made all my own. And so on through a column of solid nonpareil type. Altogether, his panegyric placed me in a more ridiculous light than any amount of abuse could have done. His sentiment was a thousand times more deadly than his satire.

Though my vacation was not at an end by several weeks, I quietly packed my valise that night, and fled from the friend of my youth.

—

I find that I am using the capital letter *I* rather freely in this sketch—a reprehensible habit, into which many people who write autobiography are very apt to fall; but really, my intention is to give as little of myself and as much of my friend as possible.

In the two or three years that followed this ignominious flight from my native town, I frequently heard of Governor Dorr indirectly. He had become famous now, in his modest way. I heard of him in New Orleans and in some of the Western cities. Once, at least, he reappeared in Rivermouth, where he got into some difficulty with a number of non-combatant turkeys prepared for Thanksgiving, the result of which was he spent that day of general festivity at the Hôtel d'Adams. But New York was, I believe, his favorite field of operations, as well as mine.

I cannot explain why the man so often came uppermost in my mind in those days; but I thought of him a great deal at intervals, and was thinking of him very particularly one dismal November afternoon in 185–, as I sat alone in the editorial room of the *Saturday Press*, where I had remained to write after the departure of my *confrères*.

It was a melancholy, small room, up two flights of stairs, in the rear of a building used as a warehouse by a paper firm doing business in the basement. Though bounded on all sides by turbulent streams of traffic, this room was as secluded and remote as if it had stood in the middle of the Desert of Sahara. It would have made an admirable scenic background for a noiseless midday murder in a melodrama. But it was an excellent place in which to write, in spite of the cobwebbed rafters overhead and the confirmed symptoms of scrofula in the plastering.

I did not settle down to work easily that afternoon; my fancy busied itself with everything except the matter in hand. I fell to thinking of old times and Rivermouth, and what comical things boys are with their hero-worship and their monkey-shines; and how I used to regard Governor Dorr as a cross between Sir Philip Sidney and Sir Walter Raleigh; and what a pitiable, flimsy hero he was in reality—a king of shreds and patches. "Why were such men born?" I said to myself. "Nature in her severe economy creates nothing useless, unless it be the ruminative moth or the New Jersey mosquito: the human species alone is full of failures monstrous and inexplicable."

In the midst of this the door opened, and Governor Dorr stood before me. I have had pleasanter surprises.

There was a certain deprecating air about him as he raised his hat in a feeble attempt at his old-time manner, a tacit confession that he couldn't do it. With his closely cropped hair, he looked like a prize-fighter retired from business. He was unshaven and pathetically shabby. His features were out of drawing, and wore that peculiar retributive pallor which gin and water in unfair proportions are said to produce. The dye had faded from his heavy mustache, leaving it of a dark greenish tint not becoming to his style of beauty. His threadbare coat was buttoned unevenly across his chest close up to the throat, and was shiny at the cuffs and along the seams. His hat had a weed on it, which struck me as being strange, as I did not remember that anybody had been hanged recently. I afterwards formed a theory touching that weed, based on the supposition that the hat was somebody else's property. Altogether, the Governor looked as if he had fallen upon evil days since our last meeting. There was a hard, cold look in his eyes which, in spite of his half-apologetic attitude, was far from reassuring.

Given a voice in the matter, I would not have chosen to have a private conference with him that dull November afternoon in that lonely room in the old barracks on Spruce Street.

The space occupied by the editorial tables was shut off from the rest of the office by a slight wooden rail extending across the apart-ment. In the centre of this rail was a gate, which my visitor, after a moment's hesitation, proceeded to open.

As I noted down all the circumstances of the interview while it was fresh in my mind, I am able to reproduce the Governor's words and manner pretty faithfully.

He closed the gate behind him with laborious care, advanced a few steps, rested one hand upon the back of a chair, and fixed a pair of fishy eyes upon me. If he intended to fascinate me, he failed; if he intended to make me feel extremely nervous, his success was complete.

"Telemachus," he said, at length, in a voice that had lost its old music, and may be succinctly described as ropy—"you know I used to call you Telemachus in those happy days when I was your 'guide, philosopher and friend'—you see before you a reformed man."

I suppose I was not entirely successful in concealing my inward conviction.

"So help me Bob!" exclaimed the Governor, "I am going to reform, and get some decent clothes"—casting a look of unutterable scorn on his coat-sleeve.

The idea of connecting a reformatory measure with an increase of wardrobe struck me as neat, and I smiled.

"I am going to be honest," continued Governor Dorr, not heeding my unseemly levity; " 'Honest Iago.' I am going to turn over a new leaf. I don't like the way things have been going. I wasn't intended to be a low fellow. I ain't adapted to being an outcast from society. 'We know what we are, but we don't know what we may be,' as the sublime Shakespeare remarks. Now, I know what I am, and I know what I'm going to be. I'm going to be another man. But I must get out of New York first. The boys wouldn't let me reform. 'The little dogs and all, Tray, Blanch and Sweetheart, see, they bark at me!' I know too many people here and too many people know me. I am going to New Orleans. My old friend Kendall of the *Picayune* knows my literary qualifications, and would give me an engagement on his paper at sight; but I'm not proud, and if worst came to worst I could get advertisements or solicit subscribers, and work my way up. In the bright lexicon of a man who means what he says, 'there's no such word as fail.' He doesn't know how to spell it."

The Governor paused and looked at me for a reply; but as I had nothing to say, I said it.

"I've been down to Rivermouth," he resumed, a trifle less spiritedly, "to see what my old chums would do towards paying my way to New Orleans. They gave me a good deal of good advice, especially Colonel B——; but I am out just twenty dollars, traveling expenses. Advice, however excellent, doesn't pay a fellow's passage to New Orleans in the present disordered state of society. I have collected some money, but not enough by a few dollars; and presuming on the memory of those days—those Arcadian days, when we wandered hand in hand through the green pastures of American poesy—I have come to you for a temporary loan—however small," he added hastily, "to help me in becoming an honest citizen and a useful member of society."

I listened attentively to the Governor's statement, and believed not a syllable of it, not so much as a hyphen. It had a fatally familiar jingle; I had helped to reform people before. Nevertheless, the man's misery was genuine, and I determined not to throw him over altogether. But I did not wish him to consider me the victim of his cleverness; so I frankly told him that I did not believe a word about his reforming, and that if I gave him a little pecuniary assistance, it was solely because I used to think kindly of him when I was a boy.

The Governor was so affected by this that he searched in several pockets for a handkerchief, but not finding one, he wiped away what I should call a very dry tear with the cuff of his sleeve.

" 'Had I but served my God,' " he remarked, " 'with half the zeal' I have fooled away my chances, 'he would not have left me in mine age' to solicit financial succor in this humiliating fashion."

It was the mendaciousness of Jeremy Diddler toned down by the remorse of Cardinal Wolsey.

"I am well aware," I said coldly, "that the few dollars I intend to give you will be staked at the nearest faro-table or squandered over the bar of some drinking-shop. I want you to understand distinctly that you are not imposing on me."

Now the journal of which I was part proprietor had a weekly circulation of less than forty thousand copies, and at the end of the week, when we had paid a sordid printer and an unimaginative paper-maker, we were in a condition that entitled us to rank as objects of charity rather than as benefactors of the poor. A five-dollar bill was all my available assets that November afternoon, and out of this I purposed to reserve two dollars for my dinner at Mataran's. I stated the case plainly to the Governor, suggesting that I could get the note changed at the *Tribune* office.

He picked up the bill which I had spread out on the table between us, remarking that he thought he could change it. Whereupon he produced a portly pocket-book from the breast of his coat, and from the pocket-book so fat a roll of bank-notes that I glowed with indignation to think he had the coolness to appropriate three-fifths of my slender earnings.

"New Orleans, you know," he remarked, explanatorily.

The Governor was quite another man now, running dexterously over the bills with a moist forefinger in the gayest of spirits. He handed me my share of the five-dollar bill with the manner of a benevolent prince dispensing his bounties, accorded me the privilege of grasping his manly hand, raised his hat with a good deal of his old quasi aristocratic flourish, and was gone.

There is this heavenly quality in a deed of even misplaced charity: it makes the heart of the doer sit lightly in his bosom. I treated myself handsomely that afternoon at dinner, regarding myself, in the abstract, as a person who ought to dine well, and was worthy of at least half a pint of table claret. I tested the delicacies of Mataran's *cuisine* as far as my purse would allow; but when I stepped to the desk to pay the reckoning, those two one-dollar bills rather awkwardly turned out to be counterfeits!

Well, I suppose I deserved it.

———

The frequency with which Governor Dorr's name figured in the local police reports during the ensuing twelve months leads me to infer that he did not depart for New Orleans as soon as he expected.

Time rolled on, and the *Saturday Press*, being loved by the gods, died early, and one morning in 1861 I found myself at liberty to undertake a long-deferred pilgrimage to Rivermouth.

On arriving at my destination, cramped with a night's ride in the cars, I resolved to get the kinks out of me by walking from the station. Turning into one of the less-frequented streets, in order not to meet too many of my townsfolk, I came abruptly upon a hearse jogging along very pleasantly, and followed at a little distance by a single hack. When all one's friends can be put into a single hack, perhaps it is best that one should be buried expeditiously.

A malign urchin stood at the corner whistling shrilly through his fingers, which he removed from his lips with an injured air long enough to answer my question. "Who's dead? Why, Guvner Dorr's dead. That's 'im," curving a calliopean thumb in the direction of the hearse. The pity of it! The forlornness of the thing touched me, and a feeling of gratitude went out from my bosom towards the two or three hacks which now made their appearance around the corner and joined the funeral train.

Broken down in his prime with careless living, Governor Dorr a few months previously has straggled back to the old place to die; and thus had chance—which sometimes displays a keen appreciation of dramatic effect—once more, and for the last time, brought me in contact with the friend of my youth. Obeying the impulse, I turned and followed the procession until it came to the head of that long, unbuilt street which, stretching in a curve from the yawning gate of the cemetery into the heart of the town, always seemed to me like a great siphon draining the life from Rivermouth. Here I halted, and watched the black carriages as they crawled down the road, growing smaller and smaller, until they appeared to resolve themselves into one tiny coach, which, lessening in the distance, finally vanished through a gateway that seemed about a foot high.

The gratest bores in the world are those who are eternally trieing to prove to yu that 2 and 2 allwuss makes 4.

JOSH BILLINGS

THE CAMEL AND THE ZEBRA

AMBROSE BIERCE

"What have you there on your back?" said a zebra, jeeringly, to a "ship of the desert" in ballast.

"Only a bale of gridirons," was the meek reply.

"And what, pray, may you design doing with them?" was the incredulous rejoinder.

"What am I to do with gridirons?" repeated the camel, contemptuously. "Nice question for *you*, who have evidently just come off one!'

People who wish to throw stones should not live in glass houses; but there ought to be a few in their vicinity.

"Success with Small Fruits"

R. J. BURDETTE

"I just rolled out here from the grocery store," said the little green apple, as it paused on the sidewalk for a moment's chat with the banana peel; "I am waiting here for a boy. Not a small, weak, delicate boy," added the little green apple, proudly, "but a great big boy, a great hulky, strong, leather-lunged, noisy fifteen-year-older, and little as I am, you will see me double up that boy to-night, and make him wail and howl and yell. Oh, I'm small, but I'm good for a ten acre field of boys, and don't you forget it! All the boys in Burlington," the little green apple went on, with just a shade of pitying contempt in its voice, "couldn't fool around me as any one of them fools around a banana."

"Boys seems to be your game," drawled the banana peel, lazily; "well, I suppose they are just about strong enough to afford you a little amusement. For my own part, I like to take somebody of my size. Now, here comes the kind of a man I usually do business with. He is large and strong, it is true, but—"

And just then a South Hill merchant, who weighs about 231 pounds when he feels right good, came along, and the banana peel just caught him by the foot, lifted him about as high as the awning post, turned him over, banged him down on a potato basket, flattening it out until it looked like a splint door-mat, and the shock jarred everything loose in the show-window. And then, while the fallen merchant, from various quarters of the globe, fished his silk hat from the gutter, his spectacles from the cellar, his handkerchief from the tree-box, his cane from the show-window, and one of his shoes from the eaves-trough, and a little boy ran for the doctor, the little green apple blushed red and shrank a little back out of sight, covered with awe and mortification.

"Ah," it thought, "I wonder if I can ever do that? Alas, how vain I was, and yet how poor and weak and useless I am in this world."

But the banana peel comforted it, and bade it look up and take heart, and do well what it had to do, and labor for the good of the cause in its own useful sphere. "True," said the banana peel, "you cannot lift up a two hundred pound man and break a cellar door with him, but you can give him the cholera morbus, and if you do your part, the world will feel your power and the medical colleges will call you blessed."

And then the little green apple smiled and looked up with grateful blushes on its face, and thanked the banana peel for its encouraging counsel. And that very night, an old father who writes thirteen hours a day, and a patient mother who was almost ready to sink from weariness, and a nurse and a doctor, sat up until nearly morning with a thirteen-year-old boy, who was all twisted up into the shape of a figure 3, while all the neighbors on that block sat up and listened, and pounced their pillows, and tried to sleep, and wished that boy would either die or get well.

And the little green apple was pleased, and its last words were, "At least I have been of some little use in this great wide world!"

Natral and Unnatral Aristokrats

JOSH BILLINGS

Natur furnishes all the nobleman we hav.

She holds the pattent.

Pedigree haz no more to do in making a man aktually grater than he iz, than a pekok's feather in his hat haz in making him aktually taller.

Thiz iz a hard phakt for some tew learn.

This mundane earth iz thik with male and femail ones who think they are grate bekauze their ansesstor waz luckey in the sope or to-bacco trade; and altho the sope haz run out sum time since, they try tew phool themselves and other folks with the suds.

Sope suds iz a prekarious bubble.

Thare ain't nothing so thin on the ribs az a sope suds aristokrat.

When the world stands in need ov an aristokrat, natur pitches one into it, and furnishes him papers without enny flaw in them.

Aristokrasy kant be transmitted—natur sez so—in the papers.

Titles are a plan got up bi humans tew assist natur in promulgating aristokrasy.

Titles ain't ov enny more real use or nesessity than dog collars are.

I hav seen dog collars that kost 3 dollars on dogs that want worth, in enny market, over 87½ cents.

This iz a grate waste ov collar; and a grate damage tew the dog.

Natur don't put but one ingredient into her kind ov aristokrasy, and that iz virtew.

She wets up the virtew, sumtimes, with a little pepper sass, just tew make it lively.

She sez that all other kinds are false; and i beleave natur.

I wish every man and woman on earth waz a bloated aristokrat—bloated with virtew.

Earthly manufaktured aristokrats are made principally out ov munny.

Forty years ago it took about 85 thousand dollars tew make a good-sized aristokrat, and innokulate his family with the same disseaze, but it takes now about 600 thousand tew throw the partys into fits.

Aristokrasy, like all other bred stuffs, haz riz.

It don't take enny more virtew tew make an aristokrat now, nor clothes, than it did in the daze ov Abraham.

Virtew don't vary.

Virtew iz the standard ov values.

Clothes ain't.

Titles aint.

A man kan go barefoot and be virtewous, and be an aristokrat.

Diogoneze waz an aristokrat.

His brown stun front waz a tub, and it want on end, at that.

Moneyed aristokrasy iz very good to liv on in the present hi kondishun ov kodphis and wearing apparel, provided yu see the munny, but if the munny kind of tires out and don't reach yu, and you don't git ennything but the aristokrasy, you hav got to diet, that's all.

I kno ov thousands who are now dieting on aristokrasy.

They say it tastes good.

I presume they lie without knowing it.

Not enny ov this sort ov aristocrasy for Joshua Billings.

I never should think ov mixing munny and aristokrasy together; i will take mine seperate, if yu pleze.

I don't never expekt tew be an aristokrat, nor an angel; i dont kno az i want tew be one.

I certainly should make a miserable angel.

I certainly never shall hav munny enuff tew make an aristokrat.

Raizing aristokrats iz a dredful poor bizzness; yu don't never git your seed back.

One democrat iz worth more tew the world than 60 thousand man-ufaktured aristokrats.

An Amerikan aristokrat iz the most ridikilus thing in market. They are generally ashamed ov their ansesstors; and, if they hav enny, and live long enuff, they generally hav cauze tew be ashamed ov their pos-terity.

I kno ov sevral familys in Amerika who are trieing tew liv on their aristokrasy. The money and branes giv out sum time ago.

It iz hard skratching for them.

Yu kan warm up kold potatoze and liv on them, but yu kant warm up aristokratik pride and git even a smell.

Yu might az well undertake tew raze a krop ov korn in a deserted brik yard by manuring the ground heavy with tan bark.

———

Yung man, set down, and keep still—yu will hav plenty ov chances yet to make a phool ov yureself before yu die.

JOSH BILLINGS

EXAMPLES OF TURKISH JUSTICE

S. S. COX

In Egypt, long before the Turkish rule in that region, there were strug-gles between the Mamelukes and the Circassians. A Circassian chief, through the advice of a servant, who, though ignorant, was naturally astute, happened by accident to discover the weak points of the ruling government in Egypt. Upon these points, as upon the rounds of a ladder, he ascended to the throne. Formerly, the Circassian had promised the servant that if ever he obtained that eminence the servant should receive the appointment of Chief Judge. The servant's name was Caracoush, meaning "black bird." So, as soon as the chief was enthroned, he gave Caracoush the promised post. Among the many cases that came before him was the following petition:

"Being a burglar by profession, and compelled by want to rob a house, I select that of a tailor. To enter it I must make my way through the courtyard. This is surrounded by a high wall. In jumping from this wall I am caught on the spikes the tailor had fixed in the wall to suspend ropes for the washing. The result is, I lose an eye. I now demand that my eye be restored, and that the fellow who drove the spike shall be punished."

The judge reads the petition, and concludes that justice is due the petitioner. He summons the tailor, to whom the matter is explained. The tailor argues that the thief has no business to jump into his yard in the night, so that if he lost an eye, it is his own fault. But the judge remarks:

"The thief is only practicing his profession, and the law only punishes robbers."

"If," he says to the tailor, "you had not driven the spikes in the walls, the thief would not have lost his eye; therefore your eye must pay the forfeit."

The poor tailor begs and cries in vain. The verdict is pronounced. It must be executed. After a long struggle, the tailor seizes the knees of the judge, kisses them vigorously, and with tears in his eyes, exclaims:

"Oh! mighty judge. Your decision is sound, but consider. Am I not supporting a large family—my old mother, my wife, and my seven young children? They all depend on me, and I myself depend on my two eyes. Am I not a tailor? Do I not need my two eyes? If I lose one, how can I pass the thread into the needle's eye? How can I do my fine sewing? My reputation will suffer and all of us starve!"

Seeing some sign of relenting in the judicial countenance, the tailor is encouraged. He resumes, brightening:

"I have a neighbor who is a sportsman. When he aims at the game he shuts one eye. Why, great judge, his two eyes are an embarrassment to him! Had he but one, it would save him the trouble of shutting the other. Moreover, what difference does it make to this robber? All he wants is an eye pulled out. Whether it be mine or that of the sportsman's, what matter? It is all one to him."

The argument sounds plausible. The judge considers a moment, and then sends for the sportsman. In spite of protests, he decrees the loss of the sportsman's superfluous eye. The verdict is carried into execution, and judicial logic is vindicated!

—

In the interior of Hungary a Turkish agent is sent to buy cavalry horses to recruit for the then probable war with Bulgaria and Greece. While there the agent desires that the proprietor of a village, with whom he was contracting, should show him a specimen of the Hungarian mode of proceeding.

"Wait a few moments," says the proprietor, who is also a magistrate, "and I will see who is in the town jail."

Calling his constable, he is informed by that officer that a goose thief had been apprehended during the night, and is in confinement. He sends for the criminal.

"Are there any witnesses?" asks the judge.

"Two," is the answer; "the man who owns the goose, and a man who saw the theft."

After hearing the evidence, the judge, in his fierce and harsh Hungarian-Finnish-Tartaric tongue, calls up the culprit and says:

"You have been found guilty, and I fine you ten kreutzers and ten days' imprisonment for stealing the goose!"

Thereupon the judge summons the owner of the bird:

"I fine you ten kreutzers and ten days' imprisonment for allowing your goose to be stolen!"

Having thus disposed of the parties, the judge, turning to the witness, says:

"Sirrah! I fine you ten kreutzers and ten days' imprisonment for not minding your own business!"

Hilmi Effendi listens with interest to this story of Slavonic justice, and remarks that almost as odd a case recently came before one of the courts of Stamboul.

A creditor comes to the judge to have a note sued. It is for 1,500 piastres, and not due until three years after the complaint is made. The judge entertains the suit, and condemns the creditor to confinement for three years.

"For," said his honor: "How do I know where you will be three years hence, so as to pay you the piastres, unless I hold you?"

We agree that this is an improvement on the American custom of the imprisonment of witnesses in criminal cases.

A Great Fit

ORPHEUS C. KERR

Robert Henry Newell, the *Orpheus C. Kerr* of every one's acquaintance, is a veteran editor and a prolific author. He was born in New York, December 13, 1836.

"There was a man in Arkansaw
    As let his passions rise,
And not unfrequently picked out
    Some other varmint's eyes.

"His name was Tuscaloosa Sam,
    And often he would say,
'There's not a cuss in Arkansaw
    I can't whip any day.'

"One morn, a stranger, passin' by,
    Heard Sammy talkin' so,
When down he scrambled from his hoss,
    And off his coat did go.

"He sorter kinder shut one eye,
    And spit into his hand,
And put his ugly head one side,
    And twitched his trowsers' band.

" 'My boy,' says he, 'it's my belief,
    Whomever you may be,
That I kin make you screech, and smell
    Pertikler agony.'

" 'I'm thar,' says Tuscaloosa Sam,
    And chucked his hat away;
'I'm thar,' says he, and buttoned up
    As far as buttons may.

"He thundered on the stranger's mug,
    The stranger pounded he;
And oh! the way them critters fit
    Was beautiful to see.

"They clinched like two rampageous bears,
    And then went down a bit;
They swore a stream of six-inch oaths
    And fit, and fit, and fit.

"When Sam would try to work away,
    And on his pegs to git,
The stranger'd pull him back; and so,
    They fit, and fit, and fit!

"Then like a pair of lobsters, both
    Upon the ground were knit,
And yet the varmints used their teeth,
    And fit, and fit, and fit!!

"The sun of noon was high above,
    And hot enough to split,
But only riled the fellers more,
    That fit, and fit, and fit!!!

"The stranger snapped at Sammy's nose,
    And shortened it a bit;
And then they both swore awful hard,
    And fit, and fit, and fit!!!!

"The mud it flew, the sky grew dark,
    And all the litenins lit;
But still them critters rolled about,
    And fit, and fit, and fit!!!!!

"First Sam on top, then t'other chap;
    When one would make a hit,
The other'd smell the grass; and so,
    They fit, and fit, and fit!!!!!!

"The night came on, the stars shone out
    As bright as wimmen's wit;
And still them fellers swore and gouged,
    And fit, and fit, and fit!!!!!!!

"The neighbors heard the noise they made,
    And thought an earthquake lit;
Yet all the while 'twas him and Sam
    As fit, and fit, and fit!!!!!!!!

"For miles around the noise was heard;
    Folks couldn't sleep a bit,
Because them two rantankerous chaps
    Still fit, and fit, and fit!!!!!!!!!

"But jist at cock-crow, suddenly,
    There came an awful pause,
And I and my old man run out
    To ascertain the cause.

"The sun was rising in the yeast,
    And lit the hull concern;
But not a sign of either chap
    Was found at any turn.

"Yet, in the region where they fit,
    We found, to our surprise,
One pint of buttons, two big knives,
    Some whiskers, and four eyes!"

Artemus Ward and
the Prince of Wales

ARTEMUS WARD

I was drawin' near to the Prince, when a red-faced man in Millingtery close grabd holt of me and axed me whare I was goin' all so bold?

"To see Albert Edard, the Prince of Wales," sez I; "who are you?"

He sed he was the Kurnal of the Seventy Fust Regiment, Her Magisty's troops. I told him I hoped the Seventy Onesters was in good helth, and was passin' by when he ceased hold of me agin, and sed in a tone of indigent cirprise:

"What? Impossible! It kannot be! Blarst my hize, sir, did I understan' you to say that you was actooally goin' into the presents of his Royal Iniss?"

"That's what's the matter with me," I replied.

"But blarst my hize, sir, its onprecedented. It's orful sir. Nothin' like it hain't happened sins the Gun Power Plot of Guy Forks. Owdashus man, who air yu?"

"Sir, sez I, drawin' myself up & puttin' on a defiant air, "I'm a Amerycan sitterzen. My name is Ward. I'm a husband, & the father of twins, which I'm happy to state thay look like me. By perfession I'm a exhibiter of wax works & sich."

"Good God!" yelled the Kurnal; "the idee of a exhibiter of wax figgers goin' into the presents of Royalty! The British Lion may well roar with raje at the thawt!"

Sez I, "Speakin' of the British Lion, Kurnal, I'd like to make a bargin with you fur that beast fur a few weeks to add to my Show." I didn't meen nothin' by this. I was only gettin' orf a goak, but you orter hev seen the Old Kurnal jump up and howl. He actooally foamed at the mowth.

"This can't be real," he showtid. "No, no. It's a horrid dream. Sir, you air not a human bein'—you hav no existents—yu're a Myth!"

"Wall," sez I, "old hoss, yule find me a ruther oncomfortable Myth ef you punch my inards in that way agin." I began to git a little riled, fur when he called me a Myth he puncht me putty hard. The Kurnal now comments showtin fur the Seventy Onesters. I at fust thawt I'd stay & becum a Marter to British Outraje, as sich a course mite git my name up & be a good advertisement fur my Show, but it occurred to me that ef enny of the Seventy Onesters shood happen to insert a baronet into my stummick it mite be onplesunt; & I was on the pint of runnin' orf when the Prince hisself kum up & axed me what the matter was. Sez I, "Albert Edard, is that you?" & he smilt & sed it was. Sez I, "Albert Edard, hears my keerd. I cum to pay my respecks to the futer King of Ingland. The Kurnal of the Seventy Onesters hear is ruther smawl pertaters, but of course you ain't to blame fur that. He puts on as many airs as tho he was the Bully Boy with the glass eye."

"Never mind," sez Albert Edard, "I'm glad to see you, Mister Ward, at all events," & he tuk my hand so plesunt like, & larfed so sweet that I fell in love with him to onct. He handid me a segar, & we sot down on the Pizarro & commenst smokin' rite cheerful.

"Wall," sez I, "Albert Edard, how's the old folks?"

"Her Majesty & the Prince are well," he sed.

"Duz the old man take his Lager beer reglar?" I inquired.

The Prince larfed, & intermatid that the old man didn't let many kegs of that bevridge spile in the sellar in the coarse of a year. We sot & tawked there sum time abowt matters & things, & bimeby I axed him how he liked bein' Prince, as fur as he'd got.

"To speak plain, Mister Ward," he sed, "I don't much like it. I'm sick of all this bowin' & scrapin' & crawlin' & hurrain over a boy like me. I would rather go through the country quietly & enjoy myself in my own way, with the other boys, & not be made a Show of to be gaped at by everybody. When the *peple* cheer me I feel pleesed, fur I know they meen it; but if these one-horse offishuls cood know how I see threw all their moves & understan' exactly what they air after, & knowd how I larft at 'em in private, thayd stop kissin' my hands & fawnin' over me as thay now do. But you know, Mister Ward, I can't help bein' a Prince, & I must do all I kin to fit myself for the persishun I must sumtime ock-epy."

"That's troo," sez I; "sickness & the docters will carry the Queen orf one of these dase, sure's yer born."

The time hevin' arove fur me to take my departer, I rose up & sed: "Albert Edard, I must go, but previs to doin' so, I will obsarve that you soot me. Yure a good feller, Albert Edard, & tho I'm agin Princes as a gineral thing, I must say I like the cut of your Gib. When you git to be King, try & be as good a man as your muther has bin! Be just & be Jenerus, espeshully to showmen, who have allers bin aboosed sins the dase of Noah, who was the fust man to go into the Menagery bizniss, & ef the daily papers of his time air to be beleeved, Noah's colleck-shun of livin' wild beests beet ennything ever seen sins, tho I make bold to dowt ef his snaiks was ahead of mine. Albert Edard, adoo!" I tuk his hand, which he shook warmly, & givin' him a perpetooal free pars to my show, & also parses to take hum for the Queen & Old Al-bert, I put on my hat and walkt away.

"Mrs. Ward," I solilerquized as I walkt along—"Mrs. Ward, ef you could see your husband now, just as he prowdly emerjis from the pre-sunts of the futer King of Ingland, you'd be sorry you called him a Beest jest becaws he cum home tired 1 nite & wantid to go to bed with-out takin' off his boots. You'd be sorry for tryin' to deprive yure hus-band of the priceless Boon of liberty, Betsy Jane!"

Jest then I met a long perseshun of men with gownds onto 'em. The leader was on horseback, & ridin' up to me, he sed:

"Air you Orange?"

Sez I, "Which?"

"Air you a Orangeman?" he repeated, sternly.

"I used to peddle lemins," sed I, "but never delt in oranges. They are apt to spile on yure hands. What particler Loonatic Asylum hev you & yure friends escaped frum, if I may be so bold?" Just then a suddent thawt struck me, & I sed, "Oh, yure the fellers who air worryin' the Prince so, & givin' the Juke of Noocastle cold sweats at nite, by yure infernal catawalins, air you? Wall, take the advice of a Amerykin sit-terzen, take orf them gownds & don't try to get up a religious fite, which is 40 times wuss nor a prize fite, over Albert Edard, who wants to receive you all on a ekal footin' not keerin' a tinker's cuss what meetin'-house you sleep in Sundays. Go home & mind yure bisness, & not make noosenses of yourselves." With which observashuns I left 'em.

I shall leave British sile 4thwith.

BRILLIANT DRUNKARDS

CHARLES DUDLEY WARNER

It is a temptation to a temperate man to become a sot, to hear what tal-ent, what versatility, what genius, is almost always attributed to a mod-erately bright man who is habitually drunk. Such a mechanic, such a mathematician, such a poet he would be if he were only sober; and then he is sure to be the most generous, magnanimous, friendly soul, conscientiously honorable, if he were not so conscientiously drunk. I suppose it is now notorious that the most brilliant and promising men have been lost to the world in this way. It is sometimes almost painful to think what a surplus of talent and genius there would be in the world if the habit of intoxication should suddenly cease; and what a slim chance there would be for the plodding people who have always had tolerable good habits. The fear is only mitigated by the observation that the reputation of a person for great talent sometimes ceases with his reformation.

TRAIN MANNERS

R. J. BURDETTE

Genesee.—A woman with three bird-cages and a little girl has just got on the train. She arranges the three bird-cages on a seat, and then she and the little girl stand up in the aisle, and she glares around upon the ungallant men who remain glued to their seats, and look dreamily out of the window. I bend my face down to the tablet and write furiously, for I feel her eyes fastened upon me. Somehow or other, I am always the victim in cases of this delicate nature. Just as I expected! She speaks, fastening her commanding gaze upon me:

"Sir, would it be asking too much if I begged you to let myself and my little girl have that seat? A gentleman can always find a seat so much more easily than a lady."

And she smiled. Not the charmingest kind of a smile. It was too triumphant to be very pleasing. Of course I surrendered. I said:

"Oh, certainly, certainly! I could find another seat without any trouble."

She thanked me, and I crawled out of my comfortable seat, and gathered up my overcoat, my manuscript, my shawl-strap package, my valise, and my overshoes, and she and the little girl went into the vacant premises; the writ of ejectment had been served, and they looked happy and comfortable.

Then I stepped across the aisle; I took up those bird-cages and set them along on top of the coal box, and sat down in the seat thus vacated. I apologetically remarked to the woman, who was gazing at me with an expression that boded trouble, that "it was much warmer for the canaries up by the stove." She didn't say anything, but she gave me a look that made it much warmer for me, for about five minutes, than the stove can make it for the canaries.

Belvidere.—A woman has just gone out of the car and left the door wide, wide open, and the wind is blowing through the coach a hundred miles a minute. Why is it that a woman never shuts a car door? Also, why does a man always leave it open? And indeed, why nobody ever shuts it except the brakeman, and he only closes it for the sake of the noise he can make with it.

Yesterday morning, I saw a man go out of a car, and shut the door after him. I have traveled very constantly for nearly three years, and this was the first man I ever saw shut the car door after him as he went out.

And he only shut it because I was right behind him, trying to get out, with a big valise in each hand. When I set down my valises to open the door, I made a few remarks on the general subject of people who would get up in the night to do the wrong thing at the wrong time, but the man was out on the platform, and failed to catch the drift of my remark.

I was not sorry for this, because the other passengers seemed to enjoy it quite as well by themselves, and the man whose action called forth this impromptu address was a forbidding looking man, as big as a hay wagon, and looked as though he would have banged me clear through the side of a box car if he had heard what I said.

I suppose these people who invariably do the wrong things at the wrong time are necessary, but they are awfully unpleasant.

Cuba.—A woman gets on the train and says a very warm-hearted good-bye to a great cub of a sixteen-year-old boy who sets down her bundles, and turns to leave the car with a gruff grunt that may mean good-bye or anything else. There is a little quiver on her lip as she calls after him, "Be a good boy, write to me often, and do as I tell you." He never looks around as he leaves the car. He looks just like the kind of a boy who will do just as she tells him, but she must be careful to tell him to do just as he wants to. I have one bright spark of consolation as the train moves on, and I see that boy performing a clumsy satire on a clog dance on the platform. Some of these days he will treat some man as gruffly and rudely as he treats his mother. Then the man will climb onto him and lick him; pound the very sawdust out of him. Then the world will feel better and happier for the licking he gets. It may be long deferred, but it will come at last. I almost wish I had pounded him myself, while he is young and I felt able to do it. He may grow up into a very discouragingly rugged man, extremely difficult to lick, and the world may have to wait a very long time for this act of justice. It frequently happens that these bad boys grow up into distressingly "bad" men.

We have got as far as Hinsdale, and here we have ceased to progress. The experienced passengers sit as patiently as the train itself. The inexperienced ones fly around and tramp in and out, and leave the door open, and ply the train men and the operator with numerous questions. Sometimes the train men answer their questions, and then sometimes they do not answer them. When they do reply to the eager conundrums, somehow or other the passenger always feels as though he knew a little less than he did before. It is a cruel, deceitful old world, in snow time.

A man has gone to the front seat, and is warming his feet by planting the soles of his boots against the side of the stove. As he wears India rubber boots, the effect is marked but not pleasant.

As usual, the drinking boy is on the car. He has laid regular siege to the water tank, and, I think, will empty it before we get to Salamanca. I wish to call the attention of the temperance societies to this class of intemperates. There should be a pledge drawn up and some color of ribbon—a bit of watered silk would be appropriate, I suppose—for boys of six and seven years, who are addicted to drinking water at the rate of eighteen tin-cupfuls a minute. Ten or twelve boys of this class can drink a creek dry when they are feeling comfortably thirsty.

A friendly passenger wants to talk. I am not feeling particularly sociable this morning, and consequently I do not propose to talk to anybody. He asks how I like this kind of weather, and I say, "Splendidly."

He laughs feebly, but encouragingly, and says there has been a little too much snow. I say, "Not for health; it was just what we needed."

He asks if I heard of the accident on the Central Railroad, and I say, "Yes."

Then he asks me how it was, and I tell him, "I don't know; didn't read it."

He wants to know what I think of Hayes, and I say, "I think he made a very good constable."

"Constable?" he says; "I mean President Hayes."

I say I thought he meant Dennis Hays, of Peoria.

Then he asks if I "am going far?"

I say, "No."

"How far?" he asks.

"Fourteen hundred miles," I say, unblushingly.

He thinks that is what he would call "far," and I make no response. Two babies in the car are rehearsing a little, and in rather faulty time, but with fine expression. And the man, with one or two "dashes," asks if it doesn't bother me to write with a lot of "brats squalling around?"

I looked up at him very severely, for it always makes me angry to hear a man call a baby a "brat," and I say to him, in a slow, impressive manner, that "I would rather listen to a baby cry than hear a man swear."

This eminently proper and highly moral rebuke has its effect. The man forsakes me, and he is now wreaking a cheap, miserable revenge on the smiling passengers by whistling "My Grandfather's Clock," accompanying himself by drumming on the window with his fingers.

THEIR FIRST QUARREL

W. D. HOWELLS

"We shall have time for the drive round the mountain before dinner," said Basil, as they got into their carriage again; and he was giving the order to the driver, when Isabel asked how far it was.

"Nine miles."

"O, then we can't think of going with one horse. You know," she added, "that we always intended to have two horses for going round the mountain."

"No," said Basil, not yet used to having his decisions reached without his knowledge. "And I don't see why we should. Everybody goes with one. You don't suppose we're too heavy, do you?"

"I had a party from the States, ma'am, yesterday," interposed the driver; "two ladies, real heavy ones, two gentlemen, weighin' two hundred apiece, and a stout young man on the box with me. You'd 'a' thought the horse was drawin' an empty carriage, the way she darted along."

"Then his horse must be perfectly worn out to-day," said Isabel, refusing to admit the poor fellow directly even to the honors of a defeat. He had proved too much, and was put out of court with no hope of repairing his error.

"Why, it seems a pity," whispered Basil, dispassionately, "to turn this man adrift, when he had a reasonable hope of being with us all day, and has been so civil and obliging."

"O, yes, Basil, sentimentalize him; do! Why don't you sentimentalize his helpless, overworked horse?—all in a reek of perspiration."

"Perspiration! Why, my dear, it's the rain!"

"Well, rain or shine, darling, I don't want to go round the mountain with one horse; and it's very unkind of you to insist now, when you've tacitly promised me all along to take two."

"Now, this is a little too much, Isabel. You know we never mentioned the matter till this moment."

"It's the same as a promise, your not saying you wouldn't. But I don't *ask* you to keep your word. *I* don't want to go round the mountain. I'd *much* rather go to the hotel. I'm tired."

"Very well, then, Isabel, I'll leave you at the hotel."

In a moment it had come, the first serious dispute of their wedded life. It had come as all such calamities come—from nothing; and it was on them in full disaster ere they knew. Such a very little while ago, there in the convent garden, their lives had been drawn closer in sympathy than ever before; and now that blessed time seemed ages since, and they were further asunder than those who have never been friends. "I thought," bitterly mused Isabel, "that he would have done anything for me!" "Who would have dreamed that a woman of her sense would be so unreasonable!" he wondered. Both had tempers, as I know my dearest reader has (if a lady), and neither would yield; and so, presently, they could hardly tell how, for they were aghast at it all, Isabel was alone in her room amidst the ruins of her life, and Basil alone in the one-horse carriage, trying to drive away from the wreck of his happiness. All was over; the dream was past; the charm was broken. The sweetness of their love was turned to gall; whatever had pleased them in their loving moods was loathsome now, and the things they had praised a moment before were hateful. In that baleful light, which seemed to dwell upon all they ever said or did in mutual enjoyment, how poor and stupid and empty looked their wedding-journey! Basil spent five minutes in arraigning his wife and convicting her of every folly and fault. His soul was in a whirl:

> "For to be wroth with one we love,
> Doth work like madness in the brain."

In the midst of his bitter and furious upbraidings he found himself suddenly become her ardent advocate, and ready to denounce her judge as a heartless monster. "On our wedding journey, too! Good heavens, what an incredible brute I am!" Then he said, "What an ass I am!" And the pathos of the case having yielded to its absurdity, he was helpless. In five minutes more he was at Isabel's side, the one-horse carriage driver dismissed with a handsome *pour-boire*, and a pair of lusty bays with a glittering barouche waiting at the door below. He swiftly accounted for his presence, which she seemed to find the most natural thing that could be, and she met his surrender with the openness of a heart that forgives but does not forget, if indeed the most gracious art is the only one unknown to the sex.

She rose with a smile from the ruins of her life, amidst which she had heart-brokenly sat down with all her things on. "I knew you'd come back," she said.

"So did I," he answered. "I am much too good and noble to sacrifice my preference to my duty."

"I didn't care particularly for the two horses, Basil," she said, as they descended to the barouche. "It was your refusing them that hurt me."

"And I didn't want the one-horse carriage. It was your insisting so that provoked me."

"Do you think people *ever* quarreled before on a wedding journey?" asked Isabel, as they drove gayly out of the city.

"Never! I can't conceive of it! I suppose, if this were written down, nobody would belive it."

"No, nobody could," said Isabel, musingly; and she added, after a pause, "I wish you would tell me just what you thought of me, dearest. Did you feel as you did when our little affair was broken off, long ago? Did you hate me?"

"I did, most cordially; but not half so much as I despised myself the next moment. As to its being like a lover's quarrel, it wasn't. It was more bitter; so much more love than lovers ever give had to be taken back. Besides, it had no dignity, and a lover's quarrel always has. A lover's quarrel always springs from a more serious cause, and has an air of romantic tragedy. This had no grace of the kind. It was a poor, shabby little squabble."

"Oh, don't call it so, Basil! I should like you to respect even a quarrel of ours more than that. It was tragical enough with me, for I didn't see how it could ever be made up. I knew *I* couldn't make the advances. I don't think it is quite feminine to be the first to forgive, is it?"

"I'm sure I can't say. Perhaps it *would* be rather unladylike."

"Well, you see, dearest, what I am trying to get at is this: whether we shall love each other the more or the less for it. *I* think we shall get on all the better, for a while, on account of it. But I should have said it was totally out of character. It's something you might have expected of a very young bridal couple; but after what we've been through, it seems too improbable."

"Very well," said Basil, who, having made all the concessions, could not enjoy the quarrel as she did, simply because it was theirs; "let's behave as if it had never happened."

"Oh no; we can't. To me, it's as if we had just won each other."

THE NEAT PERSON

JOSH BILLINGS

Neatness, in my opinyun iz one ov the virtews. I hav alwus konsidered it twin sister to chastity. But while I almost worship neatness in folks, i hav seen them who did understand the bizzness so well az tew acktually make it fearful tew behold. I hav seen neatness that want satisfied in being a common-sized virtew, but had bekum an ungovernable pashun, enslaving its possesser, and making everyboddy un eazy who kum in kontackt with it.

When a person finds it necessary to skour the nail heds in the cellar stairs evry day, and skrub oph the ducks' feet in hot water, it iz then that neatness haz bekum the tyrant of its viktim.

I hav seen individuals who wouldn't let a tired fly light on the wall paper ov their spare room enny quicker than they would let a dog mix up the bread for them, and who would hunt a single cockroach up stairs and down until his leggs were wore oph clear up to his stummuk but what they would hav him. I kan't blame them for being a little lively with the cockroach, for i don't like cockroaches miself—espeshily in mi soup.

Thare iz no persons in the world who work so hard and so eternally az the vicktims ov extatick neatness; but they don't seem tew do mutch after all, for they don't get a thing fairly cleaned to their mind before the other end ov it gits dirty, and they fall tew skrubbing it awl over agin.

If you should shut one ov these people up in a hogshed, they would keep bizzy skouring all the time, and would clean a hole right thru the side ov the hogshed in less than 3 months.

They will keep a whole house dirty the year round cleaning it, and the only peace the family can hav iz when mother iz either bileing soap or making dip kandles.

They rize before daylight, so az to begin skrubbing early, and go tew bed before dark for fear things will begin tew git dirty. These kind ov excessiv neat folks are not alwus very literary, but they know soft water from hard bi looking at it, and they kan tell what kind ov soap will fetch oph the dirt best. They are sum like a kitchin gardin—very regularly laid out, but not planted yet.

If mi wife waz one ov these kind ov neatnesses, I would love her more than ever, for i do luv the different kind ov neatness; but i think we would keep house by traveling round awl the time, and not stay but one night in a place, and i don't think she would undertake tew skrub up the whole ov the United States ov Amerika.

RAILWAY VOLAPÜK

R. J. BURDETTE

To him who, in the love of nature, holds communion with the railway trains, she speaks in various languages. Sometimes she speaks through the conductor, and says, briefly: "Tix!" or, "Fare!" Sometimes the train butcher interprets for her, and then she talks of books that nobody reads; and fruit that nobody eats; and things that nobody buys. Sometimes, again, the brakeman interprets, and then she voices her thoughts in a weird, mysterious patois, that sounds like something you never heard; and you learn, when it is miles too late, that "Kyordltpnnn! Chair car fp Bdroomfld!" meant, "Carrollton! Change cars for Bradford!" Again, she employs the hackman at the station, and he roars: " 'Bus forrup town! Going ritup! Hack? Kavallack? kavahack? kavahack? 'Bus for Thamerica Nouse! Merchant Sotel! This sway for the Planter Souse!" And still again, the passengers hold converse with you, and one man asks you "Whyn't you going to stop off at Enver?" which you understand to mean, "Why, are you not going to stop off at Denver?" And yet another begins his narrative: "Devtell you 'bout the time," etc., which, by interpretation is: "Did I ever tell you," etc. And so, the way of the traveler is Polyglot.

SIMON SUGGS GETS A "SOFT SNAP" ON HIS DADDY

JOHNSON J. HOOPER

Johnson J. Hooper, prominent among the early Southern humorists, was born in North Carolina in 1815. He early removed to Alabama, studied law, became judge, and in 1861 was Secretary of the Provisional Confederate Congress. He died in 1863.

The shifty Captain Suggs is a miracle of shrewdness. He possesses, in an eminent degree, that tact which enables man to detect the *soft spots* in his fellow, and to assimilate himself to whatever company he may fall in with. Besides, he has a quick, ready wit, which has extricated him from many an unpleasant predicament, and which makes him, whenever he chooses to be so—and that is always—very companionable. In short, nature gave the Captain the precise intellectual outfit most to be desired by a man of his propensities. She sent him into the world a sort of he-Pallas, ready to cope with his kind, from his infancy, in all the arts by which men "*get along*" in the world; if she made him, in respect to his moral conformation, a beast of prey, she did not refine the cruelty by denying him the fangs and the claws.

But it is high time we were beginning to record some of those specimens of the worthy Captain's ingenuity, which entitle him to the epithet "*Shifty.*" We shall therefore relate the earliest characteristic anecdote which we have been able to obtain; and we present it to our readers with assurance that it has come to our knowledge in such a way as to leave upon our mind not "a shadow of doubt" of its perfect genuineness. It will serve, if no other purpose, at least to illustrate the precocious development of Captain Sugg's peculiar talent.

Until Simon entered his seventeenth year, he lived with his father, an old "hard-shell" Baptist preacher; who, though very pious and remarkably austere, was very avaricious. The old man reared his boys—or endeavored to do so—according to the strictist requisitions of the moral law. But he lived, at the time to which we refer, in middle Georgia, which was then newly settled; and Simon, whose wits, from the time he was a "shirt-tail boy," were always too sharp for his father's, contrived to contract all the coarse vices incident to such a region. He stole his mother's roosters to fight them at Bob Smith's grocery, and his father's plough-horses to enter them in "quarter" matches at the same place. He pitched dollars with Bob Smith himself, and could "beat him into doll rags" whenever it came to a measurement. To crown his accomplishments, Simon was tip-top at the game of "old sledge," which was the fashionable game of that era; and was early initiated in the mysteries of "stocking the papers." The vicious habits of Simon were, of course, a sore trouble to his father, Elder Jedediah. He reasoned, he counselled, he remonstrated, and he lashed—but Simon was an incorrigible, irreclaimable devil. One day the simple-minded old man returned rather unexpectedly to the field where he had left Simon, and Ben, and a negro boy named Bill, at work. Ben was still following his plough, but Simon and Bill were in a fence corner very earnestly engaged at "seven up." Of course the game was instantly suspended as soon as they spied the old man sixty or seventy yards off, striding towards them.

It was evidently a "gone case" with Simon and Bill; but our hero determined to make the best of it. Putting the cards into one pocket, he coolly picked up the small coins which constituted the stake, and fobbed them in the other, remarking, "Well, Bill, this game's blocked; we'd as well quit."

"But, Mass Simon," remarked the boy, "half dat money's mine. Ain't you gwine to lemme hab 'em?"

"Oh, never mind the money, Bill; the old man's going to take the bark off both of us—and besides, with the hand I helt when we quit, I should 'a' beat you and won it all, any way."

"Well, but Mass Simon, we nebber finish de game, and de rule—"

"Go to an orful h—l with your rule," said the impatient Simon— "don't you see daddy's right down upon us, with an armful of hickories? I tell you I helt nothin' but trumps, and could 'a' beat the horns off of a billygoat. Don't that satisfy you? Somehow or another you're d——d hard to please!" About this time a thought struck Simon, and in a low tone—for by this time the Reverend Jedediah was close at hand—he continued, "But maybe daddy don't know, *right down sure*, what we've been doin'. Let's try him with a lie—'twon't hurt, no way— let's tell him we've been playin' mumble-peg."

Bill was perforce compelled to submit to this inequitable adjustment of his claim to a share of the stakes; and of course agreed to swear to the game of mumble-peg. All this was settled and a peg driven into the ground, slyly and hurriedly, between Simon's legs as he sat on the ground, just as the old man reached the spot. He carried under his left arm, several neatly trimmed sprouts of formidable length, while in his left hand he held one which he was intently engaged in divesting of its superfluous twigs.

"Soho, youngsters!—*you* in the fence corner, and the *crap* in the grass; what saith the Scriptur', Simon? 'Go to the ant, thou sluggard,' and so forth and so on. What in the round creation of the yeath have you and that nigger been a-doin'?"

Bill shook with fear, but Simon was cool as a cucumber, and answered his father to the effect that they had been wasting a little time in the game of mumble-peg.

"Mumble-peg! mumble-peg!" repeated old Mr. Suggs; "what's that?"

Simon explained the process of *rooting* for the peg; how the operator got upon his knees, keeping his arms stiff by his sides, leaned forward, and extracted the peg with his teeth.

"So you git *upon your knees*, do you, to pull up that nasty little stick? you'd better git upon 'em to ask mercy for your sinful souls and for a dyin' world! But let's see one o' you git it up now."

The first impulse of our hero was to volunteer to gratify the curiosity of his worthy sire; but a glance at the old man's countenance changed his "notion," and he remarked that "Bill was a long ways the best hand." Bill, who did not deem Simon's modesty an omen very favorable to himself, was inclined to reciprocate compliments with his young master; but a gesture of impatience from the old man sent him instantly upon his knees; and, bending forward, he essayed to lay hold with his teeth of the peg, which Simon, just at that moment, very wickedly pushed a half inch further down. Just as the breeches and hide of the boy were stretched to the uttermost, old Mr. Suggs brought down his longest hickory, with both hands, upon the precise spot where the tension was greatest. With a loud yell, Bill plunged forward, upsetting Simon, and rolled in the grass; rubbing the castigated part with fearful energy. Simon, though overthrown, was unhurt; and he was mentally complimenting himself upon the sagacity which had prevented his illustrating the game of mumble-peg for the paternal amusement, when his attention was arrested by the old man's stooping to pick up something—what is it?—a card upon which Simon had been sitting, and which, therefore, had not gone with the rest of the pack into his pocket. The simple Mr. Suggs had only a vague idea of the pasteboard abomination called *cards*; and though he decidedly inclined to the opinion that this was one, he was by no means certain of the fact. Had Simon known this he would certainly have escaped; but he did not. His father, assuming the look of extreme sapiency which is always worn by the interrogator who does not desire or expect to increase his knowledge by his questions, asked:

"What's this, Simon?"

"The Jack-a-dimunts," promptly responded Simon, who gave up all as lost after this *faux pas*.

"What was it doin' down thar, Simon, my sonny?" continued Mr. Suggs, in an ironically affectionate tone of voice.

"I had it under my leg, thar, to make it on Bill, the first time it come trumps," was the ready reply.

"What's trumps?" asked Mr. Suggs, with a view of arriving at the import of the word.

"Nothin' ain't trumps *now*," said Simon, who misapprehended his father's meaning; "but *clubs* was, when you come along and busted up the game."

A part of this answer was Greek to the Reverend Mr. Suggs, but a portion of it was full of meaning. They had, then, most unquestionably, been "throwing" cards, the scoundrels! the "audacious" little hellions!

"To the 'mulberry' with both on ye, in a hurry," said the old man sternly. But the lads were not disposed to be in a "hurry," for "the mulberry" was the scene of all formal punishment administered during work hours in the field. Simon followed his father, however, but made, as he went along, all manner of "faces" at the old man's back; gesticulated as if he were going to strike him between the shoulders with his fists, and kicking at him so as almost to touch his coat-tail with his shoe. In this style they walked on to the mulberry-tree, in whose shade Simon's brother Ben was resting.

It must not be supposed that, during the walk to the place of punishment, Simon's mind was either inactive, or engaged in suggesting the grimaces and contortions wherewith he was pantomimically expressing his irreverent sentiments toward his father. Far from it. The movements of his limbs and features were the mere workings of habit—the self-grinding of the corporeal machine—for which his reasoning half was only remotely responsible. For while Simon's person was thus, on its own account, "making game" of old Jed'diah, his wits, in view of the anticipated flogging, were dashing, springing, bounding, darting about, in hot chase of some expedient suitable to the necessities of the case; much after the manner in which puss—when Betty, armed with the broom, and hotly seeking vengeance for pantry robbed or bed disturbed, has closed upon her the garret doors and windows—attempts all sorts of impossible exits, to come down at last in the corner, with panting side and glaring eye, exhausted and defenseless. Our unfortunate hero could devise nothing by which he could reasonably expect to escape the heavy blows of his father. Having arrived at this conclusion and the "mulberry" about the same time, he stood with a dogged look awaiting the issue.

The old man Suggs made no remark to any one while he was seizing up Bill—a process which, though by no means novel to Simon, seemed to excite in him a sort of painful interest. He watched it closely, as if endeavoring to learn the precise fashion of his father's knot; and when at last Bill was swung up a-tiptoe to a limb, and the whipping commenced, Simon's eye followed every movement of his father's arm; and as each blow descended upon the bare shoulders of his sable friend, his own body writhed and "wriggled" in involuntary sympathy.

"It's the devil—it's hell," said Simon to himself, "to take such a walloppin' as that. Why, the old man looks like he wants to git to the holler, if he could—rot his old picter! It's wuth, at the least, fifty cents—je-e-miny how that hurt!—yes, it's wuth three-quarters of a dollar to take that 'ere lickin'! Wonder if I'm "predestinated," as old Jed'diah says, to git the feller to it? Lord, how daddy blows! I do wish to —— he'd bust-wide open, the durned old deer-face! If 'twa'n't for Ben helpin' him, I b'lieve I'd give the old dog a tussel when it comes to my turn. It couldn't make the thing no wuss, if it didn't make it no better. 'D rot it! what do boys have daddies for, any how? 'Tain't for nuthin' but to beat 'em and work 'em. There's some use in mammies—I kin poke my finger right in the old 'oman's eye, and keep it thar, and if I say it aint thar, she'll say so too. I wish she was here to hold daddy off. If 'twa'n't so fur, I'd holler for her, any how. How she would cling to the old fellow's coat-tail!"

Mr. Jedediah Suggs let down Bill and untied him. Approaching Simon, whose coat was off, "Come, Simon, son," said he, "cross them hands; I'm gwine to correct you."

"It aint no use, daddy," said Simon.

"Why so, Simon?"

"Jist bekase it ain't. I'm gwine to play cards as long as I live. When I go off to myself, I'm gwine to make my livin' by it. So what's the use of beatin' me about it?"

Old Mr. Suggs groaned, as he was wont to do in the pulpit, at this display of Simon's viciousness.

"Simon," said he, "you're a poor ignunt creetur. You don't know nuthin', and you've never bin no whars. If I was to turn you off, you'd starve in a week—"

"I wish you'd try me," said Simon, "and jist see. I'd win more money in a week than you can make in a year. There ain't nobody round here kin make seed corn off o' me at cards. I'm rale smart," he added with great emphasis.

"Simon! Simon! you poor unlettered fool. Don't you know that all card-players, and chicken-fighters and horse-racers go to hell? You cracked-brained creetur you! And don't you know that them that plays cards always loses their money, and—"

"Who win's it all, then, daddy?" asked Simon.

"Shet your mouth, you imperdent, slack-jawed dog. Your daddy's a-tryin' to give you some good advice, and you a-pickin' up his words that way. I knowed a young man once, when I lived in Ogletharp, as went down to Augusty and sold a hundred dollars worth of cotton for his daddy, and some o' them gambollers got him to drinkin', and the *very first* night he was with 'em they got every cent of his money."

"They couldn't get my money in a *week*," said Simon. "Any body can git these here green fellers' money; them's the sort I'm a-gwine to watch for myself. Here's what kin fix the papers jist about as nice as anybody."

"Well, it's no use to argify about the matter," said old Jed'diah; "What saith the Scriptur'! 'He that begetteth a fool, doeth it to his sorrow.' Hence, Simon, you're a poor, misubble fool—so cross your hands!"

You'd jist as well not, daddy; I tell you I'm gwine to follow playin' cards for a livin', and what's the use o' bangin' a feller about it? I'm as smart as any of 'em, and Bob Smith says them Augusty fellers can't make rent off o' me."

The Reverend Mr. Suggs had once in his life gone to Augusta; an extent of travel which in those days was a little unusual. His consideration among his neighbors was considerably increased by the circumstance, as he had all the benefit of the popular inference, that no man could visit the city of Augusta without acquiring a vast superiority over all his untraveled neighbors, in every department of human knowledge. Mr. Suggs, then, very naturally felt ineffably indignant that an individual who had never seen any collection of human habitations larger than a log-house village—an individual, in short, no other or better than Bob Smith—should venture to express an opinion concerning the manners, customs, or anything else appertaining to, or in any wise connected with, the *ultima Thule* of backwoods Georgians.

There were two propositions which witnessed their own truth to the mind of Mr. Suggs—the one was, that a man who had never been at Augusta could not know any thing about that city, or any place, or any thing else; the other, that one who *had* been there must, of necessity, not only be well informed as to all things connected with the city itself, but perfectly *au fait* upon all subjects whatsoever. It was, therefore, in a tone of mingled indignation and contempt that he replied to the last remark of Simon.

"*Bob Smith* says, does he? And who's *Bob Smith*? Much does *Bob Smith* know about Augusty! he's *been thar*, I reckon! Slipped off yerly some mornin', when nobody warn't noticin', and got back afore night! It's *only* a hundred and fifty mile. Oh, yes, *Bob Smith* knows *all* about it! *I* don't know nothin' about it! *I* a'n't never been to Augusty—I couldn't find the road thar, I reckon—ha! ha! *Bob—Smi-th!* The eternal stink! if he was only to see one o' them fine gentlemen in Augusty, with his fine broad-cloth, and bell-crown hat, and shoe-boots a-shinin' like silver, he'd take to the woods and kill himself a-runnin'. Bob Smith! that's whar all your devilment comes from, Simon."

"Bob Smith's as good as anybody else, I judge; and a heap smarter than some. He showed me how to cut Jack," continued Simon, "and that's more nor some people can do, if they *have* been to Augusty."

"If Bob Smith kin do it," said the old man, "I kin, too. I don't know it by that name; but if it's book knowledge or plain sense, and Bob kin do it, it's reasonable to s'pose that old Jed'diah Suggs won't be bothered *bad*. Is it any ways similyar to the rule of three, Simon?"

"Pretty much, daddy, but not adzactly," said Simon, drawing a pack from his pocket, to explain. "Now daddy," he proceeded, "you see these here four cards is what we calls the Jacks. Well, now the idee is, if you'll take the pack and mix 'em all up together, I'll take off a passel from top, and the bottom one of them I take off will be one of the Jacks."

"Me to mix 'em fust?" said old Jed'diah.

"Yes."

"And you not to see but the back of the top one, when you go to 'cut,' as you call it?"

"Jist so, daddy."

"And the backs all jist as like as can be?" said the senior Suggs, examining the cards.

"More alike nor cow-peas," said Simon.

"It can't be done, Simon," observed the old man, with great solemnity.

"Bob Smith kin do it, and so kin I."

"It's agin nater, Simon; thar a'n't a man in Augusty, nor on top of the yeath that kin do it!"

"Daddy," said our hero, "ef you'll bet me—"

"What!" thundered old Mr. Suggs. "*Bet*, did you say?" and he came down with a *scorer* across Simon's shoulders—"me, Jed'diah Suggs, that's been in the Lord's sarvice these twenty years—*me* bet, you nasty, sassy, triflin' ugly—"

"I didn't go to say *that*, daddy; that warn't what I meant adzactly. I went to say that ef you'd let me off from this here maulin' you owe me, and *give me* 'Bunch,' ef I cut Jack, I'd *give you* all this here silver, ef I didn't—that's all. To be sure, I allers knowed *you* wouldn't *bet*."

Old Mr. Suggs ascertained the exact amount of the silver which his son handed him, in an old leathern pouch, for inspection. He also, mentally, compared that sum with an imaginary one, the supposed value of a certain Indian pony, called "Bunch," which he had bought for his "old woman's" Sunday riding, and which had sent the old lady into a fence corner, the first and only time she ever mounted him. As he weighed the pouch of silver in his hand, Mr. Suggs also endeavored to analyze the character of the transaction proposed by Simon. "It sartinly *can't* be nothin' but *givin'*, no way it kin be twisted," he murmured to himself. "I *know* he can't do it, so there's no resk. What makes bettin'? The resk. It's a one-sided business, and I'll jist let him give me all his money, and that'll put all his wild sportin' notions out of his head."

"Will you stand it, daddy?" asked Simon, by way of waking the old man up. "You mought as well, for the whippin' won't do you no good, and as for Bunch, nobody about the plantation won't ride him but me."

"Simon," replied the old man, "I agree to it. Your old daddy is in a close place about payin' for his land; and this here money—it's jist eleven dollars, lacking of twenty-five cents—will help out mightily. But mind, Simon, ef anything's said about this, herearter, remember, you *give* me the money."

"Very well, daddy; and ef the thing works up instid o' down, I s'pose we'll say you give *me* Bunch—eh?"

"You won't never be troubled to tell how you come by Bunch; the thing's agin nater, and can't be done. What old Jed'diah Suggs knows, he knows as good as anybody. Give me them fixments, Simon."

Our hero handed the cards to his father, who, dropping the plough-line with which he had intended to tie Simon's hands, turned his back to that individual, in order to prevent his witnessing the operation of *mixing.* He then sat down, and very leisurely commenced shuffling the cards, making, however, an exceedingly awkward job of it. Restive *kings* and *queens* jumped from his hands, or obstinately refused to slide into the company of the rest of the pack. Occasionally a sprightly *knave* would insist on *facing* his neighbor; or, pressing his edge against another's, half double himself up, and then skip away. But Elder Jed'diah perseveringly continued his attempts to subdue the refractory, while heavy drops burst from his forehead, and ran down his cheeks. All of a sudden an idea, quick and penetrating as a rifle-ball, seemed to have entered the cranium of the old man. He chuckled audibly. The devil had suggested to Mr. Suggs an *impromptu* "stock," which would place the chances of Simon, already sufficiently slim, in the old man's opinion, without the range of possibility. Mr. Suggs forthwith proceeded to cull out all the *picter ones*, so as to be certain to include the *Jacks*, and place them at the bottom, with the evident intention of keeping Simon's fingers above these when he should cut. Our hero, who was quietly looking over his father's shoulders all the time, did not seem alarmed by this disposition of the cards; on the contrary, he smiled as if he felt perfectly confident of success, in spite of it.

"Now, daddy," said Simon, when his father had announced himself ready, "narry one of us ain't got to look at the cards while I'm a cuttin'; if we do it'll spile the conjuration."

"Very well."

"And another thing—you've got to look me right dead in the eye, daddy—will you?"

"To be sure—to be sure," said Mr. Suggs; "fire away!"

Simon walked up close to his father, and placed his hand on the pack. Old Mr. Suggs looked in Simon's eye, and Simon returned the look for about three seconds, during which a close observer might have detected a suspicious working of the wrist of the hand on the cards, but the elder Suggs did not remark it.

"Wake, snakes! day's a-breakin'! Rise, Jack!" said Simon, cutting half a dozen cards from the top of the pack, and presenting the face of the bottom one for the inspection of his father.

It was the Jack of hearts.

Old Mr. Suggs staggered back several steps with uplifted eyes and hands!

"Marciful master!" he exclaimed, "ef the boy hain't—well, how in the round creation of the—! Ben, did you ever? to be sure and sartin, Satan has power on this yeath!" and Mr. Suggs groaned in very bitterness.

"You never seed nothin' like that in *Augusty*, did ye, daddy?" asked Simon, with a malicious wink at Ben.

"Simon, how *did* you do it?" queried the old man, without noticing his son's question.

"Do it, daddy? Do it? 'Tain't nothin'. I done it jist as easy as— shootin'."

Whether this explanation was entirely, or in any degree, satisfactory to the perplexed mind of Elder Jed'diah Suggs, cannot, after the lapse of time which has intervened, be sufficiently ascertained. It is certain, however, that he pressed the investigation no farther, but merely requested his son Benjamin to witness the fact, that in consideration of his love and affection for his son Simon, and in order to furnish the donee with the means of leaving that portion of the State of Georgia, he bestowed upon him the impracticable pony, "Bunch."

"Jist so, daddy; jist so; I'll witness that. But it 'minds me mightily of the way mammy *give* old Trailler the side of bacon, last week. She a-sweepin' up the hath; the meat on the table— old Trailler jumps up, gethers the bacon and darts! mammy arter him with the broom-stick, as fur as the door—but seein' the dog has got the start, she shakes the stick at him and hollers, 'You sassy, aig-sukkin', roguish, gnatty, flop-eared varmint! take it along! I only wish 'twas full of a'snic, and ox-vomit, and blue vitrul, so as 'twould cut your interls into chitlins!' That's about the way you give Bunch to Simon."

"Oh, shuh! Ben," remarked Simon, "I wouldn't run on that way; daddy couldn't help it, it was *predestinated*—'whom he hath, he will,' you know;" and the rascal pulled down the under lid of his left eye at his brother. Then addressing his father, he asked, "Warn't it, daddy?"

"To be sure—to be sure—all fixed aforehand," was old Mr. Suggs's reply.

"Didn't I tell you so, Ben?" said Simon—"I knowed it was all fixed aforehand;" and he laughed until he was purple in the face.

"What's in ye? What are ye laughin' about?" asked the old man wrothily.

"Oh, it's so funny that it could all a' been *fixed aforehand!*" said Simon, and laughed louder than before.

The obtusity of the Reverend Mr. Suggs, however, prevented his making any discoveries. He fell into a brown study, and no further allusion was made to the matter.

FOUND

JOSH BILLINGS

A Malteese soprano kat, about 12 months old, singing old hundred on a picket fence, late last thursda nite, whichever person owns sed kat will find him (or her, according to circumstansis) in a vakant lot, just bak ov our hous, still butiful in death.

COLONEL SELLERS AT HOME

MARK TWAIN

Washington was greatly pleased with the Sellers mansion. It was a two-story-and-a-half brick, and much more stylish than any of its neighbors. He was borne to the family sitting-room in triumph by the swarm of little Sellerses, the parents following with their arms about each other's waists.

The whole family were poorly and cheaply dressed; and the clothing, although neat and clean, showed many evidences of having seen long service. The Colonel's "stovepipe" hat was napless, and shiny with much polishing, but nevertheless it had an almost convincing expression about it of having been just purchased new. The rest of his clothing was napless and shiny, too; but it had the air of being entirely satisfied with itself, and blandly sorry for other people's clothes. It was growing rather dark in the house, and the evening air was chilly, too. Sellers said:

"Lay off your overcoat, Washington, and draw up to the stove and make yourself at home—just consider yourself under your own shingles, my boy—I'll have a fire going in a jiffy. Light the lamp, Polly, dear, and let's have things cheerful—just as glad to see you, Washington, as if you'd been lost a century and we'd found you again!"

By this time the Colonel was conveying a lighted match into a poor little stove. Then he propped the stove door to its place by leaning the poker against it, for the hinges had retired from business. This door framed a small square of isinglass, which now warmed up with a faint glow. Mrs. Sellers lit a cheap, showy lamp, which dissipated a good deal of the gloom, and then everybody gathered into the light and took the stove into close companionship.

The children climbed all over Sellers, fondled him, petted him, and were lavishly petted in return. Out from this tugging, laughing, chattering disguise of legs and arms and little faces, the Colonel's voice worked its way, and his tireless tongue ran blithely on without interruption; and the purring little wife, diligent with her knitting, sat near at hand, and looked happy and proud and grateful; and she listened as one who listens to oracles and gospels, and whose grateful soul is being refreshed with the bread of life. By and by the children quieted down to listen: clustered about their father, and resting their elbows on his legs, they hung upon his words as if he were uttering the music of the spheres.

A dreary old hair-cloth sofa against the wall; a few damaged chairs; the small table the lamp stood on; the crippled stove—these things constituted the furniture of the room. There was no carpet on the floor; on the wall were occasionally square-shaped interruptions of the general tint of the plaster, which betrayed that there used to be pictures in the house—but there were none now. There were no mantel ornaments—unless one might bring himself to regard as an ornament a clock which never came within fifteen strokes of striking the right time, and whose hands always hitched together at twenty-two minutes past anything, and traveled in company the rest of the way home.

"Remarkable clock!" said Sellers, and got up and wound it. "I've been offered—well, I wouldn't expect you to believe what I've been offered for that clock. Old Governor Hager never sees me but he says,

'Come, now, Colonel, name your price—I *must* have that clock!' But, my goodness! I'd as soon think of selling my wife! As I was saying to— silence in the court, now, she's begun to strike! You can't talk against her—you have to just be patient and hold up till she's said her say. Ah—well, as I was saying, when—she's beginning again! Nineteen, twenty, twenty-one, twenty-two, twen—ah, that's all. Yes, as I was saying to old Judge ——, go it, old girl, don't mind me. Now, how is that?—isn't that a good, spirited tone? She can wake the dead! Sleep? Why, you might as well try to sleep in a thunder factory. Now just listen at that. She'll strike a hundred and fifty now without stopping— you'll see. There ain't another clock like that in Christendom."

Washington hoped that this might be true, for the din was distracting—though the family, one and all, seemed filled with joy; and the more the clock "buckled down to her work," as the Colonel expressed it, and the more insupportable the clatter became, the more enchanted they all appeared to be. When there was silence, Mrs. Sellers lifted upon Washington a face that beamed with a childlike pride, and said:

"It belonged to his grandmother."

The look and the tone were a plain call for admiring surprise, and, therefore, Washington said (it was the only thing that offered itself at the moment):

"Indeed!"

"Yes, it did; didn't it, father?" exclaimed one of the twins. "She was my great-grandmother—and George's, too; wasn't she, father? *You* never saw her, but Sis has seen her, when Sis was a baby—didn't you, Sis? Sis has seen her most a hundred times. She was awful deef—she's dead, now. Ain't she father?"

All the children chimed in now, with one general Babel of information about deceased—nobody offering to read the riot act, or seeming to discountenance the insurrection, or disapprove of it in any way— but the head twin drowned all the turmoil, and held his own against the field.

"It's our clock, now—and it's got wheels inside of it, and a thing that flutters every time she strikes—don't it, father! Great-grandmother died before hardly any of us was born—she was an Old-School Baptist, and had warts all over her—you ask father if she didn't. She had an uncle once that was bald-headed and used to have fits; he wasn't *our* uncle; I don't know what he was to us—some kin or another, I reckon—father seen him a thousand times—hain't you, father! We used to have a calf that et apples, and just chawed up dish-rags like nothing; and if you stay here you'll see lots of funerals—won't he, Sis? Did you ever see a house afire? *I* have! Once me and Jim Terry—"

But Sellers began to speak now, and the storm ceased. He began to tell about an enormous speculation he was thinking of embarking some capital in—a speculation which some London bankers had been over to consult with him about—and soon he was building glittering pyramids of coin, and Washington was presently growing opulent under the magic of his eloquence. But at the same time Washington was not able to ignore the cold entirely. He was nearly as close to the stove as he could get, and yet he could not persuade himself that he felt the slightest heat, notwithstanding the isinglass door was still gently and serenely glowing. He tried to get a trifle closer to the stove, and the consequence was, he tripped the supporting poker, and the stove-door tumbled to the floor. And then there was a revelation—there was nothing in the stove but a lighted tallow candle.

The poor youth blushed, and felt as if he must die with shame. But the Colonel was only disconcerted for a moment—he straightway found his voice again:

"A little idea of my own, Washington—one of the greatest things in the world! You msut write and tell your father about it—don't forget that, now! I have been reading up some European Scientific reports—friend of mine, Count Fugier, sent them to me—sends me all sorts of things from Paris—he thinks the world of me, Fugier does. Well, I saw that the Academy of France had been testing the properties of heat, and they came to the conclusion that it was a non-conductor, or something like that, and of course its influence must necessarily be deadly in nervous organizations with excitable temperaments, especially where there is any tendency toward rheumatic affections. Bless you, I saw in a moment what was the matter with us, and says I, out goes your fires!—no more slow torture and certain death for me, sir. What you want is the *appearance* of heat, not the heat itself—that's the idea. Well, how to do it was the next thing. I just put my head to work, pegged away a couple of days, and here you are! Rheumatism? Why, a man can't any more start a case of rheumatism in this house than he can shake an opinion out of a mummy! Stove with a candle in it, and a transparent door—that's it—it has been the salvation of this family.

Don't you fail to write your father about it, Washington. And tell him the idea is mine—I'm no more conceited than most people, I reckon, but you know it is human nature for a man to want credit for a thing like that."

Washington said with his blue lips that he would, but he said in his secret heart that he would promote no such iniquity. He tried to believe in the healthfulness of the invention, and succeeded tolerably well; but, after all, he could not feel that good health in a frozen body was any real improvement on the rheumatism.

The supper at Colonel Sellers's was not sumptuous, in the beginning, but it improved on acquaintance. That is to say, that what Washington regarded at first sight as mere lowly potatoes, presently became awe-inspiring agricultural productions that had been reared in some ducal garden beyond the sea, under the sacred eye of the duke himself, who had sent them to Sellers; the bread was from corn which could be grown in only one favored locality in the earth, and only a favored few could get it; the Rio coffee, which at first seemed execrable to the taste, took to itself an improved flavor when Washington was told to drink it slowly and not hurry what should be a lingering luxury in order to be fully appreciated—it was from the private stores of a Brazilian nobleman with an unrememberable name. The Colonel's tongue was a magician's wand that turned dried apples into figs and water into wine as easily as it could change a hovel into a palace and present poverty into imminent future riches.

Washington slept in a cold bed in a carpetless room, and woke up in a palace in the morning; at least the palace lingered during the moment that he was rubbing his eyes and getting his bearings—and then it disappeared, and he recognized that the Colonel's inspiring talk had been influencing his dreams. Fatigue had made him sleep late; when he entered the sitting-room he noticed that the old hair-cloth sofa was absent; when he sat down to breakfast the Colonel tossed six or seven dollars in bills on the table, counted them over, said he was a little short, and must call upon his banker; then returned the bills to his wallet with the indifferent air of a man who is used to money. The breakfast was not an improvement upon the supper, but the Colonel talked it up and transformed it into an Oriental feast. Bye and bye, he said:

"I intend to look out for you, Washington, my boy. I hunted up a place for you yesterday, but I am not referring to that, now—that is a

mere livelihood—mere bread and butter; but when I say I mean to
look out for you, I mean something very different. I mean to put things
in your way that will make a mere livelihood a trifling thing. I'll put
you in a way to make more money than you'll ever know what to do
with. You'll be right here where I can put my hand on you when anything turns up. I've got some prodigious operations on foot; but I'm
keeping quiet; mum's the word; your old hand don't go around pow-
wowing and letting everybody see his k'yards and find out his little
game. But all in good time, Washington, all in good time! You'll see!
Now, there's an operation in corn that looks well. Some New York men
are trying to get me to go into it—buy up all the growing crops, and
just boss the market when they mature—ah, I tell you it's a great thing.
And it only costs a trifle; two millions or two and a half will do it. I
haven't exactly promised yet—there's no hurry—the more indifferent
I seem, you know, the more anxious those fellows will get. And then
there is the hog speculation—that's bigger still. We've got quiet men at
work" [He was very impressive here.] "mousing around, to get propositions out of all the farmers in the whole West and Northwest for the
hog crop, and other agents quietly getting propositions and terms out
of all the manufactories—and don't you see, if we can get all the hogs
and all the slaughter-houses into our hands on the dead quiet—whew!
it would take three ships to carry the money. I've looked into the
thing—calculated all the chances for and all the chances against, and
though I shake my head, and hesitate, and keep on thinking, apparently, I've got my mind made up that if the thing can be done on a capital of six millions, that's the horse to put up money on! Why,
Washington—but what's the use of talking about it? any man can see
that there's whole Atlantic oceans of cash in it, gulfs and bays thrown
in. But there's a bigger thing than that, yet—a bigger—"

"Why Colonel, you can't want anything bigger!" said Washington,
his eyes blazing. "Oh, I wish I could go into either of those speculations—I only wish I had money—I wish I wasn't cramped and kept
down and fettered with poverty, and such prodigious chances lying
right here in sight! Oh, it is a fearful thing to be poor. But don't throw
away those things—they are so splendid, and I can see how sure they
are. Don't throw them away for something still better, and maybe fail
in it! I wouldn't, Colonel. I would stick to these. I wish father were
here, and were his old self again—Oh, he never in his life had such

chances as these are. Colonel, you *can't* improve on these—no man can improve on them!"

A sweet, compassionate smile played about the Colonel's features, and he leaned over the table with the air of a man who is "going to show you," and do it without the least trouble:

"Why, Washington, my boy, these things are nothing. They *look* large—of course they look large to a novice, but to a man who has been all his life accustomed to large operations—shaw! They're well enough to while away an idle hour with, or furnish a bit of employ-ment that will give a trifle of idle capital a chance to earn its bread while it is waiting for something to *do*, but—now just listen a mo-ment—just let me give you an idea of what we old veterans of com-merce call 'business.' Here's the Rothschilds' proposition—this is between you and me, you understand—"

Washington nodded three or four times impatiently, and his glow-ing eyes said, "Yes, yes—hurry—I understand—"

"—for I wouldn't have it get out for a fortune. They want me to go in with them on the sly—agent was here two weeks ago about it—go in on the sly" [Voice down to an impressive whisper, now.] "and buy up a hundred and thirteen wild-cat banks in Ohio, Indiana, Ken-tucky, Illinois and Missouri—notes of these banks are at all sorts of discount now—average discount of the hundred and thirteen is forty-four per cent—buy them all up, you see, and then all of a sudden let the cat out of the bag! Whiz! the stock of every one of those wild-cats would spin up to a tremendous premium before you could turn a handspring—profit on the speculation not a dollar less than forty mil-lions!" [An eloquent pause, while the marvelous vision settled into W.'s focus.] "Where's your hogs now! Why, my dear innocent boy, we would just sit down on the front door-steps and peddle banks like lucifer matches!"

Washington finally got his breath and said:

"Oh, it is perfectly wonderful! Why couldn't these things have hap-pened in father's day? And I—it's of no use; they simply lie before my face and mock me. There is nothing for me but to stand helpless and see other people reap the astonishing harvest."

"Never mind, Washington, don't you worry. I'll fix you. There's plenty of chances. How much money have you got?"

In the presence of so many millions, Washington could not keep from blushing when he had to confess that he had but eighteen dollars in the world.

"Well, all right—don't despair. Other people have been obliged to begin with less. I have a small idea that may develop into something for us both, all in good time. Keep your money close and add to it. I'll make it breed. I've been experimenting (to pass away the time) on a little preparation for curing sore eyes—a kind of decoction nine-tenths water and the other tenth drugs that don't cost more than a dollar a barrel; I'm still experimenting: there's one ingredient wanted yet to perfect the thing, and somehow I can't just manage to hit upon the thing that's necessary, and I don't dare talk with a chemist, of course. But I'm progressing, and before many weeks I wager the country will ring with the fame of Beriah Sellers' Infallible Imperial Oriental Optic Liniment and Salvation for Sore Eyes—the Medical Wonder of the Age! Small bottles fifty cents, large ones a dollar. Average cost, five and seven cents for the two sizes. The first year sell, say, ten thousand bottles in Missouri, seven thousand in Iowa, three thousand in Arkansas, four thousand in Kentucky, six thousand in Illinois, and say twenty-five thousand in the rest of the country. Total, fifty-five thousand bottles; profit clear of all expenses, twenty thousand dollars at the very lowest calculation. All the capital needed is to manufacture the first two thousand bottles—say a hundred and fifty dollars—then the money would begin to flow in. The second year, sales would reach 200,000 bottles— clear profit, say, $75,000—and in the mean time the great factory would be building in St. Louis, to cost, say, $100,000. The third year we could easily sell 1,000,000 bottles in the United States and—"

"O, splendid!" said Washington. "Let's commence right away— let's—"

"—1,000,000 bottles in the United States—profit at least $350,000—and *then* it would begin to be time to turn our attention toward the *real* idea of the business."

"The *real* idea of it! Ain't $350,000 a year a pretty real—"

"Stuff! Why, what an infant you are, Washington—what a guileless, short sighted, easily contented innocent you are, my poor little country-bred know-nothing! Would I go to all that trouble and bother for the poor crumbs a body might pick up in *this* country? Now, do I look like a man who—does my history suggest that I am a man who deals in trifles, contents himself with the narrow horizon that hems in the common herd, sees no further than the end of his nose? Now *you* know that that is not me—couldn't *be* me. *You* ought to know that if I throw my time and abilities into a patent medicine, it's a patent medicine whose field of operations is the solid earth! its clients the swarming nations that inhabit it! Why, what is the Republic of America for an eyewater country? Lord bless you, it is nothing but a barren highway, that you've got to cross to get *to* the true eyewater market! Why, Washington, in the Oriental countries people swarm like the sands of the desert; every square mile of ground upholds its thousands of struggling human creatures—and every separate and individual devil of them's got the ophthalmia! It's as natural to them as noses are—and sin. It's born with them, it stays with them, it's all that some of them have left when they die. Three years of introductory trade in the Orient, and what will be the result? Why, our headquarters would be in Constantinople and our hindquarters in Farther India! Factories and warehouses in Cairo, Ispahan, Bagdad, Damascus, Jerusalem, Yedo, Peking, Bangkok, Delhi, Bombay and Calcutta! Annual income—well, God only knows how many millions and millions apiece!"

Washington was so dazed, so bewildered—his heart and his eyes had wandered so far away among the strange lands beyond the seas, and such avalanches of coin and currency had fluttered and jingled confusedly down before him, that he was now as one who has been whirling round and round for a time, and, stopping all at once, finds his surroundings still whirling and all objects a dancing chaos. However, little by little the Sellers family cooled down and crystallized into shape, and the poor room lost its glitter and resumed its poverty. Then the youth found his voice, and begged Sellers to drop everything and hurry up the eyewater; and he got his eighteen dollars and tried to force it upon the Colonel—pleaded with him to take it—implored him to do it. But the Colonel would not; said he would not need the capital (in his native magnificent way he called that eighteen dollars Capital) till the eyewater was an accomplished fact. He made Washington easy in his mind, though, by promising that he would call for it just as soon as the invention was finished; and he added the glad tidings that nobody but just they two should be admitted to a share in the speculation.

When Washington left the breakfast-table he could have worshiped that man. Washington was one of that kind of people whose hopes are in the very clouds one day and in the gutter the next. He walked on air now. The Colonel was ready to take him around and introduce him to the employment he had found for him, but Washington begged for a few moments in which to write home: with his kind of people, to ride to-day's new interest to death and put off yesterday's till another time, is nature itself. He ran up-stairs and wrote glowingly, enthusiastically, to his mother about the hogs and the corn, the banks and the eye-water—and added a few inconsequential millions to each project. And he said that people little dreamed what a man Colonel Sellers was, and that the world would open its eyes when it found out. And he closed his letter thus:

"So make yourself perfectly easy, mother—in a little while you shall have everything you want, and more. I am not likely to stint *you* in any-thing, I fancy. This money will not be for me alone, but for all of us. I want all to share alike; and there is going to be far more for each than one person can spend. Break it to father cautiously—you understand the need of that—break it to him cautiously, for he has had such cruel hard fortune, and is so stricken by it, that great good news might pros-trate him more surely than even bad, for he is used to the bad but is grown sadly unaccustomed to the other. Tell Laura—tell all the chil-dren. And write to Clay about it, if he is not with you yet. You may tell Clay that whatever I get he can freely share in—freely. He knows that that is true—there will be no need that I should swear to that to make him believe it. Good-bye—and mind what I say: Rest perfectly easy, one and all of you, for our troubles are nearly at an end."

Poor lad! he could not know that his mother would cry some loving, compassionate tears over his letter, and put off the family with a syn-opsis of its contents which conveyed a deal of love to them but not much idea of his prospects or projects. And he never dreamed that such a joyful letter could sadden her and fill her night with sighs, and troubled thoughts, and bodings of the future, instead of filling it with peace and blessing it with restful sleep.

When the letter was done, Washington and the Colonel sallied forth, and as they walked along, Washington learned what he was to be. He was to be a clerk in a real estate office. Instantly, the fickle youth's dreams forsook the magic eyewater and flew back to the Tennessee Land. And the gorgeous possibilities of that great domain straightway began to occupy his imagination to such a degree that he could scarcely manage to keep even enough of his attention upon the Colonel's talk to retain the general run of what he was saying. He was glad it was a real estate office—he was a made man now, sure.

The Colonel said that General Boswell was a rich man, and had a good and growing business; and that Washington's work would be light, and he would get forty dollars a month, and be boarded and lodged in the General's family—which was as good as ten dollars more; and even better, for he could not live as well even at the "City Hotel" as he would there, and yet the hotel charged fifteen dollars a month where a man had a good room.

General Boswell was in his office; a comfortable looking place, with plenty of outline-maps hanging about the walls and in the windows, and a spectacled man was marking out another one on a long table. The office was in the principal street. The General received Washington with a kindly but reserved politeness. Washington rather liked his looks. He was about fifty years old, dignified, well preserved and well dressed. After the Colonel took his leave, the General talked a while with Washington—his talk consisting chiefly of instructions about the clerical duties of the place. He seemed satisfied as to Washington's ability to take care of the books, he was evidently a pretty fair theoretical book-keeper, and experience would soon harden theory into practice. By and by dinner-time came, and the two walked to the General's house; and now Washington noticed an instinct in himself that moved him to keep not in the General's rear, exactly, but yet not at his side—somehow the old gentleman's dignity and reserve did not inspire familiarity.

Two months had gone by, and the Hawkins family were domiciled in Hawkeye. Washington was at work in the real estate office again, and was alternately in paradise or the other place, just as it happened that Louise was gracious to him or seemingly indifferent—because indifference or preoccupation could mean nothing else than that she was thinking of some other young person. Col. Sellers had asked him, several times, to dine with him, when he first returned to Hawkeye, but Washington, for no particular reason, had not accepted. No particular reason except one which he preferred to keep to himself—viz., that he could not bear to be away from Louise. It occurred to him, now, that the Colonel had not invited him lately—could he be offended? He resolved to go that very day, and give the Colonel a pleasant surprise. It was a good idea; especially as Louise had absented herself from break-fast that morning, and torn his heart; he would tear hers, now, and let her see how it felt.

The Sellers family were just starting to dinner when Washington burst upon them with his surprise. For an instant the Colonel looked nonplussed, and just a bit uncomfortable; and Mrs. Sellers looked ac-tually distressed; but the next moment the head of the house was him-self again, and exclaimed:

"All right, my boy, all right—always glad to see you—always glad to hear your voice and take you by the hand. Don't wait for special invi-tations—that's all nonsense among friends. Just come whenever you can, and come as often as you can—the oftener the better. You can't please us any better than that, Washington; the little woman will tell you so herself. We don't pretend to style. Plain folks, you know—plain folks. Just a plain family dinner, but such as it is, our friends are *always* welcome; I reckon you know that yourself, Washington. Run along, children, run along; Lafayette,* stand off the cat's tail, child; can't you see what you're doing! Come, come, come, Roderick Dhu! it isn't nice for little boys to hang onto young gentlemen's coat-tails—but never mind him, Washington, he's full of spirits, and don't mean any harm. Children will be children, you know. Take the chair next to Mrs. Sell-ers, Washington—tut, tut! Marie Antoinette, let your brother have the fork if he wants it; you are bigger than he is."

Washington contemplated the banquet, and wondered if he were in his right mind. Was this the plain family dinner? And was it all present? It was soon apparent that this was indeed the dinner: it was all on the table; it consisted of abundance of clear, fresh water, and a basin of raw turnips—nothing more.

Washington stole a glance at Mrs. Seller's face, and would have given the world, the next moment, if he could have spared her that.

---

*In those old days the average man called his children after his most revered literary and historical idols; consequently there was hardly a family, at least in the West, but had a Wash-ington in it—and also a Lafayette, a Franklin, and six or eight sounding names from Byron, Scott and the Bible, if the offspring held out. To visit such a family, was to find one's self con-fronted by a congress made up of representatives of the imperial myths and the majestic dead of all the ages. There was something thrilling about it, to a stranger, not to say awe-inspiring.

The poor woman's face was crimson, and the tears stood in her eyes. Washington did not know what to do. He wished he had never come there and spied out this cruel poverty, and brought pain to that poor little lady's heart and shame to her cheek; but he was there, and there was no escape. Colonel Sellers hitched back his coat-sleeves airily from his wrists, as who should say, "*Now* for solid enjoyment!" seized a fork, flourished it, and began to harpoon turnips and deposit them in the plates before him.

"Let me help you, Washington—Lafayette, pass this plate to Washington—ah, well, my boy, things are looking pretty bright, now, *I* tell you. Speculation—my! the whole atmosphere's full of money. I wouldn't take three fortunes for one little operation I've got on hand now—have anything from the casters? No? Well, you're right; you're right. Some people like mustard with turnips, but—now there was Baron Poniatowski—lord! but that man did know how to live!—true Russian, you know, Russian to the back bone; I say to my wife, give me a Russian every time, for a table comrade. The Baron used to say, 'Take mustard, Sellers, try the mustard—a man *can't* know what turnips are in perfection without mustard,' but I always said: 'No, Baron, I'm a plain man, and I want my food plain—none of your embellishments for Beriah Sellers—no made dishes for me! And it's the best way—high living kills more than it cures in this world, you can rest assured of that. Yes, indeed, Washington, I've got one little operation on hand that—take some more water—help yourself, won't you?—help yourself, there's plenty of it—you'll find it pretty good, I guess. How does that fruit strike you?"

Washington said he did not know that he had ever tasted better. He did not add that he detested turnips, even when they were cooked—loathed them in their natural state. No, he kept this to himself, and praised the turnips to the peril of his soul.

"I thought you'd like them. Examine them—examine them—they'll bear it. See how perfectly firm and juicy they are; they can't start any like them in this part of the country, I can tell you. These are from New Jersey—I imported them myself. They cost like sin, too; but lord bless me! I go in for having the best of a thing, even if it does cost a little more—its the best economy, in the long run. These are the Early Malcolm—it's a turnip that can't be produced except in just one orchard, and the supply never is up to the demand. Take some more water,

Washington—you can't drink too much water with fruit—all the doctors say that. The plague can't come where this article is, my boy!"

"Plague? What plague?"

"What plague, indeed! Why, the Asiatic plague that nearly depopulated London a couple of centuries ago!"

"But how does that concern us? There is no plague here, I reckon."

"Sh! I've let it out! Well, never mind—just keep it to yourself. Perhaps I oughtn't said anything, but it's *bound* to come out sooner or later, so what is the odds? Old McDowells wouldn't like me to—to—bother it all, I'll just tell the whole thing and let it go! You see, I've been down to St. Louis, and I happened to run across old Dr. McDowells—thinks the world of me, does the doctor. He's a man that keeps himself to himself, and well he may, for he knows that he's got a reputation that covers the whole earth—he won't condescend to open himself out to many people, but Lord bless you! he and I are just like brothers; he won't let me go to a hotel when I'm in the city—says I'm the only man that's company to him; and I don't know but there's some truth in it, too, because, although I never like to glorify myself and make a great to-do over what I am, or what I can do, or what I know, I don't mind saying, here among friends, that I am better read up in most sciences, maybe, than the general run of professional men in these days. Well, the other day he let me into a little secret, strictly on the quiet, about this matter of the plague.

"You see, it's booming right along in our direction—follows the Gulf Stream, you know, just as all those epidemics do—and within three months it will be just waltzing through this land like a whirlwind! And whoever it touches can make his will and contract for the funeral. Well, you can't *cure* it, you know, but you can prevent it. How? Turnips! that's it! Turnips and water! Nothing like it in the world, old McDowells says; just fill yourself up two or three times a day, and you can snap your fingers at the plague. Sh!—keep mum, but just you confine yourself to that diet and you're all right. I wouldn't have old McDowells know that I told about it for anything—he never would speak to me again. Take some more water, Washington—the more water you drink, the better. Here, let me give you some more of the turnips. No, no, no, now, I insist. There, now. Absorb those. They're mighty sustaining—brim full of nutriment—all the medical books say so. Just eat from four to seven good-sized turnips at a meal, and drink from a pint and a half to a quart of water, and then just sit around a couple of hours and let them ferment. You'll feel like a fighting-cock next day."

Fifteen or twenty minutes later the Colonel's tongue was still chattering away—he had piled up several future fortunes out of several incipient "operations" which he had blundered into within the past week, and was now soaring along through some brilliant expectations born of late promising experiments upon the lacking ingredient of the eyewater. And at such a time Washington ought to have been a rapt and enthusiastic listener, but he was not, for two matters disturbed his mind and distracted his attention. One was, that he discovered, to his confusion and shame, that in allowing himself to be helped a second time to the turnips, he had robbed those hungry children. He had not needed the dreadful "fruit," and had not wanted it; and when he saw the pathetic sorrow in their faces when they asked for more, and there was no more to give them, he hated himself for his stupidity and pitied the famishing young things with all his heart. The other matter that disturbed him was the dire inflation that had begun in his stomach. It grew and grew, it became more and more insupportable. Evidently the turnips were "fermenting." He forced himself to sit still as long as he could, but his anguish conquered him at last.

He rose in the midst of the Colonel's talk, and excused himself on the plea of a previous engagement. The Colonel followed him to the door, promising over and over again that he would use his influence to get some of the Early Malcolms for him, and insisting that he should not be such a stranger, but come and take pot-luck with him every chance he got. Washington was glad enough to get away and feel free again. He immediately bent his steps toward home.

In bed he passed an hour that threatened to turn his hair gray, and then a blessed calm settled down upon him that filled his heart with gratitude. Weak and languid, he made shift to turn himself about and seek rest and sleep; and as his soul hovered upon the brink of unconsciousness, he heaved a long, deep sigh, and said to himself that in his heart he had cursed the Colonel's preventive of rheumatism before, and now *let* the plague come if it must—he was done with preventives; if ever any man beguiled him with turnips and water again, let him die the death.

If he dreamed at all that night, no gossiping spirit disturbed his visions to whisper in his ear of certain matters just then in bud in the East, more than a thousand miles away, that after the lapse of a few years would develop influences which would profoundly effect the fate and fortunes of the Hawkins family.

INTERVIEW WITH PRESIDENT LINCOLN

ARTEMUS WARD

I hav no politics. Nary a one. I'm not in the bisniss. If I was, I spose I should holler versiffrusly in the streets at nite, and go home to Betsy Jane smellen of coal ile and gin in the mornin'. I should go to the Poles arly. I should stay thare all day. I should see to it that my nabers was thare. I should git carriges to take the kripples, the infirm and the indignant thar. I should be on guard agin frauds and sich. I should be on the look-out for the infamus lise of the enemy, got up jest be4 elecshun for perlitical effeck. When all was over and my candydate was elected, I should move heving & erth—so to speak—until I got orfice, which if I didn't git a orfice I should turn round and abooze the Administration with all my mite and maine. But I'm not in the bisniss. I'm in a far more respectful bisniss nor what pollertics is. I wouldn't giv two cents to be a Congresser. The wuss insult I ever received was when sertin citizens of Baldinsville axed me to run fur the Legislater. Sez I, "My frends, dostest think I'd stoop to that there?" They turned as white as a sheet. I spoke in my most orfullest tones, & they knowd I wasn't to be trifled with. They slunked out of site to onct.

   There4, havin' no politics, I made bold to visit Old Abe at his humstid in Springfield. I found the old feller in his parler, surrounded by a perfeck swarm of orfice seekers. Knowin' he had been capting of a flatboat on the roarin' Mississippy, I thought I'd address him in sailor lingo, so I sez, "Old Abe, ahoy! Let out yer main-suls, reef hum the forecastle & throw yer jib-poop overboard! Shiver my timbers, my harty!" [N. B.—This is ginuine mariner langwidge. I know, becawz I've seen sailor plays acted out by them New York theatre fellers.] Old Abe lookt up quite cross & sez: "Send in yer petition by & by. I can't possibly look at it now. Indeed, I can't. It's onpossible, sir!"

   "Mr. Linkin, who do you s'pect I air?" sed I.

   "A orfice-seeker, to be sure!" sed he.

"Wall, sir," sed I, "you's never more mistaken in your life. You hain't gut a orfiss I'd take under no circumstances. I'm A. Ward. Wax figgers is my perfeshun. I'm the father of Twins, and they look like me—*both of them*. I cum to pay a frendly visit to the President eleck of the United States. If so be you wants to see me, say so—if not, say so, & I'm orf like a jug handle."

"Mr. Ward, sit down. I'm glad to see you, Sir."

"Repose in Abraham's Buzzum!" sed one of the orfiss seekers: his idee bein' to git orf a goak at my expense.

"Wall," sez I, "ef all you fellers repose in that there Buzzum, there'll be mity poor nussin for some of you!" whereupon Old Abe buttoned his weskit clear up and blusht like a maidin of sweet 16. Just at this pint of the conversation another swarm of orfice-seekers arove & cum pilin' into the parler. Sum wanted post orfices, sum wanted collector-ships, sum wanted furrin missions, and all wanted sumthin. I thought Old Abe would go crazy. He hadn't more than had time to shake hands with 'em, before another tremenjis crowd cum porein onto his premises. His house and dooryard was now perfeckly overflowed with orfice seekers, all clameruss for a immegit interview with Old Abe.

One man from Ohio, who had about seven inches of corn whisky into him, mistook me for Old Abe and addrest me as "The Prahayrie Flower of the West!" Thinks I, *you* want a offiss putty bad. Another man, with a gold heded cane and a red nose, told Old Abe he was "a seckind Washington & the Pride of the Boundliss West."

Sez I, "Squire, you wouldn't take a small post-offiss if you could git it, would you?"

Sez he, "a patrit is abuv them things, sir!"

"There's a putty big crop of patrits this season, ain't there, Squire?" sez I, when *another* crowd of offiss-seekers poured in. The house, door-yard, barn and woodshed was now all full, and when another crowd cum, I told 'em not to go away for want of room, as the hog-pen was still empty. One patrit from a small town in Michygan went up on top the house, got into the chimney, and slid down into the parler, where Old Abe was en-deverin to keep the hungry pack of orfiss-seekers from chawin' him up alive without benefit of clergy. The minit he reached the fireplace he jumpt up, brusht the soot out of his eyes, and yelled: "Don't make eny pintment at the Spunkville postoffiss till you've read my papers. All the respectful men in our town is signers to that thare dockyment!"

"Good God!" cried Old Abe; "they cum upon me from the skize—down the chimneys, and from the bowels of the yerth!" He hadn't more'n got them words out of his delikit mouth before two fat offiss-seekers from Wisconsin, in endeverin to crawl atween his legs for the purpuss of applyin' for the toll-gateship at Milwawky, upsot the President eleck, & he would hev gone sprawlin' into the fire-place if I hadn't caught him in these arms. But I hadn't more'n stood him up strate before another man cum crashin down the chimney, his head strikin' me vilently agin the inards and prostratin' my voluptoous form onto the floor. "Mr. Linkin," shoutid the fatooated being, "my papers is signed by every clergyman in our town, and likewise the skoolmaster!"

Sez I, "You egrejis ass!" gittin' up & brushin' the dust from my eyes. "I'll sign your papers with this bunch of bones, if you don't be a little more keerful how you make my bread-basket a depot in the futer. How do you like that air perfumery?" sez I, shuving my fist under his nose. "Them's the kind of papers I'll give you! Them's the papers *you* want!"

"But I workt hard for the ticket; I toiled night and day! The patrit should be rewarded!"

"Virtoo," sed I, holdin' the infatooated man by the coat-collar, "virtoo, sir, is its own reward. Look at me!" He did look at me, and qualed be4 my gase. "The fact is," I continued, lookin' round on the hungry crowd, "there is scacely a offiss for every ile lamp carrid round durin' this campane. I wish thare was. I wish thare was furrin' missions to be filled on varis lonely Islands where eppydemics rage incessantly, and if I was in Old Abe's place I'd send every mother's son of you to them. What air you here for?" I continnered, warmin' up considerable; "can't you giv' Abe a minit's peace? Don't you see he's worrid most to death? Go home, you miserable men; go home & till the sile! Go to peddlin' tinware—go to choppin' wood—go to bilin' sope—stuff sassengers—black boots—git a clerkship on sum respectable manure cart—go round as origenal Swiss Bell Ringers—becum 'origenal and only' Campbell Minstrels—go to lecturin' at 50 dollars a nite—imbark in the peanut bizniss—*write for the Ledger*—saw off your legs and go round givin' concerts, with tuchin' appeals to a charitable public printed on your handbills—anything for a honest living, but don't come round here drivin' Old Abe crazy by your outrajis cuttings up! Go home. Stand not upon the order of your goin', but go to onct! Ef in five minits from this time," sez I, pullin' out my new sixteen dollar huntin' cased watch and branishin' it before their eyes, "Ef in five minits from this time a single sole of you remains on these here premises, I'll go out to my cage near by, and let my Boy Constructor loose! & ef he gits among you, you'll think old Solferino has cum again, and no mistake!" You ought to hev seen them scamper, Mr. Fair. They run orf as tho Satun hisself was arter them with a red-hot ten-pronged pitchfork. In five minits the premises was clear.

"How kin I ever repay you, Mr. Ward, for your kindness?" sed Old Abe, advancin' and shakin' me warmly by the hand. "How kin I ever repay you, sir?"

"By givin' the whole country a good, sound administration. By poerin' ile upon the troubled waturs, North and South. By pursooin' a patriotic, firm and just course, and then if any State wants to secede, let 'em Sesesh!"

"How 'bout my Cabinit, Mister Ward?" sed Abe.

"Fill it up with Showmen, sir! Showmen is devoid of politics. They hain't got any principles. They know how to cater for the public. They know what the public wants, North & South. Showmen, sir, is honest men. Ef you doubt their literary ability, look at their posters, and see small bills! Ef you want a Cabinit as is a Cabinit, fill it up with show-men, but don't call on me. The moral wax figger perfeshun mustn't be permitted to go down while there's a drop of blood in these vains! A. Linkin, I wish you well! Ef Powers or Walcutt wus to pick out a model for a beautiful man, I scarcely think they'd sculp you; but ef you do the fair thing by your country you'll make as putty an angel as any of us! A. Linkin, use the talents which Nature has put into you judishusly and firmly, and all will be well! A. Linkin, adoo!"

The Alarmed Skipper

J. T. FIELDS

"It was an Ancient Mariner."

Many a long, long year ago,
Nantucket skippers had a plan

Of finding out, though "lying low,"
How near New York their schooners ran.

They greased the lead before it fell,
And then, by sounding through the night,
Knowing the soil that stuck, so well,
They always guessed their reckoning right.

A skipper gray, whose eyes were dim,
Could tell, by *tasting*, just the spot,
And so below he'd "dowse the glim"—
After, of course, his "something hot."

Snug in his berth, at eight o'clock,
This ancient skipper might be found;
No matter how his craft would rock,
He slept—for skippers' naps are sound!

The watch on deck would now and then
Run down and wake him, with the lead;
He'd up, and taste, and tell the men
How many miles they went ahead.

One night, 't was Jotham Marden's watch.
A curious wag—the peddler's son—
And so he mused (the wanton wretch),
"To-night I'll have a grain of fun.

"We're all a set of stupid fools
To think the skipper knows by *tasting*
What ground he's on—Nantucket schools
Don't teach such stuff, with all their basting!

And so he took the well-greased lead
And rubbed it o'er a box of earth
That stood on deck—a parsnip-bed—
And then he sought the skipper's berth.

"Where are we now, sir? Please to taste."
The skipper yawned, put out his tongue,
Then oped his eyes in wondrous haste,
And then upon the floor he sprung!

The skipper stormed, and tore his hair,
Thrust on his boots, and roared to Marden,

*"Nantucket's sunk, and here we are
Right over old Marm Hackett's garden!"*

How I Killed a Bear

CHARLES DUDLEY WARNER

So many conflicting accounts have appeared about my casual encounter with an Adirondack bear last summer, that in justice to the
public, to myself and to the bear, it is necessary to make a plain statement of the facts. Besides, it is so seldom I have occasion to kill a bear,
that the celebration of the exploit may be excused.

The encounter was unpremeditated on both sides. I was not hunting for a bear, and I have no reason to suppose that a bear was looking
for me. The fact is, that we were both out black-berrying and met by
chance—the usual way. There is among the Adirondack visitors always a great deal of conversation about bears—a general expression of
the wish to see one in the woods, and much speculation as to how a
person would act if he or she chanced to meet one. But bears are
scarce and timid, and appear only to a favored few.

It was a warm day in August, just the sort of a day when an adventure of any kind seemed impossible. But it occurred to the housekeepers at our cottage—there were four of them—to send me to the
clearing, on the mountain back of the house, to pick blackberries. It
was, rather, a series of small clearings, running up into the forest, much
overgrown with bushes and briers, and not unromantic. Cows pastured
there, penetrating through the leafy passages from one opening to another, and browsing among the bushes. I was kindly furnished with a
six-quart pail, and told not to be gone long.

Not from any predatory instinct, but to save appearances, I took a
gun. It adds to the manly aspect of a person with a tin pail if he also
carries a gun. It was possible I might start up a partridge; though how
I was to hit him, if he started up instead of standing still, puzzled me.
Many people use a shot-gun for partridges. I prefer the rifle: it makes
a clean job of death, and does not prematurely stuff the bird with
globules of lead. The rifle was a Sharps, carrying a ball cartridge (ten

to the pound)—an excellent weapon belonging to a friend of mine, who had intended, for a good many years back, to kill a deer with it. He could hit a tree with it—if the wind did not blow, and the atmosphere was just right, and the tree was not too far off—nearly every time. Of course, the tree must have some size. Needless to say that I was at that time no sportsman. Years ago I killed a robin under the most humiliating circumstances. The bird was in a low cherry-tree. I loaded a big shot-gun pretty full, crept up under the tree, rested the gun on the fence, with the muzzle more than ten feet from the bird, shut both eyes and pulled the trigger. When I got up to see what had happened, the robin was scattered about under the tree in more than a thousand pieces, no one of which was big enough to enable a naturalist to decide from it to what species it belonged. This disgusted me with the life of a sportsman. I mention the incident to show, that although I went blackberrying armed, there was not much inequality between me and the bear.

In this blackberry-patch bears had been seen. The summer before, our colored cook, accompanied by a little girl of the vicinage, was picking berries there one day, when a bear came out of the woods and walked towards them. The girl took to her heels, and escaped. Aunt Chloe was paralyzed with terror. Instead of attempting to run, she sat down on the ground where she was standing, and began to weep and scream, giving herself up for lost. The bear was bewildered by this conduct. He approached and looked at her; he walked around and surveyed her. Probably he had never seen a colored person before, and did not know whether she would agree with him: at any rate, after watching her a few moments, he turned about and went into the forest. This is an authentic instance of the delicate consideration of a bear, and is much more remarkable than the forbearance towards the African slave of the well-known lion, because the bear had no thorn in his foot.

When I had climbed the hill, I set up my rifle against a tree, and began picking berries, lured on from bush to bush by the black gleam of fruit (that always promises more in the distance than it realizes when you reach it); penetrating farther and farther, through leaf-shaded cow-paths flecked with sunlight, into clearing after clearing. I could hear on all sides the tinkle of bells, the cracking of sticks, and the stamping of cattle that were taking refuge in the thicket from the flies.

Occasionally, as I broke through a covert, I encountered a meek cow, who stared at me stupidly for a second, and then shambled off into the brush. I became accustomed to this dumb society, and picked on in silence, attributing all the wood-noises to the cattle, thinking nothing of any real bear. In point of fact, however, I was thinking all the time of a nice romantic bear, and, as I picked, was composing a story about a generous she-bear who had lost her cub, and who seized a small girl in this very wood, carried her tenderly off to a cave, and brought her up on bear's milk and honey. When the girl got big enough to run away, moved by her inherited instincts, she escaped, and came into the valley to her father's house (this part of the story was to be worked out, so that the child would know her father by some family resemblance, and have some language in which to address him), and told him where the bear lived. The father took his gun, and, guided by the unfeeling daughter, went into the woods and shot the bear, who never made any resistance, and only, when dying, turned reproachful eyes upon her murderer. The moral of the tale was to be, kindness to animals.

I was in the midst of this tale, when I happened to look some rods away to the other edge of the clearing, and there was a bear! He was standing on his hind-legs, and doing just what I was doing—picking blackberries. With one paw he bent down the bush, while with the other he clawed the berries into his mouth—green ones and all. To say that I was astonished is inside the mark. I suddenly discovered that I didn't want to see a bear, after all. At about the same moment the bear saw me, stopped eating berries, and regarded me with a glad surprise. It is all very well to imagine what you would do under such circumstances. Probably you wouldn't do it: I didn't. The bear dropped down on his fore-feet, and came slowly towards me. Climbing a tree was of no use, with so good a climber in the rear. If I started to run, I had no doubt the bear would give chase; and although a bear cannot run down hill as fast as he can run uphill, yet I felt that he could get over this rough, brush-tangled ground faster that I could.

The bear was approaching. It suddenly occurred to me how I could divert his mind until I could fall back upon my military base. My pail was nearly full of excellent berries—much better than the bear could pick himself. I put the pail on the ground, and slowly backed away from it, keeping my eye, as beast tamers do, on the bear. The ruse succeeded.

The bear came up to the berries, and stopped. Not accustomed to eat out of a pail, he tipped it over, and nosed about in the fruit, "gorming" (if there is such a word) it down, mixed with leaves and dirt, like a pig. The bear is a worse feeder than the pig. Whenever he disturbs a maple-sugar camp in the spring, he always upsets the buckets of syrup, and tramples round in the sticky sweets, wasting more than he eats. The bear's manners are thoroughly disagreeable.

As soon as my enemy's head was down, I started and ran. Somewhat out of breath, and shaky, I reached my faithful rifle. It was not a moment too soon. I heard the bear crashing through the brush after me. Enraged at my duplicity, he was now coming on with blood in his eye. I felt that the time of one of us was probably short. The rapidity of thought at such moments of peril is well known. I thought an octavo volume, had it illustrated and published, sold fifty thousand copies, and went to Europe on the proceeds, while that bear was loping across the clearing. As I was cocking the gun, I made a hasty and unsatisfactory review of my whole life. I noted that, even in such a compulsory review, it is almost impossible to think of any good thing you have done. The sins come out uncommonly strong. I recollected a newspaper subscription I had delayed paying years and years ago, until both editor and newspaper were dead, and which now never could be paid to all eternity.

The bear was coming on.

I tried to remember what I had read about encounters with bears. I couldn't recall an instance in which a man had run away from a bear in the woods and escaped, although I recalled plenty where the bear had run from the man and got off. I tried to think what is the best way to kill a bear with a gun, when you are not near enough to club him with the stock. My first thought was to fire at his head; to plant the ball between his eyes: but this is a dangerous experiment. The bear's brain is very small; and, unless you hit that, the bear does not mind a bullet in his head; that is, not at the time. I remembered that the instant death of the bear would follow a bullet planted just back of his foreleg, and sent into his heart. This spot is also difficult to reach, unless the bear stands off, side towards you, like a target. I finally determined to fire at him generally.

The bear was coming on.

The contest seemed to me very different from anything at Creedmoor. I had carefully read the reports of the shooting there; but it was not easy to apply the experience I had thus acquired. I hesitated whether I had better fire lying on my stomach; or lying on my back, and resting the gun on my toes. But in neither position, I reflected, could I see the bear until he was upon me. The range was too short; and the bear wouldn't wait for me to examine the thermometer, and note the direction of the wind. Trial of the Creedmoor method, therefore, had to be abandoned; and I bitterly regretted that I had not read more accounts of off-hand shooting.

For the bear was coming on.

I tried to fix my last thoughts upon my family. As my family is small, this was not difficult. Dread of displeasing my wife, or hurting her feelings, was uppermost in my mind. What would be her anxiety as hour after hour passed on, and I did not return! What would the rest of the household think as the afternoon passed, and no blackberries came! What would be my wife's mortification when the news was brought that her husband had been eaten by a bear! I cannot imagine anything more ignominious than to have a husband eaten by a bear. And this was not my only anxiety. The mind at such times is not under control. With the gravest fears the most whimsical ideas will occur. I looked beyond the mourning friends, and thought what kind of an epitaph they would be compelled to put upon the stone. Something like this:

HERE LIE THE REMAINS

OF

——— ———

EATEN BY A BEAR

AUG. 20, 1877.

It is a very unheroic and even disagreeable epitaph. That "eaten by a bear" is intolerable. It is grotesque. And then I thought what an inadequate language the English is for compact expression. It would not answer to put upon the stone simply "eaten," for that is indefinite, and requires explanation: it might mean eaten by a cannibal. This difficulty could not occur in the German, where *essen* signifies the act of feeding by a man, and *fressen* by a beast. How simple the thing would be in German!—

HIER LIEGT
HOCHWOHLGEBOREN
HERR —— ——,
GEFRESSEN
AUG. 20, 1877.

That explains itself. The well-born one was eaten by a beast, and presumably by a bear—an animal that has a bad reputation since the days of Elisha.

The bear was coming on; he had, in fact, come on. I judged that he could see the whites of my eyes. All my subsequent reflections were confused. I raised the gun, covered the bear's breast with the sight, and let drive. Then I turned, and ran like a deer. I did not hear the bear pursuing. I looked back. The bear had stopped. He was lying down. I then remembered that the best thing to do after having fired your gun is to reload it. I slipped in a charge, keeping my eyes on the bear. He never stirred. I walked back suspiciously. There was a quiver in the hind-legs, but no other motion. Still, he might be shamming: bears often sham. To make sure, I approached, and put a ball into his head. He didn't mind it now; he minded nothing. Death had come to him with a merciful suddenness. He was calm in death. In order that he might remain so, I blew his brains out, and then started for home. I had killed a bear!

Notwithstanding my excitement, I managed to saunter into the house with an unconcerned air. There was a chorus of voices:

"Where are your blackberries?"

"Why were you gone so long?"

"Where's your pail?"

"I left the pail."

"Left the pail? What for?"

"A bear wanted it."

"Oh, nonsense!"

"Well, the last I saw of it a bear had it."

"Oh, come! You didn't really see a bear?"

"Yes, but I did really see a real bear."

"Did he run?"

"Yes; he ran after me."

"I don't believe a word of it! What did you do?"

"Oh! nothing particular—except kill the bear."

Cries of "Gammon!" "Don't believe it!" Where's the bear?"

"If you want to see the bear, you must go up into the woods. I couldn't bring him down alone."

Having satisfied the household that something extraordinary had occurred, and excited the posthumous fear of some of them for my own safety, I went down into the valley to get help. The great bear-hunter, who keeps one of the summer boarding-houses, received my story with a smile of incredulity; and the incredulity spread to the other inhabitants and to the boarders, as soon as the story was known. However, as I insisted in all soberness, and offered to lead them to the bear, a party of forty or fifty people at last started off with me to bring the bear in. Nobody believed there was any bear in the case; but every-body who could get a gun carried one; and we went into the woods, armed with guns, pistols, pitchforks and sticks, against all contingencies or surprises—a crowd made up mostly of scoffers and jeerers.

But when I led the way to the fatal spot, and pointed out the bear, lying peacefully wrapped in his own skin, something like terror seized the boarders, and genuine excitement the natives. It was a no-mistake bear, by George! and the hero of the fight—well, I will not insist upon that. But what a procession that was, carrying the bear home! and what a congregation was speedily gathered in the valley to see the bear! Our best preacher up there never drew anything like it on Sunday.

And I must say that my particular friends, who were sportsmen, be-haved very well on the whole. They didn't deny that it was a bear, al-though they said it was small for a bear. Mr. Deane, who is equally good with a rifle and a rod, admitted that it was a very fair shot. He is prob-ably the best salmon-fisher in the United States, and he is an equally good hunter. I suppose there is no person in America who is more de-sirous to kill a moose than he. But he needlessly remarked, after he had examined the wound in the bear, that he had seen that kind of a shot made by a cow's horn.

This sort of talk affected me not. When I went to sleep that night, my last delicious thought was, "I've killed a bear!"

A milkman was lately seeking the aid of the police to trace the where-abouts of a family who had left the neighborhood owing him eighteen dollars. "Well, I suppose there was nine dollars' worth of water in that milk account" remarked the policeman. "That's where it galls me—that's where it hurts," replied the dealer. "They were new customers, and I hadn't commenced to water the milk yet!"—*Newspaper*

THE GRASSHOPPER AND THE ANT

G. T. LANIGAN

A frivolous Grasshopper, having spent the Summer in Mirth and Revelry, went, on the Approach of the inclement Winter, to the Ant, and implored it of its charity to stake him. "You had better go to your Uncle," replied the prudent Ant; "had you imitated my Forethought and deposited your Funds in a Savings Bank, you would not now be compelled to regard your Duster in the light of an Ulster." Thus saying, the virtuous Ant retired, and read in the Papers next morning that the Savings Bank where he had deposited his Funds had suspended.

Moral.—Dum Vivimus, Vivamus.

A SLEEPING-CAR EXPERIENCE

BRET HARTE

It was in a Pullman sleeping-car on a Western road. After that first plunge into unconsciousness which the weary traveler takes on getting into his berth, I awakened to the dreadful revelation that I had been asleep only two hours. The greater part of a long winter night was before me to face with staring eyes.

Finding it impossible to sleep, I lay there wondering a number of things: why, for instance, the Pullman sleeping-car blankets were unlike other blankets; why they were like squares cut out of cold buckwheat cakes, and why they clung to you when you turned over, and lay heavy on you without warmth; why the curtains before you could not have been made opaque, without being so thick and suffocating; why it would not be as well to sit up all night half asleep in an ordinary passenger-car as to lie awake all night in a Pullman. But the snoring of my fellow-passengers answered this question in the negative.

With the recollection of last night's dinner weighing on me as heavily and coldly as the blankets, I began wondering why, over the whole extent of the continent, there was no local dish; why the bill of fare at restaurant and hotel was invariably only a weak reflex of the metropolitan hostelries; why the *entrées* were always the same, only more or less badly cooked; why the traveling American always was supposed to demand turkey and cold cranberry sauce; why the pretty waiter-girl apparently shuffled your plates behind your back, and then dealt them over your shoulder in a semicircle, as if they were a hand at cards, and not always a good one. Why, having done this, she instantly retired to the nearest wall, and gazed at you scornfully, as one who would say, "Fair sir, though lowly, I am proud; if thou dost imagine that I would permit undue familiarity of speech, beware!" And then I began to think of and dread the coming breakfast; to wonder why the ham was always cut half an inch thick, and why the fried egg always resembled a glass eye that visibly winked at you with diabolical dyspeptic suggestions; to wonder if the buckwheat cakes, the eating of which requires a certain degree of artistic preparation and deliberation, would be brought in, as usual, one minute before the train started. And then I had a vivid recollection of a fellow-passenger who, at a certain breakfast station in Illinois, frantically enwrapped his portion of this national pastry in his red bandana handkerchief, took it into the smoking-car, and quietly devoured it *en route*.

Lying broad awake, I could not help making some observations which I think are not noticed by the day traveler. First, that the speed of a train is not equal or continuous. That at certain times the engine apparently starts up, and says to the baggage train behind it, "Come, come, this won't do! Why, it's nearly half-past two; how in h—ll shall we get through! Don't you talk to *me*. Pooh, pooh!" delivered in that rhythmical fashion which all meditation assumes on a railway train. *Exempli gratia:* One night, having raised my window-curtain to look over a moonlit snowy landscape, as I pulled it down the lines of a popular comic song flashed across me. Fatal error! The train instantly took it up, and during the rest of the night I was haunted by this awful refrain: "Pull down the bel-lind, pull down the bel-lind; somebody's klink klink, O don't be shoo-shoo!" Naturally this differs on the different railways. On the New York Central, where the road-bed is quite perfect and the steel rails continuous, I have heard this irreverent train give the words of a certain popular revival hymn after this fashion: "Hold the fort, for I am Sankey; Moody slingers still. Wave the swish swash back from klinky, klinky klanky kill." On the New York and New Haven, where there are many switches, and the engine whistles at every cross-road, I have often heard, "Tommy, make room for your whoopy! that's a little clang; bumpity, bumpity, booby, clikitty, clikitty clang." Poetry, I fear, fared little better. One starlit night, coming from Quebec, as we slipped by a virgin forest, the opening lines of "Evangeline" flashed upon me. But all I could make of them was this: "This is the forest primeval-eval; the groves of the pines and the hemlocks-locks-locks-locks-loooock!" The train was only "slowing" or "braking" up at a station. Hence the jar in the metre.

I had noticed a peculiar Æolian-harp-like cry that ran through the whole train as we settled to rest at last after a long run—an almost sigh of infinite relief, a musical sigh that began in C and ran gradually up to F natural, which I think most observant travelers have noticed day and night. No railway official has ever given me a satisfactory explanation of it. As the car, in a rapid run, is always slightly projected forward of its trucks, a practical friend once suggested to me that it was the gradual settling back of the car body to a state of inertia, which, of course, every poetical traveler would reject. Four o'clock—the sound of boot-blacking by the porter faintly apparent from the toilet-room. Why not talk to him? But, fortunately, I remembered that any attempt at extended conversation with conductor or porter was always resented by them as implied disloyalty to the company they represented. I recalled that once I had endeavored to impress upon a conductor the absolute folly of a midnight inspection of tickets, and had been treated by him as an escaped lunatic. No, there was no relief from this suffocating and insupportable loneliness to be gained then. I raised the window-blind and looked out. We were passing a farm-house. A light, evidently the lantern of a farm-hand, was swung beside a barn. Yes, the faintest tinge of rose in the far horizon. Morning, surely, at last!

We had stopped at a station. Two men had got into the car, and had taken seats in the one vacant section, yawning occasionally and conversing in a languid, perfunctory sort of way. They sat opposite each other, occasionally looking out of the window, but always giving the strong impression that they were tired of each other's company. As I looked out of my curtains at them the One Man said, with a feebly concealed yawn:

"Yes, well, I reckon he was at one time as pop'lar an ondertaker ez I knew."

The Other Man (inventing a question rather than giving an answer, out of some languid, social impulse): "But was he—this yer ondertaker—a Christian—hed he jined the church?"

The One Man (reflectively): "Well, I don't know ez you might call him a purfessin' Christian; but he hed—yes, he hed conviction. I think Dr. Wylie hed him under conviction. Et least, that was the way I got it from *him*."

A long, dreary pause. The Other Man (feeling it was incumbent upon him to say something): "But why was he pop'lar ez an ondertaker?"

The One Man (lazily): "Well, he was kinder pop'lar with widders and widderers—sorter soothen 'em a kinder keerless way; slung 'em suthin' here and there, sometimes outer the Book, sometimes outer hisself, ez a man of experience as hed hed sorror. Hed, they say *(very cautiously)*, lost three wives hisself, and five children by this yer new disease—dipthery—out in Wisconsin. I don't know the facts, but that's what's got round."

The Other Man: "But how did he lose his pop'larity?"

The One Man: "Well, that's the question. You see, he interduced some things into ondertaking that waz new. He hed, for instance, a way, as he called it, of manniperlating the features of the deceased."

The Other Man (quietly): "How manniperlating?"

The One Man (struck with a bright and aggressive thought): "Look yer; did ye ever notiss how, generally speakin', onhandsome a corpse is?"

The Other Man had noticed this fact.

The One Man (returning to his fact): "Why, there was Mary Peebles, ez was daughter of my wife's bosom friend—a mighty pooty girl and a professing Christian—died of scarlet fever. Well, that gal—I was one of the mourners, being my wife's friend—well, that gal, though I hedn't, perhaps, oughter say—lying in that casket, fetched all the way from some A1 establishment in Chicago, filled with flowers and furbelows—didn't really seem to be of much account. Well, although my wife's friend, and me a mourner—well, now, I was—disappointed and discouraged."

The Other Man (in palpably affected sympathy): "Sho, now!"

"Yes, *sir!* Well, you see, this yer ondertaker, this Wilkins, hed a way of correctin' all thet. And just by manniperlation. He worked over the face of the deceased ontil he perduced what the survivin' relatives called a look of resignation—you know, a sort of smile, like. When he wanted to put in any extrys, he perduced what he called—hevin' reg'lar charges for this kind of work—a Christian's hope."

The Other Man: "I want to know!"

"Yes. Well, I admit, at times it was a little startlin'. And I've allers said (a little confidentially) that I had my doubts of its being Scriptooral or sacred, we being, ez you know, worms of the yearth; and I relieved my mind to our pastor, but he didn't feel like interferin', ez long ez it was confined to church membership. But the other day, when Cy Dunham died—you disremember Cy Dunham?"

A long interval of silence. The Other Man was looking out of the window, and had apparently forgotten his companion completely. But as I stretched my head out of the curtain I saw four other heads as eagerly reached out from other berths to hear the conclusion of the story. One head, a female one, instantly disappeared on my looking around, but a certain tremulousness of her window-curtain showed an unabated interest. The only two utterly disinterested men were the One Man and the Other Man.

The Other Man (detaching himself languidly from the window): "Cy Dunham?"

"Yes; Cy never hed hed either convictions or purfessions. Uster get drunk and go round with permiscous women. Sorter like the prodigal son, only a little more so, ez fur ez I kin judge from the facks ez stated to me. Well, Cy one day petered out down at Little Rock, and was sent up yer for interment. The fammerly, being proud-like, of course didn't spare no money on that funeral, and it waz—now between you and me—about ez shapely and first-class and prime-mess affair ez I ever saw. Wilkins hed put in his extrys. He hed put onto that prodigal's face the A 1 touch—hed him fixed up with a 'Christian's hope.' Well, it waz

514 · *Mark Twain's Library of Humor*

about the turning-point, for thar waz some of the members and the pastor hisself thought that the line oughter be drawn somewhere, and thar waz some talk at Deacon Tibbett's about a reg'lar conference meetin' regardin' it. But it wazn't thet which made him onpop'lar."

Another silence; no expression nor reflection from the face of the Other Man of the least desire to know what ultimately settled the unpopularity of the undertaker. But from the curtains of the various berths several eager, and one or two even wrathful, faces, anxious for the result.

The Other Man (lazily recurring to the fading topic): "Well, what made him onpop'lar?"

The One Man (quietly): "Extrys, I think—that is, I suppose, not knowin' (cautiously) all the facts. When Mrs. Widdecombe lost her husband, 'bout two months ago, though she'd been through the valley of the shadder of death twice—this bein' her third marriage, hevin' been John Barker's widder—"

The Other Man (with an intense expression of interest): "No; you're foolin' me!"

The One Man (solemnly): "Ef I was to appear before my Maker tomorrow, yes! she was the widder of Barker."

"The Other Man: "Well, I swow!"

The One Man: "Well, this Widder Widdecombe, she put up a big funeral for the deceased. She hed Wilkins, and thet ondertaker just laid hisself out. Just spread hisself. Onfort'nately—perhaps fort'nately in the ways of Providence—one of Widdecombe's old friends, a doctor up thar in Chicago, comes down to the funeral. He goes up with the friends to look at the deceased, smilin' a peaceful sort o' heavinly smile, and everybody sayin' he's gone to meet his reward, and this yer friend turns round, short and sudden on the widder settin' in her pew, and kinder enjoyin', as wimen will, all the compliments paid the corpse, and he says, says he:

" 'What did you say your husband died of, marm?'

" 'Consumption,' she says, wiping her eyes, poor critter. 'Consumption—gallopin' consumption.'

" 'Consumption be d—d,' sez he, bein' a profane kind of Chicago doctor, and not bein' ever under conviction. 'Thet man died of strychnine. Look at thet face. Look at thet contortion of them fashal muscles.

Thet's strychnine. Thet's *risers Sardonikus'* (thet's what he said; he was always sorter profane).

" 'Why, doctor,' says the widder, 'thet—thet is his last smile. It's a Christian's resignation.'

" 'Thet be blowed; don't tell me,' sez he. 'Hell is full of thet kind of resignation. It's pizon. And I'll'—why, dern my skin, yes we are; yes, it's Joliet. Wall, now, who'd hev thought we'd been nigh onto an hour."

Two or three anxious passengers from their berths: "Say; look yer, stranger! Old Man! What became of—"

But the One Man and the Other Man had vanished.

THE SHOPPER

R. J. BURDETTE

> Tramp, tramp, tramp!
> With the morning clocks at ten,
> She skimmed the street with footsteps fleet,
> And hustled the timid men;
> Tramp, tramp, tramp!
> She entered the dry goods store,
> And with echoing tread the dance she led
> All over the crowded floor.
> She charged the throng where the bargains were,
> And everybody made way for her;
> Wherever she saw a painted sign,
> She made for that spot a prompt bee-line;
> Whatever was old, or whatever was new,
> She had it down and she looked it through;
> Whatever it was that caught her eye,
> She'd stop, and price, and pretend to buy.
> But 'twas either too bad, too common, or good,
> So she did, and she wouldn't, and didn't, and would.
> And round the counters and up the stairs,
> In attic, and basement, and everywheres.
> The salesmen fainted and cash-boys dropped,

But still she shopped, and shopped, and shopped,
And round, and round, and round, and round,
Like a winding toy with a key that's wound,
She'd weave and wriggle and twist about,
One way in and the other way out,
Till men grew giddy to see her go.
And by and by, when the sun was low,
Homeward she dragged her weary way,
And had sent home the spoils of the day:
A spool of silk and a hank of thread—
Eight hours—ten cents—and a dame half dead.

THE BUMBLE BEE

JOSH BILLINGS

The bumble bee iz a kind ov big fly who goes muttering and swareing around the lots, during the summer, looking after little boys to sting them, and stealing hunny out ov the dandylions and thissells. He iz mad all the time about sumthing, and don't seem to kare a kuss what people think ov him. A skool boy will studdy harder enny time to find a bumble bees nest than he will to get hiz lesson in arithmetik, and when he haz found it, and got the hunny out ov it, and got badly stung into the bargin, he finds thare aint mutch margin in it. Next to poor molassis, bumble bee hunny iz the poorest kind ov sweetmeats in market. Bumble bees hav allwuss been in fashion, and probably allwuss will be, but whare the fun or proffit lays in them, i never could cypher out. The proffit don't seem to be in the hunny, nor in the bumble bee neither. They bild their nest in the ground, or enny whare else they take a noshun too, and ain't afrade to fite a whole distrikt skool, if they meddle with them. I don't blame the bumble bee, nor enny other fellow, for defending hiz sugar: it iz the fust, and last Law ov natur, and i hope the law won't never run out. The smartest thing about the bumble bee iz their stinger.

ANOTHER CHANCE FOR SOROSIS

R. J. BURDETTE

Mrs. Ewing says in the *Woman's Journal* that "she believes 50,000 women could earn a living in this country by the manufacture and sale of home-made bread." We believe so, too. There's a fortune in it. A paving material that will be yielding to the horse's foot, comparatively noiseless, and yet more durable than Belgian block, is something that has not yet been discovered.

AFTER THE FUNERAL

J. M. BAILEY

It was just after the funeral. The bereaved and subdued widow, enveloped in millinery gloom, was seated in the sitting-room with a few sympathizing friends. There was that constrained look so peculiar to the occasion observable on every countenance. The widow sighed.

"How do you feel, my dear?" observed her sister.

"Oh! I don't know," said the poor woman, with difficulty restraining her tears. "But I hope everything passed off well."

"Indeed it did," said all the ladies.

"It was as large and respectable a funeral as I have seen this winter," said the sister, looking around upon the others.

"Yes, it was," said the lady from next door. "I was saying to Mrs. Slocum, only ten minutes ago, that the attendance couldn't have been better—the bad going considered."

"Did you see the Taylors?" asked the widow faintly, looking at her sister. "They go so rarely to funerals, that I was surprised to see them here."

"Oh, yes! the Taylors were all here," said the sympathizing sister. "As you say, they go but a little: they are *so* exclusive!"

"I thought I saw the Curtises also," suggested the bereaved woman droopingly.

"Oh, yes!" chimed in several. "They came in their own carriage too," said the sister animatedly. "And then there were the Randalls, and the Van Rensselaers. Mrs. Van Rensselaer had her cousin from the city with her; and Mrs. Randall wore a very heavy black silk, which I am sure was quite new. Did you see Col. Haywood and his daughters, love?"

"I thought I saw them; but I wasn't sure. They were here, then, were they?"

"Yes, indeed!" said they all again; and the lady who lived across the way observed:

"The colonel was very sociable, and inquired most kindly about you, and the sickness of your husband."

The widow smiled faintly. She was gratified by the interest shown by the colonel.

The friends now rose to go, each bidding her good-bye, and expressing the hope that she would be calm. Her sister bowed them out. When she returned, she said:

"You can see, my love, what the neighbors think of it. I wouldn't have had anything unfortunate to happen for a good deal. But nothing did. The arrangements couldn't have been better."

"I think some of the people in the neighborhood must have been surprised to see so many of the up-town people here," suggested the afflicted woman, trying to look hopeful.

"You may be quite sure of that," asserted the sister. "I could see that plain enough by their looks."

"Well, I am glad there is no occasion for talk," said the widow, smoothing the skirt of her dress.

And after that the boys took the chairs home, and the house was put in order.

CANNIBALISM IN THE CARS

MARK TWAIN

I visited St. Louis lately, and on my way west, after changing cars at Terre Haute, Indiana, a mild, benevolent-looking gentleman of about forty-five, or maybe fifty, came in at one of the way-stations and sat down beside me. We talked together pleasantly on various subjects for an hour, perhaps, and I found him exceedingly intelligent and entertaining. When he learned that I was from Washington, he immediately began to ask questions about various public men, and about Congressional affairs; and I saw very shortly that I was conversing with a man who was perfectly familiar with the ins and outs of political life at the Capital, even to the ways and manners and customs of procedure of Senators and Representatives in the Chambers of the National Legislature. Presently two men halted near us for a single moment, and one said to the other:

"Harris, if you'll do that for me, I'll never forget you, my boy."

My new comrade's eyes lighted pleasantly. The words had touched upon a happy memory, I thought. Then his face settled into thoughtfulness—almost into gloom. He turned to me and said, "Let me tell you a story; let me give you a secret chapter of my life—a chapter that has never been referred to by me since its events transpired. Listen patiently, and promise that you will not interrupt me."

I said I would not, and he related the following strange adventure, speaking sometimes with animation, sometimes with melancholy, but always with feeling and earnestness.

THE STRANGER'S NARRATIVE

"On the 19th of December, 1853, I started from St. Louis on the evening train bound for Chicago. There were only twenty-four passengers, all told. There were no ladies and no children. We were in excellent spirits, and pleasant acquaintanceships were soon formed. The journey bade fair to be a happy one; and no individual in the party, I think, had even the vaguest presentiment of the horrors we were soon to undergo.

"At 11 P.M. it began to snow hard. Shortly after leaving the small village of Welden, we entered upon that tremendous prairie solitude that stretches its leagues on leagues of houseless dreariness far away towards the Jubilee Settlements. The winds, unobstructed by trees or hills, or even vagrant rocks, whistled fiercely across the level desert, driving the falling snow before it like spray from the crested waves of a stormy sea. The snow was deepening fast; and we knew, by the diminished speed of the train, that the engine was ploughing through it with steadily increasing difficulty. Indeed, it almost came to a dead halt sometimes, in the midst of great drifts that piled themselves like colossal graves across the track. Conversation began to flag. Cheerfulness gave place to grave concern. The possibility of being imprisoned in the snow, on the bleak prairie, fifty miles from any house, presented itself to every mind, and extended its depressing influence over every spirit.

"At two o'clock in the morning I was aroused out of an uneasy slumber by the ceasing of all motion about me. The appalling truth flashed upon me instantly—we were captives in a snowdrift! 'All hands to the rescue!' Every man sprang to obey. Out into the wild night, the pitchy darkness, the billowy snow, the driving storm, every soul leaped, with the consciousness that a moment lost now might bring destruction to us all. Shovels, hands, boards—anything, everything, that could displace snow, was brought into instant requisition. It was a weird picture, that small company of frantic men fighting the banking snows, half in the blackest shadow and half in the angry light of the locomotive's reflector.

"One short hour sufficed to prove the utter uselessness of our efforts. The storm barricaded the track with a dozen drifts while we dug one away. And, worse than this, it was discovered that the last grand charge the engine had made upon the enemy had broken the fore-and-aft shaft of the driving-wheel! With a free track before us, we should still have been helpless. We entered the car wearied with labor, and very sorrowful. We gathered about the stoves, and gravely canvassed our situation. We had no provisions whatever—in this lay our chief distress. We could not freeze, for there was a good supply of wood in the tender. This was our only comfort. The discussion ended at last in accepting the disheartening decision of the conductor, viz., that it would be death for any man to attempt to travel fifty miles on foot through snow like that. We could not send for help; and even if we could, it could not come. We must submit, and await, as patiently as we might, succor or starvation! I think the stoutest heart there felt a momentary chill when those words were uttered.

"Within the hour conversation subsided to a low murmur here and there about the car, caught fitfully between the rising and falling of the blast; the lamps grew dim; and the majority of the castaways settled themselves among the flickering shadows to think—to forget the present, if they could—to sleep, if they might.

"The eternal night—it surely seemed eternal to us—wore its lagging hours away at last, and the cold gray dawn broke in the east. As the light grew stronger the passengers began to stir and give signs of life; one after another, and each in turn, pushed his slouched hat up from his forehead, stretched his stiffened limbs, and glanced out at the windows upon the cheerless prospect. It was cheerless indeed!—not a living thing visible anywhere, not a human habitation; nothing but a vast white desert; uplifted sheets of snow drifting hither and thither before the wind—a world of eddying flakes shutting out the firmament above.

"All day we moped about the cars, saying little, thinking much. Another lingering, dreary night—and hunger.

"Another dawning—another day of silence, sadness, wasting hunger, hopeless watching for succor that could not come. A night of restless slumber, filled with dreams of feasting—wakings distressed with the gnawings of hunger.

"The fourth day came and went—and the fifth! Five days of dreadful imprisonment! A savage hunger looked out at every eye. There was in it a sign of awful import—the foreshadowing of a something that was vaguely shaping itself in every heart—a something which no tongue dared yet to frame into words.

"The sixth day passed—the seventh dawned upon as gaunt and haggard and hopeless a company of men as ever stood in the shadow of death. It must out now! That thing which had been growing up in every heart was ready to leap from every lip at last! Nature had been taxed to the utmost—she must yield. RICHARD H. GASTON, of Minnesota, tall, cadaverous and pale, rose up. All knew what was coming.

All prepared—every emotion, every semblance of excitement was smothered—only a calm, thoughtful seriousness appeared in the eyes that were lately so wild.

" 'Gentlemen—It cannot be delayed longer! The time is at hand! We must determine which of us shall die to furnish food for the rest!'

"Mr. JOHN J. WILLIAMS, of Illinois, rose and said: 'Gentlemen—I nominate the Rev. James Sawyer, of Tennessee.'

"Mr. WM. R. ADAMS, of Indiana, said: 'I nominate Mr. Daniel Slote, of New York.'

"Mr. CHARLES J. LANGDON: 'I nominate Mr. Samuel A. Bowen, of St. Louis.'

"Mr. SLOTE: 'Gentlemen—I desire to decline in favor of Mr. John A. Van Nostrand, Jun., of New Jersey.'

"Mr. GASTON: 'If there be no objection, the gentleman's desire will be acceded to.'

"Mr. VAN NOSTRAND objecting, the resignation of Mr. Slote was rejected. The resignations of Messrs. Sawyer and Bowen were also offered, and refused upon the same grounds.

"Mr. A. L. BASCOM, of Ohio: 'I move that the nominations now close, and that the House proceed to an election by ballot.'

"Mr. SAWYER: 'Gentlemen—I protest earnestly against these proceedings. They are, in every way, irregular and unbecoming. I must beg to move that they be dropped at once, and that we elect a chairman of the meeting, and proper officers to assist him, and then we can go on with the business before us understandingly.'

"Mr. BELL, of Iowa: 'Gentlemen—I object. This is no time to stand upon forms and ceremonious observances. For more than seven days we have been without food. Every moment we lose in idle discussion increases our distress. I am satisfied with the nominations that have been made—every gentleman present is, I believe—and I, for one, do not see why we should not proceed at once to elect one or more of them. I wish to offer a resolution—'

"Mr. GASTON: 'It would be objected to, and have to lie over one day, under the rules, thus bringing about the very delay you wish to avoid. The gentleman from New Jersey—'

"Mr. VAN NOSTRAND: 'Gentlemen—I am a stranger among you; I have not sought the distinction that has been conferred upon me, and I feel a delicacy—'

"Mr. MORGAN, of Alabama (interrupting): 'I move the previous question.'

"The motion was carried, and further debate shut off, of course. The motion to elect officers was passed, and under it Mr. Gaston was chosen chairman, Mr. Blake secretary, Messrs. Holcomb, Dyer and Baldwin a committee on nominations, and Mr. R. M. Howland purveyor, to assist the committee in making selections.

"A recess of half an hour was then taken, and some little caucussing followed. At the sound of the gavel the meeting reassembled, and the committee reported in favor of Messrs. George Ferguson, of Kentucky, Lucien Herrman, of Louisiana, and W. Messick, of Colorado, as candidates. The report was accepted.

"Mr. ROGERS, of Missouri: 'Mr. President—The report being properly before the House now, I move to amend it by substituting for the name of Mr. Herrman that of Mr. Lucius Harris, of St. Louis, who is well and honorably known to us all. I do not wish to be understood as casting the least reflection upon the high character and standing of the gentleman from Louisiana—far from it. I respect and esteem him as much as any gentleman here present possibly can; but none of us can be blind to the fact that he has lost more flesh during the week that we have lain here than any among us—none of us can be blind to the fact that the committee has been derelict in its duty, either through negligence or a graver fault, in thus offering for our suffrages a gentleman who, however pure his own motives may be, has really less nutriment in him—'

"THE CHAIR: 'The gentleman from Missouri will take his seat. The Chair cannot allow the integrity of the Committee to be questioned save by the regular course, under the rules. What action will the House take upon the gentleman's motion.'

"Mr. HALLIDAY, of Virginia: 'I move to further amend the report by substituting Mr. Harvey Davis, of Oregon, for Mr. Messick. It may be urged by some gentlemen that the hardships and privations of a frontier life have rendered Mr. Davis tough; but, gentlemen, is this a time to cavil at toughness? is this a time to be fastidious concerning trifles? is this a time to dispute about matters of paltry significance? No, gentlemen: bulk is what we desire—substance, weight, bulk—these are the supreme requisites now—not talent, not genius, not education. I insist upon my motion.'

"Mr. MORGAN (excitedly): 'Mr. Chairman—I do most strenuously object to this amendment. The gentleman from Oregon is old, and, furthermore, is bulky only in bone—not in flesh. I ask the gentleman from Virginia if it is soup we want instead of solid sustenance? if he would delude us with shadows? if he would mock our suffering with an Oregonian spectre? I ask him if he can look upon the anxious faces around him, if he can gaze into our sad eyes, if he can listen to the beating of our expectant hearts, and still thrust this famine-stricken fraud upon us? I ask him if he can think of our desolate state, of our past sorrows, of our dark future, and still unpityingly foist upon us this wreck, this ruin, this tottering swindle, this gnarled and blighted and sapless vagabond from Oregon's inhospitable shores? Never!' [Applause.]

"The amendment was put to vote, after a fiery debate, and lost. Mr. Harris was substituted on the first amendment. The balloting then began. Five ballots were held without a choice. On the sixth, Mr. Harris was elected, all voting for him but himself. It was then moved that his election should be ratified by acclamation, which was lost, in consequence of his again voting against himself.

"Mr. RADWAY moved that the House now take up the remaining candidates, and go into an election for breakfast. This was carried.

"On the first ballot there was a tie, half the members favoring one candidate on account of his youth, and half favoring the other on account of his superior size. The President gave the casting vote for the latter, Mr. Messick. This decision created considerable dissatisfaction among the friends of Mr. Ferguson, the defeated candidate, and there was some talk of demanding a new ballot; but in the midst of it, a motion to adjourn was carried, and the meeting broke up at once.

"The preparations for supper diverted the attention of the Ferguson faction from the discussion of their grievance for a long time, and then, when they would have taken it up again, the happy announcement that Mr. Harris was ready, drove all thought of it to the winds.

"We improvised tables by propping up the backs of car-seats, and sat down with hearts full of gratitude to the finest supper that had blessed our vision for seven torturing days. How changed we were from what we had been a few short hours before! Hopeless, sad-eyed misery, hunger, feverish anxiety, desperation, then—thankfulness, serenity, joy too deep for utterance now. That I know was the cheeriest hour of my eventful life. The winds howled, and blew the snow wildly about our prison-house, but they were powerless to distress us any more. I liked Harris. He might have been better done, perhaps, but I am free to say that no man ever agreed with me better than Harris, or afforded me so large a degree of satisfaction. Messick was very well, though rather high-flavored, but for genuine nutritiousness and delicacy of fibre, give me Harris. Messick had his good points—I will not attempt to deny it, nor do I wish to do it—but he was no more fitted for breakfast than a mummy would be, sir—not a bit. Lean?—why, bless me!—and tough? Ah, he was very tough! You could not imagine it— you could never imagine anything like it."

"Do you mean to tell me that—"

"Do not interrupt me, please. After breakfast we elected a man by the name of Walker, from Detroit, for supper. He was very good. I wrote his wife so afterwards. He was worthy of all praise. I shall always remember Walker. He was a little rare, but very good. And then the next morning we had Morgan, of Alabama, for breakfast. He was one of the finest men I ever sat down to—handsome, educated, refined, spoke several languages fluently—he was a perfect gentleman, and singularly juicy. For supper we had that Oregon patriarch, and he *was* a fraud, there is no question about it—old, shaggy, tough—nobody can picture the reality. I finally said, gentlemen, you can do as you like, but I will wait for another election. And Grimes, of Illinois, said, 'Gentlemen, *I* will wait also. When you elect a man that has *something* to recommend him, I shall be glad to join you again.' It soon became evident that there was general dissatisfaction with Davis, of Oregon, and so, to preserve the good-will that had prevailed so pleasantly since we had had Harris, an election was called, and the result of it was that Baker, of Georgia, was chosen. He was splendid! Well, well—after that we had Doolittle, and Hawkins, and McElroy (there was some complaint about McElroy, because he was uncommonly short and thin), and Penrod, and two Smiths, and Bailey (Bailey had a wooden leg, which was clear loss, but he was otherwise good), and an Indian boy, and an organ grinder, and a gentleman by the name of Buckminster—a poor stick of a vagabond that wasn't any good for company and no account for breakfast. We were glad we got him elected before relief came."

"And so the blessed relief *did* come at last?"

"Yes, it came one bright, sunny morning, just after election. John

Murphy was the choice, and there never was a better, I am willing to testify; but John Murphy came home with us, in the train that came to succor us, and lived to marry the widow Harris—"

"Relict of—"

"Relict of our first choice. He married her, and is happy and respected and prosperous yet. Ah, it was like a novel, sir—it was like a romance. This is my stopping-place, sir; I must bid you good-bye. Any time that you can make it convenient to tarry a day or two with me, I shall be glad to have you. I like you, sir; I have conceived an affection for you. I could like you as well as I liked Harris himself, sir. Good day, sir, and a pleasant journey."

He was gone. I never felt so stunned, so distressed, so bewildered in my life. But in my soul I was glad he was gone. With all his gentleness of manner and his soft voice, I shuddered whenever he turned his hungry eye upon me; and when I heard that I had achieved his perilous affection, and that I stood almost with the late Harris in his esteem, my heart fairly stood still!

I was bewildered beyond description. I did not doubt his word; I could not question a single item in a statement so stamped with the earnestness of truth as his; but its dreadful details overpowered me, and threw my thoughts into hopeless confusion. I saw the conductor looking at me. I said, "Who is that man?"

"He was a member of Congress once, and a good one. But he got caught in a snowdrift in the cars, and like to been starved to death. He got so frost-bitten and frozen up generally, and used up for want of something to eat, that he was sick and out of his head two or three months afterwards. He is all right now, only he is a monomaniac, and when he gets on that old subject, he never stops till he has eat up that whole car-load of people he talks about. He would have finished the crowd by this time, only he had to get out here. He has got their names as pat as A.B.C. When he gets them all eat up but himself, he always says: 'Then the hour for the usual election for breakfast having arrived, and there being no opposition, I was duly elected, after which, there being no objections offered, I resigned. Thus I am here.' "

I felt inexpressibly relieved to know that I had only been listening to the harmless vagaries of a madman instead of the genuine experiences of a bloodthirsty cannibal.

Pie

CHARLES DUDLEY WARNER

There has come over this country within the last generation, as everybody knows, a great wave of condemnation of pie. It has taken the character of a "movement," though we have had no conventions about it, nor is any one, of any of the several sexes among us, running for president against it. It is safe almost anywhere to denounce pie, yet nearly everybody eats it on occasion. A great many people think it savors of a life abroad to speak with horror of pie, although they were very likely the foremost of the Americans in Paris who used to speak with more enthusiasm of the American pie at Madame Busque's than of the Venus of Milo. To talk against pie and still eat it is snobbish, of course; but snobbery, being an aspiring failing, is sometimes the prophecy of better things. To affect dislike of pie is something. We have no statistics on the subject, and cannot tell whether it is gaining or losing in the country at large. Its disappearance in select circles is no test. The amount of writing against it is no more test of its desuetude, than the number of religious tracts distributed in a given district is a criterion of its piety. We are apt to assume that certain regions are substantially free of it. Herbert and I, traveling north one summer, fancied that we could draw in New England a sort of diet line, like the sweeping curves on the isothermal charts, which should show at least the leading pie sections. Journeying towards the White Mountains, we concluded that a line passing through Bellows Falls, and bending a little south on either side, would mark, northward, the region of perpetual pie. In this region pie is to be found at all hours and seasons, and at every meal. I am not sure, however, that pie is not a matter of altitude rather than latitude, as I find that all the hill and country towns of New England are full of those excellent women, the very salt of the housekeeping earth, who would feel ready to sink in mortification through their scoured kitchen floors, if visitors should catch them without a pie in the house. The absence of pie would be more noticed than a scarcity of Bible even. Without it the housekeepers are as distracted as the boarding-house keeper who declared that if it were not for canned tomato she should have nothing to fly to. Well, in all this great agitation I find Herbert unmoved, a conservative, even to the under-crust. I dare not ask him if he eats pie at breakfast. There are some tests that the dearest friendship may not apply.

Almost enny phool kan prove that the bible aint true: it takes a wize man to beleave it.

JOSH BILLINGS

BUTTERWICK'S LITTLE GAS BILL

ANONYMOUS

During one of those few cold snaps which we had last winter the gas meter in Mr. Butterwick's house was frozen. Mr. Butterwick attempted to thaw it out by pouring hot water over it, but after spending an hour upon the effort, he emerged from the contest with the meter with his feet and trousers wet, his hair full of dust and cobwebs, and his temper at fever heat. After studying how he should get rid of the ice in the meter, he concluded to use force for the purpose; and so, seizing a hot poker, he jammed it through a vent hole, and stirred it around inside the meter with a considerable amount of vigor. He felt the ice give way, and he heard the wheels buzz around with rather more vehemence than usual. Then he went up-stairs.

He noticed for three or four days that the internal machinery of that meter seemed to be rattling around in a remarkable manner. It could be heard all over the house. But he was pleased to find that it was working again in spite of the cold weather, and he retained his serenity.

About two weeks afterwards his gas bill came. It accused him of burning, during the quarter, 1,500,000 feet of gas, and it called on him to settle to the extent of nearly $350,000. Before Mr. Butterwick's hair had time to descend after the first shock, he put on his hat and went down to the gas office. He addressed one of the clerks:

"How much gas did you make at the works last quarter?"

"Dunno; about a million feet, I reckon."

"Well, you've charged me in my bill for burning half a million more than you made. I want you to correct it."

"Let's see the bill. Mm-m-m—this is all right. It's taken off the meter. That's what the meter says."

"S'pose'n it does; I couldn't have burned more'n you made!"

"Can't help that. The meter can't lie."

"Well, but how d' you account for the difference?"

"Dunno; 'tain't our business to go poking and nosing around after scientific truth. We depend on the meter. If that says you burned six million feet, why, you must have burned it, even if we never made a foot of gas out at the works."

"To tell you the honest truth," said Butterwick, "that meter was frozen, and I stirred it up with a poker, and set it whizzing around."

"Price just the same," said the clerk. "We charge for pokers just like we do for gas."

"You ain't actually going to have the audacity to ask me to pay $350,000 on account of that poker?"

"If it was $700,000 I'd take it with a calmness that would surprise you. Pay up, or we'll turn off your gas."

"Turn it off and be hanged!" exclaimed Butterwick, as he emerged from the office, tearing his bill to fragments. Then he went home, and grasping that too lavish poker, he approached the meter. It had registered another million feet since the bill was made out. It was running up a score of a hundred feet a minute. In a month Butterwick would have owed the gas company more than the United States Government owes its creditors. So he beat the meter into a shapeless mass, tossed it into the street, and turned off the gas inside the cellar.

He is now sitting up at nights writing an essay on "Our Grinding Monopolies," by the light of a kerosene lamp.

PISTOL SHOOTING—
A COUNTER CHALLENGE

JOHN PHŒNIX

SAN DIEGO, CAL., *September 1, 1854.*

I copy the following paragraph from the *Spirit of the Times*, for July 15th:

PISTOL SHOOTING—A CHALLENGE

Owing to the frequent and urgent solicitations of many of my friends, I am induced to make the following propositions:

1. I will fit a dollar to the end of a twig two inches long, and while a second person will hold the other end in his mouth, so as to bring the coin within an inch and a half of his face, I engage to strike the dollar, three times out of five, at the distance of ten paces, or thirty feet. I will add, in explanation, that there are several persons willing and ready to hold the twig or stick described above, when required.

2. I will hit a dollar tossed in the air, or any other object of the same size, three times out of five, *on a wheel and fire.*

3. At the word, I will split three balls out of five, on a knife blade, placed at the distance of thirty feet.

4. I will hit three birds out of five, sprung from the trap, standing thirty feet from the trap when shooting.

5. I will break, at the word, five common clay pipe stems out of seven, at the distance of thirty feet.

6. I engage to prove, by fair trial, that no pistol-shot can be produced who will shoot an apple off a man's head, at the distance of thirty feet, oftener than I can. Moreover, I will produce two persons willing and ready to hold the apple on their heads for me, when required to do so.

7. I will wager, lastly, that no person in the United States can be produced who will hit a quarter of a dollar, at the distance of thirty feet, oftener than I can, *on a wheel and fire.*

I am willing to bet $5,000 on any of the above propositions, one fourth of that amount forfeit. So soon as any bet will be closed, the money shall be deposited in the Bank of the State of Missouri, until paid over by the judges, or withdrawn, less forfeit. I will give the best and most satisfactory references that my share will be forthcoming when any of my propositions are taken up. Any one desiring to take up any of my propositions must address me by letter, through the St. Louis Post Office, as the advertisements or notices of newspapers might not meet my eye. Propositions will be received until the first of September next.

EDMUND W. PAUL
140 Sixth Street, between Franklin Avenue and
Morgan Street, St. Louis, Missouri.

I am unable to see anything very extraordinary in the above propositions, by Mr. Edmund W. Paul. Any person acquainted with the merest rudiments of the pistol, could certainly execute any or all of the proposed feats without the slightest difficulty.

"Owing" to my entertaining these opinions, "without solicitation from friends, and unbiased by unworthy motives," *I* am induced to make the following propositions:

1. I will suspend *two* dollars by a ring from a second person's nose, so as to bring the coins within three-fourths of an inch from his face, and with a double barrelled shot-gun, at a distance of thirty feet, will blow dollars, nose and man at least thirty feet further, four times out of five. I will add, in explanation, that, San Diego containing a rather intelligent community, I can find, at present, no one here willing or ready to have his nose blown in this manner; but I have no manner of doubt I could obtain such a person from St. Louis, by Adams & Co.'s Express, in due season.

2. I will hit a dollar, or anything else that has been tossed in the air (of the same size), on a wheel, *on a pole or axletree, or on the ground*, every time out of five.

3. At the word, I will place five balls on the blade of a penknife, and split them all!

4. I will hit three men out of five, sprung from obscure parentage, and stand within ten feet of a steel trap (properly set) while shooting!

5. I will break, at the word, a whole box of common clay pipes, with a single brick, at a distance of thirty feet.

6. I engage to prove, by a fair trial, that no pistol-shot (or other per-

son) can be produced who will throw more apples at a man's head than I can. Moreover, I can produce in this town more than sixty persons willing and ready to hold an apple on their heads for me, provided they are allowed to eat the apple subsequently.

7. I will wager, lastly, that no person in the United States can be produced, who, with a double barrelled shot-gun, while throwing a back-handed summerset, can hit oftener a dollar and a half, on the perimeter of a *revolving* wheel *in rapid motion*, than I can.

Any one desiring to take up any of my propositions, will address me through the columns of *The Pioneer Magazine*. Propositions will be received on the first of April next.

JOHN PHŒNIX.

1384 Seventeenth Street, Valecitos.
Se compra oro aqui, up-stairs.
P. S.—Satisfactory references given and required. A bet from a steady, industrious person, who will be apt to pay if he loses, will meet with prompt attention.

J.P.

BOSTON

A.W. to His Wife

ARTEMUS WARD

Dear Betsy: I write you this from Boston, "the Modern Atkins," as it is denomyunated, altho' I skurcely know what those air. I'll giv you a kursoory view of this city. I'll klassify the paragrafs under seprit headin's, arter the stile of those Emblems of Trooth and Poority, the Washington correspongdents:

COPPS' HILL

The winder of my room commands a exileratin' view of Copps' Hill, where Cotton Mather, the father of the Reformers and sich, lies berrid.

There is men even now who worship Cotton, and there is wimin who wear him next their harts. But I do not weep for him. He's bin ded too lengthy. I ain't goin' to be absurd, like old Mr. Skillins, in our nabor-hood, who is ninety-six years of age, and gets drunk every 'lection day, and weeps Bitturly because he hain't got no Parents. He's a nice Or-phan, *he* is.

MR. FANUEL

Old Mr. Fanuel is ded, but his Hall is still into full blarst. This is the Cradle in which the Goddess of Liberty was rocked, my Dear. The Goddess hasn't bin very well durin' the past few years, and the num'ris quack doctors she called in didn't help her any; but the old gal's physicians now are men who understand their bisness, Major-generally speakin', and I think the day is near when she'll be able to take her three meals a day, and sleep nights as comf'bly as in the old time.

THE LEGISLATUR

The State House is filled with Statesmen, but sum of 'em wear queer hats. They buy 'em, I take it, of hatters who carry on hat stores down-stairs in Dock Square, and whose hats is either ten years ahead of the prevalin' stile, or ten years behind it—jest as a intellectooal person sees fit to think about it. I had the pleasure of talkin' with sevril mem-bers of the legislatur. I told 'em the Eye of 1,000 ages was onto we American peple of to-day. They seemed deeply impressed by the re-mark, and wantid to know if I had seen the Grate Orgin.

HARVARD COLLEGE

This celebrated institootion of learnin' is pleasantly situated in the Bar-room of Parker's, in School Street, and has poopils from all over the country.

I had a letter, yes'd'y, by the way, from our mootual son, Artemus, Jr., who is at Bowdoin College, in Maine. He writes that he is a Bowdoin Arab. & is it cum to this? Is this Boy, as I nurtered with a Parent's care into his childhood's hour—is he goin' to be a Grate American humorist? Alars! I fear it is too troo. Why didn't I bind him out to the Patent Travelin' Vegetable Pill Man, as was struck with his appearance at our last County Fair, & wanted him to go with him and be a Pillist? Ar, these Boys—they little know how the old folks worrit about 'em. But my father he never had no occasion to worrit about me. You know, Betsy, that when I fust commenced my career as a moral exhibitor with a six-legged cat and a Bass drum, I was only a simple peasant child—skurce 15 Summers had flow'd over my yoothful hed. But I had sum mind of my own. My father understood this. "Go," he said—"go, my son, and hog the public!" (He ment, "knock em," but the old man was allus a little given to slang.) He put his withered han' tremblin'ly onto my hed, and went sadly into the house. I thought I saw tears tricklin' down his venerable chin, but it might hav' been tobacker jooce. He chaw'd.

WHERE THE FUST BLUD WAS SPILT

I went over to Lexington yes'd'y. My Boosum hove with sollum emotions. "& this," I said to a man who was drivin' a yoke of oxen, "this is where our Revolootionary forefathers asserted their independence and spilt their Blud. Classic ground!"

"Wall," the man said, "it's good for white beans and potatoes, but as regards raisin' wheat, 't ain't worth a damn. But hav' you seen the Grate Orgin?"

THE POOTY GIRL IN SPECTACLES

I returned in the Hoss Cars, part way. A pooty girl in spectacles sot near me, and was tellin' a young man how much he reminded her of a man she used to know in Waltham. Pooty soon the young man got out; and, smilin' in a seductiv' manner, I said to the girl in spectacles, "Don't *I* remind you of somebody you used to know?"

"Yes," she said, "you do remind me of one man, but he was sent to the penitentiary for stealin' a Bar'l of mackril—he died there, so I conclood you ain't *him*." I didn't pursoo the conversation. I only heard her silvery voice once more durin' the remainder of the jerney. Turnin' to a respectable lookin' female of advanced summers, she asked her if she had seen the Grate Orgin.

RICHMOND, MAY 18, 1865

The old man finds hisself once more in a Sunny climb. I cum here a few days arter the city catterpillertulated.

My naburs seemed surprised & astonisht at this darin' bravery onto the part of a man at my time of life, but our family was never know'd to quale in danger's stormy hour.

My father was a sutler in the Revolootion War. My father once had a intervoo with Gin'ral La Fayette.

He asked La Fayette to lend him five dollars, promisin' to pay him in the Fall; but Lafy said "he couldn't see it in those lamps." Lafy was French, and his knowledge of our langwidge was a little shaky.

Immejutly on my 'rival here I perceeded to the Spotswood House, and callin' to my assistans a young man from our town who writes a good runnin' hand, I put my ortograph on the Register, and handin' my umbrella to a bald-heded man behind the counter, who I s'posed was Mr. Spotswood, I said, "Spotsy, how does she run?"

He called a cullud purson, and said:

"Show the gen'l'man to the cowyard, and giv' him cart number 1."

"Isn't Grant here?" I said. "Perhaps Ulyssis wouldn't mind my turnin' in with him."

"Do you know the Gin'ral?" inquired Mr. Spotswood.

"Wal, no, not 'zacky; but he'll remember me. His brother-in-law's Aunt bought her rye meal of my uncle Levi all one winter. My uncle Levi's rye meal was—"

"Pooh! pooh!" said Spotsy, "don't bother me," and he shuv'd my umbrella onto the floor. Obsarvin' to him not to be so keerless with that wepin, I accompanid the African to my lodgin's.

"My brother," I sed, "air you aware that you've been 'mancipated? Do you realize how glorus it is to be free? Tell me, my dear brother, does it not seem like some dreams, or do you realize the great fact in all its livin' and holy magnitood?"

He sed he would take some gin.

I was show'd to the cowyard, and laid down under a one-mule cart.

The hotel was orful crowded, and I was sorry I hadn't gone to the Libby Prison. Tho' I should hav' slept comf'ble enuff if the bed-clothes hadn't bin pulled off me durin' the night, by a scoundrul who cum and hitched a mule to the cart and druv it off. I thus lost my cuverin', and my throat feels a little husky this mornin'.

Gin'ral Hullock offers me the hospitality of the city, givin' me my choice of hospitals.

He has also very kindly placed at my disposal a small-pox amboolance.

There is raly a great deal of Union sentiment in this city. I see it on ev'ry hand.

I met a man to-day—I am not at liberty to tell his name, but he is a old and inflooential citizen of Richmond, and sez he, "Why! we've bin fightin' agin the Old Flag! Lor' bless me, how sing'lar!" He then borrer'd five dollars of me and bust into a flood of teers.

Sed another (a man of standin', and formerly a bitter rebuel), "Let us at once stop this effooshun of Blud! The Old Flag is good enuff for me. Sir," he added, "you air from the North! Have you a doughnut or a piece of custard pie about you?"

I told him no; but I knew a man from Vermont who had just organized a sort of restaurant, where he could go and make a very comfortable breakfast on New England rum and cheese. He borrowed fifty cents of me, and askin' me to send him Wm. Lloyd Garrison's ambrotype as soon as I got home, he walked off.

Said another: "There's bin a tremendious Union feelin' here from the fust. But we was kept down by a rain of terror. Have you a dagerretype of Wendell Phillips about your person? and will you lend me four dollars for a few days till we air once more a happy and united people?"

Robert Lee is regarded as a noble feller.

He was opposed to the war at the fust, and draw'd his sword very reluctant. In fact, he wouldn't hav' draw'd his sword at all, only he had a large stock of military clothes on hand, which he didn't want to waste. He sez the colored man is right, and he will at once go to New York and open a Sabbath School for negro minstrels.

Feelin' a little peckish, I went into a eatin' house to-day, and encountered a young man with long black hair and slender frame. He didn't wear much clothes, and them as he did wear looked onhealthy.

He frowned on me, and sed, kinder scornful, "So, Sir—you cum here to taunt us in our hour of trouble, do you?"

"No," sed I, "I cum here for hash!"

"Pish-haw," he sed, sneerin'ly, "I mean, you air in this city for the purpuss of gloatin' over a fallen peple. Others may basely succumb, but as for me, I will never yield—*never, never!*"

"Hav' suthin' to eat?" I pleasantly suggested.

"Tripe and onions!" he sed furcely; then he added, "I eat with you, but I hate you. You're a low-lived Yankee!"

To which I pleasantly replied, "How'll you have your tripe?"

"Fried, mudsill! with plenty of ham-fat!"

He et very ravenus. Poor feller! He had lived on odds and ends for several days, eatin' crackers that had bin turned over by revelers in the bread tray at the bar.

He got full at last, and his hart softened a little to'ards me. "After all," he sed, "you hav sum peple at the North who air not wholly loathsum beasts!"

"Well, yes," I sed, "we hav' now and then a man among us who isn't a cold-bluded scoundril. Young man," I mildly but gravely sed, "this crooil war is over, and you're lickt! It's rather necessary for sumbody to lick in a good, square, lively fite, and in this 'ere case it happens to be the United States of America. You fit splendid, but we was too many for you. Then make the best of it, & let us all give in, and put the Republic on a firmer basis nor ever.

"I don't gloat over your misfortins, my young fren'. Fur from it. I'm a old man now, & my hart is softer nor it once was. You see my spectacles is misten'd with suthin' very like tears. I'm thinkin' of the sea of good rich Blud that has bin spilt on both sides in this dreadful war! I'm thinkin' of our widders and orfuns North, and of your'n in the South. I kin cry for both. B'leeve me, my young fren', I kin place my old hands tenderly on the fair yung hed of the Virginny maid whose lover was laid low in the battle-dust by a fed'ral bullet, and say, as fervently and piously as a vener'ble sinner like me kin say anythin', God be good to you, my poor dear, my poor dear."

I riz up to go, & takin' my yung Southern fren', kindly by the hand, I sed, "Yung man, adoo! You Southern fellers is prob'ly my brothers, tho' you've occasionally had a cussed queer way of showin' it! It's over now. Let us all jine in and make a country on this continent that shall giv' all Europe the cramp in the stummuck ev'ry time they look at us! Adoo, adoo!"

And as I am through, I'll likewise say adoo to you, jentle reader, merely remarkin' that the Star Spangled Banner is wavin' round loose agin, and that there don't seem to be anything the matter with the Goddess of Liberty, beyond a slite cold.

SEWING-MACHINE-
FELINE ATTACHMENT

Circular. To the Public

JOHN PHŒNIX

Permit me to call your undivided attention to an invention lately made and patented by myself, which is calculated to produce the most beneficial results, and prove of inestimable value to mankind. It is well known that the sewing-machines now so generally in use, are the most important invention and greatest blessing of the age. Every lady considers this instrument indispensable to her happiness; it has completely usurped the place of the piano-forte and harp in all well-regulated families; and she who once purchased materials for clothing by the yard, now procures them by the piece or bolt, to enjoy the rational pleasure of easily making them into garments.

In the humble cabin of the laborer, and in the halls of the rich and great, now resounds from morning until night, the whir of the sewing-machine. The result of this universal grinding, although eminently gratifying to the sellers of dry goods, and the philanthropic fathers and husbands who discharge their bills, has not been of a favorable nature to our ladies in a physical point of view. It is found that the constant use of the crank has brought on rheumatic and neuralgic affections in the shoulder, and a similar application of the treadle has a tendency to produce hip diseases and white swelling of the knee-joint, accompanied by nervous complaints of a painful character. The undersigned is acquainted with a most estimable single lady of middle age, who, having procured one of the fast-running machines, was so enchanted with it, that she persisted in its use for thirty-six hours without cessation, and found, on endeavoring to leave off, that her right leg had acquired the motion of the treadle in such a painful manner, that it was impossible to keep it still, and her locomotion therefore assumed a species of polka step exceedingly ludicrous to witness, and particularly mortifying to herself. I regret to add that she was compelled, by a vote of the society, to withdraw from the Methodist Church, on a charge of dancing down the broad aisle on a Communion Sunday. A more melancholy instance was the case of Mrs. Thompson, of Seekonk, a most amiable lady, beloved and respected by all around her, but who, by constant use of the crank, lost all control of the flexors and extensors of her right arm, and inadvertently punched her husband in the eye, which, he being a man of suspicious and unforgiving disposition, led to great unhappiness in the family, and finally resulted in the melancholy case of Thompson *vs.* Thompson, so familiar to most of the civilized world. A turn for mechanism, and an intense desire to contribute to the happiness of the female sex, have ever been distinguished traits in my character. On learning these facts, therefore, I devoted myself to a thorough investigation of the subject, and after a month of close application, have at last made an invention which will at once do away with everything objectionable in the use of the sewing-machine.

This beautiful discovery is now named

"Phœnix's Feline Attachment"

Like most great inventions, the Attachment is of great simplicity. An upright shaft is connected with the machine by a cogwheel and pinion, and supported below by a suitable frame-work. Two projecting arms are attached to the shaft, to one of which a large cat is connected by a light harness, and from the other, a living mouse is suspended by the tail, within a few inches of the nose of the *motor*. As the cat springs toward the mouse, the latter is removed, and keeping constantly at the original distance, the machine revolves with great rapidity. The prodigious velocity produced by the rapacity of the cat in its futile endeavors to overtake the mouse, can only be imagined by one who has seen the Attachment in full operation.

It is thus that man shows his supremacy over the brute creation, by making even their rapacious instincts subservient to his use.

Should it be required to arrest the motion of the machine, a hand-kerchief is thrown over the mouse, and the cat at once pauses, disgusted.

Remove the handkerchief, and again she springs forward with renewed ardor. The writer has seen one cat (a tortoise-shell) of so ardent and unwearying disposition, that she made eighteen pairs of men's pantaloons, two dozen shirts, and seven stitched shirts, before she lay down exhausted. It is to be hoped that the ladies throughout the land will avail themselves of this beautiful discovery, which will entirely supersede the use of the needle, and make the manufacture of clothing and household materials a matter of pleasure to themselves, and exciting and healthy exercise to their domestic animals. The Attachment will be furnished, to families having sewing-machines, on the most reasonable terms and at the shortest notice. Young and docile cats supplied with the Attachment, by application at 348 Broadway, New York—office of the Patent Back-Action Hen Persuader.

"Phœnix's Feline Attachment"

Sewing-Machine, Box-pattern,	$75 00
Cat, at various prices, say,	$2½ to 10 00
Vertical Shaft,	5 00
H. Projecting arms,	50
Mouse,	12½
Total cost of Machine and Attachment,	$90 62½

Fables

The Merchant of Venice

G. T. LANIGAN

A Venetian merchant, who was lolling in the lap of Luxury, was accosted upon the Rialto by a Friend who had not seen him for many months. "How is this?" cried the latter; "when I last saw you your Gaberdine was out at elbows, and now you sail in your own Gondola!"

True," replied the Merchant, "but since then I have met with serious losses, and been obliged to compound with my Creditors for ten Cents on the Dollar.

Moral.—Composition is the Life of Trade.

The Good Samaritan

G. T. LANIGAN

A certain Man went from Jerusalem to Jericho, and fell among Thieves, who beat him and stripped him and left him for dead. A Good Samaritan, seeing this, clapped Spurs to his Ass and galloped away, lest he should be sent to the House of Detention as a Witness, while the Robbers were released on Bail.

Moral.—The Perceiver is worse than the Thief.

Preaching v. Practice

R. J. BURDETTE

A Sea Cliff, L.I., audience was dreadfully shocked last Sunday night. Just as a local temperance leader was about to begin his address, he leaned too closely over the candle and his breath caught fire. He afterwards explained, however, that he had been using camphor for the toothache. The amendment was accepted, and the talk went on.

THE SOCIETY UPON THE STANISLAUS

BRET HARTE

I reside at Table Mountain, and my name is Truthful James;
I am not up to small deceit, or any sinful games;
And I'll tell in simple language what I know about the row
That broke up our society upon the Stanislow.

But first I would remark, that it is not a proper plan
For any scientific gent to whale his fellow-man,
And, if a member don't agree with his peculiar whim,
To lay for that same member for to "put a head" on him.

Now nothing could be finer, or more beautiful to see,
Than the first six months' proceedings of that same society,
Till Brown of Calaveras brought a lot of fossil bones
That he found within a tunnel, near the tenement of Jones.

Then Brown he read a paper, and he reconstructed there,
From those same bones, an animal that was extremely rare;
And Jones then asked the Chair for a suspension of the rules,
Till he could prove that those same bones was one of his lost mules.

Then Brown he smiled a bitter smile, and said he was at fault.
It seemed he had been trespassing on Jones's family vault:
He was a most sarcastic man, this quiet Mr. Brown,
And on several occasions he had cleaned out the town.

Now I hold it is not decent for a scientific gent
To say another is an ass—at least, to all intent;
Nor should the individual who happens to be meant
Reply by heaving rocks at him to any great extent.

Then Abner Deal, of Angel's, raised a point of order—when
A chunk of old red sandstone took him in the abdomen,
And he smiled a kind of sickly smile, and curled up on the floor,
And the subsequent proceedings interested him no more.

For, in less time than I write it, every member did engage
In a warfare with the remnants of a palæozoic age;
And the way they heaved those fossils in their anger was a sin,
Till the skull of an old mammoth caved the head of Thompson in.

And this is all I have to say of these improper games,
For I live at Table Mountain, and my name is Truthful James;
And I've told, in simple language, what I know about the row
That broke up our society upon the Stanislow.

What He Wanted It For

J. M. Bailey

Those who attended the sale of animals from Barnum's hippodrome in Bridgeport, the other day, report the following occurrence. A tiger was being offered. The bid run up to forty-five hundred dollars. This was made by a man who was a stranger, and to him it was knocked down. Barnum, who had been eyeing the stranger uneasily during the bidding, now went up to him, and said:

"Pardon me for asking the question; but will you tell me where you are from?"

"Down South a bit," responded the man.

"Are you connected with any show?"

"No."

"And are you buying this animal for yourself?"

"Yes."

Barnum shifted about uneasily for a moment, looking alternately at the man and the tiger, and evidently trying his best to reconcile the two together.

"Now, young man," he finally said, "you need not take this animal unless you want to; for there are those here who will take it off your hands."

"I don't want to sell," was the quiet reply.

Then Barnum said, in his desperation:

"What on earth are you going to do with such an ugly beast, if you have no show of your own, and are not buying for some one who is a showman?"

"Well, I'll tell you," said the purchaser. "My wife died about three weeks ago. We had lived together for ten years, and—and I miss her." He paused to wipe his eyes, and steady his voice, and then added: "So I've bought this tiger."

"I understand you," said the great showman in a husky voice.

Ants, Etc.

Josh Billings

Ants are older than Adam.

Man *(for very wise reasons)* want bilt untill all other things were finished, and pronounced good.

If man had bin made fust he would hav insisted upon bossing the rest of the job.

He probably would hav objekted to having enny little bizzy aunts at all, and various other objekshuns would have bin offered, equally green.

I am glad that man waz the last thing made.

If man hadn't hav bin made at all, you would never hav heard me find enny fault about it.

The Romance of the Carpet

R. J. Burdette

Basking in peace in the warm spring sun,
South Hill smiled upon Burlington.

The breath of May! and the day was fair,
And the bright motes danced in the balmy air.

And the sunlight gleamed where the restless breeze
Kissed the fragrant blooms on the apple-trees.

His beardless cheek with a smile was spanned,
As he stood with a carriage whip in his hand.

And he laughed as he doffed his bobtail coat,
And the echoing folds of the carpet smote.

And she smiled as she leaned on her busy mop,
And said she'd tell him when to stop.

So he pounded away till the dinner-bell
Gave him a little breathing spell.

But he sighed when the kitchen clock struck one,
And she said the carpet wasn't done.

But he lovingly put in his biggest licks,
And he pounded like mad till the clock struck six.

And she said, in a dubious kind of way,
That she guessed he could finish it up next day.

Then all that day, and the next day, too,
That fuzz from the dirtless carpet flew.

And she'd give it a look at eventide,
And say, "Now beat on the other side."

And the new days came as the old days went,
And the landlord came for his regular rent.

And the neighbors laughed at the tireless broom,
And his face was shadowed with clouds of gloom.

Till at last, one cheerless winter day,
He kicked at the carpet and slid away.

Over the fence and down the street,
Speeding away with footsteps fleet.

And never again the morning sun
Smiled on him beating his carpet-drum.

And South Hill often said with a yawn,
"Where's the carpet-martyr gone?"

Years twice twenty had come and passed
And the carpet swayed in the autumn blast.

For never yet, since that bright spring-time,
Had it ever been taken down from the line.

Over the fence a gray-haired man
Cautiously clim, clome, clem, clum, clamb.

He found him a stick in the old woodpile,
And he gathered it up with a sad, grim smile.

A flush passed over his face forlorn
As he gazed at the carpet, tattered and torn.

And he hit it a most resounding thwack,
Till the startled air gave his echoes back.

And out of the window a white face leaned,
And a palsied hand the pale face screened.

She knew his face; she gasped, and sighed,
"A little more on the other side."

Right down on the ground his stick he throwed,
And he shivered and said, "Well, I am blowed!"

And he turned away, with a heart full sore,
And he never was seen not more, not more.

MR. SIMPKINS'S DOWNFALL

W. L. ALDEN

Man is the only animal that wears short socks. This is not only a more accurate definition than any hitherto devised by scientific persons, but it shows the inferiority of man to all other animals, and ought to have even more effect in humbling our wicked pride than has the famous story of the little girl who was excessively proud of her silk dress until she was told that it was spun, woven, cut out, made up, and trimmed by a loathsome worm.

The great trouble with the short sock is, that it will not keep its place. There being nothing whatever to hold it, the force of gravitation necessarily drags it down about the ankle. This causes an amount of misery which is appalling. There is no man who can feel any confidence in his socks. Whether he is walking or sitting, he knows that his socks are slowly but surely slipping down. Garters being out of the question, since the shortness of the sock does not permit a garter to be placed in a position where it will not slip, there is absolutely no remedy for what we may fairly call the giant evil of the age. Pins and mucilage have both been tried by desperate men, but they have proved useless, and have merely added to the misery of the user. In these circumstances there is nothing left for man to do except to bear the sock in silence, or to boldly cast it aside and adopt the full-grown stocking.

The latter alternative was recently chosen by that eloquent but unfortunate clergyman, Rev. Charles Simpkins, of Westbridge, Pennsylvania. Previous to the catastrophe which lately overtook him, the Church did not possess a more popular and promising young clergyman. He could repeat the opening exhortation all the way from "Dearly beloved" to "forgiveness for the same," without once pausing for breath; and it has been asserted that he could monotone the entire Apostles' Creed while breathing only three times. As he was unmarried, and not yet twenty-seven years old, he was regarded with peculiar reverence by the unmarried ladies of his parish, and he received more annual slippers than any other clergyman in the United States.

Neatness was one of the distinguishing characteristics of Mr. Simpkins, and there are probably few men who have suffered more keenly from short socks. When walking through the village, he was in continual dread lest his socks should descend into public view, and even while preaching his most eloquent sermons, the perspiration would gather on his brow as he felt that one of his socks was gradually slipping down. This wore upon him to that extent that his massive intellect threatened to totter, and on the morning of the eighty-first Sunday after Trinity, he deliberately paused, after remarking "here endeth"—and stooped down to repair damages. That night he resolved that vigorous measures must be taken, and he accordingly wrote a confidential letter to his sister's husband, who resided in this city, and inclosed the necessary measurements. Shortly afterward he received, ostensibly from the husband, but really from the affectionate sister, two dozen pair of Balbriggan hose, together with a pair of scarlet elastics an inch in width, and of precisely the right size.

As soon as Mr. Simpkins had learned, by repeated experiment, how to wear the scarlet appliances, his spirits began to rise. He was no longer a prey to doubt and despair. His stockings firmly kept their place, and he felt that he could even attend a church picnic and climb over a fence without fear of consequences. Accordingly, for the first time during his residence at Westbridge, he consented to attend the Sunday-school picnic of the 21st of October last, and thereby filled with unutterable delight the souls of all the unmarried teachers of the church.

Mr. Simpkins, being free from care, entered into the sports of the picnic with great zest, and the children insisted that he, together with their teachers, should take part in a game of blindman's buff. The request was acceded to, and the usual running, laughing and shrieking followed. It was while Mr. Simpkins was fleeing, in company with six excited teachers, from the pursuit of a blindfolded small boy, that he suddenly noticed that one of his elastics had become unclasped, and had fallen to the ground. At the same moment it was perceived by the prettiest of the teachers, who made a frantic effort to seize it, but was anticipated by the unhappy clergyman. It was bad enough for him to know that the teacher had discovered his misfortune; but what was his horror and amazement when, with every appearance of anger, she demanded that he should "hand her that" instantly. He was so astonished at her evident desire to make sport of him that he did not deign to answer her, but put the disputed article in his pocket and walked away. Whereupon the teacher burst into tears, and informed her confidential friends that Mr. Simpkins had had the inconceivable audacity to steal one of her—in fact, her private property.

The scandal spread rapidly and widely, and grew as rapidly as it spread. At the end of half an hour every lady at the picnic had cut the clergyman in the most marked manner. Burning with shame and indignation, he forgot to repair the deficiencies of his toilet, and went home feeling rather more crestfallen than did the prophet Daniel when he found that the lions would not recognize his existence. It was not until he was on the point of seeking a sleepless pillow that he discovered that both his scarlet elastics were in their proper place, while the one which he had picked up at the picnic lay on his table. The full horror of his situation flashed upon him. The teacher had really dropped a scarlet elastic, and he had seized it under the impression that it was his own.

The utter hopelessness of ever making any satisfactory explanation of the affair was only too apparent. Early the next morning Mr. Simpkins fled from Westbridge a ruined man. The fatal articles which had caused his downfall he left behind him, and they teach with mute but powerful eloquence the lesson that we should bear the socks we have, and never dream of flying to stockings, of which we know nothing except by hearsay.

Mr. Rabbit Grossly Deceives
Mr. Fox

UNCLE REMUS

One evening when the little boy, whose nights with Uncle Remus are as entertaining as those Arabian ones of blessed memory, had finished supper and hurried out to sit with his venerable patron, he found the old man in great glee. Indeed, Uncle Remus was talking and laughing to himself at such a rate that the little boy was afraid he had company. The truth is, Uncle Remus had heard the child coming, and, when the rosy-cheeked chap put his head in at the door, was engaged in a monologue, the burden of which seemed to be:

> "Ole Molly Har',
> W'at you doin' dar,
> Settin' in de cornder
> Smokin' yo' seegyar?"

As a matter of course, this vague allusion reminded the little boy of the fact that the wicked Fox was still in pursuit of the Rabbit, and he immediately put his curiosity in the shape of a question.

"Uncle Remus, did the Rabbit have to go clean away when he got loose from the Tar-Baby?"

"Bless grashus, honey, dat he didn't! Who? Him? You dunno nuthin' 'tall 'bout Brer Rabbit ef dat's de way you puttin' 'em down. W'at he gwine 'way fer? He mouter stayed sorter close twel de pitch rub off'n his ha'r, but twern't menny days 'fo' he wuz lopin' up en down de naberhood same ez ever, en I dunno ef he wern't mo' sassier dan befo'.

"Seem like dat de tale 'bout how he got mixt up wid de Tar-Baby got 'roun' 'mongst de nabers. Leas'ways, Miss Meadows en de gals got win' un' it, en de nex' time Brer Rabbit paid um a visit Miss Meadows tackled 'im 'bout it, en de gals sot up a monstus gigglement. Brer Rabbit, he sot up des ez cool ez a cowcumber, he did, en let 'em run on."

"Who was Miss Meadows, Uncle Remus?" inquired the little boy.

"Don't ax me, honey. She wuz in de tale, Miss Meadows en de gals wuz, en de tale I give you like hi't wer' gun ter me. Brer Rabbit, he sot dar, he did, sorter lam' like, en den bimeby he cross his legs, he did, and wink his eye slow, en up en say, sezee:

" 'Ladies, Brer Fox wuz my daddy's ridin' hoss fer thirty year; maybe mo', but thirty year dat I knows un', sezee; en den he paid um his 'specks, en tip his beaver, en march off, he did, des ez stiff en ez stuck up ez a fire-stick.

"Nex' day, Brer Fox cum a callin', and w'en he 'gun fer ter laff 'bout Brer Rabbit, Miss Meadows en de gals, dey ups en tells 'im 'bout w'at Brer Rabbit say. Den Brer Fox grit his toof sho' nuff, he did, en he look mighty dumpy, but w'en he riz fer ter go he up en say, sezee:

" 'Ladies, I ain't 'sputin' w'at you say, but I'll make Brer Rabbit chaw up his words en spit um out right yer whar you kin see 'im', sezee, en wid dat off Brer Fox marcht.

"En w'en he got in de big road, he shuck de dew off'n his tail, en made a straight shoot fer Brer Rabbit's house. W'en he got dar, Brer Rabbit wuz spectin' un 'im, en de do' wuz shet fas'. Brer Fox knock. Nobody ain't ans'er. Brer Fox knock. Nobody ans'er. Den he knock agin—blam! blam! Den Brer Rabbit holler out mighty weak:

" 'Is dat you, Brer Fox? I want you ter run en fetch de doctor. Dat bait er pusly w'at I e't dis mawnin' is gittin' 'way wid me. Do, please, Brer Fox, run quick,' sez Brer Rabbit, sezee.

" 'I come atter you, Brer Rabbit,' sez Brer Fox, sezee. 'Dere's gwineter be a party up at Miss Meadows's,' sezee. 'All de gals 'll be dere, en I promus' dat I'd fetch you. De gals, dey 'lowed dat hit wouldn't be no party 'ceppin' I fotch you,' sez Brer Fox, sezee.

"Den Brer Rabbit say he wuz too sick, en Brer Fox say he wuzzent, en dar dey had it up and down, 'sputin' en contendin'. Brer Rabbit say he can't walk. Brer Fox say he tote 'im. Brer Rabbit say how? Brer Fox Fox say in his arms. Brer Rabbit say he drap 'im. Brer Fox 'low he won't. Bimeby Brer Rabbit say he go ef Brer Fox tote 'im on his back. Brer Fox say he would. Brer Rabbit say he can't ride widout a saddle. Brer Fox say he git de saddle. Brer Rabbit say he can't set in saddle less he have bridle fer ter hol' by. Brer Fox say he git de bridle. Brer Rabbit say he can't ride widout bline bridle, kaze Brer Fox be shyin' at stumps 'long de road, en fling 'im off. Brer Fox say he git bline bridle. Den Brer Rabbit say he go. Den Brer Fox say he ride Brer Rabbit mos' up ter

BRER RABBIT'S HORSE.

Miss Meadows's, en den he could git down en walk de balance er de way. Brer Rabbit 'greed, en den Brer Fox lipt out atter de saddle en de bridle.

"Co'se Brer Rabbit know de game dat Brer Fox wuz fixin' fer ter play, en he 'termin' fer ter outdo 'im, en by de time he koam his ha'r en twis' his mustarsh, en sorter rig up, yer come Brer Fox, saddle en bridle on, en lookin' ez peart ez a circus pony. He trot up ter de do' en stan' dar pawin' de ground en chompin' de bit same like sho 'nuff hoss, en Brer Rabbit he mount, he did, en dey amble off. Brer Fox can't see behime wid de bline bridle on, but bimeby he feel Brer Rabbit raise one er his foots.

" 'W'at you doin' now, Brer Rabbit?' sezee.

" 'Short'nin' de lef' stir'p, Brer Fox,' sezee.

"Bimeby Brer Rabbit raise up de udder foot.

" 'W'at you doin' now, Brer Rabbit?' sezee.

" 'Pullin' down my pants, Brer Fox,' sezee.

"All de time, bless grashus, honey, Brer Rabbit wer puttin' on his spurrers, en w'en dey got close to Miss Meadows's, whar Brer Rabbit wuz to git off, en Brer Fox made a motion fer ter stan' still, Brer Rabbit slap de spurrers inter Brer Fox's flanks, en you better b'leeve he got over de groun'. W'en dey got ter de house, Miss Meadows' en all de gals wuz settin' on de peazzer, en stidder stoppin' at de gate, Brer Rabbit rid on by, he did, en den come gallopin' down de road en up ter de hoss-rack, w'ich he hitch Brer Fox at, en den he santer inter de house, he did, en shake han's wid de gals, en set dar, smokin' his seegyar same ez a town man. Bimeby he draw in long puff, en den let hit out in a cloud, en squar hisse'f back en holler out, he did:

" 'Ladies, ain't I done tell you Brer Fox wuz de ridin'-hoss for our fambly? He sorter losin' his gait' now, but I speck I kin fetch 'im all right in a mont' er so,' sezee.

"En den Brer Rabbit sorter grin, he did, en de gals giggle, en Miss Meadows, she praise up de pony, en dar wuz Brer Fox hitch fas' ter de rack, en couldn't he'p hisse'f."

"Is that all, Uncle Remus?" asked the little boy as the old man paused.

"Dat ain't all, honey, but 'twon't do fer ter give out too much cloff fer ter cut one pa'r pants," replied the old man sententiously.

When "Miss Sally's" little boy went to Uncle Remus the next night to hear the conclusion of the adventure in which the Rabbit made a riding-horse of the Fox, to the great enjoyment and gratification of Miss Meadows and the girls, he found the old man in a bad humor.

"I ain't tellin' no tales ter bad chilluns," said Uncle Remus curtly.

"But, Uncle Remus, I ain't bad," said the little boy plaintively.

"Who dat chunkin' dem chickens dis mawnin'? Who dat knockin' out fokes's eyes wid dat Yallerbammer sling des 'fo' dinner? Who dat sickin' dat pinter puppy atter my pig? Who dat scatterin' my ingun sets? Who dat flingin' rocks on top er my house, w'ich a little mo' on one un em would er drap spang on my head?"

"Well, now, Uncle Remus, I didn't go to do it. I won't do so any more. Please, Uncle Remus, if you will tell me, I'll run to the house and bring you some tea-cakes."

"Seein' um's better'n hearin' tell un um," replied the old man, the severity of his countenance relaxing somewhat; but the little boy darted out, and in a few minutes came running back with his pockets full and his hands full.

"I lay yo' mammy 'll 'spishun dat de rats' stummucks is widenin' in dis naberhood w'en she come fer ter count up 'er cakes," said Uncle Remus, with a chuckle. "Deze," he continued, dividing the cakes into two equal parts—"deze I'll tackle now, en deze I'll lay by fer Sunday.

"Lemme see. I mos' dis'member wharbouts Brer Fox en Brer Rabbit wuz."

"The rabbit rode the fox to Miss Meadows's, and hitched him to the horse-rack," said the little boy.

"W'y co'se he did," said Uncle Remus. "Co'se he did. Well, Brer Rabbit rid Brer Fox up, he did, en tied 'im to de rack, en den sot out in de peazzer wid de gals a smokin' er his seegyar wid mo' proudness dan w'at you mos' ever see. Dey talk, en dey sing, en dey play on de peaner, de gals did, twel bimeby hit come time fer Brer Rabbit fer to be gwine, en he tell um all good-by, en strut out to de hoss-rack samo's ef he wuz de king er de patter-rollers, en den he mount Brer Fox en ride off.

"Brer Fox ain't sayin' nuthin' 'tall. He des rack off, he did, en keep his mouf shet, en Brer Rabbit know'd der waz biznezz cookin' up fer him, en he feel monstus skittish. Brer Fox amble on twel he git in de long lane, outer sight er Miss Meadows's house, an den he tu'n loose, he did. He rip en he r'ar, en he cuss en he swar, he snort en he cavort."

"What was he doing that for, Uncle Remus?" the little boy inquired.

"He wuz tryin' fer ter fling Brer Rabbit off'n his back, bless yo' soul! But he des might ez well er rastle wid his own shadder. Every time he hump hisse'f Brer Rabbit slapp de spurrers in 'im, en dar dey had it, up en down. Brer Fox fa'rly to' up de groun', he did, en he jump so high en he jump so quick dat he mighty nigh snatch his own tail off. Dey kep' on gwine on dis way twel bimeby Brer Fox lay down en roll over, he did, en dis sorter onsettle Brer Rabbit, but by de time Brer Fox got back on his footses again, Brer Rabbit wuz gwine thro de underbresh mo' samer dan a race-hoss. Brer Fox he lit out after 'im, he did, en he push Brer Rabbit so close dat it wuz 'bout all he could do fer ter git in a holler tree. Hole too little fer Brer Fox fer ter git n, en he hatter lay down en res' en gedder his mine tergedder.

"While he wuz layin' dar, Mr. Buzzard come floppin' 'long, en seein' Brer Fox stretch out on the groun', he lit en view de premusses. Den Mr. Buzzard sorter shake his wing, en put his head on one side, en say to hisse'f like, sezee:

" 'Brer Fox dead, en I so sorry,' sezee.

" 'No, I ain't dead, nudder,' sez Brer Fox, sezee. 'I got ole man Rabbit pent up in yer,' sezee, 'en I'm a gwineter git 'im dis time ef it take twel Chris'mus', sezee.

"Den, atter some mo' palaver, Brer Fox make a bargain dat Mr. Buzzard wuz ter watch de hole, en keep Brer Rabbit dar wiles Brer Fox went after his axe. Den Brer Fox he lope off, he did, en Mr. Buzzard he tuck up his stan' at the hole. Bimby, w'en all git still, Brer Rabbit sorter scramble down close to der hole, he did, en holler out:

" 'Brer Fox! Oh, Brer Fox!'

"Brer Fox done gone, en nobody say nuthin'. Den Brer Rabbit squall out like he wuz mad; sezee:

" 'You needn't talk less you wanter,' sezee; 'I knows youer dar, en I ain't keerin',' sezee. 'I des wanter tell you dat I wish mighty bad Brer Tukkey Buzzard wuz here,' sezee.

"Den Mr. Buzzard try ter talk like Brer Fox:

" 'W'at you want wid Mr. Buzzard?' sezee.

" 'Oh, nuthin' in 'tickler, 'cep' dere's de fattes' gray squir'l in yer dat ever I see,' sezee, 'en ef Brer Tukkey Buzzard wuz 'roun', he'd be mighty glad fer ter git 'im,' sezee.

" 'How Mr. Buzzard gwine ter git 'im?' sez de Buzzard, sezee.

" 'Well, dars a little hole roun' on the udder side er de tree,' sez Brer Rabbit, sezee, 'en ef Brer Tukkey Buzzard wuz here, so he could take up his stan' dar,' sezee, 'I'd drive dat squir'l out,' sezee.

" 'Drive 'im out, den,' sez Mr. Buzzard, sezee, 'en I'll see dat Brer Tukkey Buzzard gits 'im,' sezee.

"Den Brer Rabbit kick up a racket, like he wer' drivin' sum'in' out, en Mr. Buzzard he rush 'roun' fer ter ketch de squir'l, en Brer Rabbit he dash out, he did, en he des fly fer home."

At this point Uncle Remus took one of the tea-cakes, held his head back, opened his mouth, dropped the cake in with a sudden motion, looked at the little boy with an expression of astonishment, and then closed his eyes and begun to chew, mumbling, as an accompaniment, the plaintive tune of "Don't you Grieve atter Me."

The *séance* was over; but before the little boy went into the "big house," Uncle Remus laid his rough hand tenderly on the child's shoulder, and remarked, in a confidential tone:

"Honey, you mus' git up soon Chris'mus mawnin' en open de do'; kase I'm gwineter bounce in on Marse John en Miss Sally en holler Chris'mus gif' des like I useter endurin' de fahmin' days fo' de war, w'en ole Miss wuz 'live. I boun' dey don't fergit de ole nigger, nudder. W'en you hear me callin' de pigs, honey, you des hop up en onfassen de do'. I lay I'll give Marse John wunner deze yer 'sprize parties."

How I Edited an

Agricultural Paper

MARK TWAIN

I did not take temporary editorship of an agricultural paper without misgivings. Neither would a landsman take command of a ship without misgivings. But I was in circumstances that made the salary an object. The regular editor of the paper was going off for a holiday, and I accepted the terms he offered, and took his place.

The sensation of being at work again was luxurious, and I wrought all the week with unflagging pleasure. We went to press, and I waited a day with some solicitude to see whether my effort was going to attract any notice. As I left the office, toward sundown, a group of men and boys at the foot of the stairs dispersed with one impulse, and gave me passage-way, and I heard one or two of them say, "That's him!" I was naturally pleased by this incident. The next morning I found a similar group at the foot of the stairs, and scattering couples and individuals standing here and there in the street, and over the way, watching me with interest. The group separated and fell back as I approached, and I heard a man say, "Look at his eye!" I pretended not to observe the notice I was attracting, but secretly I was pleased with it, and was purposing to write an account of it to my aunt. I went up a short flight of stairs, and heard cheery voices and a ringing laugh as I drew near the door, which I opened, and caught a glimpse of two young rural-looking men, whose faces blanched and lengthened when they saw me, and then they both plunged through the window with a great crash. I was surprised.

In about half an hour an old gentlemen, with a flowing beard and a fine but rather austere face, entered, and sat down at my invitation. He seemed to have something on his mind. He took off his hat and set it on the floor, and got out of it a red silk handkerchief and a copy of our paper.

He put the paper on his lap, and while he polished his spectacles with his handkerchief, he said, "Are you the new editor?"

I said I was.

"Have you ever edited an agricultural paper before?"

"No," I said; "this is my first attempt."

"Very likely. Have you had any experience in agriculture practically?"

"No; I believe I have not."

"Some instinct told me so," said the old gentleman, putting on his spectacles, and looking over them at me with asperity, while he folded his paper into a convenient shape. "I wish to read you what must have made me have that instinct. It was this editorial. Listen, and see if it was you that wrote it:

" 'Turnips should never be pulled; it injures them. It is much better to send a boy up and let him shake the tree.'

"Now, what do you think of that?—for I really suppose you wrote it?"

"Think of it? Why, I think it is good. I think it is sense. I have no doubt that every year millions and millions of bushels of turnips are spoiled in this township alone by being pulled in a half-ripe condition, when, if they had sent a boy up to shake the tree—"

"Shake your grandmother! Turnips don't grow on trees!"

"Oh, they don't, don't they? Well, who said they did? The language was intended to be figurative—wholly figurative. Anybody that knows anything will know that I meant that the boy should shake the vine."

Then this old person got up, and tore his paper all into small shreds, and stamped on them, and broke several things with his cane, and said I did not know as much as a cow, and then went out and banged the door after him; and, in short, acted in such a way that I fancied he was displeased about something. But not knowing what the trouble was, I could not be any help to him.

Pretty soon after this a long, cadaverous creature, with lanky locks hanging down to his shoulders, and a week's stubble bristling from the hills and valleys of his face, darted within the door and halted, motionless, with finger on lip, and head and body bent in listening attitude. No sound was heard. Still he listened. No sound. Then he turned the key in the door, and came elaborately tiptoeing toward me till he was within long reaching distance of me, when he stopped, and after scanning my face with intense interest for a while, drew a folded copy of our paper from his bosom, and said:

"There, you wrote that! Read it to me—quick! Relieve me! I suffer!"

I read as follows; and as the sentences fell from my lips I could see the relief come; I could see the drawn muscles relax, and the anxiety go out of the face, and rest and peace steal over the features like the merciful moonlight over a desolate landscape:

"The guano is a fine bird, but great care is necessary in rearing it. It should not be imported earlier than June or later than September. In the winter it should be kept in a warm place, where it can hatch out its young.

"It is evident that we are to have a backward season for grain. Therefore it will be well for the farmer to begin setting out his cornstalks and planting his buckwheat cakes in July instead of August.

"Concerning the pumpkin.—This berry is a favorite with the natives of the interior of New England, who prefer it to the gooseberry for the making of fruit-cake, and who likewise give it the preference over the raspberry for feeding cows, as being more filling and fully as satisfying. The pumpkin is the only esculent of the orange family that will thrive in the North, except the gourd and one or two varieties of the squash. But the custom of planting it in the front yard with the shubbery is fast going out of vogue, for it is now generally conceded that the pumpkin as a shade tree is a failure.

"Now, as the warm weather approaches, and the ganders begin to spawn—"

The excited listener sprang toward me to shake hands, and said:

"There, there—that will do! I know I am all right now, because you have read it just as I did, word for word. But, stranger, when I first read it this morning, I said to myself, I never, never believed it before, notwithstanding my friends kept me under watch so strict, but now I believe I *am* crazy; and with that I fetched a howl that you might have heard two miles, and started out to kill somebody—because, you know, I knew it would come to that sooner or later, and so I might as well begin. I read one of them paragraphs over again, so as to be certain, and then I burned my house down and started. I have crippled several people, and have got one fellow up a tree, where I can get him if I want him. But I thought I would call in here as I passed along and make the thing perfectly certain; and now it *is* certain, and I tell you it is lucky for the chap that is in the tree. I should have killed him, sure, as I went back. Good-bye, sir, good-bye; you have taken a great load off my mind. My reason has stood the strain of one of your agricultural articles, and I know that nothing can ever unseat it now. *Good*-bye, sir."

I felt a little uncomfortable about the cripplings and arsons this per-

son had been entertaining himself with, for I could not help feeling remotely accessory to them. But these thoughts were quickly banished,
for the regular editor walked in! [I thought to myself. Now if you had
gone to Egypt, as I recommended you to, I might have had a chance to
get my hand in; but you wouldn't do it, and here you are. I sort of expected you.]

The editor was looking sad and perplexed and dejected.

He surveyed the wreck which that old rioter and these two young
farmers had made, and then said, "This is a sad business—a very sad
business. There is the mucilage bottle broken, and six panes of glass,
and a spittoon and two candlesticks. But that is not the worst. The reputation of the paper is injured—and permanently, I fear. True, there
never was such a call for the paper before, and it never sold such a large
edition or soared to such celebrity,—but does one want to be famous
for lunacy, and prosper upon the infirmities of his mind? My friend, as
I am an honest man, the street out here is full of people, and others are
roosting on the fences, waiting to get a glimpse of you, because they
think you are crazy. And well they might, after reading your editorials.
They are a disgrace to journalism. Why, what put it into your head that
you could edit a paper of this nature. You do not seem to know the first
rudiments of agriculture. You speak of a furrow and a harrow as being
the same thing; you talk of the moulting season for cows; and you recommend the domestication of the pole-cat on account of its playful-
ness and its excellence as a ratter? Your remark that clams will lie quiet
if music be played to them was superfluous—entirely superfluous.
Nothing disturbs clams. Clams *always* lie quiet. Clams care nothing
whatever about music. Ah, heavens and earth, friend! if you had made
the acquiring of ignorance the study of your life, you could not have
graduated with higher honor than you could to-day. I never saw anything like it. Your observation that the horse-chestnut as an article of
commerce is steadily gaining in favor, is simply calculated to destroy
this journal. I want you to throw up your situation and go. I want no
more holiday—I could not enjoy it if I had it. Certainly not with you
in my chair. I would always stand in dread of what you might be going
to recommend next. It makes me lose all patience every time I think of
your discussing oyster-beds under the head of "Landscape Gardening." I want you to go. Nothing on earth could persuade me to take an-

other holiday. Oh! why didn't you *tell* me you didn't know anything about agriculture?"

"*Tell* you, you cornstalk, you cabbage, you son of a cauliflower? It's the first time I ever heard such an unfeeling remark. I tell you I have been in the editorial business going on fourteen years, and it is the first time I ever heard of a man's having to know anything in order to edit a newspaper. You turnip! Who write the dramatic critiques for the second-rate papers? Why, a parcel of promoted shoemakers and apprentice apothecaries, who know just as much about good acting as I do about good farming, and no more. Who review the books? People who never wrote one. Who do up the heavy leaders on finance? Parties who have had the largest opportunities for knowing nothing about it. Who criticise the Indian campaigns? Gentlemen who do not know a war-whoop from a wigwam, and who never have had to run a footrace with a tomahawk, or pluck arrows out of the several members of their families to build the evening camp-fire with. Who write the temperance appeals, and clamor about the flowing bowl? Folks who will never draw another sober breath till they do it in the grave. Who edit the agricultural papers, you—yam? Men, as a general thing, who fail in the poetry line, yellow-covered novel line, sensation-drama line, city-editor line, and finally fall back on agriculture as a temporary reprieve from the poor-house. *You* try to tell *me* anything about the newspaper business! Sir, I have been through it from Alpha to Omaha, and I tell you that the less a man knows, the bigger the noise he makes and the higher the salary he commands. Heaven knows if I had but been ignorant instead of cultivated, and impudent instead of diffident. I could have made a name for myself in this cold, selfish world. I take my leave, sir. Since I have been treated as you have treated me, I am perfectly willing to go. But I have done my duty. I have fulfilled my contract as far as I was permitted to do it. I said I could make your paper of interest to all classes—and I have. I said I could run your circulation up to twenty thousand copies, and if I had had two more weeks I'd have done it. And I'd have given you the best class of readers that ever an agricultural paper had—not a farmer in it, nor a solitary individual who could tell a water-melon tree from a peach-vine to save his life. *You* are the loser by this rupture, not me, Pie-plant! Adios."

I then left.

A NOTE ON THE TYPE

The principal text of this Modern Library edition
was set in a digitized version of Janson,
a typeface that dates from about 1690 and was cut by Nicholas Kis,
a Hungarian working in Amsterdam. The original matrices have
survived and are held by the Stempel foundry in Germany.
Hermann Zapf redesigned some of the weights and sizes for Stempel,
basing his revisions on the original design.